AF334929

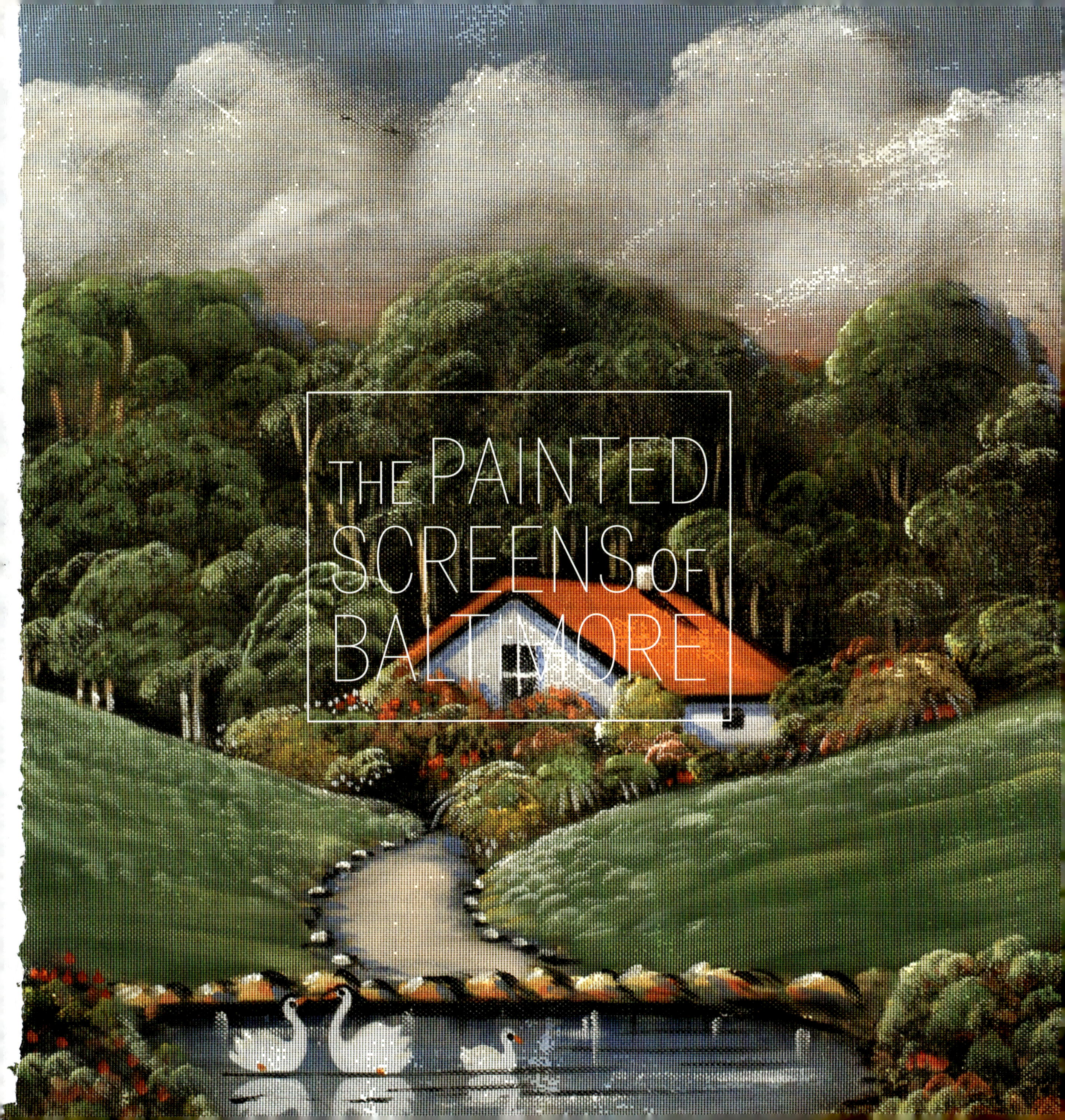

THE PAINTED
SCREENS OF
BALTIMORE

www.upress.state.ms.us

The University Press of Mississippi
is a member of the Association
of American University Presses.

Publication of this book is supported by a grant
from the Andrew W. Mellon Foundation.

Copyright © 2013 by
University Press of Mississippi
All rights reserved

Design by Kristen Spilman

Printed in Canada
First printing 2013

∞

Library of Congress Cataloging-in-
Publication Data

Eff, Elaine
    The painted screens of Baltimore : an urban
folk art revealed / Elaine Eff.
        pages cm (Folklore studies in a multicul-
        tural world)
    Includes bibliographical references and
    index.
    ISBN 978-1-61703-891-4 (hardback)
    — ISBN 978-1-61703-892-1 (ebook) 1.
    Painted wire screens—Maryland—Baltimore.
    2. Folk art—Maryland—Baltimore. I. Title.
    NK838.B35E39 2013
    745.09752'6—dc23   2013015880

British Library Cataloging-in-
Publication Data available

FOLKLORE STUDIES IN A MULTICULTURAL WORLD

The *Folklore Studies in a Multicultural World* series is a
collaborative venture of the University of Illinois Press,
the University Press of Mississippi, the University of
Wisconsin Press, and the American Folklore Society,
made possible by a generous grant from the Andrew W.
Mellon Foundation. The series emphasizes the inter-
disciplinary and international nature of current folklore
scholarship, documenting connections between communities and their cultural production. Series volumes
highlight aspects of folklore studies such as world folk
cultures, folk art and music, foodways, dance, African
American and ethnic studies, gender and queer studies,
and popular culture.

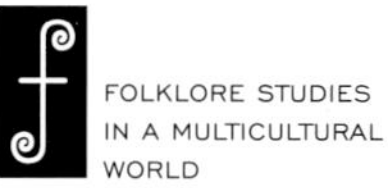

THE JUMBIES' PLAYING GROUND
Old World Influences on Afro-Creole Masquerades
in the Eastern Caribbean
Robert Wyndham Nicholls
Foreword by John Nunley
UNIVERSITY PRESS OF MISSISSIPPI

THE LAST LAUGH
Folk Humor, Celebrity Culture, and Mass-Mediated
Disasters in the Digital Age
Trevor J. Blank
UNIVERSITY OF WISCONSIN PRESS

THE PAINTED SCREENS OF BALTIMORE
An Urban Folk Art Revealed
Elaine Eff
UNIVERSITY PRESS OF MISSISSIPPI

SQUEEZE THIS!
A Cultural History of the Accordion in America
Marion Jacobson
UNIVERSITY OF ILLINOIS PRESS

THE PAINTED SCREENS OF BALTIMORE

AN URBAN FOLK ART REVEALED

ELAINE EFF

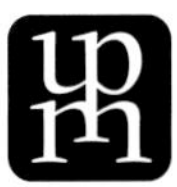

UNIVERSITY PRESS OF MISSISSIPPI — JACKSON

This book is dedicated to my parents,
Milton and Ann Goldberg.

Especially to my mother, who advised
me never to talk to strangers.

To the strangers of East Baltimore whose
kindnesses made this work possible.

And to my husband, John Fairhall,
whose guidance and patience carried
me through.

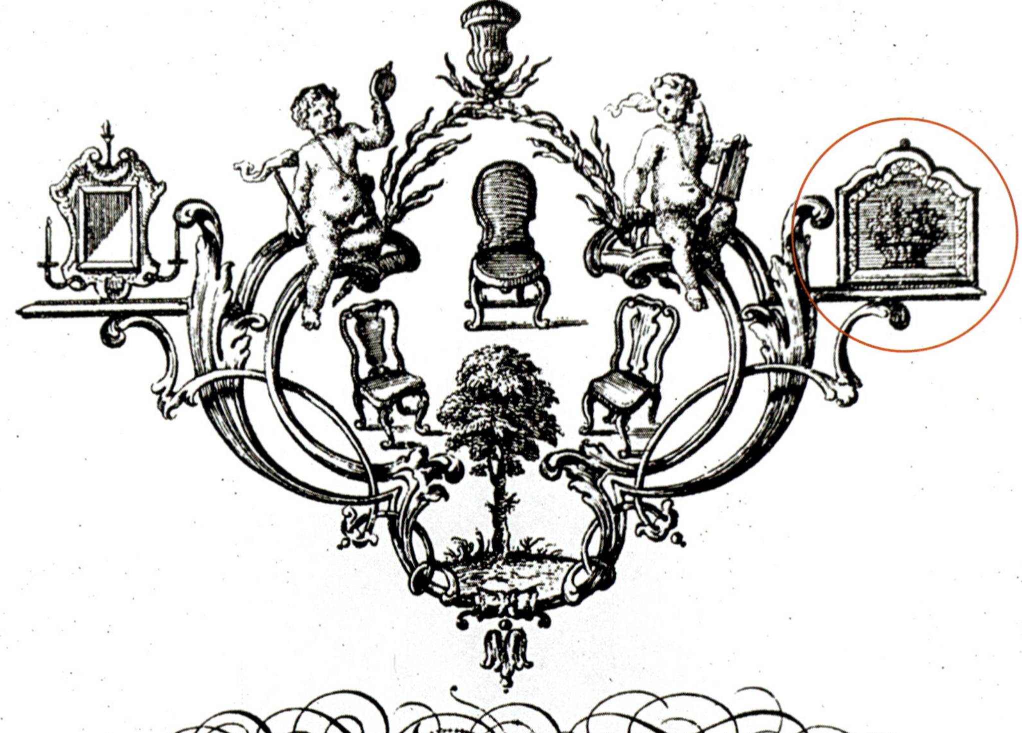

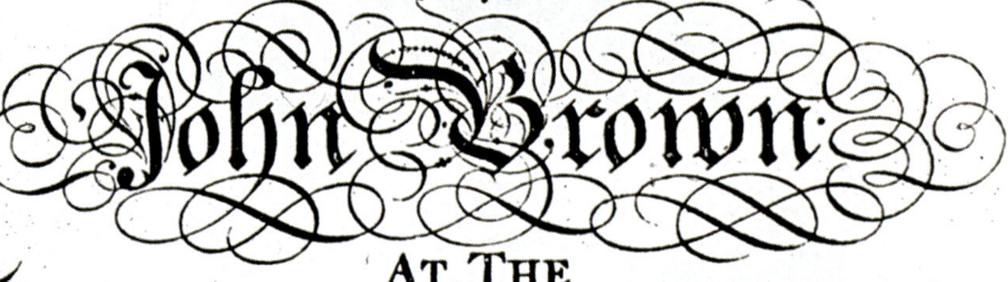

John Brown

AT THE

Three Cover'd Chairs & Walnut-Tree,
the East Side of S.ᵗ Paul's Church Yard, near the School.
LONDON

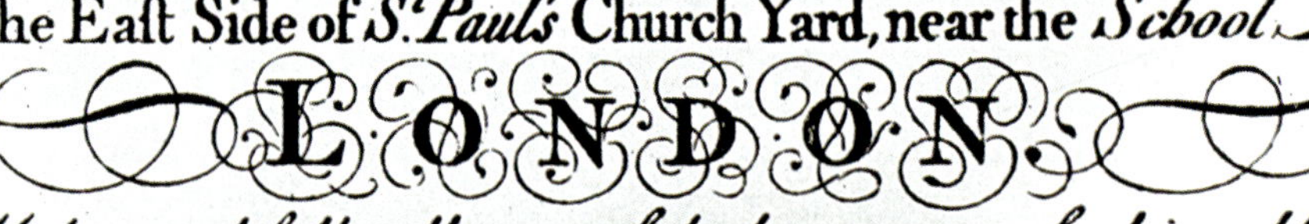

Makes and sells all sorts of the best & most fashionable
Chairs, either Cover'd, Matted, or Cand: Likewise all Sorts of
Cabinet-Work, with Sconces, Pier & Chimney-Glasses, Mohogany
and other Tables: Blinds for Windows made & Curiously
Painted on Canvas, Silk, or Wire: Where is good Choice, &
best painted of any in London, none excepted
N.B. Upholsters work of all Sorts neat & Cheap.

The earliest depiction of a painted screen was illustrated on John Brown's trade card. Many of his contemporaries offered similar wares. *Heal Collection of the British Museum.*

1987

"You see out, no one sees in." Screen owner Estelle Figinski at her home on Bank Street, near Patterson Park. *Erick Hoopes photograph, 1987.*

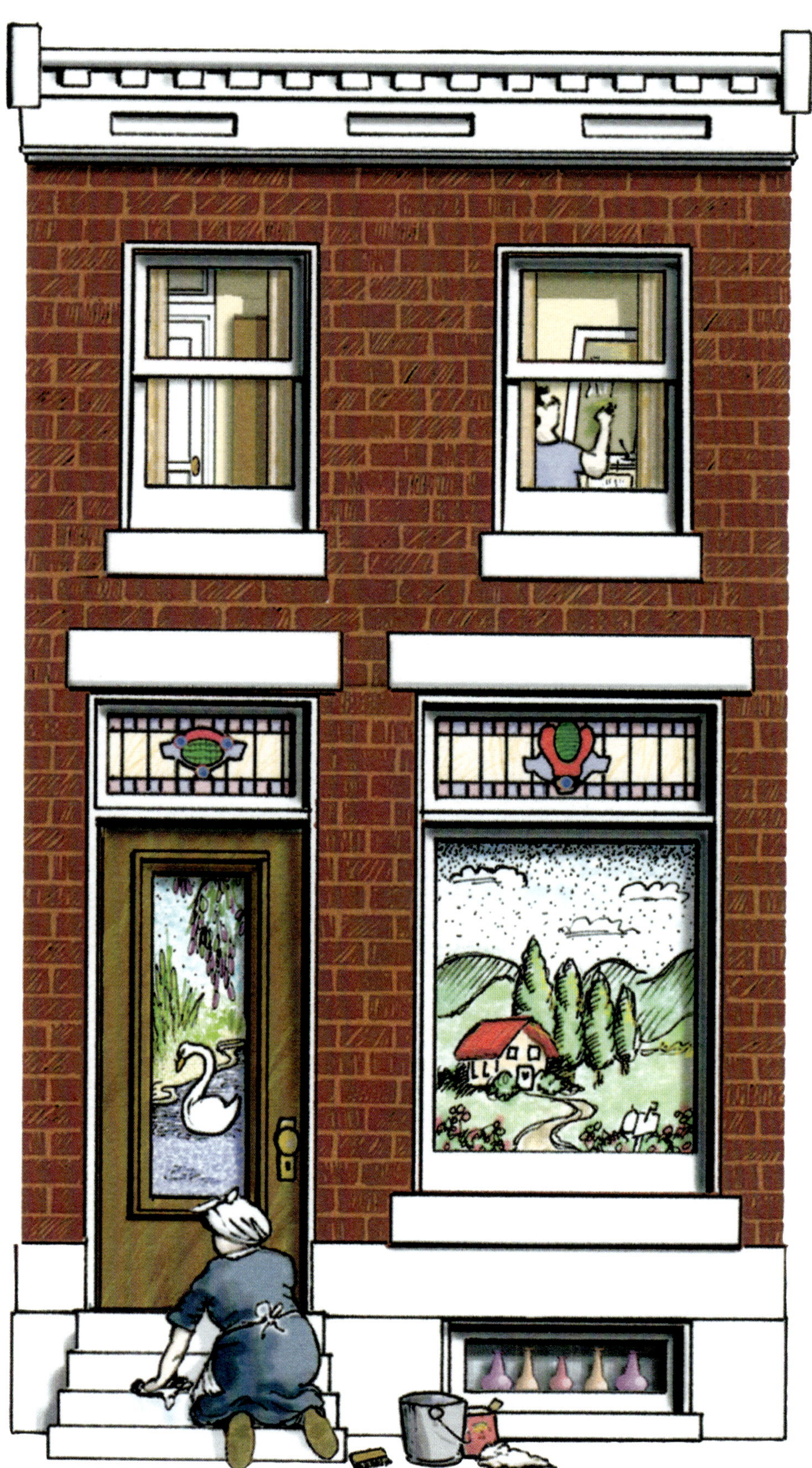

Illustration by Tim Goecke.

CONTENTS

■ SIDEBAR ■ HOW-TO

PAINTED SCREENS:
THE HOLE-Y ART OF BALTIMORE

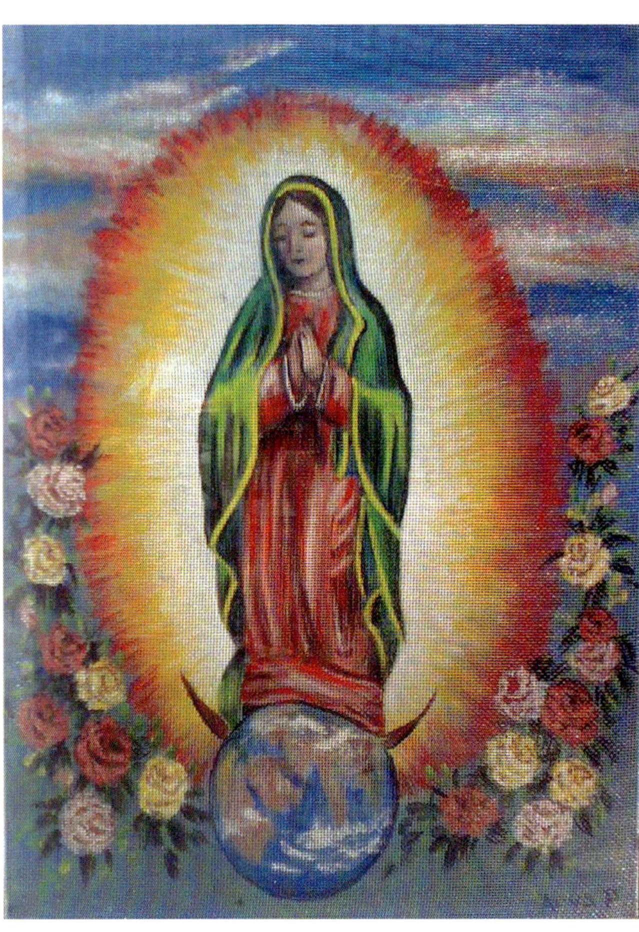

Our Lady of Guadalupe screen, painted by Anna Pasqualucci, 2012. *Courtesy of the artist.*

PAINTED SCREENS CONSTITUTE A HOLE-Y ART PRODUCED BY colorful pigments dancing on the edge of the void of each individual window and door screen mesh—to become, well, HOLY, in the best *Merriam-Webster On-line Dictionary* definition of the word, as in: "Exalted or worthy of complete devotion as one perfect in goodness and righteousness," to which I can only say a very sincere, "Amen."

If screen painting were to be classified as a kind of religion, surely Elaine Eff would constitute both its most ardent scribe and patron saint. No one is more wholeheartedly devoted to the gospel of paint on wire and to the bearers of the tradition. This book is the bible on the subject. Decades of meticulous research in effect provide a guide to enable us, and future generations, to carry on the faith. All we need to do is pick up the creative gauntlet laid down by this art's true first high priest, William Oktavec.

As a museum founder and director, I am aware of how few art forms are surrounded by such popular adoration, celebration, and sensory delight. I saw my first painted screens in Baltimore while walking hand-in-hand with my parents and big sister, on my sixth birthday, back in 1952. Only for the rare, very special family occasion did my parents leave their suburban home in Maryland's leafy Greenspring Valley for the nearly hour-long car trip to the city's East Baltimore neighborhoods, winding our way through blocks of tightly spaced red-brick rowhouses to our ultimate destination. Haussner's Restaurant was a dining Nirvana unlike any other, with its encyclopedic menu offering everything from alligator cutlets to sauerbraten and the unforgettable ten-inch-high fresh strawberry pie dessert. This eatery was itself a museum, far more fun than most, and absolutely chock full, floor to ceiling, with classical European art in gilded frames, marble statues, rare porcelains, the world's largest ball of string (incidentally made of bulk cloth napkin wraps provided by the restaurant's laundry), and a stag bar of voluptuous nudes off to one side that we children could only glimpse at the entry. The line to get into Haussner's would circle the otherwise residential blocks. Patient, eager, hungry families weathered cold and snow, heat and rain, just to get in. Haussner's took no reservations and the wait could be as long as two hours. So savvy families arrived long before the dinner hour to find good parking spaces and to walk among the rowhouse streets, taking in the locals' various devotions.

I was captivated by the variety of window arts. First the revered painted screens, which back then were a storied source of public pride—a unique, Baltimore-born, grassroots art phenomenon. The shrines were another constant. We were not Catholics, so the many parlor window displays in this mostly Eastern European immigrant neighborhood intrigued us. The colorful plaster Mother Marys stood in communing distance of crowned and cape-wearing boy Jesus gilded figurines that I later learned were Infant of Prague reproductions. Together they guaranteed a pretty darn exotic and fascinating visual feast. Many of these street facing window shrines were festooned with fabric and plastic flowers and year-round Christmas lights. They appeared as magical collections of fragile toys, lovingly put on display for all who passed by to see.

The neighborhood was immaculately clean and orderly with each house having the same rhythmic entry formed by three white marble steps, a brick façade, and a repeat pattern of windows, and yet the flash of the one-of-a-kind shrines and the brightly painted screens exalting country life gave expression to the beliefs and cultural values of the individuals who made up this city neighborhood.

It was incomprehensible to me that there was an art that could take a screen—a commodity we had in spades at our modest suburban rancher—and create an attraction that would stop an entire family in its tracks. This was duly noted, permanently engraved on my birthday-loving, young celebratory soul as part and parcel of those days of great shared family joy.

Flash forward to the 2004 expansion of our American Visionary Art Museum with its Visionary Village welcoming the public to our new Jim Rouse Visionary Center. We jumped at the chance to invest in constructing, with the expert help of Baltimore's last remaining Formstone craftsmen, a row of our own realistic brick and faux stone rowhouse façades to appropriately showcase the art of Baltimore's masters of screen painting. This dream, born on a childhood outing, was made real in collaboration with Elaine Eff and the Painted Screen Society (PSS) she had founded almost twenty years earlier.

In these past five decades, my love of visual wonders, both home-grown and naturally occurring, has increased exponentially. I especially adore the aesthetic revelations derived from observations in science and nature. I spent years poring over microscopic images and macro ones, too, sent back to earth from the Hubble telescope. Physicists, mystics, and philosophers have long contemplated this primal notion of the void. In fact, our visible material universe is built of atoms that are themselves composed primarily of holes (empty space), like the cosmos itself. Is it any surprise that an earthbound art form that surrounds voids to reveal its own beauty would arise from an immigrant's eye to practicality? And who would have imagined that a century ago and today painted screens would be on the forefront of green technologies, far ahead of the environmental movement? Such is the nature of things truly divine—that they keep revealing new layers of meaning and inspiration.

Rebecca Alban Hoffberger
Founder and Director, American Visionary Art Museum
Baltimore, Maryland
November 2012

ACKNOWLEDGMENTS

THIS BOOK REPAYS SOME LONG OUTSTANDING DEBTS. IF NOT FOR an initial query by my mother, Ann Goldberg, the history of screen art might be relegated to dog-eared articles in the vertical files of the Enoch Pratt Free Library. The first person who enthusiastically endorsed the need to chronicle the painters and their prodigious output was Ted Schuchat, a cub reporter for the *East Baltimore Guide* in the 1940s.[1] When we met, during the first stage of my investigations, he recognized a kindred spirit with a passion for local traditions, and I felt he was reading my mind when he told me, "You know, someone needs to research those painted screens." I was already on it, but his encouragement was crucial as the road took unexpected but fruitful detours: articles, a dissertation, films, exhibitions, and at long last this book.

Bruce Johnson was the first arts professional outside of Baltimore to recognize the screens' value. His support as the director of New York's (then) Museum of American Folk Art opened many doors and convinced me of the need for further exploration of this urban folk art *in situ* and the need to share the story with a larger audience. His enthusiasm was shared by Bert Hemphill, Kristina (Barbara) and Kookie Johnson, Robert Bishop, Gerard Wertkin, and Stacey Hollander of what is now the American Folk Art Museum.

My biggest regret is that this book will not grace the rowhouse coffee tables of so many proud and patient East Baltimoreans who lived through the exciting era when screen painters set up studios on their street corners. They shared invaluable observations with the inquisitive "screen lady," particularly during the 1970s and 1980s when my ambition rose, at best, to a modest research paper. Had these generous contributors survived, they would see themselves in these pages; though, walking today's streets, they might barely recognize their beloved neighborhoods.

This volume is an overdue gift to the denizens of Highlandtown, Canton, Fell's Point, Little Bohemia, and Little Italy. This is their art and their story. Local experts—my teachers—welcomed me to their community as early as 1974. First the Oktavecs—Richard, William Jr.,

Albert, Bernard, and John—and then other painters—Frank Deoms, Johnny Eck, Ben Richardson, Ted Richardson, Charles Bowman, Tom Lipka, Dee Herget, Frank Cipolloni, Leroy Bennett, Al Baldwin, Frank Abremski, James Trocki, Robin Eshelman, Ruth Chrysam Fahey, Greg Reillo, Darlene Grubb, Tilghman Hemsley, and Monica Broere. Along with their families, customers, and admirers, these artists embraced their native art form as a part of the annual cycle of life, the way they would welcome a seasonal visitor.

When I came to live in Highlandtown, Sandy Ewing McCollum and her fellow business owners Ron Borowy and Bill Scofield opened doors to the Merchants Association and to storekeepers and friends. We cracked crabs, drank National Boh at bull and oyster roasts, and marched in the I Am an American Day Parade. Richard Sause, Dorothy Barron, and Henry and Linda Smit provided homes that put me in the heart of screen country. The Baynes family of Kenwood Avenue— Barbara, Nelson, Kevin, Randy, and Lisa—showed me how the generations passed on their traditions in Canton, as did Lil Sims, who answered the Lipka family door each time I popped into town to ask one more question. Estelle Figinski, our "poster grandmother," was claimed by everyone and never tired of boasting about her home's exterior touches. In "Upper" Fell's Point, "Turkey Joe" and Sherry "Mrs. Rockefeller" Trabert shared their investigative spirit and many a meal as the wandering folklorist found herself at their doorstep precisely at their dinner hour. Bill Steinmetz took me back in time to his boyhood haunts in the "alphabet streets." Genevieve Donelson at the Abbott Center; Hannaleis Penner, Elaine Hall, Richard Orban, and Ottsie McJilton at the Hatton Center; and Margaret Majors, senior doyenne of Highlandtown, all provided the keys to the wisdom of the elders. *Baltimore Guide* editors Helen Przybylski, John Cain, and Jackie Watts shared archives that covered screen painting's every move. Captain Bill and Helen Phillips and my neighbors on the 700 block of South Ellwood Avenue deserve special thanks for enduring the presence of an inquisitive folklorist and her guests and press retinue for a decade. Gloria Aull, Bill Kelch, Steve Oney, Betty Piskor, Tom and Dolores Canoles, Pastor Lee Hudson of Messiah Lutheran Church, Tiny Postherer, Joe Poodles, Hillary Figinski, and beauty salon stylist and source Jackie Zajdel were among my Canton guides. Father Peter Lyons of St. Wenceslaus Church and his predecessors opened the doors many times to share the Oktavec handiwork in plain sight and well hidden. Chris Ryer, Amanda Smit, and Phyllis Yakim of Southeast Community Development Corporation, and Ellen Von Karajan of Fell's Point Preservation Society were always enthusiastic collaborators.

For sharing their recollections and scrapbooks over the decades, I owe much to the Oktavec family: Therese, David, Darla, Sarah, Chris, Charlotte, Mary, Pete, Ronnie, Bob, Joan, and Barbara and Bill Dewar. Thanks also to screen painters and their families: Rob Eckhardt; Rita Bennett; Mary, Frank D., Franny, and Gina Cipolloni; Jane Fahey Saunders and Farrell Fahey; Ramona and Anna Lipka, Julia Walther, and Lisa Weissner; Jerry Seaton and the family of Alonzo Parks; Gladys Richardson and Violet Felicio; Ginny Milstead, Vicki Edgerton, Edna Barney, and Ron McCulley; Veronika and Dolores Soul; as well as Carl Herget, John Iampieri, Catherine "Pat" Michalski, Anna Pasqualucci, Jacobus "Dutch" Philipoom, Jean Pula, Joseph Schlecter, Brenda Foehrkolb, and Tom Whittington. To those who are missing from this list, I regret the omission and hope that this book will lead to discovery of painters whose work escaped my research.

Eva Slezak provided invaluable research on the Czech community at the drop of a hat, on behalf of the Czech and Slovak Heritage Association of Maryland and the Enoch Pratt Free Library along with Jeffrey Korman, Linda Merican, and the Maryland Room staff. Mary Louise DeSarran of the Maryland Historical Trust Library and Simonna Simmons of UMBC's Albin O. Kuhn Library pulled research rabbits from hats.

Baltimore historians and curators Mary Ellen Hayward, Dean Krimmel, and Barry Kessler, formerly affiliated with Baltimore's regretta- bly vanished Peale and City Life Museums, and Tom Hollowak and Aidan Faust of the University of Baltimore's Langsdale Library and Baltimore City Archives, Nancy Davis and Eben Dennis of the Maryland Historical Society, Kathleen Kotarba and Eric Holcomb of the Commission for Historic and Architectural Preservation (CHAP), and Bill Pencek and Johns Hopkins of Baltimore Heritage. Frank Bittner, Wayne Schaumburg, Joseph Maguire and Francis O'Neill enthusiastically shared their epiphanies, time, and research over the decades. I count among my teachers the collectors and stewards of Baltimoreana Jeffrey Pratt Gordon, who cherishes all things Johnny Eck, and Jennifer Bodine, who has preserved the photographic legacy of her father, A. Aubrey Bodine. Lillian Bowers, Fred Schruefer, and Bob Ibex likewise made sure that Formstone would not soon be forgotten.

My academic debt is deep. It begins at the Cooperstown Graduate Programs and the New York State Historical Association, where I worked with Louis Jones, Agnes Halsey Jones, Minor Wine Thomas, Bruce Buckley, and C. R. Jones. My research continued in that region over the years with encouragement from Gail Andrews, Jack Braunlein, David Horvath, Connie Jones, Ellen White Weir, Richard Slavin, Ron and Wanda Burch, Catherine Raddatz, Gretchen Sorin, Paul D'Ambrosio, John Hart, and Ginny Reynolds. At the University of Pennsylvania, my research blossomed under the tutelage of Kenny Goldstein, Don Yoder, Barbara Kirshenblatt-Gimblett, Henry Glassie, and my Philadelphia classmates and family, Bonnie Blair, Malachi O'Connor, Maggie Holtzberg, Robert Blair St. George, LeeEllen Friedland, Rochelle, Diane, Rhoda, and Scott Goldstein, Nancy and James Glazer, Marylou and Frank Kavaler, and Dan and Harriet Berger. A Hagley-Winterthur fellowship in Arts and Industries allowed me to benefit from the wisdom of historian Roger Horowitz and curators Donald Fennimore, Wendy Cooper, Anne Verplanck, Charles Hummel, Linda Eaton, and librarians Neville Thompson, Cate Cooney, Jeanne Solensky, E. Richard McKinstry, Beatrice Taylor, and the resources of the Joseph Downs Collection.

Research institutions opened their doors before the digital world made it less necessary: Carl Nold at Historic New England (the Society for the Preservation of New England Antiquities); the Philadelphia Athenaeum; Anita Wright, Carolyn Ibbotson, and Mindy Leisenring at the Cortland County (New York) Historical Society; Sean Cummins at Cortland's 1890 House and Museum; William Ryan of Cayuga Lake National Bank; Sheila Edmunds and Judy Furness in Aurora, New York; John Dumville of the Vermont Division for Historic Preservation; Andersen Thorp, Gwenda Smith, and Sue Cain of the Friends of Justin Morrill Homestead; Marjorie Carr, at the Historical Society Museum and the Enfield (New Hampshire) Public Library; Millicent Library, Fairhaven (Massachusetts); Peabody Essex Museum, Salem (Massachusetts); Nahant (Massachusetts) Historical Society; and David Lintz at the Red Men Museum.

In Germany, Wilhelm Bleicher; in Sweden, Barbaro Klein, Elisabet Hidemark of Nordiskemuseet, and Hannes Carlsson, Thomas Nilsson and Ulla Tortenson in Gusum, James Ayres in Britain and Denise Kozikowski, Ondrej Simon, Jana Kopelentova Rehak, and Thomas Canavan and Tomas Prchlik in Czechoslovakia offered on-site investigations.

In Louisiana's Cajun country, folklorists Maida Owens, Carolyn Ware, and Carl Lindahl facilitated memorable visits with Mardi Gras mask makers Allen and Georgie Manuel, Russell "Potic" Rider, and J. B. LeBlue and family.

At the Baltimore Museum of Art, Brenda Richardson, Robert Zimmerman, Kate Sellers Markert, Dan Sellers, Duane Suter, Randi Ash, Faith Holland, Martha Parkhurst, Ann Boyce Harper, Karen Neilsen, and Melanie Harwood helped further research and planning for an unrealized exhibition and catalog that formed the basis of my doctoral dissertation; helpful also were Dennis Zambala and Anne Steele at the Baltimore Museum of Industry. The many-hatted George Ciscle, now curator-in-residence at Maryland Institute College of Art (MICA), has been a consummate advisor since our collaborations alongside Lisa Corrin and Jed Dodds at The Contemporary. Jody Albright, Bill Gilmore, Randi Vega, Roz Healy, and Andrea Vernot at the Baltimore Office of Promotion and the Arts, formerly the Mayor's Advisory Council on Art and Culture offered support. Megan Hamilton and Margaret Footner at the Creative Alliance at The Patterson have always been game to honor and celebrate hometown arts. The American Visionary Art Museum's (AVAM) Rebecca Hoffberger found a way to share the vision of William Oktavec's "outside" (i.e., found on the exteriors), not Outsider (the name applied to non-mainstream artists), art with a wider public. Her staff, Marcia Semmes, Mark Ward, Donna Katrinic, Katie Adams, and Ted Frankel of Sideshow, made us welcome. John Turner of the San Francisco Craft and Folk Art Museum and Sarah Leavitt of the National Building Museum in Washington, D.C., helped introduce the screens to wider audiences.

In Baltimore, many people made this work possible over three decades. Even screens have a political constituency: Senator Barbara Mikulski, former mayor and governor William Donald Schaefer, Mark Wasserman, Anthony Pompa, Marion Pines, state senators American Joe Miedusiewski and Perry Sfikas, delegates Donald and Peter Hammen, Carolyn Krysiak, and Councilman (aka Canton historian and *Baltimore Guide* editor) John Cain.

Steve Ziger, David Naill of Ziger/Snead Architects and Roland Hill of Contra Vision, Rob Ivers, Liam Tomlinson of Van Wagner, J. David Carduff of GKD, and Louis M. Brill helped bring screens as signage into the twenty-first century while Calvin Hill and George Berkner of Gila River Products, Roger Wright of Rensselaer Polytechnic Institute, Marc Murray of the Wire Association International, and Stephan McCandliss of the Johns Hopkins University Applied Physics Laboratory simplified technical mysteries.

Kelly Morais Abramson, Ruth "Posey" Pincoffs Boicourt, and Ann and Milton Goldberg took time as sidewalk surveyors to conduct an annual census. My sister, Jo-ann Stadtmauer, pitched in whenever she came home. Photographers Edwin Remsberg, Christine Lundquist Fillat, Bill McAllen, Jim Burger, Lisa Mason-Chaney, Steven Mroczek, Jacqueline

(Farlow) Conderacci, and Ainsley Buckner had cameras ready, and Robert Cronan helped with early illustrations. Bill Thompson, Jaimes Mayhew, and Ali Seley helped with organization and digitization, and Xiaotian Yang tended to myriad details. Ulrika Leander and Peter Von Pawel translated exotic texts. Jane Selden turned hand-scrawled charts into the ultimate screen painters' genealogy. Peter Morin and Andrew Todd kept the computers running.

Editor Kim Carlin heroically wrestled the manuscript into a coherent form. Readers who teased out early pieces include Trish Thomas, Eric Collum, Roz Tunis, Pravina Shukla, Mary Yakush, Marcia Semmes, Mary Ellen Hayward, Dean Krimmel, Cindy Byrd, John H. Lawrence, Eugenie Nable, and John Fairhall. Barry Kessler stepped in miraculously at the eleventh hour to fill illusive blanks. I am especially grateful to Jeff Todd Titon for steering me to Craig Gill at the University Press of Mississippi and his assistant, Katie Keene. A grant from the Mellon Foundation to the American Folklore Society made it possible for a first-time author like me to make good through the support of the Folklore Studies in a Multi-Cultural World initiative, managed by Laurie Matheson with Judy McCulloh of the University of Illinois Press and Sheila Leary of the University Wisconsin Press. Designer Kristen Spilman's vision elevated this volume from an idea to a work of art.

Without the good humor of friends and colleagues who played supporting roles in visible and invisible ways over the decades, this book would neither have been begun nor completed. Assistance in many forms came from Elroy Quenroe, Gil Ravenal and Frances Smythe, Louise Harper, Barry Brown, Lynn Goldsmith, Lee Morais, Luki Morin, Zena and Arnie Lerman, Joanie Boughner, Gil Anderson, Susan Russell, Maureen "Mo" and Bill Jones, Margo Downing, Bonny Wolf, Susan Magsamen, Cynthia Saunders, Nancy Forgione, Michael Hill, and Howard Stevens. Marilyn, Keith and Ted of Rehoboth's Back Porch and Nick Georgolas, Joyce Snyder, Lois Kasaberis, and Tammy Gunther Posluszny of Samos Restaurant gave me months of encouragement and sustenance on the patio and at the counter as I nursed early drafts on paper.

Dan Ward, Jim Hardin, Richard Chisolm, Alix Litwack, Penny Trams, Stephanie Shapiro, Michael Wentzel, Alex Castro, David Dudley, and John Lewis championed the cause in film and print. Colleagues Rory Turner, Bill Ferris, Roger Welsch, George Carey, Agnes Jones, Dell Upton, Orlando Ridout V, Chuck and Nancy Purdue, Marjorie Hunt, Jane Beck, Marsha MacDowell, Kurt Dewhurst, Ed Orser, Nicole King, Kathy O'Dell, William Woys Weaver, Roger Moss, Allan and Karen Jabbour, Steve Zeitlin, Molly Garfinkel, and Ladies Aid Society sisters Amy Skillman, Peggy Bulger, and Rita Moonsammy contributed in countless ways.

My research was enabled through the generosity of the Rockefeller Foundation, National Endowment for the Arts, the Baltimore City Foundation, Hagley-Winterthur Fellowship in Arts and Industries, Baltimore Office of Promotion and the Arts' Community Arts Program, Lois and Philip Macht Family Philanthropic Fund of the Associated Jewish Community Federation of Baltimore, Maryland Humanities Council, Maryland State Arts Council, and Preservation Maryland Heritage Fund.

At the Maryland State Arts Council, I owe much to my most able successor, folklorist Cliff Murphy, for knowing it was time for me to leave Maryland Traditions in his capable hands and to executive director Theresa Colvin for reminding me that "others could run a folklore program, but only you can write this book." If not for my husband, John Fairhall, who made good on his promise of time and space, the story of painted screens would never have seen the light of day.

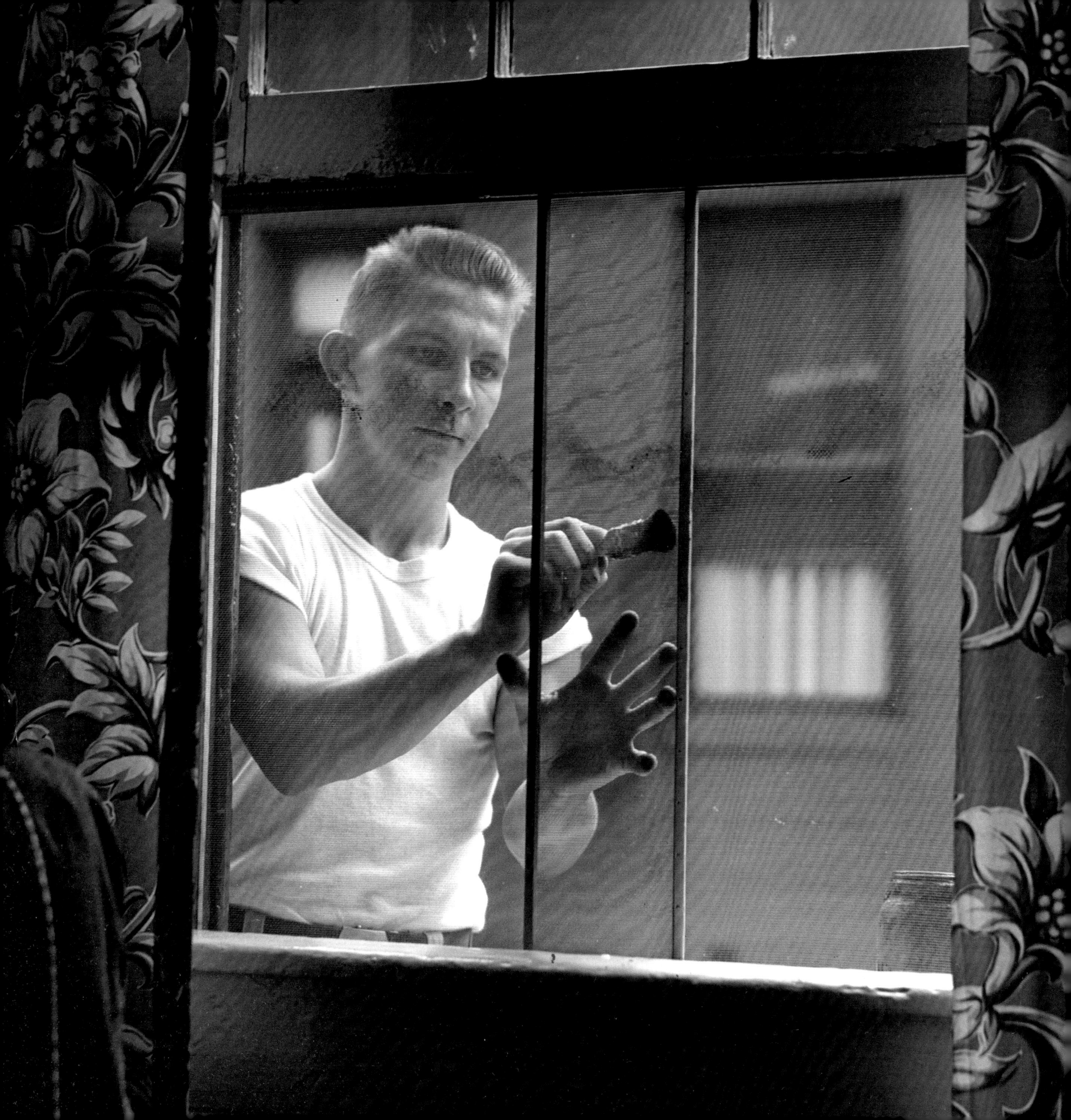

INTRODUCTION

When is a window screen more
than a piece of utilitarian hardware?

When it is also a work of art.

FOR MOST OF THE TWENTIETH CENTURY, VIVID PAINTINGS HAVE ADORNED window and door screens in Baltimore's rowhouse neighborhoods. In no other place would a walk down any random street cause passersby to wonder how they had stumbled into an outdoor art gallery. Only in Baltimore is an enticement to enjoy bright landscapes on woven wire window screens simultaneously an invitation and an act of exclusion. The beloved homegrown art form known as "painted screens" was a twentieth-century commonplace found only in this one American city. Painted screens are a gift to the streets. The art is free for the taking, but the show stops there. From inside, the screen is unadorned, the view to the street unobstructed. From the outside, all that's visible is the artwork. The privacy of rowhouse denizens is guarded by the artists' handiwork. Painted screens are one community's way of saying, "Enjoy the view, but keep moving."

While Baltimore has been the sole preserve of this folk art expression in recent history, a kindred decorative art enjoyed popularity beginning two centuries earlier in London. Both traditions are rooted in the availability of wire and woven cloth, artists' inclination to embellish any surface, and the need for privacy among homeowners and businesses. The early art form found favor in England, Europe, and Victorian America then seemed to vanish, only to be "invented" anew by William Oktavec (pronounced Ahk-tuh-vek, emphasis on the first syllable), a grocer in Baltimore's Little Bohemia neighborhood who claimed to be unaware of any precedent.[2]

OPPOSITE

Tom Lipka, when a senior at Patterson Park High School, painted directly on the slider screen in the window of his family's South Kenwood Avenue home. *Hans Marx photograph, August 9, 1953. Reprinted with permission of the Baltimore Sun Media Group. All rights reserved.*

This volume examines two threads in the history of painted screens. The narrative of this book is a multitextured warp and weft, moving back and forth between the past and the present; between a popular folk expression of Baltimore and decorative landscape-painted wire cloth found in other cities in America and abroad; between fabrication techniques first of wire then of new-age materials. It is related in two voices—the colloquial speech of the people and the facts and observations of the folklore scholar.

Though the historic and the Baltimore versions of painted screens are linked by similar materials, function, and technique, they exist as distinct expressions among different geographic and socioeconomic milieus. Similarly, late-twentieth-century inventions adapt the concept of one-way optics, applying modern materials and technology to new surfaces. Buildings, vehicles, transit and tour buses, scaffold covers for construction projects, and advertising media remind us how little is new, how a good idea survives over time, and how art forms evolve to keep up with advances in media and the demands of the marketplace. It also suggests that the one-way scrim applied to transparent surfaces is an example of polygenesis, the same idea emerging independently in multiple times and venues.

Variously known as painted blinds, landscape screens, painted screens, and more recently seen as patterned frit glass for window walls, billboards, or window graphics, the many approaches to transparency and one-way surfaces offer a surprising enhancement to everyday life and a glimpse into the creative spirit.

In Baltimore, painted screens are iconic. We have claimed them as our own for a century, in times of plenty and in times of scarcity. From a single screen that started the trend in 1913 to the glory days when tens of thousands of similarly themed scenes dazzled rowhouse windows and doors, they have sent a vibrant message of neighborliness to strangers and friends alike. What few people know, however, is that painted screens share a long and fascinating lineage abroad and in America.

In large part, the surprising associations of landscape painted screens' roots in eighteenth-century England and Victorian Europe and America parallel my own discoveries. Unearthing an early example led me right back to Baltimore and ultimately to this book. Since their twentieth-century Baltimore debut, painted screens have ridden a rollercoaster of appreciation and disdain. Beloved or reviled, they have been embraced by the city's urban rowhouse dwellers as surely as the sidewalk runs alongside the front window. I caught up to them at a time when they were recoiling from the tug of war between window air conditioners and the arrival of vinyl as the newest must-have material for replacement windows and door frames.

Painted screens are my Rosebud. I literally stumbled over them enough times that I could not help but submit to them. I never imagined I might stake my career on learning their story and sharing it with a larger audience.

My journey began when I left for graduate school, detouring from a career in law to study folk art in Cooperstown, New York. As the door to the Volkswagen van containing all my worldly possessions slid shut in a suburban Baltimore driveway, my mother queried, "Folk art? Is that like the painted screens of Baltimore?" I shrugged my shoulders, climbed behind the wheel, and headed north. Hours later I was enjoying a welcome beverage in the parlor of Louis Jones, the gentleman scholar who would become my mentor in folk art. He registered delight that a Baltimorean was sitting before him, one who might finally address his questions about that city's famed painted screens. Barely three weeks later I was toiling in the basement art storage collections of the New York State Historical Association. My job was to separate paintings from their frames, the curatorial vogue at the time. I spied a pair of misplaced artifacts. What were aged wood-framed window screens doing among the artworks? As I tilted the surface to catch the light, I noticed faded monochromatic landscape scenes on the finely woven mesh.

The catalog cards revealed that I had unearthed two late-nineteenth-century landscape screens from nearby Fort Plain, New York—no artist, no provenance. Spinning origin theories in my head—same form, earlier time, different place—I hopped into my less-than-trusty VW van and headed back down the highway, straight to northeast Baltimore and the Oktavec Art Shop, established 1922. This was in the autumn of 1974—the first of many miles in a journey that would bring people, place, and tradition in closer focus through a single creative object native to my hometown.

The research for this book was indeed more than half the fun. Meeting the screen painters, one by one, was like peeling and savoring the history embedded in the layers of wallpaper, paint, and paneling in a city rowhouse, each one more vividly patterned and unanticipated than the next. And around every corner I found an outdoor museum whose creator or curator lived just behind each street-front gallery.

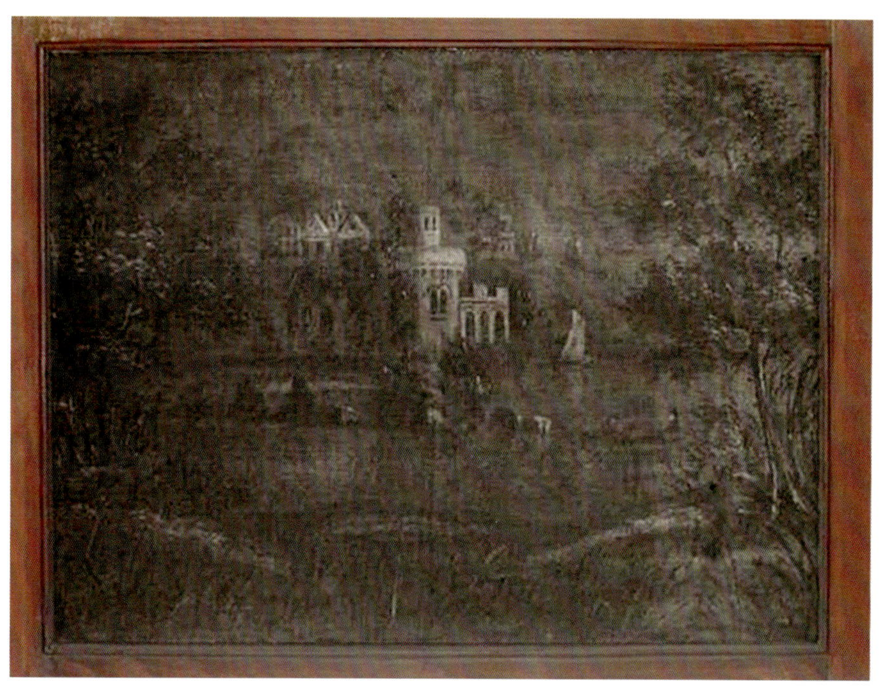

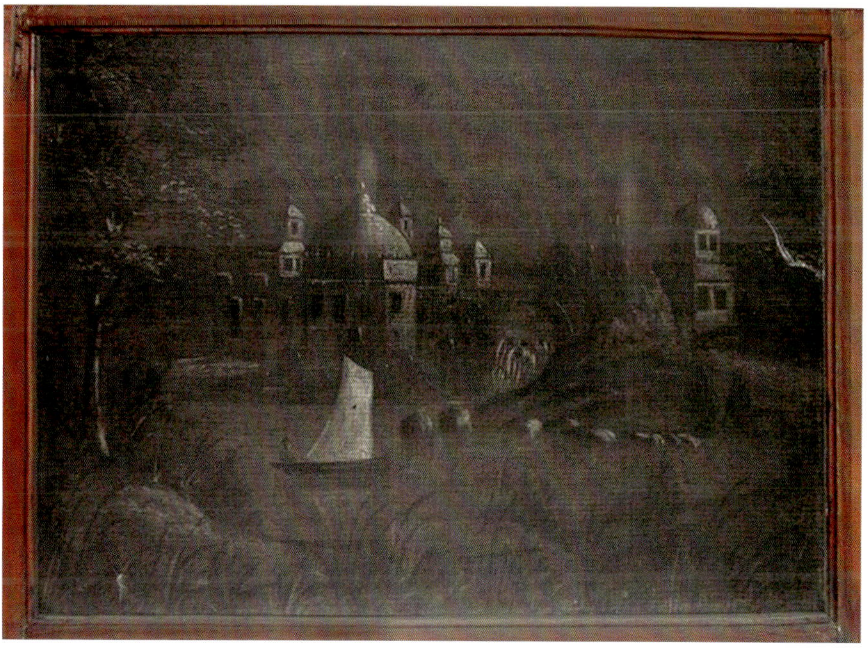

A pair of fine-meshed, late-nineteenth-century, monochromatic landscape screens from a stately home in Fort Plain, New York, after 1875. *Collection of the New York State Historical Association, Cooperstown.*

When screens came into my life that first year, they were very much a part of the urban fabric of daily life in Baltimore. From the eastern reaches of the county line at Dundalk to Morrell Park in the west, from Little Bohemia in the north to the harbor in the south, attached homes' eyes on the world were covered in vibrant landscapes. Classified ads in daily and weekly papers, flyers, and hardware store window displays offered an array of artists from whom to choose.

My search was interrupted by stints in Philadelphia pursuing a doctorate in folklore and a mission to the Smithsonian's Renwick Gallery to unearth a world of folk art stored in dark cubbies and basements of the "nation's attic." While I was investigating other peoples' art for a major exhibition, the news came that Richard Oktavec, tradition bearer of screen painting's first family, had died, leaving a fifteen-year-old son at home and unfinished work on his easel. I realized at that moment, six years into my career as a folklorist, that other people's exhibitions could be done by others, but Baltimore's painters and screens needed a chronicler before another generation perished.

It could not have been a better time to go home. In 1980 the city's inferiority complex was lifting with the shared excitement of the gleaming new Harborplace, the festival marketplace created by local visionary James Rouse on the previously invisible working waterfront. Pride of place was being restored by a mayor who wanted everyone to love Baltimore. As the city's number-one booster, William Donald Schaefer valued people, neighborhoods, creative solutions, and getting the job done. Screens and opportunities to showcase them and their makers figured on his list.

A year of dedicated fieldwork sponsored by the Baltimore Museum of Art allowed me to search for screens and named painters on two fronts—Baltimore in real time and the rest of the world in previous centuries. At home, all I needed to do was peer at a window and obliging neighbors proudly shared all they knew about these objects of mutual affection. Women of a certain age would tell you exactly who painted their screens or, at minimum, where he worked, what equipment he carried, and how he dressed. The men would relate vivid stories of sidewalk artists going house to house, street to street, on foot or by car, painting every door and window screen, front and back, for the mere price of a growler of beer. All agreed, "They used to be everywhere. Everyone had them."

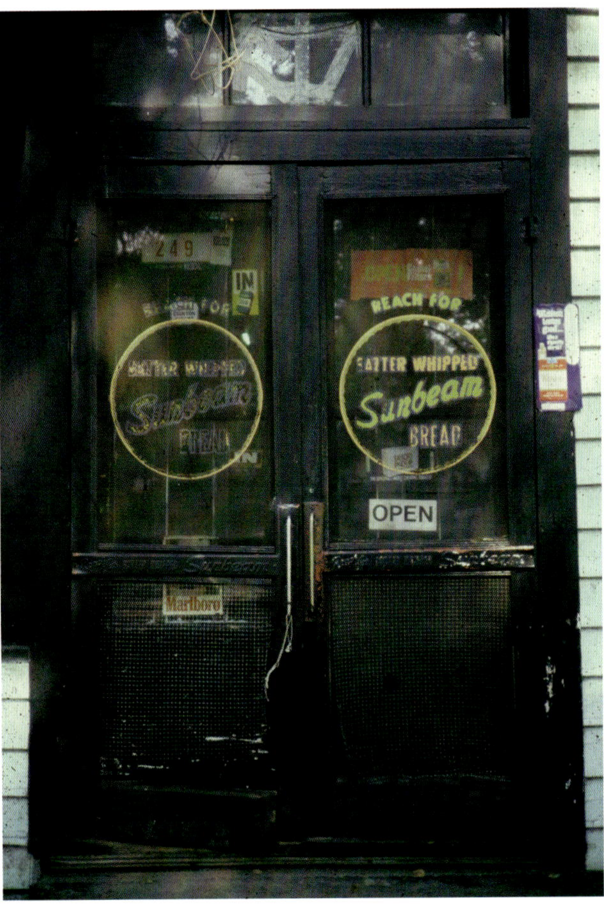

Painted signs like this Sunbeam Bread advertisement on the door of Thomas' Grocery in Savannah, Georgia, could be found on screen doors of country stores and urban markets nationwide well into the 1960s. The more durable rubberized decals that replaced them lacked both the craftsmanship and the benefits of ventilation of the painted screens. *Author photograph, 1981.*

By all accounts, a painting on wire should be an ephemeral work of art. And in many locations this would be the case. "How long do they last?" is the most frequently asked question. If well executed, the painting might outlive the screen itself. Cars became ubiquitous but their exhaust was not corrosive enough to cause serious damage, except on bus and truck routes where fumes caused considerable damage if screens were not cared for properly—removed, cleaned, stored, and replaced seasonally.

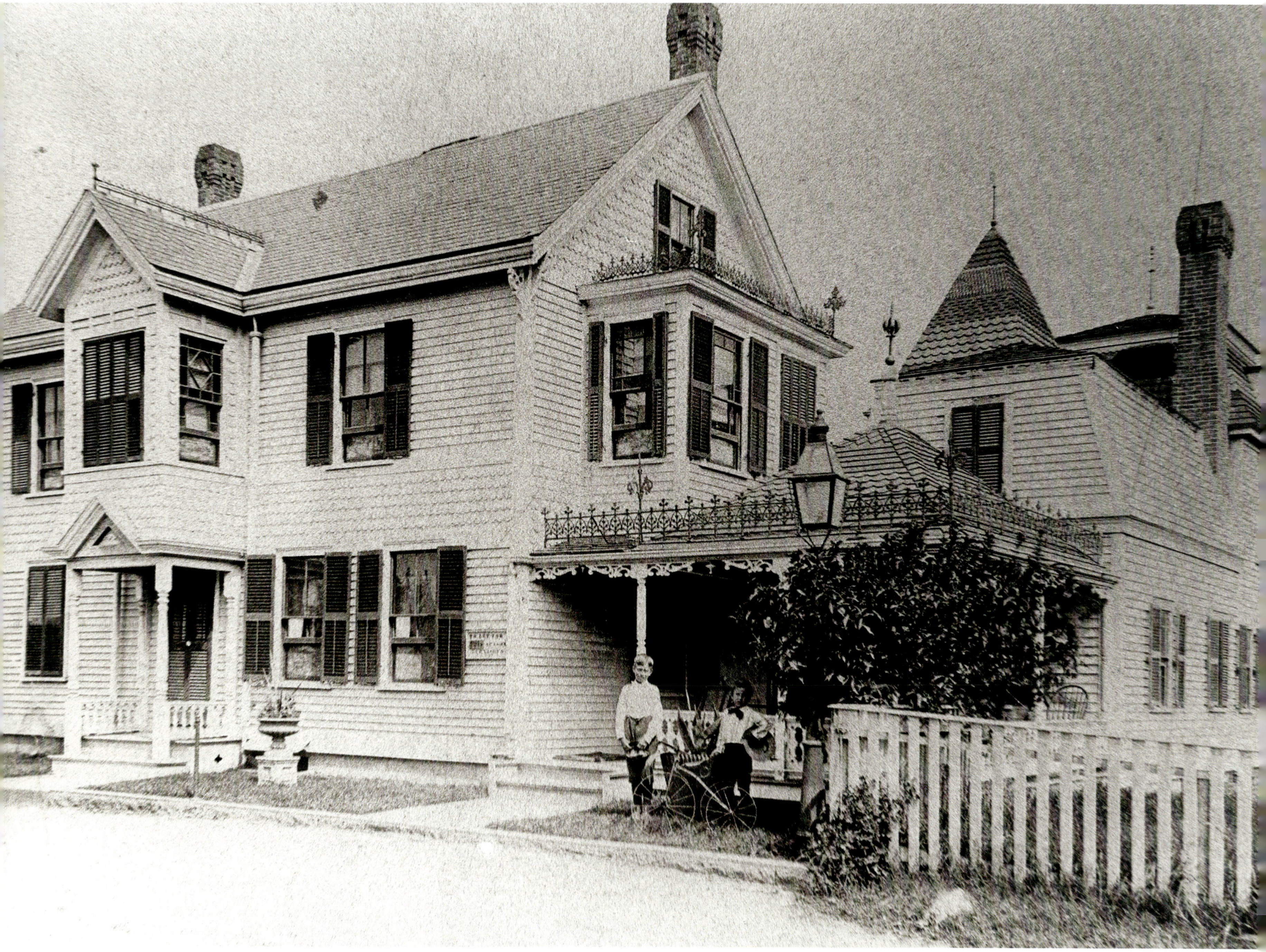

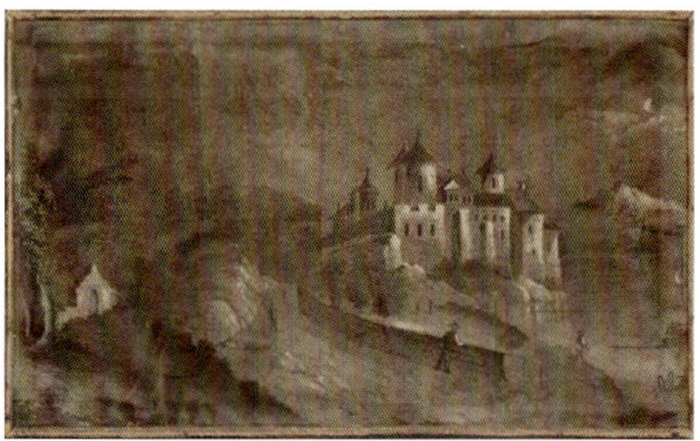

Haywood House or Cerro Gordo, as it was known in its Victorian era glory days, was a seaside boardinghouse in southern New Hampshire's New Castle-by-the-Sea, circa 1890. Landscape painted half screens, including the one to the left, were installed on every window to enhance guests' privacy.
Courtesy Douglas R. and Geraldine H. Woodward.

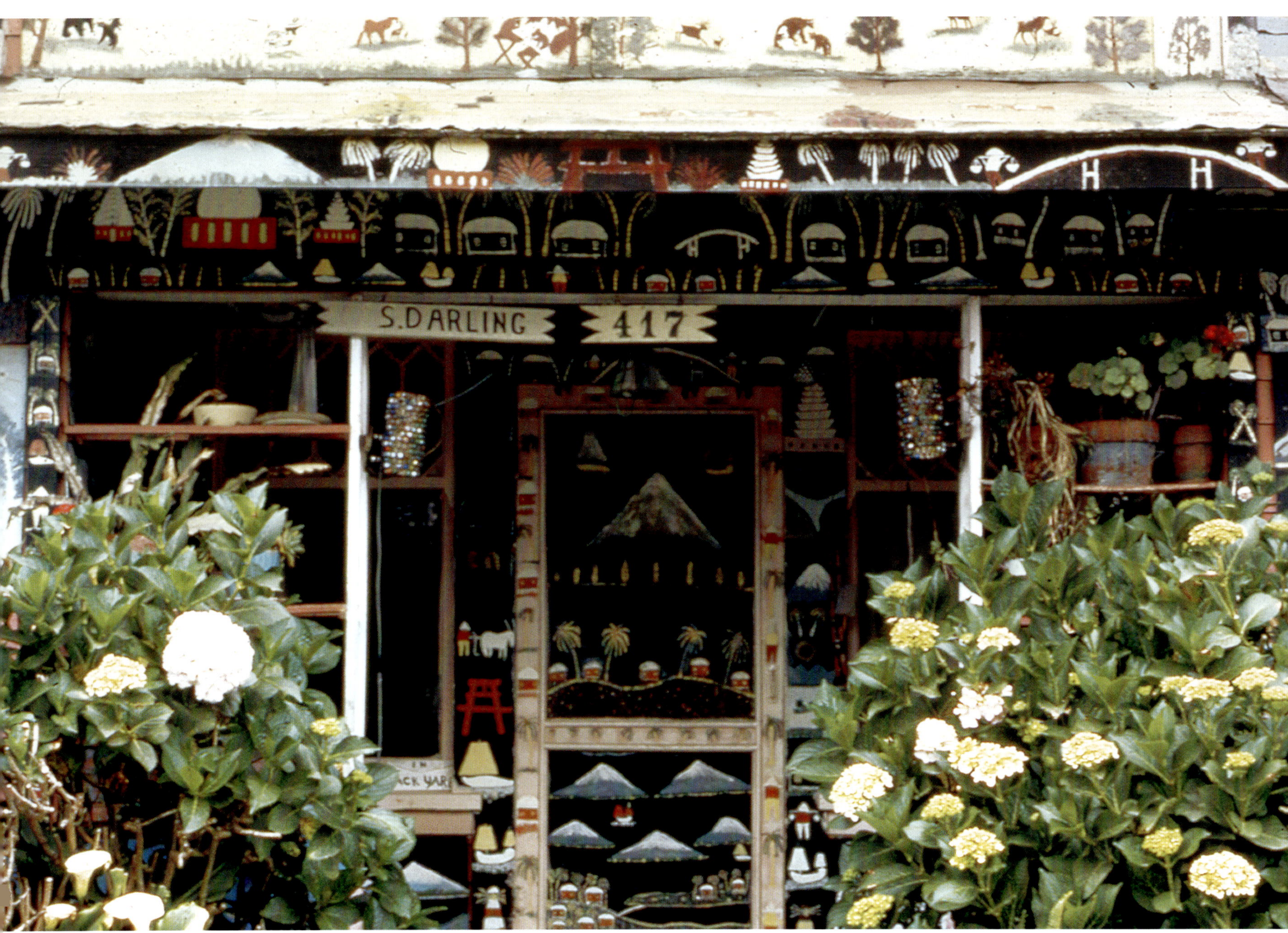

Nothing was spared when Sanford "Sam" Darling painted every surface of his Santa Barbara, California, bungalow, with scenes recalled from his travels by tramp steamer. *Courtesy Michael E. Bell and John Turner, 1978.*

Efforts to track down painted screens farther afield took me throughout the United States. The weather may be hot and humid in Baltimore, but it was not as oppressive as in the Deep South where the heat and humidity tended to destroy the wire. In Charleston, Savannah, and New Orleans, the trail grew colder as the temperature and moisture soared and it became painfully clear that landscape screens did not survive southern summers. No amount of probing turned up any survivals other than the famously flapping mid-twentieth-century rusted screen doors of country stores and corner groceries. They held on longest to the highly visible bread and soda ads supplied by distributors and hinged to well-trafficked, well-worn entrances.

A strategically placed advertisement in New England's revered *Yankee* magazine yielded a bonanza of memories and surviving screens in cities, villages, and remote rural areas. I tracked down every one—and was stunned by each nineteenth-century monochromatic landscape screen I saw and touched. The fragile, finely woven wire cloth was as alluring as the depictions of sturdy castles, fortresses, and bridges with lakes and strolling couples—no two identical, but remarkably similar (*See APPENDIX B, Recollections of Screens Past, page 231*).

The original windows of a stunning Victorian brownstone residence in Charlestown, Massachusetts, now an attorney's office, still held their solid mahogany-framed landscape screens.[3] An elderly woman conjured up World War I memories of "the times I would go to the 17th of June Parades in [Charlestown] on Bunker Hill Street. As I walked along the sidewalk the houses flush with the street would have windows at eye level and I remember the screens with painted scenes on them."[4]

Haywood House, or Cerro Gordo was a seaside boardinghouse in southern New Hampshire's Victorian playground, New Castle-by-the-Sea. Over the years, the simple vernacular one-story guest house was transformed by a riot of additions, porches, and bays, and walnut-framed painted screens were a fixture on every window. They not only protected the guests from prying eyes, but allowed ocean breezes into every room and kept pesky insects out.[5] Several landscape screens were salvaged from first-floor medical offices in Connecticut, and one from circa 1915, Springfield, Massachusetts, featured a life-like "short haired dog…a little like the RCA Victor dog…in a seated position and looking out toward the street."[6]

Throughout the country, random examples of more recent vintage were brought to my attention. Sanford "Sam" Darling, an eccentric homeowner, attached his paintings of exotic locales to the house's walls and continued to paint every exterior surface of his Santa Barbara, California, bungalow—screens included. On the East Coast, everyone who traveled the seaside route seemed to know the house in Beverly, Massachusetts, with primitive painted screens and the nearby Youngman mansion in Manchester, now a private school, that still had its monochromatic landscape screens intact.

By the time I took to the streets of Baltimore to trace the routes of the city's rowhouse Rembrandts and tease out their identities and signature works, screens were on another of their cyclical downturns. Old-timers had put away their brushes and paints, certain their days of plenty had passed. Senior center habitués offered up names of once-anonymous artists of prodigious output. Vivid descriptions of a harmonica-playing itinerant filled in blanks and linked at least one longtime painter to his unknown mentor. The attention brought several painters out of retirement and a resurgence of the local art was afoot.

One by one the artists and their patrons shared their stories and their secrets, carrying on the lineage directly from William Oktavec to his neighbors and sons and imitators to his grandson, John, who is still active today. John Oktavec is as likely to complete a commission for a scene of an imagined cosmos for a beauty salon door in gentrified Canton as he is to render his own version of his grandfather's time-tested red bungalow for a neighbor. He might be found at an art fair alongside Anna Pasqualucci, a committed screen painter for the twenty-first century who cherishes her chosen art form's past as dearly as she anticipates its future.

The screen painters of Baltimore fashioned their legacy from paint on wire. The next generation will carry on in the medium of its day with subjects it deems apropos. The urge to create is ever present. Standards of beauty are always in flux. The rowhouses of Baltimore are here to stay. Likewise, painted screens go back a long way. Their story begins here.

PAINTED SCREENS OF BALTIMORE

HISTORIC & CONTEMPORARY SITES

This map shares sites and landmarks associated with screen painting primarily throughout East Baltimore. Some are historic. Others are contemporary. Together they tell the story of 100 years of painted screens.

LITTLE BOHEMIA / MIDDLE EAST

1. Oktavec Grocery & home, 847 N Collington
2. St. Wenceslaus, Ashland & N Collington
3. St. Wenceslaus School (now MICAPlace)
4. Slavie Savings & Loan, N Collington & Madison
5. Northeast Market
6. Oktavec Art Shop, 2409 E Monument
7. Johnny Eck home/future museum, 622 N Milton
8. Ruth Chrysam (Fahey) home, 141 N Montford
9. Joe Sconga home, 801 N Chester
10. Frank Deoms home, 2426 Ashland
11. William Oktavec home, 906 N Luzerne
12. Al Oktavec home, 611 N Luzerne
13. Richard & John Oktavec home, 613 N Glover
14. Ted Richardson home, 526 N Potomac
15. Leroy Bennett home, 535 N Potomac

HIGHLANDTOWN

16. Frank Abremski home, 136 N Ellwood
17. St. Elizabeth of Hungary
18. Pagoda
19. St. Michael's Catholic Ukrainian
20. Patterson Theater, 400 block S East Ave, Eastern Ave. 2nd floor windows
21. Haussner's Restaurant
22. Monica Broere studio, 422 S Highland
23. Our Lady of Pompei
24. Southeast Anchor Library
25. Highlandtown Healthy Living Center
26. Sacred Heart of Jesus
27. National Brewery

CANTON

28. Former Beeche's Tavern, Elliott at S Clinton
29. Kozmic Scizzors, 1200 S Clinton
30. Elliott Street
31. Enoch Pratt Free Library, Canton Branch
32. O'Donnell Square
33. Alonzo Parks home, 933 S Linwood
34. Hatton Senior Center
35. Betty Piskor home, 2903 Fait Ave
36. Lil Sims / Lipka Family home, 832 S Kenwood
37. St. Casimir Catholic

FELLS POINT

38. Boston Street
39. Ted Richardson shop
40. Holy Rosary
41. Charles Bowman home & studio / Darlene Grubb studio / 1813–15 Fleet
42. "Lady Day Way," 200 block S Durham
43. St. Stanislaus Kostka
44. Thames Street
45. Broadway Market

LITTLE ITALY

46. St. Leo's
47. Frank Cipolloni home, 239 S Albemarle
48. Bocce courts

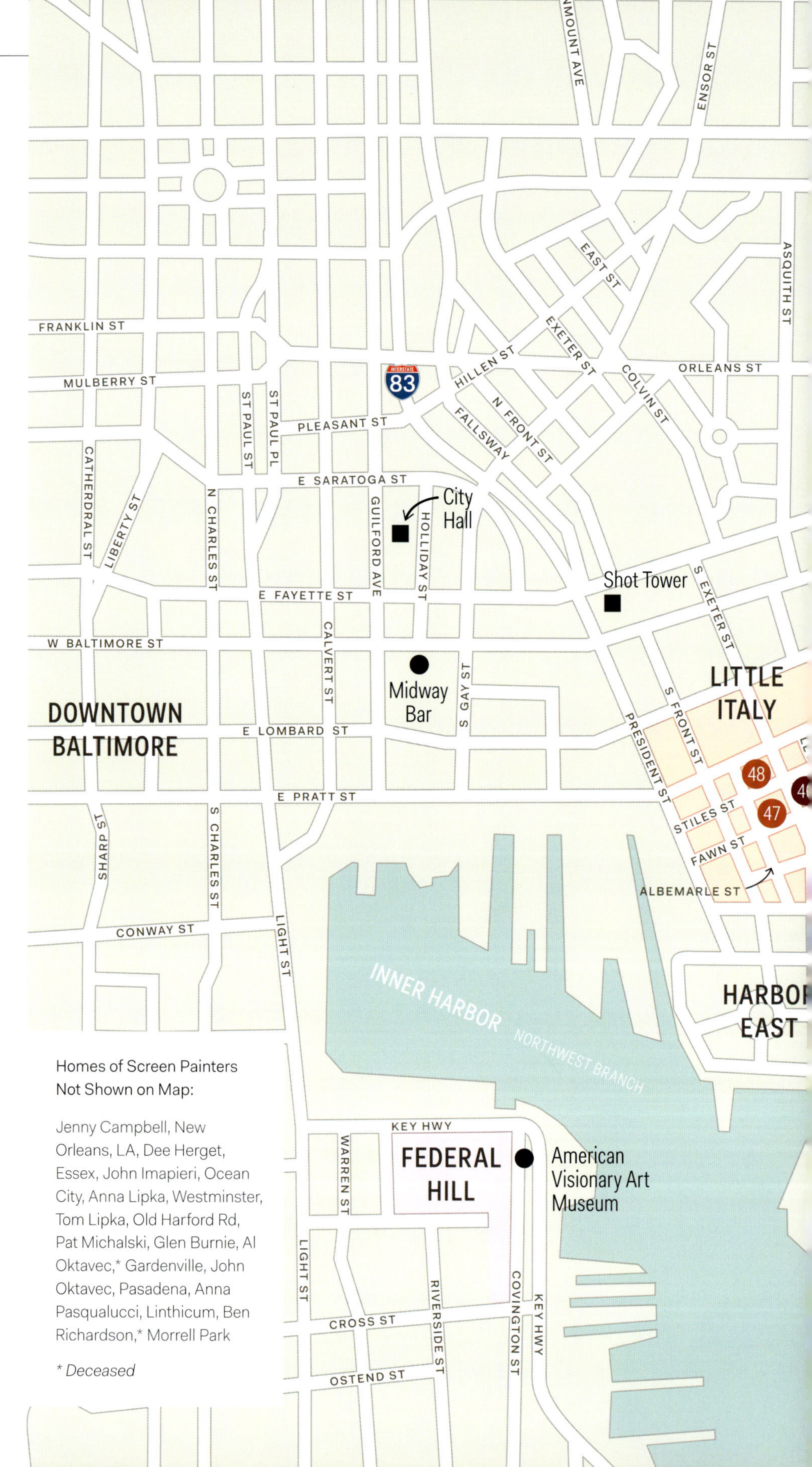

Homes of Screen Painters Not Shown on Map:

Jenny Campbell, New Orleans, LA, Dee Herget, Essex, John Imapieri, Ocean City, Anna Lipka, Westminster, Tom Lipka, Old Harford Rd, Pat Michalski, Glen Burnie, Al Oktavec,* Gardenville, John Oktavec, Pasadena, Anna Pasqualucci, Linthicum, Ben Richardson,* Morrell Park

* Deceased

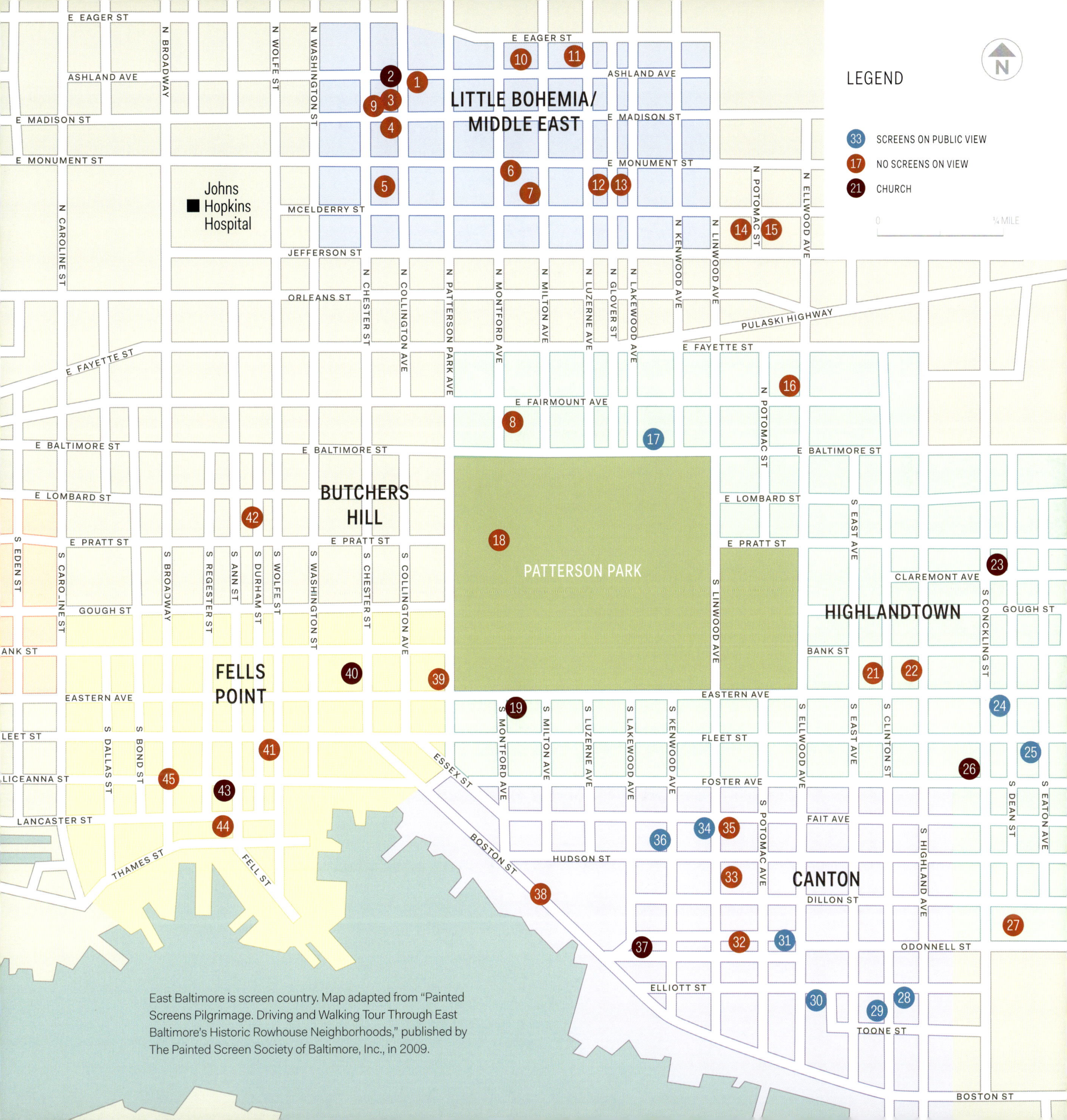

East Baltimore is screen country. Map adapted from "Painted Screens Pilgrimage. Driving and Walking Tour Through East Baltimore's Historic Rowhouse Neighborhoods," published by The Painted Screen Society of Baltimore, Inc., in 2009.

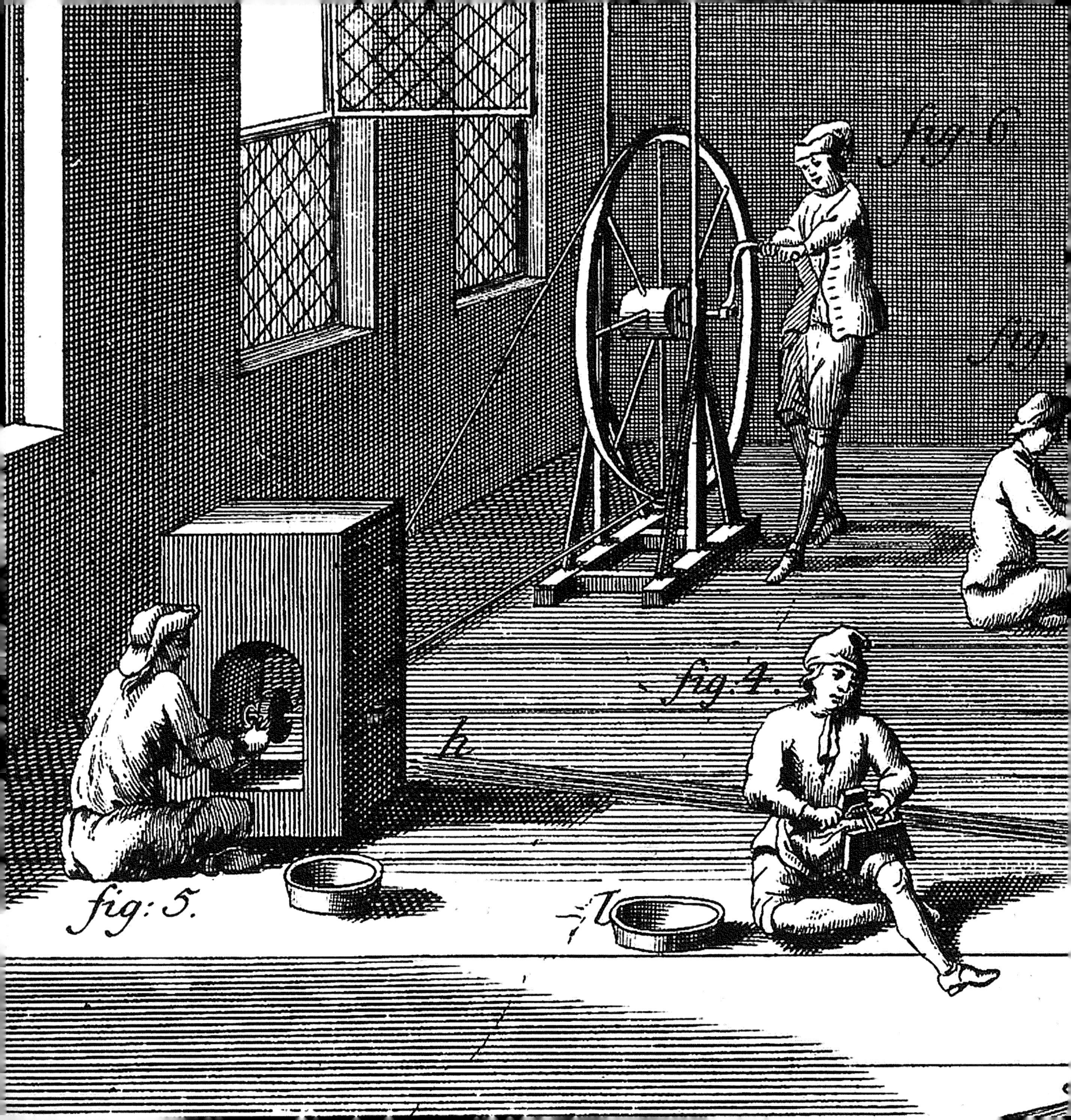

fig. 6.
fig. 4.
h
i
fig. 5.

fig. 3.
THE
THREADS
k
i
d
e
h

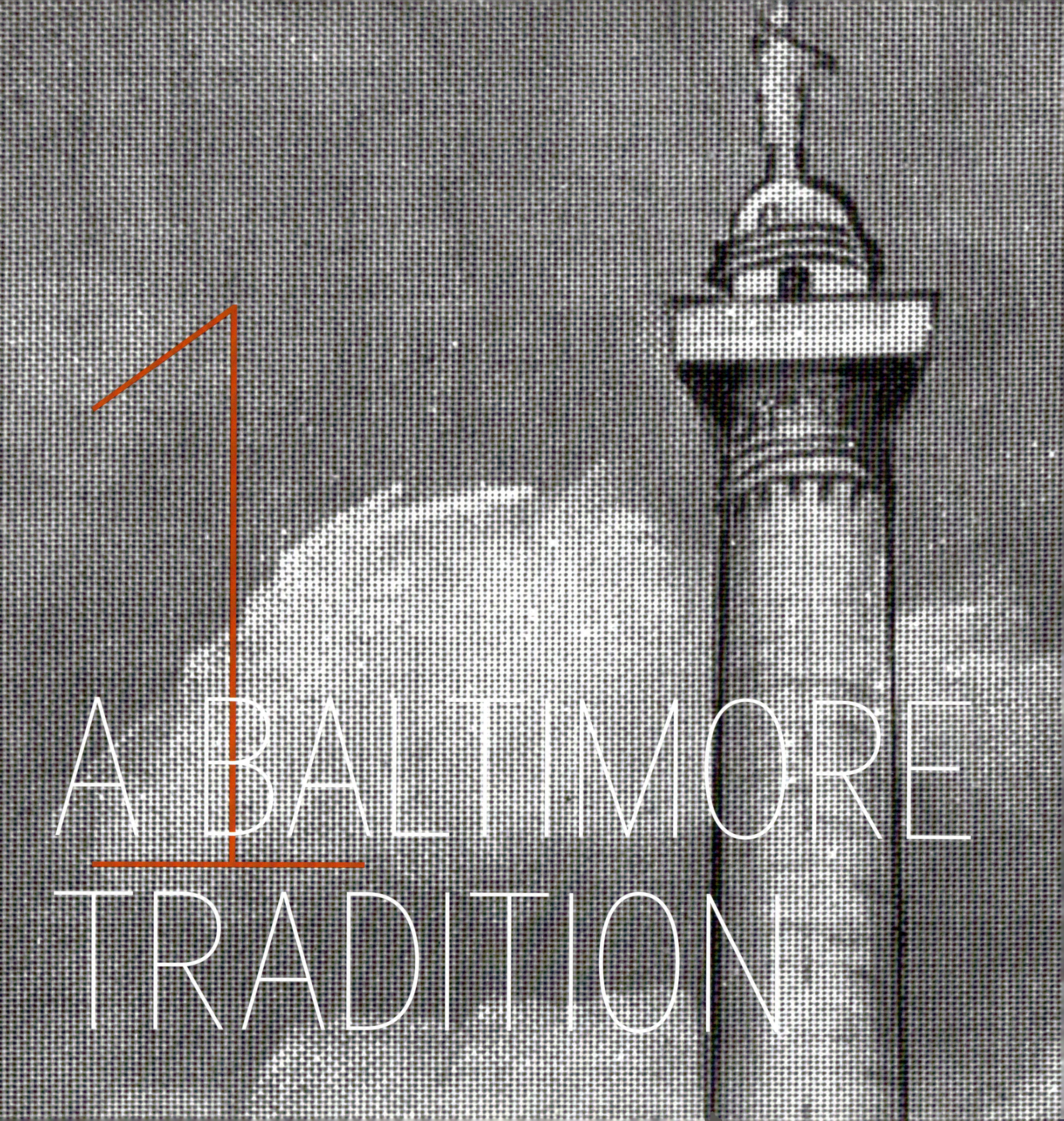
1
A BALTIMORE
TRADITION

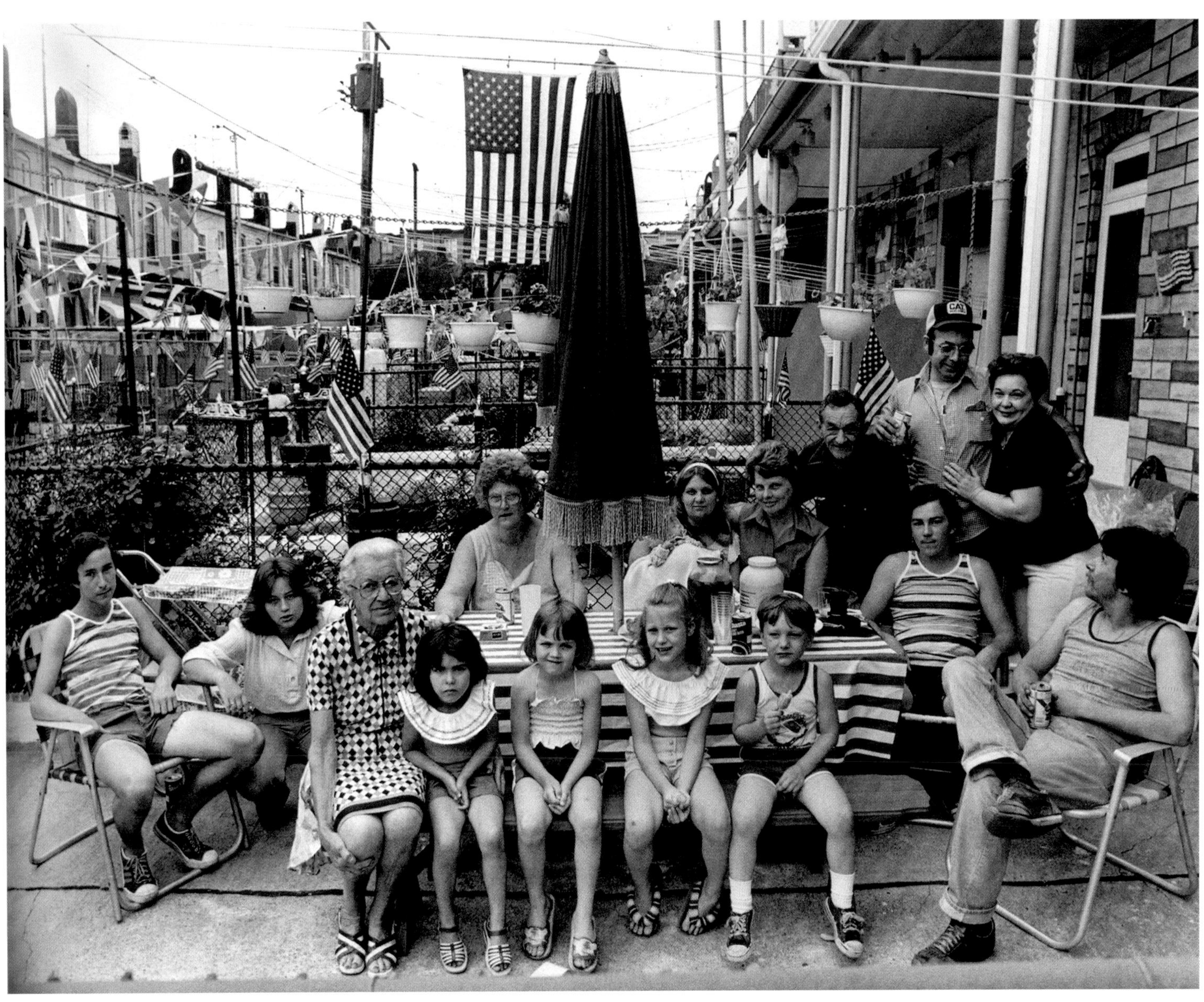

The Marski family and neighbors celebrate the Fourth of July in their Highlandtown backyard. The tradition lasted for decades and expanded to include the entire block on both sides of the alley. *Photograph by Linda G. Rich, circa 1979, The East Baltimore Documentary Photography Project. Accession Number P83-11-063. Courtesy of the Photography Collections, University of Maryland, Baltimore County.*

IN THE SUMMER OF 1913, AN ENTERPRISING GROCER MOMENTARILY EXCHANGED HIS butcher's apron for paint and brushes. His intention was strictly commercial—the act of replicating the produce and meats sold in his shop on his screen door attracted the attention of nearby residents. He called it advertising. They considered it art. In an instant, "William Oktavec the Grocer" became "William Oktavec the Artist."

The sidewalk art critics appreciated the lifelike quality of Oktavec's original rendering. But they appreciated the colorful distraction even more when they realized that they could not see inside his store, while from indoors they could see unimpeded out to the street. Flying insects stayed out. Breezes passed through. Neighbors soon requested screens by the houseful—for doors and windows, upstairs and down, front and back, block after block. Oktavec redefined the humdrum function of woven wire fly screen by treating it like a canvas with holes. The useful was made beautiful. His invention spread from rowhouse to rowhouse with lightning speed, like a juicy tidbit of gossip passed over the backyard fence.

Over time, painted screens transformed parts of Baltimore into outdoor art galleries. They were a trademark feature of the city's rowhouse neighborhoods for almost a century. Only the signature white marble steps were a more widespread and permanent presence in the rowhouse landscape. With a few brush strokes, an urban folk art was born.

In short order, demand far exceeded the good grocer's ability to supply his growing client base. Seeing there was money to be made in painted screens, amateurs and sign painters with artistic inclinations and an itch for a quick buck, joined the ranks of dabblers and handymen who called themselves "screen painters."[7] Most started at home with their own screens and, finding approval, gradually expanded their territory. Oktavec's students and imitators plied their trade from backyards, basements, and even a shop or two. Itinerants with beer boxes for seats, easels, and paint cans took to the street corners to drum up business.

By the time Oktavec closed his grocery, opened an art shop, and became a full-time artist, a profusion of painted screens by many hands overlooked the sidewalks of East Baltimore. The number of painters swelled and contracted over the decades, as did the number of screens. When the art form reached its zenith in midcentury, few windows had escaped adornment. Success in this itinerant trade was consumer driven. The painters sought little more than the cost of paint, brushes, or a cold drink. Their talents varied, as did their fees and the durability of their work. The master grocer-painter set a high standard, but beauty was in the eye of the beholder. The price—affordable to the people of the neighborhood, inexpensive enough so they could cover every window in the house—sealed the new icon's status as a people's art.

As for durability, some painted screens have lasted for decades, depending on location and care. Direct sunlight and exhaust from trucks and buses took a toll. The rise of air conditioners threatened to eliminate them. The call to arms disrupted the trade for prolonged periods, but postwar nesting was especially favorable to the rise of new artists and fluorescence of the art. The introduction of new window styles and materials every decade made replacement windows increasingly desirable and provided a convenient excuse to order new screen paintings. With every innovation, the old screens made their way to the basement for safekeeping or into the alley trash bins. Yet the unabated need for privacy from the adjacent sidewalk, and, later, nostalgia for a neighborhood tradition, continued to keep painted screens firmly affixed to Baltimore windows.

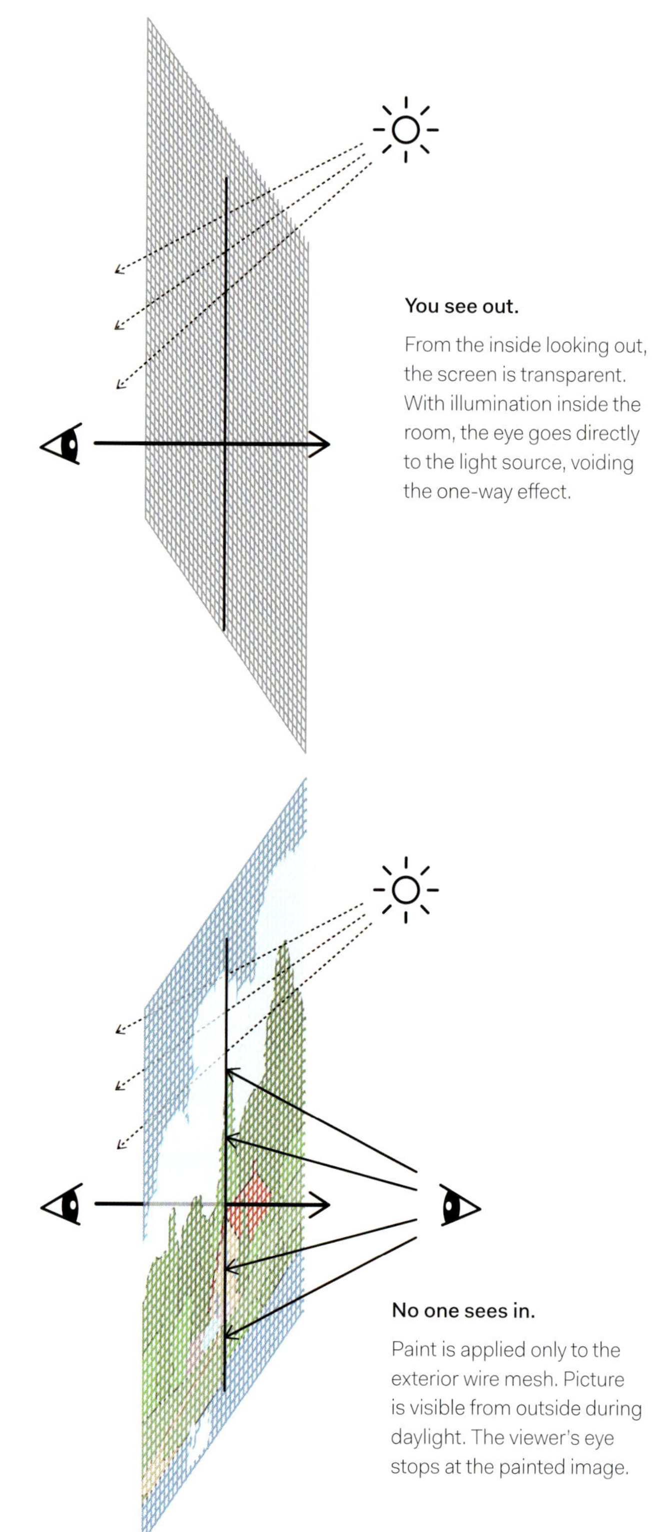

You see out.

From the inside looking out, the screen is transparent. With illumination inside the room, the eye goes directly to the light source, voiding the one-way effect.

No one sees in.

Paint is applied only to the exterior wire mesh. Picture is visible from outside during daylight. The viewer's eye stops at the painted image.

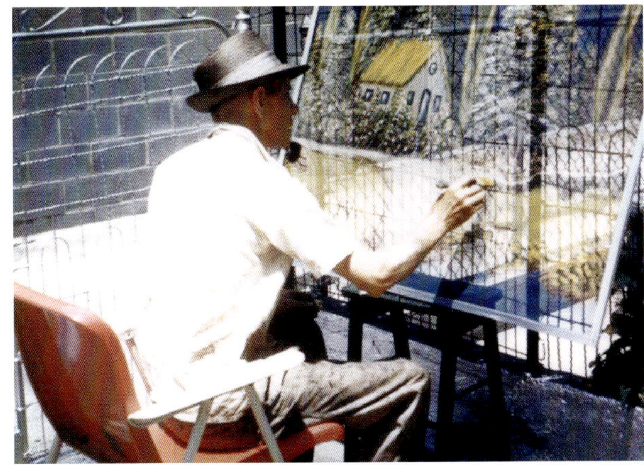

James Soul took up screen painting in the 1960s and painted for his neighbors in the backyard of his North Belnord Avenue home. *Courtesy of Delores and Veronika Soul.*

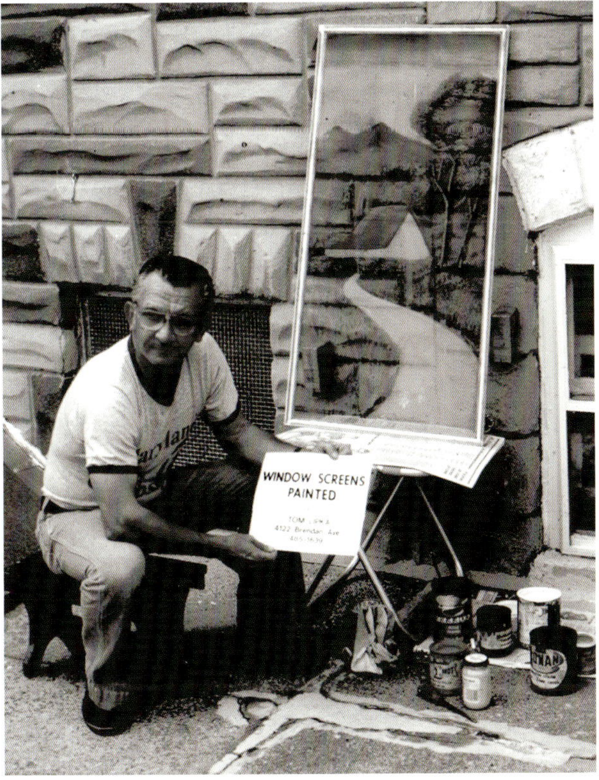

Tom Lipka began painting screens from his family's Canton home as a young boy. His career spanned six decades, with occasional time off for service in the military, work, and to raise a family. *Author photograph, 1982.*

THE PAINTED SCREENS OF BALTIMORE WERE NOT ART FOR art's sake, but a practical amenity for a densely built man-made environment. Although they are a feast for the eyes, they are made for immediate and everyday use. The screens have meaning and logic because of their physical context. They are an integral part of the architectural infrastructure, a product of place.

As an art form, painted screens succeeded due to the overwhelming presence of rowhouses, an architectural style built to provide comfortable dwellings for Baltimore's laboring and middle classes throughout the nineteenth and twentieth century. The city's relentless profile of attached two- and three-story brick façades filled contiguous blocks as far as the eye could see. These regimented house fronts provided a perfect exhibition venue with a built-in audience.

European immigrants flocked to the communities of affordable homes where familiar institutions, jobs, and their countrymen welcomed them. In East Baltimore in particular, Germans, Poles, Czechs, Ukrainians, Irish, and Italians clustered in self-imposed, church-centered enclaves. Their homes, more often purchased than rented, were their proudest possessions.

Whether situated on the main street or on a narrow alley street, Baltimore's rowhouses share basic characteristics, especially in relation to the outdoors. There is no barrier between the front window and the sidewalk. No porches, no grassy buffers, no lawns, no fences, no gardens define the exterior space. Double-hung sash windows dominate the structure and provide light, air, and views. Because of its dominant position, the first-floor window is the mediator of home life and street life. In many cases, the Baltimore rowhouse has more square footage dedicated to glazing than to actual brick and mortar. With shutters open or curtains or blinds drawn back for air or light, the front parlor, in particular, is fully exposed to the street. From within, the window offers an unobstructed view.

The window screen, a late addition to the workingman's home, and at first purely seasonal, was contemporary with Mr. Oktavec's innovation. Nowhere but in East Baltimore was the urge to embellish that screen so irresistible. As objects made, above all, for use by untrained, self-taught artists, they are an authentic folk art, of, by, and for the community in which they are found. Since Oktavec painted his first screen a hundred years ago at the behest of his next-door neighbor, Mrs. Emma Schott, they have been designed, produced, and consumed within the rowhouse communities of Baltimore.[8] They are valued for their utility, but experienced as art.

A community is both a physical, tangible location and a group of people sharing a common experience. Painted screens have long defined and provided a source of identity for residents of East Baltimore.

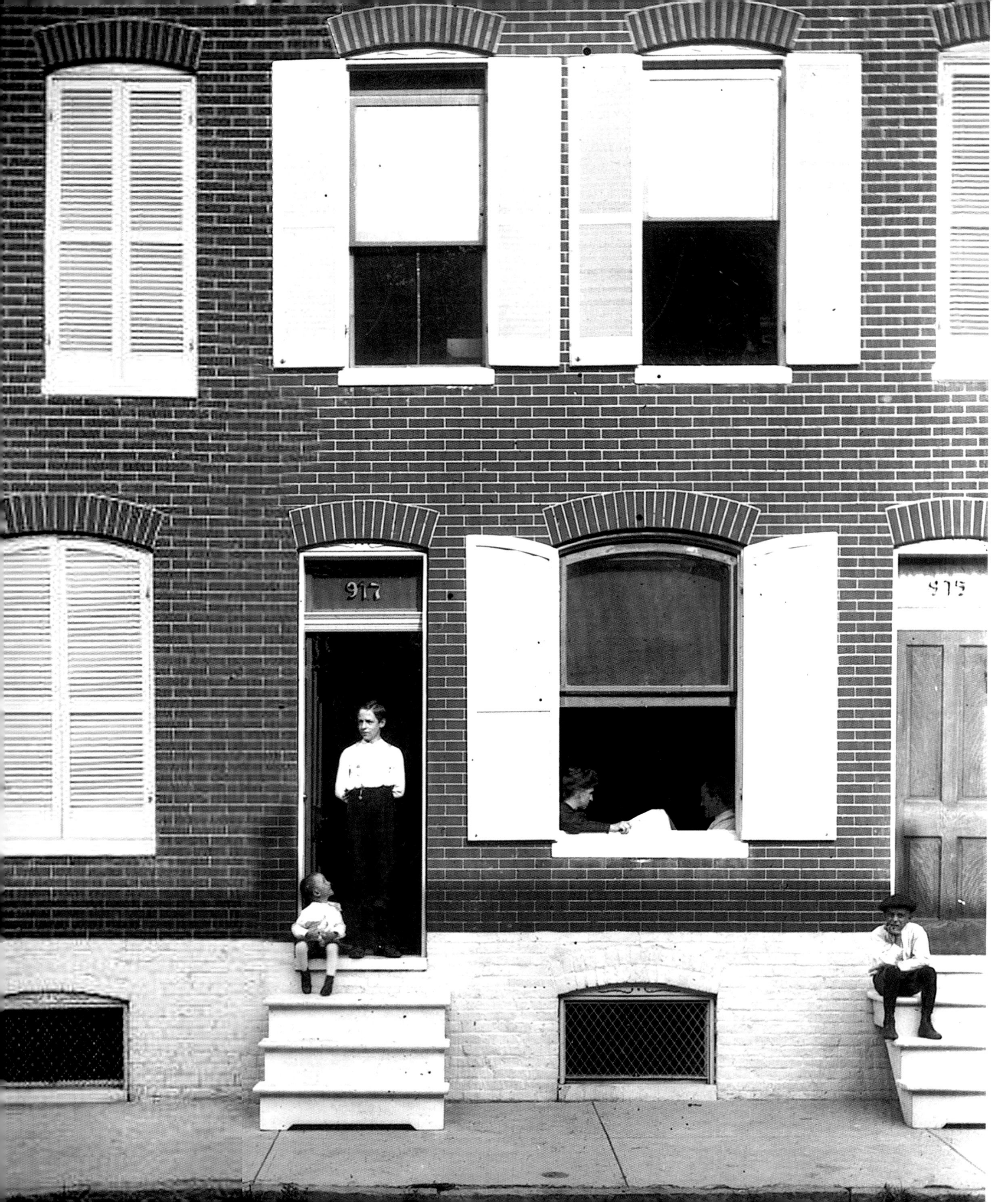

As Upper Fell's Point resident and proud owner of numerous painted screens Estelle Figinski noted, "I can't do it. You can't do it. It must be art."[9] One of Baltimore's best-known tastemakers, John Waters, agrees, observing, in an interview for the 1988 film, *The Screen Painters*:

> What amazed me is how cheap they are. That is the thing I can't believe, and nobody takes them seriously. If they would make their price a thousand dollars they would be written up in *The New York Times*. But because they are thirty dollars, people say, "They can't be art."[10]

Although today their rarity relegates painted screens to the realm of the quirky or even kitsch, three generations of eastsiders "grew up and got old seeing painted screens as something usual."[11] Painting colorful scenes on window and door screens was a summer ritual in the rowhouse neighborhoods of East Baltimore through most of the twentieth century. They were as much a part of the hot weather landscape as the brick and Formstone rowhouse façades, the white marble steps, and corner taverns and confectionaries. They were as familiar as the calls of the once-omnipresent Arabbers (pronounced A-rabbers, emphasis on the first syllable), the local term for produce vendors working from horse-drawn carts, as popular as sidewalk snowball stands selling cones of crushed ice and syrup refreshment. They were far more evident than the intermittent flowering trees rising from patches of earth carved from the curbside concrete. They provided a comforting predictable presence and offered the perfect backdrop for the camaraderie shared among neighbors escaping from the heat by sitting out on their stoops on summer evenings.

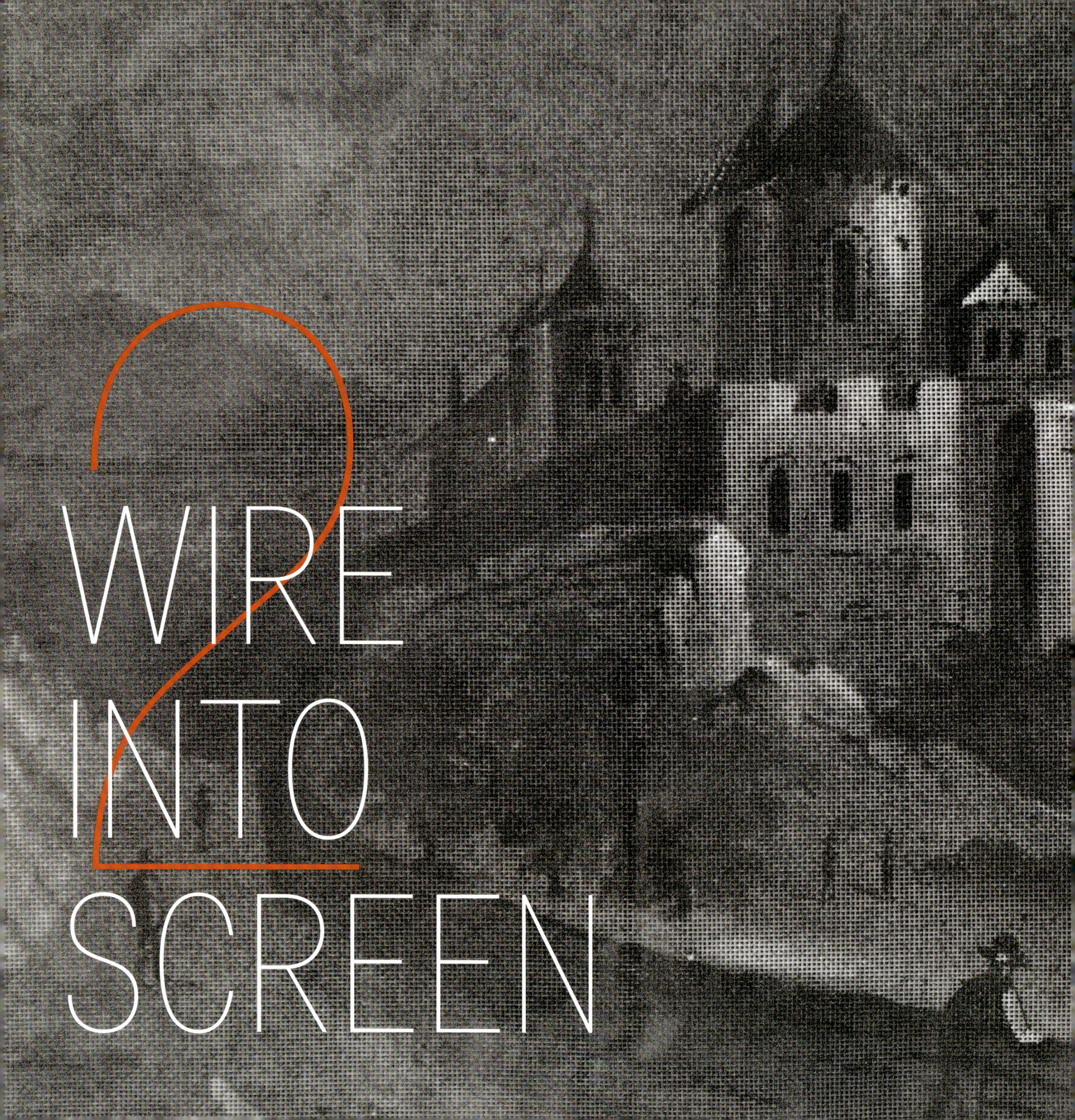

2
WIRE
INTO
SCREEN

ENTHRONED ON A FOLDING CHAIR BESIDE HER ROWHOUSE'S GLEAMING MARBLE STEPS, longtime East Baltimore resident Mildred Gottsch observed, "Screens go way back, before you were even born." Mrs. Gottsch didn't know how right she was. The painted screens on her Patterson Park rowhouse have their roots in a long evolutionary process of wire and windows. As sash windows became commonplace in homes for all classes in the middle of the nineteenth century, the need arose to cover those windows for privacy, seasonal warmth, cooling, and ventilation. In the early twentieth century, the revelation that insects carried deadly diseases instantly changed people's attitudes toward the outdoors—specifically what the air might carry into their homes. Trade catalogs began marketing window screens as an essential commodity for the masses. And almost as quickly, woven wire cloth transcended its purely utilitarian function to find its way into artists' repertoires.

WIRE

Throughout history, wherever the raw materials and the inclination toward industry prevailed, people made wire. The rise of ductile materials such as gold, copper, silver, and, later, iron, brass, and aluminum made it possible for craftsmen to draw out metal into wire of diminishing diameters. In the beginning, wire making was solitary work. A single wire drawer sat at a bench, swing, anvil, or table and forced bars or strips into fibers.

Wire for wool cards, pins, and fish hooks required minimal lengths. As new applications required longer stretches and increasing amounts of wire, shops began to appear. Throughout Europe, the process was veiled in extreme secrecy, often conducted in remote "little cracks in the hills with a stream and tributaries furnishing power."[12]

Because iron and wire production paved the way for economic self-sufficiency, Britain did everything possible to prevent the development of this industry in her American colonies. Nonetheless, Jamestown, Virginia, and Lynn, Massachusetts, claimed modest iron works by the mid-1600s. Norwich, Connecticut, became the first city in the colonies to produce and widely distribute iron wire in 1755. The War of 1812 was a major catalyst to domestic output, as independent means of production were critical to the young country's success. An 1815 treaty with Britain finally allowed the duty-free transport of iron in both directions across the Atlantic,[13] but by this date, the production of iron wire from native ores had become a well-established industry in the United States.[14]

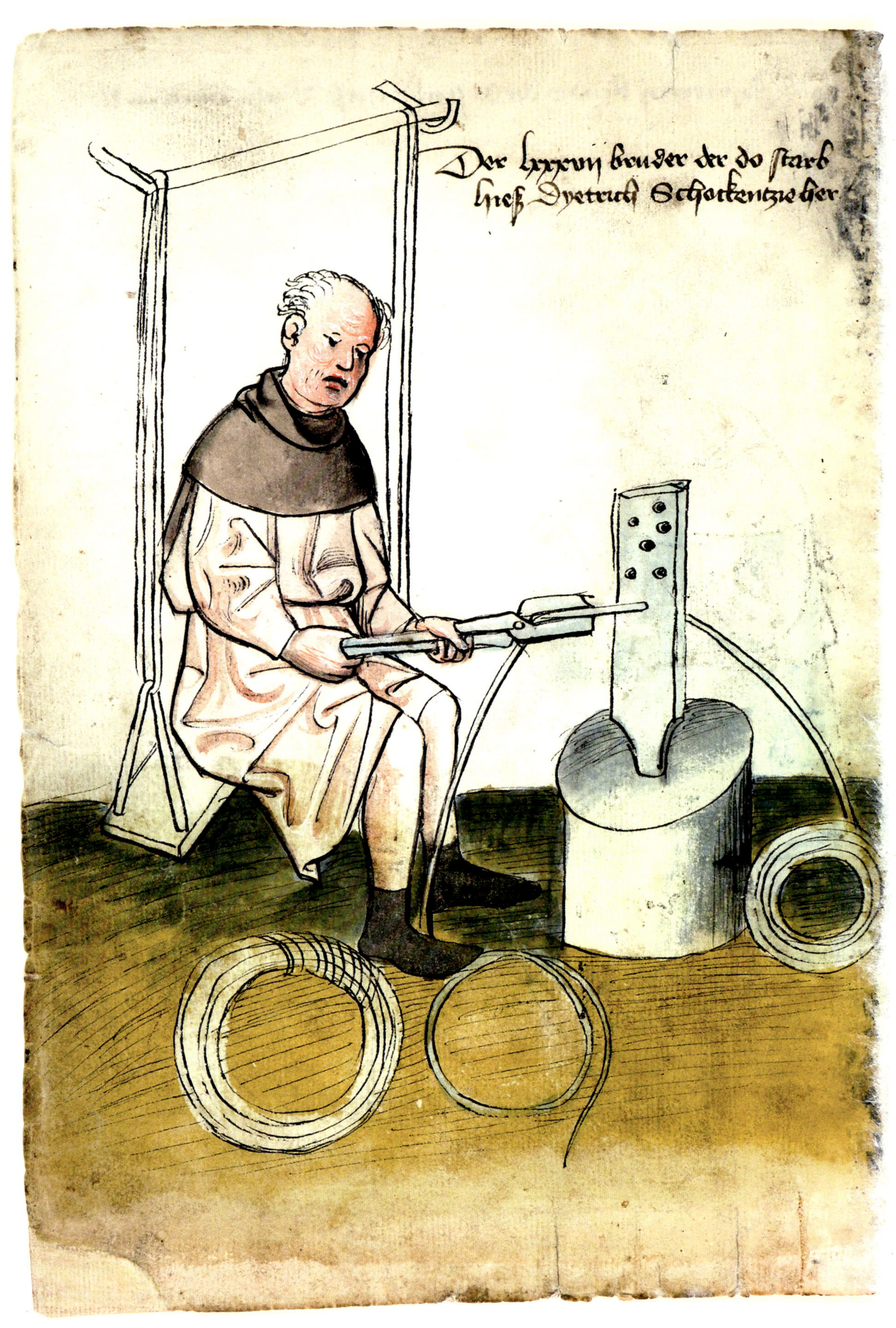

A solitary German monk known as Dyetrich Schockentzieher (shock puller) uses the back-and-forth action of a swing to draw wire through smaller and smaller dies. His was one among many trades practiced by religious men living in Nuremberg, Germany, and documented by anonymous monks in the fifteenth century. *Mendel Brothers, Hausbuch der Meldelscheb Zwölfbroderstiftung du Nurnberg, 1435-6 [House Book of the 12 Mendel Brothers Foundation]. Courtesy of the Municipal Library in Nuremberg. Stadtbibliothek Nürnberg, Amb. 317.2°, f.40r (Mendel I).*

WIRE CLOTH

The first evidence of large-scale wire cloth manufacture in America appears in 1784. John Sellers (1728–1804) of Darby Township, near Philadelphia, advertised a "Manufactory of Wire Work" that produced handmade screens for sieves and windows.[15] He inherited and built upon the woolen weaving enterprise that his father, Samuel Sellers Sr. (1655–1732), had brought from England.

In 1834 Gilbert & Bennett Wire Company of Georgetown, Connecticut, adapted a neighbor's power carpet loom to weave wire into screen, becoming the first firm in America to produce wire cloth mechanically. Gilbert & Bennett's earlier stock-in-trade was hand-woven horsehair in various mesh sizes used in wood-framed sifters for grains, meal, coffee, and sugar. With the start of the Civil War in 1861, after it had begun converting its products from horsehair to wire, the market for sieves in the South abruptly ended. Finding itself with large amounts of excess woven wire cloth, the company added a protective coating of gray paint, and began to manufacture window screening. A great improvement over the cheesecloth used earlier, these new screens met with immediate favor.[16] The company boasted that its operation was "the only establishment in

Though often located in remote areas to protect the secrecy of the process, large shops of wire drawers were common by the 1700s. *deReaumur and Duhamel du Monceau,* Art et Metiers, *"Art de Reduire le Fer en Fil," Paris 1766. Hagley Museum and Library.*

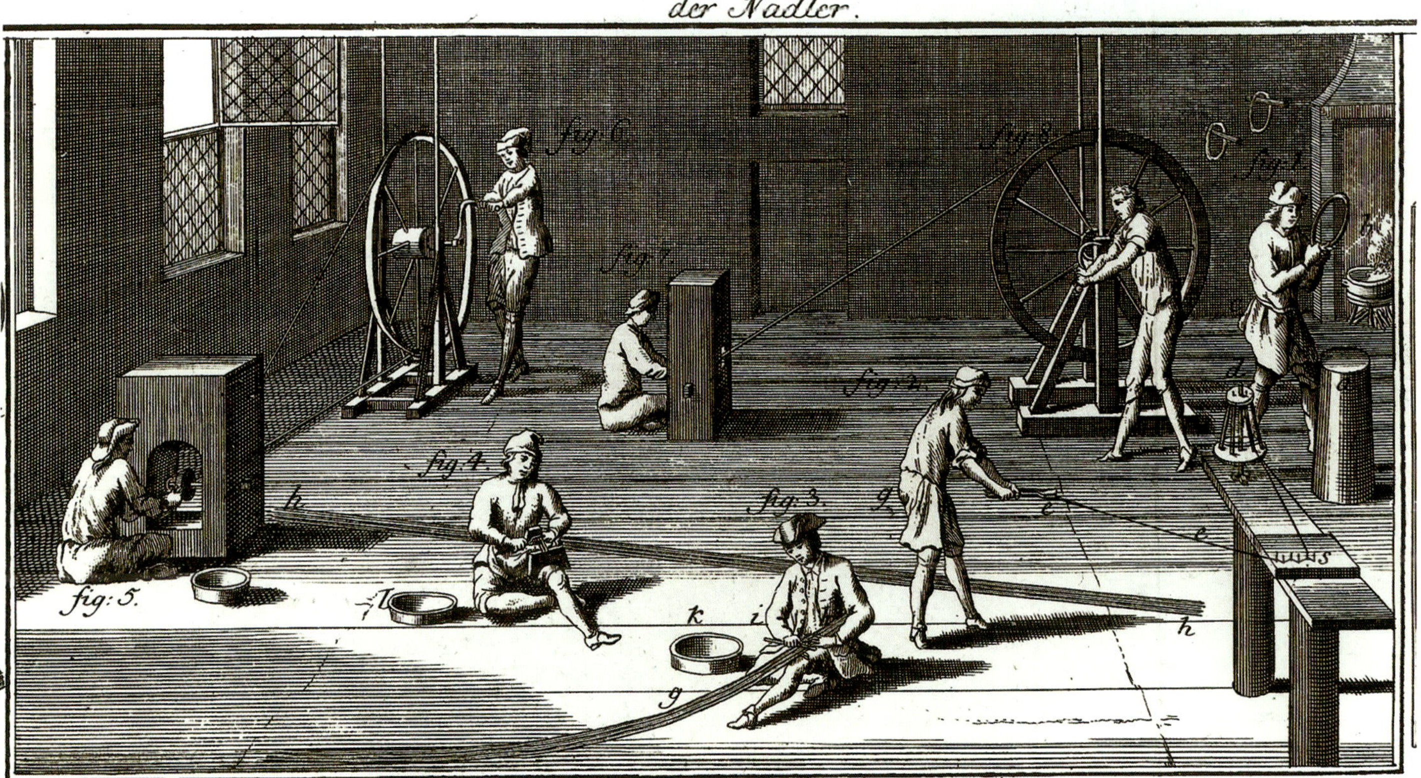

America which is complete to take the wood in the forest, to make the wire, to weave by automatic power machinery, to galvanize and to tin wire both in the strand and also in the fabric, thus enabling us to bring out, step by step, finished goods from the raw material at the lowest cost."[17]

At least three American wire manufacturers including Gilbert & Bennett claim the introduction of mechanized wire weaving. Many patents for power wire looms were granted in the mid-nineteenth century. Erastus Bigelow, best known today as the originator of Bigelow Carpets, was an inveterate inventor who had at least fifty patents to his name, and he adapted his carpet looms to produce wire cloth in 1856.[18] Soon thereafter his Clinton Wire Cloth mills offered "many different patterns for window screens, corn poppers and a great variety of other things."[19]

Wickwire Brothers, established in 1866 in Cortland, New York, had imported screen cloth from England as part of their general hardware business. When a bad debt was paid off with a second-hand carpet loom, the company's president, Chester Wickwire repurposed the prize for wire weaving and took the first step to building one of the most successful wire empires in the country. An enterprising inventor, he designed and secured patents for the looms that would supply screen cloth throughout much of the country after converting and patenting his first loom for wire cloth in 1873.[20]

Within three years, Wickwire's "manufacture of wire cloth has so grown…and is so profitable, that they wish to devote their entire time and capitol [*sic*] to that business."[21] As the company evolved into one of America's largest wire producers, its double-selvage woven wire cloth began to outsell its wire flower stands, sieves, food covers, and corn poppers. Just one among the company's many innovations, the wire cloth came in expanded widths up to forty-eight inches, and was used for food safes, doors, and large shop windows.[22]

By the late 1890s, wire screens were being promoted by manufacturers from coast to coast, and competition for the domestic market was fierce. E. T. Burrowes & Co. of Portland, Maine, billed its operation as the LARGEST SCREEN FACTORIES IN THE WORLD claiming in an early advertisement:

WIRE WINDOW & DOOR SCREENS ARE A NECESSITY in every class of dwellings, where comfort and cleanliness are desired they are indispensible. A good housekeeper and a swarm of flies cannot live happily in the same house. PROBABLY NO MONEY EXPENDED upon the fixtures of a house will make so large a return in saving repairs, in comfort, and in satisfaction, as that paid for GOOD WIRE SCREENS. They save more than their COST IN A SINGLE YEAR by keeping flies from disfiguring the interior of a house, its decorations and fixtures; by holding mosquitoes and other insect pests at a distance, and by preventing destructive moths from ruining carpets, clothing, drapery, upholstery, and bedding.[23]

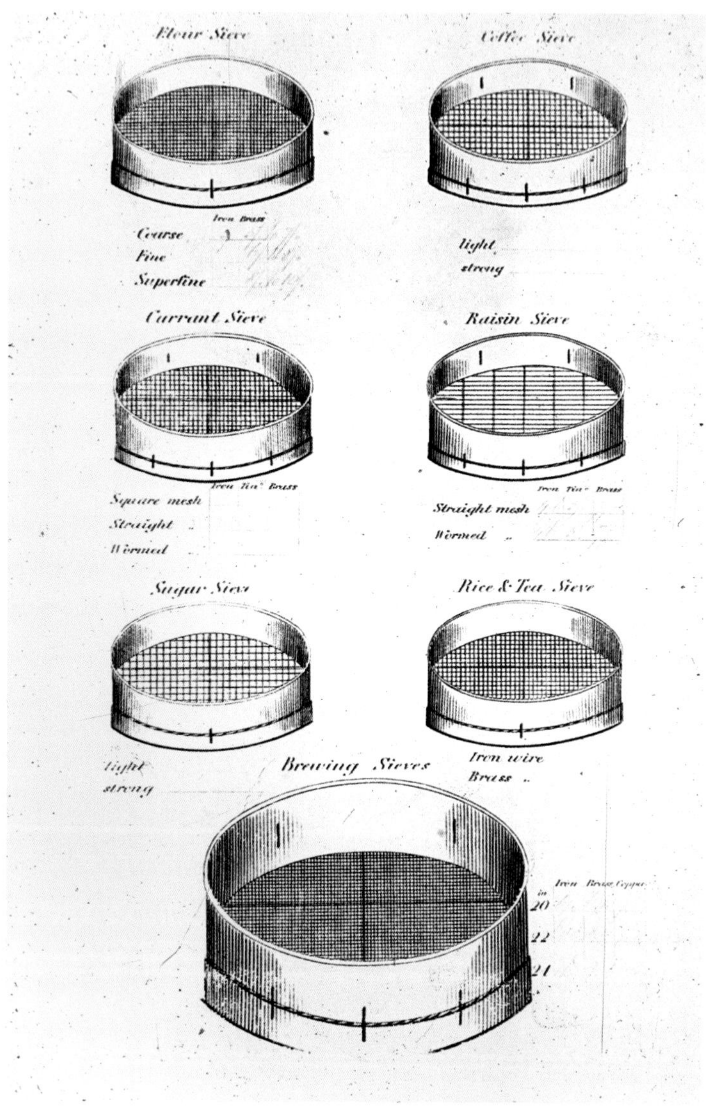

Sieves made first of woven horsehair and later of sturdier wire flooded the market during the Civil War. The surplus wire cloth was later framed and converted for use on windows. *Birmingham Trade Catalog, 1827. Courtesy of The Winterthur Library: Printed Book and Periodical Collection.*

THE SCREENING OF AMERICA

The difference between misery and comfort—a mere membrane of woven wire cloth, framed on windows and doors—was a popular selling point in trade catalogs distributed nationwide. *E. T. Barnum's Catalog of Wire Goods, 1874. Warshaw Collection of Business Americana, Smithsonian Institution Museum of American History.*

At the turn of the twentieth century, only the wealthy could afford window screens—luxury items framed in mahogany and other exotic woods. As screen production and demand increased they became more readily available and affordable, the population was making the connection between flying insects and disease. Ladies' magazines drummed the virtues of cleanliness into the conscience of the concerned—if not obsessive—housewife whose primary charge was the maintenance of home and family. Illustrated hardware catalogs heightened public awareness of new products and public health agencies promoted the dangers of insect-borne illnesses including malaria. Organized networks of regional and local retailers were using direct advertising to reach out for the first time to a new class of homeowner. Trade catalogs were the marketing miracle of the era.

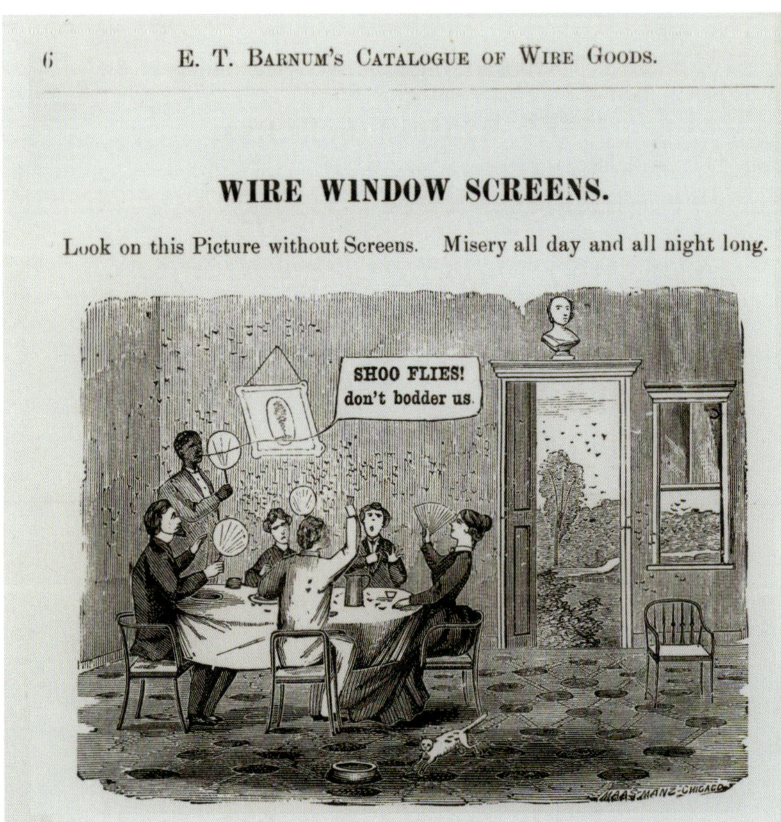

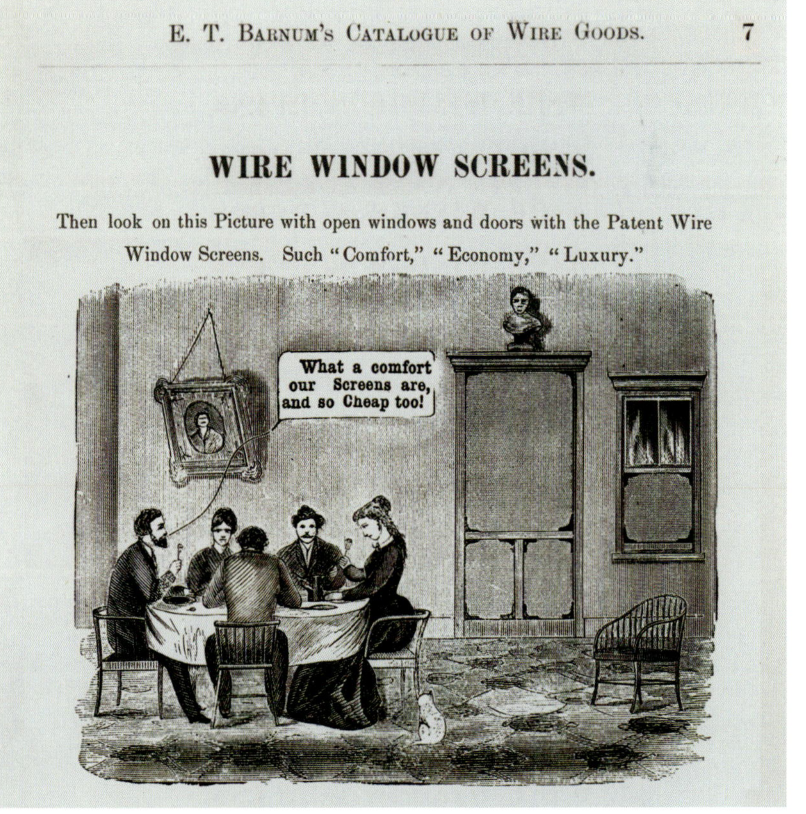

In addition to providing memorable images, catalogs played upon a woman's fears in her role as caretaker. Continental Screen Goods Co. warned, "flies produce typhoid fever and infantile diseases. She will therefore do well to make a large investment in window and door screens for the coming season."[24] A broadside from Roebling's New Jersey Wire Company affirmed the medical proof of insects' role in cholera, sleeping sickness, pinkeye, typhoid fever—even tuberculosis—and the urgent need to screen the home rather than individual furnishings. Catalogs defined domestic contentment in terms of the absence or presence of household screens, particularly at bedtime.[25] Boughton's Adjustable Mosquito and Fly Screen, patented July 8, 1873, would "make the difference between absolute misery and sweetest comfort…[are] suited to people living in rented houses and can [fit any size and] be used in different windows of the same house."[26]

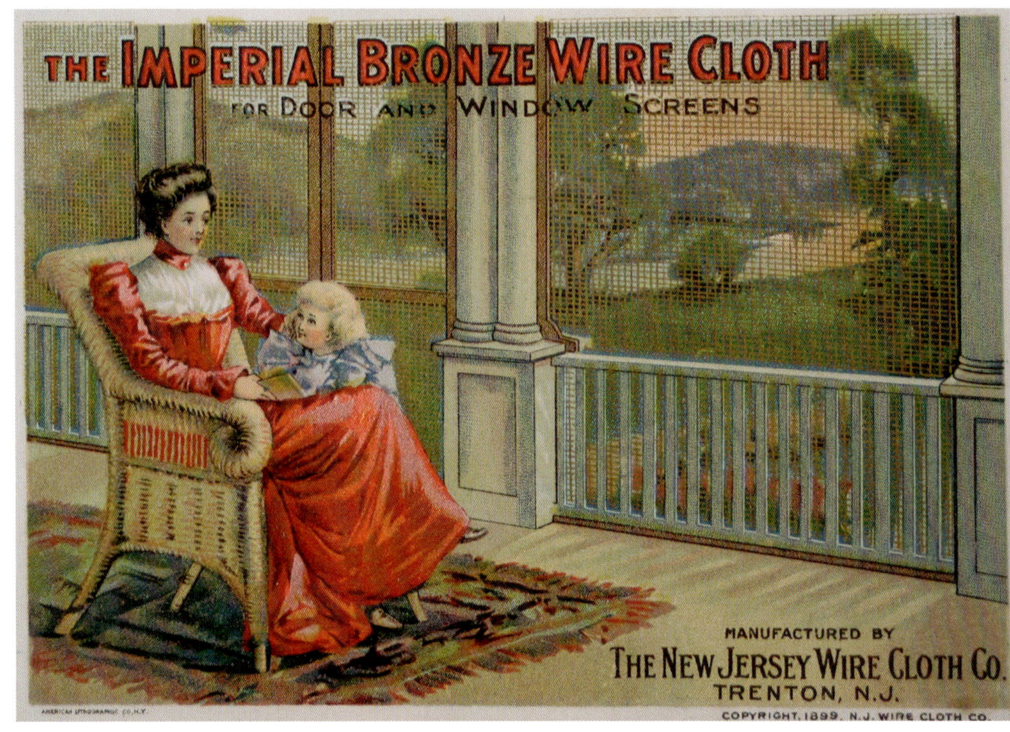

The virtues of screening for a healthy and peaceful life among people of means became evident as the nineteenth century drew to a close. Trade card for Imperial Bronze Wire Cloth, manufactured by New Jersey Wire Cloth Company, 1899. *Courtesy of Historic New England.*

Unrelenting summer visits by mosquitoes, more than any other factor, deserve the credit for the screening of America. Yellow Fever, a mysterious and deadly affliction, decimated populations in the coastal cities of the eastern and southern United States. For most of the nineteenth century, people believed it to be transmitted by strangers, exotic plants, trade goods from the West Indies, poor sanitation, hot weather, passing meteors, or poisoned air referred to as "the vapors" and "miasma," poisonous particles floating in the air.[27] As early as 1830, a New Haven doctor bravely encouraged the use of "wire gauze windows [as] a suggested protection against the effects of malaria and aerial poison."[28]

Open windows were unthinkable. The confusion as to the exact source of disease, the rising mortality rate and the hysteria of helplessness, caused residents of southern cities, in particular, to keep their dwellings tightly sealed, especially to the night air. New Orleans had a dozen epidemics over three decades, and thousands of citizens perished in each outbreak. Memphis lost a sixth of its residents to the fever, and solutions discussed included leveling the town, salting the earth, and starting over elsewhere.[29] Wealthy urban dwellers fled to outlying areas from summer through the first frost. The search for the cause of Yellow Fever resulted in the wholesale burning of houses, quarantine, death, and, on the positive side, the development of sewer systems.

Those who sought explanations and cures for what they called "stranger's fever" tried everything from "sniffing rags dipped in vinegar" to "smelling pieces of camphor or tarred rope." Men used snuff, and women resorted to smoking cigars, "sometimes to their discomfiture," while others "chewed garlic," put "garlic in their shoes," "lighted fires," or burned gunpowder. Some "whitewashed walls," while others fired "muskets from their windows."[30]

Occasionally, visionaries tried window screens. The few medical and science professionals who correctly identified the fever's sources had to wait for verification of their hypotheses until Major Walter Reed of the U.S. Army Medical Corps and Cuban physician Carlos Finlay made a historic announcement from Havana in 1900: Yellow Fever had been conclusively shown to be transmitted from person to person by the bite of the *Aedes aegypti* mosquito.

In 1903 a respected rice planter, James Troup Dent (1848–1913), screened every door and window of Hofwyl Plantation in Darien, Georgia, and spent the season there with his family instead of moving them inland for the summer. Dent's well-documented experiment in the use of screens, the first in coastal Georgia, comprised the first test of the connection between malaria and the *Anopheles* mosquito in the United States—a link that Sir Ronald Ross had established six years earlier in India.[31] Dent's experience convinced other southerners of the importance of protecting the house against flying insects, particularly mosquitoes. Successive summers saw more and more families staying safely at home.[32]

Window screens were no longer a luxury. They had become a necessity.

GALVANIZATION

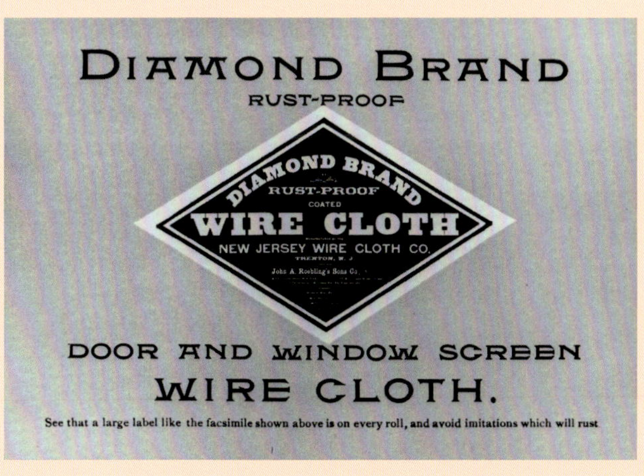

Screen cloth was made to be exposed to the elements. But unless it was fabricated from brass or copper, it was subject to rust and corrosion. Iron and steel screens required a coat of paint to prevent deterioration. Electrochemical or molten baths of zinc provided more enduring protection whether the wire was coated before or after it was woven into cloth. When dipped and then heated (annealed), the fabric was protected for the long term. The earliest patent to protect ferrous metals from oxidation was granted to Parisian Modeste Sorel in 1837. Galvanization is named for Bologna's Luigi Galvani (1737–1798), a physiologist, who in unrelated experiments discovered that electricity can result from chemical action.[33]

For manufacturers of wire cloth, galvanization became a major selling point—marketed the way they would later promote the decorative painting available from their art departments. In 1886 Massachusetts's Wright Wire Company boasted that its galvanized or "White Metal Screen Wire Cloth" was "made from specially prepared Hot Galvanized wire from our own mills, and all the experience of galvanizing wire and cloths has been brought to bear in the equipment and methods of manufacture necessary to produce a Rust Proof Screen Wire Cloth second to none on the market." Even their "Bronze Screen Wire Cloth woven from the best grade of bronze wire, drawn in our own mills, had been especially prepared for the resistance of the action of salts, acids, gases and all kinds of atmospheric conditions."[34]

Worcester brand's Black Painted Cloth was "finished in the best jet black enamel paint, put on by our own special process. We use the best materials obtainable and manufactured to our own specifications, presenting a brilliant glossy surface. The paint will not flake off, a trouble too common with many brands."[35]

3
THE CANVAS:
A CITY OF
ROWHOUSES

HARPER'S, 1911

"On a modest working man's income you may live in a delightful toy-like little red brick home with fresh paint, green shutters, and the whitest of white steps. Your house may be only ten feet wide and a story and a half high, but it is a dignified, self-respecting habitation, and your castle as no flat can ever be." [36]

SUNDAY SUN MAGAZINE, 1953

"They poured into the cities of America in the last century. refugees from oppression or from the age-old systems under which a poor man could not hope to better himself. And when they came, they paradoxically settled together in the same neighborhoods, for the new country was as strange as it was promising." [37]

THE CITY PAPER, 2005

"Hail the mighty little waterfront neighborhood rowhouse … strung together you formed instant neighborhoods for the people … German, African-American, Irish, Polish, Greek … if they worked hard for a living, they came home to you. … you are the mighty building that defined the city, and defied the city … but … you are still just a rowhouse." [38]

"RED BRICK ROWHOUSES ARE THE MORTAR OF BALTIMORE'S NEIGHBORHOODS,"[39] observed Jacques Kelly, longtime chronicler of the city's traditions and history. Although not a house type unique to the city, rowhouses are unquestionably entrenched and at home here. The style was borrowed from London's "terraces," named and introduced by Scots brothers Robert and James Adam in 1769. By the end of the century, rowhouses had found their way to Baltimore. Their design maximized the ratio of structure to lot, greatly enriching builders without sacrificing quality of life for residents. Other American cities—Washington, Wilmington, Philadelphia, New York, Boston, and Richmond—also favored this style of living. But no other place elevated its stock housing to the status of a canvas and gallery for a singular art form.

Had this building type never come to dominate Baltimore, painted screens would neither have existed nor endured. The ubiquitous attached vernacular houses provided the essentials for like-minded newcomers to build a community, a secure and welcoming environment at human scale. The new tradition of painted window screens coincided with a spectacular period of industrial development, population growth, and demographic change during the early twentieth century. What was then America's seventh-largest city welcomed newcomers from abroad in record numbers. Here, urban life met simple values from the old country.

Screen painting wove all of these threads together into an art form found nowhere else in such abundance. William Oktavec, one of the many immigrants who poured into Baltimore at this time, merged a provincial Old World aesthetic with pride in his adopted country, family, and home—to create work that was beautiful and also practical. Oktavec's neighbors, unlikely art patrons, seized upon painted window screens as a way to express their shared experience, and to assure their privacy while a purposeful street life unfolded right outside their windows.

MR. OKTAVEC'S NEIGHBORHOOD

In 1910, like so many recent arrivals, the Hradsky family took possession of a tidy red-brick rowhouse on North Collington Avenue. It had been constructed in 1902 by a fellow Bohemian immigrant, Frank Novak, a young builder who would rise to become one of Baltimore's most successful developers. The twelve-foot wide, two-story, Italianate-style home was identical in almost every way to the two dozen other connected dwellings that completed their block and the thousands of similar houses nearby. It had a basement faced in the front with marble, wood-grained window frames, and front door with a stained-glass transom.[40] The large round-arched front parlor window offered an unimpeded view of the street.

As the family's daughters, Josephine and Mary Hradsky, exited the front door and bounded down their three white marble steps, they paused to glance at the weekly Czech language paper, *The Telegraf,* resting on the stoop. Not a single blade of grass, flower, or garden gate interrupted their short trip across the paved street to the unbroken line of structures that defined their community.

The corner of North Collington and Ashland Avenues was anchored—as was all of Little Bohemia—by a substantial school and church, newly built in the Romanesque style and named for Bohemia's patron, Saint Wenceslaus.[41] Without crossing a curb, and speaking only their native language, parishioners could visit the sanctuary, rectory, and convent, and the school, gymnasium, bowling alley, rooftop dance floor, theater, and library.

Across Madison Avenue to the south stood Slavie, the Bohemian Building Loan and Savings Association. Its establishment in 1900 increased the number of Czech institutions that catered to the city's Bohemian émigrés and enabled the more recent arrivals to buy their first homes. The city's mammoth Northeast Market, known for its old country products, lay a few blocks farther south. Eastern European merchants on each corner and all along the

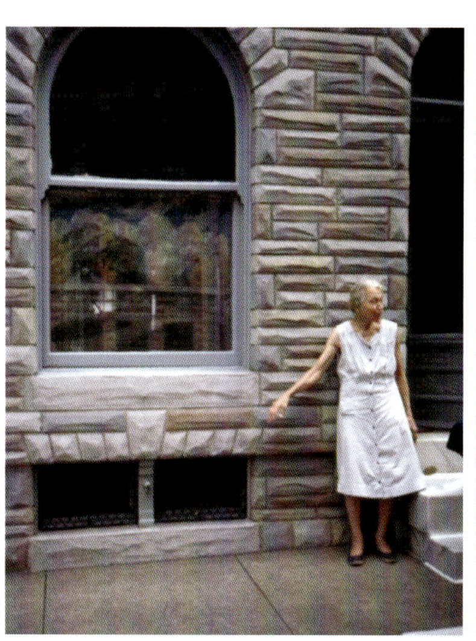

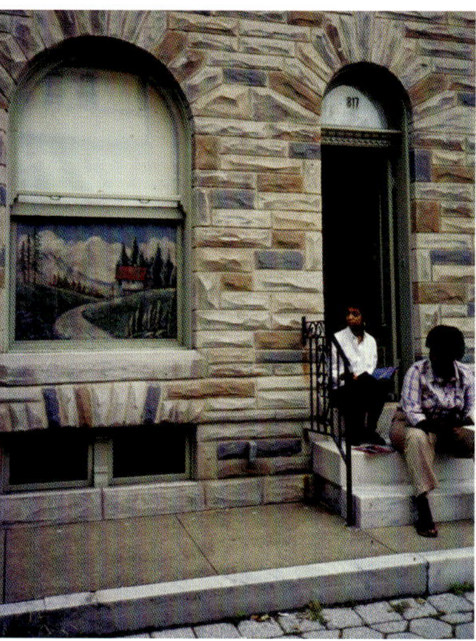

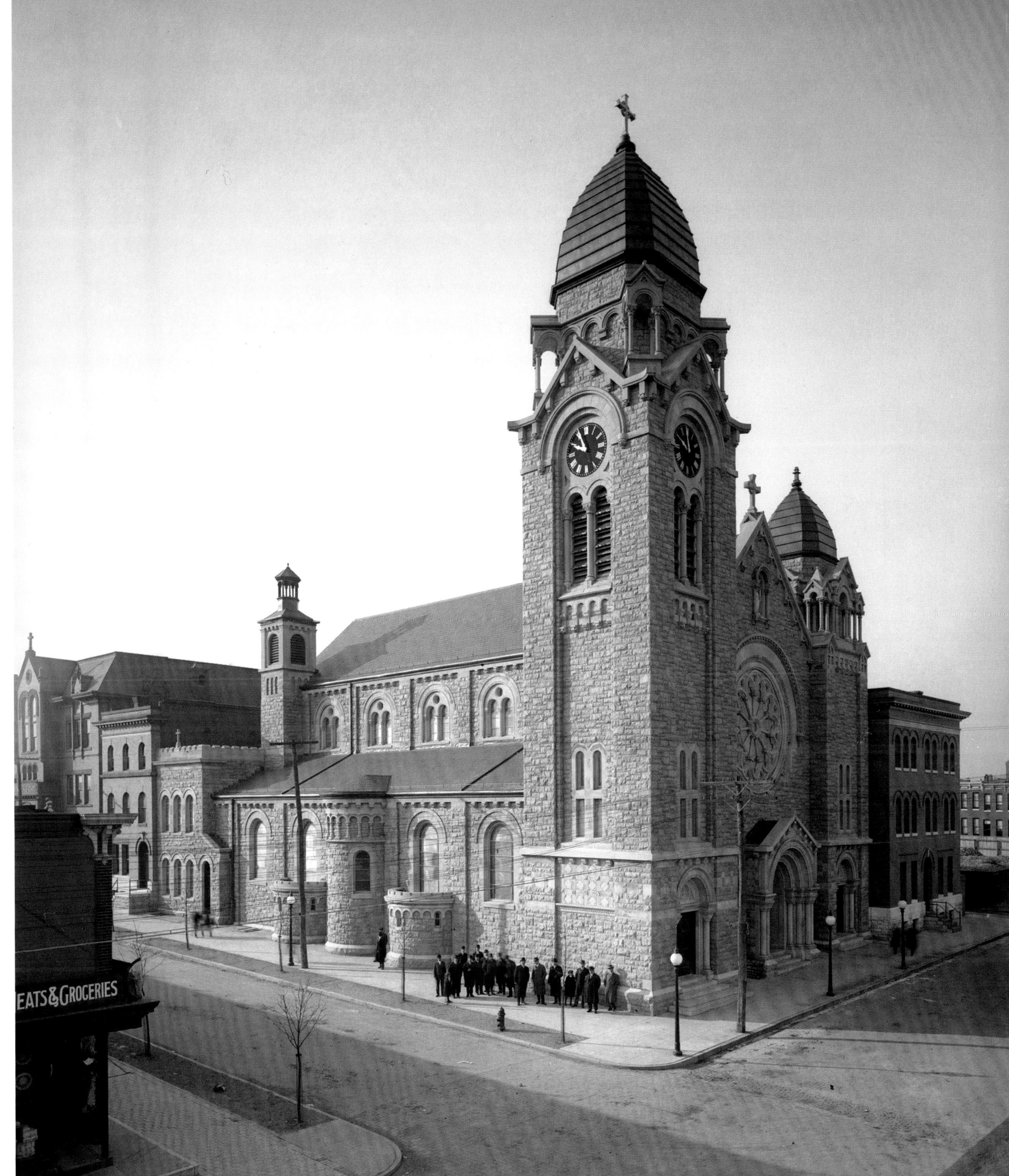
EATS & GROCERIES

East Monument Street commercial corridor sold everything else: Bauer's hardware, Petrouka's Northeast Meat Market, "Oktavec's [Meats &] Grocery (formerly Cermak's, then Prucha's), Blazek's confectionary, Peter Nozek and Klecka's saloons and Bujsinsky's dry goods. Mrs. Mary Toula ran the drugstore and her brother William Rysanek was the community physician. Emyl Mynar's orchestra entertained at Shimek's Hall."[42]

The Shimek family, who had arrived with the first wave of Czechs in 1865, took an active role in the new community, welcoming newcomers and starting and maintaining the fledgling Sokol Society movement, "dedicated to the improvement of mind and body through education and physical exercise." When the Shimeks' organ-making business expanded in 1882 they offered space for the Sokol at Broadway and Barnes Street, as part of their new factory's ground-floor saloon and upstairs meeting rooms. Here the Bohemians held parties, wedding receptions, gymnastic practices and events, labor meetings, concerts, dances, and Czech-language classes. In 1902 the Sokol group constructed its own building immediately to the north, at Preston and North Ann Streets, where they added theater and singing competitions.[43] To the west, Johns Hopkins Hospital claimed the northern reaches of Broadway, the grand boulevard that runs from the Fell's Point waterfront and delineated other immigrant enclaves on its trajectory to the former city line on North Avenue. Each neighborhood was defined by the presence of its central institutions—church, school, post office, theater, firehouse. An Enoch Pratt Free Library branch served adjoining communities.

To the south of Little Bohemia lay Patterson Park. It began as six acres of Hampstead Hill donated to the city by William Patterson (1752–1835) in 1827 for a "Public walk." The park grew until, at its height in 1917, it boasted one hundred and fifty acres, more than two thousand trees, fourteen hundred benches, lakes for boating and ice skating, a conservatory, a music pavilion, an observatory known as the Pagoda, a children's playground, athletic fields, a pool, fifty-five acres of lawn, and four miles of paths reached by twenty pedestrian entrances and five carriage entrances.[44] In 1903 the Olmsted Brothers—successors to the designers of Manhattan's Central Park and Boston's Emerald Necklace—were invited to plan an expansion for the park. They observed:

> For the most part laboring people and artizans [sic] of small means, they have little time or opportunity for recreation of any sort, and so little experience of the healthful refreshment of rural scenery that they do not realize its value, and are not often inclined to overcome many obstacles for the sake of getting it.[45]

The firm proposed to improve the park by adding 123 acres, extending it south across Eastern Avenue to Canton (now O'Donnell) Square "because the area was about to be encroached upon by houses."[46] They wanted to "offer to the working people of East Baltimore a conveniently accessible body of refreshing scenery, retired to a great degree from the turmoil of the city."[47] Easily viewed from the highest point in the park, row upon row of modest two-story red-brick homes rapidly filled the stick-straight street grid that made its way south to the harbor that started it all.

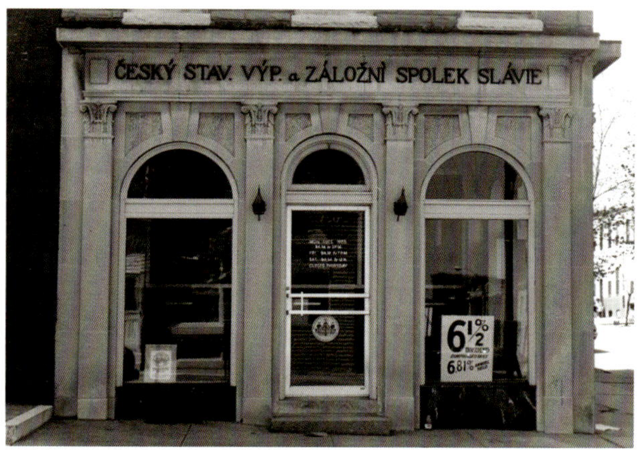

The Bohemian Building Loan and Savings Association, known to all as Slavie, was established in Little Bohemia in 1900. The membership organization enabled Bohemians to buy their own homes by paying modest weekly installments. Today its offices are in Overlea and Belair, north of Baltimore. *Baltimore City Life Museums photograph, circa 1970, courtesy of Mary Ellen Hayward.*

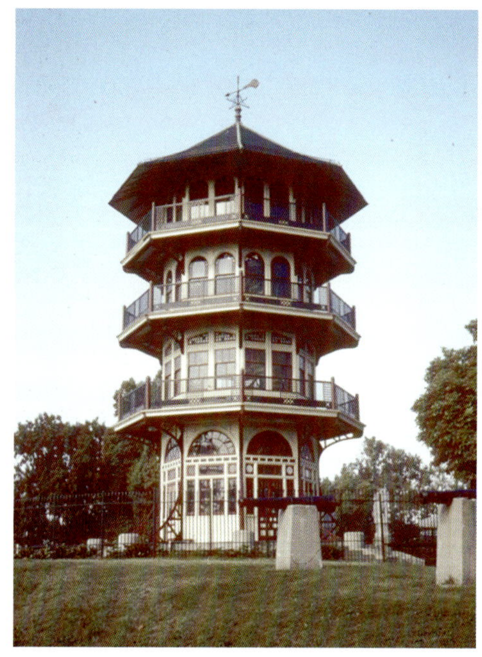

The Patterson Park Pagoda was designed by park superintendent Charles H. Latrobe and completed in 1892. Its form reflected the popularity of all things Asian. The Observatory has always been a major attraction of the park and the area, with expansive views in every direction to the harbor and the city. *Author photograph, 1996.*

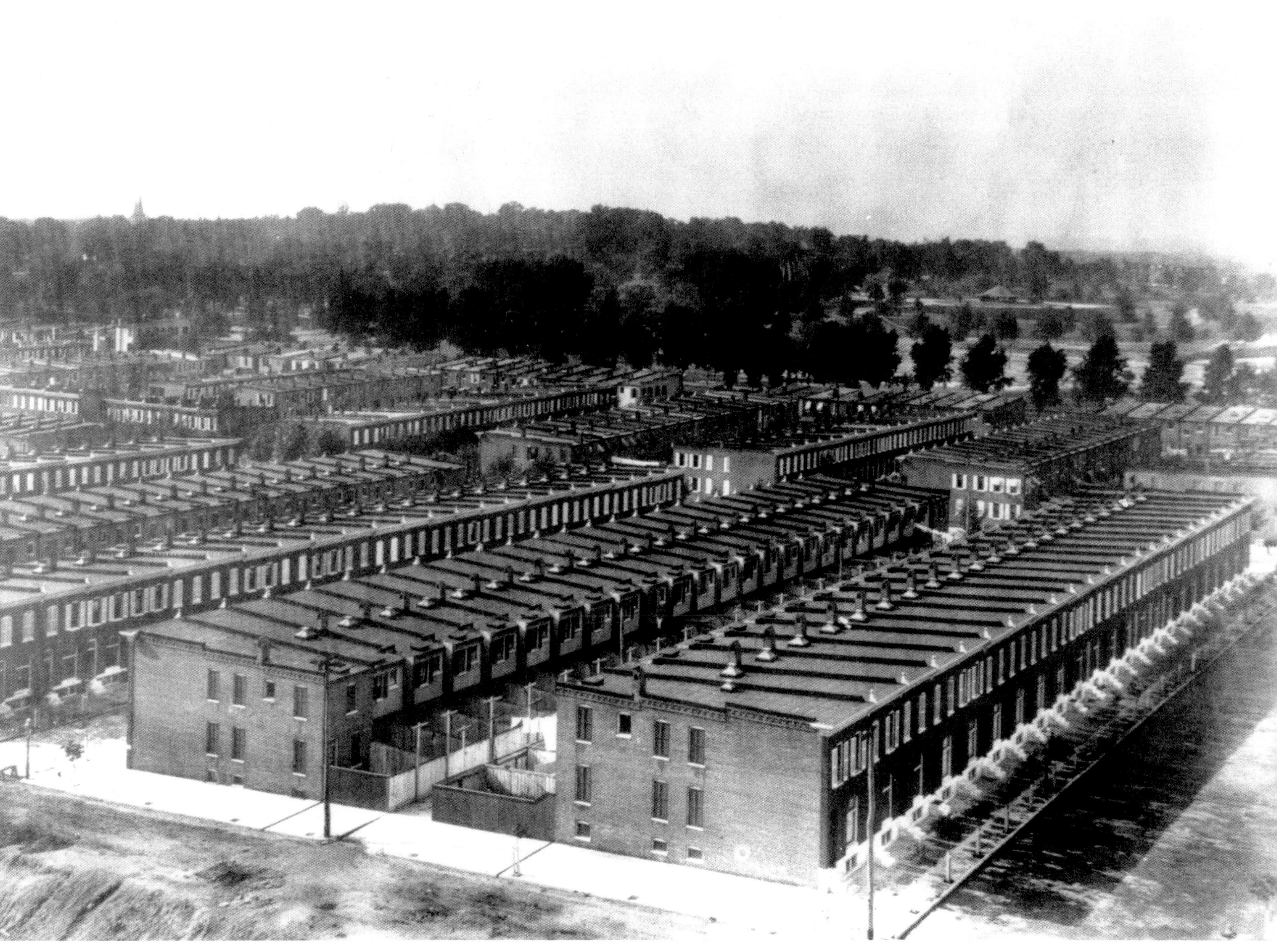

Park Side homes by Gallagher. Aerial view toward Patterson Park.
John Dubas photograph, circa 1911, courtesy of Mary Ellen Hayward.

BUILDING A CITY

The town of Baltimore took shape in 1729 on the banks of the northwest branch of the Patapsco River, twelve nautical miles from the Chesapeake Bay. Here a protected harbor basin, access to a deep-water port (at Fell's Point), and water power combined to offer rich mercantile possibilities. The town thrived and by 1797 was incorporated as a city, merging with the two adjoining settlements of Old Town (founded 1732, on the east bank of the Jones Falls, a raging stream that rushed to the harbor from the north), and Fell's Point (established in 1763 as a shipbuilding community). By 1800 only New York and Philadelphia had larger populations than Baltimore. The city continued to annex land in all directions, until it achieved its present boundaries in 1918.[48]

The Jones Falls originally bisected the city east and west. The early engine of water-powered grist and flour mills drove new textile factories north of the city by the middle of the nineteenth century. Over time it was tamed and submerged by public infrastructure, rerouted, filled, and bridged.[49]

As the city grew in the mid-eighteenth century, merchants extended wharves into the sheltered harbor basin, lining them with warehouses to store the grain and flour they were shipping to Europe and the Caribbean and to hold the fine goods they imported. Soon a thriving downtown business district extended northward from the waterfront, surrounded by rows of attached houses, often with ground-floor shops or counting houses facing the street. To maximize their profits, private landowners began dividing their property into long narrow building lots, following a development model found in London. Baltimore also adopted Britain's equally enterprising system of perpetual leases known as "ground rents." That system enriched local land developers by rewarding them for subdividing their property into as many units as possible, since each new lot earned an annual return.

In East Baltimore, Quaker shipping merchants Edward Fell (1686–1743) and his brother William (1697–1748) acquired land located along the deepest part of the harbor they named Fells Prospect (later Fell's Point). To the east, China trade merchant John O'Donnell (1749–1805) acquired two thousand acres for his country seat, which he named Canton. In 1828, in partnership with William Patterson and Peter Cooper, O'Donnell's son Columbus (1792–1873) developed the Canton Company, an industrial behemoth, where rail lines eventually met the sea. Iron and charcoal works, copper smelters, shipyards, cargo piers, grain elevators, and oil refineries were but a few of the contributors to the area's sustained productivity. The Fell brothers' heirs began to lay out building lots in 1763, and soon streets were being filled by single or paired houses, some brick, but many of frame construction. Few builders in this era could afford to erect more than two houses at a time, but as wealth increased after the Revolutionary War and into the early nineteenth century, speculative builders might put up a row of three or four or even five houses.[50] After the first freestanding structures were built, abutting structures filled in vacant lots. Soon entire blocks of attached homes were being constructed at once.

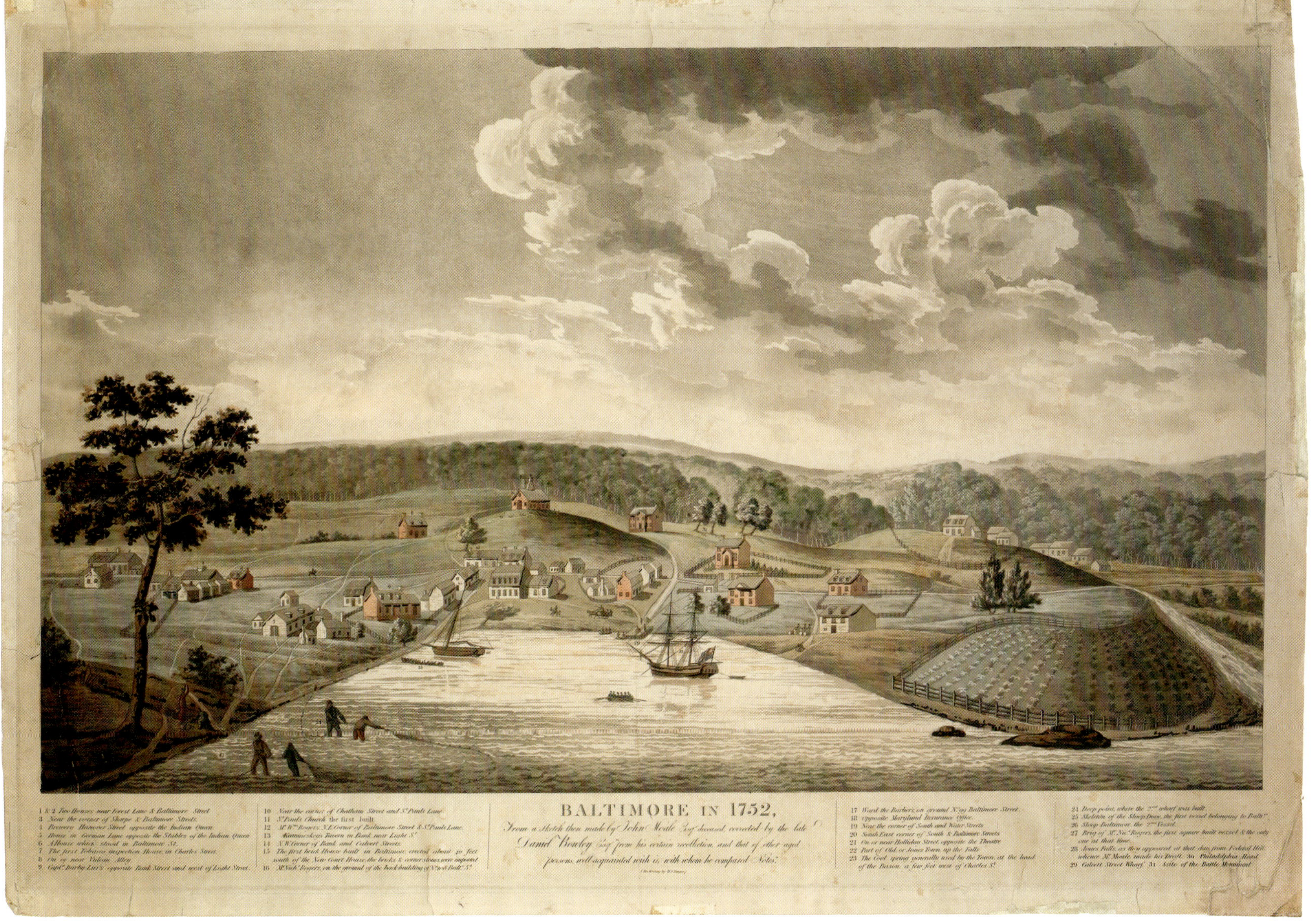

"Baltimore in 1752," William Strickland color engraving, 1817, based on a John Moale Esq. drawing, 1752. © Enoch Pratt Free Library. Maryland's State Library Resource Center. All rights reserved. Used with permission. Unauthorized reproduction or use prohibited.

The earliest houses in Fell's Point and Old Town, built of wood, were vulnerable to fire.[51] Regulations were put in place requiring that buckets, and ladders that reached the rooftops, be kept at the ready. The city levied steep fines for chimney fires. After 1799 any material for home construction other than brick was banned by law.[52] Abundant clay deposits made this city of brick possible. Maps reveal strategically located brickyards throughout the city, at first in seemingly distant locations, but soon flanking the new housing that consumed their output.[53] As builders exhausted the supply of clay in one spot, they moved elsewhere, leaving behind a barren landscape. Rows of homes soon filled in the empty spaces, as new sources for the raw material were revealed elsewhere.

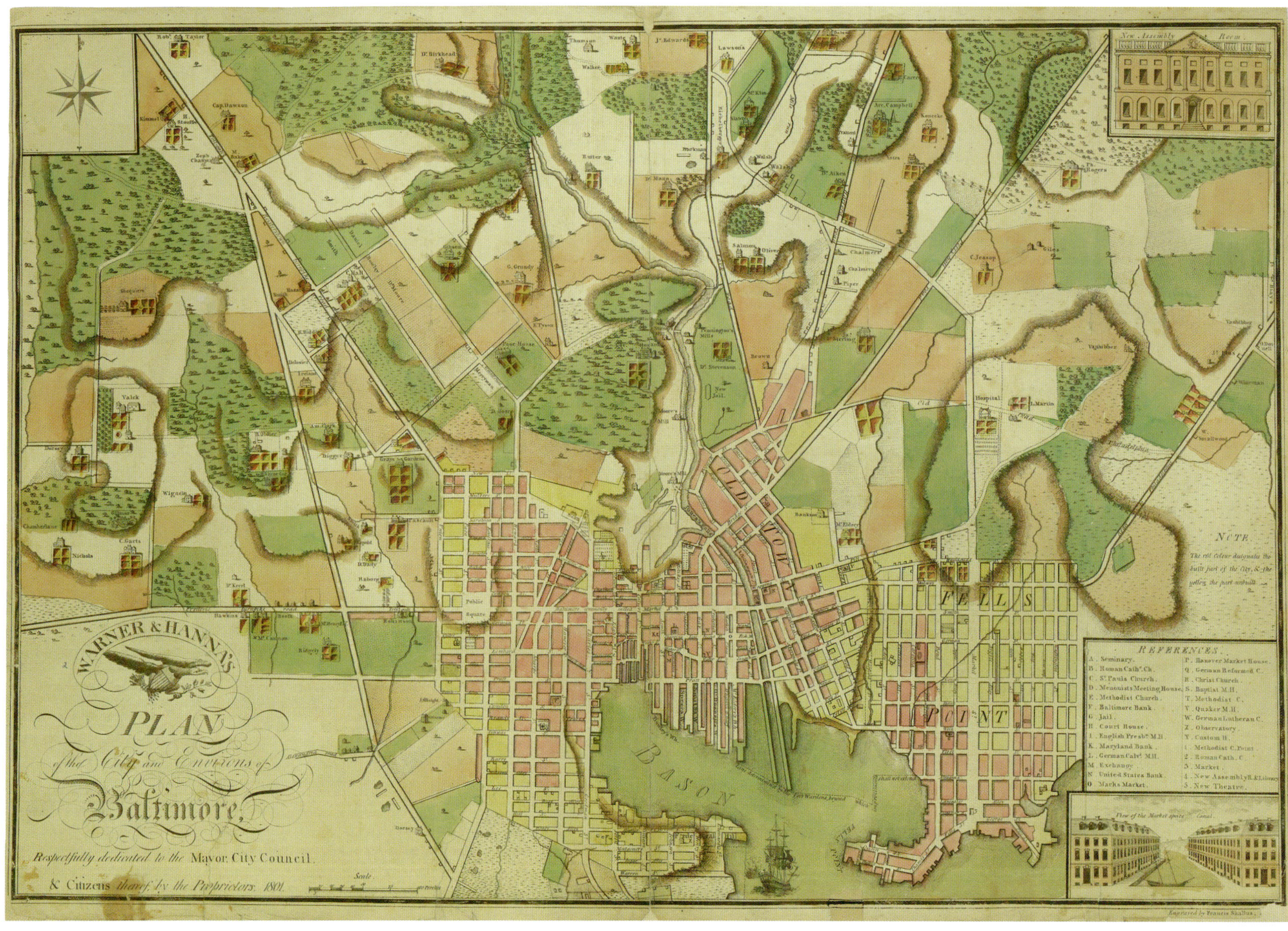

Warner & Hanna's Plan of the City and Environs of Baltimore, 1801. *The George Peabody Library, The Sheridan Libraries of The Johns Hopkins University.*

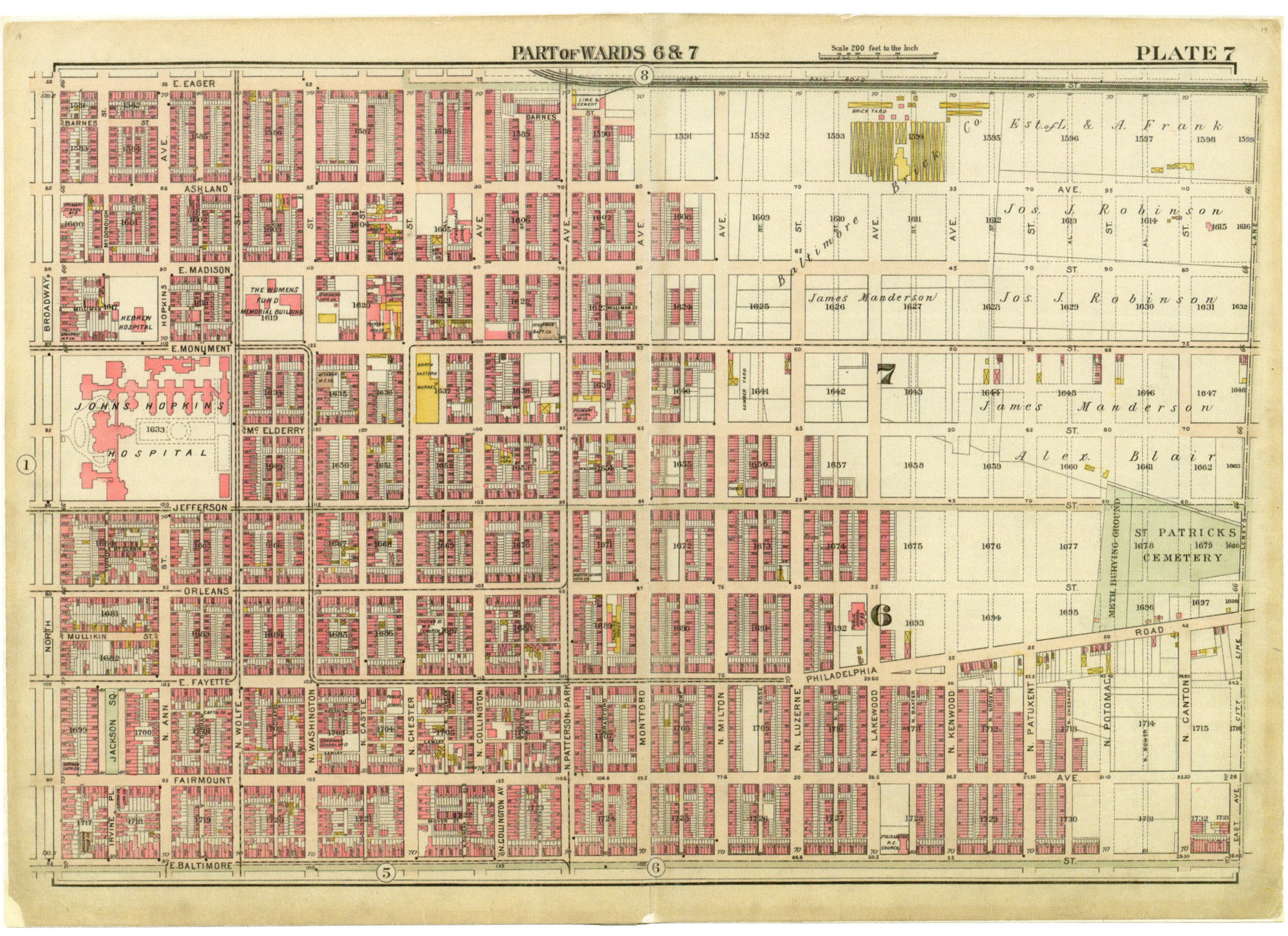

Note vacant plats occupied by Baltimore Brick Co. yards east of North Glover Street and north of Ashland Avenue. Construction replaced brickyards as the rows of Little Bohemia were built. *George W. and Walter S. Bromley's "Atlas of the City of Baltimore Maryland from Actual Surveys and Official Plans, Part of Wards 6 & 7, 1906."* © Enoch Pratt Free Library, Maryland's State Library Resource Center. All rights reserved. Used with permission. Unauthorized reproduction or use prohibited.

"From small scale builders, building a few houses at a time…to large scale developers, with access to large amounts of capital and land, filling whole tracts in the twentieth century," Baltimore took shape.[54] Rowhouses became the dominant housing type for all classes. While wealthy Baltimoreans lived in grand, often architect-designed four-story townhomes built along main thoroughfares and on public squares, more ordinary citizens made their homes in smaller models crafted by builders in simpler vernacular styles.

As the developers began completing entire blocks of rowhouses, building the streets became their responsibility as well. The city required them to lay out, excavate, and pave. Behind the houses, alleys of varying widths provided access to the private spaces that accommodated the back side of daily life—tradesmen's carts, trash, privies, gardens, laundry, and garages for carriages and, later, cars.[55] The happy and practical result of these improvements, or as some might insist, necessities, was a livable domestic environment, based like its British antecedents on a human scale.

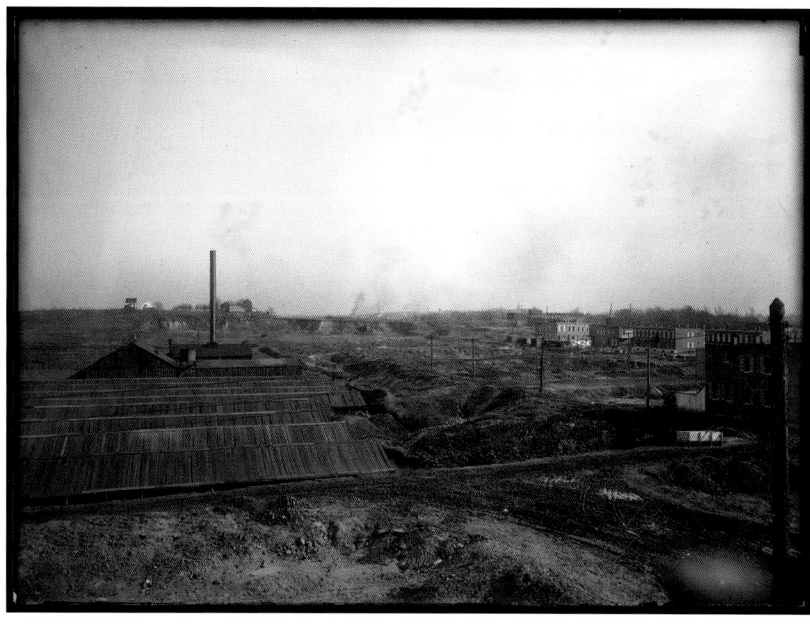

As undeveloped land gave way to neat rows of attached homes west of North Kenwood Avenue above Ashland Avenue, so did the brickyards that had sprung up to support their construction. *John Dubas photograph, 1913. Arthur U. Hooper Memorial Collection, Baltimore City Life Museums Collection. Maryland Historical Society. MC9164-2.*

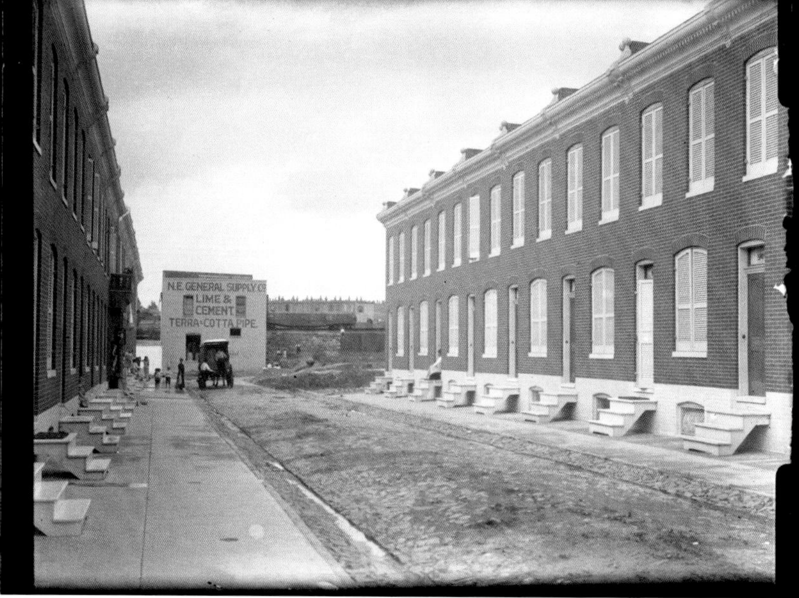

Alley houses like these on the 900 block of North Bradford Street were built alongside the resources—like lime, cement and terra-cotta pipe—used in their construction. *John Dubas photograph, 1905. Arthur U. Hooper Memorial Collection, Baltimore City Life Museums Collection. Maryland Historical Society. MC9178.*

MAKING A HOME
IN LITTLE BOHEMIA

By 1910, Baltimore's population included tens of thousands of immigrants from Ireland, Germany, and Eastern Europe. The Bohemians, from the present-day Czech Republic, constituted one of the largest groups to settle in East Baltimore. They crossed the Atlantic on the North German Lloyd Lines from the port of Bremerhaven to Fell's Point and later Locust Point directly across the harbor in South Baltimore. They chose Baltimore for the availability of factory jobs and the promise of economic advancement, both severely lacking abroad. As the Eastern European population grew, new arrivals moved northeast from the original center of this community, just above Fell's Point at Central Avenue and Baltimore Street, to the area soon to be called Little Bohemia.[56] Modest rowhouses, some aged, others freshly built, awaited the new arrivals. As the city became more industrialized, developers began to create entire neighborhoods near new factories for newly ar-

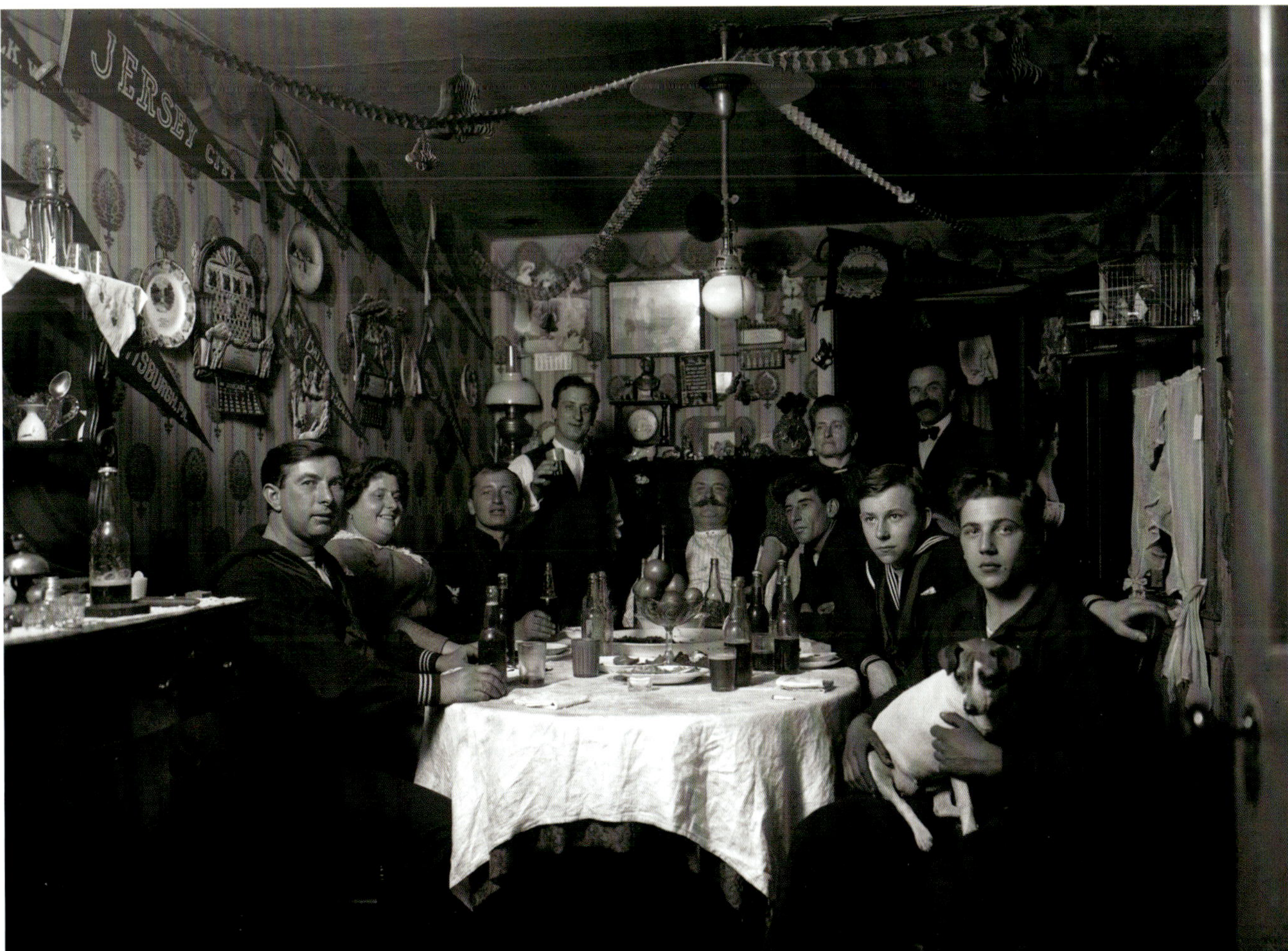

Bohemian sailors celebrate the New Year in a proudly furnished rowhouse dining room reflecting Old and New World values. *John Dubas photograph, 1915. Arthur U. Hooper Memorial Collection, Baltimore City Life Museums Collection. Maryland Historical Society. MC9449.*

rived immigrant workers.[57] By 1844, it was widely known that in Baltimore, "every industrious individual, whether the humble mechanic or the lonely widow, enjoys a cheerful and happy home of their own."[58]

In another move that contributed to Baltimore's specific profile, builders explicitly chose to create a low-rise city, foregoing crowded multifamily, multifloor walk-up tenement houses with rooms that lacked daylight. They sought to avoid the rundown, overcrowded conditions, crime, and disease notorious in New York and elsewhere. "There is little or no inclination to crowd into large and noxious tenements. The individual home for each individual is the rule. And the effect is wholesome."[59] Homeownership, rather than rental, became the norm, and a rowhouse would be the dwelling of choice. The *Daily Record* reported in 1891 that "Baltimore is becoming more and more, preeminently a city of homes and the apartment idea will never become popular with the masses of our people."[60] Within two decades it was a city of 114,000 homes and 49 apartment buildings.[61]

Baltimore's industrial output peaked in the years leading up to World War I. At the start of this period, immigrants had to live within walking distance of their work because there was no affordable transportation network. On salaries of only a few dollars a week, they could ill afford to pay a nickel each way, or sixty cents per week, to travel by horse-car. Most worked in the slaughterhouses, breweries, and rail yards close to home and family. Later, streetcars transported Bohemian workers greater distances to employment at shipyards, steel mills, and canneries, while tailors took streetcars to the garment district in the city center.[62]

In response to a housing shortage in these years, contractors built even more houses, in "jig time," to keep pace with demand.[63] In 1911 a New York writer noted, "Baltimore among great cities would seem to be the paradise of the small income. Nothing is perhaps really cheap in this country nowadays, but by comparison life in this Maryland metropolis is actually within the reach of all."[64] Another New York writer added, "There are hundreds of blocks of little one-family houses…'Two-story houses,' as they are called, though they make many streets long stretches of monotony, [yet] provide decent and comfortable homes for wage earners. For $15 or $20 a month a man can have his own house, of six or eight rooms, with bath, and often with stationary

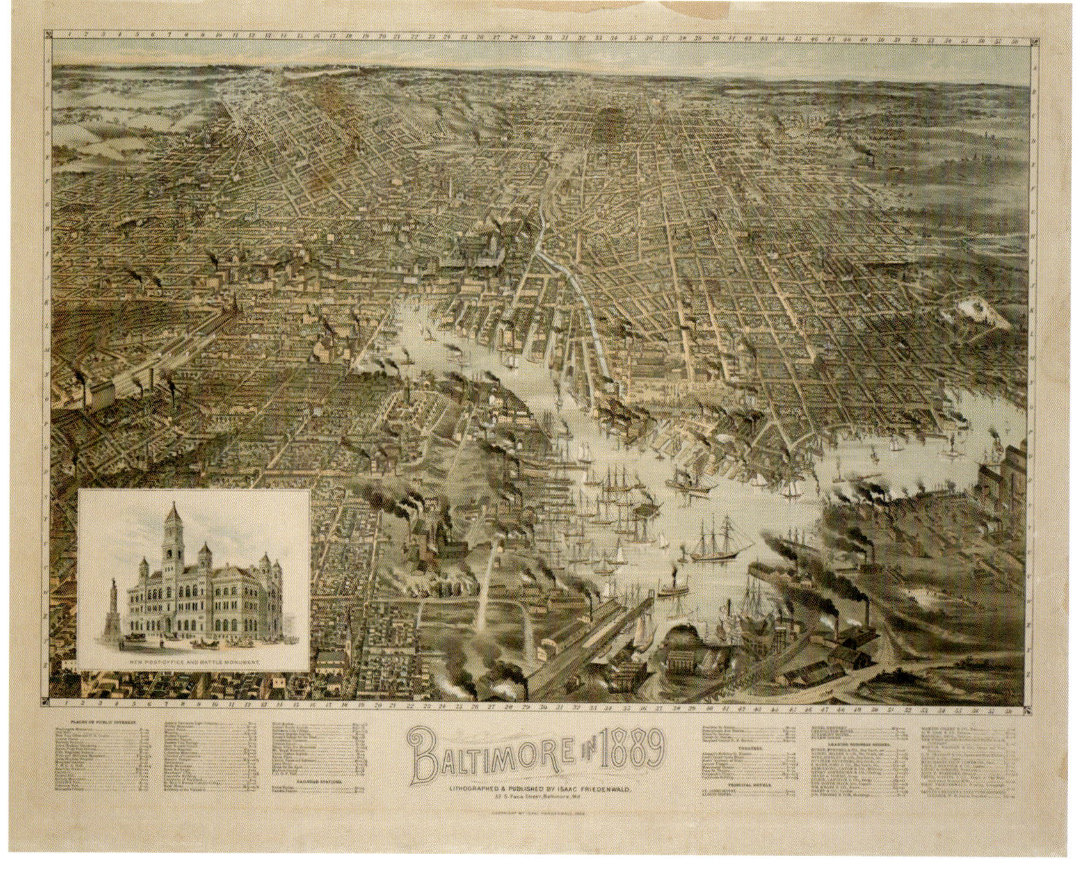

Industrial growth meant jobs, and jobs meant housing as the city spread northward from the harbor. Baltimore in 1889 by Isaac Friedenwald. *©Enoch Pratt Free Library, Maryland's State Library Resource Center. All rights reserved. Used with permission. Unauthorized reproduction or use prohibited.*

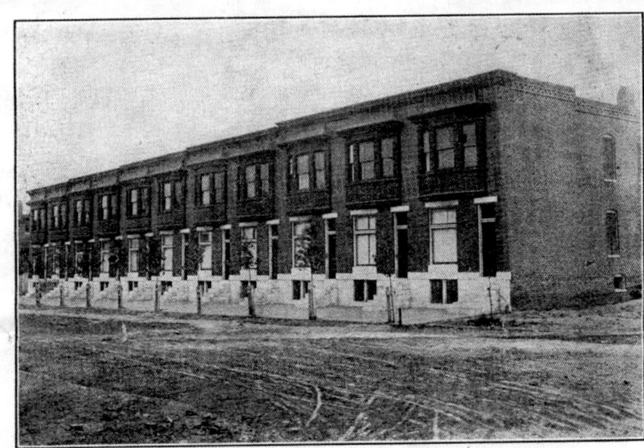

DO YOU WANT A HOME?

IF so, it will be to your advantage to inspect the homes illustrated hereon, before purchasing elsewhere. You will find them ideal houses in every respect, having every modern up-to-the-minute improvement, many of which you will NOT find in other houses. They were built by skilled mechanics, only the very best material being used in their construction, which was under the personal supervision of Mr. Edward J. Gallagher, who has erected more houses in East Baltimore than any other builder and can refer you to thousands of satisfied buyers.

If desired, our representative, Mr. John A. Becker, will call to see you at any time you may suggest, and we feel confident that terms can be arranged entirely satisfactory to you. The prices range from $900 to $1,750, and the expenses are very low.

CALL TODAY.   REPRESENTATIVE ON PREMISES.

EDWARD J. GALLAGHER, Builder.

PHONES:

Monument and Rose Sts., Wolfe 1429.   Lakewood and Eastern Aves., Wolfe 1278.

If you are not interested, do your neighbor or friend, who IS interested, a "good turn" by handing him or her this circular.

A Gallagher-built home included every amenity the new homeowner could imagine, inside and out, 1907. *Courtesy Langsdale Library, University of Baltimore.*

washtubs, cemented cellars and conveniences that in other cities the poor cannot hope for. He can take his basket and go to Lexington or one of the other big markets and get his meats, vegetables, fruits, and entire food supply for less than in almost any other city... These two-story houses are built steadily at the rate of 2,000 a year."[65]

In 1910, a typical twelve- to fourteen-foot-wide house could be purchased for $1,200 to $1,500. The humbler "alley houses," rarely exceeding twelve feet wide, built on narrow streets behind the main avenues, were available for as little as $700.[66] Affordable prices were made possible with the help of ethnic neighborhood building and loan associations. Grateful homeowners dutifully hand-carried weekly cash loan installments and association dues, accompanied by the appropriate coupon. Builders' advertisements touted their value.

It is easier for a man to save money than to find a safe place to invest it. A man should select a building loan association in his own neighborhood in which to deposit his savings and get acquainted with its directors and officers, and to satisfy himself of the security of his money.[67]

Further incentive to homeownership came from Baltimore's system of ground rents, based on the English practice, which allowed for the rental rather than purchase "in fee" of the land on which the building stood. A small sum paid annually to the builder or investor for the privilege of using a piece of land kept a home's purchase price low. After a period of years an option to buy the land could sometimes be exercised by the homeowner.

Two builders in particular, Frank Novak (1877–1945) and Edward J. Gallagher (1864–1933), vied for the title of the "Two-Story King of East Baltimore." Novak, a Bohemian, worked his way up from house construction laborer at the age of thirteen to become the developer of major parts of East Baltimore, including most of the quadrant that became known as Little Bohemia. His employer and mentor, August Hanneman, a German-born builder, died as they were constructing tidy neoclassical rows in 1899. The ambitious young man, then twenty-one, not only finished building the incomplete rows, but managed their sale and helped prospective buyers find financing from local building associations.

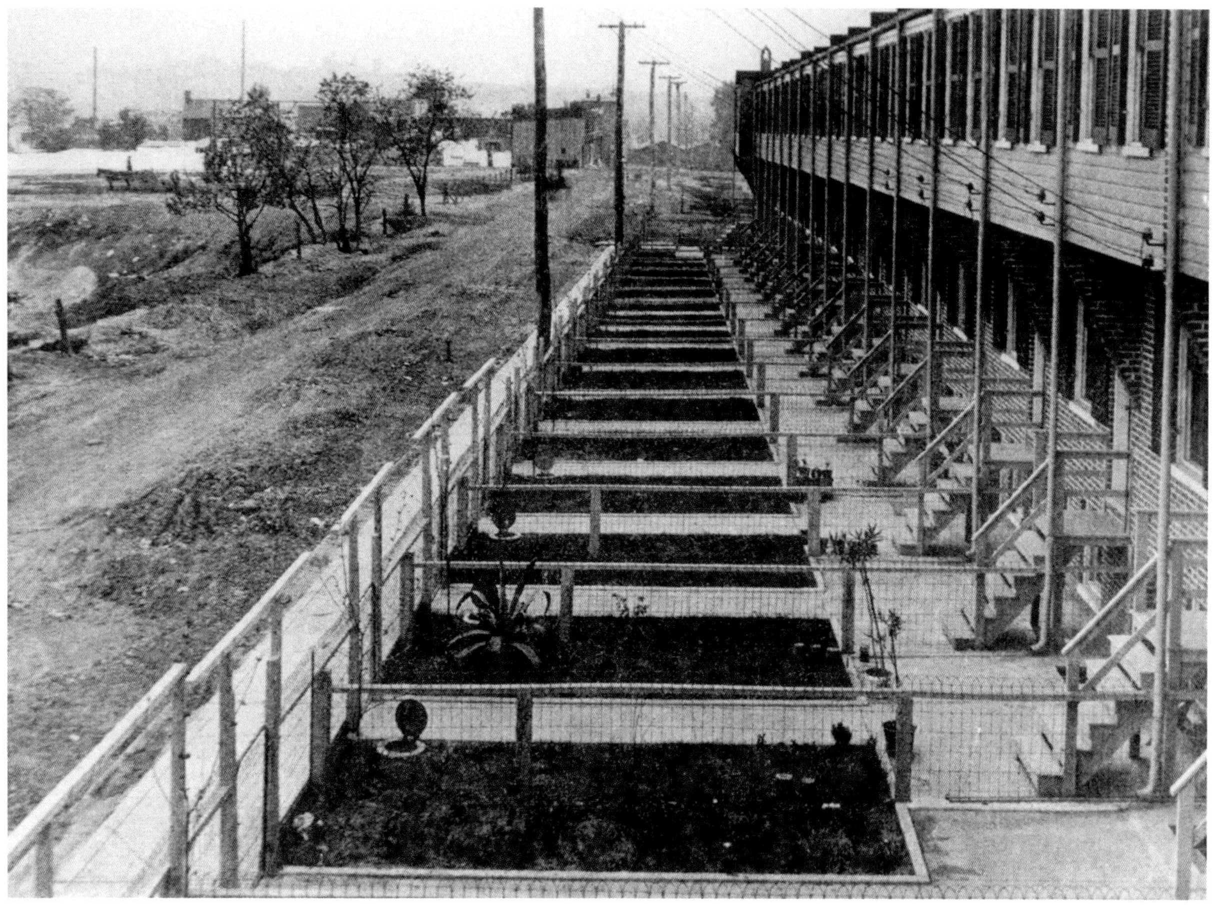

Soon Novak joined in partnership with another, more experienced German builder named Joseph Hirt. Together they purchased vacant parcels of land in Little Bohemia and in 1901 built their first homes on the east side of the 800 block of North Collington Avenue.[68] Even in these first houses Novak added the extra "touch of class" that became his trademark. His "marble houses" featured marble steps and basement fronts of white marble, as well as windows with marble lintels and sills. Wide first-floor windows were fashioned of the newly available large single sheets of plate glass. Colorful leaded-glass transoms topped the front door and front window. His homes like his name were meant to inspire trust, as his company's broadsheets affirmed:

> Over more than a quarter century the most severe test has been applied to Novak construction. Time alone can tell whether a home is well built, whether it is a wise investment. The answer with Novak homes is found in the ever-increasing readiness of the Baltimore home-buyer to accept even blindly, the name Novak as a stamp of sound construction and lasting value.[69]

"Parklike" backyards of the 500 block of North Robinson Street by Gallagher were completed in 1911 and featured prominently in advertising flyers. *Courtesy of Langsdale Library, University of Baltimore.*

Like most of the builders of his day Novak built larger homes facing main streets and smaller, more affordable homes along the alley streets that bisected most city blocks. He accumulated building capital by selling the ground rents he created to investors. With these profits he bought more land, built more houses, and created and sold more ground rents, in a continuous cycle. In East Baltimore alone, Novak built and sold, and then helped finance upwards of 7,500 homes, most to his fellow Bohemians, before expanding his reach to newer suburbs within the city limits.[70]

In 1919, as Novak's empire grew, he engineered a record-breaking deal to acquire the Baltimore Brick Company, which had by this time acquired most of the city's smaller brick-making concerns. He now owned the land, controlled the design and construction process, oversaw sales, and firmly integrated the building materials into his company's operations.[71]

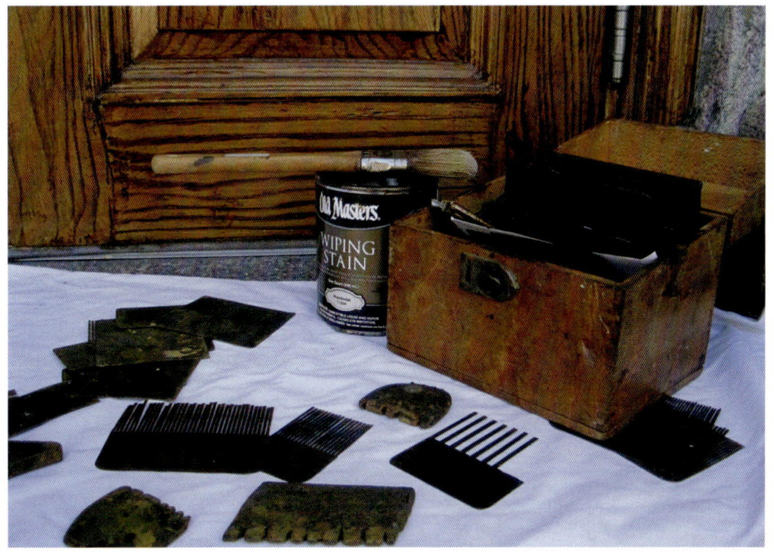

Edward J. Gallagher, Novak's chief competitor, was the son of Irish immigrants. He, too, began his building career in East Baltimore as a house carpenter. In the late 1880s Gallagher built stylish rows north of Patterson Park, expanding his enterprise east and south of the park in the early years of the new century. By his death in 1933 he was credited with having built more than 4,000 rowhomes for working Baltimoreans. Concentrated in the undeveloped areas surrounding Patterson Park, his "Lifetime Homes" often shared adjacent blocks with Novak's. By buying parcels, building modest homes, and collecting and selling ground rents, he made his fortune and helped build a city.

Both Novak and Gallagher added immediately visible but subtle exterior and interior embellishments to their houses: arching curves for windows and doors, decorative keystones, and stained-glass transoms. White marble steps uncompromised by railings or exterior lights spoke eloquently of strength and permanence.[72] Artisans grain-painted pine window frames and front doors to replicate finer wood such as oak and mahogany. Exterior shutters, the earliest and most common solution to the need for privacy and ventilation, were standard on windows and doors, front and back. "Parklike" backyards featured raised garden beds. Meanwhile, practical amenities such as permanent laundry lines, below-ground garbage containers, and rear cement slabs were among the more prosaic features included with every home.

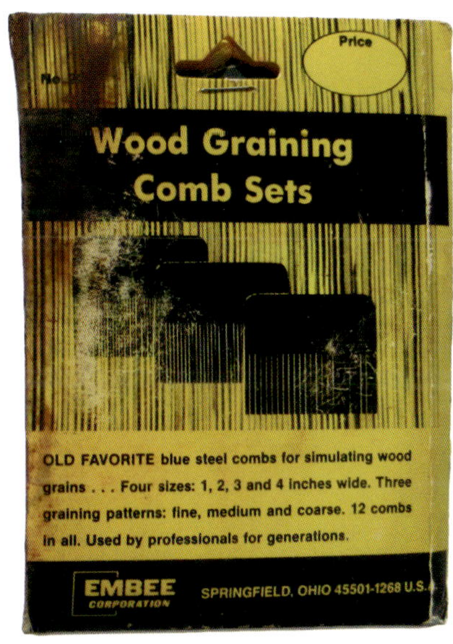

Frank Bittner, a former East Baltimore grainer, inherited the tools for faux-wood graining from his grandfather, who had plied the trade in the Curtis Bay area of Baltimore. A straw-colored door was an invitation to bring his equipment and turn pine to oak. Flexible metal combs, homemade rubber heels, and rags were the mainstay of the trade. Kits could be acquired from Henry Taylor of Sheffield, England, active 1850s–1900 and Embee Corporation of Springfield, Ohio, the last American manufacturer, active 1930s–1980s. Bittner now works his magic throughout Maryland's Eastern Shore. *Collection of Frank Bittner, Hurlock, Maryland.*

FORMSTONE:
NEVER NEEDS PAINTING

In 1937 Albert Knight of Baltimore's Lasting Products Company patented a product called FormStone, a hand-molded cement product replicating individual stonework with mortar joints.[73] Its precursor and longtime competitor Perma-Stone in Columbus, Ohio, dates from 1929. Though originally intended for exteriors of freestanding suburban homes, the product that transformed brick to (faux) stone overnight was unexpectedly and overwhelmingly embraced by rowhouse owners throughout the city of Baltimore. Dozens of companies mimicked the process, slightly varying the formula, shape, or colors for a distinctive look. For some, molds negated the hand-crafted finish. Though it carried a trademark until the 1960s, Formstone became the generic term for any number of brands of simulated masonry or hand-sculpted stone cladding. It was also applied in a fair number of interior "club cellars."

Knight's Lasting Products employed door-to-door salesmen who pitched their product as an all-in-one solution to insulation, leaks, and annual pointing, painting, or striping. Adjacent neighbors who signed their contracts together could get sizable discounts. The process could be completed in a matter of days. Wire lath attached to the brick formed the base layer for concrete that was built up with hand-formed or molded blocks of stone and then colored or sprinkled with sparkling mica. The finishing touch, once the mortar lines were incised, was the placement of the small metal plaque beside the front door identifying the company. (The plaques are now largely missing.)

Competition was fierce. Artificial stone enjoyed a hefty payday in the 1950s and 1960s. It was eclipsed by aluminum and vinyl siding a decade later, but not before most of East Baltimore's red brick had been covered with gray and golden "stone." The sales force merely updated their spiels and became "tin men," carrying their product to the suburbs. Today, more sculptured stone is removed than applied to Baltimore rowhomes. The indelible nail holes and pocked surfaces dotting brick façades where lath was once secured are sure indicators of a mid-twentieth-century remodeling job.[74]

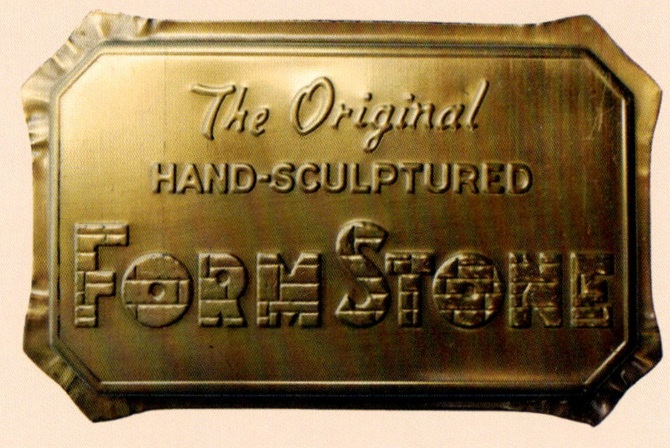

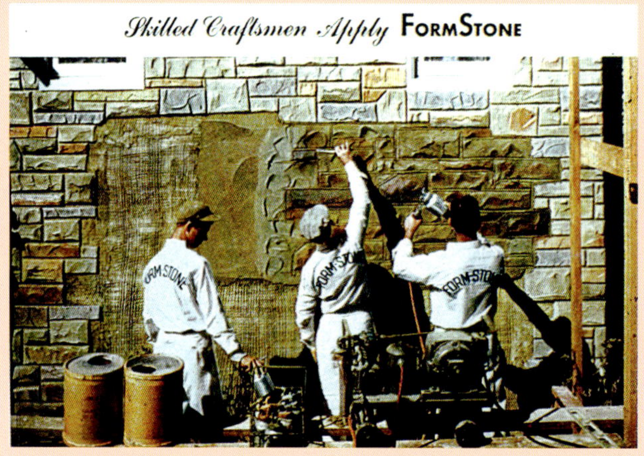

Crews worked swiftly to sculpt the wet, cement-like layers atop chicken wire to build up and complete the characteristic handcrafted appearance of FormStone. *Lasting Products brochure, circa 1950, courtesy of Dean Krimmel.*

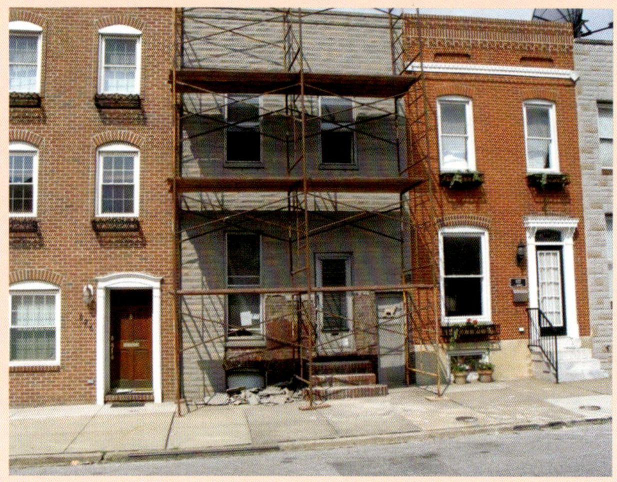

Formstone removal, a sign of changing tastes and demographics, in progress on the 800 block of South Kenwood Avenue, 2008. *Author photograph.*

ROMANCING THE BRICK

Many people, including native Baltimoreans, would say that all row-houses look alike. It was incumbent on the builder to ensure that that was not the case.

You will find them Ideal houses in every respect, having every modern up-to-the minute improvement, many of which you will NOT find in other houses. They were built by skilled mechanics, only the very best material being used in the construction which was under the personal supervision of Mr. Edward J. Gallagher, who has erected more houses in East Baltimore than any other builder and can refer you to thousands of satisfied customers.[75]

By the early twentieth century, builders had access to a new kind of brick that looked more stylish and required less exterior maintenance. New York architects McKim, Mead & White introduced a "light brown 'Roman' brick, low and narrow" for the exterior of Louis Comfort Tiffany's Manhattan mansion in 1883. In wide distribution soon after, it changed the face of the Baltimore rowhouse. Gallagher's Lifetime Homes boasted iron brick among numerous firsts in his East Baltimore rows. Similarly, Golden Spot, Roman, Pompeii, tapestry brick, and iron spot, which "need never be painted," all required less upkeep for the homeowner. Their use led to the demise of a singular occupation that went hand-in-hand with the city's own but inferior brick.[76]

Notorious for being soft and prone to flaking, the red Baltimore brick used for most houses built before the mid-1890s required constant maintenance. Pointing, painting, and penciling were the available fixes to seal moisture out and prevent walls from bulging. Anchor plates with stars decorating the exterior helped keep walls from buckling. Remortaring or pointing was costly. The latter solutions spurred a small group of house painters to take to the streets with scaffolds and highly specialized tools. One of the longer-lasting and most-economical alternatives was to paint the entire masonry surface with a single color (usually brick red or brown). If finances and taste allowed, a further option was to detail the look of mortar with "striping" or "penciling."

Henry "Sonny" Crowley (1926–1994) was among the half dozen "stripers" who worked throughout the city at any given time. During the winter he worked as a piano tuner. He mixed his own paint of "red oxide, linseed oil, turpentine and driers which contained lead,"

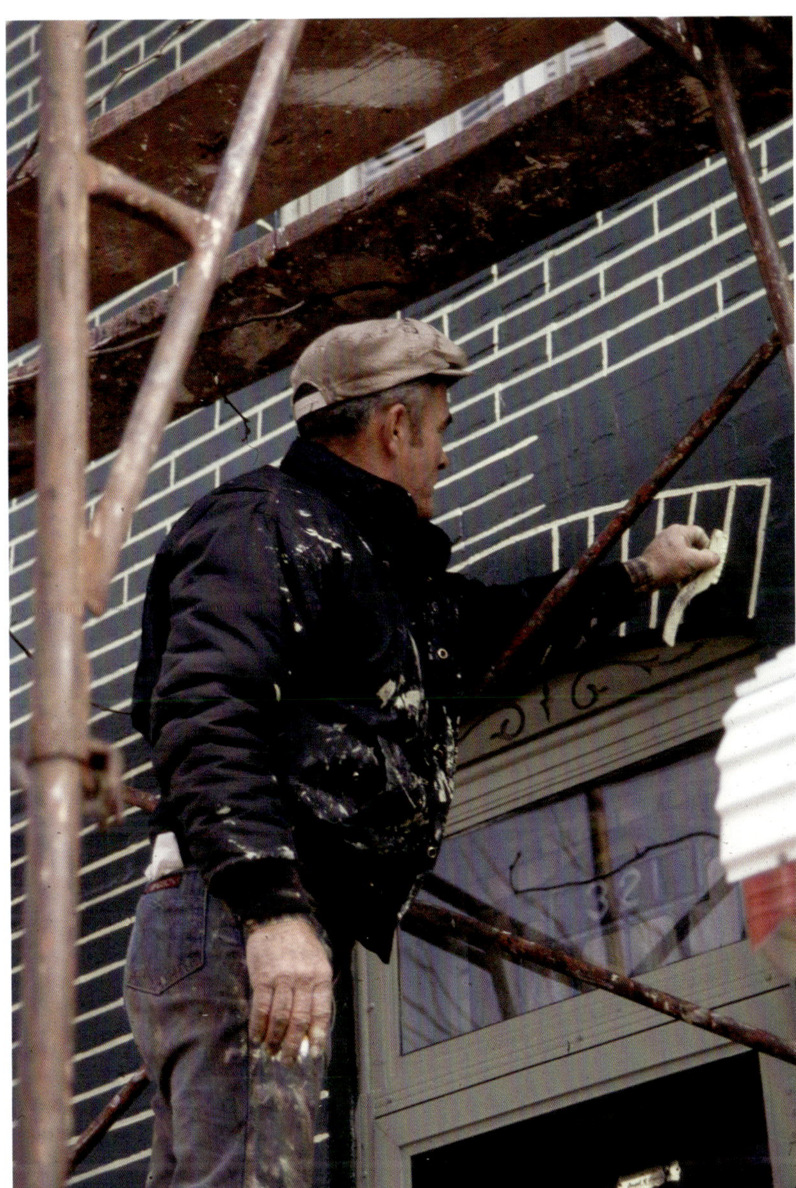

Sonny Crowley stripes the front of the Trabert home on South Chester Street, 1986. Author photograph.

until its use was banned in 1977. Self-taught, he admitted that when he started in the 1940s, for most of the first decade, his houses looked crooked. It took him that long to learn his craft. When asked why there were so few stripers in the city, he mused, "You could learn to be a lawyer faster than you could be a striper."[77] He was probably the last to work the streets of East Baltimore—getting work always by referral, word of mouth, one neighbor to the next, no advertising. A two-story rowhouse was a two-day job. He installed his own scaffolding (in order to save money for his customers) and painted the exterior on the first day. Once the whole house surface had dried, usually the second day, he worked sidewalk to roof, course by course, marking clean white horizontal lines with a tool of his own design that scored the surface with the proper brick width, then applied vertical strokes to simulate cleanly mortared bricks. He removed the scaffolding as he descended and was gone. Cash and carry.[78] This occupation born of necessity required innovative solutions. All of his tools, including his paintbrushes, were of his own invention. Methods and equipment varied with each artisan and from job to job. Crowley was able to size up a house from the street. Over the years he found that he could no longer trust the natural mortar lines for his template: "If I follow the lines, the house will look like it's falling over."

Decades before Sonny Crowley put away his scaffolding, rulers, and brushes in the late 1980s Formstone challenged brick's dominance in Baltimore. Although this artificial stone veneer was guaranteed to improve with age, and touted as economical, weatherproof, self-insulating, permanent, and, above all, beautiful, Crowley's customers chose to ignore it.[79]

WHITE MARBLE STEPS

Beyond the front door, a narrow piece of sidewalk the width of the living area was all the outdoor space the rowhouse dweller could claim. And if not for the three or four steps jutting out from the façade, leading to the front door, there would be no delineation between public and personal space.

The lack of privacy that was part and parcel of rowhouse living had long ago become an accepted feature, if not a virtue, of the housing style. No lawn to mow. No fence to paint. No garden to weed. But passersby could easily peer into the parlor, while life unfolded on the front "stoop." This was no ordinary threshold. The white marble steps were "a fad, a style, a convention, a tradition, a mark of respectability."[80] They provided a place to catch a breeze, the news or the latest gossip, smoke a cigar, slurp a snowball, drink a beer. They afforded a spot to meet and greet friends and strangers. They offered a seat, a perch for a single foot while standing and visiting. A great deal could be learned by observing who sat and who stood during a conversation. Many a courtship began there.

Before there was marble, steps were built of wood and painted white. Brick, stone, or cement would do as replacements (wooden stairs could be turned upside down overnight to discourage trespassers). But the white marble steps were so widely used that they became a

A typical Saturday almost anywhere in Baltimore found the women, and the occasional young boys, out scrubbing their marble steps. *"Washday," 1948. Photograph by A. Aubrey Bodine ©Jennifer B. Bodine. Courtesy of www.aaubreybodine.com.*

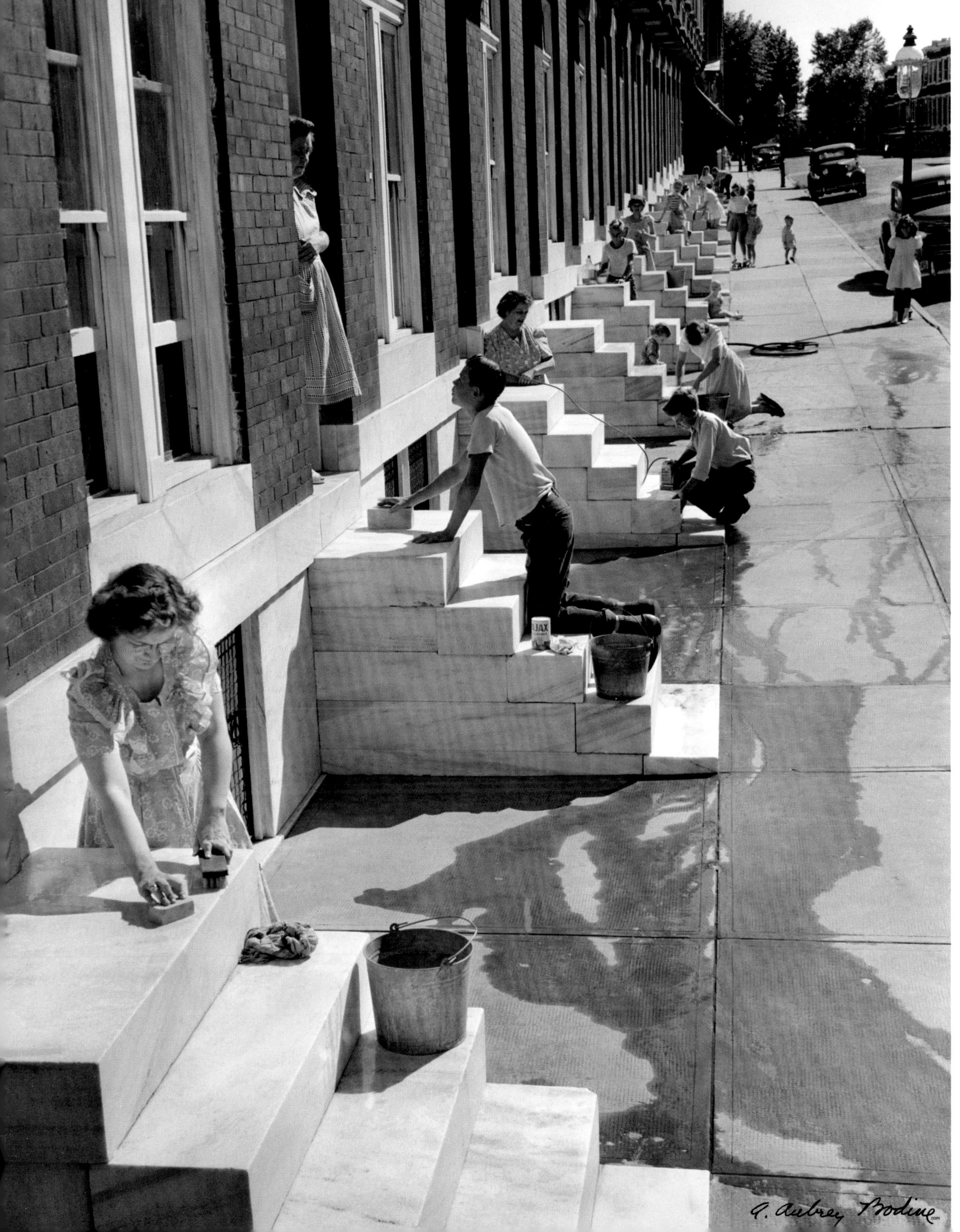
JAX

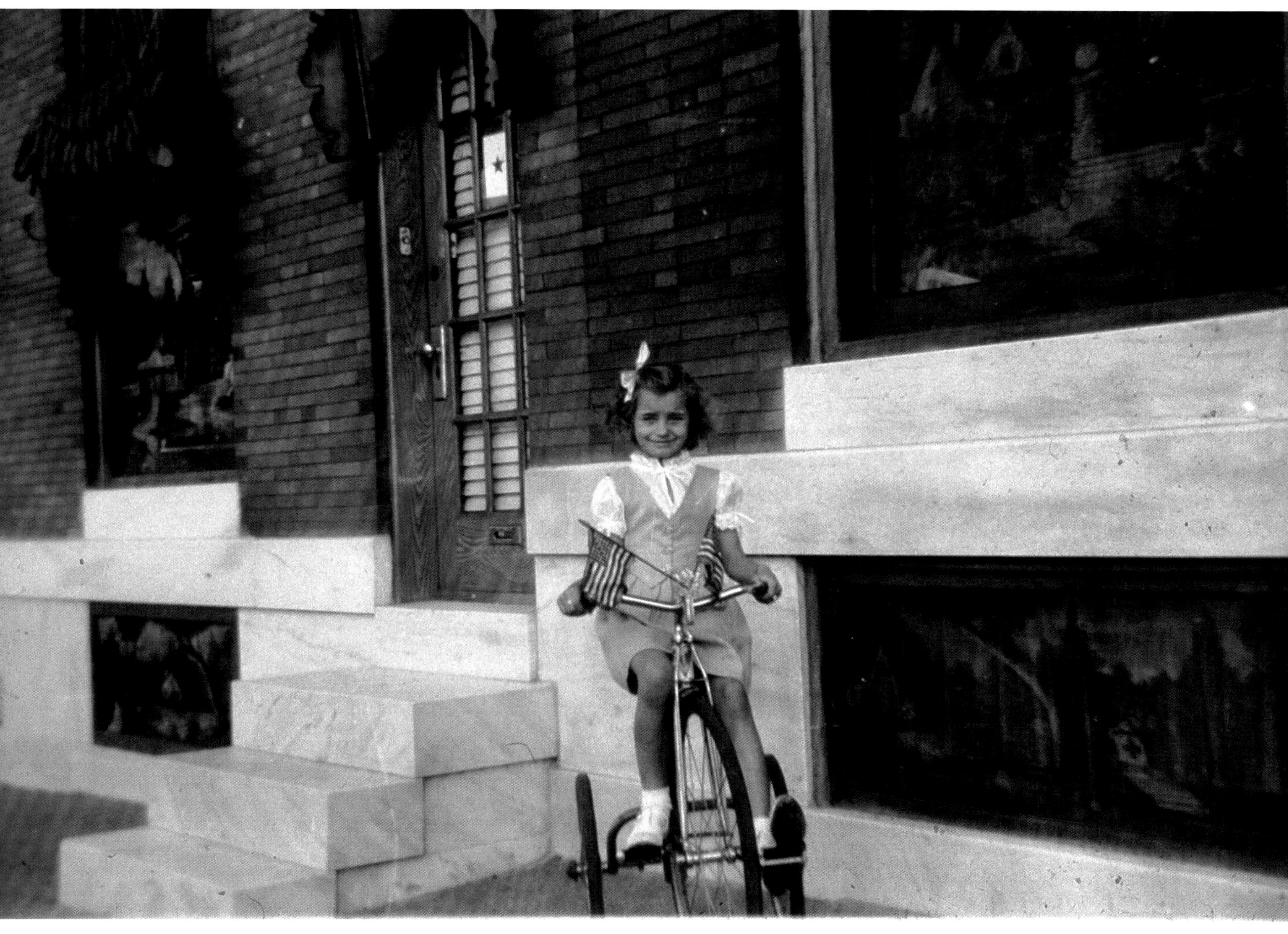

Carol Sealover Doroff of 249 South Ellwood Avenue shows off her new tricycle while painted screens and awnings protect the house from sun and prying eyes, circa 1940. *Photograph courtesy of Bruce Doroff and John Cain.*

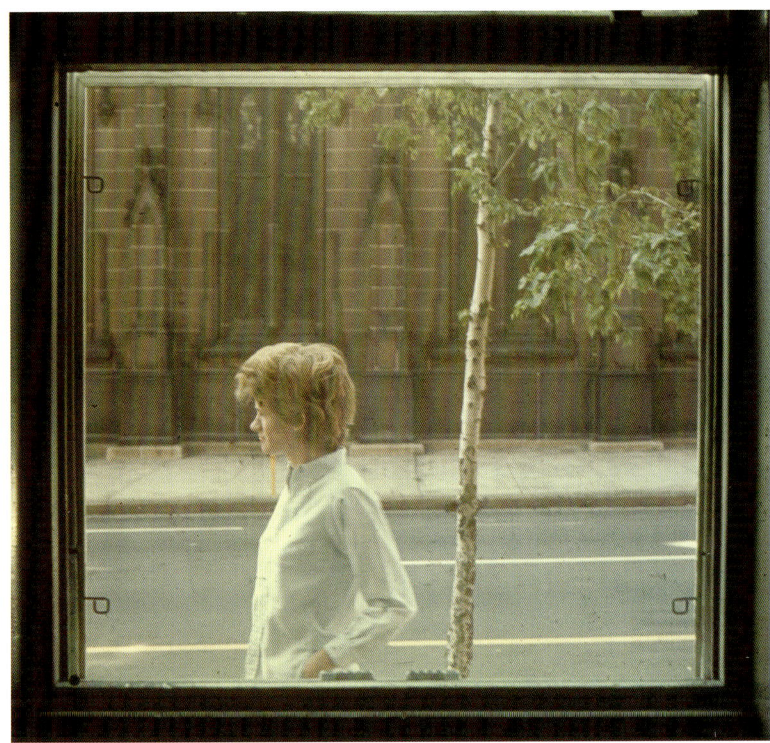

"You see out..." A. Aubrey Bodine snapped this shot of his daughter Jennifer passing by one of their Richard Oktavec screens in 1963 to demonstrate its transparency from indoors. *Photograph by A. Aubrey Bodine ©Jennifer B. Bodine. Courtesy of www.aaubreybodine.com.*

slice of Baltimoreana. Their prevalence was due to a nearby supply, both plentiful and economical. Beaver Dam quarry in Cockeysville, Baltimore County, was one of many sources in the region with a remarkably abundant vein of white dolomite marble, valued for its density, strength, and permanence. Fracturing was rare. The seemingly endless supply was used to build Baltimore's Washington Monument in Mount Vernon Place in 1815, Washington's version in 1879, Baltimore City Hall in 1876, and, with its final extraction, the University of Maryland's Art and Science Hall in 1934. When railroad spurs were directed straight from the quarry to Baltimore, it was not unusual for contractors to purchase half a carload of four-foot white steps at a time.[81]

In the city's Highlandtown neighborhood, Miller's brick and marble yard not only did the brickwork for Edward J. Gallagher but also supplied and set the marble for steps and house fronts. They chose to import a harder marble from Georgia. Their stock arrived by rail in twenty-foot-long shafts as thick as a step.[82] "Because that stone was at hand, and relatively cheap, Baltimore became a town of red brick and white marble that travelers never forgot."[83]

Housewives took tremendous pride in their steps, scrubbing them daily or at minimum each Saturday. It was widely agreed that "the whitest steps as a group belonged to East Baltimore."[84] Women were always the dominant caretakers of the steps. A youthful male might be spotted helping out, but likely for a fee. Ladies clad in printed cotton house dresses knelt on the sidewalk over their sparkling thresholds, as if in prayer. They considered it their duty and a measure of their domestic accomplishment to claim the brightest steps on the block.

Enterprising individuals came forward to capitalize on the chore. "The little girl who goes from house to house with a bucket—or without one—offering to scrub white steps for a dime" was in evidence in 1913.[85] Even Eleanora Fagan, later known as Billie Holliday (1915–1959), who as a teenager lived in Fell's Point in "a little old house on the 200 block of S. Durham Street," recalled "scrubbing those damn white steps all over Baltimore."

"When families in the neighborhood used to pay me a nickel for scrubbing them down, I decided I had to have more money, so I figured out a way. I bought me a brush of my own, a bucket, some rags, some Octagon soap, and a big white bar of that stuff I can't ever forget—Bon Ami. The first time I stood on a white doorstep and asked this woman for fifteen cents for the job, she like to had a fit." Billie figured that bringing her own supplies plus scrubbing the bathroom or kitchen floor allowed her to ask for fifteen cents instead of the usual five [cents].[86]

Journeymen laid off from the steel mill in Sparrows Point offered semiannual muriatic acid whitening treatments—a delicate procedure.[87] Decades later, one enterprising pharmacist in search of outdoor employment took note of the steps surrounding him and created a new service for at least "six East Baltimore householders, scrubbing their steps two or three times a week, the year round, at fixed rates."[88] In an effort to develop the perfect cleansing formula that would result in "a grade A job," he interviewed marble workers in the area to learn their secrets and recommendations. The spit polish marked his work "as if I'd written my signature on it."[89] The door-to-door business of cleaning and re-grouting steps sprang up seasonally well into the 1980s. Contributing to a diminished presence of diehard scrubbers was the inability of hardware and corner groceries to acquire, at any cost, the custom cleansing stones required for the job.

The best method to gain maximum shine and brilliance was a much-debated topic. Tools and methods were closely guarded. Should pumice in a solid, gritty, or powdered form be used? From what source? If commercial cleansers were used, each housewife had her absolute favorite. And never ask to borrow the prized scrubbing blocks of sandstone or marble. They were rowhouse gold. They can still be discovered in secured spots in homes throughout the city. No one questioned that the steps needed regular attention to keep up appearances, but consensus on the best method has yet to be reached. One point of agreement was that the marble was always cool and that once the afternoon sun passed over, the front stoop was the only place to be.

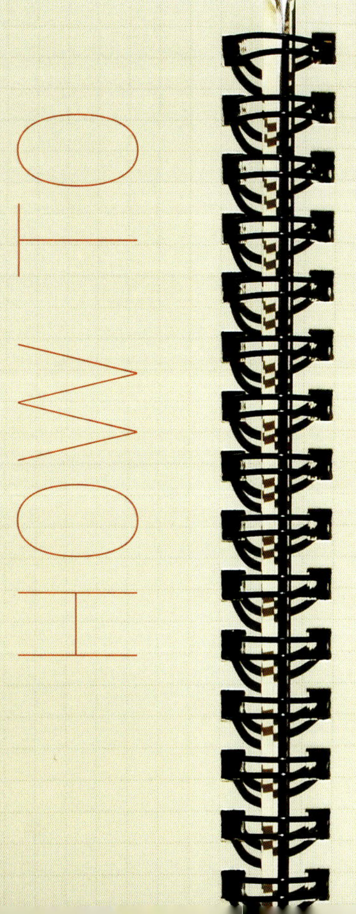

HOW TO

HOW TO CLEAN MARBLE STEPS

The marble steps of Baltimore have inspired younger generations who may never have experienced the heyday of step-scrubbing. A performance piece by artist Megan Hildebrand involved teaching twenty-first-century East Baltimore rowhouse residents the art of caring for their steps. Baltimore's Stoop Storytelling series, created by writers Jessica Henkin and Laura Wexler, tries to recapture the city's congenial tradition of passing the day's stories from house to house. A folk tradition passed down by example or word of mouth, the process and materials suggested below were compiled by the author from personal experience and many neighborly sources:

· 1 bucket of warm water
· Clean rag. Dip in warm water and wipe down.
· Cleanser—Bon Ami™, Dutch Boy™, Borax™ soap or powder. Sprinkle on step.
· Scouring stone, pumice, or a stiff bristle or metal brush. Scrub in circular motion.
· Rinse with rag or water from bucket.
· Repeat weekly.

WINDOW DRESSING

Steps were either sparkling or not, populated or empty. They might hold, however briefly, the daily newspaper (morning and evening), milk, eggs, and donuts delivered by the milkman. Not much more. But the window, a large single expanse of clear glass conveniently located at eye level, presented infinite possibilities. Shutter it, drape it, open it, close it, use it for display. Why the windows of East Baltimore were not called picture windows is anyone's guess. Instead, Americans waited fifty years for suburbia to rediscover that windows of tract houses allowed people to observe and survey one another on a daily basis.[90] From mom's rocker or dad's upholstered chair, perfectly placed by the wall, but turned just enough to command a view both inside and out, residents watched the changing scene outdoors.

The first floor front of the typical East Baltimore two-bay house had only one window and one door. Some houses featured a vestibule that opened off the front portal to an interior door, limiting light and air. Many of the houses built after 1900 featured fixed exterior shutters on doors and windows, with louvers aimed downward to repel rainwater. They were painted white to match the steps and repel heat. Shutters attached to window and door casings could be closed from inside or, in the case of first-floor windows, from the pavement. During the hottest days of summer, entire blocks appeared sealed from the outside. Windows and doors were actually wide open to permit the flow of air through the vented shutters, keeping the house dark and cool inside. As money or inclination came to homeowners, they added handsome striped exterior awnings to east- and west-facing windows to deflect most of the sun but still allow an unobstructed view. Conscientious about caring for their awnings, residents drew them in each evening as the heat of the day ebbed.

Most East Baltimore rowhouses had three rooms on each floor. Alley houses often had only two. Kitchens were in the basement, guaranteed to be cooler than the living space upstairs. The entry crossed the marble threshold either directly into the parlor or through a tiled vestibule tiny enough to make it impossible to accommodate the passage of large items of furniture or caskets. The windows were routinely removed and used for that purpose. Within the house, residents met new challenges for bringing light and air in. The front and back rooms had generous windows, but the central room required synthetic light until the "Daylight" or "Sunlight" house debuted in 1915, offering a rear cut-in allowing natural light into interior rooms (excluding the bathroom). Opposing front and rear windows and doors were meant to facilitate cross ventilation. Before fans became common and long before the introduction of window-unit room air conditioners made

A cutaway of 913 North Luzerne Street shows the practical simplicity of the Baltimore rowhouse. *Illustration by Gloria Mikolajczyk, for Root & Chester Design, and Jane Selden. Courtesy of Mary Ellen Hayward.*

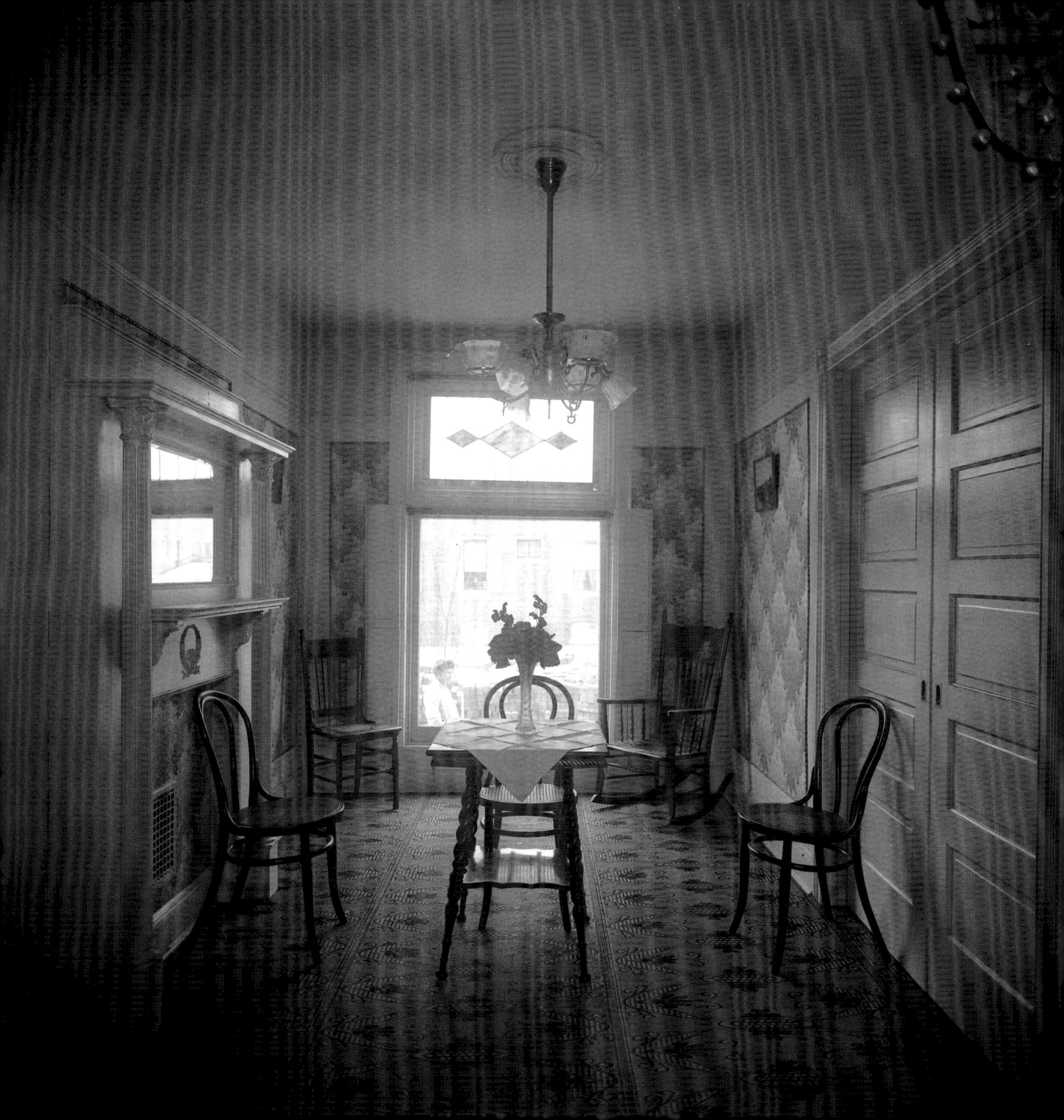

their way to these humble dwellings in the 1950s and 1960s, builders and residents tried a variety of improvements to cope with rising (and falling) temperatures of Baltimore's four seasons.[91]

Two-story homes in East Baltimore had features that mimicked larger and more expensive houses built in the Renaissance Revival or neoclassical style in Baltimore in the 1890s and early 1900s.[92] Novak and Gallagher used fashionable touches like vestibules, pilasters between the front and middle rooms, highly decorative wallpaper, and mirrored overmantels as marketing devices to make their houses more appealing. Another borrowed amenity, folding interior wooden shutters, either louvered for ventilation, or solid for insulation, might be tall enough, when closed, to cover all or part of the parlor and bedroom windows. They were unobtrusive, tucked away neatly, and provided privacy and security. However, they also reduced the amount of daylight and air that flowed into the room, and they were finicky and in need of constant repair. These drawbacks and the arrival of air conditioners would cause the shutters to be tossed out by the thousands.

With seasonal regularity, the meticulous housekeepers of East Baltimore took special pains to maintain the parts of their homes' interiors that overlooked the sidewalk. Windows were dutifully covered with heavy drapes in winter, which were swapped for lightweight lacy curtains in spring and summer.

> If you were in step with your neighbors, you'd have the winter window shades rolled up and put away, the screens up and the summer shades in place. In the month of May, you took down the white or ecru window shades…of the light color to admit all possible sunlight through the dull winter months. You then put up the dark blue shades to keep the intense summer sun from fading your furniture upholstery. You'd have the heavy winter rugs beaten clean and stored, and your floors covered with grass summer rugs to keep the house cool.[93]

It was always a mystery where the housewives found space in these closet-compromised, storage-limited homes to stash this rotating supply of dry goods. Even more bewildering were the variety of ephemera and porcelain saints and collectibles that found their way to the front sill, the domestic equivalent of a shop window. Women kept a constantly changing array of goods in basements or under beds as a way of countering their own *horror vacui*.[94] The huge expanse of the front window—up to a mammoth fifty inches on a side—could not be unadorned. The space called out for attention, possibly for admiration, even if the displays were only to be savored at a glance by pedestrians moving along the sidewalk.

If all the homes looked alike from the outside, the front window presented an opportunity for individuation. It hung precisely at eye level. Similarly, the elongated horizontal basement window was positioned at the right height to greet a child's gaze. Decorated windows became an exclusive showcase for the lady of the house to express herself, to communicate, to make a personal statement, or to signify domestic accomplishment.

The decorated rowhouse window was the equivalent of the flower garden in a suburban neighborhood. Some displays were perennials, some annuals, some monthlies. The statuary

The oversized parlor window maximized incoming light. *John Dubas photograph for Frank Novak Realty Co. flyer, December 8, 1912. Arthur U. Hooper Memorial Collection, Baltimore City Life Museums Collection. Maryland Historical Society. MC9246.*

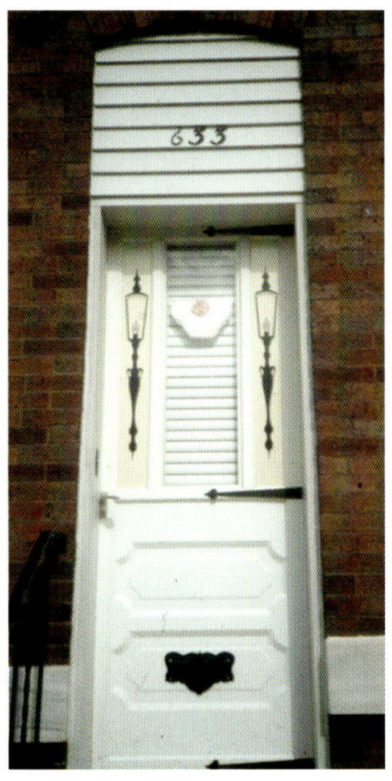

installed there was the urban equivalent of a gazing ball or a pink flamingo on a well-manicured lawn. Selecting the perfect piece of pottery, glass, or ephemera for these windows was—and in some neighborhoods still is—a cyclical task and a cause for competition among neighbors, as one husband explained:

She loves to do it. See this [the fall leaves and jack-o-lantern lights] will be up for a few more weeks and then as soon as Halloween is over, it will come down and she'll decorate for Thanksgiving. Then it'll be Christmas. See that house across the street? He used to decorate his windows too and they'd try to beat each other out. He'd call up and say to my wife, "So why do I have my decorations up before you?"[95]

Where functional interior shutters once made three-dimensional window displays impossible, and closed exterior shutters made them unnecessary, once the shutters were removed the bare window presented an opportunity to share a precious object, a specific interest, or even news. Shelves were customarily installed to deepen the sill and allow items of greater size and weight to sit at the bottom or climb up to the top. In wartime it was not unusual to find handwritten odes, patriotic colors, and framed photographs of absent servicemen. A modeler of many-masted ships or harbor tugs showed off his latest completed work. The Black Madonna Our Lady of Czestochowa or the Virgin Mary were always in style. A window full of prized African violets might reveal a resident's green thumb. Handwritten and printed announcements tucked in a corner signaled births, church suppers, bingo, and golden wedding anniversaries or offered crocheted afghans, coddies (codfish cakes), or Avon cosmetics for sale. The front window was also the only spot to post "For Sale" or "For Rent" signs, express a political preference, or remind loiterers to "Keep off the Steps."

Neighbors as well as tourists looked forward to walking by the "Elvis shrine" overflowing from the living room to fill Elizabeth Wozniak's Fell's Point front window. Maintained in loving memory since the King "left the building" in 1977 was a display of Elvis-related busts, statues, news clippings, bumper stickers, rhinestone and gilded jewelry, alongside a statue of the Blessed Virgin. It was shocking to many when this South Ann Street landmark vanished after its curator and number-one Elvis fan passed away.

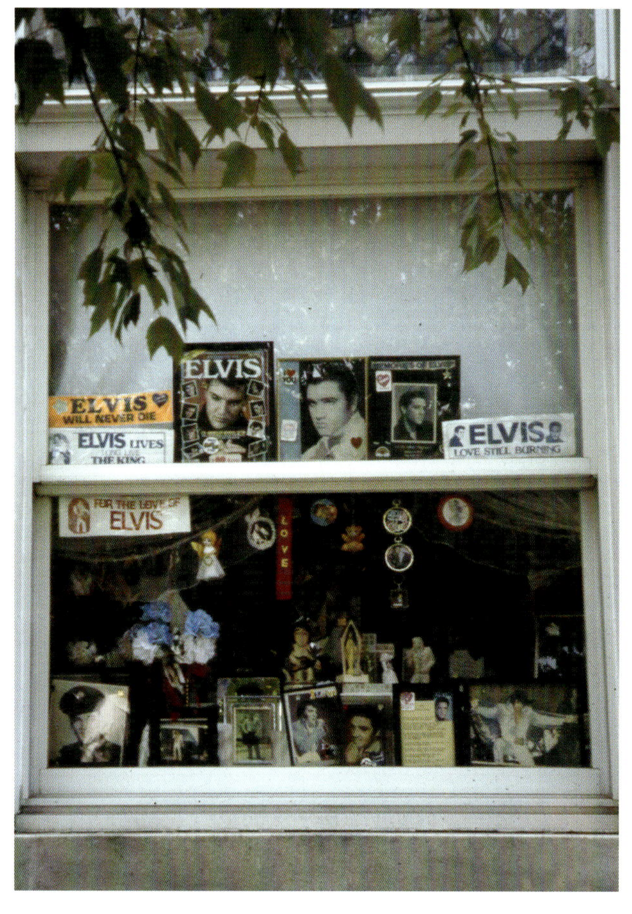

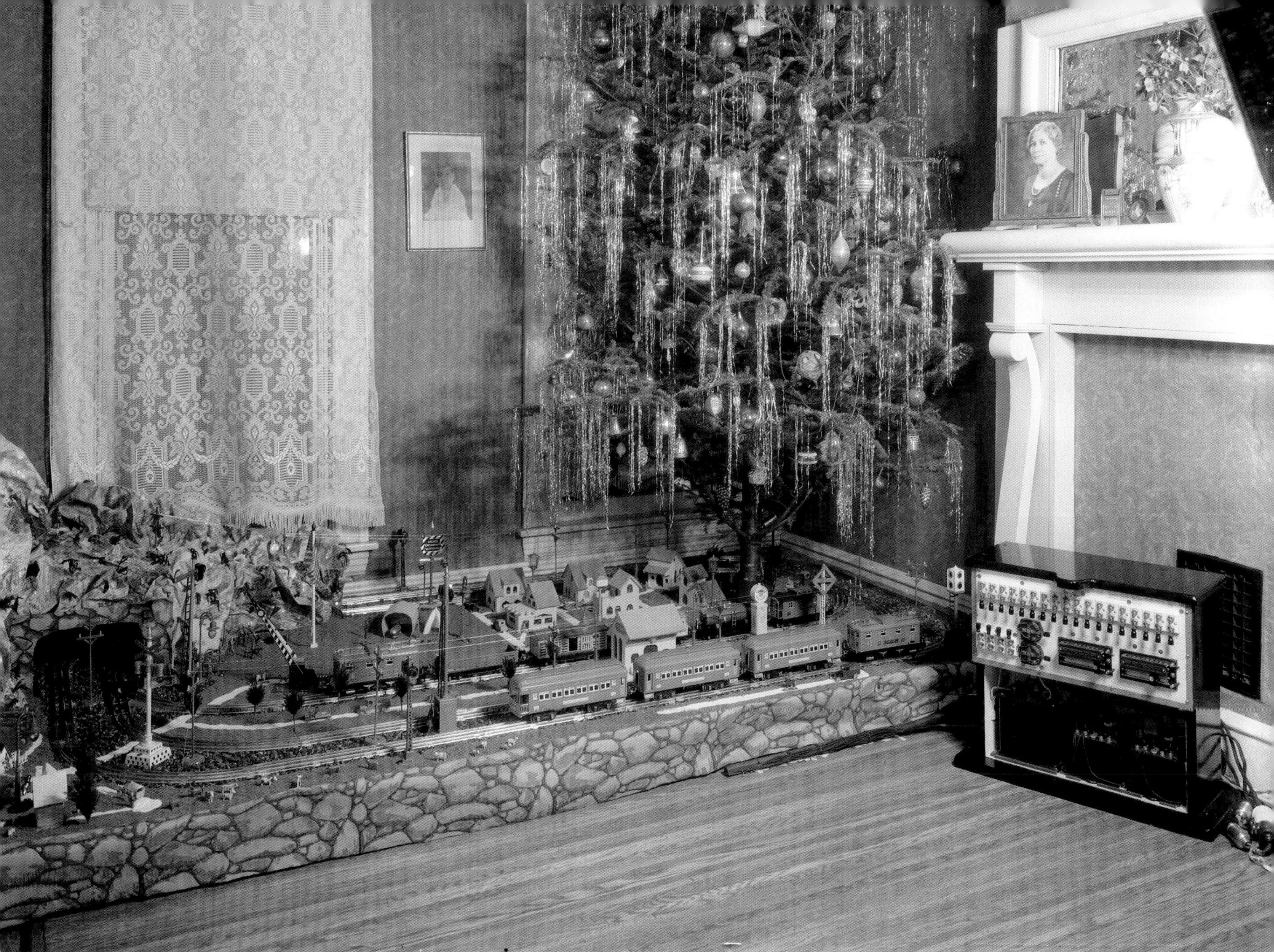

Baltimore's Christmas (or train) gardens were adapted from the German tradition. *John Dubas photograph, circa 1930. Arthur U. Hooper Memorial Collection, Baltimore City Life Museums Collection. Maryland Historical Society. MC9268-B.*

Few displays were redundant, but there were a few familiar themes. Ceramic jardinières in the shape of women's heads (a potted plant formed a leafy chapeau) appeared at entertaining intervals. Christmas train gardens, their assembly a local ritual on Thanksgiving Day, allowed men full, if brief, participation in window dressing. Parlors were converted to staging areas. A layout or table placed at the window's interior ledge often held the decorated tree at its center, surrounded by miniature replicas of villages, tunnels, and snow-covered mountains, ringed by tracks with trains steaming along for all to enjoy. In a major transformation of otherwise prized private space, the train gardeners miraculously converted the window to a public display.

Christmas gardens were a rare invitation to approach and look inside. For those few festive weeks between Thanksgiving and the New Year, residents and strangers were encouraged to get close and be awed and inspired by the view beyond the glass barrier—the domestic version of downtown department stores' holiday displays in communities where residents might not make the annual pilgrimage into the city.[96]

SCREENS

Reserved exclusively for the warm weather months, window and door screens only became a staple of the Baltimore workingman's home around 1910. Prior to that time they were found strictly on residences of the well-to-do and in commercial settings. In an instant, following discoveries in public health, woven wire screens to deter airborne pests and promote ventilation were deemed essential and demanded by all classes of homeowners. Their prices dropped to accommodate the wage earners. They began to displace shutters for those purposes. Retrofitting them to existing windows kept local carpenters and handymen busy. Factories boasted monumental output. Screens were a boon to neighborhood hardware stores, which catered to every aspect of their fabrication, distribution, renewal, or replacement. They competed with mail-order catalogs and furniture stores for the seemingly bottomless market. Once purchased, however, a screen might experience a very long run.

To the rowhouse owner, for many decades prior to the introduction of stainless steel, aluminum, and vinyl frames and nylon and fiberglass mesh, screens were a cumbersome, custom-made wooden fixture that required special care for seasonal installation, removal, and storage lest they be damaged. Because many first-floor windows were exceedingly large—particularly in Novak and Gallagher homes—the weight of the wooden frames made their handling a job for more than one person. Placing them on upstairs windows from outside was a chore. Tending to the screens was man's work requiring heroic feats on ladders, and they required annual if not more frequent cleaning, as well as occasional re-graining of the painted frame to match the home's exterior woodwork, painting of the mesh to prevent rust, and, on occasion, patching of holes or rescreening.

When colorful landscape-painted screens were introduced to the Bohemians of East Baltimore in 1913 by William Oktavec, certain aspects of the new addition to the façade immediately became the province of the woman of the house. She determined the scene and negotiated the best price with the painter, and she received the compliments when the finished screen became an integral part of her home. One of the mysteries of Baltimore painted screens that always intrigued outsiders was why the range of subjects chosen by the buyers was so limited, or why a single house or an entire block might sport the exact same scene on every window. The secret of neighborly rowhouse living was always the willingness to embrace sameness, to build harmony. Living among people with similar backgrounds, in homes with identical floor plans, on identical streets, with identical steps, transoms, and cornices cultivated contentment based on consistency. Even change was a group activity, as evidenced by the wholesale application of Formstone, the addition of wrought-iron handrails to adjacent houses, the turning of the steps sideways on some blocks. A community's health was once measured by the whiteness of its marble steps, the sparkle of the front windowpane, the presence of a tidy display, the number of Christmas gardens, the cleanliness of the sidewalks, and the presence of painted screens. Sameness was a virtue. Imitation was considered pure flattery.

MOST ATTRACTIVE PAINTED WINDOW SCREEN IN EAST BALTIMORE CONTEST

The summer of 1940 brought a new form of competition to East Baltimore. *The East Baltimore Guide,* a local news and advertising weekly, asked their forty thousand readers to consider "Who's got the most attractive painted screen in East Baltimore?" "Housewives," it queried, "Your Window—Does it Have a Painted Screen?" Postcards and letters describing favorites flooded in. No pictures, only words. The contest was extended because "the large number of entries made it impossible to judge the contest in only one week." Ted Schuchat, a seventeen-year-old cub reporter, accompanied the editor to visit each of the nominees. He may have been one of the first journalists to take an interest in the screens, observing that the contest "was a big thing around town. This may have been the first time people paid attention. They had become so commonplace."

The winner, Mrs. Earl Harvey, happened to live on the same block on which screen painting made its first appearance in Baltimore and had taken hold twenty-seven years earlier, a fact that went unremarked by the judges and the entrant. Her screen, painted not by North Collington Avenue's master screen painter, was the work of Mr. Harvey, who had painted it nine years earlier and given it an annual touch-up. "Done in brilliant colors, [it] depicts a rolling pastoral scene. A gentle stream meanders through the foreground of the picture and shade trees are in the background."

A runner-up, Lawrence Kalb of Highlandtown, had painted screens for everyone on his block. His screens were still in place well into the 1970s. His covered porch provided the privacy that usually negated the need for a painted screen, but he was determined to show off his talents, especially after being anointed by the judges.[97]

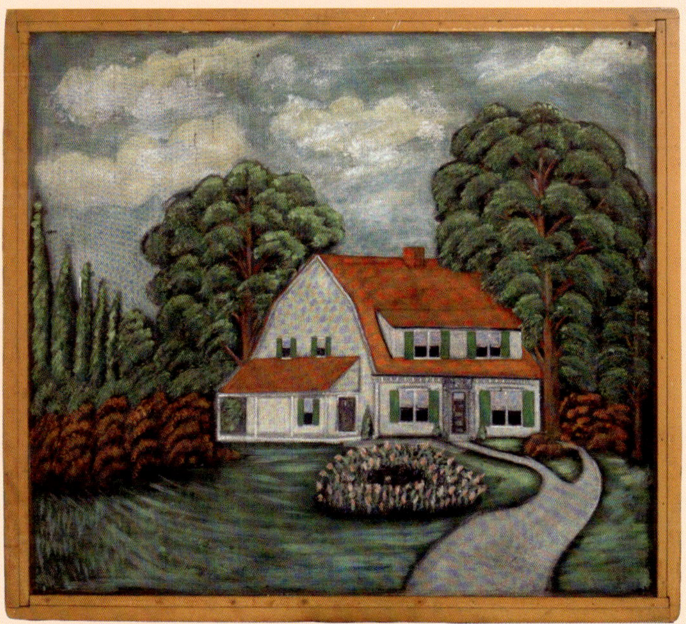

Lawrence Kalb's red-roofed dutch colonial screen painting was a fixture on his porch-front rowhouse on South Dean Street for at least four decades. *Collection of Bill Steinmetz and Betty Cooke. Edward Remsberg photograph.*

4
ORIGINS OF PAINTED SCREENS

THE PUBLICATION OF THIS BOOK IN 2013 MARKS ONE HUNDRED YEARS SINCE WILLIAM OKTAVEC painted his first screen in Baltimore. Unknown to him and the grateful city that elevated his art to signature status was the fact that landscape painted screens had a prior life. Three decades before the first painted screen appeared in Baltimore they were commonplace in many other American cities and towns. William Sumner Appleton describes the tradition in the Boston of his youth:

> Painted window screens were fairly common…when I was a boy but now I know of not one remaining in place, if I may put it that way, for it is now, I believe, out of place. In other words, on occasion there is one in a window on Bowdoin Street, but apart from that, they seem all to have disappeared.[98]

The Victorian rage for painted screens as luxury items did not bypass Baltimore. In the 1890s they could be found in fine furniture stores along the city's Charles Street shopping district or ordered from national trade catalogs. Far from the working-class rowhouse neighborhoods of East Baltimore, painted screens graced freestanding Victorian homes from coast to coast. By the water's edge they shielded vacationers in their rented quarters. In banks, they kept money handlers out of sight. In medical offices, they protected patients from prying eyes. They were custom painted with landscapes in shades of gray and drab by artists on the payrolls of wire companies in this country and abroad.

Printed evidence dates landscape-painted wire blinds to 1726 in London.[99] It can be accurately stated that Oktavec spontaneously (re)discovered the screen as a vehicle for art—which, like its simpler antecedent, derived from wire and one of its many applications, woven wire cloth.

John Brown, one of many London tradesmen who painted on wire blinds, was the first to depict the curious art form in print in 1726. Note triple-lobed frame at far right of illustration. *Heal Collection of the British Museum.*

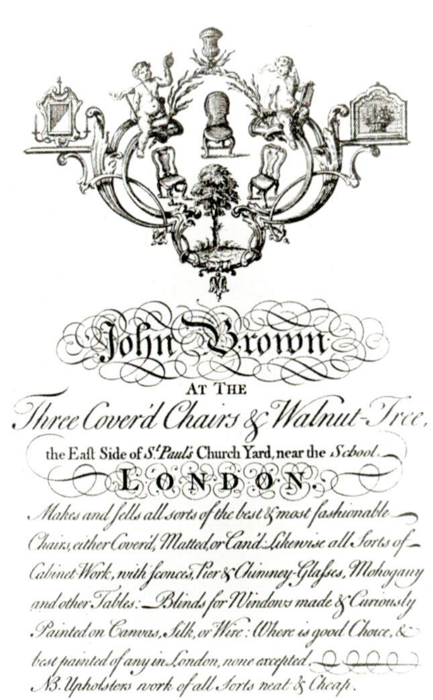

EARLY DECORATIVE SCREENS

Screen manufacturers exploited a growing market with enhanced products. The transition from window screens as a practical, even life-saving innovation, to a platform for artistic display, a source of admiration and beauty, was swift. But these manufacturers did not invent the painted screen. The practical need to coat wire to avoid rust gave rise to the extraordinary new, functional decorative art of painted "blinds" (window screens) in the first quarter of the eighteenth century in London. The earliest evidence of painted screens in print is found on the card of a London upholsterer, John Brown, who in 1726, offered "Blinds for Windows made & Curiously Painted on...Wire."[100] The card illustrates a three-lobed, free-standing window screen embellished with a pot of flowers, a common motif. According to the head of the 150-year-old Tidmarsh Company, whose business in blinds, curtains, and shutters continues to this day, "This type [and shape] of blind is one that was once made in considerable numbers being sign-written and decorated for use in shop windows, particularly of professional offices."[101]

Given the propensity to bring proven arts, technologies, and consumer goods to the colonies, it is no surprise that hand-painted screens had an early introduction in America as well. Daniel Neal, a British historian traveling in the United States in 1720, observed Bostonians' capacity for adapting the skills they had learned in England to American soil. "Their customs and manners

J. A. Tidmarsh was a 150-year-old family business in London specializing in window coverings, adapting its product lines as needs and fashion changed. It continued to make the curved top screens into the twentieth century. *J. A. Tidmarsh catalog, circa 1900.*

ILLUSTRATIONS OF DWARF WIRE BLINDS.

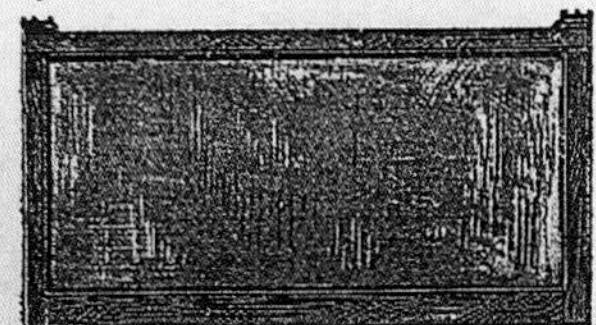

Wire Blind. In Plain Square Frame.
Pattern P.

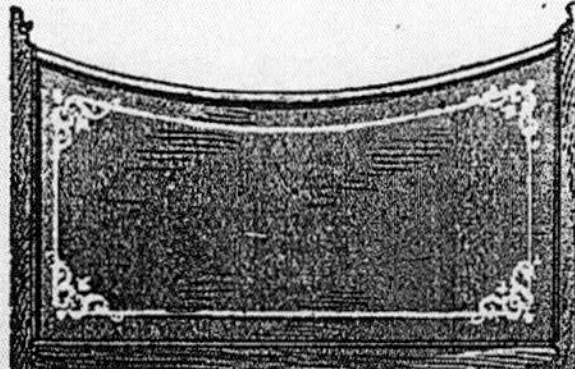

Wire Blind. With Brass Top Rail.
Pattern B.

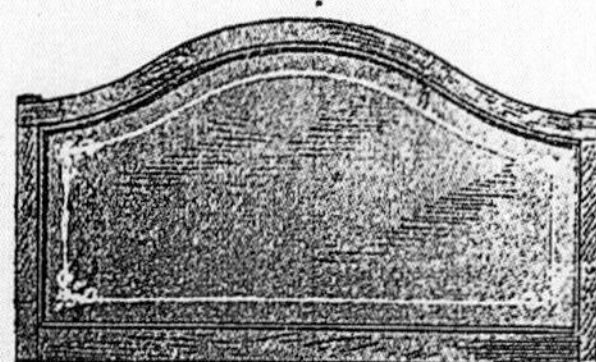

Wire Blind. With Ramped Wood.
Top Rail. **Pattern R.**

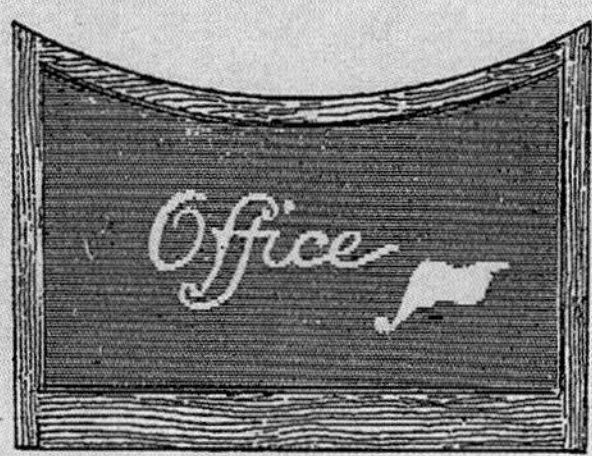

Wire Blind. With Circular Wood Top Rail.
Pattern C.

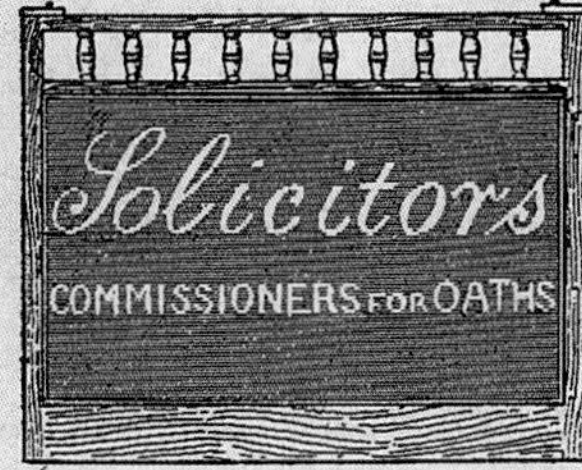

Wire Blind. With Spindle Top Rail.
Pattern S.

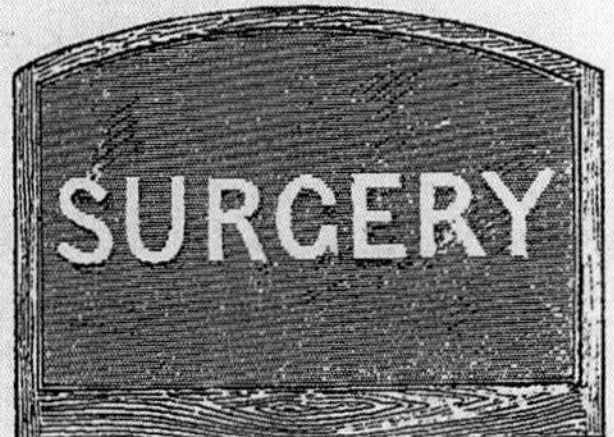

Wire Blind. With Round Wood Top Rail.
Pattern W

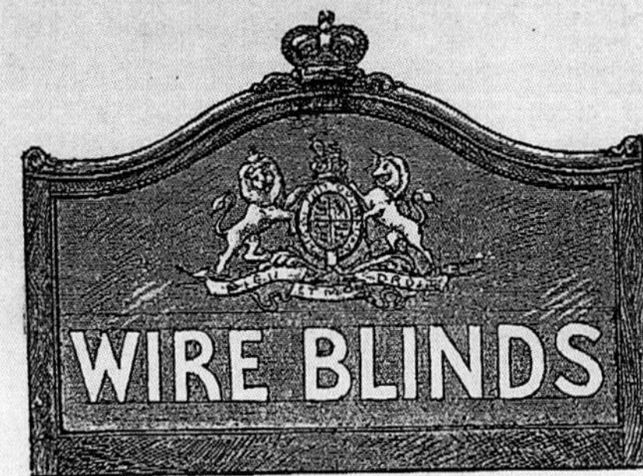

Wire Blind. With Moulded Wood Top Rail.
Pattern M.

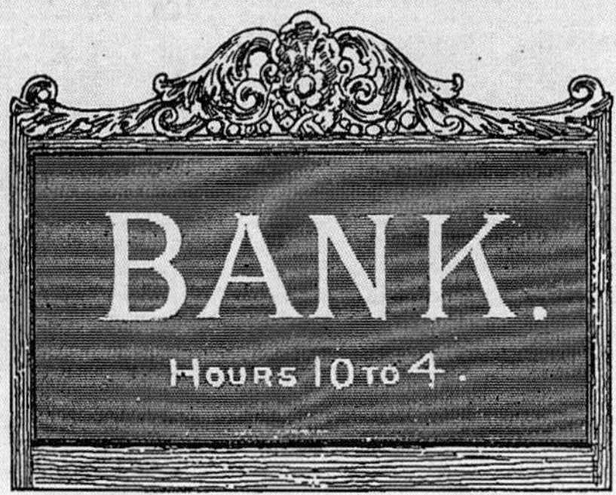

Wire Blind. With Carved Wood Top Rail
Pattern A.
37

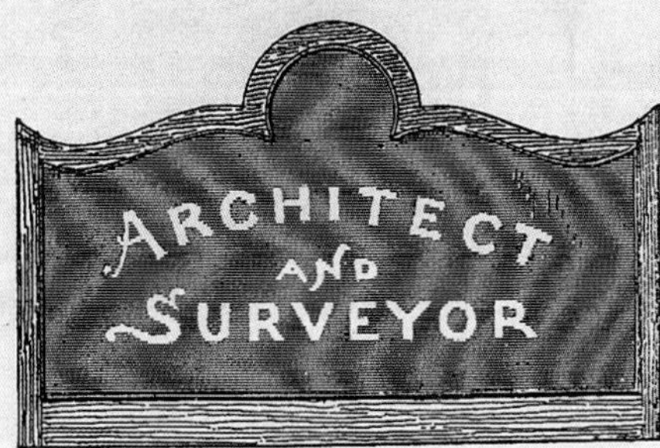

Wire Blind. With Ornamental Wood Top Rail.
Pattern O.
For Prices, see page 36.

are much the same with the English … There is no fashion in London but in three or four months is seen in Boston." It was not uncommon for merchants to travel to America and Europe and exchange habits in their houses and their furniture, with results "as showy as that of the most considerable (affluent) tradesmen in London."[102]

In 1766, at least one English painter had brought his enthusiasm for applying paint to any static surface, including window screens, to Charleston, South Carolina. In what might be the first documented commercial business in painted screens in America:

> Warwell, Painter, from London, Intending to settle in this Town begs Leave to inform the public that he has taken a House on the Point opposite to Governor Boone's, and next door to Mr. Rose's, Ship-Carpenter, where he paints History Pieces, Altar Pieces, Landscapes, Sea Pieces, Flowers, Fruit, Heraldry, Coaches, Window Blinds, Chimney Blinds, Skreens [*sic*], Gilding, Pictures, copies, cleansed or mended. Deceptive Temples, Triumphal Arches, Obelisks, Statues, and c., For Groves and Gardens.[103]

While printed ephemera confirm that a vibrant trade in painted wire blinds persisted in Britain, no vestige of actual painted screens remains from that period. Nor is there any sign of painted "screens" attributable to Warwell or other named or unnamed artists in Charleston or any southern city. The hot, wet summers alone would have made their persistence over the years unlikely. As victims of changing fashion trends and home renovations, they were surely discarded if they survived the elements and abuse of seasonal removal and replacement.[104]

Their scarcity makes the discovery of extant period screens on the continent all the more thrilling. The fact that they may have been executed by known painters both academic and self-trained adds a more personal dimension. Historic wire-producing districts in Germany, Sweden, and New York have yielded the most fruitful links between John Brown's early offerings and those of William Oktavec and his followers in Baltimore.

EUROPEAN PAINTED SCREENS

Public collections located near industrial communities are the richest source of surviving painted screens that can be definitively attributed to known painters. The archives of wire and brass factories, maintained at local historical societies and museums, yield insights into the relationship between wire, screen cloth, and artistic output. The integration of the processes—wire making and landscape painting on wire cloth—under one roof is also evident. Corporate records and artifacts confirm the presence and importance of artists to the wire manufacturers, making it possible for them to offer an impressive range of subjects to the retail market.

One of the most intact corporate collections is from Germany's Ruhr River Valley and sheds light on developments in the wire industry, as well as on the individuals who were employed exclusively to paint on wire fabric. The town of Hagen-Hohenlimburg was an early center for iron, metal, linen, and paper production. In addition, the wire industry, and particularly screen cloth manufacture, flourished there.[105] The firm Boecker and Haver introduced the mechanical weaving of wire cloth in 1818, adapting the techniques used in weaving linen to wire production.[106]

In an early effort to concentrate every aspect of the wire business under one roof, Boecker brought painter Joseph Tonnies from Berlin to Hohenlimburg "to color screens" in 1824. Tonnies received weekly wages, free meals, lodging, and laundry in return for painting "all pieces given him with the greatest industry and art."[107] Functioning like an artists' colony from 1820 to 1890, the wire company's ateliers attracted many painters to the company's payroll. Each one was reported to have a different style, expanding his individual repertoire with the application of stencils according to a "standardized system."[108]

Boecker's firm became C. M. Pieper after 1831. The plant included a richly stocked studio dedicated to creating freehand designs in addition to using a variety of templates. The workshops were well outfitted with "brushes, palettes, palette knife, easels, tables, oil varnish, lacquer, red lead, chrome yellow and red, green cinnabar, light and dark cinnabar, ochre, sulfur green, gum arabic, gold polish, zinc white and sulfur green, and stencils." One inventory notes "85 green landscapes, 82 with frames, and 36 color landscapes."[109] Although monochromatic scenes had been the norm elsewhere, the Hohenlimburg screens were noted for using a full color palette. Their most popular images featured "neo-romantic" subjects, namely, "landscapes, bridges, ponds, churches and castles… animal and flower motifs."[110]

Custom paintings and copies of pieces depicting historic places and events were produced on demand. In an 1838 letter, Mr. Zoncada from Iserlohn ordered, presumably for his home or place of business, among other things, "four Turks on horseback in onslaught," and "two paintings on wire, Limburg end of 1800" and "Dominion Limburg." These screens were considered worthy of display in the chancellery of the town hall of Rheda, sixty miles northeast of Hagen-Hohenlimburg.[111]

Surviving screens, embellished with painted scenes, dating back 175 years, are unusual enough. But the discovery of specific individuals responsible for the work is even rarer. Heinrich A. Tilmann (b. 1820) was one of Pieper's most noted resident artists. He studied art in Dusseldorf where he was influenced by the seventeenth-century Dutch landscape painters Jacob van Ruisdael and Paulus Potter, from whom he borrowed his swan pattern. Tilmann's workshop has been partially preserved, giving a glimpse into the painting process as well as the elevated status of artists within the wire factory. The painters worked on long tables in the garret above the plant. Long stencils made of thick, leather-like cardboard hung on the walls. The screens were rolled out to cover a

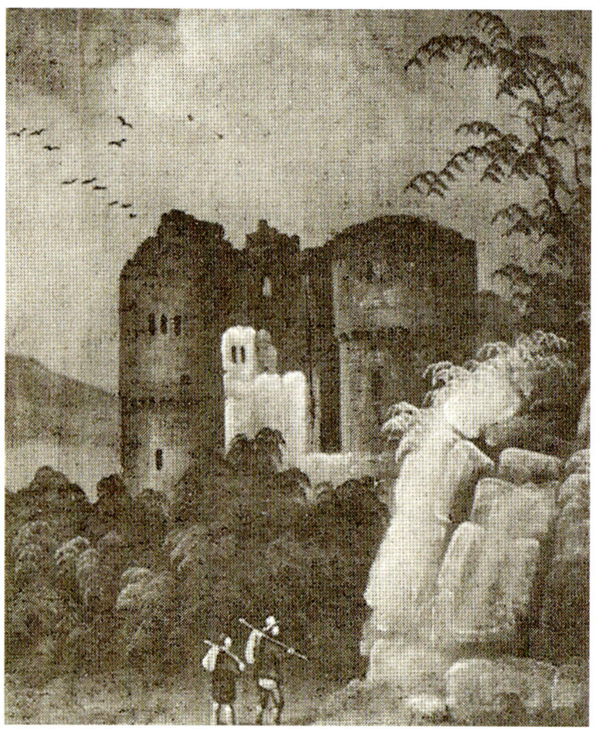

ABOVE

This screen, typical of the time, is one of several surviving works of Heinrich A. Tilmann, a highly trained artist employed in the workshops of the wire firm C. M. Pieper in Hohenlimburg, Germany, circa 1840. Wilhelm Bleicher, "Maler Tillman," *Raum Iserlohn,* 1979.

OPPOSITE, TOP

Nils Andersson painted and initialed a screen depicting Gusums Bruk, the Swedish foundry that employed him to paint custom scenes on wire between 1835 and 1840. *From Gusums Bruk, 1975.*

OPPOSITE, BOTTOM

Swedish screens, perched on small wooden feet and placed on windowsills for privacy, were offered in both monochromatic and bright hues. A view of Capetown, South Africa, other public buildings, and this possibly realistic lake scene were painted by Nils Andersson at Gusums, circa 1835. *Courtesy Gusums Bruksmuseum. Collection of Thomas Nilsson, Gusum, Sweden.*

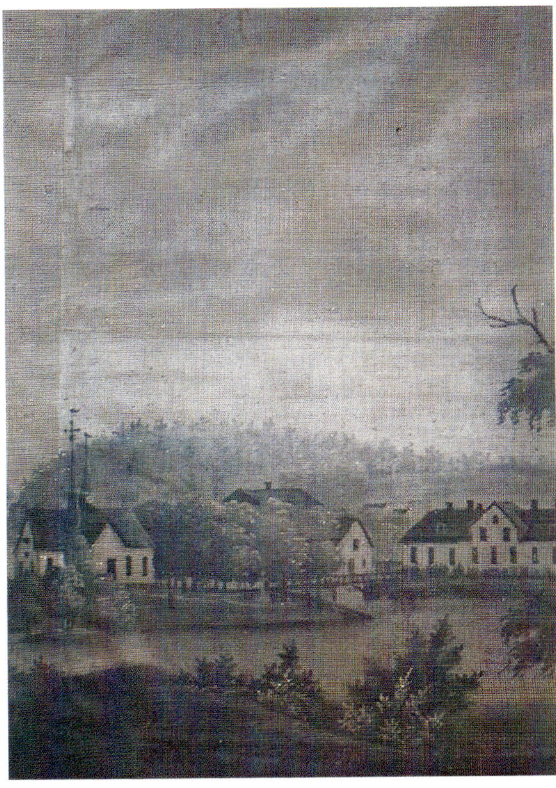

three-meter by three-meter surface. Then they were lacquered with a blue or green ground color in order to provide protection against rust. The artist's assistant would place a stencil over the wire gauze and flatten both layers with lead weights. Tillman, who worked with only one arm, having lost the other to amputation, then executed the design.[112]

According to Hohenlimburg's chronicler, Wilhelm Bleicher, "most often floral drawings in white and green were stenciled … [but] the real work of art in the age of technical reproduction had to be created by freehand painting."[113]

An order book from Pieper includes a wide range of subjects supplied by Tilmann and presumably other artists on the company payroll:

+ Swiss landscape with figures, animals, lake and boat on blue or brown or green background, also in colors,
+ Green, grey, dark blue or colored landscapes,
+ Colored Dutch landscapes with many cows, horses, and small boats,
+ Rhenish landscapes on diverse grounds or mixed— with castles, rivers, and boats etc.,
+ Hunting scenes on various grounds or colored,
+ Single flower pieces,
+ Small objects and animals,
+ Textile designs (silks, moirés) with Brazilian or Portuguese escutcheons,
+ Landscapes with fire-red ground for piano backs,
+ Imitations of curtains,
+ Single castles, peasant dwellings, ruins, bucolic scenes [114]

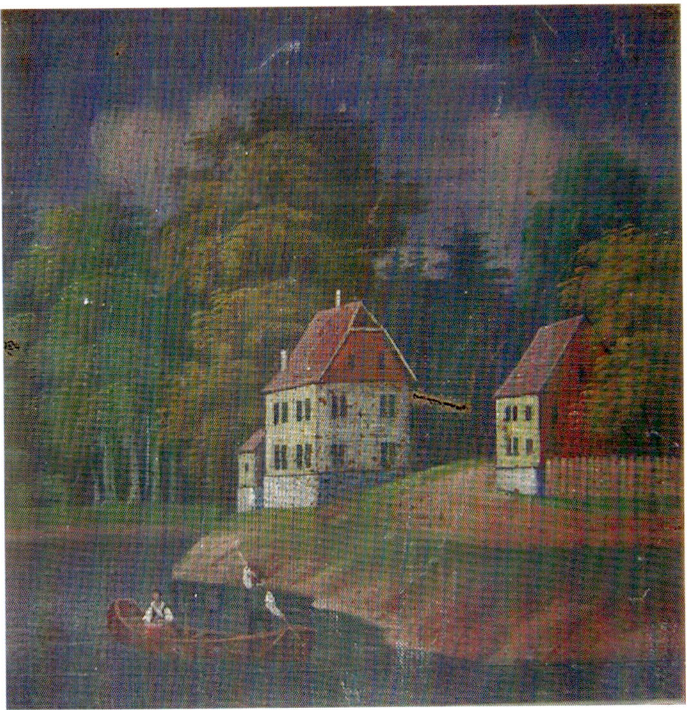

Hohenlimburg screens peaked in popularity in Germany after 1860. Their main market was homeowners eager to exclude flies from their living quarters. Correspondence indicates that grocers ordered screens with images of meats and produce for their doors and windows. While William Oktavec is reported to have painted precisely this scene on the door of his Baltimore grocery in 1913, he claimed never to have seen this type of work either in his native Bohemia or during his apprenticeship years in Germany.

Farther afield, Pieper screens found receptive markets in Holland, Africa, India, China, and "the Tropics."[115] Rising import duties and increasing competition from Austria in both resources and labor forced Pieper to close its diminished painting department by 1905, as interest in landscape-painted screens waned.

In Sweden, homemakers have long propped portable frames stretched with textiles, preferably lace, or wire cloth, in front of their windows for privacy.[116] In the mid-nineteenth century, scenic painting on woven wire screens to serve the same purpose was a vigorous tradition. The town of Gusum, south of Stockholm, was home to a factory that specialized in brass wire and objects. Founded in 1663 and active until it closed in 1988, Gusums Bruk (factory) produced "701 window screens of brass, net or iron" in 1837.[117]

Many of the early hand-painted (vs. machine printed) examples were signed by artist Nils Andersson (1817–1865). Andersson was self-taught as a youngster. Although his impoverished parents attempted to reverse his growing interest in art, he nonetheless apprenticed to a landscape painter named Backström who taught him "craft painting" on utilitarian objects. At the age of eighteen, Andersson made his way from his native East Jutland to Gusum, where he worked in the wire mill as a *jalusi målare* (wire blind painter) for five years. The range of images he applied to wire included views of Swedish manors and castles, one view of Cape Town, South Africa, and one of Gibraltar, all taken from prints. A large landscape screen that shows the Gusum Factory bears his initials, making it the only known signed example of his work.[118]

THE VICTORIAN WINDOW

The Victorian era ushered in a new emphasis on design and ornamentation in all aspects of dress and furnishing. The period lasted during Queen Victoria's reign, from 1837 to 1901. It was inspired by her predilection for unrestrained effects that turned the home into a temple of excess. The window, inside and out, became one of many showplaces for the taste of the time. The urge to adorn all available surfaces and fill every space many times over contributed to the success of the market for landscape screens in Europe and America.

Painted screens' ephemeral quality may have made them the perfect addition to the already crowded field of decorative accessories vying for a spot on the Victorian window in America. The tendency toward "over-decoration and super-elaboration" was evident in:

fringes and tassels, in somber colors and gaudy figures, in the curlicues and rosettes…In the treatment of windows it expressed itself with full eloquence. The truly well-dressed Victorian window was not permitted to go so scantily clad as to allow the ready passage of light and air. It had to wear almost as many garments as the heavily-petticoated lady of the house. In the first place, the panes themselves were embellished with a border of many-colored stained glass. Before the clear glass hung a transparency, preferably showing Niagara Falls. Within the massive moldings of the embrasure fitted folding shutters which could be deployed to keep out draughts and inquisitive glances. Heavy white lace curtains hung within the frame. A deep lambrequin or valance concealed the support of the sumptuous draperies that fell in

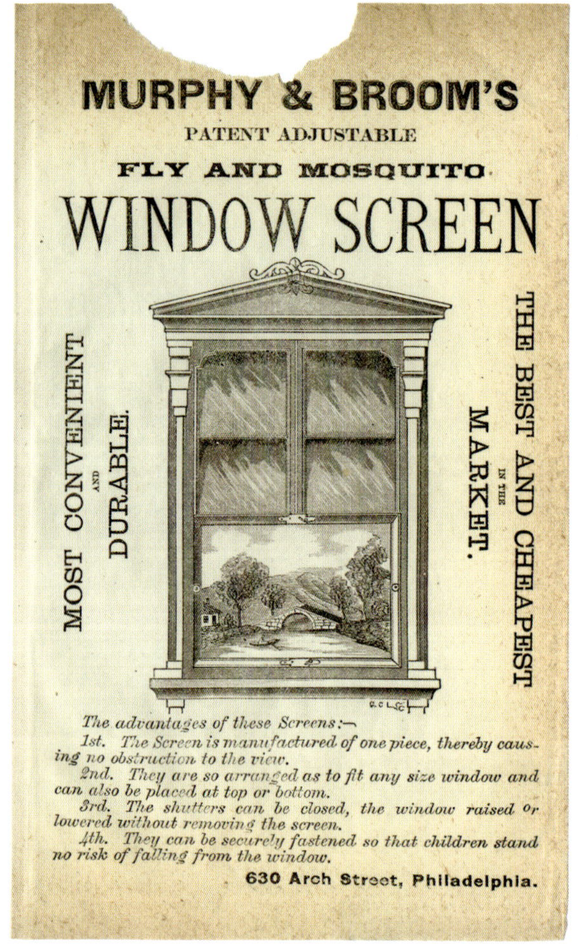

The 1876 Philadelphia Centennial Exhibition introduced Murphy & Broom's innovations in screens. *Courtesy of the Library Company of Philadelphia.*

voluminous folds to the floor and spread their fringe upon the carpet. And that was not all. Even the paper window shade could not go undecorated, but was painted in polychrome with bouquets of flowers or romantic ruins or sylvan scenes.[119]

Window shades, known in America as blinds (to add to the confusion of the English blinds, which include what we call screens) or "roller" blinds enjoyed immense popularity after the 1820s for their light-filtering quality. Their main advantages were blocking sunlight and preventing damage to furnishings, although they were also touted to enhance privacy. Their solid surface compromised ventilation, but only if screens or shutters were also in place would flying insects be excluded. The first American mention appears in Hugh Barkley and Patrick O'Meara's advertisement for "transparent Blinds for Windows" in Baltimore in 1792.[120] Made of paper or cloth, these blinds' introduction followed the success of similarly backlit parade banners and stage sets, which yielded to theater curtains known as "scrims," and operated much like painted screens, allowing one-way vision only.[121]

These early, decorated window shades drew their pictorial inspiration from the same sources as the earlier painted screens in Germany and Sweden—idyllic landscapes, gothic ruins, central medallions, and simple figured borders. Whether rendered in *grisailles*—a limited palette of grays, white, and black—to mute the light, or a riot of color to stop the light, "the Beautiful hid the Functional, disguised the Commonplace, [and] elaborated the Simple."[122] These artful offerings could be applied to face the street or be oriented indoors to be enjoyed by the home's inhabitants. "In cities, painted window shades were used basically for disguising the disagreeable but as well to create beauty where there was none before."[123] They could also be viewed after dark from outdoors with the addition of "strategically placed oil lamps" illuminating them from within the home.[124]

Samuel F. Bartol employed 150 artists in his New York City company by 1850, when shades were at the height of fashion and becoming increasingly affordable to growing numbers of Americans.[125] In great demand, having "universally adorn[ed] the best dwellings in the metropolis," hand-decorated painted shades gave way to factory-produced shades before losing favor altogether by 1860.[126]

The market for landscape shades had overshadowed the market for painted screens, but in fact were a steppingstone to the latter's acceptance. In Baltimore an influential interior decorator noted in the 1920s:

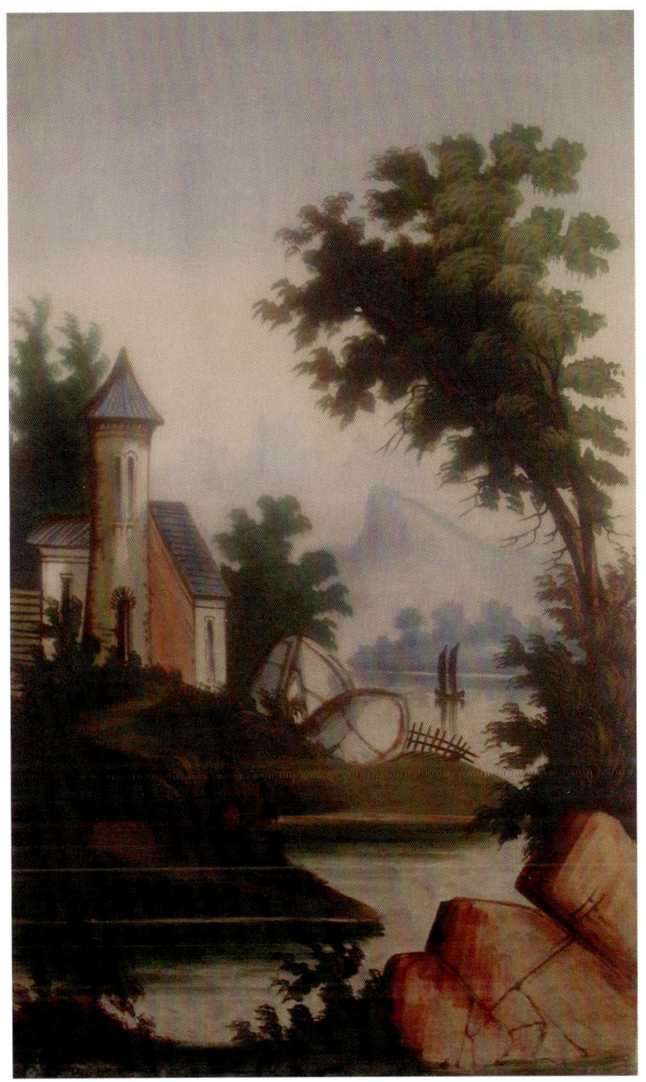

One of a pair of painted muslin window shades illustrates the romantic interest in ruins associated with the Gothic Revival in Europe and America and the Victorian desire to be surrounded by natural scenery, indoors and out. *New York State Historical Association, Cooperstown, FO264.55, 1835-1850.*

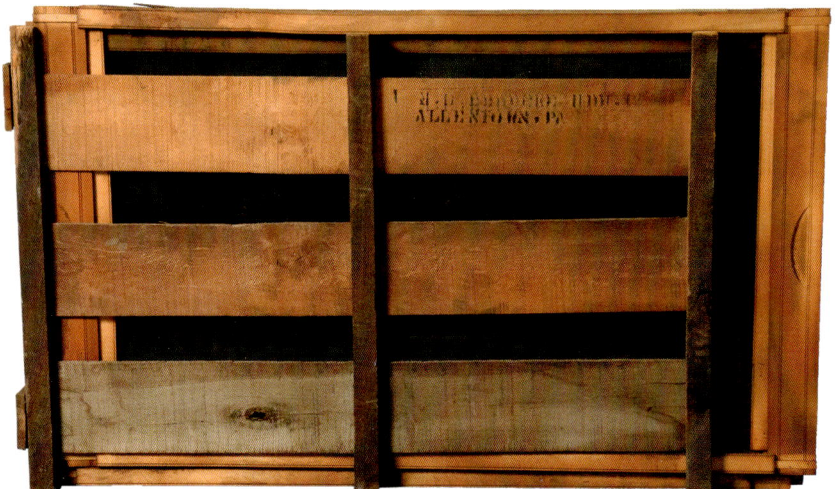 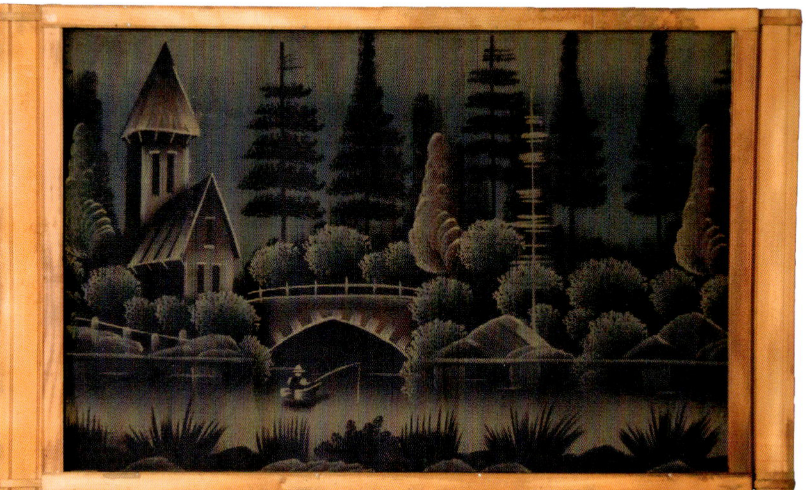

The crate above was shipped to M.C. Ebbecke Hdwe. of Allentown, Pennsylvania, a family-owned company that thrived from 1880 until late in the twentieth century. Recently discovered unopened in storage, it contained six subtly colored landscape screens in spring loaded adjustable wooden frames. The container was from an unknown source, most likely the screen fabricator that employed the painter who embellished the woven metal wire. Note the outline for the unfinished tree in white. *Courtesy of Dennis and Linda Moyer. Christine Fillat photographs.*

Decorated shades have been very fashionable for several years past, and from painted shades to painted screens is but a step. We have had painted window shades and shades of French Toile and English chintz for several years, and as summer approaches these shades, which are expensive, are taken down and plain ones are substituted. In many cases the family has grown to like the colorful window furnishings, and so in summer these painted screens are used instead of the expensive shades which were up all during the winter.[127]

Landscape screens were in their heyday by the time of the 1876 Centennial Exhibition in Philadelphia, which showcased American ingenuity and industrial innovation. The centennial may have signaled wider acceptance of this curious art form and introduced the painted screen to its largest audience. Philadelphia's own Murphy & Broom's Patent Adjustable Fly and Mosquito Window Screen offered a broadsheet featuring a screen with a romantic idyll on its cover, promising a product that was:

1st: Manufactured of one piece, causing no obstruction to the view

2nd: Arranged to fit any size window and be placed at top or bottom

3rd: Allowed shutters to be closed, and the window to be raised or lowered without removing the screen

4th: Able to be securely fastened so that children are not at risk of falling from the window.[128]

It is certain that landscape screens were available direct to the Baltimore consumer in 1893. Baltimore's Mohler & Hurlbutt, Importers at 14 North Charles Street offered "Landscape screens… for office and other windows where greater privacy is required."[129]

Landscape screens were available to Baltimoreans in 1893 at Mohler & Hurlbutt's furniture store.
Courtesy of The Winterthur Library: Joseph Downs Collection of Manuscripts and Printed Ephemera, 88x106.

THE PAINTERS

In addition to the artists employed by wire screen manufacturers, entrepreneurs at every stage of accomplishment and jacks of many trades capitalized on the popularity of painted screens in nineteenth-century America. The marketplace was filled with catalogs to capture the attention of the affluent buyer, introducing the decorating-crazed populace to yet another layer for the overdressed window. Enterprising and would-be artists sought to enter the emerging market.

William Henry Jackson (1843–1942), the famed photographer of the American West, grew up in Troy, New York. His short-lived career as a twelve-year-old roving painter of screens in his hometown may have stoked his curiosity about new places and prepared him for his illustrious career. The youngster had plenty of customers:

> I got all the window screen business I could take care of—by underselling my professional competitors. My usual fee, which had to cover the cost of paint and wear and tear on brushes was fifteen cents a screen; however, once in a while I screwed up my nerve to the point of charging a quarter if the screen turned out to be exceptionally large. If I made a profit I don't remember it; I feel safer in saying that I plowed every cent right back into the business.[130]

Judging by the size and number of pages of advertisements in trade catalogs of the period, activity in landscape-painted screens was lively—whether they were painted in factory workshops, aftermarket by artists hired by hardware vendors, or by amateurs. Landscape screens were at the height of popularity in the United States between 1870 and 1890. They were found in affluent homes and offices in large and small cities, villages, and rural outposts. The variety of subject matter grew with their popularity. When ordering, purveyors advised their customers:

> Give length and height. If the windows are large the frames are usually made by parties ordering the Screens, as they ship better and are easily tacked on. Any special designs in landscapes can be furnished to order, such as U.S. Capitol, State Capitol, U.S. Coat of Arms or any other design.…Any name or sign can be put on them in large rich gold letters if desired.[131]

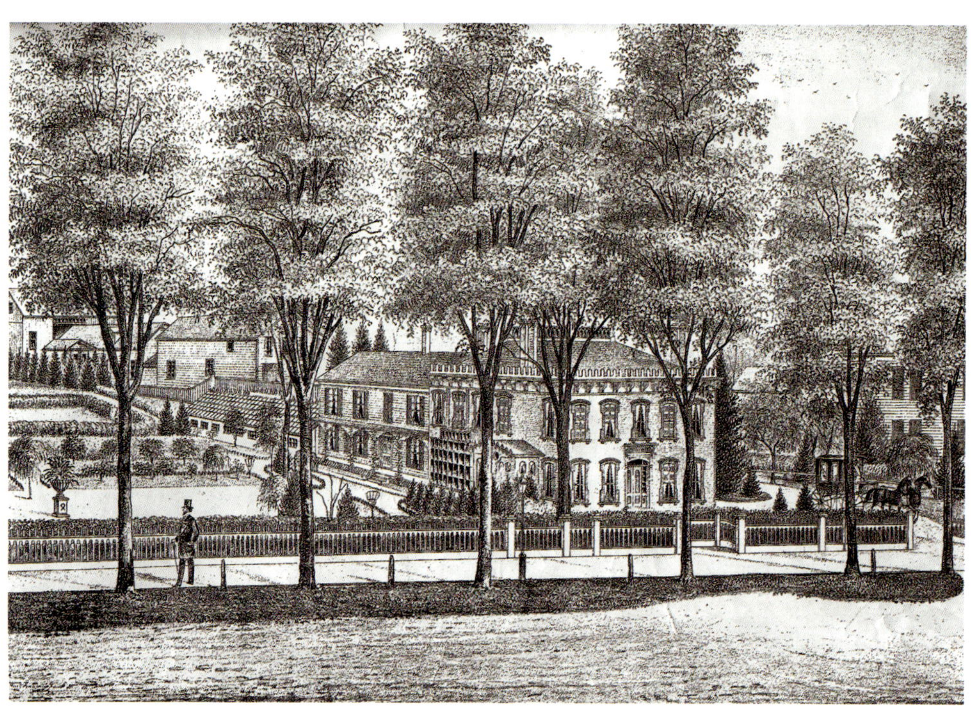

The Italianate residence of Jacob M. Schermerhorn in Homer, New York, was one of the finest and most up-to-date homes in the town. *Combination Atlas Map of Cortland County, New York. Philadelphia: Everts Ensign and Everts, 1876. 45.*

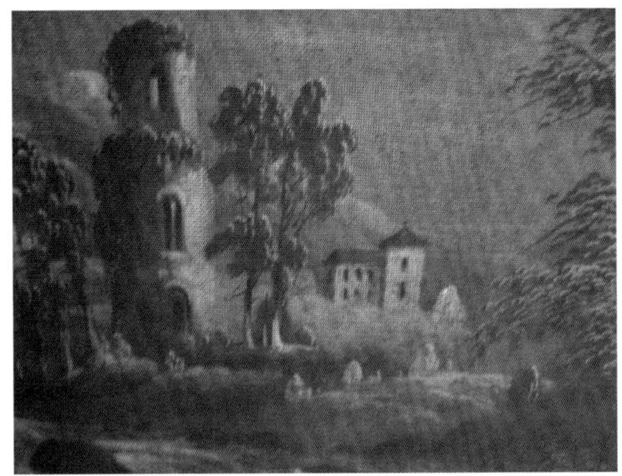

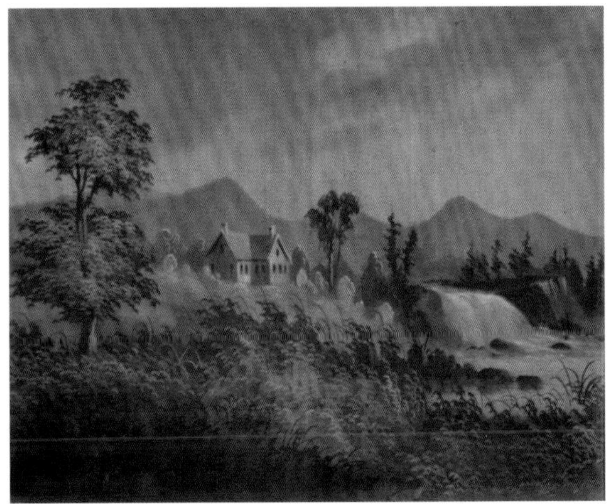

Byron Carpenter painted these landscape screens for the windows of the Schermerhorn house while employed as an artist by Wickwire Brothers in Cortland, New York, after 1877. *Courtesy of Cortland County Historical Society.*

In the United States, as in the ateliers in Hagen-Hohenlimburg and Gusum, the men who applied art to wire cloth were either employees of the wire company or pieceworkers who contracted to do the work from their own studios.

As large-scale manufacturing of screens expanded, adding decorative painting to the fabric quickly followed. Wickwire Brothers capitalized on the growing popularity of hand- and roller-painted screens. They first offered scenic wire cloth in 1878. A local observer, Horatio Ballard, called "the adornment of the wire window screen with exquisite landscape painting…by an artist here in town…well worth a visit to see." By 1882 business was "booming" and the wireworks was unable "to get orders out fast enough."[132]

Two artists, Roe Smith and Byron Carpenter, the best known of the Wickwire Company artists, executed landscape scenes there between 1877 and 1888, according to records of payment to both men for "landscapes, landscapes in color and signs."[133] Smith's name appears in the Cortland City Directory for a decade beginning in 1879 as a painter, gilder, and paint shop foreman for Cortland Wagon Company, and as overseer of Hitchcock's paint shop.[134]

Byron Ruel Carpenter (1840–1901), born in nearby Groton, New York, was a self-taught artist. His modest canvas paintings depict local scenes and family members and occasionally incorporate gold leaf. After surviving unscathed through four years of Civil War combat that included eighty-four battles and having two horses shot out from under him, he returned home to work as a carriage maker and decorator for Samson-Williams Carriage Works. He moved to Cortland in 1881 to work at the local wagon company, where artist Roe Smith was also employed. Carpenter's specialty was the application of gold leaf and scrolls.[135] He begins to appear in Wickwire's account books in January 1883, receiving up to .06 cents per square foot for scenes that were then sold to hardware stores nationwide for .10 cents per square foot, by the roll and as special orders. The next month he filled a special order for "Dr. Woods' screen," likely destined for the doctor's examining room.

Individual screens sold for $2.50 to $3.50, depending on the size and scene requested. In March 1883 Carpenter completed "2,112 sf Landscape in Color at .06 cents and 1,597 square feet" in April of "Landscape in Color."[136] His employers praised his output, "A couple of window screens [he painted] for Bushby's Steamship Ticket Office attracting much attention. The designs are attractive and appropriate and are very skillfully worked out. Carpenter had a decided genius in this direction."[137]

Carpenter's work graced the windows of homes and businesses throughout the region, including a pair of screens from the impressive home of Jacob M. Schermerhorn, on the main street of Homer, New York.[138] In May 1886 Carpenter opened a studio on Cortland's Main Street in the Wickwire Building, Room No. 8, where he advertised "portraits and painting instruction in oil watercolors, [on] velvet, banners and wire" while continuing to turn out landscapes for Wickwire.[139]

THE PATRONS

One of the best-preserved and earliest examples of American painted screens for domestic use dating from this period is found far from the population centers of the northeast, in the Strafford, Vermont, homestead of Justin Smith Morrill (1810–1898). Morrill was born in the town, the son of a blacksmith. The successful self-made, self-educated Vermont businessman and later politician is best known as the author of the Land-Grant College Bill, which he introduced to the Senate in 1857 and was enacted under President Lincoln in 1862.

At age thirty-eight, after a successful career as a merchant and a life dedicated to public service, farming, and reading—he took pride in his wide and eclectic library—Senator Morrill retired. He spent the next three years designing and building his cottage, completing it in 1851, in time to share it with his bride, Ruth Barrell Swann. Described by one twentieth-century critic as "a frivolous expression of the Gothic Revival," Morrill's cottage is a pink but practical froth, asymmetrical, with "picturesque irregularities."[140]

In 1859 he planned and supervised an addition to the Vermont house, including a new library wing that boasted etched windows imported from France depicting ruins of Scotland's Holyrood

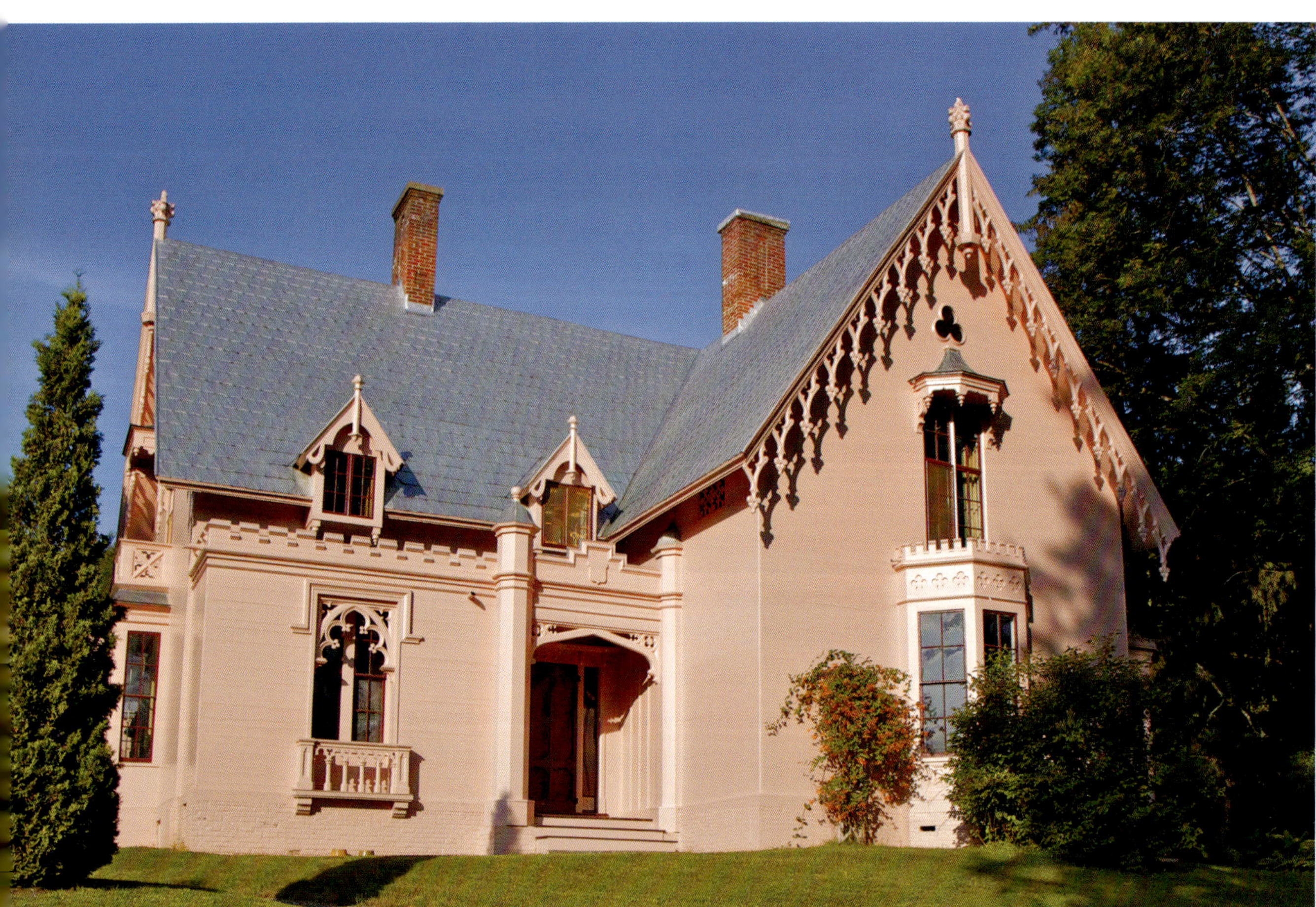

Justin Morrill's 1851 cottage and later addition, Strafford, Vermont. *Mary Louise Pierson photograph. Courtesy of Vermont Division for Historic Preservation.*

OPPOSITE
This Gothic window, added to Morrill's dining room in 1859, has held the same painted screens for more than 150 years. *Mary Louise Pierson photograph. Courtesy of Vermont Division for Historic Preservation.*

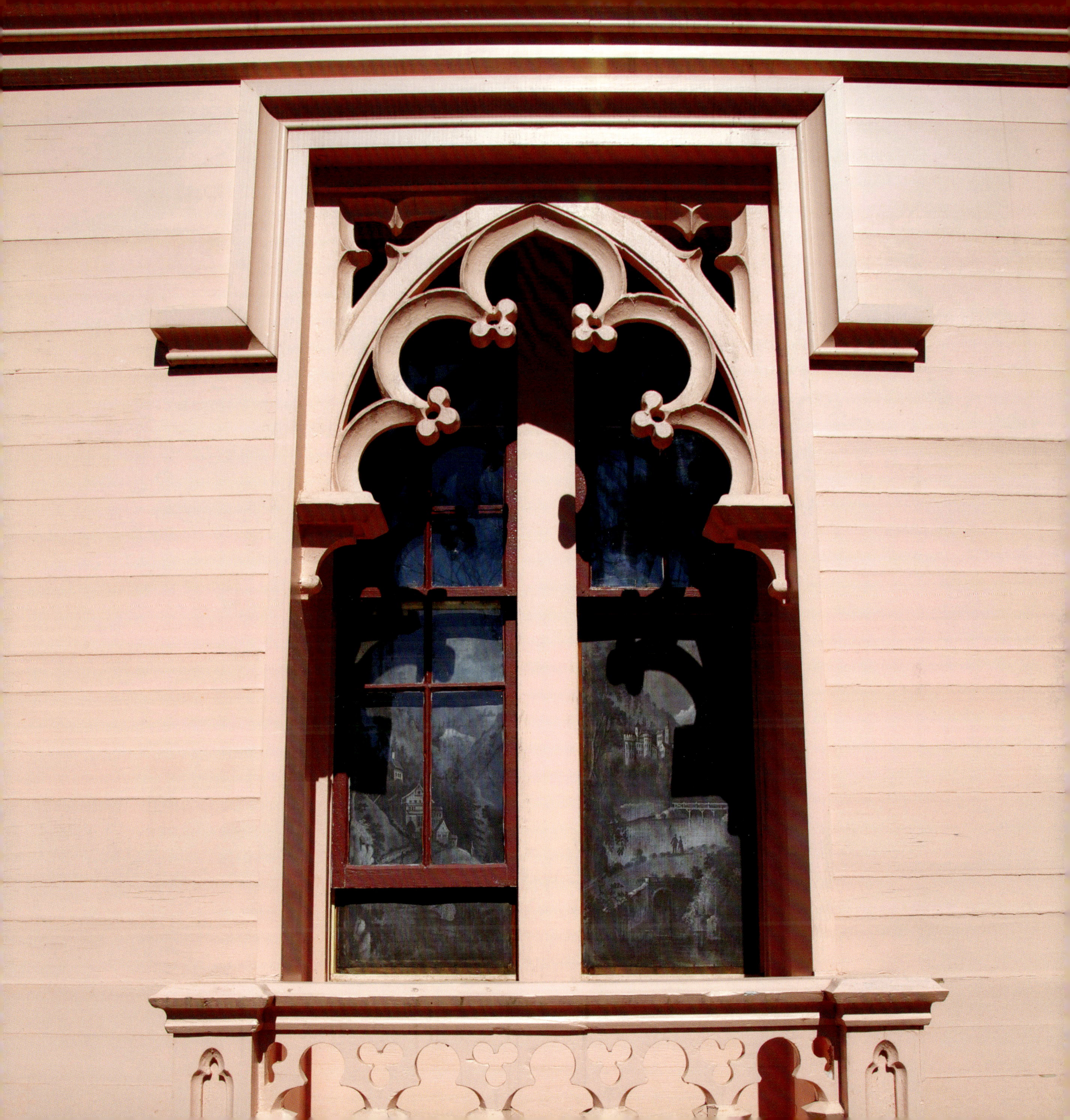

chapel. A group of five exquisitely executed window screens each featured a tall, narrow landscape painted in shades of black and gray. The distinctly European views transport the viewer into high mountain passes and alpine lakes that appear to be of Austrian, Swiss, or Bavarian origin.[141] Surely they were not intended for privacy, as the Morrill home was far from any public access atop a small hill in the rural village. The single screen in the window of Senator Morrill's library suggests his desire to be left undisturbed while poring over his beloved books.

Although the senator directed the addition, Mrs. Morrill may well have been behind the acquisition of the screens. Among her papers is a letter from a former Strafford neighbor and close friend who, after relocating to the Vermont-Canada border, wrote, "I should like to have you write me the cost of your blinds in the dining room."[142]

A pair of screens (now in the Enfield Historical Society Museum in Enfield Center) from the Johnson House in Enfield, New Hampshire, might have inspired Morrill's purchase, as she was a frequent visitor to the house. Located across the Connecticut River, it was forty miles overland from Strafford.[143] Yet another possible source of inspiration for the Morrill screens was proposed by a descendant of another Enfield resident, who noted that her "grandfather built and furnished his house shortly after the Civil War. It was lavishly decorated and furnished from Boston…I well remember the painted screens [he had]. They were landscapes. I assumed at that time that this was done so that passers-by could not see in." This building, like the Johnson house, fronted directly on Enfield's Main Street.[144]

The Morrill Homestead remained in the family until 1930. Its succeeding stewards valued the structure and the contents and kept it intact. The house and farmstead have been preserved as a National Historic Landmark since 1960. It was donated to the State of Vermont in 1969. Today, the Morrill screens remain in their original location, are removed seasonally, and appear fresh and untarnished after 150 years.[145]

The Morrill Homestead screens were unquestionably hand-painted, although the use of stencils has not been ruled out.[146] Given the screens' decidedly European flavor and the senator's willingness to employ artisans from abroad when required, a non-American source would not be surprising. That said, it is unlikely that many landscape-painted screens in America were foreign made, although late-nineteenth-century purveyors often claimed they were, to stimulate sales.

These screens are coated with a ground color of drab and afterwards beautifully decorated by hand by an experienced French artist in imitation of water, mountain, rustic and other natural scenery, making very handsome and useful screens and signs. A peculiarity of these screens apart from their great beauty is that persons inside of a room can look out without difficulty, while those from the street cannot look in, and you are thus secluded from the gaze of outsiders. This alone is of great importance to banking institutions when they have money or valuables exposed. If desired any name or sign can be lettered upon them in rich gold letters, shaded, making them very attractive and indispensable, especially in banking offices.[147]

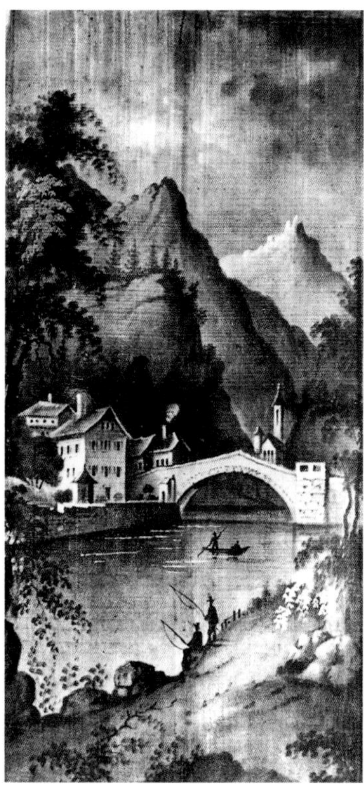

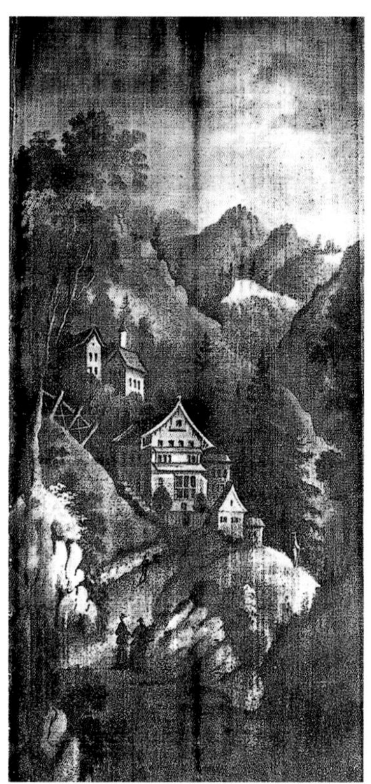

Symbols of strength and endurance were suggested for screens for banking institutions. *E. T. Barnum's Catalogue of Wire Goods, p. 8. Warshaw Collection of Business Americana, Smithsonian Institution Museum of American History.*

One of the last remaining examples of an early screen for a business remains in use in its original site. On the east side of Lake Cayuga in central New York State, the village of Aurora grew in large part owing to the wealth of a few families. The Morgans and the Wellses collaborated in establishing two great nineteenth-century institutions, Wells Fargo and American Express.

An 1840 tenant house on the Morgan property, built of local limestone, was converted to the First National Bank of Aurora (now Cayuga Lake National Bank) in 1864. The house was purchased by Henry Wells for $1,100 in his role as the bank's first president and member of the building committee. The roof on the diminutive structure was raised and bracketed cornices were applied to create the appearance of an Italian villa.[148]

Coinciding with the renovation, two tall, monochromatic landscape screens were custom made to fit the front windows facing the street, at the exact spot where the tellers handled money. Under natural or dim lighting, the screens' pictorial offerings, rather than a view of the employees, captured the attention of customers entering from outdoors. Precisely as promised in advertisements in hardware catalogs, Aurora's bankers continue to use the visual foil to shield the handling of currency from the public.

A Detroit catalog of wire goods reminded "Banks, Express, Insurance Billiard Rooms, Commission Houses and Other Office[s]" that visual exclusion "alone is of great importance to institutions when they have money exposed." E. T. Barnum's catalog offered screens painted with plain or gold leaf lettering and with or without landmark buildings or landscapes. The directors at Aurora chose not to use their windows to advertise. They also bypassed rugged landscapes suggesting America's strength, typical for financial institutions, in favor of views more commonly seen in screens intended for the home.[149] Their selections featured sturdy, fortress-like stone buildings, at least one figure gazing at a forest, a couple stopping in conversation to view rushing water, and ducks swimming in more gentle waters.

OPPOSITE

In keeping with the foreign provenance of other decorative features made for the Morrill home, European artists may have painted these alpine scenes for the Homestead's screens. *Courtesy of Vermont Division for Historic Preservation.*

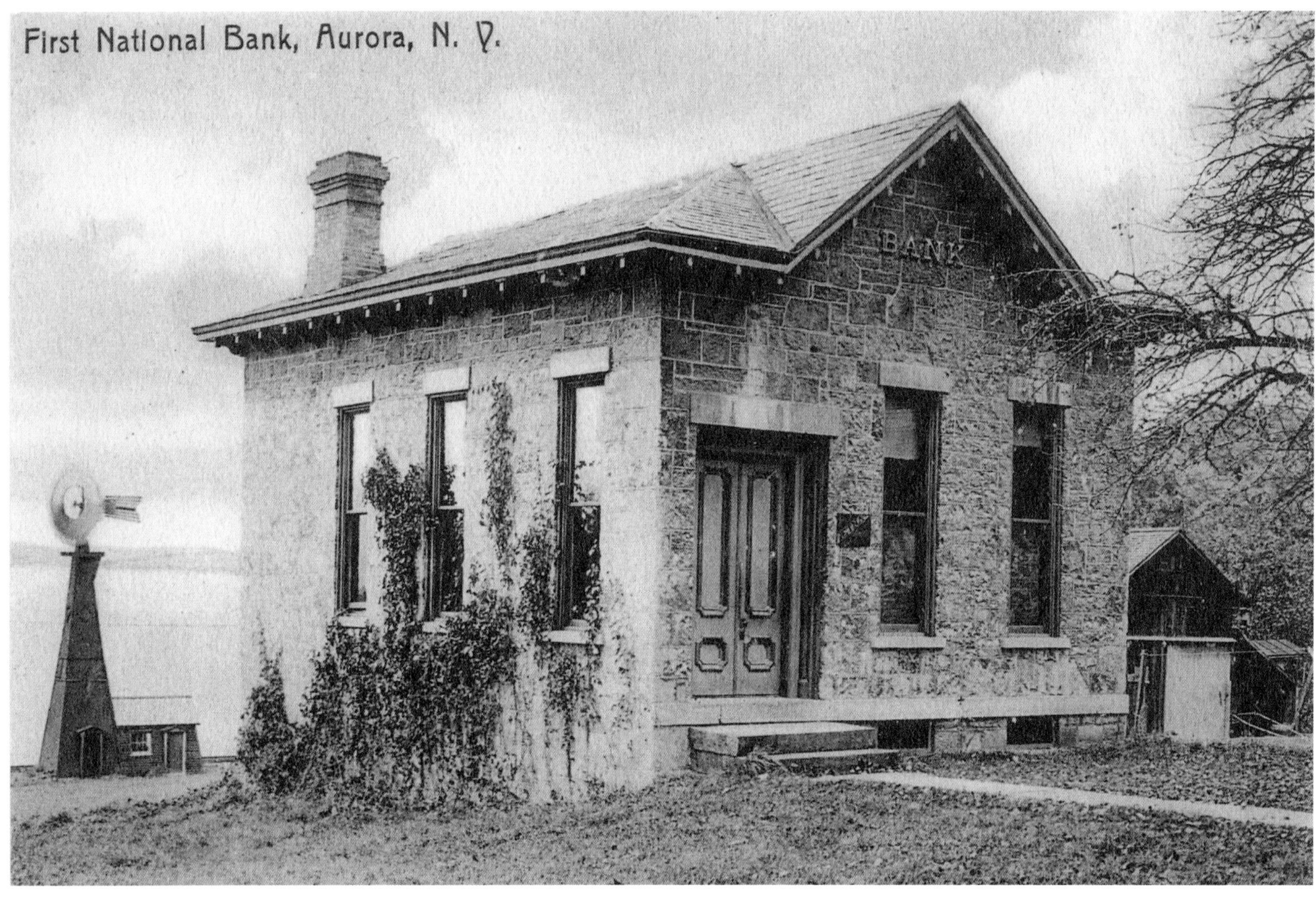

For many years, it was believed that the Aurora Bank screens were produced and decorated at Wickwire Brothers, located forty miles east in Cortland, New York. However, Wickwire didn't begin to specialize in wire cloth until more than a decade after the bank began operation. Careful inspection reveals a barely legible inscription on the bottom of one of the screens, which reads, "DeWitt 104 John St.," suggesting that the screen was made in New York City by the DeWitt Wire Cloth Company of that address. Mr. Wells often traveled to the city, where he might have seen and selected the $2.50 screens and shipped or carried them back to Aurora.[150]

Aurora Bank on New York's Lake Cayuga still has its 1864 painted screens in their original location to provide security in windows alongside the tellers' work area. *Courtesy of the Aurora Free Library.*

Many examples of remembered or extant screens and painters from the nineteenth to mid-twentieth century were discovered through research for this book and reveal the proliferation of this art form throughout the northeastern United States. Representative excerpts appear in Appendix B.

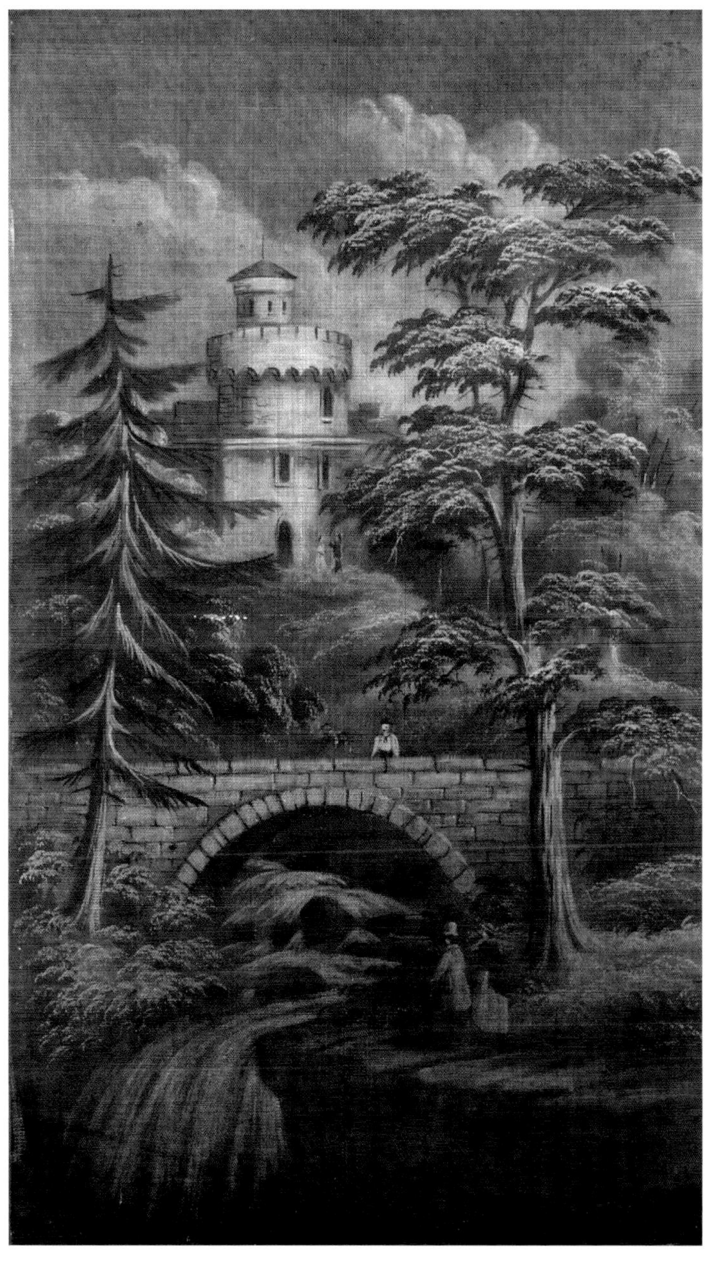

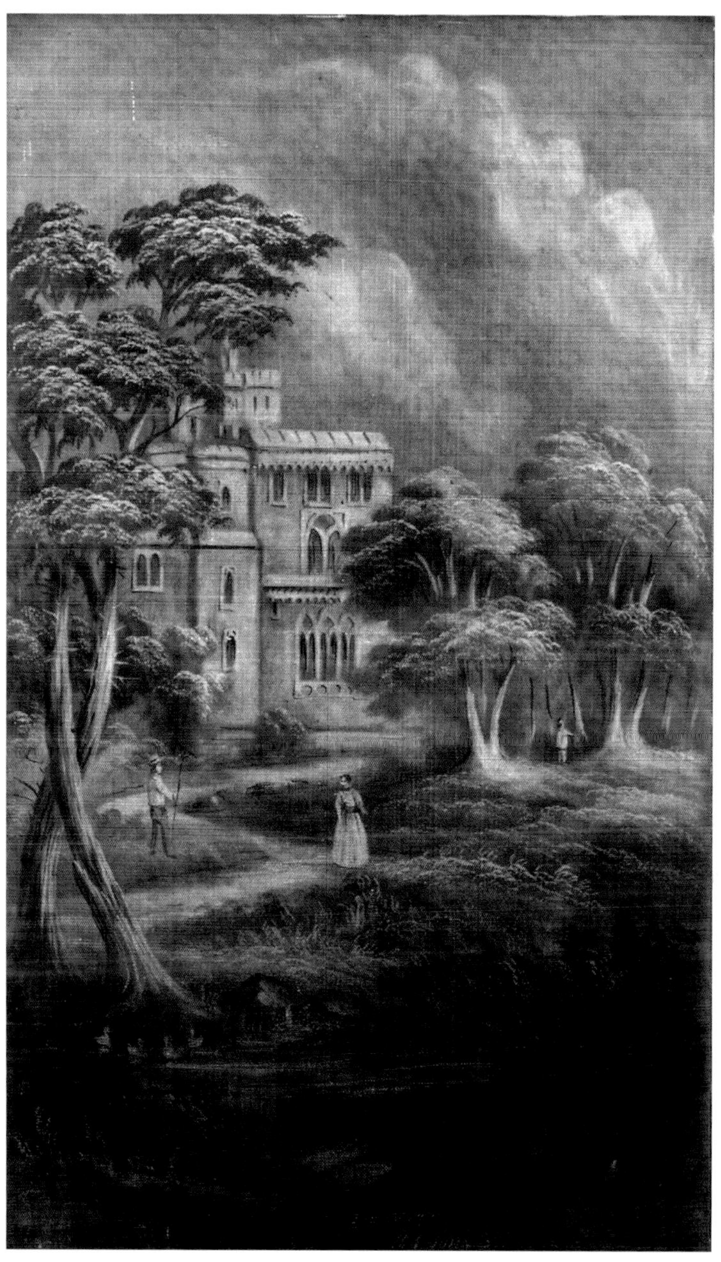

Scenes of the idylls of country life, images more commonly found on residences, were chosen for Aurora Bank's windows. *Courtesy of William Ryan, Cayuga Lake National Bank. Photographs by Jacqueline Conderacci.*

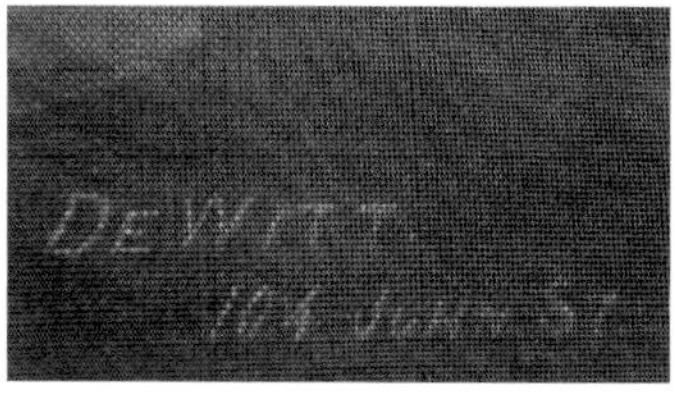

This detail in long-lasting white lead paint identifies the New York wire purveyor, "DeWitt, 104 John Street," where Henry Wells likely purchased the pair of screens for Aurora Bank in 1864. *Photograph by Jacqueline Conderacci.*

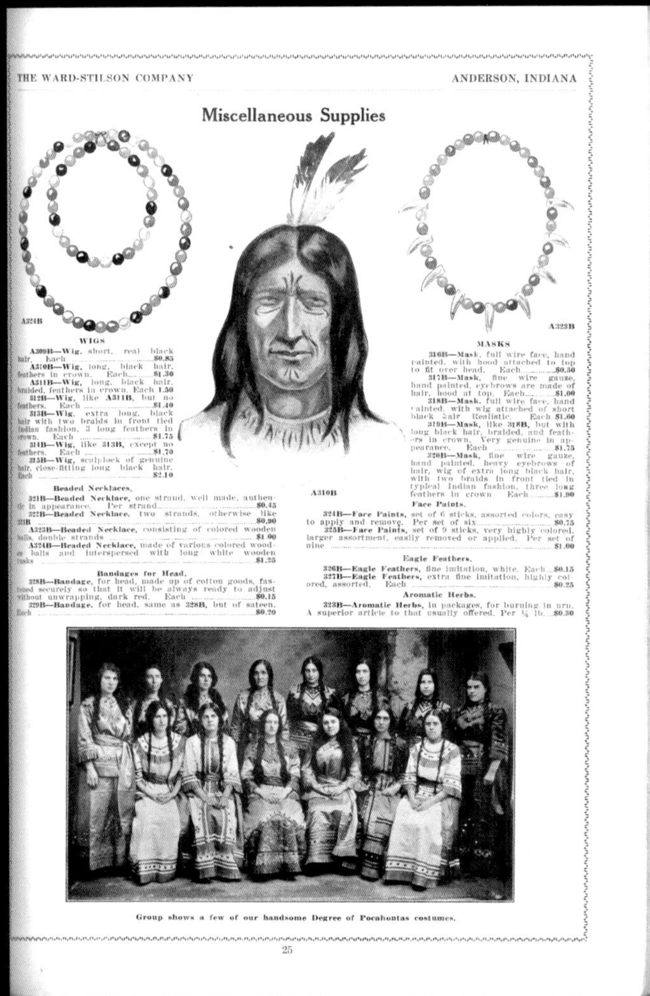

THE WARD-STILSON COMPANY   ANDERSON, INDIANA

Miscellaneous Supplies

A324B   A310B   A323B

WIGS

A309B—Wig, short, real black hair. Each $0.85

A310B—Wig, long, black hair, feathers in crown. Each $1.30

A311B—Wig, long, black hair, braided, feathers in crown. Each 1.50

312B—Wig, like A311B, but no feathers. Each $1.40

313B—Wig, extra long, black hair with two braids in front tied Indian fashion, 3 long feathers in crown. Each $1.75

314B—Wig, like 313B, except no feathers. Each $1.70

315B—Wig, scalplock of genuine hair, close-fitting long black hair. Each $2.10

Beaded Necklaces.

321B—Beaded Necklace, one strand, well made, authentic in appearance. Per strand $0.45

322B—Beaded Necklace, two strands, otherwise like 321B $0.90

A323B—Beaded Necklace, consisting of colored wooden balls, double strands $1.00

A324B—Beaded Necklace, made of various colored wooden balls and interspersed with long white wooden tusks $1.25

Bandages for Head.

328B—Bandage, for head, made up of cotton goods, fastened securely so that it will be always ready to adjust without unwrapping, dark red. Each $0.15

329B—Bandage, for head, same as 328B, but of sateen. Each $0.20

MASKS

316B—Mask, full wire face, hand painted, with hood attached to top to fit over head. Each $0.50

317B—Mask, fine wire gauze, hand painted, eyebrows are made of hair, hood at top. Each $1.00

318B—Mask, full wire face, hand painted, with wig attached of short black hair. Realistic. Each $1.60

319B—Mask, like 318B, but with long black hair, braided, and feathers in crown. Very genuine in appearance. Each $1.75

320B—Mask, fine wire gauze, hand painted, heavy eyebrows of hair, wig of extra long black hair, with two braids in front tied in typical Indian fashion, three long feathers in crown. Each $1.90

Face Paints.

324B—Face Paints, set of 6 sticks, assorted colors, easy to apply and remove. Per set of six $0.75

325B—Face Paints, set of 9 sticks, very highly colored, larger assortment, easily removed or applied. Per set of nine $1.00

Eagle Feathers.

326B—Eagle Feathers, fine imitation, white. Each $0.15

327B—Eagle Feathers, extra fine imitation, highly colored, assorted. Each $0.25

Aromatic Herbs.

323B—Aromatic Herbs, in packages, for burning in urn. A superior article to that usually offered. Per ¼ lb. $0.30

Group shows a few of our handsome Degree of Pocahontas costumes.

25

Ward-Stilson of Indiana was one of many purveyors of wire masks for initiation or welcome ceremonies by members of the Improved Order of Red Men. *Courtesy of the Red Men Museum and Library, Waco, Texas.*

MASKS TO CONCEAL. MASKS TO CELEBRATE.

For many of the same reasons that painted window screens have been used as a mediator of public and private space, painted wire masks have been incorporated in rituals throughout the world. Flexible wire cloth offers an excellent raw material for mask-making: it can easily be molded to fit the face and create a lifelike form; it takes paint well, and when only wire is painted (without filling in the spaces between the mesh), the colored surface obscures the face without compromising the wearer's breathing or vision.

Masking to conceal one's identity for combat and revelry is an ancient tradition that has experienced resurgences at different times in history. Following the explosion of fraternal lodges nationwide at about 1830, dozens of mail-order catalogs began to offer masks of delicate woven wire. These masks were used to depict the "other" in rituals to attract membership and to enliven their events and pranks. Some of these masks added embellishments such as eyebrows and wigs woven from real hair, raising both the price and the mystery. Originally homemade, such masks became especially popular in America after the 1893 Columbian Exposition introduced Americans to foreign races and ethnicities.

The catalogs of the DeMoulin Bros. & Co. of Greenville, Illinois, and Ward-Stilson of Anderson, Indiana, among others, boasted active trade in masks from 1890 until World War I.

One of the earliest secret societies in America to embrace wire masks was the Improved Order of Red Men. With a long tradition of facial obfuscation, the Order traces its roots to the Sons of Liberty in 1765 and its successor the Sons of St. Tamina (the seeds of New York's Tammany Hall). "These patriots concealed their identities and worked 'underground' to help establish freedom and liberty in the early Colonies."[151] This was the same fraternal order whose members disguised themselves as Indians in 1773 and notoriously dumped 342 chests of tea overboard into Boston Harbor. Breaking away from the larger order, a group formed the Society of Red Men in 1813 and then the Improved Order of Red Men in 1834. In 1847, the national organization was chartered. Members customarily donned full regalia for a variety of rites and reserved brightly colored masks replicating faces of Native Americans for "adoption" or

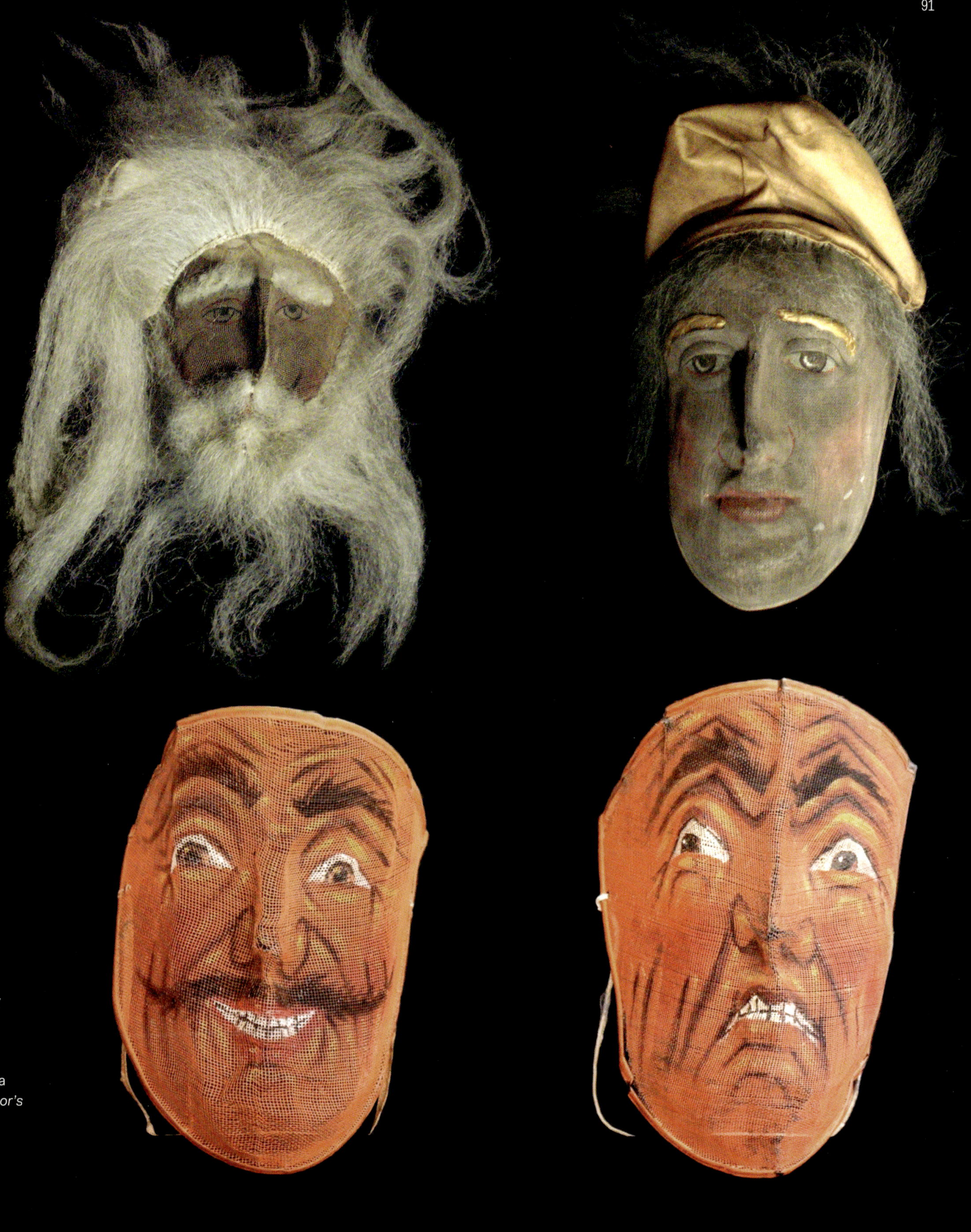

TOP ROW
Masks circa 1900. *Courtesy of Georgie Manuel.*

BOTTOM ROW
Pair of Red Men masks, circa 1900, found in Boston. *Author's collection.*

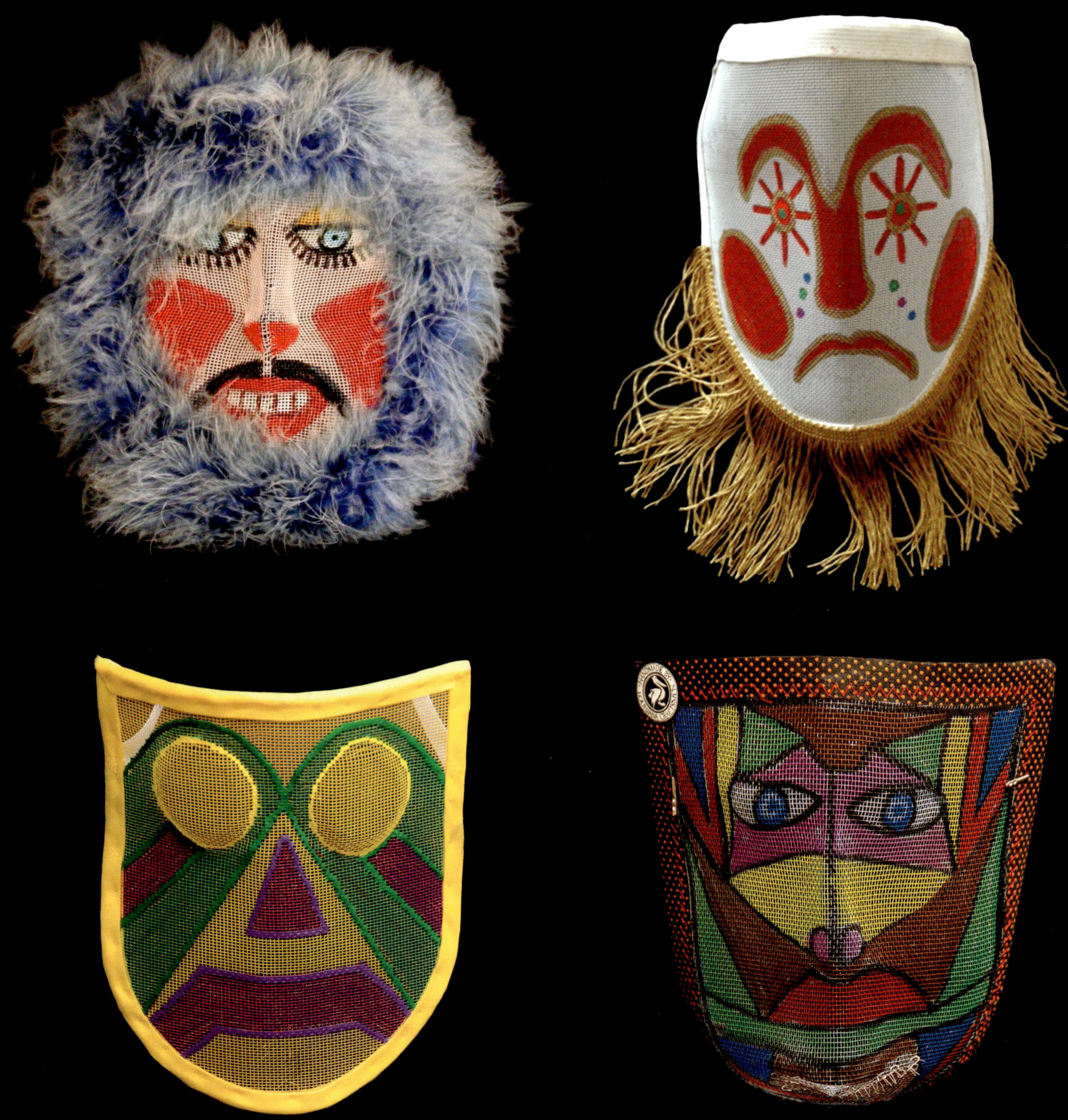

"raising up" ceremonies to welcome initiates or honor a new chief. No photography was permitted at these rituals, but many of the masks survive, sadly removed from their performance contexts. With members in all fifty states and territories, their numbers topped half a million by the late 1920s. In recent years, those numbers and range have dwindled, and masks are no longer a part of their regalia.

Simple variants of early painted-wire masks imported from Austria and Germany, dating to the last half of the nineteenth century, are still in active use today by participants in Caribbean John Canoe (known among islanders as Junkanoo, Jankunu, and many other variations) celebrations during Christmas and New Year's.[152] In southwest Louisiana's Cajun Mardi Gras, where the penchant for mayhem and mischief require anonymity, the masks are central to their revels. Wildly colorful pointed hats, ruffled pants, and shirts and painted-screen masks are defining outfits.

Georgie and Allen Manuel are credited with the revival of the masks in Eunice, Louisiana, in the 1970s as well as reintroducing the annual *Courir de Mardi Gras* ride (on horseback or hay wagons) or run that continues there as part of a huge week-long pre-Lenten attraction. The Manuels are the most prolific of the regional fabricators and are deeply committed to every aspect of the event's and the craft's roots and future. As the local expert on Cajun Mardi Gras wire screen masks, Georgie Manuel regularly receives reports of historic masks from the region, and maintains an impressive collection of early and contemporary examples.

In nearby Basile, Louisiana, Russell "Potic" (pronounced pot-see) Rider, who is the *capitan* of the local *Courir*, and J. B. "Junior" LeBlue supply local revelers with distinctive masks, either by request or as gifts. The Basile event's trademarks are "Cajun music, a flatbed trailer, its own route, live chickens (for the culminating gumbo), and authentic costumes featuring *capuchones* (cone-shaped hats) and wire screen masks."[153]

Materials have been adapted over time as new media and technologies become available. The Cajun screen makers now use nontoxic paint pens in lieu of brushes and enamel paint. Heavier meshed shale shaker cloth (called "shell shaker" locally) straight from the oil fields in a variety of mesh sizes and densities provides a firmer fabric for Rider to apply his signature technique of three layers of paint rather than the more frequently found, and more transparent, single coat employed by others. Silky store-bought fringe has replaced natural hair. Ribbon rather than crimped metal is used to trim and protect the wearer's face from the mask's rough edges. Several artists who once used wire have moved on to use plastic needlepoint canvas to serve as a base for attaching found items, thus sacrificing the virtues of the open mesh for ventilation and transparency.

The Cajun mask has yet to become a staple at New Orleans's Mardi Gras. However, the Manuels receive an annual invitation to share their creations and lore at the Jazz and Heritage Festival's craft village each spring.

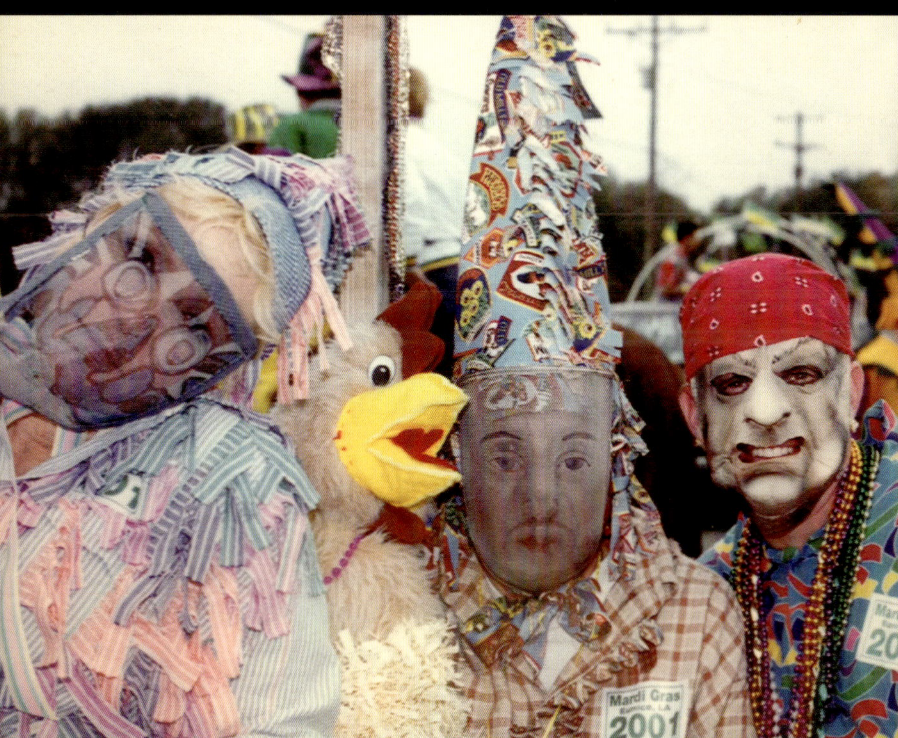

Screen masks are part and parcel of southwest Louisiana's anonymous tradition of mischief making during the Cajun Mardi Gras's *Courir* (run). *Courtesy of Georgie Manuel.*

THE DECLINE

As one of the nation's premier manufacturers of wire screens, the Wickwires took pride in their customer relations, finding no job too small or unprofitable. The company's correspondence indicates a loyal private and commercial customer base from New Orleans to San Francisco, Michigan to Vermont. It also suggests the management's accommodating service.

Messrs. A. J. Phillips & Sons, Fenton, Michigan, Feb. 25. 1889

Replying to our favor of the 22 inst. The cloth would have to be painted especially to fit your doors. We have a man that paints landscapes for us and if you would send us a draft of your door giving the size of the panels and we will make for you the pieces that will fit the doors. It has to be painted lengthwise of the roll for a door where our stock is all appointed cross-wise of the rolls. We would have to cut the cloth in Blanks so as to fit the door. As to the price we get 8 cents per square foot but we expect this would be too high for you. We could have him do the work by the job, he can put as much work as you want on the door, if you will say what price you can pay for this work we will have him do the work at that price and the cloth we will bill you the same as if in the roll. We make a figured cloth in the roll that will work either way as you will see by the sample, this we can furnish you at $2.25 per 100 square feet.

Yours respectfully,
Wickwire Brothers[154]

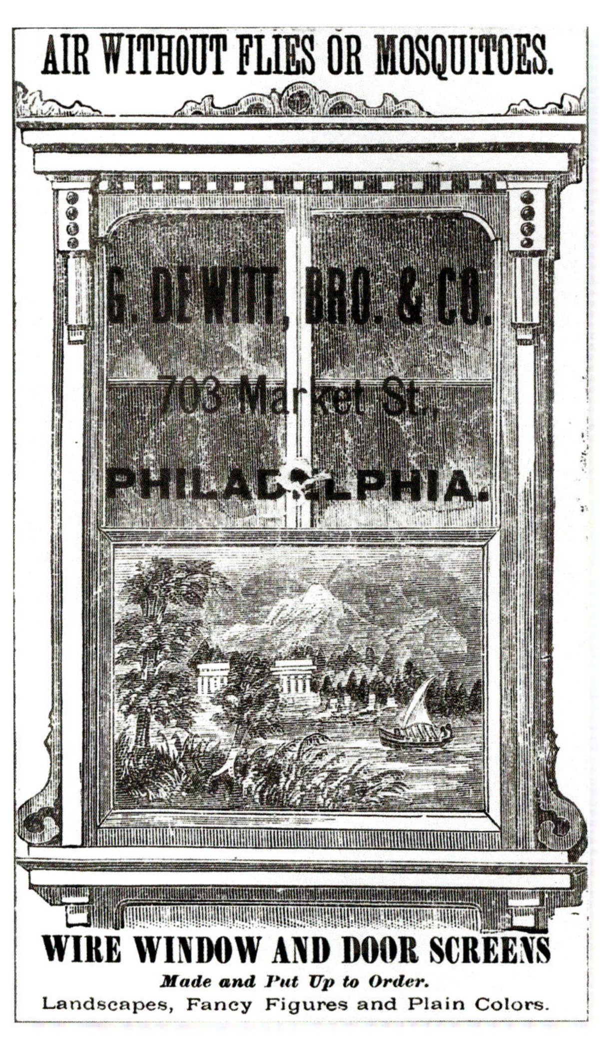

Trade catalogs made landscape screens available in all parts of the country, creating a popular trend found in fine homes during the last quarter of the twentieth century. *Warshaw Collection of Business Americana, Smithsonian Institution National Museum of American History.*

Wire producers including Wickwire Brothers had already determined a way to make a one-size-fits-most landscape by creating a central idyll with excessive amounts of sky and foreground.

Our landscape Shade Cloth is hand painted on a Drab background, in Black and White, and on opening the roll there appears a beautiful panorama of castles and ruins, wood and water, rock and meadow scenery. This cloth can be cut across the roll at any place, any position of it over a foot long being a complete picture in itself. Widths in stock 24, 48 inches.[155]

While artists toiled over custom orders, their employers continually sought novel ways to cut corners. Machinery was introduced to speed up output. In 1870, Chicago Stamping Company introduced a roller printing process capable of producing 100-foot rolls. Their "Figured Wire Screens"

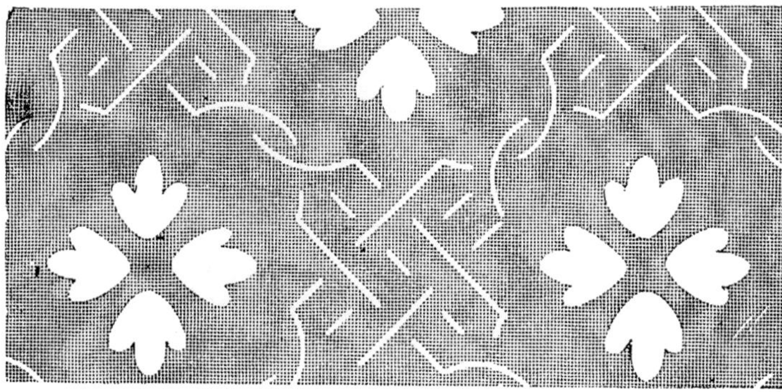

FIGURED WIRE WINDOW SCREENS.

Having a ground color of green, drab or gray, relieved by a white figure as shown in the cut below.

PRICE OF FIGURED WIRE CLOTH.

Special Figures for large orders.

Green Figured, 24, 28, 30 and 36 inches wide, per square foot------------20c.
Gray or Drab figured, 24, 28, 30 and 36 inches wide, per square foot------20c.
Imported   "   "   "   "   "   " ex. fine per square ft--25c.

These cloths are very generally used in Dwelling Houses, Offices and Banks; and on milk and provision Safes. Can be lettered etc., the same as landscape if desired. It also makes a good lining to put inside of bank railings to protect and screen money and valuables on the teller's desk. Special prices to manufacturers of safes for large orders.

In 1874, Chicago Stamping Co. offered figured screens, a less costly alternative to hand-painted screens. *Warshaw Collection of Business Americana, Smithsonian Institution National Museum of American History.*

featured "a ground color of green, drab or gray, relieved by a white figure."[156] In 1879 the Wickwire catalog added "Figured Wire Cloth" with a continuous repeat diamond pattern "black figure on drab cloth and white figure on green cloth…at $2.25 per 100 square feet…very handsome and almost excludes any object inside from outside view."[157] The geometric designs worked either vertically or horizontally, making them more versatile than a one-way floral pattern. Wickwire supplied retailers and individual clients in Chicago, St. Louis, Cleveland, and Milwaukee, while other trade catalogs from Baltimore, Detroit, and San Francisco served an expanding market.

Roller printing eliminated the need for "French" or local highly paid artists. In 1885 the San Francisco Wire Works' elaborate catalog featured pages of new designs for figured screens. Their "Vines Pattern" and "Grecian Pattern," available in tri-colored, white, and green, were lower-priced options to the more costly landscape screen at a savings of $1.50 per piece.[158]

It is no surprise that actual examples of figured screen have not survived. While a hand-painted window screen would be less likely to be consigned to the trash heap, the repetitive and cheaper figured wire screen would have little long-term aesthetic value.

The 1890 Wickwire catalog eliminated landscape-painted screens entirely. Whether this decision was due to the loss of their resident artist or to declining numbers of orders is unknown. The company advised Mrs. J. H. Crumb, a customer from nearby DeRuyter, New York, to consider alternatives.

The screens you wish made of black walnut and landscape cloth would cost you $2.50 each. We make very few landscape screens now than we used to. They used to be more fashionable than at present. Could make you hard wood frame black walnut finish covered with black wire cloth which makes a very nice job and is what is used in the finest residences now. These would cost you $1.00 each.[159]

They suggested that buyers "put the expense on the wood work and use plain black cloth" instead, ensuring their market for woven wire window and door screens but signaling the death knell for the curious art of landscape painting on wire.[160]

The reason for the rise and fall and rise of painted screens in any America city is anyone's guess. Fashions come and go. Style centers adopt and let go of the current fad in their own time. A design trend pronounced obsolete in New York gains eager adherents elsewhere.

Mary Clara Bowie, writing in the *Baltimore Sun* in 1926 with one eye in the past and another on foreign trends, describes a concentration of screen sightings in northern sections of the city. "One or two of the stucco houses in Italian Style located in that [Roland Park] suburb have placed in their windows, screens done in the old-time gray monotones with scenes copied from the Roman Forum, after the best Italian manner." She attributes painted screens' revival to "those to be seen abroad, notably in England, France and Italy. One house in Guilford has a pair of window screens painted with Japanese garden scenes, the hues…toning exactly with those…in the stone path and chimney. To further confuse the idylls, one little tearoom not far from Towson has screens painted with dancing Polish figures, the men in high boots and frogged coats and the women in full skirts and kerchiefs."[161] Bowie's only mention of painted screens in a rowhouse was in a Waverly (North Baltimore) street off York Road, renamed "Good Husbands' Row," where, in their idle hours, the "industrious mechanics" who lived in a series of attached cottages painted identical scenes of the matrimonial barque and attending Cupid taken from their marriage licenses.

Bowie addresses a 1920s "year-old" screen revival in the city's affluent Roland Park and Guilford neighborhoods, citing the few remaining screens from an earlier era with only a fleeting nod to painted screens' rapid growth in ethnic East Baltimore. She bemoans their late arrival as if unaware of their nineteenth-century appearance at Charles Street furniture emporiums and trade catalogs of the period.

"Among well-to-do conservative Baltimoreans," interior decorators along with their housewife patrons took credit in certain communities for keeping screens in the active design vocabulary. Fads thrived and perished at different rates around the country. Although the factory-based ateliers may have disappeared by the end of the 1800s, many screens survived in situ well into the twentieth century, due to a fondness for the antique or to inertia. Their once-vivid images faded, as did memories of their dominance on fine homes throughout America. Their departure was quick and thorough.

An unlikely holdover into the late twentieth century, this screen, found on South Chester Street above Fell's Point, depicts colorful ruins popular in the Victorian era. It made the transition to a time when the Red Bungalow screen was well established in Baltimore. Artist unknown. *Zelinski family screen. Author photograph, 1974.*

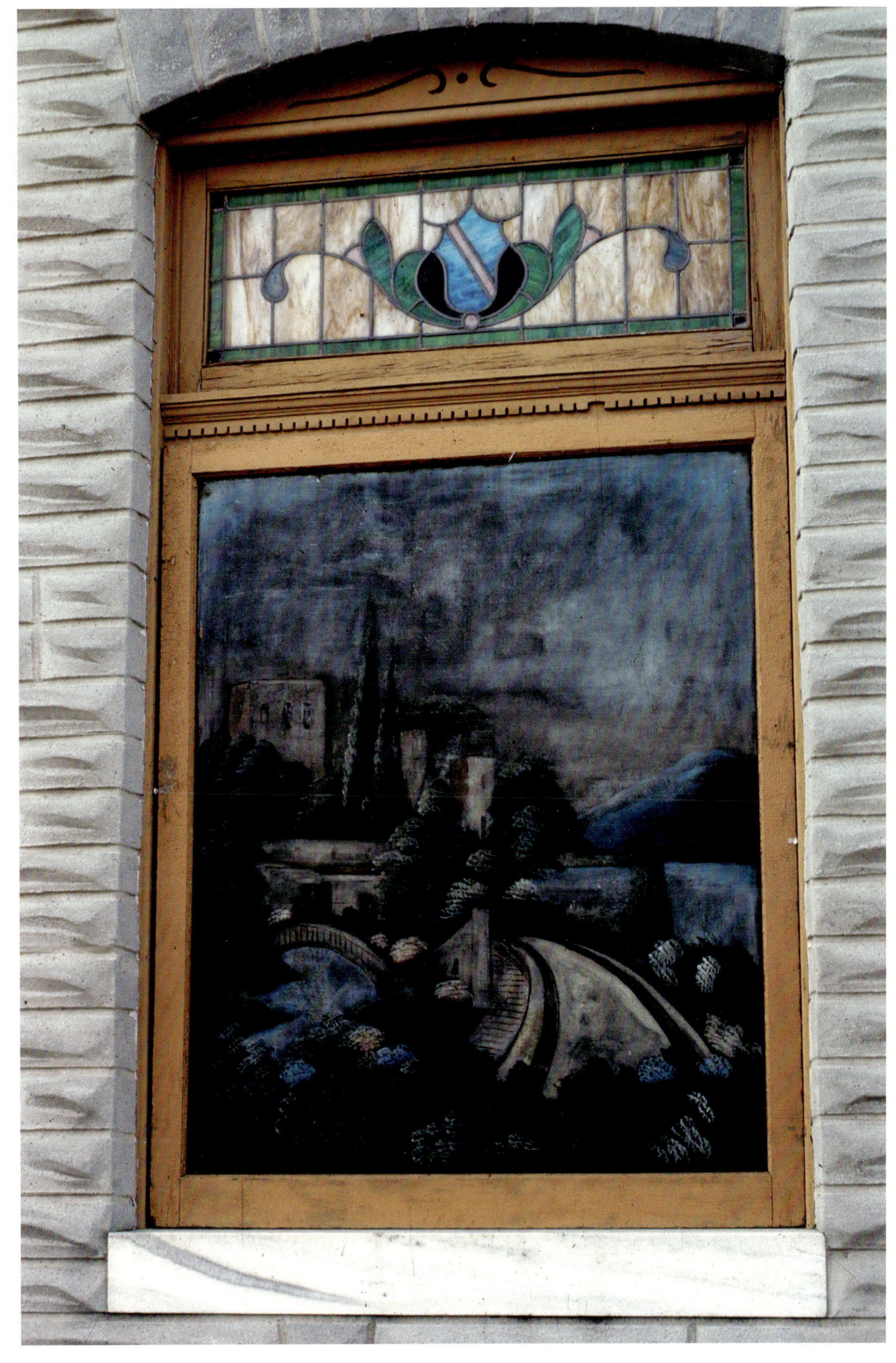

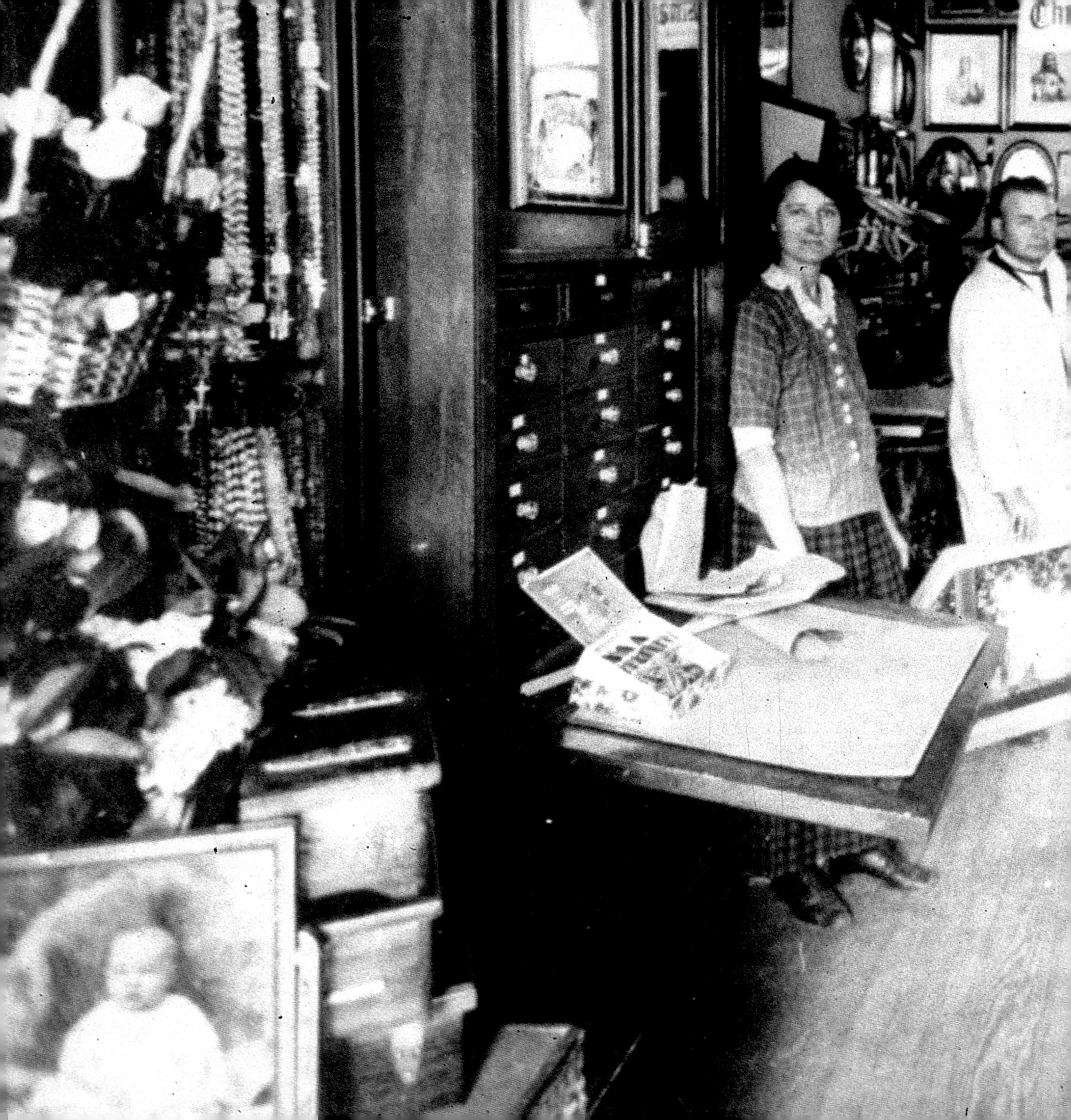

THE SCREEN PAINTERS

The Art Shop, circa 1925.

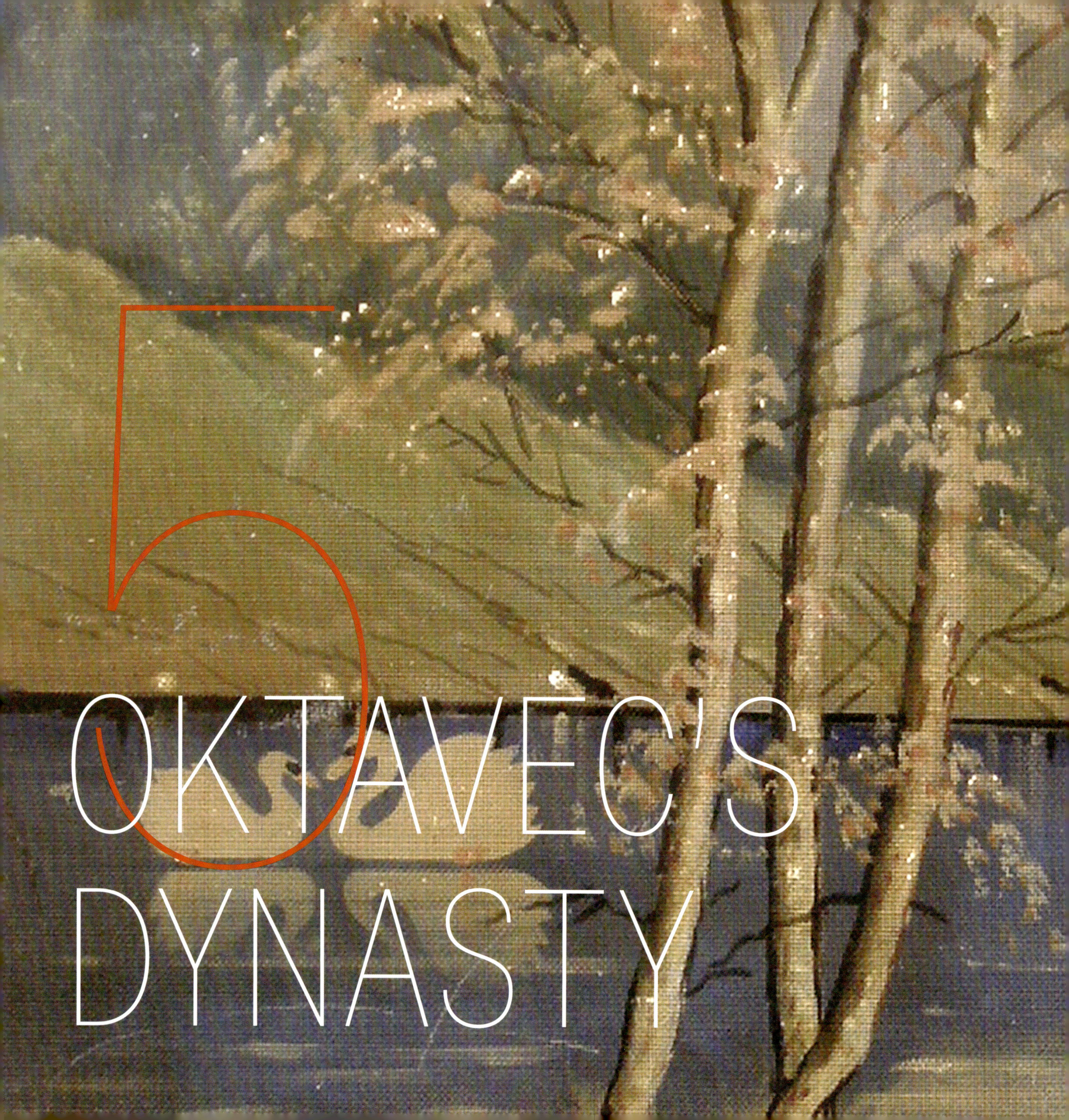
5
OKTAVEC'S
DYNASTY

Everybody claims, although I'm not mentioning any names, that they invented it. "Oh my father invented it, my mother invented it, Grandma Moses invented it." Not so.

Johnny Eck

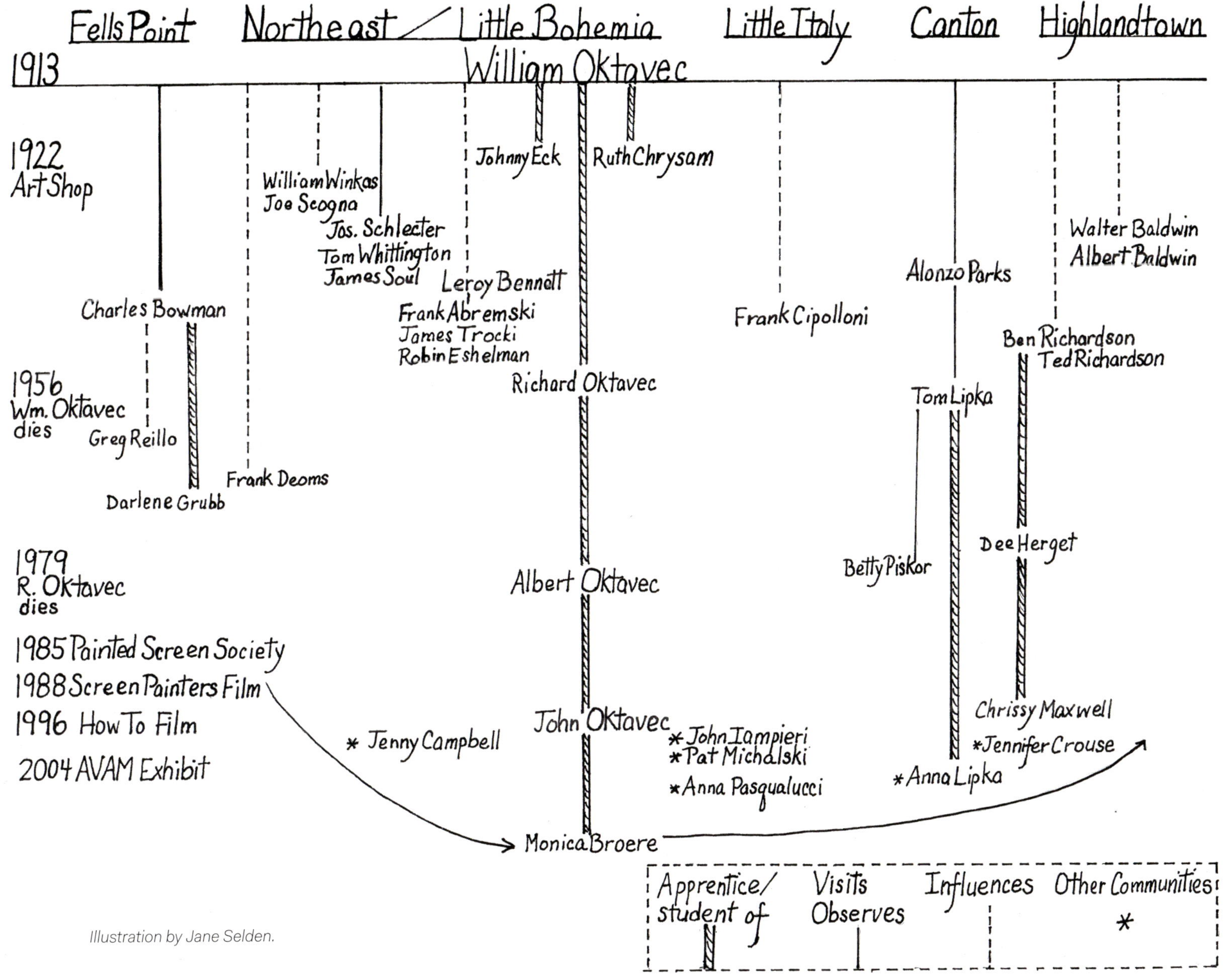

Illustration by Jane Selden.

FROM BOHEMIA TO BALTIMORE

Born in the Bohemian village of Kasejovice, then under Austrian rule, Vàclav Anton Oktavec was the fifth of eight siblings. The family lived on a four-acre farmstead, supported by their father's earnings as a nailsmith. Art and invention were Vàclav's lifelong passions. He recalled scenes from his boyhood at his father's side, watching a flock of geese in a meadow and sketching his surroundings with a sharp tool in the local clay.[162] After completing his formal education, the fourteen-year-old Vaclav left his picture-postcard, red-roofed rural village to train as a butcher in Germany. As his youngest son related years later, "all the males from thirteen to sixteen had to go to Germany and learn a trade. He didn't particularly like it, but he learned butchering. And at night he would do his artwork."[163]

He returned home with his newly acquired trade, and for two years worked to perfect his skills, but the harsh economic situation and political instability in turn-of-the-century Bohemia (now the Czech Republic) led him to pursue employment in yet another nation. In 1901, Vàclav and a younger sister, Alzbeta, sailed from Bremerhaven aboard the steamer *Kaiser Wilhelm der Grosse*, bound for New York.[164] The seven-day voyage brought the young butcher and his sister, who most likely traveled in steerage, to America, a land of unimaginable opportunity. The next year, their parents and younger brother and sister joined them in Manhattan. Eventually the entire Oktavec family, minus one sister who stayed behind, shared a sixth-floor walk-up in Yorkville, an upper East Side neighborhood densely populated by newly arrived Eastern Europeans. Alzbeta found work as a servant, probably in a wealthy German or Jewish household where her ability to speak German would have been highly prized. Finding the city "too noisy... [his parents and one sister] went back to the old country."[165] The four Oktavec brothers settled permanently in the United States. Frank, a pastry chef, candy maker, and cake decorator, found work and a career at one of the city's popular Schrafft's restaurants and confectioners. He became famous for crafting giant Easter eggs, which were displayed in Grand Central Terminal, the seasonal equivalent of the decorated department store Christmas windows along Fifth Avenue. His crowning confection was so large that delighted travelers walked around it in wonder.

Brother Albert was a "crackerjack machinist" who worked for almost fifty years at the Naval Academy in Annapolis.[166] Martin, the youngest brother, eventually trained as a Redemptorist priest and held pulpits in Baltimore and New York.

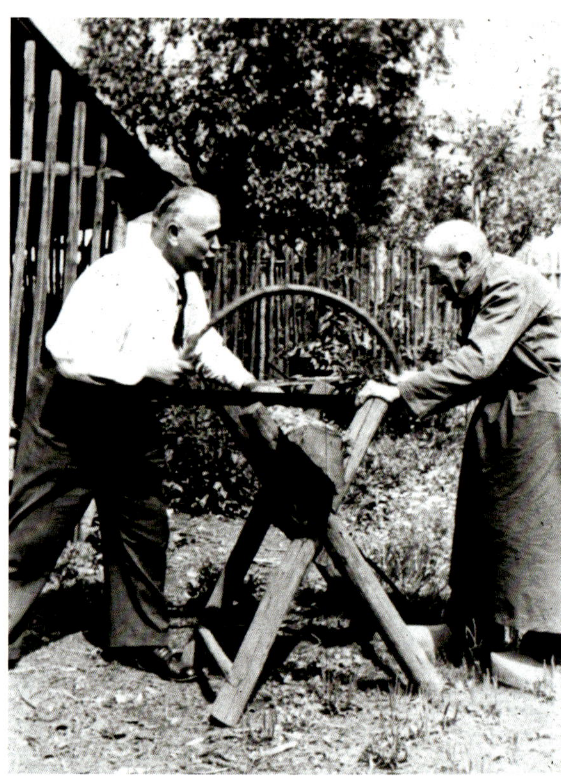

William Oktavec helps his father, who operated a small farm in Kasejovice. Taken during a 1938 visit, the first time William Oktavec returned to Bohemia after leaving for America, and the last time he would see his European family. *Oktavec family photograph.*

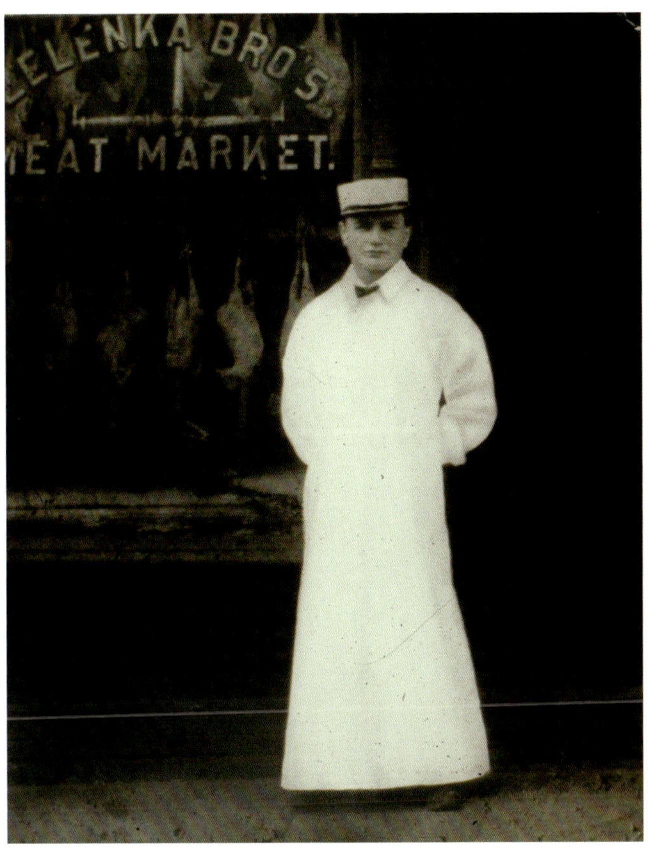

William Oktavec was trained to be a butcher in Germany as a boy and found immediate work in the Czech community of Brooklyn when he emigrated in 1901. *Oktavec family photograph.*

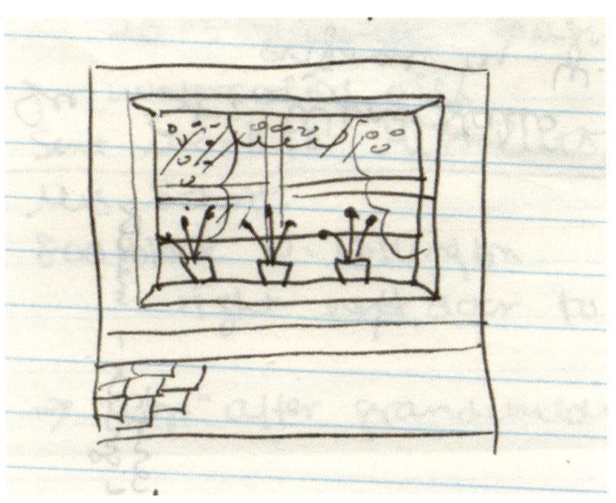

The story of the first screen that William Oktavec painted for a harried secretary at their workplace in New Jersey became part of family lore. Depicted here as remembered by his oldest son. *Illustration by William Oktavec Jr., 1985.*

Vàclav found work in the Brownsville section of Brooklyn. He apprenticed with the Zelenka brothers, also from Kasejovice, who had established a thriving enterprise in the city—a meat market. Vàclav's inner artist yearned for more creative pursuits than carving meat, and he enrolled in night classes for drafting, which, along with his growing grasp of English, propelled him toward greater opportunities.

In 1906, Oktavec found work at the newly established Eclipse Air Brush factory in Newark, New Jersey, where he quickly mastered the emerging technology of compressed-air sprayers to cover hard-to-paint surfaces. He traveled to Philadelphia and Chicago, demonstrating high-pressure painting of wicker furniture, woodwork, window screen, and other objects.[167] Eclipse quickly promoted the affable, astute young man to run their lacquering and japanning departments, where he further advanced his knowledge of painted surfaces.[168]

Within a few years, Vàclav had a job with the Western Electric Company spray-painting telephone wires and diaphragms. According to his eldest son, William Jr., it was while his father worked at Western Electric that he created his first painted screen, to help shield a coworker from distractions outside her office widow:

She worked in this office and the guys across the way from her used to see her [at her window] and whistle at her. She used to get quite shook up about it. So she told my father about it, wondered if there could be something that could be done. So he said, "Let me think about it." So he went home and he painted a window screen. The original that I remember [hearing about], he painted like a window with lace curtains on it and it had a pot of flowers. And he put it in the window and she could see out and they couldn't see in.[169]

Vàclav's success at Western Electric assured him that he could earn a living and begin a family. He and his brother Albert courted two Bohemian American, Baltimore-born sisters from the Soler family and married them in a double Valentine's Day ceremony in 1912. Vàclav and his bride, Theresa, left New York after the birth of their first son, William, the following year. They settled in northeast Baltimore's Czech enclave, Little Bohemia, to be near Theresa's family. Satisfied that America, and Baltimore in particular, were a good fit, Vaclav applied for naturalization, listing his occupation as "Artist" and anglicizing his name to William Anton Oktavec.[170]

Typical of corner groceries, Bohemian-owned Peroutka's Northeast Meat Market at North Port Street and Ashland Avenue was two blocks east of Oktavec's store, and similar to it in many ways. It was photographed by North Bradford Street resident John Dubas, who chronicled home life in Little Bohemia. *Arthur U. Hooper Memorial Collection, Baltimore City Life Museums Collection. Maryland Historical Society. MC9244.*

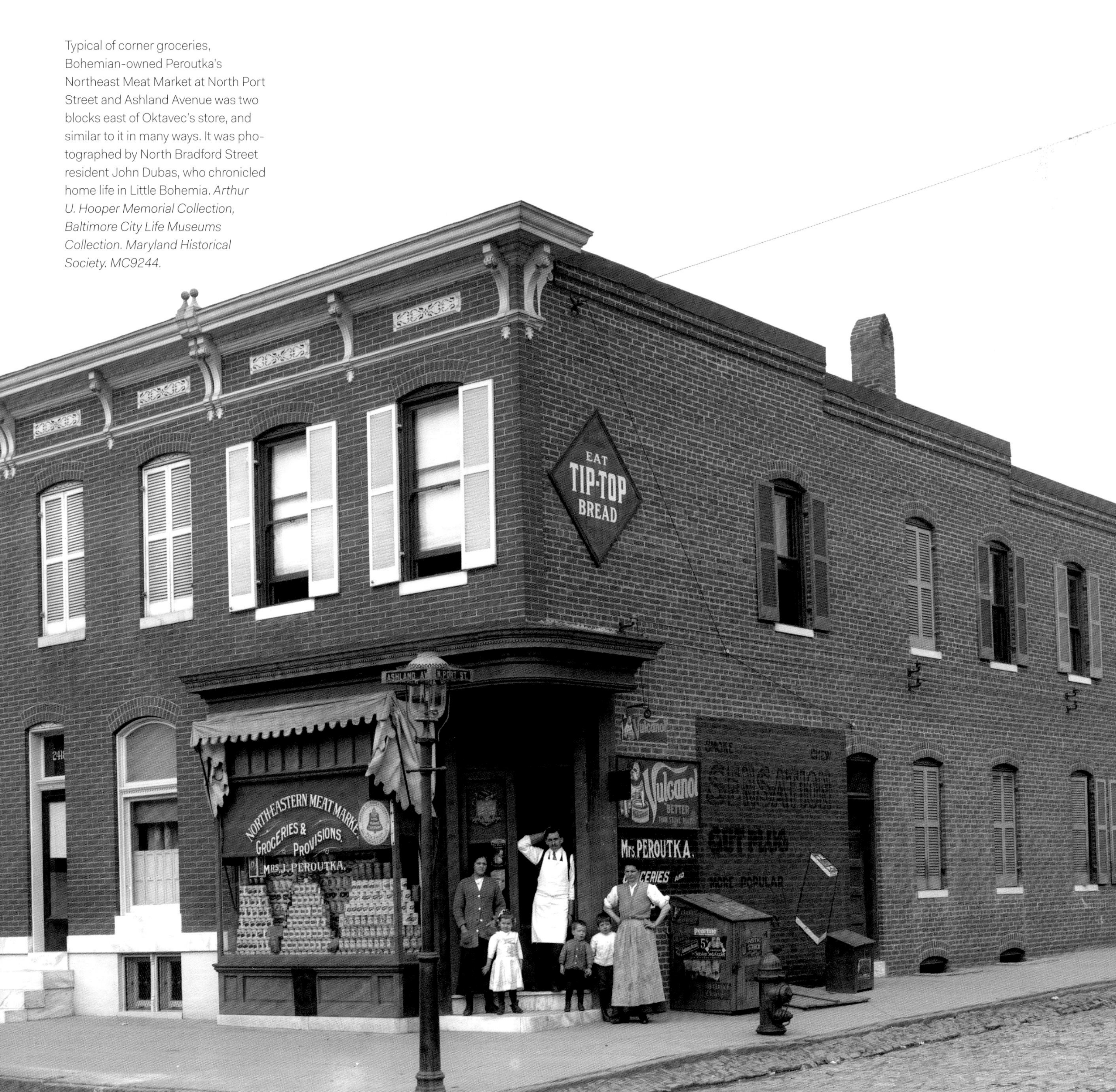

The young family could not have chosen to make Baltimore their home at a better time. It was in the midst of a building boom, and they discovered a "city of small houses, the pleasantest large settlement of the moderately rich and the moderately poor in our whole country."[171]

Oktavec purchased a corner rowhouse with an existing grocery store from James Cermak, and returned to his earlier training as a butcher. The family's second-floor living quarters and first-floor business at 847 North Collington Avenue stood in the shadow of the new St. Wenceslaus Roman Catholic Church. The butcher-draftsman-machinist-in-training sought loans for his house and store from Slavie, the nearby Bohemian Building Loan and Savings Association, one of ten such banks that catered to a Czech community now approaching 15,000 residents, 90 percent of whom were homeowners.[172]

It was at this spot, on the corner of North Collington and Ashland Avenues that the short and stocky butcher unveiled his first screen in Baltimore on a hot summer day in 1913.[173] The painting on his market's screen door showed "cuts of beef, spare ribs, lettuce, cucumbers, and carrots." He later recalled: "I used all my artistic temperament, all the art that was in me to make it as real as possible…it looked so real when I got through that customers who came in would get mad when we said we were out of lettuce because they said they saw it."[174]

FROM BUTCHER
TO ARTIST

His next-door neighbor, Emma (Mrs. John) Schott, was the first in Baltimore to notice the practical virtues of the one-way views provided by the painted screen. With a painted screen installed in her parlor, she found relief from "the bums on the corner rubbering [rubber necking] in the window"[175] of her rowhouse. For artistic inspiration, she supplied Oktavec with a scene clipped from a calendar, depicting a red mill on a pond. At first the painted screen she commissioned caused more attention than she might have desired, but the new set of gawkers were enjoying the artwork, not peering into her windows. She and her husband could relax inside, unobserved, at least in the daytime (their privacy was compromised when the interior was illuminated). As the summer simmered on, other ladies of Little Bohemia ordered their own screens from the butcher. Into his capable hands they pressed chromolithographs featuring red-roofed cottages and rustic mills with ponds and swans. He proceeded to paint the front and rear screens of their rowhouses—one after another after another.

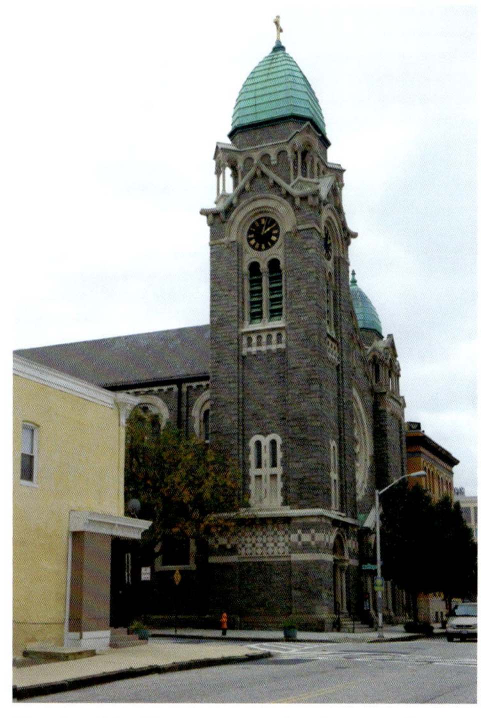

The site of the Oktavec grocery has been a private residence for many decades but still retains its profile as the corner store. It now overlooks Henderson-Hopkins School across Ashland Avenue rather than the rows of working-class homes that were demolished in 2012.

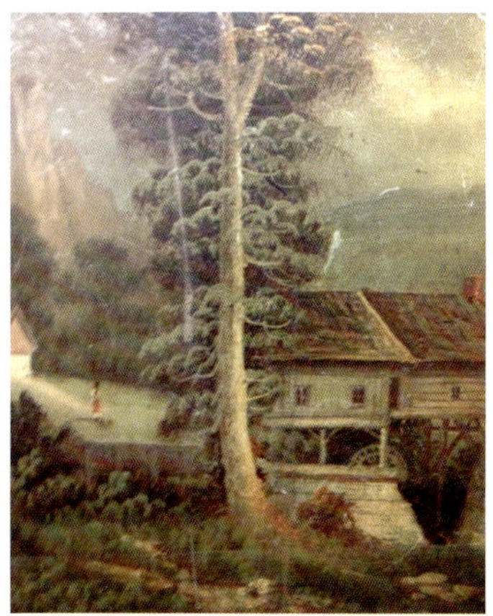

This mill scene may be the original calendar art supplied to Oktavec by Mrs. Schott for her window screen. It was found on the front of the Art Shop safe almost a century later. *Courtesy of Cash USA. Author photograph.*

That summer alone, William Oktavec claimed to have painted two hundred landscape screens. "People saw it and they wanted it. They want a lot of trees, sunshine, water, small dogs and one or two swans."[176] "After beauty, people want it so other people can't look into their house while they're waiting across the street for a trolley or their girl."[177]

Mrs. Schott had inadvertently started a fad, the popularity and endurance of which no one could have anticipated. Considering the new invention a necessity, her neighbors, however thrifty, found ways to barter or save the fifty cents or dollar that Oktavec charged per screen, receiving a discount if they ordered a houseful. Every window on the 800 block of North Collington Avenue was soon adorned. Oktavec the screen painter could have had no better advertisement. Although he never signed his screens, word of mouth brought a new stream of customers to his grocery, looking for art, not food. Thousands eyed the neighborhood's colorful scenes as they walked to and from St. Wenceslaus Church and school each day, or enjoyed an unintended gallery of landscape-painted screens en route to the city-owned Northeast Market on Monument Street, where Old World purveyors and craftspeople of every sort were found, or to the savings and loan associations to pay their mortgages. Few could resist the painted screens' unique combination of visual appeal and promise of privacy.

Within a few years of his move to Baltimore, William Oktavec found success not only as the corner grocer, a stopgap occupation, but also unexpected fame as the master of Baltimore screen painting, a fulfilling sideline. He continued the training in drafting that he had begun in New York with evening classes in mechanical drawing at Polytechnic Institute. To accommodate his growing family and with thoughts of serving his new country as World War I approached, he gave up his grocery and residence on Collington Avenue in 1915, purchased a rowhouse several blocks to the east at 906 North Luzerne Avenue, and began making a daily commute to Washington, D.C., to work as a draftsman at the Naval Gun Factory. His new residence also exposed him to a fresh supply of neighbors in need of painted screens. For the front window of the Luzerne Street house, Oktavec painted a peculiar screen featuring the Bethesda Fountain, a landmark in New York City's Central Park. Neither he nor his family ever fully explained his choice of this subject, but the idyllic spot might have been the place where he courted his future wife before 1912.

At the war's end he returned to work in Baltimore, as a draftsman-apprentice and machinist-instrument maker for the Slaysman Company, a supplier of equipment for the city's canning industry. His positions with the federal government and private industry, supplemented by income from his side business of screen painting, provided him with the confidence and capital to pursue his as-yet unrealized dream of becoming a full-time artist.

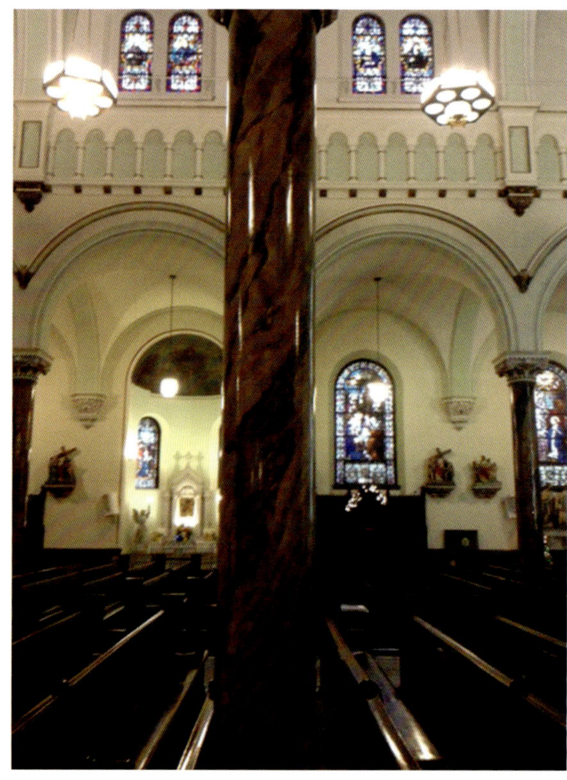

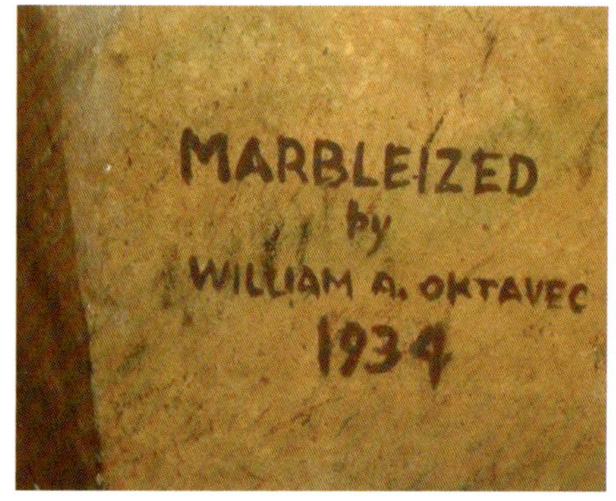

St. Wenceslaus Church was the home parish of the Oktavec family. William not only prayed and celebrated there, but also restored it inside and out as part of his church restoration business. He signed the faux marble columns as a gesture of pride in his work. *Photograph courtesy of Wayne Schaumburg.*

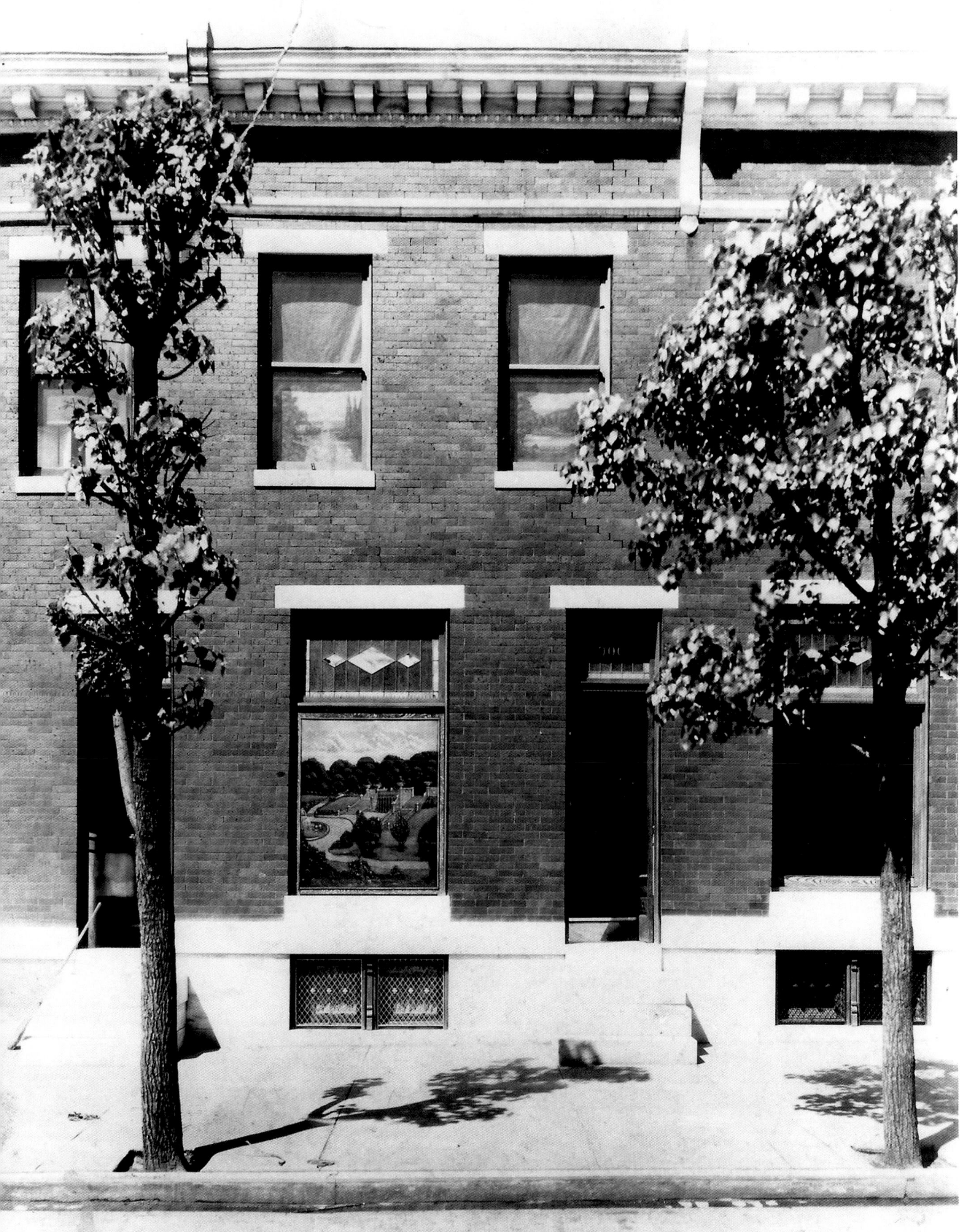

The house owned by the Oktavec family after 1915, 906 North Luzerne Avenue, sports a scene of the Bethesda Fountain in New York's Central Park, where William and his wife, Theresa, likely courted. *Oktavec family photograph.*

THE ART SHOP

In 1922 Oktavec opened the Art Shop at 2409 East Monument Street on the first floor of a single rowhouse in the heart of northeast Baltimore's bustling business corridor. The family lived upstairs, and the last of William and Theresa's four sons was born there. In the early years, peach crates served as chairs for the family and visitors who gathered to enjoy the homemade donuts, crullers, and hot coffee that "Mom" brought down to encourage good fellowship. In the backyard, "Pop" built a regulation boxing ring, where the accomplished boxer and fitness buff taught his sons the rudiments of self-defense. The proximity of their residence to the business may account for the fact that each of the boys eventually excelled in some aspect of the visual arts. In the downstairs workshop, their father specialized in painting and repairing religious statuary, as well as household objects—ornaments, china, and figurines—in need of mending. Sacred artifacts and ephemera filled the shop's shelves and showcases: Bibles, rosaries, chalices, crucifixes, statues of all sizes and descriptions, paintings, and art prints.[178] Oktavec also matted and framed pictures and diplomas, a specialty much in demand by the doctors of nearby Johns Hopkins Hospital. Oktavec sold art and office supplies, as well as greeting cards and postcards. He offered a calligraphy service for signatures and addresses on letters, cards, and envelopes, charging extra for fancy flourishes. He would even compose an original poem on request. The store was so successful that at one time six saleswomen kept the cash registers ringing.

Eventually, the Art Shop grew to fill three storefronts and included a cavernous basement classroom, where William held Saturday classes in screen painting. According to Oktavec's son Albert, "Sometimes the classes lasted all week."[179] But William was especially selective when choosing students to carry his innovation forward.

The local press covered Oktavec's output over more than four decades. The first painted screen to appear on an East Baltimore window or door was a harbinger of spring, certain to be noted in the daily papers with a story or photograph. William Oktavec's fame as the preeminent painter of woven wire screens was not limited to Baltimore. He received commissions from as far away as Washington State: one dozen copper-wire-screened panels for a room in the private residence of the chairman of Weyerhauser Lumber Corporation. The scene requested? Evergreen forests, of course. Oktavec's clients included the owner of an Atlantic City hotel and a Philadelphia apartment building. Though no record has surfaced, the family folklore supports their father's boast of a single order for more than eight hundred painted screens in ten different designs—at $6.50 each.[180]

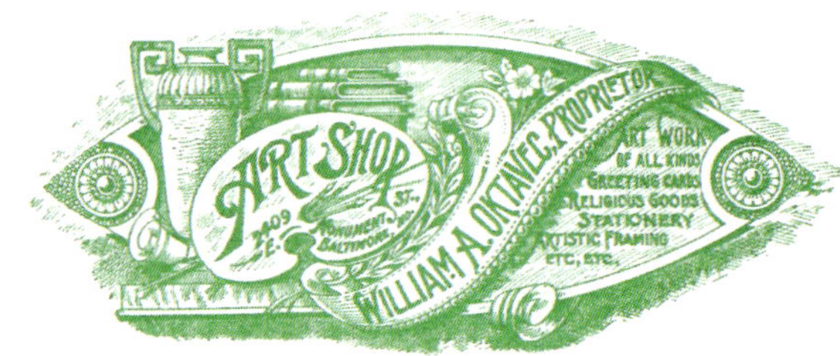

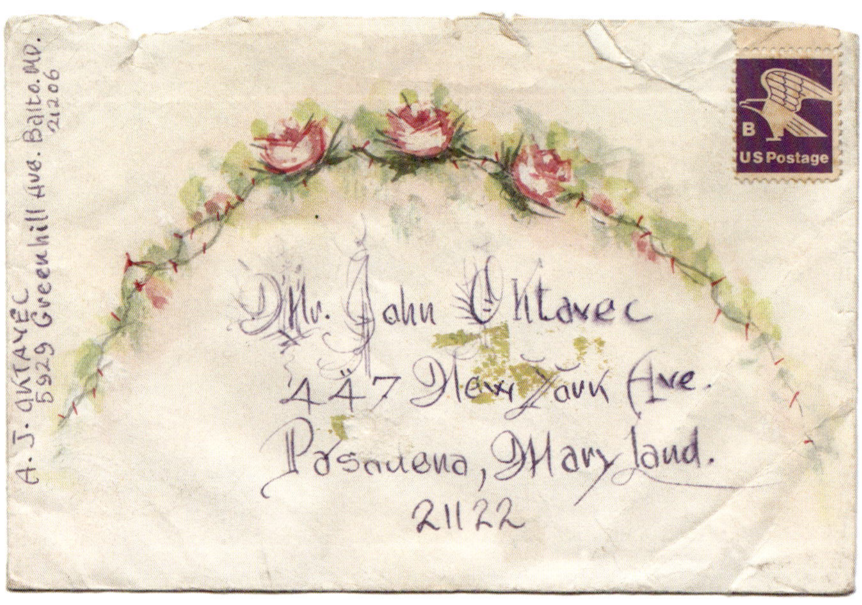

William Oktavec designed the Art Shop logo in a demonstration of his talent at engrossing (illuminated calligraphy). He and each of his sons, in turn, offered a work of art in routine correspondence, greeting cards and diplomas. Whoever the recipient, an Oktavec envelope was always a showcase for decorative penmanship. *Collection of the Painted Screen Society of Baltimore, Inc.*

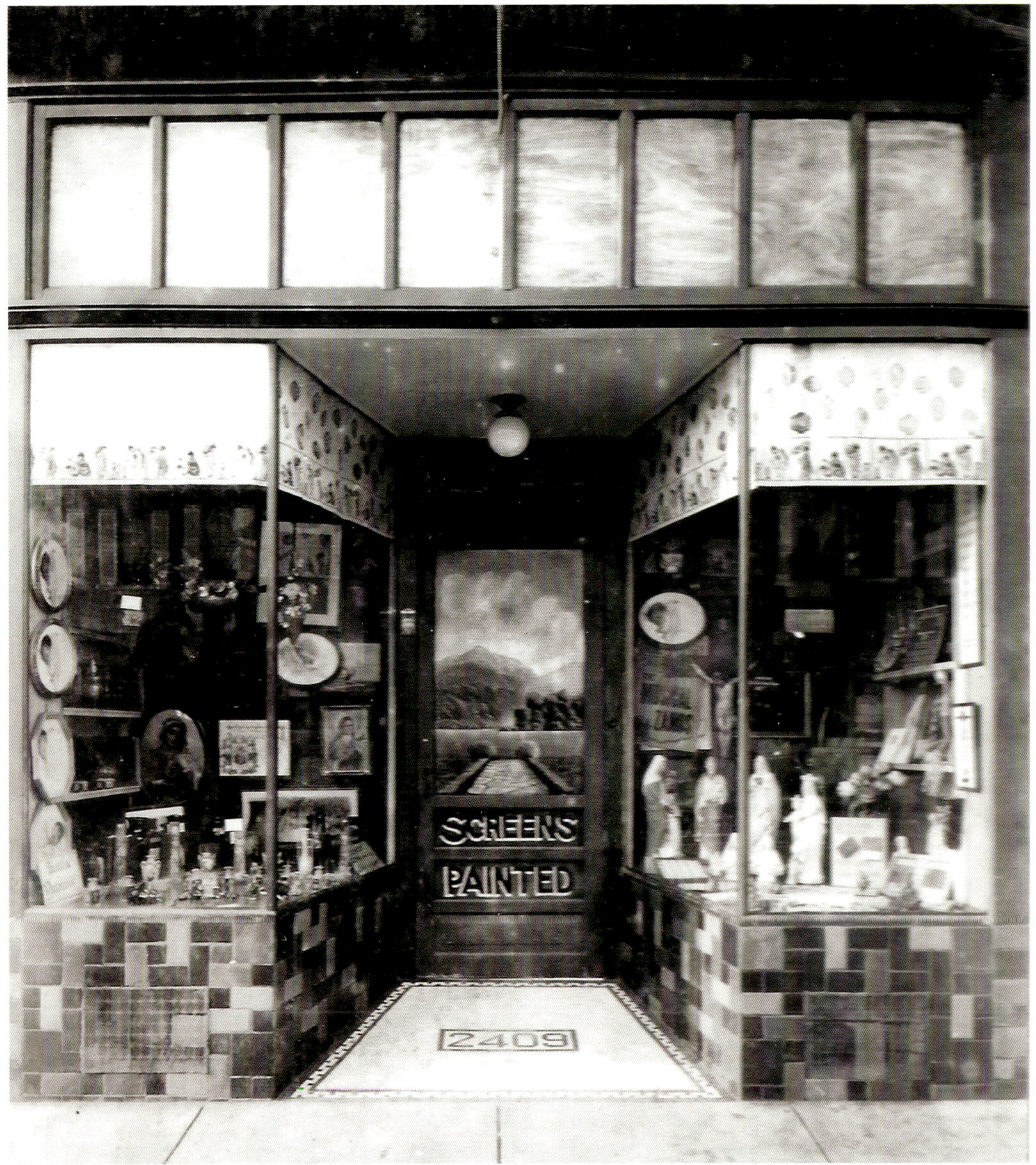

The Art Shop expanded as Oktavec's retail, screen painting, teaching and church restoration business grew. The East Monument Street corridor was a bustling commercial district catering to Bohemians early in the century and to new communities over time.

TOP: The Art Shop, circa 1922.
BOTTOM, LEFT: circa 1940.
Oktavec family photographs.

BOTTOM, RIGHT: circa 1980.
Author photograph.

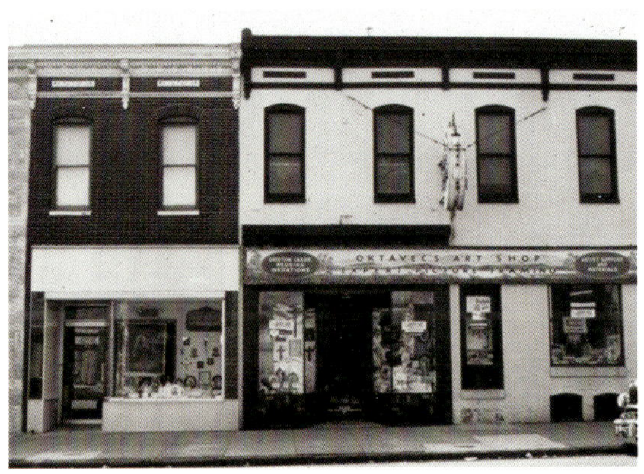

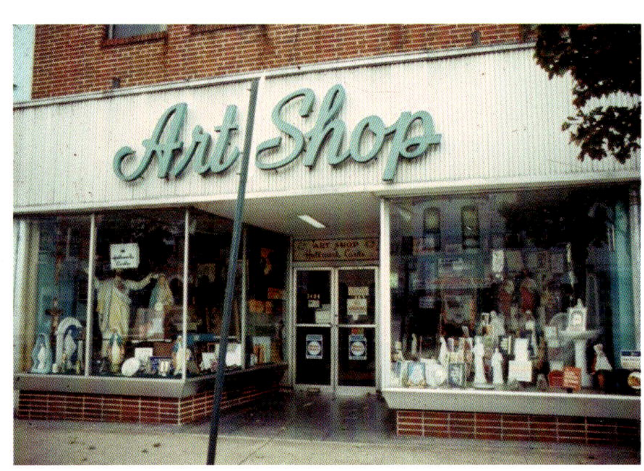

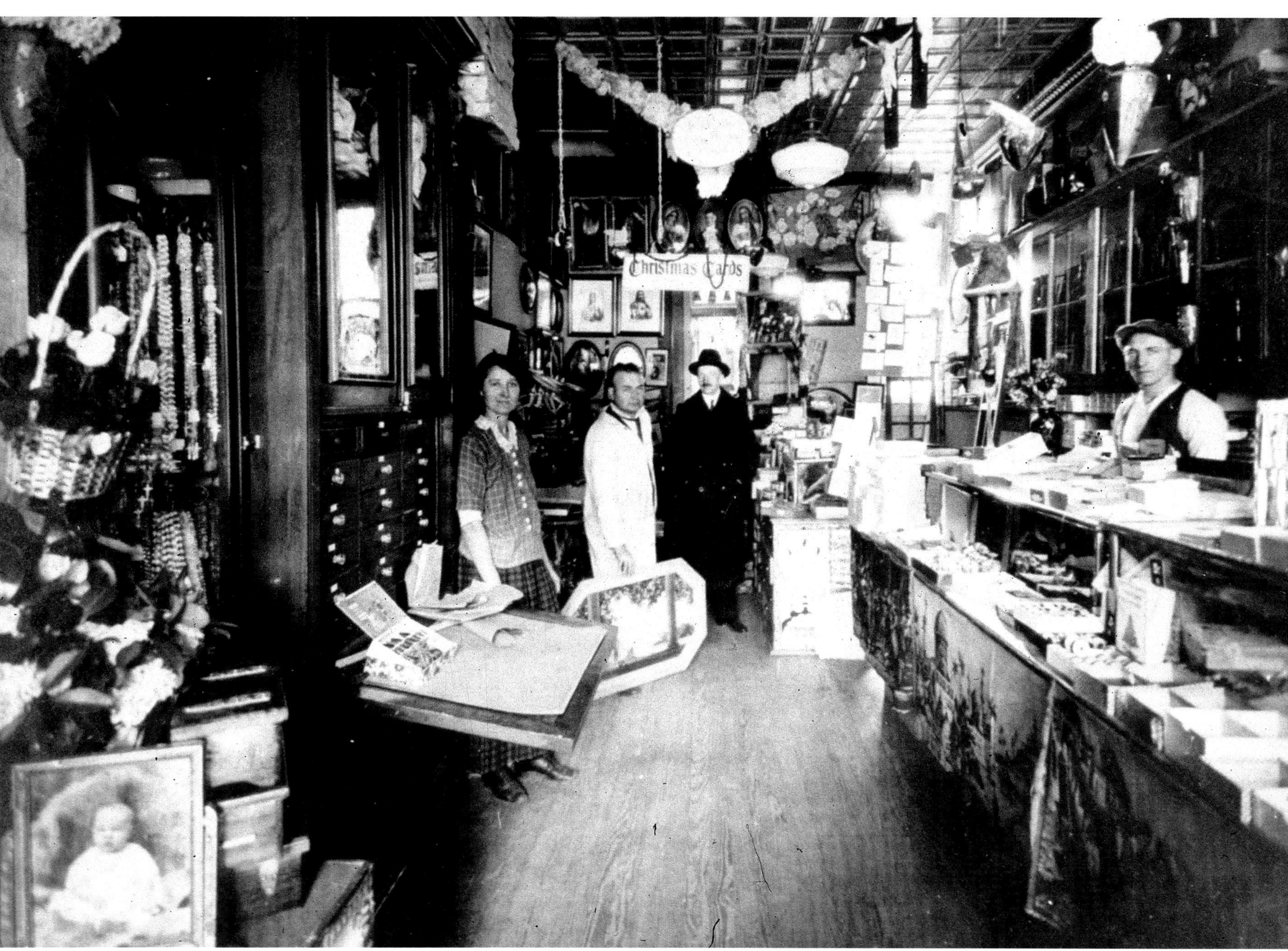

William Oktavec, in white coat, poses
inside the original Art Shop, circa 1925
with his wife Theresa, his brother Fr.
Martin in coat and hat and an employee.
Oktavec family photograph.

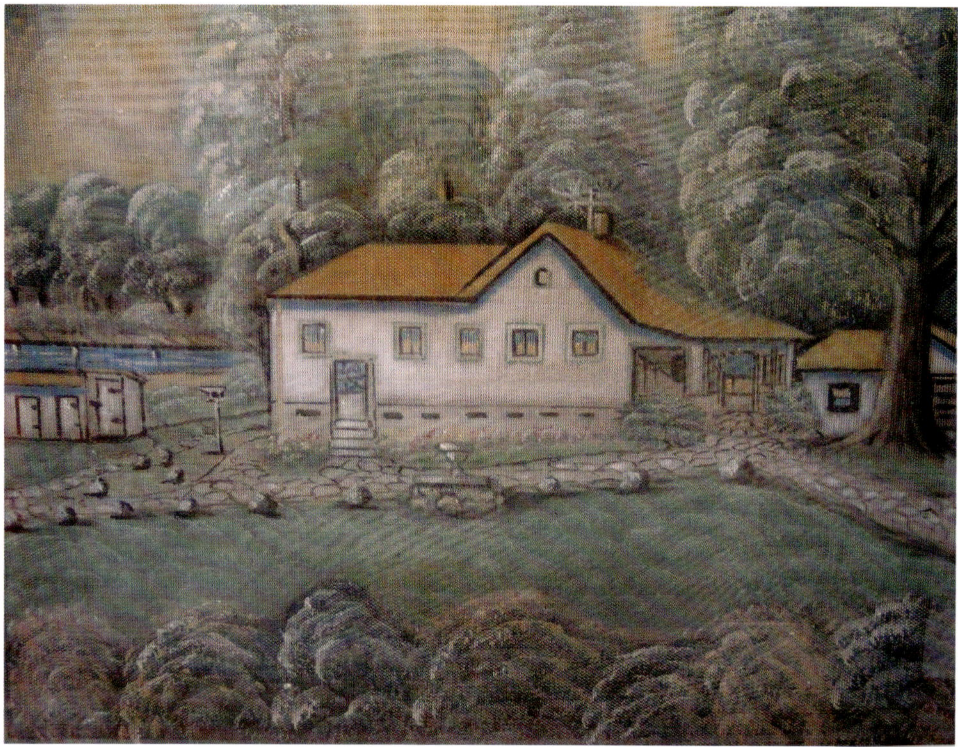

William Oktavec purchased his waterfront Boulevard Park retirement home at a tax sale in 1947. He painted the red-roofed bungalow he called his "Old Man's Nest" on screen, circa 1950. *Courtesy of the Oktavec family.*

His son Albert remembers a commission his father accepted to paint fifteen hundred screens for an apartment building in the Germantown neighborhood of Philadelphia. The job "almost killed us because we were painting them by hand. And that is not the way to do it. That's when we found out about silk screening."[181] From then on, William Oktavec used a silkscreen process on large orders, with each screen touched up by hand.[182] On other occasions, his sons recalled, he cast complicated images onto the white-coated wire screen with an opaque projector rather than rendering the designs freehand.[183] Although it was not widely known, in ongoing efforts to streamline the process, he sometimes used stencils for his trademark pair of swimming swans. He never used an airbrush or paint sprayer, even for the undercoat, preferring to have his students and sons prime the screens by hand before he began his painting.

After Oktavec's wife, Theresa, died in 1937, three days short of their silver wedding anniversary, he returned to his native village and saw his parents and siblings for the first time since they had abruptly left Manhattan decades before. As he returned to Baltimore at the end of that trip, he was painfully aware that the Czechoslovakia he visited would be forever changed by political events in the region and that he would likely never see his aged parents again. As he faced the future as a widower, he began to prepare for a new stage in his life. He knew that he would soon turn over the Art Shop to his sons. In 1947 he bought a shore house on Gray's Creek in Anne Arundel County's Boulevard Park section for $1,200 at a tax sale. He moved from the family apartment above the Art Shop to the new home. This was the first freestanding dwelling he had lived in since his childhood in Bohemia. He planned to retire there, "painting and helping the boys, teach-

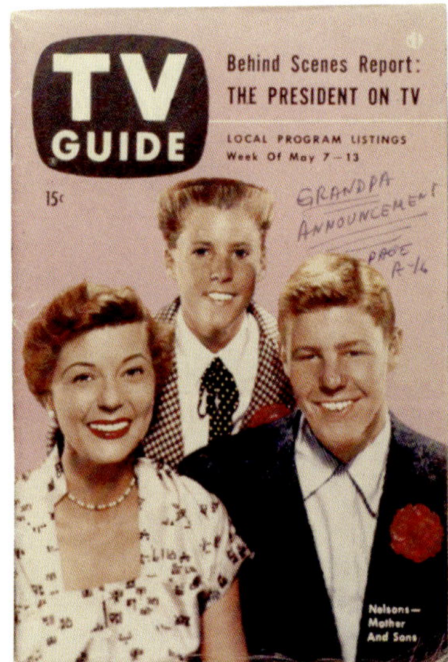

William shared his unusual talent and speed in front of a live national television audience, completing a screen in record time on *"You Asked for It"* on May 9, 1954. TV Guide, *courtesy of the Oktavec family.*

ing them all I know, and reading the book of life in nature."[184] He was fifty-three years old. Within two years he married Anna Minarik and they shared his self-described "Old Man's Nest" outside of the city. Among the screens that he completed in the basement workshop of his new home was one depicting his own red-roofed bungalow. For many years it hung in the kitchen window of his son Albert's home in Baltimore.

A high point of the elder Oktavec's long career was a feature in 1954 in the nationally circulated Sunday magazine *This Week*, followed by an invitation to paint a screen on Art Baker's nationally televised weekly show, "You Asked for It."[185] William and his wife, Anna, were flown to Hollywood and treated like visiting monarchs. They were seen off and welcomed home by admirers at Baltimore's Friendship Airport. The popular Sunday evening program, which presented "oddities of all sorts in response to requests from viewers," was broadcast live on May 9, 1954.[186] For the television appearance, he painted his typical red bungalow with winding path while the clock ticked away—fifteen minutes from start to finish. To set the scene, the studio created a dramatization of a vintage workplace and the original screen he had painted for the harried secretary in New Jersey. America's favorite source for television listings at the time, *TV Guide*, summarized the segment that Oktavec shared with a surfboard-riding dog and a boxing bout on stilts: "Optical Illusion. William Okatvec [*sic*], decorator of window screens."[187]

Demonstrating his technique for a national television audience did little to demystify the process. Despite their omnipresence, painted screens had always been both commonplace and a source of great mystery among Baltimoreans. No one ever questioned that the illusion worked. "You see out. No one sees in" was explanation enough.

William Oktavec never revealed where his idea to paint scenes on woven wire originated. His youngest son, Richard, said, simply, "Pop invented it."[188] Nor did he ever acknowledge any connection between the red-roofed village of his childhood and the predominant image of his thousands of works.[189] He denied any Old World origins, and said he had seen neither the advertisements for nor the actual landscape screens sold in New York and Baltimore furniture emporiums in the early twentieth century.

Although several Baltimore artists have on occasion attempted to claim the invention as their own, the lineage of the city's painted screens unquestionably begins in 1913 with the arrival of William Oktavec the corner butcher.

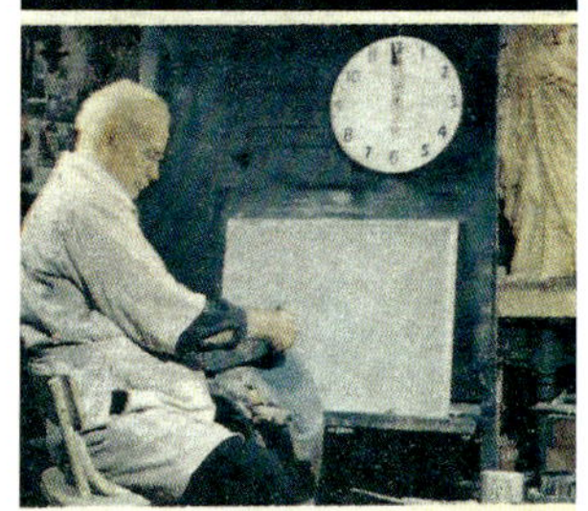

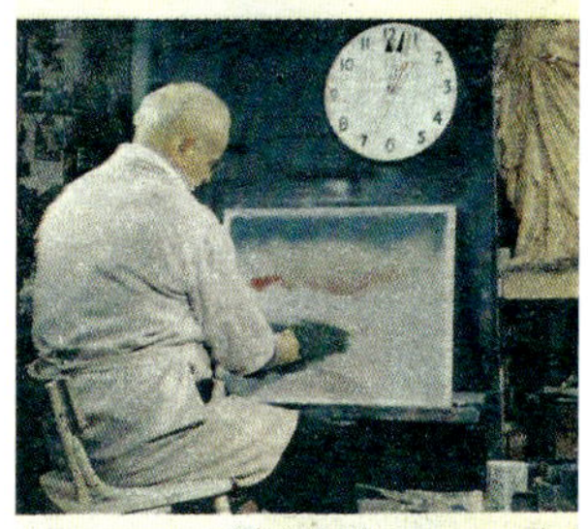

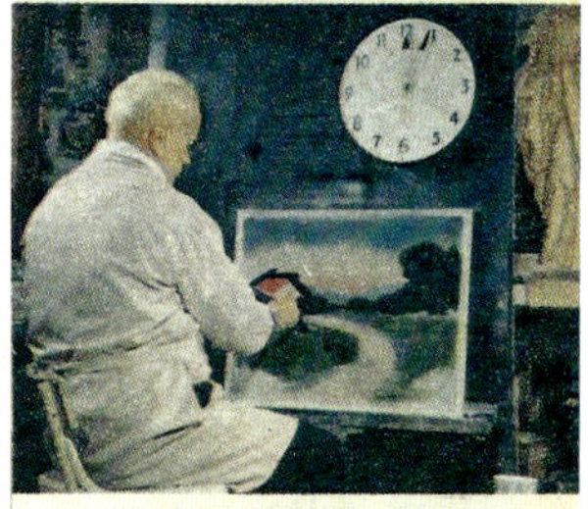

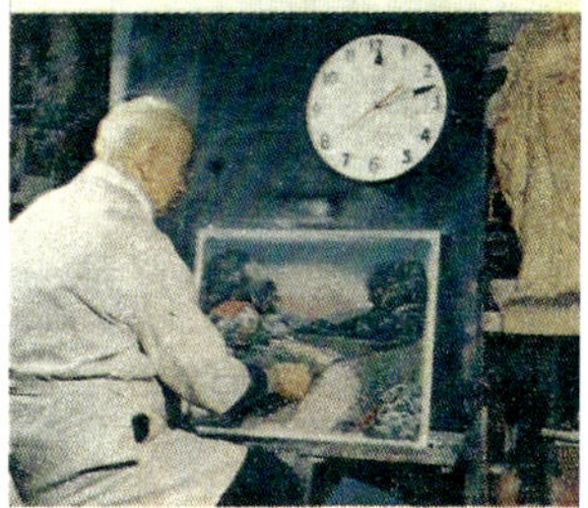

ABOVE

William became a national sensation when his ability to complete a screen in fifteen minutes was documented for a weekly magazine. This Week, *May 6, 1954.*

OPPOSITE

The basement studio in his home was William Oktavec's preferred spot to paint screens and engage in a variety of artistic endeavors after he retired from the Art Shop. *Hans Marx photograph, August 9, 1953. Reprinted with permission of the Baltimore Sun Media Group. All rights reserved.*

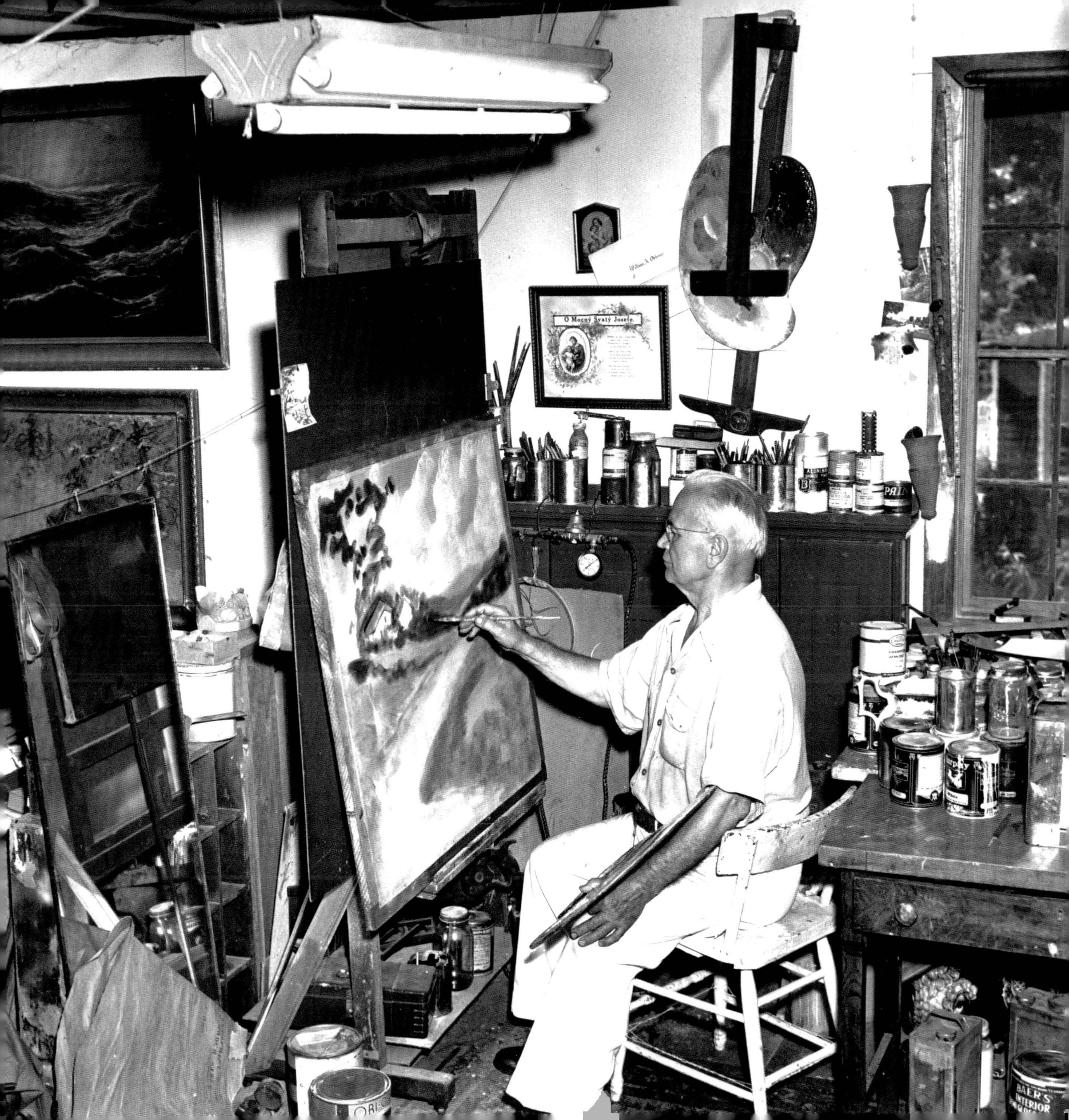

THE NEXT GENERATIONS

According to his 1956 obituary, "hours before he died, he painted his landscape, a red bungalow with a winding path leading from the house—with lots of trees and flowers everywhere."[190] Although William had schooled all of his sons in the family trade, and each participated in Saturday morning classes in the Art Shop basement, no one knew who might carry the tradition forward. It was Richard who picked up the brushes and finished the screen perched on his father's easel when he died.[191] From two studios, one in the Art Shop and later in the Boulevard Park home, Richard continued his father's work. After Richard's death in 1979, his older brother Albert wore the family mantle until he died in 1992. Now Richard's son John continues what had been firmly established as a family and a Baltimore tradition.

A rare photograph circa 1938 shows all the Oktavec men together. As family photographer, Bill was usually behind the camera. *On sofa, from left:* William, Richard, Bernard. *Standing:* Bill (William Jr.), Albert. *Oktavec family photograph.*

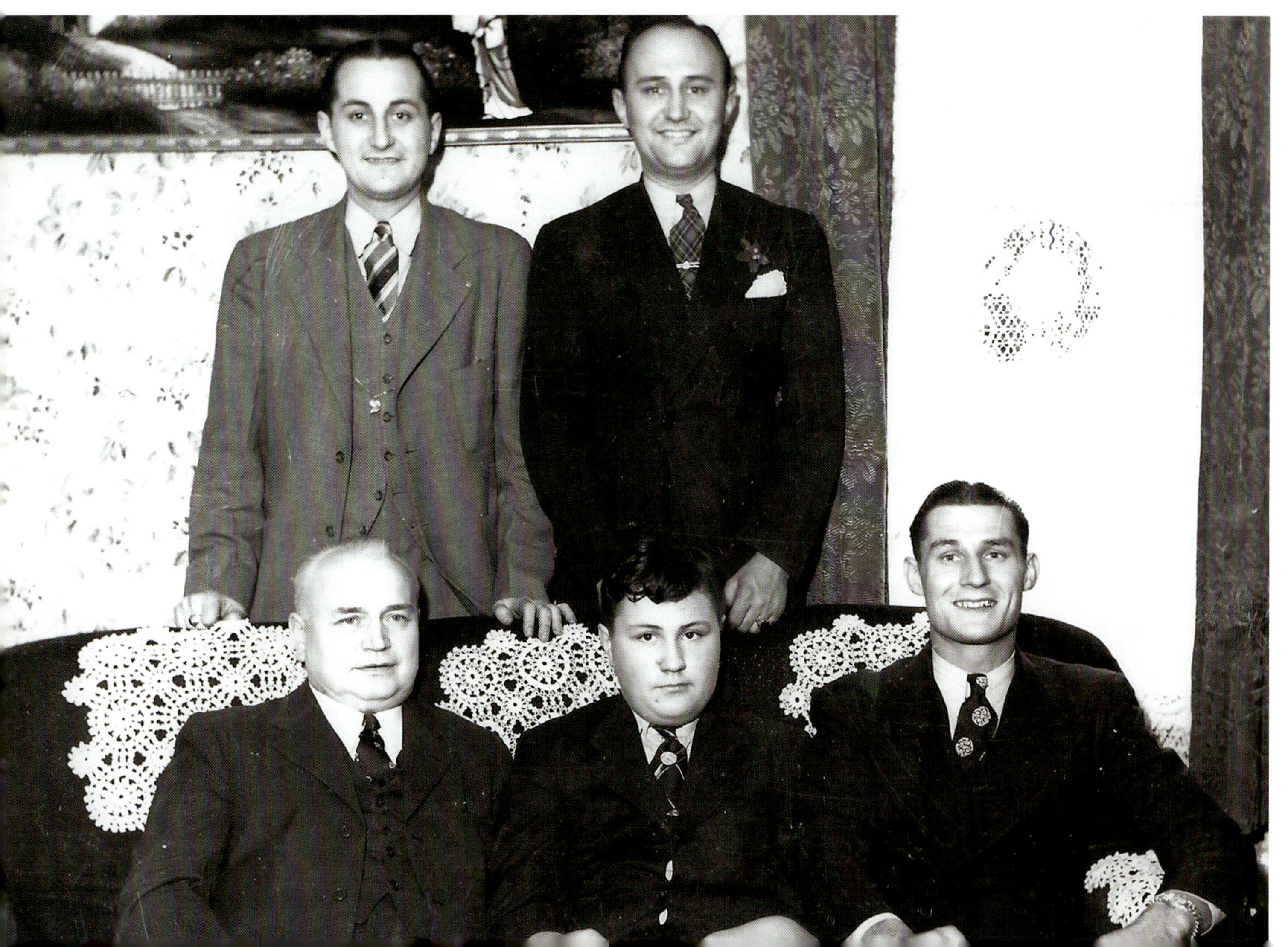

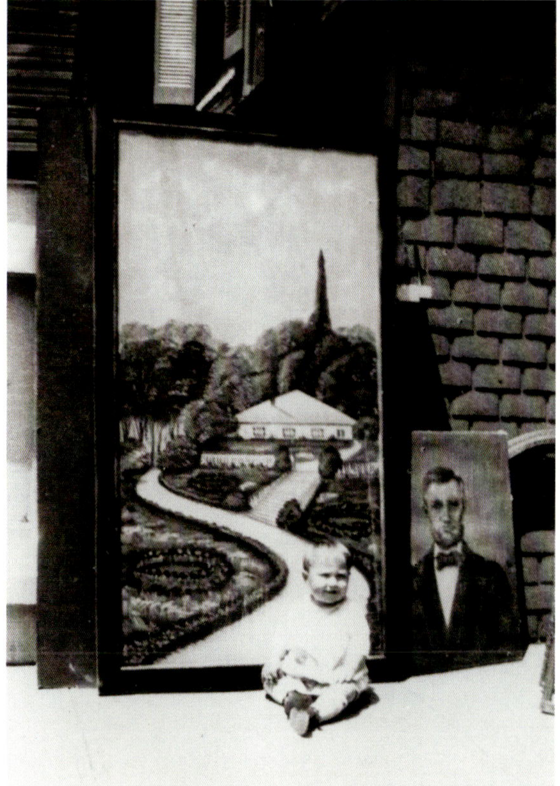

Richard Oktavec often said he was born to be a screen painter. As an infant he was steeped in the tradition, in the yard behind the Art Shop and family home. *Oktavec family photograph, 1929.*

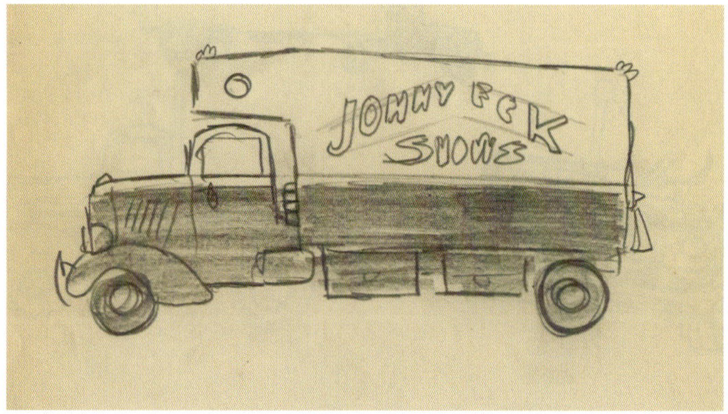

As a teenager, Rich kept blank composition notebooks for pen and pencil drawings. Among his favorite subjects were cars, World War II bombers, arms, penmanship exercises, and his fantasy sideshow trucking company with partner Johnny Eck. *"Drawings by R.S. Oktavec, No. 2, Age 17, 1944," courtesy of John Oktavec.*

RICHARD OKTAVEC

Youngest of the four Oktavec sons, Rich was born five years after his father established the Art Shop and secured his reputation as the original and preeminent Baltimore screen painter. It would be an understatement to say that Rich grew up surrounded by screens. In his early years, the shop also served as the family home. An early snapshot finds him as an infant planted beneath a towering red bungalow screen in the backyard.

From an early age, Richard was a constant at his father's art classes, whatever the medium. Along with his friend and neighbor Johnny Eck (born Eckhardt), he primed, or undercoated, the screens with a layer of white paint. Like all the Oktavec boys, art came naturally to Rich. He followed in his father's footsteps, refining his talent at vocational school and at evening classes in drafting and lettering at Baltimore City College and the Maryland Institute (later the Maryland Institute College of Art). In his high school notebooks are page after page of pencil-and-ink drawings of planes, cars, armored vehicles, battle scenes, munitions, and caricatures, with a few bungalows, penmanship exercises, and sketches of a transport for the "Johnny Eck Shows" thrown in.[192]

Rich married a neighborhood girl, Marlene Smith. They lived first with her parents and then in a rowhouse several blocks east of the shop that they rented from her family. Fascinated with the way things work, Rich owned a succession of Triumph, Harley Davidson, and BSA motorcycles, which he rebuilt and took on the road or raced with members of his bike club.[193] A man of surprising interests and talents, he did not consider himself an artist. In his typical self-deprecating way he announced, "Canvas is hard. Now if you can do that, then you're a real artist. We're all just amateurs."[194]

He joined his brothers in ownership of the Art Shop in 1947, when their father happily retired full-time to the shore. In addition to expanding the space, they designed and proudly supervised the hoisting of a signature neon sign in the shape of an artist's palette, but, according to brother Al, "the law made us take it down" due to a zoning conflict.[195] When not on the sales floor, Rich excelled at sign painting, a form of decorative calligraphy known as engrossing, gold leaf, and stained-glass fabrication and repair. Brother Bernie headed the framing division and Al was chief of the church restoration business. William Jr., the eldest, brought his talents to nearby Johns Hopkins University School of Medicine and Hospital, where he spent his career as an illustrator and photographer. When "Pop" passed away in 1956, with one unfinished screen on his easel and dozens more awaiting his brush, Rich was the son who embraced the tradition.

When he died, he had a whole pile of screens and nobody wanted to do them, so I said, "Well, I'll give it a try." So from watching him year after year, I tried to copy his technique to get as close as I could. And then after a while, I wanted to do something a little different. So I started on the Swiss type of bungalow. His was just a red bungalow with the white clouds and flowers. And I tried with the mountain and the tall pines, so that caught on pretty good. But they still like the old bungalow. That caught on and it just never let go.[196]

He inherited not only his father's easel, brushes, paints, and following, but also his home. When Rich's own family grew to include a daughter and son, they moved to Pop's bungalow on Gray's Creek in Anne Arundel County in 1972. Twenty years after his father's death, he was still using many of the same hand-me-down brushes. Rich boasted finding his newer implements in neighborhood trash cans. He sent local kids out into the alleys in search of other peoples' discards, preferring hard-bristled, seasoned ones, "the nastier the better."

Rich never came close to his father's documented record for painting a screen in fifteen minutes. To him, "fast" was an hour or more. His customers and especially the Bohemians like himself "loved art [and] deserved a painting done with care."[197] He recalled painting no fewer than twenty-five or thirty screens per season, and as many as one hundred in especially busy years.

Everyone who knew him commented on Rich's pleasant demeanor. He was calm, patient, and generous. He spent much of his leisure time visiting hospitals under another name, which obliquely referred to his trade as a screen painter. He entertained children as "Turpentine the Clown" and was a proud member of Clowns of America throughout his life.

Rich died suddenly of an aneurysm he suffered at the Art Shop in 1979, at age fifty-seven, but not before sharing with his teenage son John some of the finer points of many of the arts he practiced—stencil, gold leaf, and screen painting. Like his father before him, Rich left an unfinished screen on his easel and a raft of orders to complete. In this moment of crisis, the role of Oktavec family screen painter fell to his brother Al.

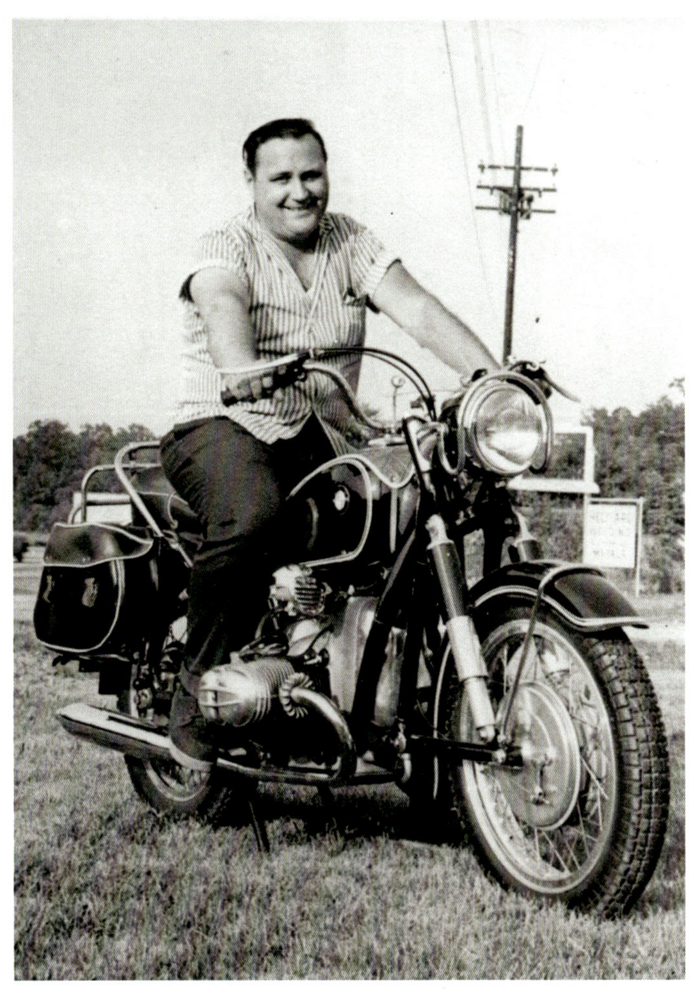

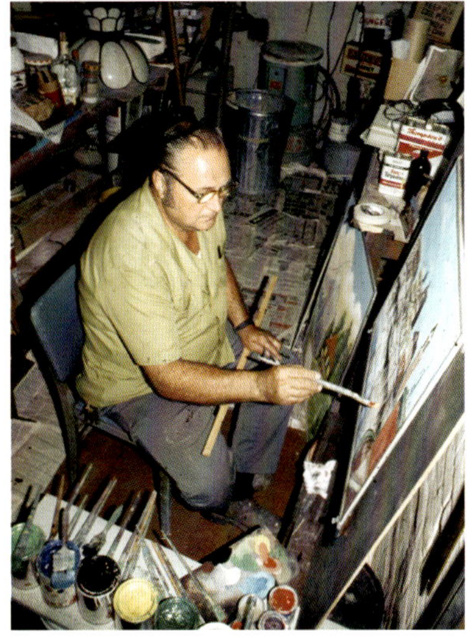

TOP
Rich loved motorcycles and owned several during his lifetime, "always black," according to his nephew Boh, who shared his love of bikes. Here Richard tests a BMW at a local dealership. *Courtesy of John Oktavec.*

BOTOM
Rich's preferred studio was the basement of the Art Shop, guaranteed to be quiet year round and, especially, cool in the summer. *Author photograph, 1974.*

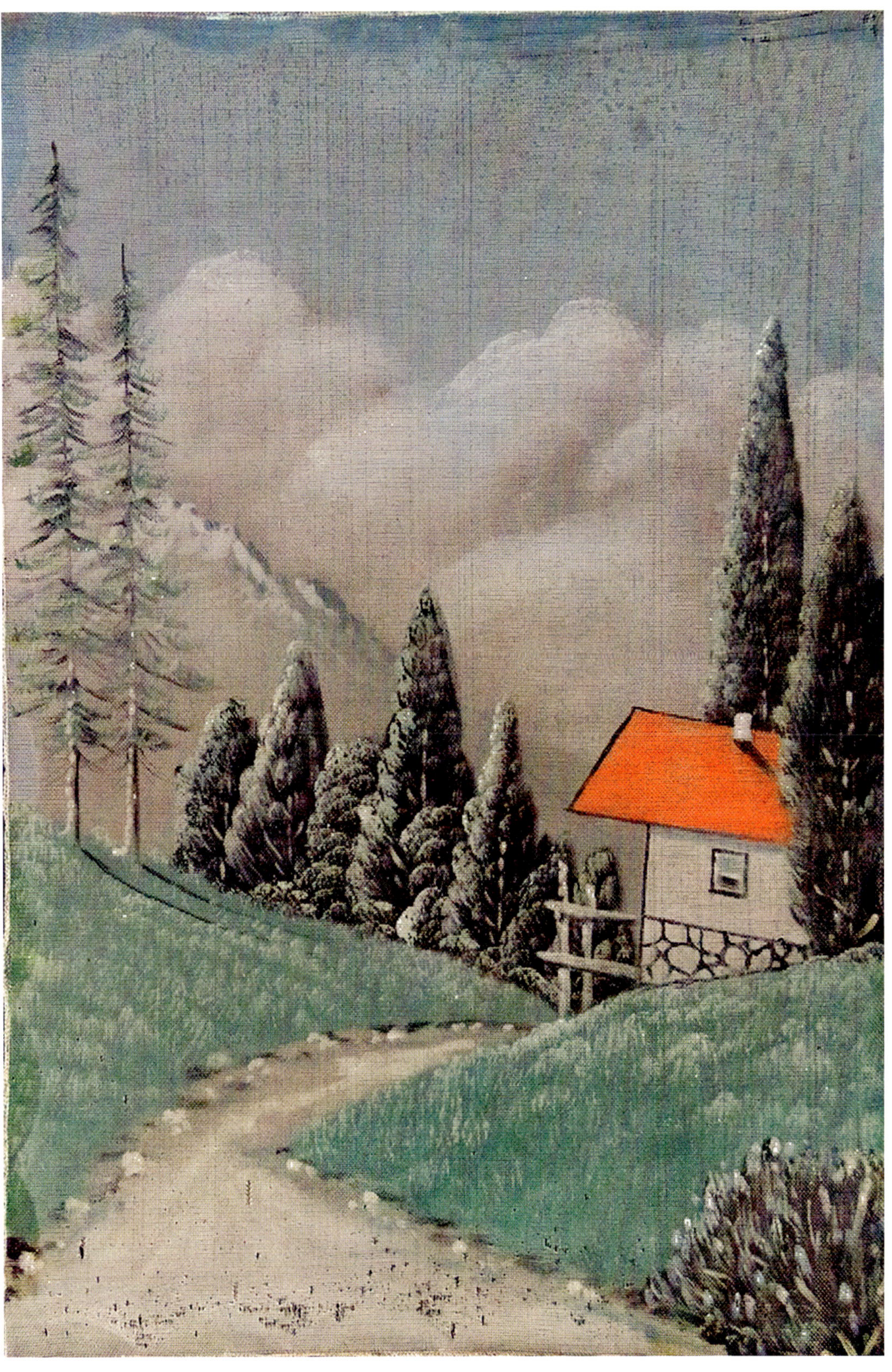

The Swiss chalet was Rich Oktavec's version of his father's Red Bungalow, created because he felt it was important to have a signature image of his own. Customers who did not make a specific request were supplied with this design from 1956 until 1979. *Collection of John Oktavec. Christine Fillat photograph.*

A. Aubrey Bodine (1906–1970), *Sunpapers'* photographer, and Baltimore's pictorialist, gave two of his well-known images of Mt. Vernon to Richard to replicate on screen. These screens graced the windows of Bodine's home in the 800 block of Park Avenue. *A. Aubrey Bodine photograph. Reprinted with permission of the Baltimore Sun Media Group. All rights reserved.*

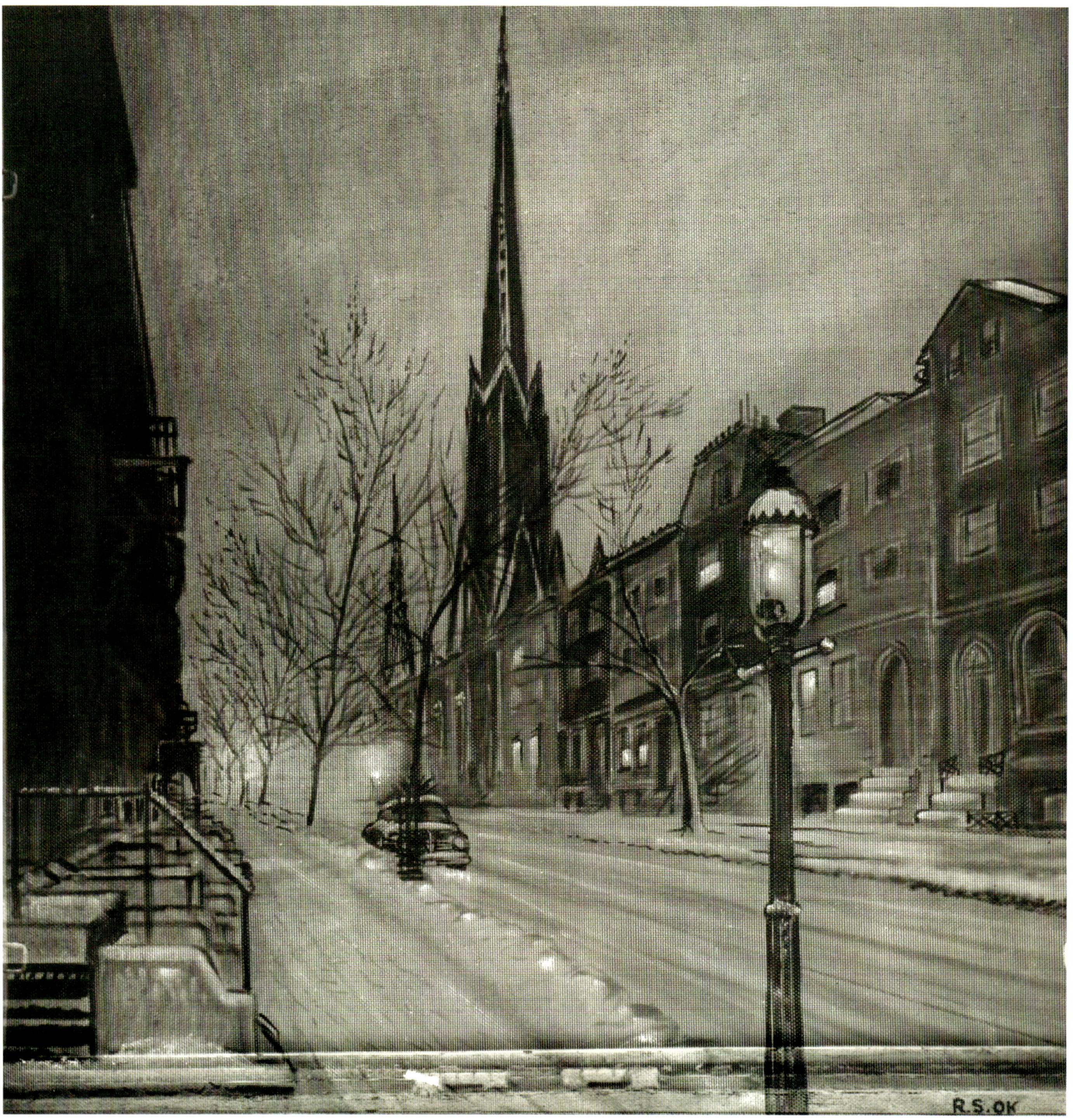

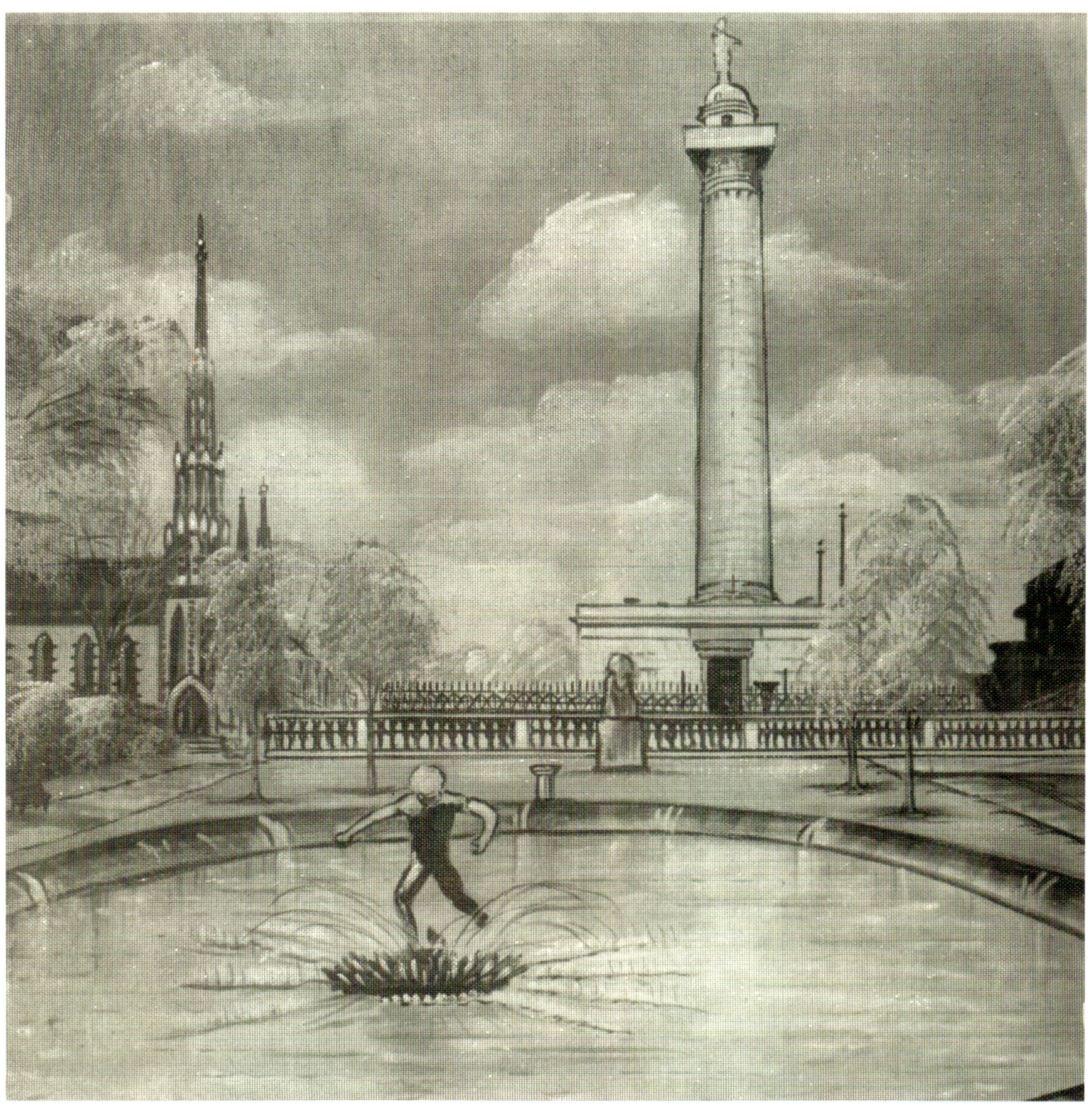

ALBERT OKTAVEC

Raised above the Art Shop, Al worked there for as long as he could remember. He began to specialize in the restoration of painting and sculpture, stained glass, wood graining, marbleizing, gold leaf and lettering, unaware that he had, without a lesson or ever trying, picked up the fine points of painting on wire as well. The second of William Oktavec's four sons, Al was the last of the brothers to take up screen painting. When the torch was passed, he was already looking toward retirement, but like his baby brother Rich, he accepted his calling without missing a beat. And like his brother before him, Al found that the Oktavec style—red bungalow, trees, clouds, lawn, rocks, path, and swans—also came naturally to him. "You don't throw it away. It's in your blood."[198] He always demurred when the subject of his expertise came up, claiming that his "father and brother were the real painters. They could do them fast if you would leave them alone. And they would get lost. Boy, you got a painting, not a decoration, a painting."[199] As a specialist in ornamental painting for church walls, altars, and ceilings, he knew the difference.

His one attempt at a formal screen-painting lesson from his father did not go well. "One time when I was real young, I got myself some tuna cans and went to Pop to pour the paints, and he sort of rebuffed me. It kind of hurt at the time. I found out later, you don't pour paint when you're working. In those days, you had to think about making a buck."[200] He learned at some personal cost that timely output was critical to success. Al was especially gregarious and could regale customers, who became friends, for hours from behind the Art Shop counter.

Al recalled his father's never-repeated "eighty-seven screen night"—part of a record 300-screen season indelibly etched in Al's memory because he had white-coated every one himself. The other brothers' job was to "drum up business [for screens] outside the Highlandtown area. One day I decided to go out to Guilford where the wealthy people lived. My father was shocked when I returned with a whole truckload of screens for him to paint. It turned out everybody wanted one." In an earlier telling, though, he "got no orders there. These people were house-poor, couldn't afford painted screens."[201] It was more likely that the setting of those mansions, far back from the sidewalk and shielded by trees and lawn, negated the need for the screens' primary virtue of providing privacy.

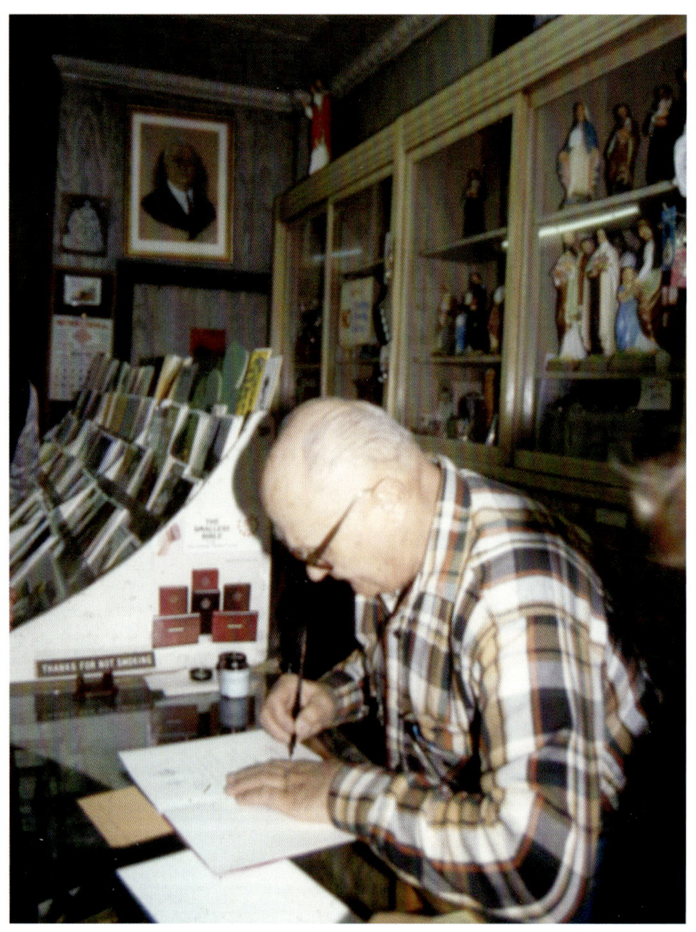

Al Oktavec ran the family church restoration business and the Art Shop (after 1979 with his brother Bernie), where, like all the Oktavec men, he embellished cards and envelopes for doctors and staff from Johns Hopkins Hospital and customers from all over the city. *Author photograph, 1985.*

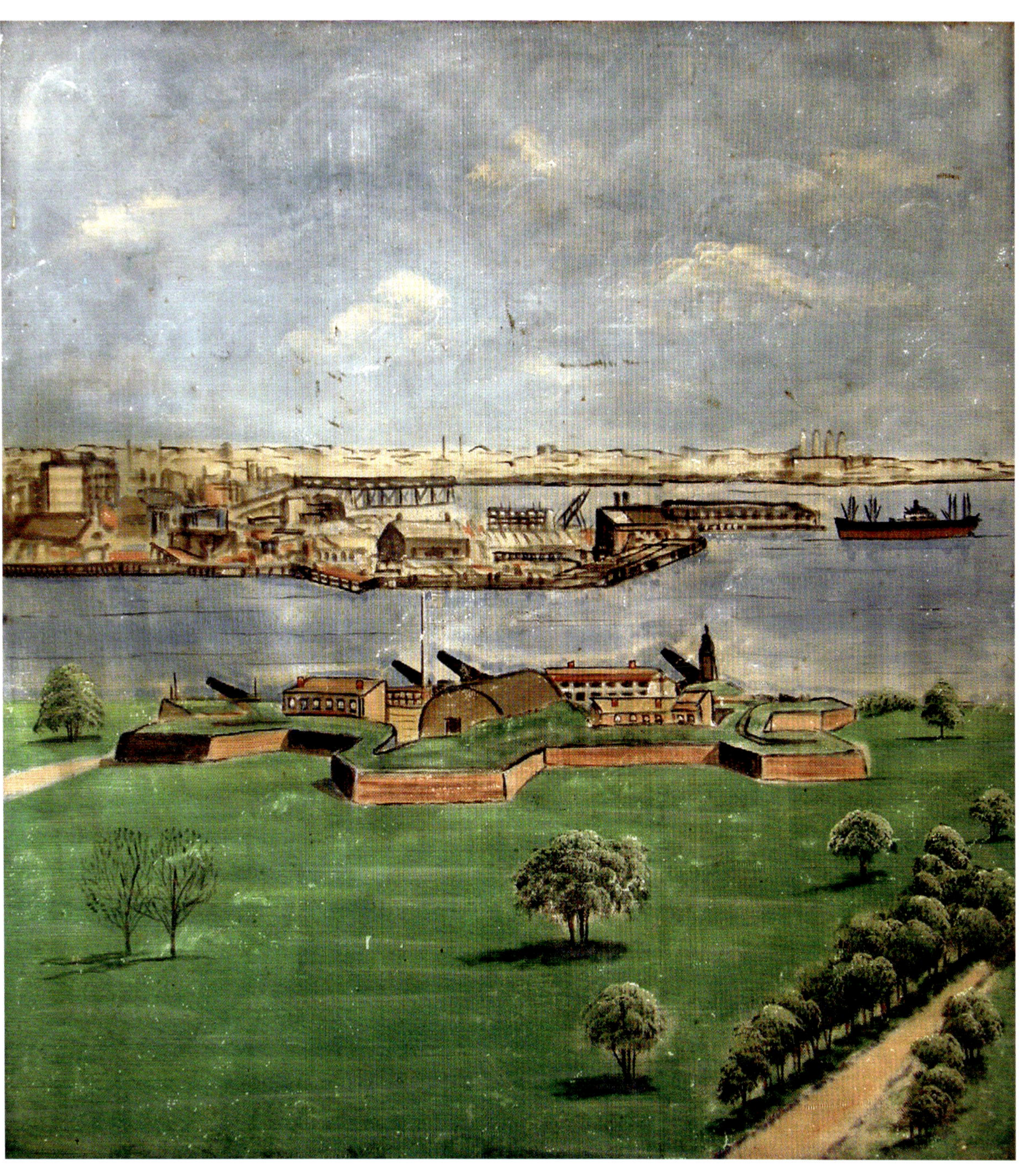

Al Oktavec's family moved to Gardenville in the 1940s, but took the city with them in the form of a screen he painted depicting Fort McHenry. It covered the picture window of their suburban home. *Author's collection. Edwin Remsberg photograph.*

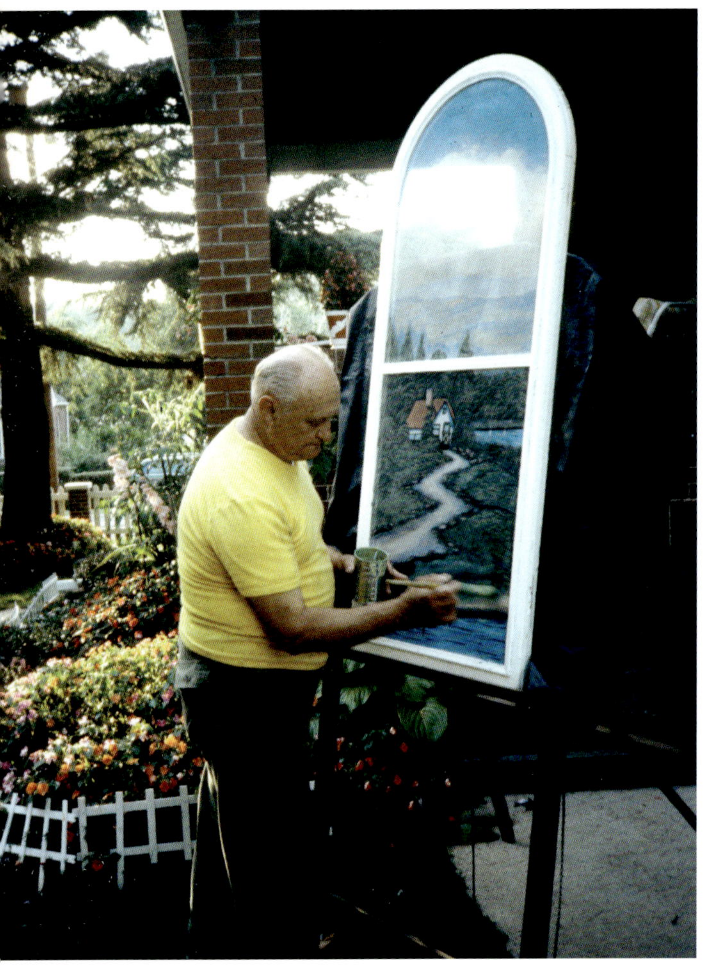

Al Oktavec painted screens at home wherever he found room, indoors and out. *Author photograph, 1987.*

At the time of Richard's untimely death, Al found as many as "eighty screens left here to be painted. We got together and painted them. Had to get them out." He likely pressed both Johnny Eck and his brother Rob Eckhardt into service, and possibly a son or two. "Then it mushroomed," with Al as the go-to screen guy.[202]

In addition, Al presided over the diminishing Art Shop business as the community rapidly changed. Brother Bernie continued to run the framing operation. Baltimore did not escape the riots that spread across the nation's cities in 1968 following the murder of Martin Luther King Jr. But despite unfounded and lingering rumors to the contrary, the Art Shop survived unscathed while much of Monument Street went up in flames. The family attributed the shop's survival to the array of saints displayed in the windows.[203]

After the riots, though, Hopkins doctors, medical students, and other employees were less inclined to walk the few blocks to have their diplomas framed or cards embellished. The ladies who customarily came in search of statuary for their backyard gardens and front window displays and the perfect Slavic language greeting card were leaving the community. Yet, the church restoration business, Oktavec Brothers of Baltimore, the successor to A. Oktavec & Sons of Baltimore, and particularly its services in the area of decorative and fancy painting, persisted. This became Al's primary occupation, and it paid the bills when the income from a neighborhood art shop did not. Al worked alongside his son Chris to ensure the succession of that business, also started by his father.

The "partial list of what Oktavec's Master Craftsmen does [*sic*] [includes] decoration, leaded glass, wooden pews and woodwork, statuary, graining, gilding, glazing, murals, carpentry, polychroming. No job too small or too large."[204] Richard's son John, an Art Shop habitué, was mesmerized by his Uncle Al's work and workplace, which he and others likened to "the Vatican's attic."[205]

A lot of times they'd bring statues back to the shop [to] my uncle in the back upstairs. He had a studio where he used to do only statues. And if there was a piece chipped off, he'd use plaster and rub it over there. And I'd smell him airbrushing…. He could get real skin tones and they'd look like real people.[206]

A reluctant master, despite always deferring to his brother and father, Al was unable to shirk his screen-painting responsibilities and birthright. He feared that neither of his remaining brothers or sons would rise to the task and that his father's legacy would die on his watch. The thought of turning down loyal customers who came screens in hand was unthinkable. In the early 1980s Al worked locally as well as through a dealer on the West Coast, who encouraged more creative scenes. "I just painted a set of louvered doors on a screen for someone in California. It had three red geraniums in flowerpots and even a handle painted on. Before I shipped it out, I set it up on my door, and this friend sat there looking at it all day. He said he didn't know it was a wire screen until he got up to go in."[207] Coincidentally, the very first screen painted by Al's father William Oktavec, for a harried New Jersey secretary, depicted a pot of flowers in a curtained window. And William's grocery store screen, his first in Baltimore, was mistaken for an actual produce display before his neighbors realized its artful and practical properties.

Al dutifully completed screens as they were carried through the door of the Art Shop until he and Bernie finally decided to close the retail business in 1987, ending its sixty-five-year run on East Monument Street. Both took occasional commissions at home, Al for screens and Bernie for framing. During the years after Rich's passing, out of a sense of duty Al acted as the screens' poster boy, posing and demonstrating for the media when asked. But, for the most part, according to his son Chris, Al "stayed in the shadows. He didn't like publicity, yet they gave it to him all the time."[208]

His 1940s Cape Cod–style detached house, with a generous front lawn and backyard in the far northeastern neighborhood of Gardenville, was festooned with painted screens. A patriot and a proud second-generation Baltimorean, Al painted a screen depicting Fort McHenry, its flag flying, on his oversized picture window facing the suburban street.[209]

When Al died in 1992, it was unclear who would carry on the screen painters' legacy. His son Chris was managing the family's church restoration business from his Bowley's Quarter waterfront retreat in eastern Baltimore County, where the fishing vied for his free time.[210] His son David, then fully employed by UPS, became a Sunday painter who created a lush Monet-inspired garden at his home in rural northern Baltimore County, near the Pennsylvania line.[211] William Oktavec's eight grandsons and granddaughters, all staying in the Baltimore region, with one exception, pursued careers and families other than screen painting, and his great-grandchildren were scattered across the country. Chris's son Pete, a talented artist, was the one member of the third generation whom many family members expected to carry on the screen-painting tradition, but he chose to balance his artistic gifts between church renovations and scenic work for film and television. The legacy fell instead to a member of the family who was not on anyone's radar.

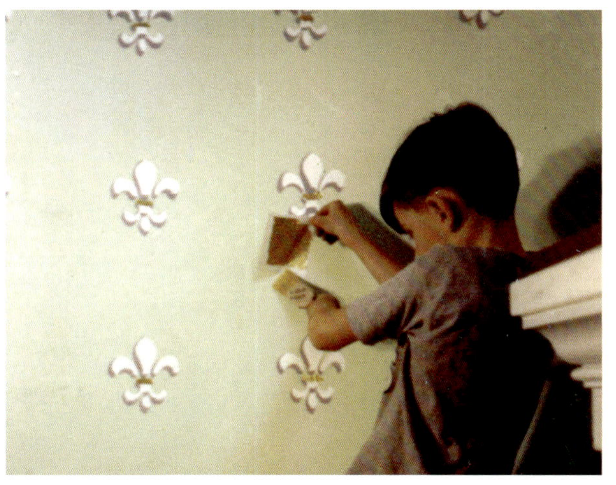

John Oktavec accompanied his father to church jobs and took on tasks appropriate to his height but far beyond what would ordinarily be expected of a youngster. He applies gold leaf at St. Wenceslaus Church. *Courtesy of John Oktavec, circa 1970.*

JOHN OKTAVEC

Among the many Oktavec grandchildren, it was John, Rich's only son, who belatedly took up where Al left off. In 1992 John was living in Pasadena, Anne Arundel County, in a little bungalow not far from his grandfather's shore home, and working for a nearby commercial sign painting company. He had inherited the Oktavec gene for excelling at commercial art as well as his father's gentle demeanor and love of all things mechanical.

As a youngster growing up within blocks of the Art Shop, John, like his father and uncles before him, was surrounded by and learned every type of art practiced in the Oktavec studios. His route from home to his father's workplace took him by "scenes done in different neighbors' windows and it always fascinated [him]," as did the street life.[212]

You could play in the alleys. We played marbles on the sidewalk. We rode bikes up and down the street. Went to the penny candy store, the snowball stand, and there was always something going on, always. A kid riding a bike or the gypsies would come through and the Arabbers [produce vendors in horse-drawn carts]. They'd be selling fruit and you could go up and pet the ponies. And when I'd walk back and forth I'd see the different scenery in the windows and you know it attracted me to 'em. [I thought] I'd love to be able to paint something like that one day.

The store and its cavernous workrooms were John's boyhood playground. He recalls the "hodgepodge of smells of ink and paper, chalk and big gum rubber erasers" and the "rosin in the middle of solder of stained glass." When not seeking places to conceal himself—"there were places for a kid to hide all day and there were friendly people coming in and out of the store"—he would "just sit on the steps and look down. It was a great view. Dad used to do stained glass in the basement."

John learned alongside his father, eagerly accompanying him to church jobs, where his tiny fingers applied gold leaf and stencils to hard-to-reach spots. Together they worked on altars and burnished many Stations of the Cross. When they brought statues back to the shop for repair, his uncle Albert performed the lifesaving interventions, replacing chipped plaster and deftly applying paint with an airbrush, a skill that he shared with his nephew and that would become a primary tool in John's professional sign-painters' toolkit.

The screens, however, held a special allure for young John. The family left the city behind and moved to Pop Oktavec's shore home in 1972 as white flight reached northeast Baltimore.

OPPOSITE, TOP

John Oktavec paints a portrait of his grandfather, William, using an airbrush, a tool they both were experts at using. *Author photograph, 2004.*

Produce vendors in horse-drawn carts, known only in Baltimore as Arabbers, were a familiar site in all parts of the city. *Martha Cooper photograph.*

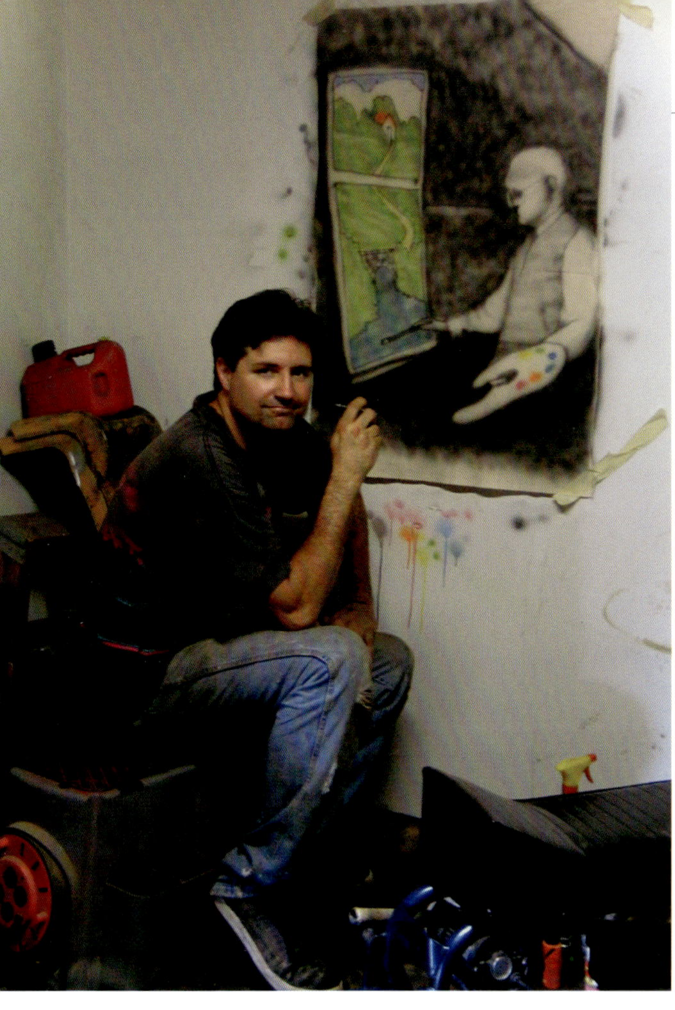

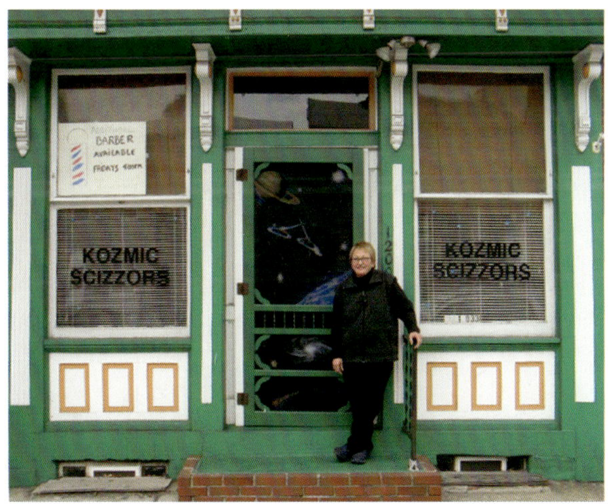

Kozmic Scizzors, a two-chair barber-beauty salon in Canton, hired John over a period of several decades to paint various versions of an otherworldly universe, a subject he especially enjoys. *Author photograph, 2008.*

And then when we moved to the country, I kind of missed them [the screens]. There was nothing like that in [the] county. So my dad brought some home and painted 'em and he trained me how to paint them. I started first coating, learned not to clog the holes and then I graduated over the weeks and months and probably years. I learned shadows and highlights and everything in between. How the sky is reflected by the water, how different colors go. Fall, winter, stuff like that.

To his lifelong dismay, John enjoyed too few years under his father's tutelage. Richard died when John was only fifteen. His widow and two children moved from the family-owned cottage and became estranged from the Oktavec family.

If Al had been a reluctant screen painter, John was flatly unwilling for years to acknowledge his esteemed lineage. Living outside of the city was a convenient excuse for a time. However, his unmistakable name made it impossible for the ever-widening outflow of Baltimoreans to overlook his connection to the familiar, beloved, and as time passed, increasingly nostalgic art form. "People kept coming up to me and saying, 'Oh, you're an Oktavec.'"

He supplied his neighbors in Baltimore County's Riviera Beach with screens on demand and often at no cost. His own home sported red bungalow screens on each front window. He sold screens at local flea markets and later online, along with his mechanical creations, R2D2 robots, chopped bikes, and rebuilt cars and trucks. It was not until 2000 that John publicly embraced his inheritance as a screen painter. He was enticed to create a series of screens for demonstration at a senior center class taught by Catherine "Pat" Michalski, a mature art student, teacher, and self-taught screen painter who had learned the techniques from a booklet she borrowed.[213]

By 2004 John was working closely with the Painted Screen Society to provide artwork for museum and special event installations, and to fulfill requests by savvy customers who valued the Oktavec name. His renderings on screen bear the unmistakable family trademarks—cottage, swans, trees, and clouds. His color palette is only slightly updated, introducing a blue-green for water and subjects his father would never commit to wire—Harley Davidson motorcycles and the Grim Reaper. When not in his garage—repairing, rebuilding, and detailing cars, trucks, and motorcycles—John continues to work on screens at home in a studio that he carved from a second-floor room under the eaves and behind a painted screen covered window. "I get swamped and I can't say no 'cause I love doing it so much, man. I get lost up here for hours. I forget everything. I'll turn classical music on and, you know, gone. I'll paint all night, doesn't matter." His muse—his dad—is with him: "He's alive in me today. Every time I paint, I know he's watching."

Despite a two-decade hiatus between lessons at his father's side and John Oktavec's appearance as a screen painter for the twenty-first century, the artistic string remains unbroken. His work holds its own alongside his grandfather's, his father's, and his uncle Al's, bearing the distinctive and deft touch of an Oktavec.[214]

RB: THE RED BUNGALOW

William Oktavec's first screen commission borrowed an image from a handy commercial calendar. The red-roofed mill set an aesthetic standard that was well received in East Baltimore. Oktavec's initial patrons were the ladies of North Collington Avenue, stalwarts of St. Wenceslaus Church. They were homemakers who raised large families in narrow houses, patronized the shopkeepers of East Monument Street, walked to the Northeast Market, and sewed in the local garment factories. Clutching calendars and greeting cards or selecting a scene from batches of artist's samples, neighbors in ever-widening arcs brought their requests and their screens to the grocer's doorstep.

They usually knew exactly what image they wanted him to paint. More often than not, they chose exactly what their neighbors had—rowhouse dwellers know better than to attract unwanted attention. Conformity has always been the key to neighborhood harmony. The most frequently selected image featured a red-roofed bungalow, with winding path, pond, stone bridge, and a pair of swans, all nestled among verdant lawns, evergreens, and bushes, beneath perfectly formed white cumulus clouds in a light blue sky.

Supply followed demand and the Red Bungalow quickly became synonymous with "painted screen." When Oktavec moved from his butcher shop to become proprietor of an art shop, centrally located on the busy main street of Little Bohemia, he included among his inventory, racks of greeting cards, containing popular bucolic scenes of cozy cottages, a staple in the industry. Clients in search of an idea for their custom-painted screen selected a card from his inventory, handed it to the painter, ordered a copy for every window, settled on a price, and returned a few days later to carry their treasures home.

Contrary to superficial appearances, the dominant scene of the Baltimore painted screen was not an idealized representation of the cottages of the patrons' homelands, as suggested time and again by outside observers. No evidence supports the notion that the pastoral scene recalled any specific place. Nor was it the spot Baltimoreans dreamed of retiring to when their rowhouse days drew to a close. Nostalgia probably played a greater role for those who chose scenes of the great buildings of their native countries—the castles, cathedrals, and town halls that constituted another popular subject matter. William Oktavec believed the red bungalow image that he and subsequent painters referred to as the RB reflected his customers' love of home.

With some subtle tweaks, the RB made an appearance on tens of thousands of windows at the peak of Baltimore painted screens' popularity in the 1940s and 1950s, before and following World War II. It was not unusual to find the same screen by the same hand on every house in a block, whether on a major thoroughfare or tucked in a narrow alley. To a stranger, all the screens might look identical, but upon more careful inspection, subtle variations on a single theme could be detected—a duck here, a pink or blue bush, heavy black outlines, curtains or a vase of flowers in the bungalows' windows. Ultimately these signature touches became associated with specific artists. Everyone agreed that an Oktavec screen was the finest, but also the most costly, and required a trip up to Monument Street.

Was the Red Bungalow a purely Baltimore phenomenon? Historical evidence suggests that the same aesthetic impulse that gave rise to the RB in Baltimore was at work in earlier iterations elsewhere.

The signature romantic imagery of the nineteenth-century painted screens described in chapter 4 was borrowed from real and imagined places. Nils Andersson's rare colored landscapes of 1830s Sweden featured red-roofed buildings. Sources for the pastoral scenery adopted by the Victorians and the early screen painters were consistent with those used to decorate a variety of functional and nonfunctional objects, including historic prints, ceramics, wallpaper, drapery fabrics, chimney and stove tiles, murals, window shades, painted chairs and tables, and canvases—all reflecting an enduring infatuation with the natural landscape and architectural follies. Solo fishermen draped themselves over stone-arched bridges. The occasional cooing couple wandered

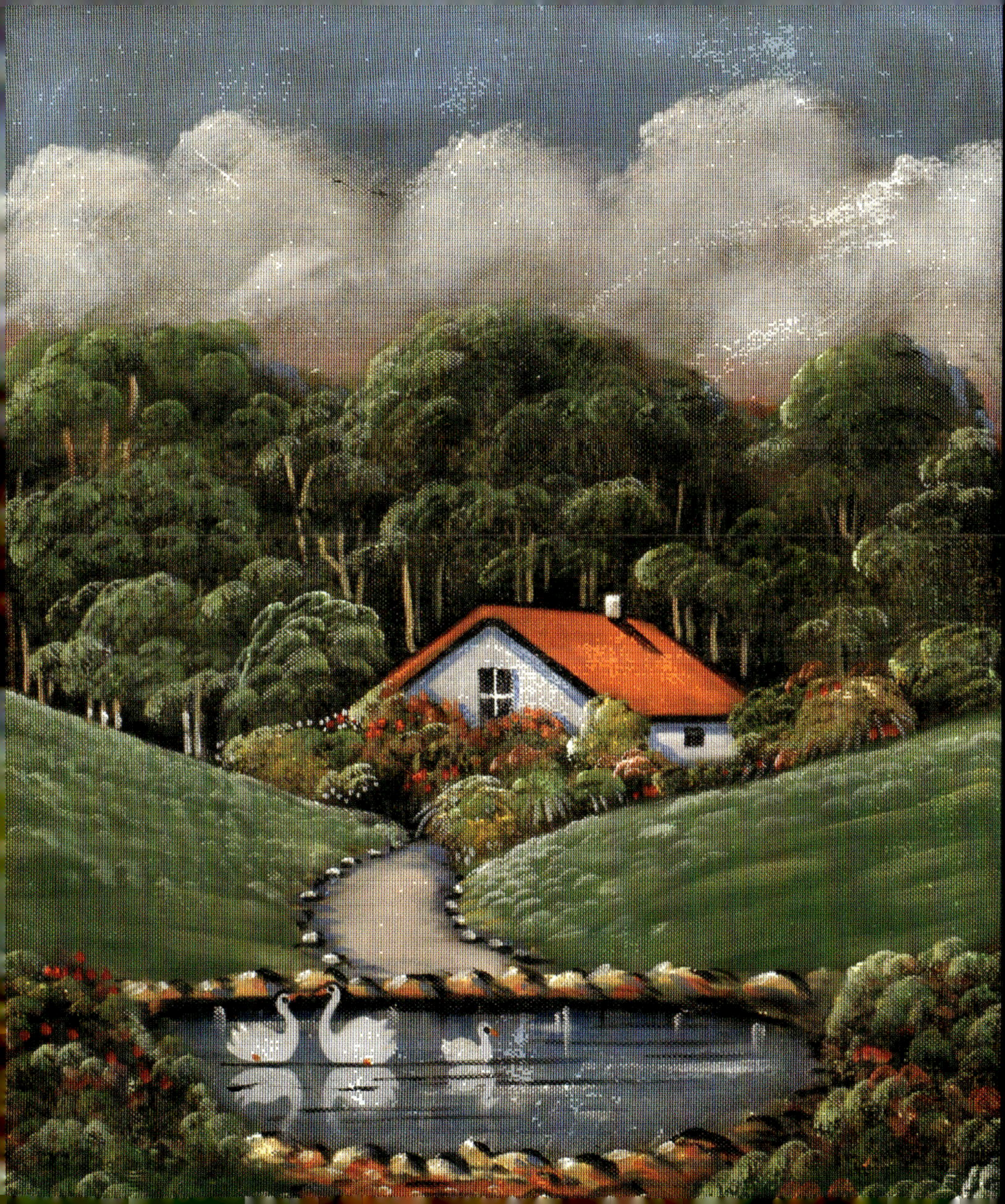

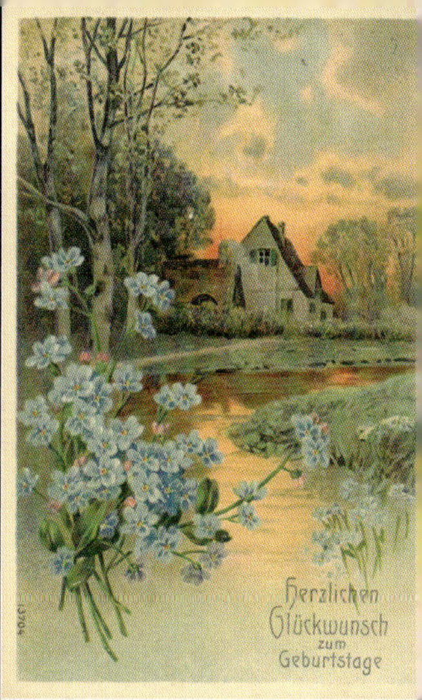

Inspiration for painted-screen iconography could be picked from the shelf at any card or paper supply store. English and foreign language calendars and greeting cards like this one expressing "Heartfelt birthday wishes" were popular sources. *American Greetings Antique Collection, ex Cleveland Public Library, circa 1913.*

along meandering lakeside paths in sight of lazy sailing barques or
paused at crenellated fortresses. A pedestrian strolling through Troy,
New York, would encounter images that were repeated in cities and
towns throughout America.

Window screens were more than mere utilitarian barriers to
houseflies and mosquitoes. They were the medium for displaying
some of the most astonishing pictorial art ever known to man. As
you walked along Fourth Street on a summer's day every open
window cried aloud for admiration. Here were Mr. Jones' parlor
windows parading the virtues of home life among the Romans,
there were Mrs. Smith's testifying to her travels through the Black
Forest and an idyllic honeymoon on Lake Lucerne; just beyond Dr.
Robinson's eloquently bespoke his love of grazing cows, old mills
and waterfalls. It was a wonderful world—and a live market for a boy
who could create it.[215]

As proof of the endurance and universality of the landscape
in popular culture, beginning in 1994, two Russian émigré artists,
Vitaly Komar and Alex Melamid, with a bit of impish wit, conducted a
'professional market research survey about aesthetic preference. Their
aim was to discover what a 'true people's art' would look like." Setting
out to systematically survey global aesthetic preference in painting, they
found a generic, all-purpose realist style "unmistakably Hudson River-
Biedermeier." That particular image of blue sky, trees, and water, "just
happens to be what the people really want."

Throughout the world the results have been strikingly congruent, in the
sense that each country's Most Wanted [painting] looks like, give or
take a few details, every other…the kind of painting whose degenerate
descendants embellish calendars from Kalamazoo to Kenya.[216]

Komar and Melamid suggest that "it is possible, of course, that
everyone's concept of art *was* formed by calendars (even in Africa), which
now constitutes a sort of paradigm of what everyone first thinks of when
they think of art. And 44 percent choose the blue landscape with water
and trees, the a priori aesthetic universal, what everyone who thinks of art
first thinks of."

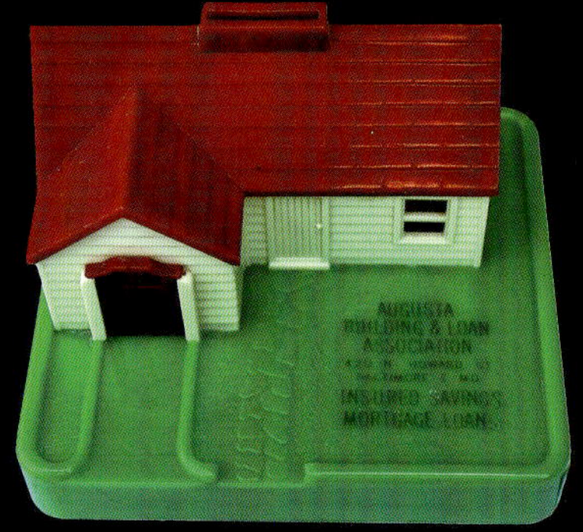

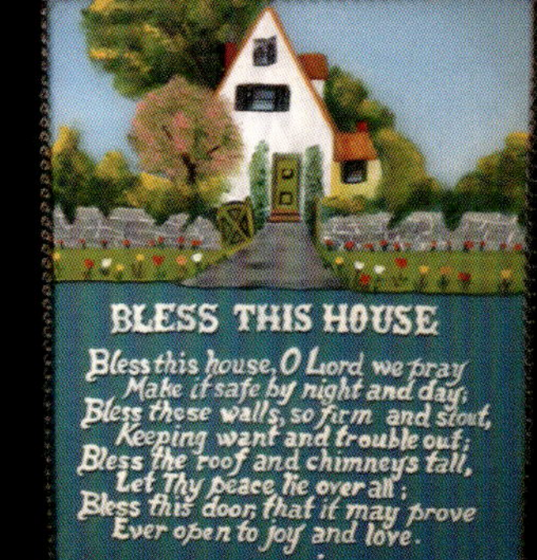

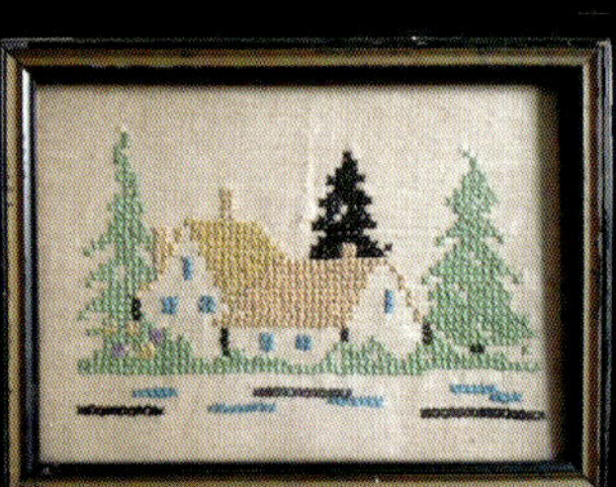

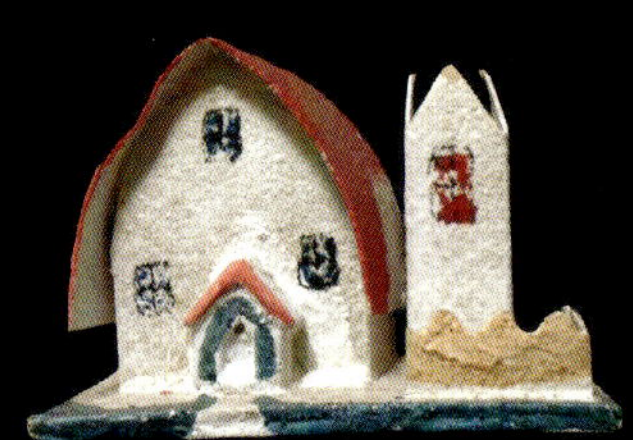

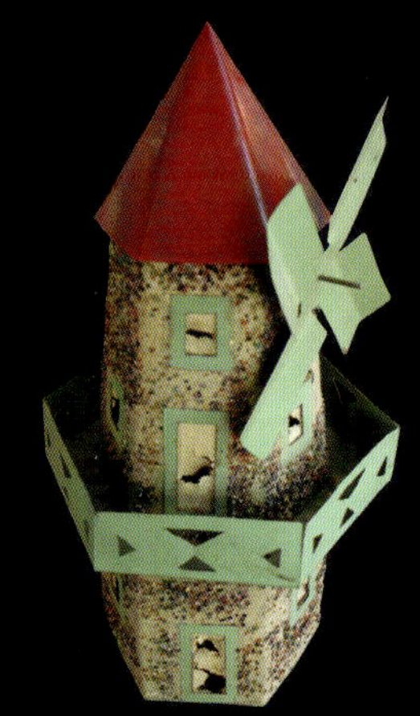

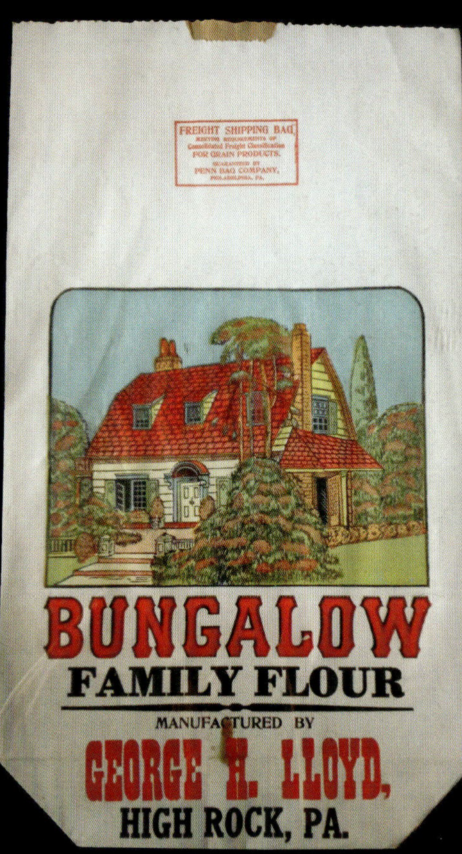

This collection represents a miniscule sampling of red
roof cottage-inspired objects made between the late
nineteenth and early twentieth centuries. Author's collection unless otherwise noted.

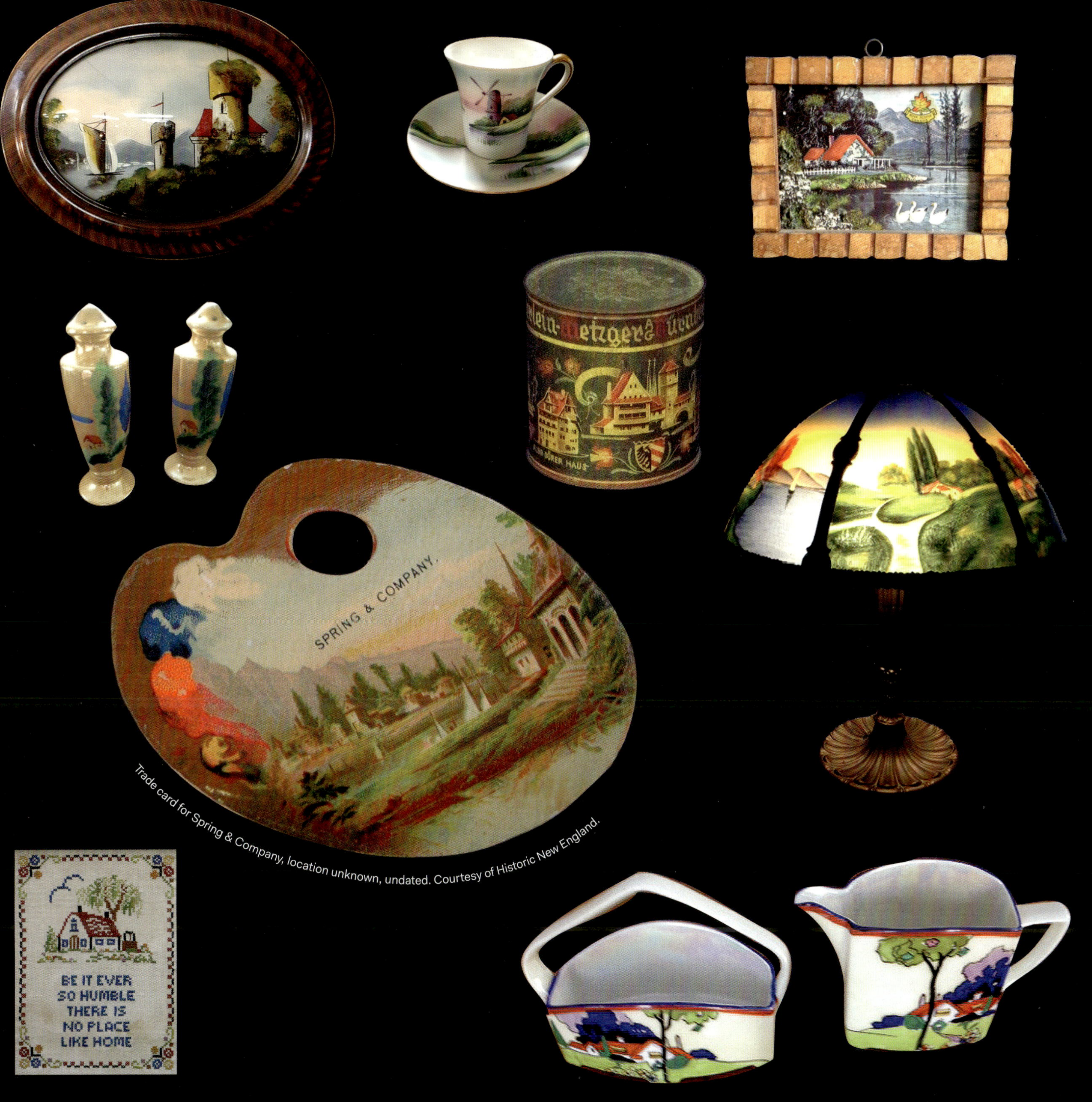

Trade card for Spring & Company, location unknown, undated. Courtesy of Historic New England.

Collection of Leah and Jerome Garchik. Robert Kaplan photograph.

Noritake sugar and cream set, Japan. Courtesy of Zena Lerman.

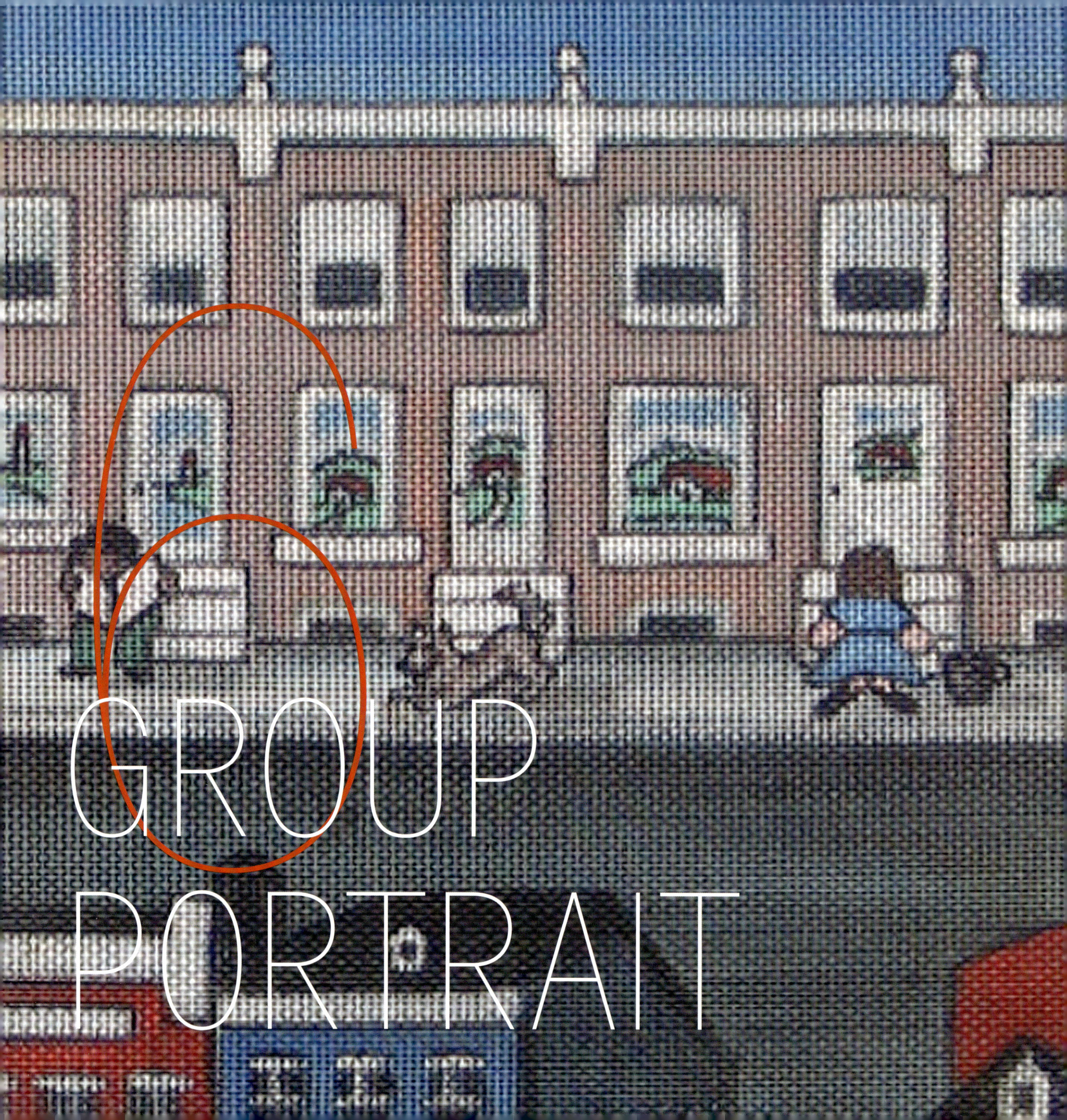

GROUP
PORTRAIT

The more screens there are out there, the more people want them, and the more work there is for everyone.

Ben Richardson

I have painted thousands and thousands of screens. I don't know how many. It's been so long and I didn't keep count of them. But I guess it would end up into the millions.

Ted Richardson

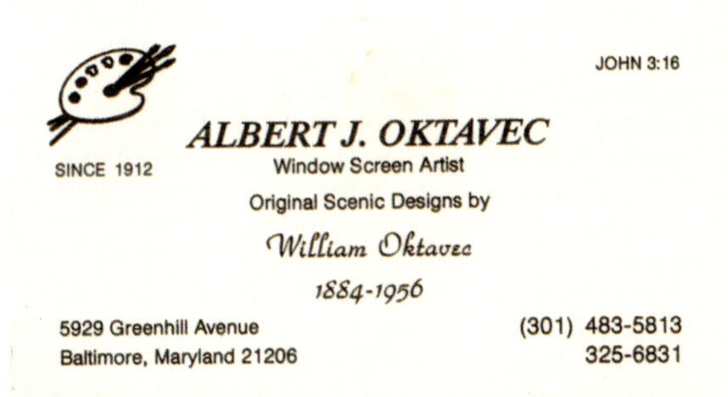

NEXT PAGE
Collage of business cards by screen painters.

Baltimoreans so fully embraced painted screens that upwards of 100,000 original works of art of varying degrees of accomplishment graced the unlikely outdoor museum of East Baltimore during the art form's heyday from the 1930s to the 1950s. It took many painters, most of them nameless, to complete that many screens. Their ranks, including one-time and Sunday painters, reached into the hundreds.

Like William Oktavec, new immigrants flooded into East Baltimore in the first decades of the twentieth century. Most initially found employment in flourishing local industries, but the decades leading up to and following World War I were tenuous economic times. The Depression years put even more men on the street desperately searching for work. When World War II ended, the country embraced the entrepreneur, the self-made man. Enter resourceful individuals on the lookout for opportunities, newcomers who spoke the same Old World languages that prevailed in these neighborhoods. Oktavec had not only pioneered an unfamiliar art form, he had introduced a new source of income, a windfall for unemployed and underemployed men at a time when jobs were hard to come by.

The original hub of screen painting was Oktavec's grocery at Collington and Ashland Avenues. As screens proliferated in ever-widening circles after the butcher's first foray in 1913, the screens themselves inspired new artists to take up the brush. In 1922, when William Oktavec opened the Art Shop in the Monument Street commercial corridor, the center of Baltimore screen painting moved a few blocks south and east, surrounded by Czech, Polish, and German enclaves.

SCREEN ARTIST

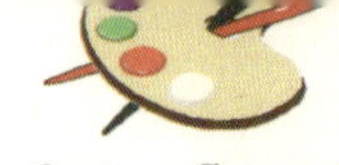

Custom Artwork by
JOHN OKTAVEC
Church Road
410-437-796
DENA, MD 21122

HAND-PAINTED WINDOW
AND DOOR SCREENS
"A Baltimore Tradition With A T
Robin Richards (410) 592-294
E-mail: robinpaints@hotmail.com

Anna Lip
Ar
Screen Painter & Creative Pai
501 S. Frizzellburg
Westminster, MD 21
443-791-1
Email me at annamlipka@yahoo.c
Website: annascreenart.

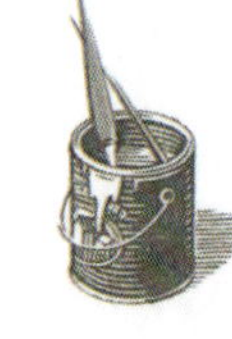

JOHN 3:16
A. Oktavec & Son Of Baltimore
Restoration, Painting & Decorating
Of Churches & Chapels
5929 Greenhill Ave.
Baltimore, MD 21206
AL 483-5813
CHRIS 325-6831

JOSEPH SCOGNA
SCREENS ARTISTICALLY PAINTED
You can see out — They can't see in
Night Clubs and Taverns Decorated
Rear of 801 N. Chester St.   Baltimore 5, Md.

PAINTED WINDOW S
BY TOM LIP
2525 FLEETWOOD A
BALTIMORE MD 2
410-319-9254
screenpainter@verizon.
screenpainter@hotmail.
screenpainterlipka@juno.
www.geocities.com/screenpainter

Scenic Windo
TOM LIPKA

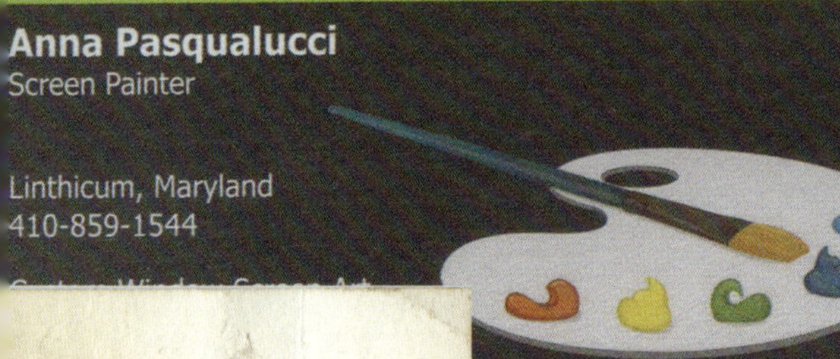
Anna's Painted Screens
Folk Art for Today's World.   Go Green with a Painted Screen.
Anna Pasqualucci
Screen Painter
Linthicum, Maryland
410-859-1544
Custom Window Screen Ar

Club Cellars   Black Light
Screen Artist
TED RICHARDSON
641 S. LEHIGH STREET
BALTIMORE, MD. 21224
CALL 327--7298   7 - 11 P. M.
"Any window can be a picture window"
2217 EASTERN AVE
Murals   Show Cards

Anna's Paint
folk ar
AnnaPasqua

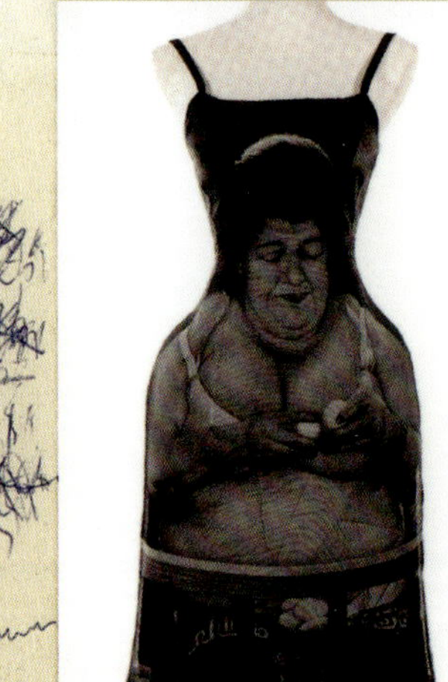

arlene
76 3
Ho
1809 7

JENNIFER CROUSE
Screen Painter/Artist
118 West Elm Avenue
Baltimore, MD 21206
Cell: (443) 838-3281
Home: (410) 663-5664

732-8634

L. W. BENNETT
SIGNS & SHO-CARDS
WINDOW SCREEN ARTIST
533
N. POTOMAC ST.   BALTO., MD.

na's Custom Painted
410-859-1
AnnaPasqualucci@gmail.com
www.PaintedScreens.synthasite.com

410-39
N@AOL.COM
DOW SCR
Traditional Folk Art
www.screenpainter.co

4107 FLEETWOOD AVENUE
BALTIMORE, MD. 21206-1534
Phone:410-254-8888

SCENIC   SCREEN
PAINTING
BY
TOM LIPKA
4122 BRENDAN AVE
485-1639

(301) 675-6075
Balti
Window S
You See Out

Darlene's
WINDOW SCREEN PAINTING STUDIO
Work Done by Expert Artists
Call 327-1847   Mon. thru Thur. 9 to 3

BALTIMORE'S TRADITIONAL
PAINTED WINDOW SCREENS
DEE HERGET
910 SUE G
BALTIMORE, M

HERGET

Painted Wi
DEE H
910 SUE G
ESSEX, MARYLAND 21221
391 - 1750

TED RICHARDSON

Jenny Campbell
410-804-6456
jennycampbellonline.com
jennycampbellonline@gmail.com
Jenny Campbell Painted Screens - facebook
Mermaid Workshop
mermaidworkshop.com
Mermaid Workshop - facebook

THE TRADITION THAT MADE BALTIMORE SMILE
Ted. Edw. Richardson
526 N. Potomac St.
Baltimore, MD 21205
WINDOW SCREEN PAINTING
"Any Window Can Be A Picture"
You See Out   No One Sees In
By Ted Richardson
Phone 675-6075

PAINTED WINDOW
Baltimo
ww
DEE HERGET

4

Pat Michalski
Artist

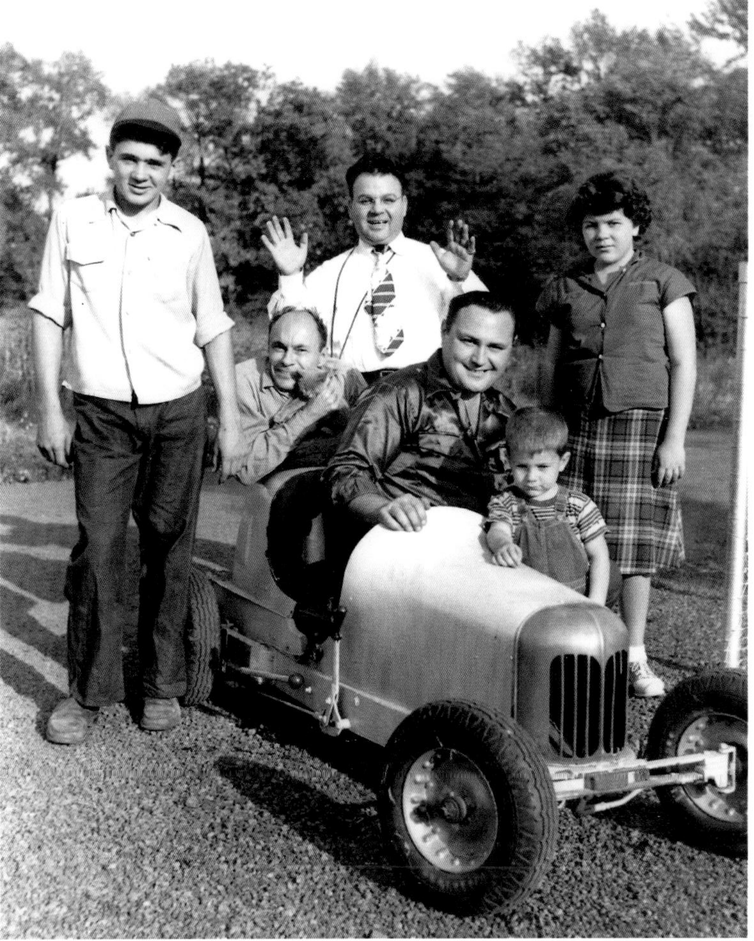

Rich Oktavec joins lifelong friend and neighbor Johnny Eck in his specially designed car while young John and unidentified friends look on. *Courtesy of the Johnny Eck Museum.*

The East Baltimore pavements teemed with activity during this period. People walked everywhere. Few had cars. The colorful screens, lined up in windows and doors chock-a-block on any given street, ensured that Oktavec would have all the business that he could handle. He would not monopolize the market for long, however.

Inevitably, screens and screen painters spread to adjoining neighborhoods, progressing toward the harbor through Highlandtown, Canton, Fell's Point, and Little Italy. For some, repainting faded screens offered an ideal entry point to the new art form. Wives insisted that their husbands try their hands at painting their own screens. Jacks-of-all-trades embraced the opportunity for acquiring a new skill or embarking on a new venture. Sign painters, already equipped with the proper materials, jumped right in. A modest expenditure for paint and brushes at the local hardware or sign supply shop would pay off in no time if the finished product were done to the satisfaction of the sidewalk critics. Relatives and neighbors placed orders. Street by street, week by week, newly minted artists adopted the art form. A willingness to work outdoors during the warm months could bring significant income to the enterprising artist.

THE ARTISTS

Dozens, if not hundreds, of artists came and went from the 1920s through the 1960s. Most painted only a few screens before moving on to the next item on the household to-do list. Their screens remained when their names were long forgotten. A few kept it up, painting thousands of screens. Oktavec called them "handymen and amateurs."[217] But they were not that easily characterized. For the most part they cared more about opportunity than art. Their names suggested that they were new arrivals or first-generation white males of European ancestry—Oktavec, Scogna, Bennett, Baldwin, Schlecter, Soul, Reillo, Bowman, Richardson, Cipolloni, Abremski, Trocki.

By the 1950s every community from Little Bohemia to the harbor boasted its own resident or traveling screen artist. Advertisements began to regularly in the *Sunpapers*, the *News American*, and the *Shoppers' Guide*. Joe Scogna, a rare painter who signed his work, catered to his Polish neighbors just blocks from the Oktavecs' businesses. The Richardson brothers, from England, added screen painting as a sideline to ventures that took them far afield. Ben offered a screen pick-up and delivery service to customers on his route as a bill collector for a local haberdasher. Ted, a natural showman who played with a hillbilly band, drummed up business door-to-door wherever he was performing or doing masonry work. Later, his distinctive sign-laden automobiles helped him widen his territory. Alonso Parks, harmonica player and local character, walked the streets of Highlandtown and Canton, offering his services on the spot in exchange for cash or a drink. He would set up an outdoor studio in front of the customer's home or tavern, which made him one of the most visible screen painters in the areas where he worked.

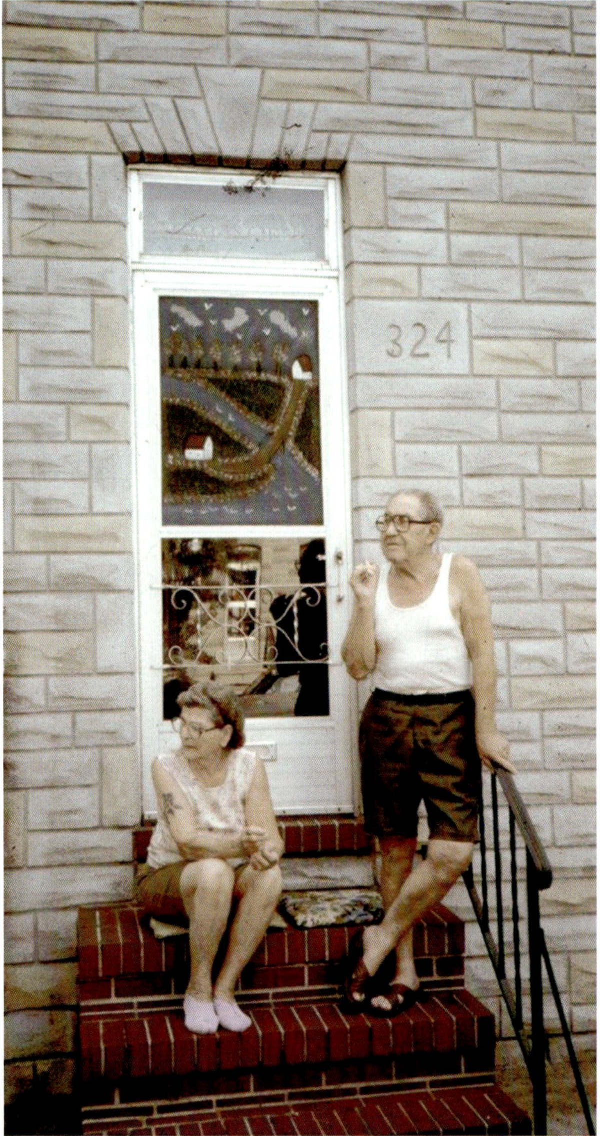

Mary and Jacobus "Dutch" Philipoom were regulars on their stoop on South Chester Street in Upper Fell's Point. Screens were merely a small part of his painting repertoire. A former merchant mariner, he painted every surface of the house. His wife insisted that if she hadn't kept moving, he would have painted her. *Author photograph, 1975.*

100,000 SCREENS? LET'S DO THE MATH.

After asking, "Painted what…why and how do they do it…how long does it take to paint one," most people want to know how many painted screens are scattered throughout Baltimore. That's not an easy question to answer, because painted screens are a moving target—their number depends on when the question is asked, the year and the season. One hundred thousand screens sounds like a huge number, but not if you consider the amount of activity at the height of screen-painting's popularity at mid-century. I arrived at that number through interpolation of data collected through door-to-door surveys. Between 1980 and 1982, during the "high season," June to September, several assistants and I walked Baltimore's streets and alleys, block by block, neighborhood by neighborhood. We counted and catalogued the screens on view, noting their placement and identifying the artists by style or by asking the resident when a hand was unfamiliar to us. I kept a handwritten gazetteer in a small looseleaf notebook that listed streets alphabetically, running from the harbor to Ashland Avenue and from Broadway to the railroad bridge that separates Highlandtown from Greektown at Haven Street. My companions made the work far more enjoyable and those additional eyes ensured an accurate census.

If a typical two-story rowhouse averages five front windows, including door and basement, and four rear windows—all of the screens would have been painted—the number of screens per rowhouse would have been nine. If every house on a block had painted screens, an average of twenty addresses per side, times two (for both sides of a street), the number of screens per block would be 180. Frank Novak, the most active builder in William Oktavec's territory between 1900 and 1915, constructed at least 10,000 rowhouses. These buildings alone might account for 90,000 painted screens. Up to 1,000 blocks in the contiguous communities of Little Bohemia, Highlandtown, Canton, Fell's Point, and Little Italy probably sported painted screens. Even using an extremely conservative count of four screens per house, the figures are staggering.

> *1,000 blocks*
>
> *x 40 houses per street (on average)*
>
> *x 4 screens per house*
>
> *= 160,000 screens*

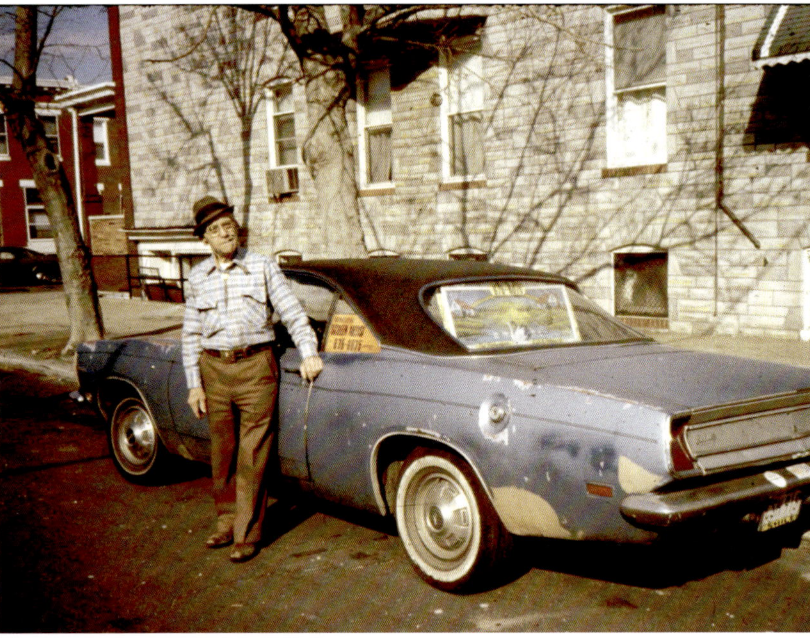

Ted Richardson was typical of the itinerant screen painters who traveled by car to extend their territories and avoid competition. His screen- and sign-bedecked car was his second-best advertisement, after the screens themselves. *Author photograph, 1983.*

Think "screen painter" and you would be hard pressed to conjure a single cohesive image save that they were almost exclusively male. With the exception of Ruth Chrysam, all known screen painters active in Baltimore between 1913 and 1974 were men. Ruth sought art lessons in the 1920s and became a screen painter because the only class offered in her neighborhood was William Oktavec's. It took fifty years for women to fully embrace the art form. Screen painting was initially considered man's work because it required heavy lifting and hauling. The housewives of North Collington Avenue often expected Oktavec the butcher to move the cumbersome wood-framed screens from parlor windows to his backyard "studio" and back again.

Miss Ruth worked strictly indoors. Ladies did not work alone outdoors in those early years, or claim the street as a workplace—although they did scrub their own marble steps and tend to the daily maintenance of their front sidewalk. They walked freely to market, church, hair salons, and relatives' rowhouses.

No other female artists were in evidence until the 1970s, when the commercial artist/screen painter Charles Bowman took on apprentice Darlene Grubb, and Dolores "Dee" Herget set her sights on screen painting. Changing cultural norms meant that women were free to work in trades that had once been inaccessible to them, and to drive cars and take buses. With frames of that period fabricated in aluminum and vinyl and screens made of fiberglass, nylon, and other synthetic fibers, the art form had become far more portable. Door and window screens could be carried away by an artist, male or female, who lived and worked at a distance, rather than painted on the spot.

SIGNATURES

Creativity had its limits in Oktavec's Baltimore. Say the words "painted screen" and only one image came to mind: the simple, red-roofed cottage borrowed from greeting cards and calendars. Yet the variations on this icon of a century ago were legion, like the hands that painted them. As Ruth Chrysam observed, "you would always detect a screen painter's work."[218] Richard Oktavec embraced the competition: "It's good. The more the merrier, 'cause everybody's got his own style."[219] Though no two screen painters produced identical screens, lineages could be traced through the paintings themselves.

Each artist may have had a signature style, but the screens were rarely signed. Ben Richardson never remembered putting his name on his work: "I was just glad to get the screen done, get it out of my hands."[220] Ironically, his brother and disciple, Ted Richardson, "was determined to have my name on them all and the date. So I used a rubber stamp when I was busy—but it was my actual signature—and when I got unbusy, I just painted it with a small tiny brush."[221] A sticker on the frame, with a current phone number, came next. Joe Scogna would have been lost to history if not for the signature he added to one bungalow scene he painted in the 1930s. Al Oktavec remembered him decades later as a handicapped young neighbor who spent time at the Art Shop coaxing tips from the elder Oktavec. The Oktavecs signed their screens only if pressed. At the request of a West Coast dealer who commissioned dozens from Al around 1982, he "started putting on just my initials, but he told me he wanted my whole name."[222] But Al never signed his Baltimore orders. The style of an Oktavec screen, soft and subtly hued, was mark enough. In contrast, Johnny Eck liked painting his last name on his screens in large capital letters, possibly a throwback to the larger-than-life banners that had announced him as a featured attraction in a previous career as a carnival entertainer. To the uninitiated, all screens look alike. But even without a signature, each painter managed, intentionally or not, to claim his brand with subtle distinctions—a particular style of rendering, consistency of color choices, thickness of line; positioning and shape of the cottage, roof pitch, chimney placement, color of the house, window, and roof; the presence or absence of shadow, type of water feature—river, lake, ocean, or falls—sky and water hues, clouds, bridge design, evergreen or deciduous trees, flowering

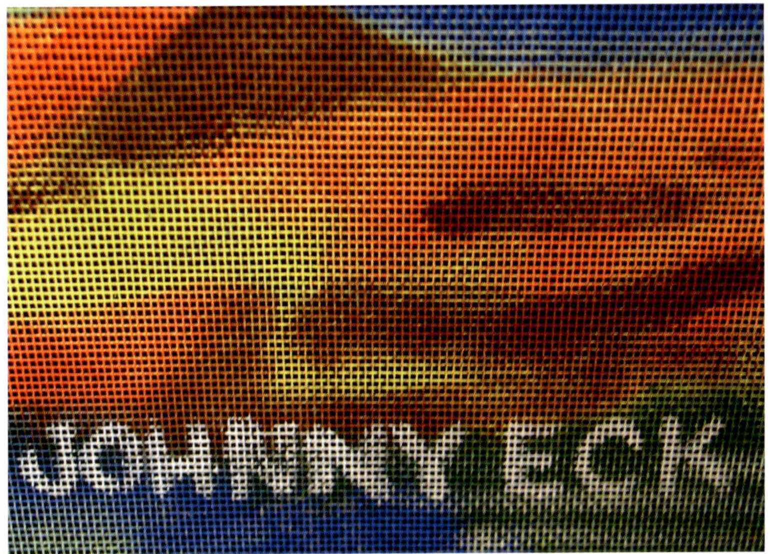

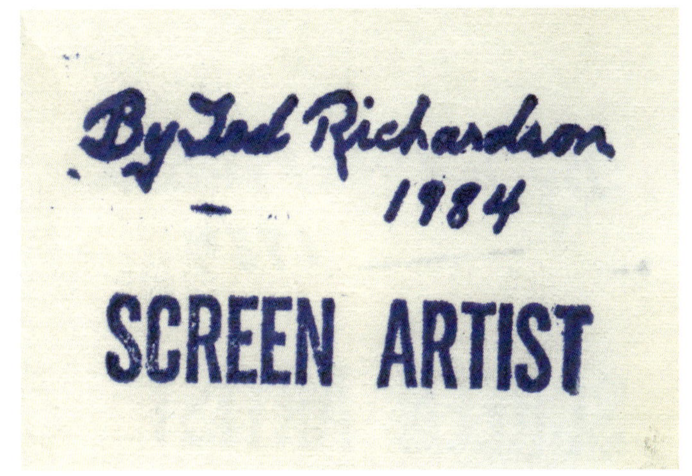

or plain bushes, straight or winding path, stones, rounded or peaked mountains, the use of outlines. Other than the Oktavecs, no two artists painted red bungalows the same way, except for one notable exception: Tom Lipka, whether through constant exposure to the artist at work in his neighborhood, or his photographic memory, was able to virtually replicate Alonzo Parks's unmistakable version of the iconic cottage when he took up painting decades later. Dee Herget made note of the small touches that differentiated one screen painter from another: "You can look at a screen and tell who painted it because no matter what is on it or how you rearrange it, my trees are my trees, and Tom's trees are his and Ben, we all have our style. Like handwriting it is all unique."[223] Adept at picking out one artist's work from another as the result of doing touch-up jobs, even years later, she regretted having painted over the signature of one now forgotten painter. Often she merely cut out the original screen and replaced it with her own version on new screening.

All the screen painters paint a cottage with a red roof because William Oktavec started that and it caught on and became sort of a tradition. But, we all paint the cottage with the red roof with a different style and with a different shape to it. There's always a little difference to it. I would no more copy Tom Lipka's cottage—which is gorgeous—than I would copy Oktavec's cottage, which is the best. So I developed my own style and have to be noted for that. Maybe in twenty years they'll say, Oh, that's a Herget![224]

ALL SCREENS LOOK ALIKE—OR DO THEY?

The Red Bungalow (RB) Style Sheet: What to Look For

As you examine the individual elements of screens by different artists, looking for the presence or absence of certain features, you will begin to see the distinctions:

THE OVERALL PALETTE

- ☐ bright
- ☐ soft
- ☐ dark

OUTLINES

- ☐ Present or absent
- ☐ heavy or light
- ☐ color

STRUCTURE (BUILDINGS)

- ☐ position
- ☐ house color
- ☐ roofline
- ☐ roof color
- ☐ shadow
- ☐ door

TYPE

- ☐ log cabin
- ☐ cottage
- ☐ Tudor
- ☐ other

WINDOWS

- ☐ shutters
- ☐ color
- ☐ curtains

LANDSCAPING

- ☐ trees
- ☐ shapes
- ☐ lawn
- ☐ shrubs
- ☐ flowers
- ☐ path
- ☐ water feature
- ☐ stones
- ☐ bridge
- ☐ mountains
- ☐ layering
- ☐ shadow
- ☐ colors

SWANS (SINGLE OR PAIR)

- ☐ relative size
- ☐ color
- ☐ other animals or birds

SKY

- ☐ color
- ☐ clouds
- ☐ style
- ☐ sunset

FIGURES

- ☐ people
- ☐ activity

SIGNATURE

- ☐ present or not
- ☐ location

UNDERCOATING

- ☐ visible
- ☐ color
- ☐ front
- ☐ back

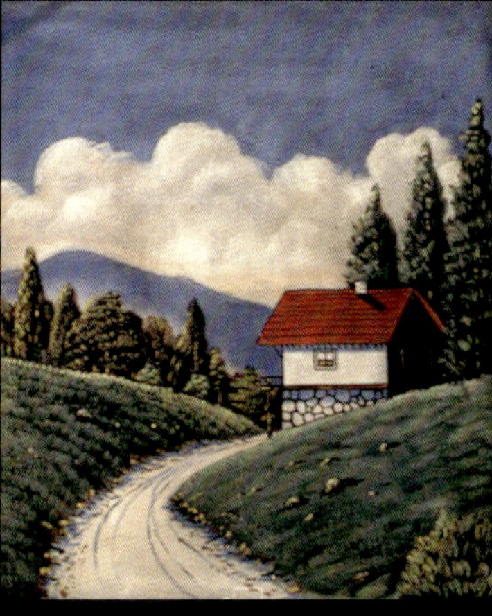

RICHARD OKTAVEC

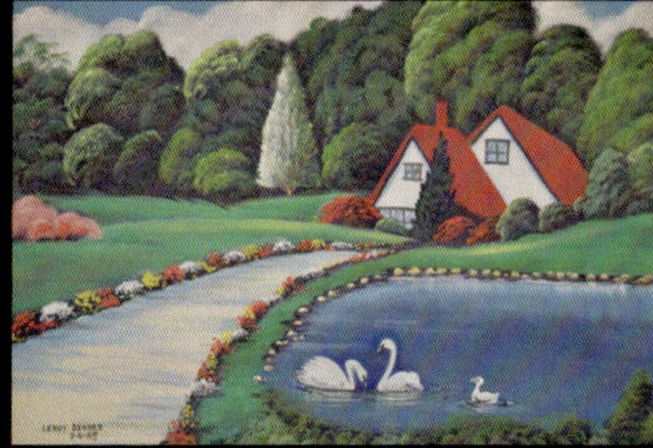

AL OKTAVEC

LEROY BENNETT

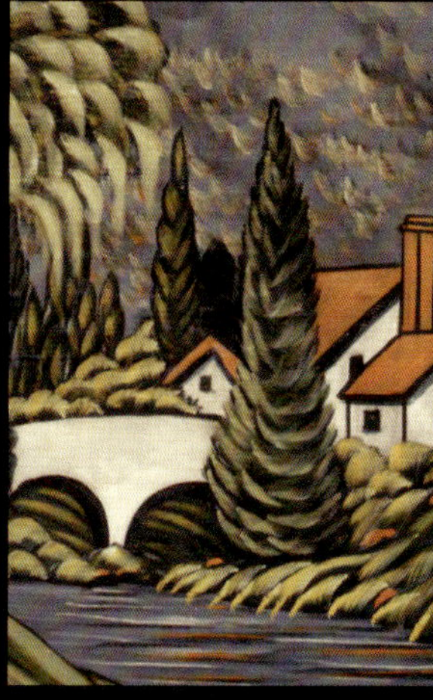

BEN RICHARDSON

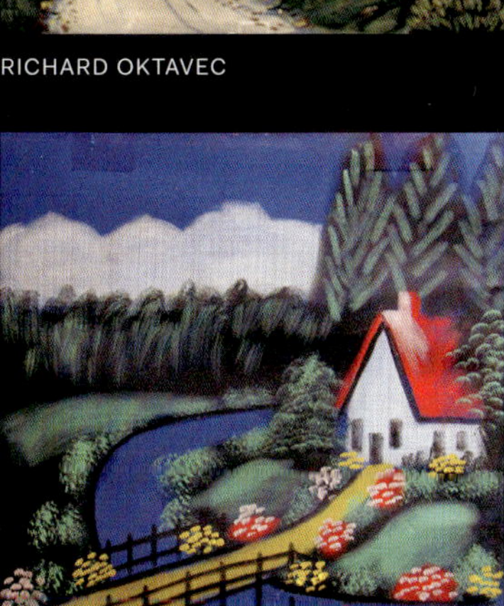

CHARLES BOWMAN

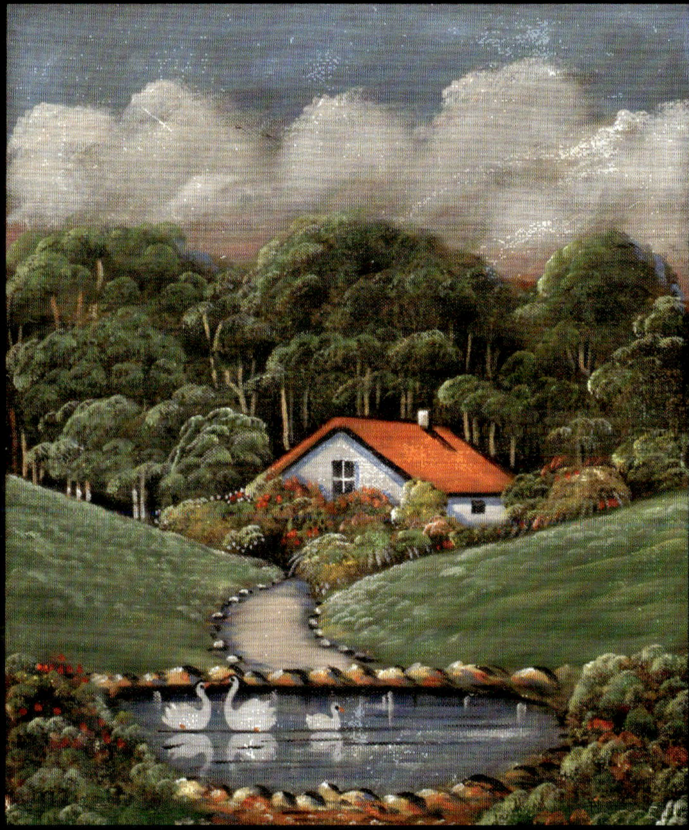

WILLIAM OKTAVEC

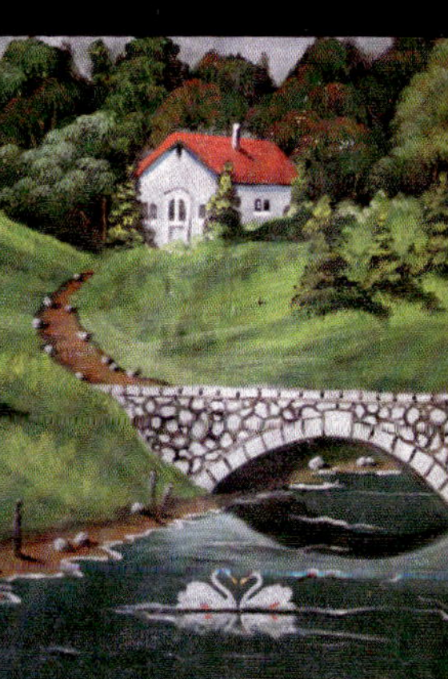

JOHN OKTAVEC

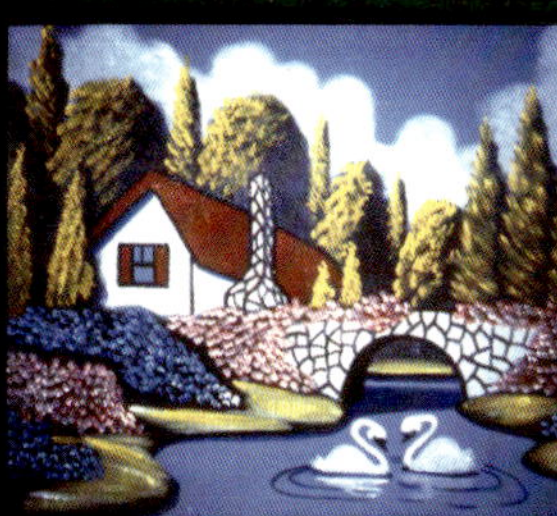

DEE HERGET

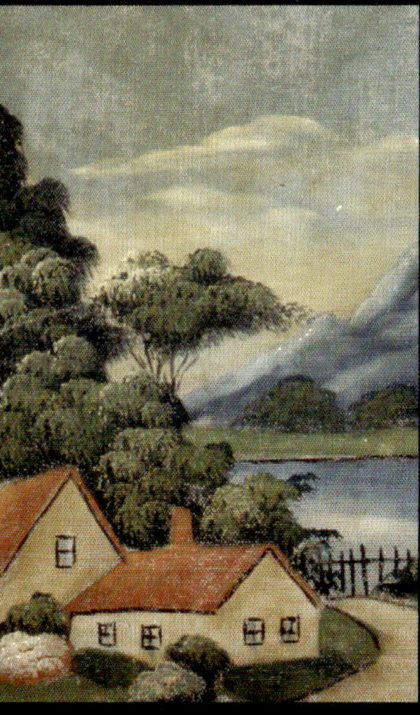

ALONZO PARKS

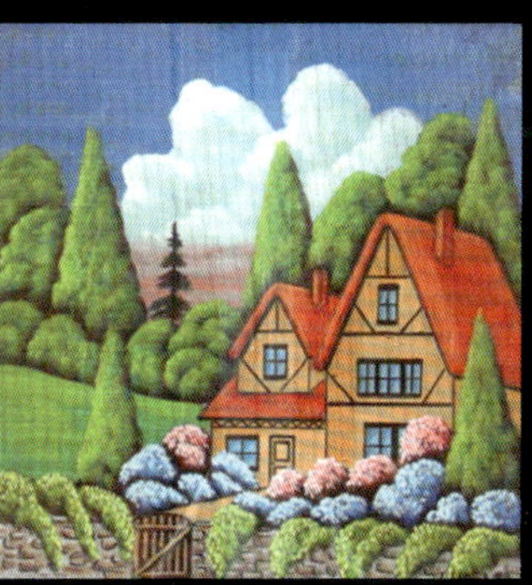

TOM LIPKA

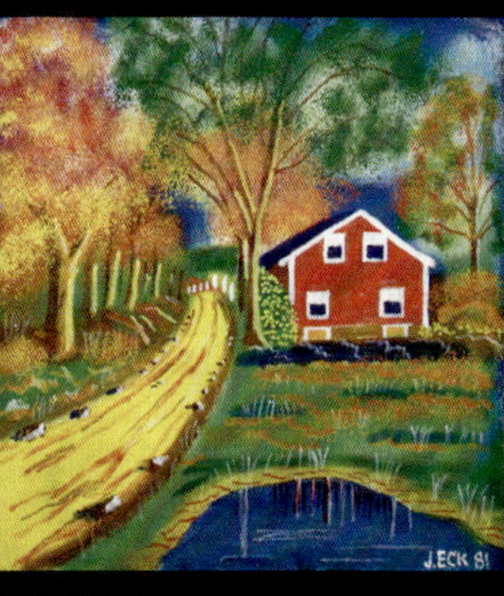

JOHNNY ECK

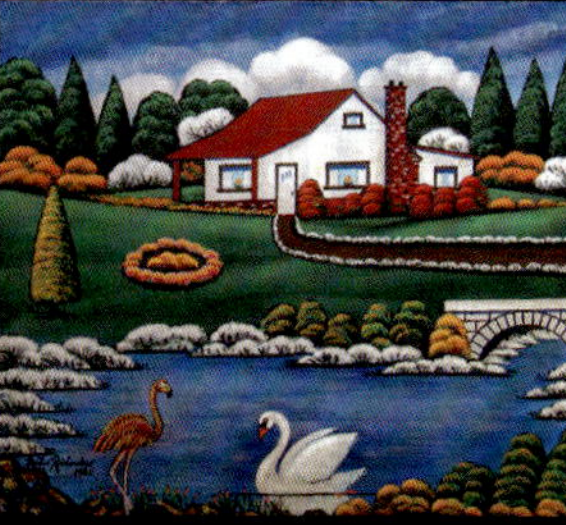

TED RICHARDSON

THE ITINERANTS

After Oktavec established the Art Shop, he ceased making house calls and asked his customers to deliver and claim their screens. Offering full service, the amateurs went directly to their clients and set up shop on the sidewalk. "Nine times out of ten [the customer] was…a woman. Like one woman who'd get it and then the next woman across the street said, I would like my house done. I want my screens done."[225]

Painting on demand, artists worked all day, in sun or shade, and installed the finished screens before collecting their fees and working their way down the block. Oktavec's imitators at first stayed close to home, claiming familiar streets and alleys as their own personal territory—and eventually their gallery. Some continually sought new turf, testing how far they could roam without running into the competition. Men who went house to house or window to window in search of business became fixtures in the rowhouse neighborhoods of East Baltimore. They staked out corners and set up their studios on the sidewalks of well-traveled routes to essential destinations like the market, bank, or church. On occasion they painted directly on the screen as it sat in the window. The open-air studio by far was the best form of advertising and certainly offered the lowest overhead. They traveled light, but their carefree, minimalist approach required that they carry a box or suitcase for paints, brushes, and solvents; a seat; and, in some cases, an easel. They straddled beer boxes or three-legged stools placed on the sidewalk, lining up the finished screens to dry along the house fronts until the light left the summer sky and they had to pack up their tools for the day.

A single block could keep a screen painter busy for days if each house had eight to ten screens, front and back. A corner house, with its additional street-facing side, provided a bonanza. Screen painting was a cash-only business, with prices beginning at fifty cents, but package deals could be arranged. Like the men who sold Formstone after its introduction in 1937, screen painters offered group rates to residents of contiguous houses—if they all had the same scenes painted at the same time by the same painter. Even as late as the 1980s, screens were painted for as little as $10 to $20 each, a remarkably affordable sum for custom art.

STREET SCHOOL

An Oktavec screen was for many considered the epitome of the form, but fulfillment of an order from the master painter could take weeks or months, given the high demand for his handiwork, as well as his commitments for church restorations, calligraphy, framing orders, classes, and the day-to-day operations of a retail store. By the time Oktavec opened the Art Shop, he had all the work he needed, but he was still reluctant to reveal any secrets to his many competitors. Aspiring artists regularly made the pilgrimage to the mecca of screen art, vainly hoping to learn something about the kinds of paint, thinner, brushes, and strokes. But no information was forthcoming. Oktavec may even have intentionally misled them. Ben Richardson swore that he told him his paints came from China when in fact he used pigments known as Japan paints.[226] William Oktavec did choose a few students, with great care. These included his sons Richard and Albert, and two neighbors.

Johnny Eck, his star pupil, was a regular at the Art Shop's Saturday classes. He continued in the master's footsteps for most of the twentieth century, maintaining possibly the longest screen-painting streak. William Oktavec chose as his apprentice Ruth Chrysam, a young woman from the neighborhood who had immense talent. In the basement of her family's home, she painted delicate, exquisitely detailed screens for family members who lived nearby. After only a few seasons with Oktavec, her skill and aspirations carried her to New York where she pursued a career in commercial art that did not include screen painting.

With the exception of the Art Shop, no school or individual offered lessons in screen painting. Though many of the painters took evening, weekend, or day classes over the years in a variety of subjects at the Maryland Institute, each one was eager to associate his practice in some way with the master. Neither manuals nor how-to postings at paint or hardware stores existed in the early years of screen painting. The only screen school available to them was the streets, and the lessons consisted of what the hopeful could pick up from studying Oktavec's work in situ, watching other painters, or from hard-won experience, trial and error. In 1928 Joe Scogna, who lived around the corner from Oktavec's market, "saw the way men were sitting on the sidewalk painting screens. That's how I got the idea. I started practicing by myself."[227] Charles Bowman observed a man in a blue apron methodically work his way through the screens of Fell's Point. Frank Deoms was amazed by the speed and carelessness of the street painters. He refused to "smack out them trees so fast."[228] Ben Richardson lost no time in converting his route as a salesman-collector into an additional source of revenue:

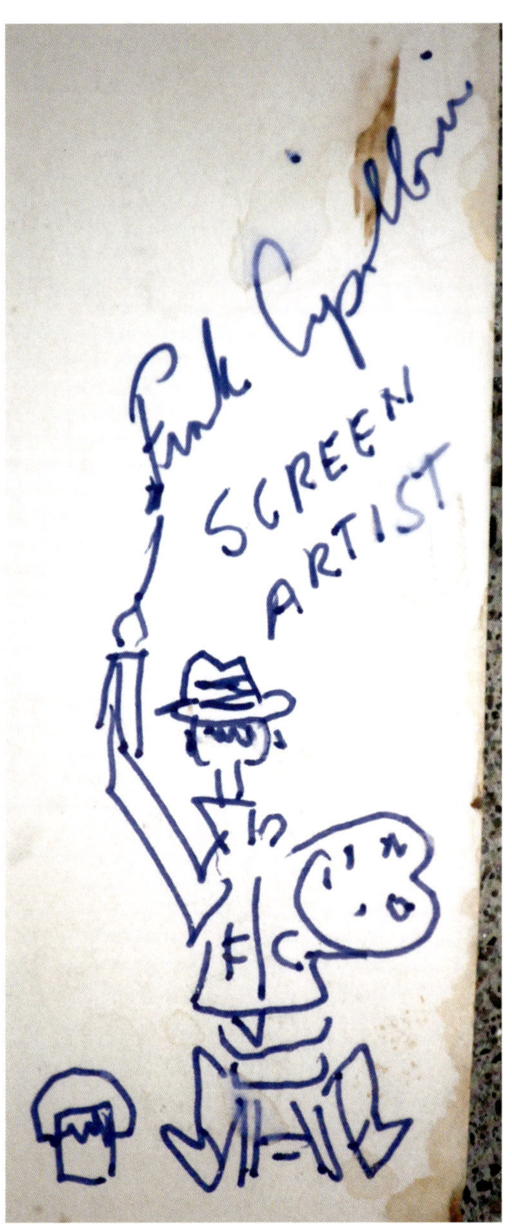

Frank Cipolloni tagged personal notes on his work in most media other than screen with a simple self-portrait of the artist at work on the sidewalks of Little Italy. *Courtesy of the Cipolloni family.*

I saw different ones on the pavement painting screens and that's what gave me the idea that I could do it too…but nobody showed me how to do it. After I learned to paint my own window screens, then I started doin' 'em on the street. They'd start talkin' about window screens and I'd say, "Do you want your window screens painted?" "Yeah. Do you do it?" And I said, "Yeah." "Alright you take 'em, bring 'em back."[229]

He realized he could double his income by capitalizing on his weekly access to East Baltimore customers, primarily housewives, offering speedy pick-up and return of their painted screens. His brother Ted claimed to

go around and watch some of these old…winos or something like that. And I watched to see how they were doing it and that is where I got the idea from. They just doctored things up quick, didn't make much of a picture. And they used to do it for about a whiskey. The person wanted them done, and they would get some money to buy a bottle of whiskey I thought that was a pretty good racket, you know? So I went around and started doing it myself.[230]

Dee Herget describes a brief childhood encounter with an anonymous, gruff screen painter who invaded her playground—the sidewalk—in Highlandtown. She may have watched only once, as he haphazardly applied paint to wire at record-breaking speed. But when, decades later, she found herself in need of a new career, she recalled that fleeting lesson. There is a certain irony that when she sought a teacher, she approached Ben Richardson, whose imagination had also been piqued by the screen painters he met working the streets. When he gave her lessons in his West Baltimore dining room, he did not demonstrate, but offered random verbal insights into his practice.

Albert Baldwin used to accompany his father, Walter, along the Eastern Avenue corridor looking for work prior to 1940. By noon they could easily clear $50, break for lunch, and return to the same area in the afternoon to do more of the same. These anecdotes shouldn't suggest that the screen painter's lot was always simple and lucrative. There were unavoidable occupational hazards associated with painting out-of-doors, as Baldwin and others related: "My father, he wanted to get off the street too. In bad weather we can't do anything. Rainy weather we can't do anything. We got tired of going to the movies. We'd have to go to the Patterson Theater on Eastern Avenue, just to get in from the weather."[231] Not only rain, but heat and wind took their toll. Painters complained of flying debris in many forms, including insects and chicken feathers. And the rambunctious youngsters whose playground was their shared sidewalk/studio were a constant annoyance. Despite these nuisances, the door-to-door approach was popular for other reasons. In addition to the screens, painters picked up odd jobs, such as decorating holiday-themed mirrors in bars and residential vestibules. During Prohibition, screen painting attracted "smokehounds," heavy drinkers who used the funds they earned to purchase ingredients to concoct their own beverages, often with a "smoky" hue. Alonzo Parks was known to do this, and later, to take his pay straight to the corner tavern. "You knew never to pay him in advance, or you'd never see your screens. He'd drink up that dollar as soon as he saw it," reminisced one Canton neighbor.[232] Artists of every stripe found a quick way to make easy money and keep busy with screens.

Teenagers like Tom Lipka would work for "date money." He started outdoors to attract business, but also because there was not much space at home. A typical rowhouse was crowded and lacked ventilation. The "airy way" (or alley way), a covered ground floor opening that ran between houses to provide access to backyards and alleys in unbroken blocks, offered shelter from the elements or a drying area in bad weather. Eventually the painters traveled between neighborhoods by car, to carry unfinished screens home for completion or to seek refuge.

'ART OUT OF NOTHING'

Resourcefulness was undoubtedly the one virtue all Baltimore screen painters had in common—the ability to seize an opportunity and more important make a buck from nothing. Frank Deoms, a magician and sideshow operator, lived blocks from Oktavec's grocery and from the Art Shop. He recalled the proliferation of painters, "Inside of a year there was ten of them."[233] Deoms lived among painted screens for decades before taking up the brush to fill his idle hours. When he started painting he was well into his seventies. The fact that he was a magician put him in a good position. Turning wire into landscape paintings was just like pulling rabbits from hats. The story of Deoms's extremely full life offers a window into the souls of the men of Baltimore who craved productive work and the luxury of being their own bosses. Many early screen painters like Deoms were moonlighters, with day jobs as paper hangers, sign painters, musicians, violin repairmen, door-to-door salesmen, day laborers, bricklayers.

Boys of high-school age sought only enough business to earn the price of a movie, bowling, or pizza. They were not looking for repeat customers, touch-up work, or local renown. The length of their tenure as screen artists was determined by their immediate financial needs. Fell's Point's Greg Reillo, active since the 1950s, was one of these: "It was never a business with me. I just did it to pick up a few bucks. With me it was strictly a sideline. Cash and carry. I figure if they need a screen they knew where to find me. I was in the neighborhood."[234] Raise the question of pricing with any screen painter, and you'll quickly realize you've hit on a sticky subject. Many screen painters simply threw out a number and if no one balked, it stuck. The price varied from painter to painter, block to block, day to day. Johnny Eck was proud to be able to "fit the bill to the patient," charging what he considered fair from one day to the next. He questioned whether he should charge his neighbors and other rowhouse dwellers the same as the couple driving their Mercedes in from New York. When his work in particular began to attract collectors from far away, he felt the need to price his work at a level that would keep screens in use locally, as they were intended.

As the market changed, no one knew what to charge. Eck steamed when he saw advertisements that undercut his prices. Customers began to shop around. "I've got competitors. Do you know what they charge? Now no names mentioned. Bargains. Special bargains. Three dollars and up. And I thought, three dollars and up, and I looked at this artist, and I said, Do you know what I charge? I charge five to ten dollars just to talk to the people."[235]

What started as a fifty-cent investment in 1913 has risen incrementally over the years. In 1987, painted screens could be purchased for $15, and today they might run $75 or more for a single window. Such rates reflect a change in perception. Increasingly, artists charge by the piece, by the square foot, or by the subject. Some base their costs on the complexity of the scene. The Patterson Park pagoda is one of the more costly views. In the early years, painted screens were everywhere, a basic necessity. And while painters were once found on every street corner, now they are scarce. Today consumers and artists value the screen's art more highly than its utility.

'INSIDER ART' SHOPS AND STUDIOS

Ted Richardson was the first screen painter to make screen painting a full-time job, and to pursue it in a dedicated retail space located on a major East Baltimore thoroughfare. Once artists went indoors, they appropriated spaces borrowed from other tasks. Ruth Chrysam's parents happily relinquished part of their basement for her art shop. As youngsters, Johnny Eck and his brother Rob used their knee-high front basement window to pass screens to and from customers on the street. Years later, when the family home became the brothers' bachelor pad, Johnny carved out space for a studio beside the stairway. He took only the area required for a single screen to rest on the floor, along with several pints of Ronan paint, his preferred brand, and some brushes. Sign painter Charles Bowman maintained his sign shop in the former front parlor of an unheated Fleet Street house (he lived in an adjacent rowhouse). There he did commercial work and screen commissions, and also repaired violins. His "Screens Painted" sign in the window drew customers to the location on a busy street, visible to passing cars and sidewalk traffic, and the door was often left open so that large items could be moved in and out easily. He shared his room-sized sign painter's easel with an apprentice. It easily accommodated screen-painting with the addition of a permanent black backdrop.

For most screen painters, a basement corner or a purloined pantry would do. A single-purpose room was a luxury. Dee Herget's ten-foot-square studio off the kitchen accommodated canned goods and the washer and dryer, as well as her custom-made painting table and a growing collection of ephemera. Tom Lipka moved between an easily accessible walk-in basement workspace, with ceilings that grazed the top of his head and, during cold weather, a second-floor spare bedroom.

Ben Richardson's screened-in backyard gazebo must have been the envy of every painter, but he was philosophical about its charms, noting, "Some painters carry paint supplies in a cardboard box. Some paint from the trunk of a car. I feel more at home in my gazebo."[236] Initially doubling as a venue for crab feasts and cookouts, his commodious, four-season homemade retreat kept him out of his wife's way and allowed him to while away the hours painting, playing music, or planning his next project. The move there also signaled the end of his personal transfer service. He remembered, "I started to pick up & deliver, for a few years. Traveling became expensive plus lost time loading and unloading. I got out of that and started cash & carry—a very good move."[237]

GETTING THE WORD OUT

It would be safe to say that except for the Oktavecs and their extended family, the painters kept to themselves. The fact that each practiced an arcane, local art form isolated them from one another rather than bringing them together. Competition among them was fierce, though it never broke out into outright animosity. Reverence for the incomparable work of the Oktavec family is unanimous, but petty jealousies and criticisms, the stuff of human nature, marked the relationships of painters beyond the founding family of Baltimore screen painting.

Brothers Ben and Ted Richardson told different versions of who painted the first screen in the family, and those stories changed with every telling. Their collaborations and break-ups were epic. Everything was fair game. The colorful work of Johnny Eck, who rarely stuck to a single subject and whose palette was unique, was never really understood by the coterie of painters who toed a more traditional line (although Ben visited Johnny late in their lives, and thereafter had only the highest praise for "that little Eck boy," at that time well into his seventies). Only the Oktavecs escaped criticism entirely. Once the painters began to meet regularly in the 1980s, at get-togethers, exhibitions, and workshops, mutual appreciation and harmony grew.

The sheer number of artists working the streets ensured that, at the height of its popularity, screen painting was a highly competitive art form. Getting screens up on more houses than other artists was as much a source of pride as of income. Screen painters, like graffiti artists, got a lot of satisfaction out of "tagging" houses around town, particularly when they could infringe on another artist's turf. But it was all legal and welcome.

Finding, or sometimes even identifying, the painter of a particular screen was always the customer's challenge. Artists were tracked down usually through word of mouth. Because they rarely signed their work, they relied on leafleting and strategically placed business cards, of various sizes, to bring in customers. Joe Scogna distributed printed cards in the 1940s. While working as a bricklayer, Ted Richardson attracted attention to his screen painting by displaying his work at his

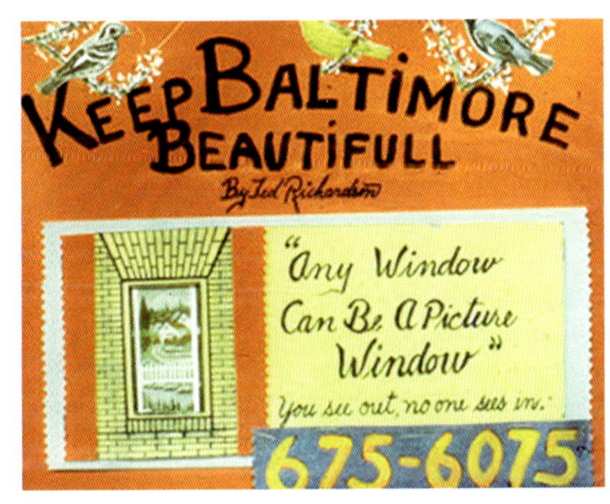

Ted Richardson created his own advertisements and displayed them wherever he might encounter a crowd. *Collection of the Painted Screen Society of Baltimore, Inc.*

job sites. Later he topped his ever-changing fleet of sedans and station wagons with handmade signs and exhibited painted screens emblazoned with his phone number or address in his car and home windows.

Ben Richardson advised future screen painters "How to Advertise" in an unpublished, unedited manual he wrote in 1982, entitled, *How to Paint Window Screens*:

· Paint a sample with phone # on it. Show in Shoping centers and etc. (Neighborhood hardware stores have been the venue of choice for many painters.) Make a Leterd Sighn on a screen with black letters. Name-Phone.

· Newspappers where screen painting is popular.

· Attend Art Shows.

· Remember—A 1 year add in the phone book can keep you on the phone instead of your workshelf.[238]

By the 1970s, the *Baltimore Guide* was the place to find painters. Dee Herget unwisely placed her first ad in the citywide *Baltimore Sun,* then teeming with other ads for sales and services. She received not a single response and quickly switched to advertising in the "Miscellaneous Services" column of the *Guide's* classifieds, where she vied for top billing with Ted Richardson and Darlene Grubb, who regularly ran unfathomable notices such as "$7 Window Specials" and "$12 Special Design of Standard Size Door-3 weeks only." Ads appeared into the 1990s in the *Guide* and nearby county weeklies. When no notices were placed, residents panicked, "They've disappeared. Where can I find a screen painter?"

PASSING IT ON

Some of the screen painters who, like Oktavec, had art training, picked up weekend or evening classes at the Maryland Institute, which at that time was everyman's art school. But no one took courses in screen painting, as there were none to be had. When the Painted Screen Society began to offer workshops in 1985 the painters of the old school—the Richardson brothers, Frank Cipolloni, Frank Abremski, and Leroy Bennett—began to work alongside next-generation screen painters like Tom Lipka and Dee Herget. The Society's day-long classes at the Canton branch of the Enoch Pratt Free Library, the Hatton Senior Center, and at other locations by invitation throughout the city and county always were filled to capacity. Students came from throughout Baltimore and the suburbs as well as from New York, New Jersey, and Vermont. Most nursed memories of painted screens in their parents' and grandparents' homes in the old neighborhood and had long been curious about the techniques. At least one, a curator from a historic New England house museum, sought to understand the works in her own institution's collections. Special classes

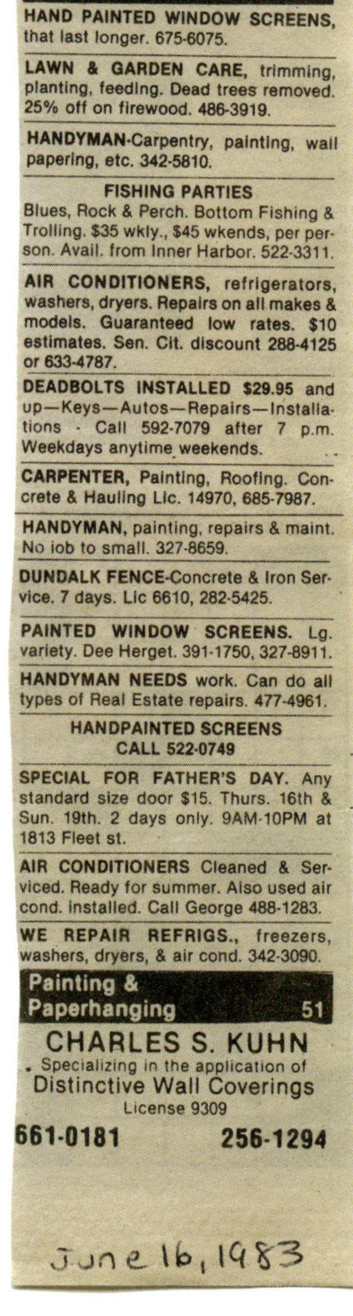

The *Baltimore Guide* was the go-to place to find a screen painter in the city.

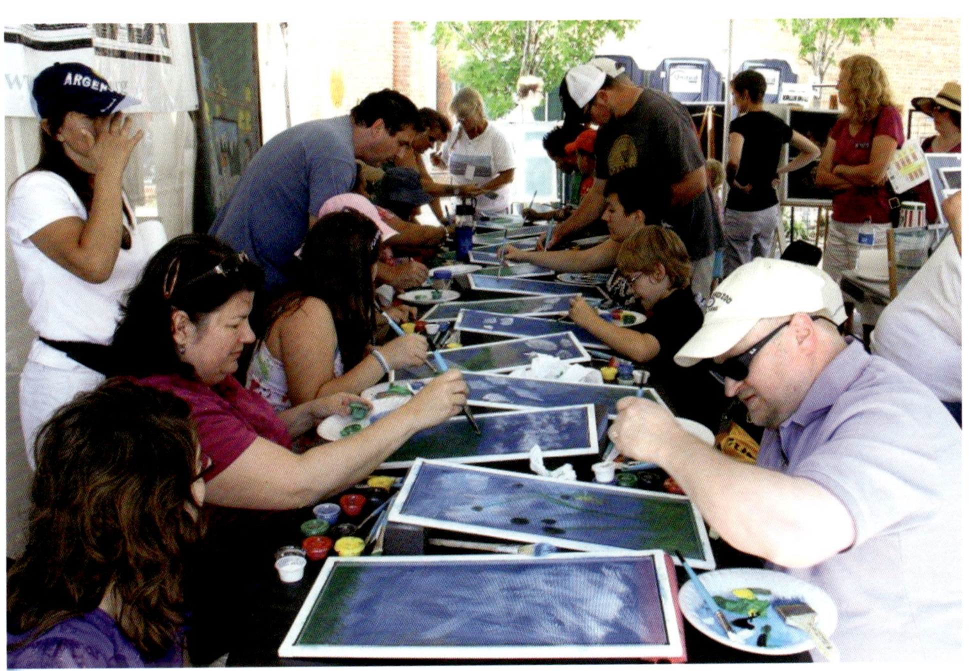

Visitors to the 2012 Maryland Traditions Folklife Festival at the Creative Alliance at the Patterson enjoy a free workshop offered by the Painted Screen Society taught by Anna Pasqualucci. *Michael Stewart photograph.*

were held for Baltimore City art teachers in hopes of spurring awareness, if not a revival, of the indigenous art form. Screen painters always attracted future students and built a strong volunteer base for the Society through participation in festivals from Hopkins to Highlandtown, Patterson Park, Fell's Point, the Flower Mart, and the Inner Harbor. Staying local had its benefits, but Dee Herget was particularly energetic in finding venues and making new friends farther afield. On occasion, all of the painters would paint in a single venue, inspiring youngsters and teasing recollections from the old-timers. *Windowscapes* was a highlight of the 1984 Artscape, Baltimore's annual citywide arts festival. All of the active painters assembled for that exhibition of their work, which filled the lobby of the Lyric Opera House.

The audience for screen paintings and classes grew exponentially with the 1988 release of the documentary film *The Screen Painters.* The film unleashed a demand for even more hands-on classes, screen-painting demonstrations and public events.

From the mid-1980s to the mid-1990s, painters new to the art form were drawn to Society-sponsored workshops. Many became active as volunteers. Unable to keep up with the demand for classes requested by schools and senior centers, the Society produced a video, *How to Paint a Baltimore Screen*, featuring Dee Herget.[239] With the release of the video and later a DVD version, the art of screen painting was popularized once more, its secrets at last revealed and available to all. Sold in specialty shops and museums, at festivals, and by mail order, these films detailed the tools and techniques of screen painting to a national and international audience. Today, screen painters are turning up in storefronts in hip Baltimore shopping districts, on the Eastern Shore and in Western Maryland, in Iowa, Florida, Massachusetts, and Arizona. The how-to video generated legions of instant experts who pop up as instructors in schools, craft shops, community and senior centers. New screen painters emerging from these classes either teach others or complete work for their own enjoyment. Their screens are likely to be framed and hung indoors or on wraparound porches in vacation homes in Ocean City, Maryland, the Outer Banks of North Carolina, and on lanais (pool and patio enclosures) in Florida—bringing the art full circle to its roots, not in Baltimore, but in Victorian seaside homes. The new artists identify less with William Oktavec and other early Baltimore screen painters than with their students who have gone on to teach. They learn not by observing the art on the street, but through magazines and YouTube videos.

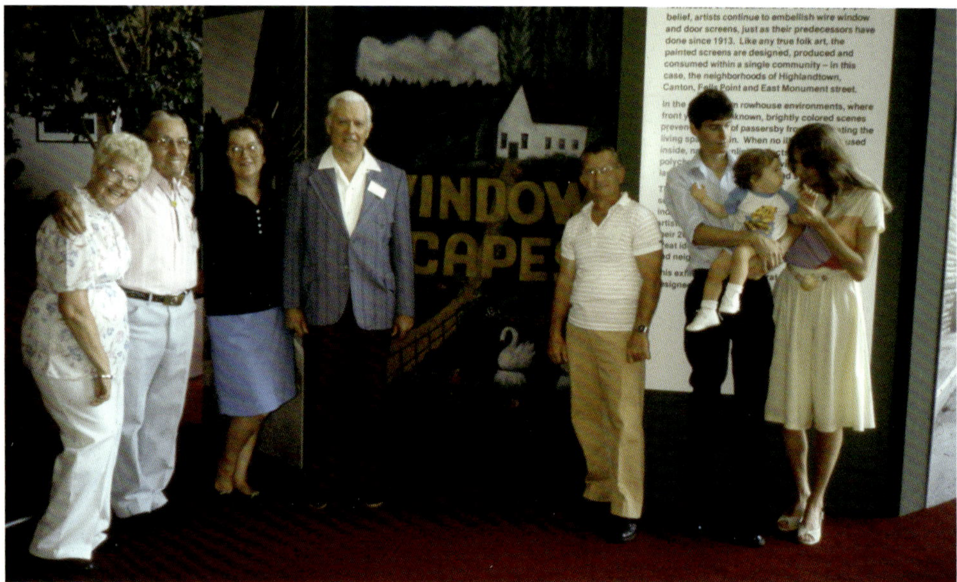

Windowscape, a screen-painting exhibition held as part of Baltimore's annual arts festival, Artscape, in 1984, brought together painters and confirmed to thousands of visitors that screen painting was alive and well. *Shown, left-to-right:* Ginny Milstead, Ted Richardson, Dee Herget, Frank Abremski, Tom Lipka, and Tilghman, Will, and Sonny Hemsley.

Tom Lipka has offered multi-week continuing education courses through Baltimore County Community College since 1996. Over the years screen painters such as Anna Pasqualucci and Lipka's apprentice (and daughter-in-law), Anna Lipka, have emerged from Tom's classes and gone on to teach in new venues and find untapped avenues for the distribution of their work. Dee Herget teaches workshops at senior centers and in elementary schools, hoping to return screen painting to its East Baltimore roots.

Those who proudly identify themselves as "screen painters" share, above all, an unwavering passion for Baltimore, its history, and its neighborhoods. Baltimore's conservative nature, holding onto and valuing its distinctive housing stock, has played a significant role in giving new generations of painters an uninterrupted context for their work. The persistence of ethnic enclaves and traditions created a constant reference point. Dee Herget noted that people prefer screens less for their privacy or art value than because their grandmothers had them. The past with which these artists choose to connect remains very present. Thirty years after William Oktavec's death, his oldest son and namesake noted, "One of these days, you'll probably see these things all around Baltimore again and you can think back and say, who started all of this? It's just like Babe Ruth and baseball. That's one thing I like about Baltimore, because things like this can exist and endure."[240]

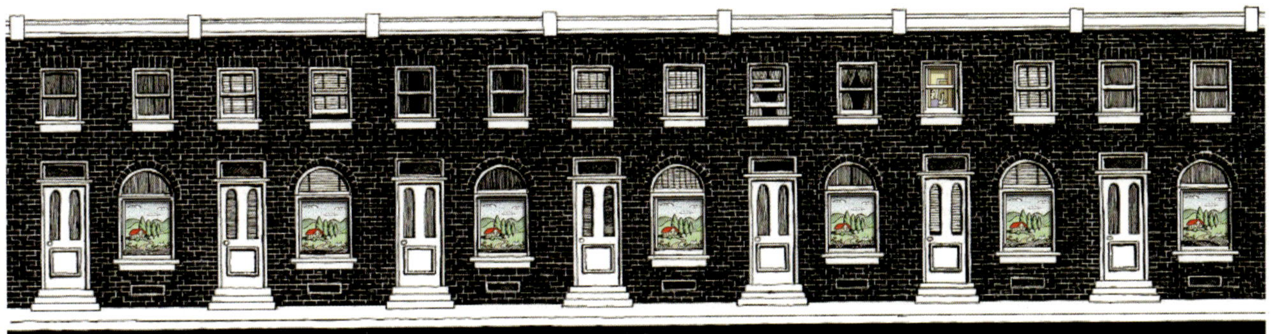

The Painted Screen Society of Baltimore

Design by Tim Goecke

Within a decade of Dee Herget's embrace of screen painting, and coinciding with my return to Baltimore to research the art form fulltime, I began to visit with each of the artists individually. It became clear that the painters did not know their counterparts, despite oblique encounters with one another over the years. The exceptions were those who had visited the Oktavec Art Shop and Dee Herget, who had gotten her start by visiting Ben Richardson. I was the single point of connection among the artists, and now they were eager to know one another.

An afternoon gathering at my Canton rowhouse brought together a group who became the nucleus of an informal guild of screen painters. Meeting informally for several years at local spots relevant to their work—a restaurant with an Alonzo Parks mural (since painted over), for example—the screen painters began to share information, agreeing at long last that they had much to learn from one another. Dee and I helped them develop what ultimately became the Painted Screen Society, a membership organization. Founded originally as the tongue-tying Society for the Preservation of Painted Screens, it became a nonprofit in 1985. As neighbors and former residents learned about the fledgling organization, they, too, wanted to be a part of it. At its height, as many as five hundred individuals and families claimed membership.

Owners, aficionados, and future painters of screens flocked to lectures, conversations, demonstrations, tours, and workshops. One of the earliest classes brought a half-dozen seasoned painters together to advise a classroom full of students at a local community center.

By the mid-1980s it was becoming increasingly difficult to keep up with the requests for presentations about painted screens. Slide lectures were the dominant format then. In late 1986, Ted Richardson went into Bayview Hospital where he was diagnosed with terminal prostate cancer, and we talked in his hospital room about making a film. He was ready to share his story, and particularly his love of screen painting. Although he had left his false teeth on a meal tray, never to be seen again, he was not deterred. Within a week of his return home, we assembled a crew to film a pilot. By the time grants were in hand, Ted had passed away, but seven other artists—Johnny Eck, Ben Richardson, Albert Oktavec, Frank Cipolloni, Tom Lipka, and Dee Herget—told their stories. Many others were also filmed at the time.[241]

The documentary, *The Screen Painters,* traces the art form's roots in interviews with William Oktavec's sons in the Art Shop shortly before it was shuttered. Artists at home and in their studios, screen owners, and admirers on the street add their voices to the twenty-eight-minute film, which premiered at Highlandtown's Patterson Theater on June 7 and 8, 1988. Two showings were required to accommodate the crowds. The governor and Maryland's Congressional delegation from Washington attended. Mounted police were stationed at the doors. It was a big night in East Baltimore. The film started its own publicity landslide and screen-painting renaissance, with articles in the *New York Times, Washington Post, Preservation News,*[242] and other national and international periodicals. The documentary was shown regionally on public television stations and in Canada, England, Scotland, Ireland, South Africa, and Australia. It won numerous awards including Cine Golden Eagle, UCLA Vitas, and American Association of State and Local History (AASLH) Award of Merit. It is available on DVD from the Painted Screen Society.

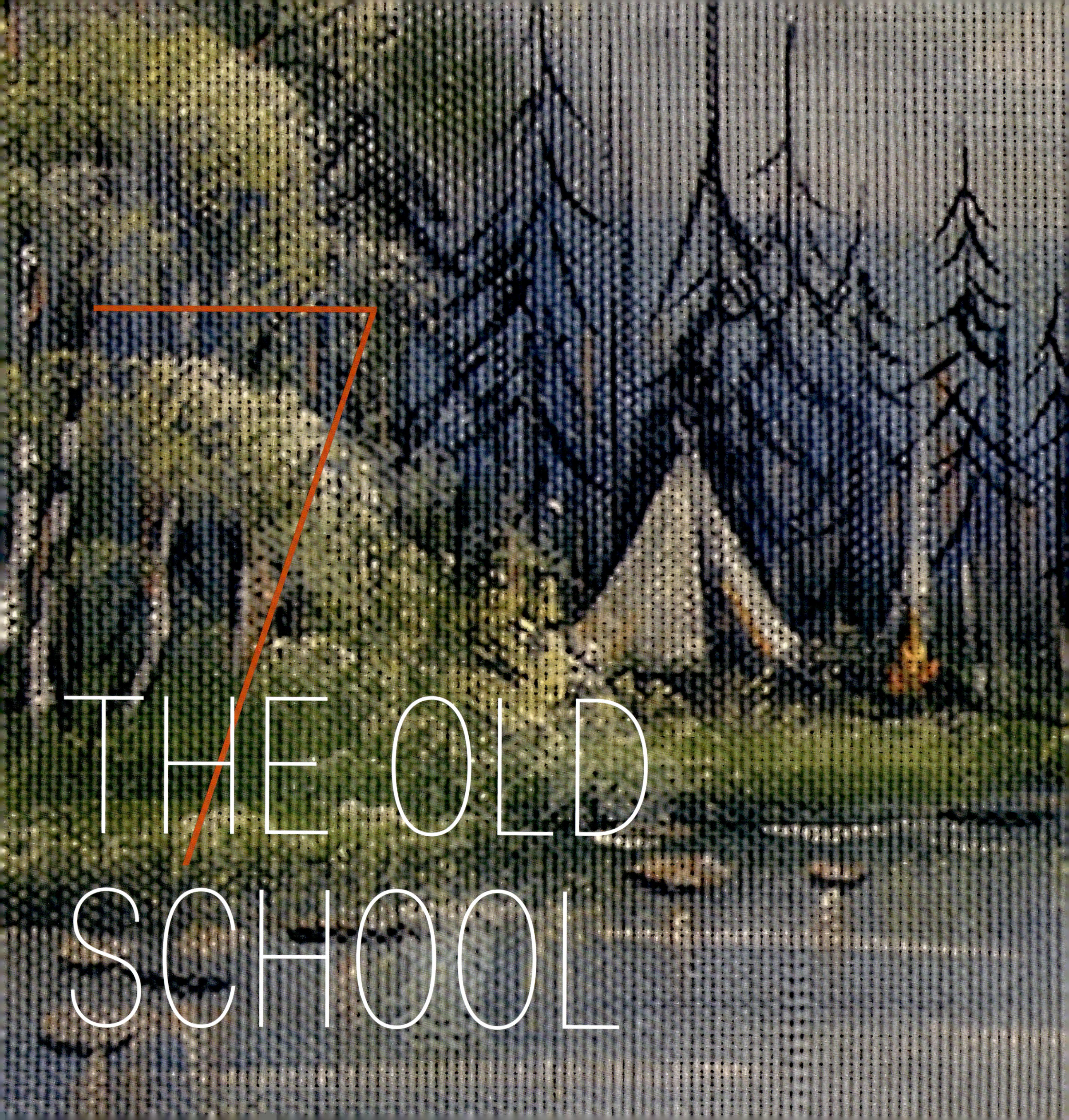
7
THE OLD
SCHOOL

THE MEN AND WOMEN WHO BUILT ON WILLIAM OKTAVEC'S LEGACY TO MAKE PAINTED SCREENS a staple of mid-twentieth-century Baltimore arrived at the art form via different paths. This group was drawn to the master and either knew or visited him in order to learn his tools and technique. For many, the urge to paint screens came and, as quickly, passed. It might occupy a lean time in transition to another moneymaking enterprise. For some it was in their blood, for others it felt like a calling.

THE INDEPENDENTS

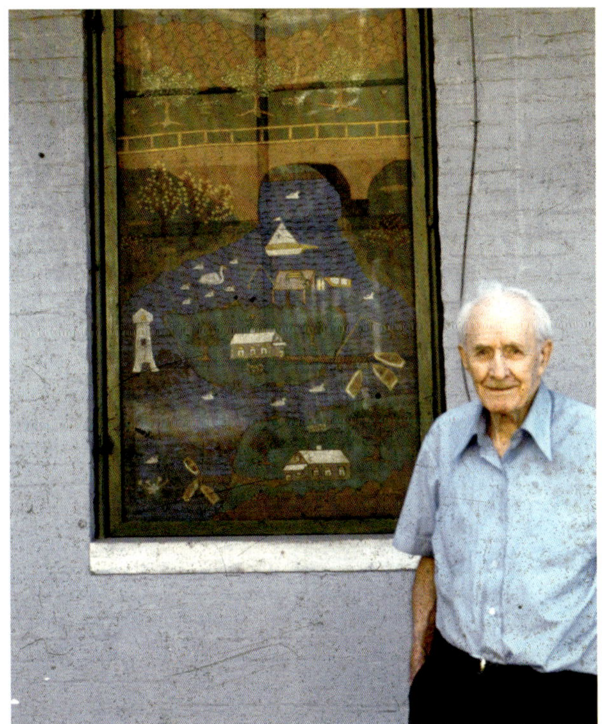

Frank Deoms was a paperhanger, crabber, printer, magician, and Punch-and-Judy show man who found work in unexpected places. Painted screens happened to be his neighborhood art form. He lived across Ashland Avenue from their birthplace and found an appreciative audience nearby. *Author photograph, 1974.*

FRANK DEOMS

(FEBRUARY 28, 1893–AUGUST 1979)

"Uh, oh, I got a job," said Frank Deoms, jack of many trades, who lived across Ashland Avenue from Oktavec's Grocery. He considered wallpaper hanging his primary occupation but, as was typical of many men of his era and of his class, he did not shy away from creative and independent work. Depending on the day or decade, he might admit to being a magician, crabber, printer, clown, or window screen painter. "I been everything, anything to make money. The first job I had I worked for a boss setting type and fixing presses. I never worked for any boss after that. I made up my own work and kept busy all the time."[243] "I been everywhere," he boasted, "All the way to New York, Brooklyn and Canada." His resourcefulness, typical of Depression-era survivors, knew no bounds, whether it was developing a Punch-and-Judy show or a carnival attraction out of nothing, or running bingo games or dances, he was eternally engaged in keeping himself and others entertained. He claimed to have taken "little" Johnny Eck around to tent shows before Eck had made a name for himself as a sideshow performer. One of his prouder midway cons centered on man's willingness to be fleeced. He intoned, "Tell your friends about it. See Lizzie Stripped." He separated men from their admission fees, filling fairground tents to capacity many times, to reveal behind a red-velvet curtain, a Model T Ford, known to all as a Tin Lizzie—stripped to its meager frame.[244]

For twenty-seven years he crabbed in season, using a simple trotline, from his weekend getaway, a shore house on the nearby Chesapeake Bay. When he sold that house, he needed another way to bring in easy money. "I was riding around the block and I see the numbers on the houses and some of them were half wore out and all. And I looked…a job." He imagined a future in much-needed nocturnal house identification. His "illuminization" project never saw the light of day since he insisted it required a family member to double-team the whole block. The idea that a helper would leave and start a competing business was a constant fear.

He watched the colorful screens proliferate all around him from his youth into his later years and was keenly aware of their benefits, but why, he pondered, should he "pay Oktavec fifty cents when I could do it myself?" And why would he paint the redundant red bungalow when he "could paint scenes of people swimming and fishing and having a good time?" He made his way to the Art Shop for insights into the art and came away empty.

Deoms's classroom instead was the sidewalk; his teachers, the itinerants.

Fellow used to sit there on the street about an hour and a half and he's done. But he painted a little teeny house, red roof, white, you know, everything, trees…so fast. Buncha trees. Little clouds up there. Maybe something with a little bit of water. And he's doin' it so fast. You gotta get a little experience in it. If I were to do it all the time, I'd be getting different ideas all the time…and practice on it and go faster. That's the main thing. 'Cause the way I do 'em, what I do takes a real while. You take a house out here with that porch all around it. You can't smack it out like a tree. A tree is easy to make. But when you're drawing a house like that you gotta put those windows in and different colors and all. It takes a little while.

Deoms painted in the privacy of his rowhouse cellar, a crowded space he did not readily share with visitors. He fabricated his own fancifully colored wooden strip frames for rectangular basement screens or added his signature bright hues to aluminum models and distributed them to his neighbors, who were happy to receive them. He was downright impish and admitted that he neglected to tell his friends who lived behind him that the privacy feature did not work when lights were on inside their daughters' upstairs bedroom.

By the mid-1970s, Richard Oktavec was charging $18 for a standard-sized window screen that today might cost $75 to $100. Deoms claimed he would "do them for nothing until I get my hand in 'em. I'd go nuts if I didn't get some screens for the winter." He vowed that the next season he would begin to charge, "No more free stuff." After all, his neighbors were getting all new replacement windows and screens so he'd have plenty of business, but he would "charge for the paint only."

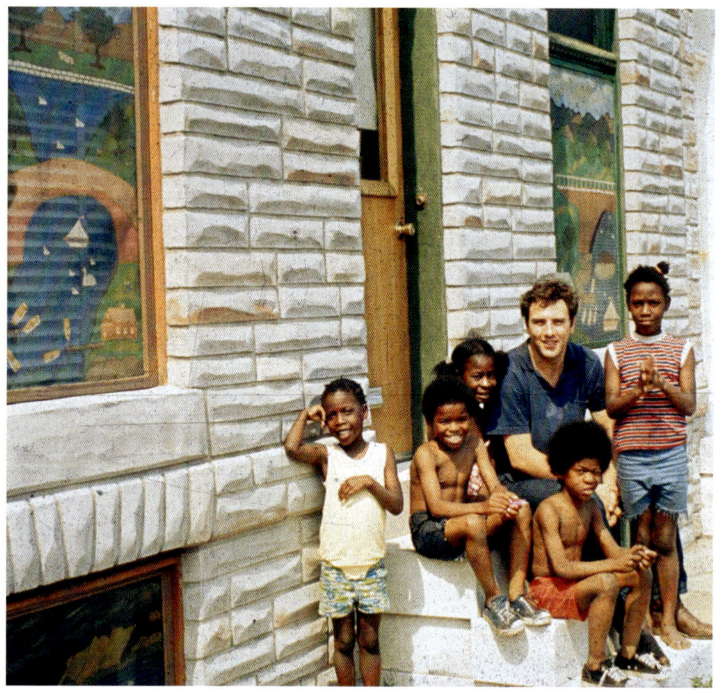

Deoms's screens brought joy to the blocks he decorated. Bruce Johnson, former director of the Museum of American Folk Art in New York, found them the perfect backdrop with companions for afternoon stoop sitting. *Author photograph, 1975.*

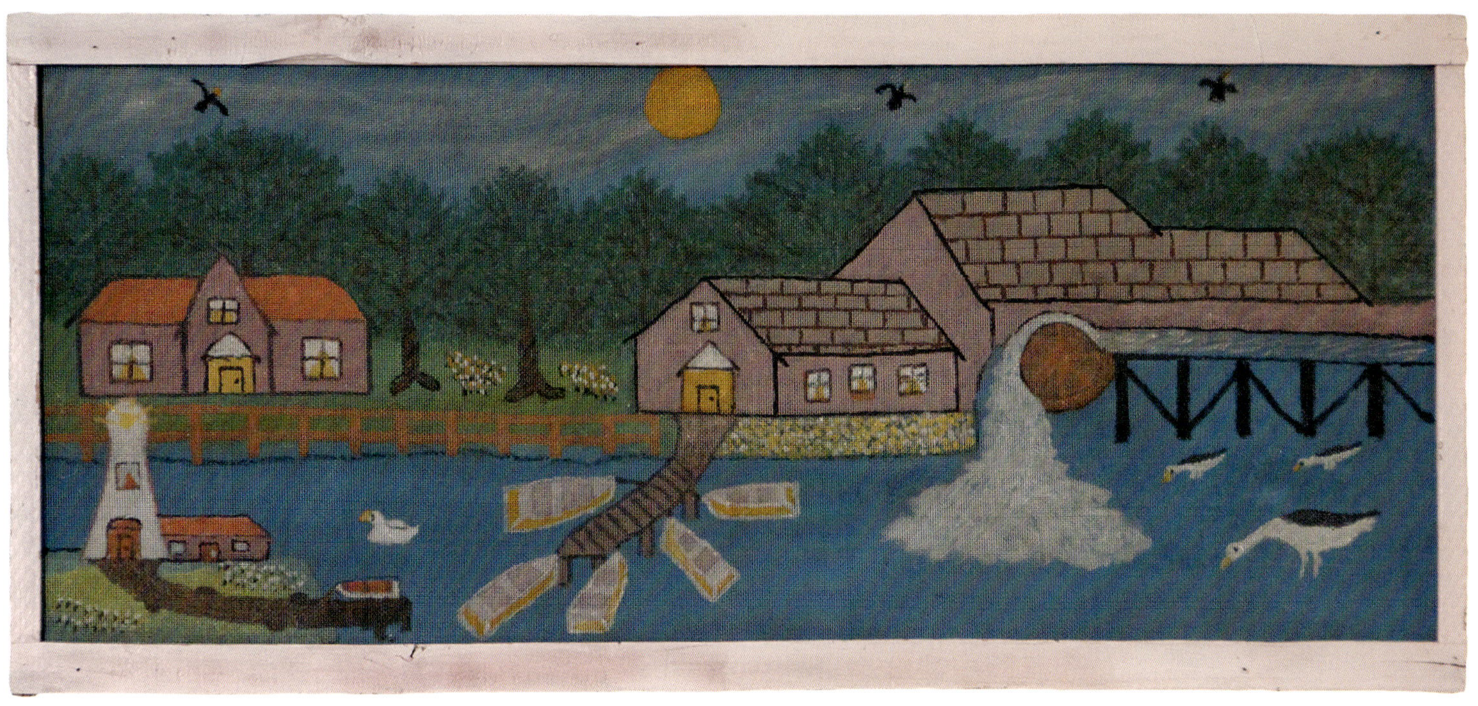

Deoms crafted his own frames out of strips of wood when necessary for his one-of-a-kind screens like this basement screen. His "ideas come from everywhere." *Author's collection. Christine Fillat photograph.*

Like most of the screen painters, Deoms was self-taught and averse, if not downright hostile, to the idea of using someone else's method. Unable to coax any information from the Oktavecs, he walked down the block from the Art Shop to Bauer's Hardware, one of the dozens in East Baltimore, to learn about paints. He used no primer. "I take chalk and draw it up on a screen, get it right where it belongs. Draw the house first or what I want in the center. Nice and neat. The ground where you want, the water, clouds. Chalk it all out first. It's nothing to it." As for the paint, he was advised "to use white semi gloss enamel to thin paint and color with tube paint, make paint thin and use driers on the side to help it dry faster." He advised taking "an ice pick to punch out holes. Varnish for shine. No turpentine. Never."

His work was unlike anyone else's. He railed against the little red-roofed cottage in the midst of the painting. "I like a house with something on it." Instead, he envisioned the screen as a place of constant human activity, whether on land or water. "If you once get a thing looks good for the center, the rest comes to you. Gotta have a house, little roads . . ." Nothing from his own experience but "ideas out of books and from television...a long open drawbridge for the center and a yacht coming down. Ducks and launches and the green all around. White and pink." His scenes fit the expectations of admirers steeped in the work of Grandma Moses or the emerging primitive folk art genre of the 1970s. In East Baltimore, his work was the exception and found no adherents other than his Ashland Avenue neighbors. "It seems like what I do, they like them." And the price was right.

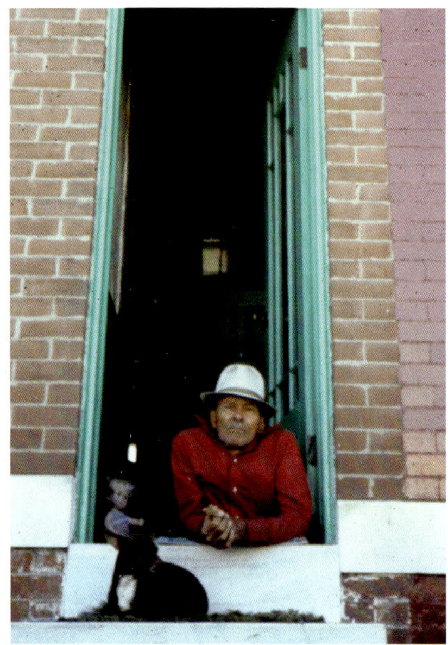

Johnny Eck could be found most days holding court on his front steps. When guests arrived, his stoop became a salon. Reds, his dog, was always in attendance. *Author photograph, 1979.*

JOHNNY ECK

(AUGUST 27, 1911–JANUARY 5, 1991)

Among the services offered at Oktavec's Art Shop were classes in a variety of hands-on techniques central to their business. Students were selected for their likelihood to continue working on site or on custom jobs as part of Oktavec's one-screen-at-a-time neighborhood beautification program and on church contracts around the region. His protégés rarely traveled farther than a few blocks to attend the classes.

Johnny Eck, who lived around the corner, described his "natural condition to be an artist." He was eleven when the Art Shop opened its doors in 1922. The Eckhardts, Alsatian-American mother, German-American shipyard carpenter father, two sons, and daughter, lived a few houses below the Monument Street commercial corridor at 622 North Milton Avenue. John and his twin brother Rob ("born twenty minutes earlier") were forbidden from becoming "wallpaper artists around the house. Crayons and stuff like that was taboo."[245] Their early works were limited to watercolor on paper. "Excellent penmen" as well, the boys began classes with Oktavec as soon as the sign advertising "Art Lessons" appeared in the converted rowhouse storefront's "one big window." Mother Emelia frequented the shop to buy supplies for her own paper and fiber craft projects, and she took her son along. A prescient aunt, aware of the boys' need "sooner or later to make a living," encouraged them to take classes. "She could see the future," Johnny remarked.

[Oktavec] had a class and he offered me to come around and to teach me. Having nothing to lose and everything to gain, I went. I went and took art lessons, fifty cents a class…[painting] on hard cover compoboard [masonite]. The canvas glued on heavy poster board hadn't come out yet, but there were some beautiful colors. I got a darn good set of oil tubes from Mr. Oktavec at a good discount. I got a rebate on my art lessons even though he had two or three of us at one time. That's how I started painting pictures…I went around there about two or three weeks and he looked at me one time and he said, "Look, I am not taking your money. I've got five here that they don't know what they are doing. You already know the answers. You can come around and it is entirely up to you."

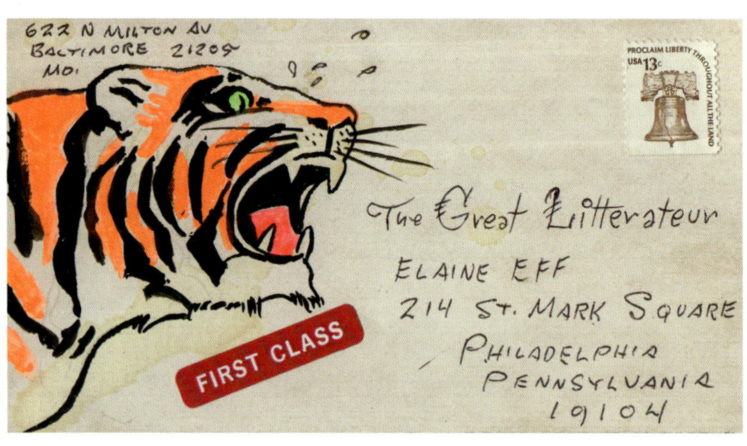

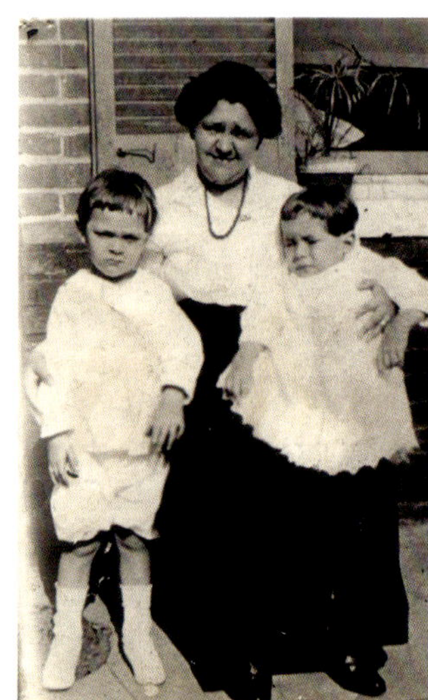

LEFT
Johnny Eck began drawing at an early age with materials supplied by his father. He rarely sent a piece of mail without elaborating it in some way. *Author's collection.*

RIGHT
Emelia Eckhardt, "the most wonderful mother in the world," and twin sons Rob and John in the backyard of their Milton Avenue home, circa 1914. *Courtesy of the Johnny Eck Museum.*

Johnny Eck's formal training at Oktavec's side lasted but two seasons. "His hours around there were nine in the morning to nine at night, six days a week…He would teach us how to paint and then he'd wait on the store at the same time. And in the back of the store, up on a higher level, that was his studio." Oktavec "was just beginning to get into screens in a big way. He was the only one. But they kept everything under wraps. Everything was secret."

John was torn between a life in art and life as an entertainer, another area where he considered himself a "natural" because he was born "different from the rest," without the lower half of his body. Perfectly healthy otherwise, what he lacked in limbs he more than made up for in personality. He was eighteen inches tall. He walked on his hands before his twin was on two feet. He propelled himself with his well-developed arms, wearing gloves when warranted, and used homemade wheeled transports akin to present-day skateboards. As he matured, he owned miniature hand-operated cars. When he complained to his mother that he might never climb a tree, she assured him that, as an artist, he "could always paint one."

Prone to action rather than self-pity as a youngster, he capitalized upon his condition by volunteering at a church-sponsored magic show. He recalled how "a white figure with a little white sweater come down the aisle on two hands, climbed up over the crowd" and he "flew up on that stage like a big bird, grabbed the magician's tablecloth and took off," as his "dear mother fainted." "The magician said to my brother, 'Why, he is worth a fortune.'" His career as a magician, mud show, circus, and sideshow performer and movie star was launched that day. Eck's formal education ended at about the same time. By age twelve he had already skipped ahead two grades and become an accomplished typist. "The educators agreed that I knew it all." The elder Eckhardts' notion that their son might have a career as a stenographer was quickly dashed.

Johnny thought otherwise. "I have seen too many of these unusual people called 'freaks.' And back in those days you had to exhibit yourself to make a living. There was no welfare, no free food. No free milk, you had to go out and work." He and Rob left Baltimore with their parents' blessings to join Peerless Shows and later, Ringling Brothers Barnum and Bailey, Cole Brothers, and Ripley's Believe it or Not! At one point, John traveled from town to town in his own train car. Though far from home, he found himself among "his people" for the first time. He crossed North America with freaks and carnies as well as unscrupulous managers. His act capitalized on his skills as a juggler, animal handler, acrobat, trapeze artist, Punch-and-Judy man, cartoonist, typist, and screen painter. Rob was almost always by his side. His banners dubbed him "King of the Freaks" and "Johnny Eck, the Half Boy [later Half Man], Eighth Wonder of the World." By 1932 he was discovered by Hollywood agents and featured in early *Tarzan* films and Tod Browning's 1932 cult classic *Freaks*.

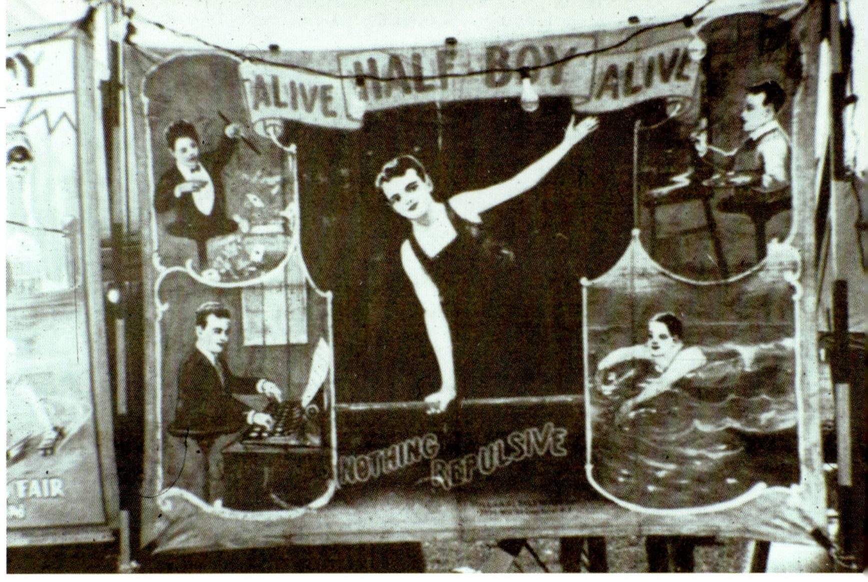

Eck's dream was to have his own side-show and professionally made banners. His dream came true when he joined Ringling Brothers Barnum and Bailey, Cole Brothers, and Ripley's Believe it or Not! shows. *Courtesy of the Johnny Eck Museum.*

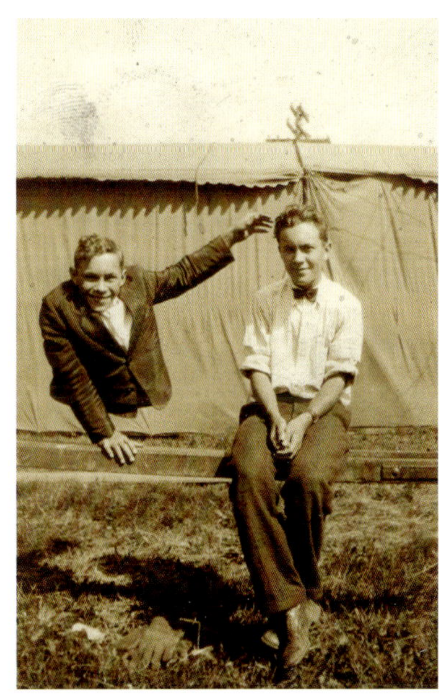

Johnny Eck and brother Rob were rarely apart. They worked together, toured together, and lived together their entire lives. *Courtesy of the Johnny Eck Museum.*

Disheartened by his motion picture experience and by disreputable managers who left him feeling violated and without control of his career, he and Rob returned to Baltimore and their North Milton Avenue home in the mid-1930s. During this period the brothers spent a short time painting scenes on screens at the behest of "people up the street. We got the magnificent sum of two dollars [and] it was an immediate success." "I love to make people happy. Whether it is stories or illustrating or doing magic." They learned an early lesson in their rendering of an exquisite sailing boat.

It was a big screen, of about three by four feet. But we weren't too good on picking the colors. We used the colors we had down in our paint department—far from what I am using today. We painted this huge sailing ship and then we forgot…. We failed to varnish it. Which the result was, after being weathered by the sunlight, naturally it bleached. It started to fade. But after that we got on to it. We went around to Mr. Oktavec, even though they were reluctant to let you know any of the secrets, and they would also give you bum steers. They would not tell you what paint to use. They wouldn't tell about the background or type of paint—trial and error.

Despite John's early training at Oktavec's side, the brothers quickly learned that "screen painting is all secrets, the same as magic. It was a family secret."

For that first screen they had chosen a maritime scene because their "father worked all his life on the waterfront and naturally we were always interested in painting boats and building model boats, which was to change in later years, when we got away from the boats and started to collect trains."

Among the creative enterprises that took them out of Baltimore between the 1930s and 1950s was a portable penny arcade they purchased and a miniature "big magnificent streamliner" train they toured locally. In addition, the pair conducted an orchestra and painted screens, many for the Art Shop.

The relationships established from boyhood visits to the Art Shop, however, sustained Eck for a lifetime. Johnny's considerable talents were nurtured and invigorated there. Both he and Rob became a part of Oktavec's growing family of four sons, both at work and at play. While Rob went on to specialize in stained glass, John was tapped early on to apply the white undercoat on screen commissions. He eventually worked alongside the youngest of Oktavec's four sons, Richard, who became his closest friend and mentor. Years later when the seasonal backlog of screens overwhelmed him, Pop carried the boys to his shore home to help out. As Eck remembered, "Oh, he had a big place down there, down the country…he had a big barn down there." Oktavec's invitation was informal: "I'll tell you what. If you want,

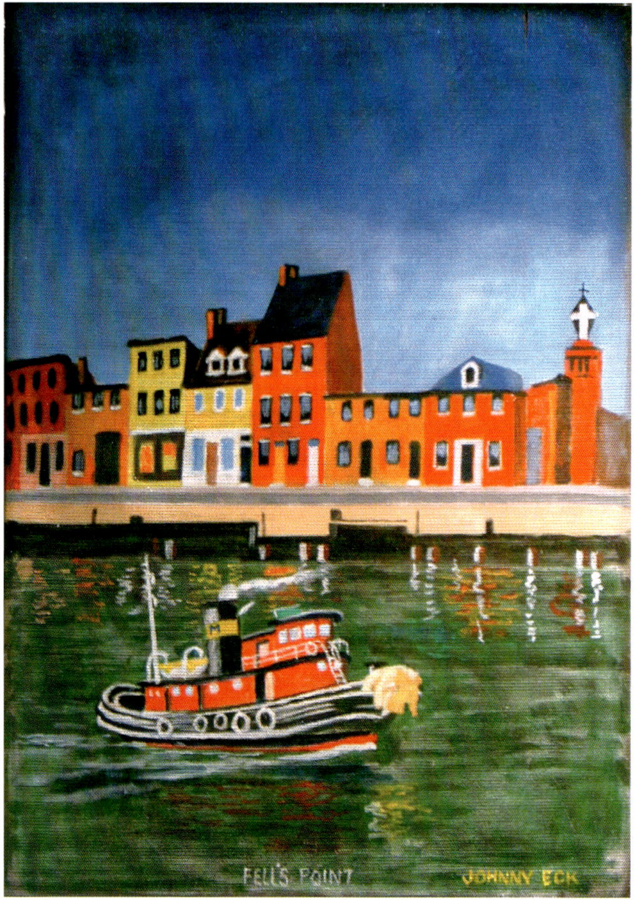

The resident tugboats of Fell's Point's Thames Street were a popular subject for screens by every artist. Johnny Eck's reputation as the *fauve* of screen painting is evident here. *Johnny Eck Museum Collection.*

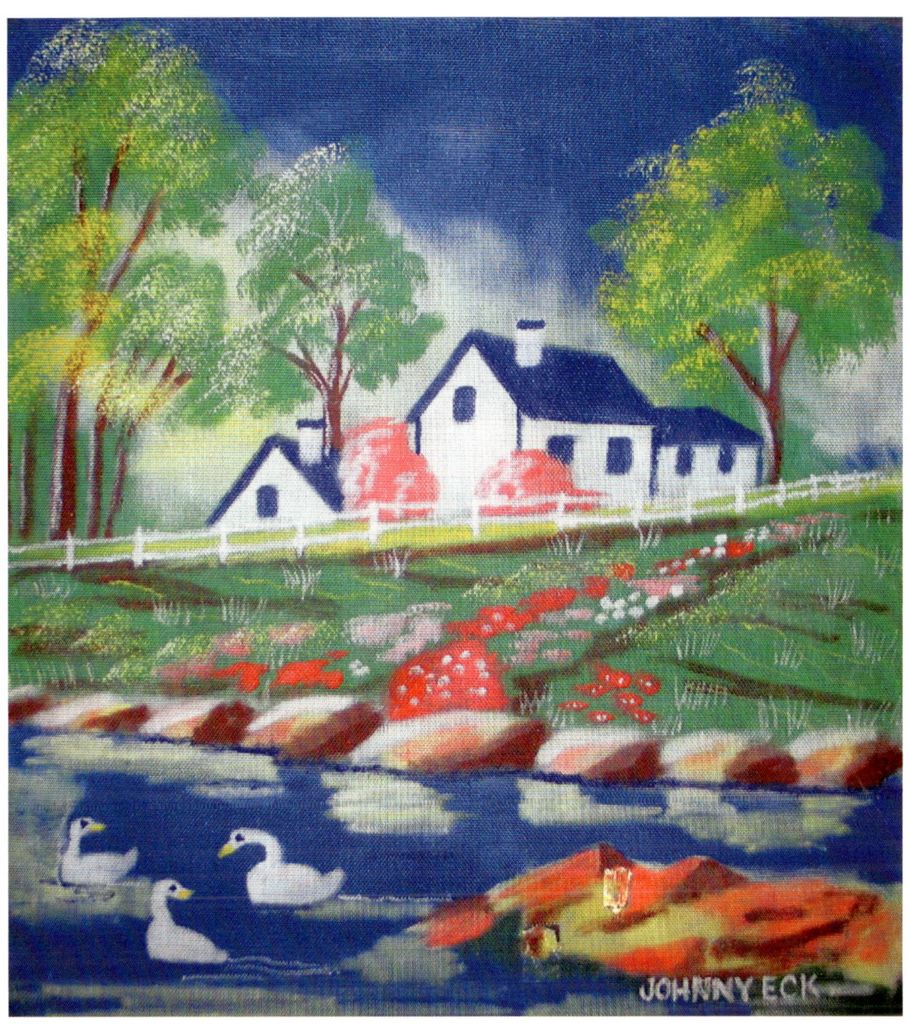

Eck enjoyed shaking things up by offering a blue roof on his bungalow if his customers did not specify a preference. *Author's collection. Edwin Remsberg photograph.*

when Richard comes down to the country place, I've got a lot of screens down there. How would you like to help me down there?"

"White coat?" And I said, "I'm your man." He was a wonderful man. He made you feel like you were wanted. Every time I went down there the first thing he would say was, "Son, I am so glad you came. It is kind of lonesome down here." This was prior to his second marriage in 1947. He said, "I know you fellows are kind of tired and hungry but that is alright. I'll get your dinner ready. But now is refreshment time. Richard, I have something for you." He would bring him out a quart of ice cream. And then Mr. Oktavec would say, "John, you and I sit over here under this tree. We are the men. You have a cold beer and I will drink with you." Never once did I go down there that that man didn't treat us. It was always one cold beer to start. And then we would have dinner.

When the elder Oktavec died in 1956, Rich became the screen painter in the family. Johnny and Rob came back from the road permanently about that time, and the Art Shop, then owned by the four Oktavec brothers, pressed Johnny into service to keep up with the backlog of screen orders. Now under Rich's tutelage he was summoned to complete the entire scene, and the buyer never suspected that it was not an original Oktavec, despite its distinctive flamboyant style and palette.

Many times I came to his [Oktavec's] aid and helped when he got into a jackpot. I used to do his backgrounds and do his white coat. Nobody wanted to do that. That's the most dull part of painting. Even Rich wouldn't do it. Richard wouldn't do a winter scene either, a snow scene. He would send them all over to me. Then towards the last, he was sending me all kinds of work, which I appreciate.

Johnny noted that he lived "on the poorest block in East Baltimore," one so lacking in amenities that at the height of the fad "there were only about six screens on Milton Avenue and only in the front windows"—a stark contrast to the typical blocks in adjacent Little Bohemia and Highlandtown, where every window and door, front and back, sported a handmade work of art by Oktavec or any of the multiplying corps of artists who plied the streets in search of commissions. Eck's screen-painting career started in earnest in the 1950s when a neighbor suffering from a disfiguring illness sought privacy from sidewalk oglers.

We got a call. It was for a man up the street. He was not long for the world, so the woman come here and said, "You fellows, would you paint a picture? It's a rush job." I think he had something like the elephant man disease where you get all kind of bumps all over your face and arms and hands. He enjoyed sitting in the window. He was living on borrowed time, and the woman comes up and asked Rob if he could help her do something that her husband could look out the window and enjoy the summer and cool breeze without the people looking and gawking in at him. Rob said, "I got just the thing for you." So he came in and we went through our catalog of pictures and he picked that one out. It was a mountain with a log cabin and water and everything…And in two days' time it was ready. It took in the whole window. Perfect. For two years, that man looked out at the people and the traffic and the sights, but they couldn't look in and see him.

Screen painting would occupy Johnny Eck the remainder of his life. Though trained by the masters, whose subdued style defined their work, Johnny could not help but deviate from the prescribed Red Bungalow format. The colors he chose were unusually vibrant. He credited a banner artist he had met at a big carnival in Pennsylvania with introducing him to "Ronan. The House of Color" brand, sign painters' bulletin colors that he affectionately likened to "painting with a can of syrup." Though costly, he swore by their luscious jewel-like hues throughout his career. His buildings, trees, lawns, and animals seemed to fly off the screen. Bold, brilliant shots of color covering large areas, nothing delicate, identified his singular style. Not confined by outlines, his orgy of color might be compared to the *Fauves*, the "wild beasts" of the Impressionist era. Just to prove he was not bound by rules, despite his training, he slapped pure royal blue roofs on his bungalows for approving customers who might also be willing to buck the Red (roof) Bungalow tradition.

I like bright colors. Most of my clouds are yellow with just a touch of white and sometimes, if I am in a good mood, I will have the sun going down or coming up. It depends on if you just got out of bed or are just going to bed. The red streaks will make it really good. And of course, the flowers…I have a book in here that shows you all the colored pictures. It is a seed catalogue. But I am not interested in seeds, I am interested in flowers. So that is where the flowers come from.

For the most part, his colors came "right out of the can. Why? Saves time. It takes time to put a stick in there and drop it down and put another one there and then take a palette knife, that little blade, and stir it. For the highly technical colors that actually

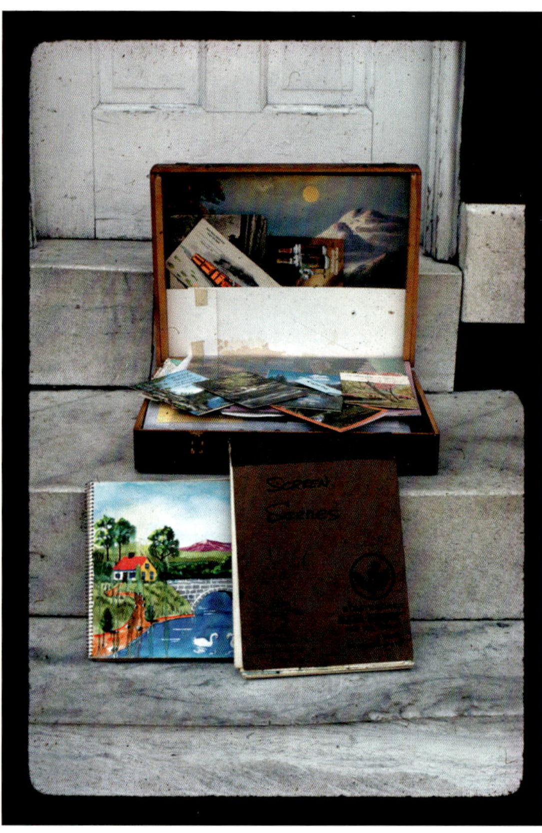

Johnny Eck's "idea box" was an easily portable briefcase in which he collected clippings and cards for future painting or drawing projects and notebooks for his own artwork. *Author photograph, 1979.*

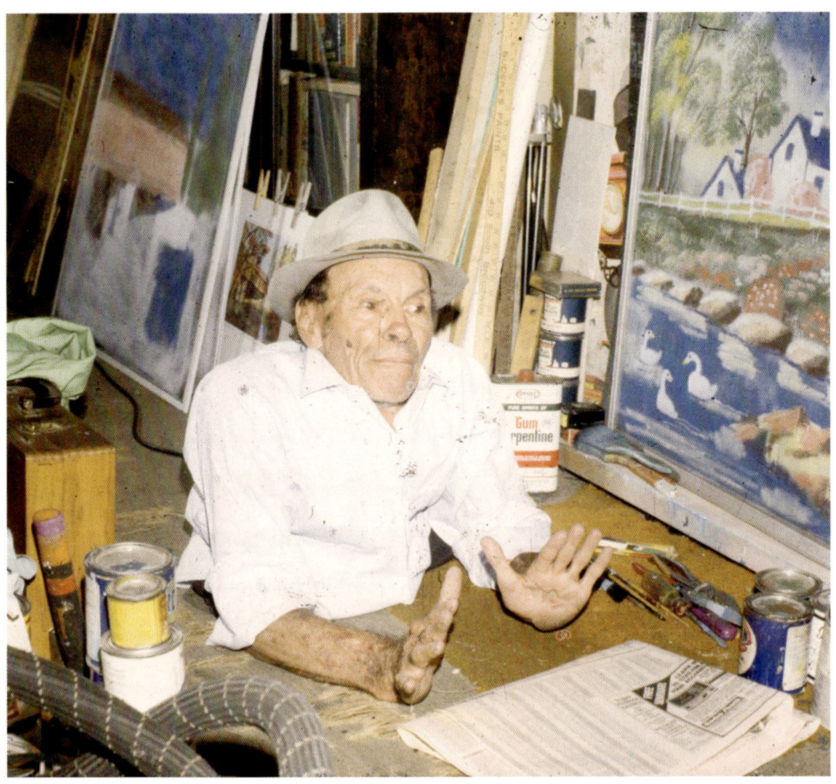

Eck created a space at the foot of the stairs at the entrance to the house for his painting studio. The wall was his easel. *Author photograph, 1984.*

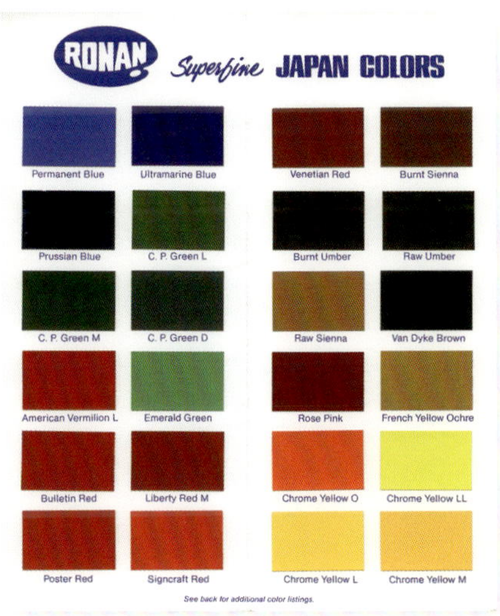

Eck never scrimped on materials. He chose costly Ronan brand Pure Japan colors, valued by sign painters for their brightness and sheen. *Edwin Remsberg photograph.*

need mixing, I can mix my own. There is one color that no man can ever mix. Violet. Purple. You must buy it."

Rather than using a palette, and "to keep the 'fast-drying paint' from drying in the can, I only open up three cans at one time, no more. And I put so much paint out on the newspaper and immediately cover the cans, hand tight so the air don't start a skin."

His studio was "wherever I put the screen. That is where I would paint. In the front room against the front door, in the middle room, against the stairwell, against the door inside I am completing one right now in back of me. I just put newspaper down and use it as a palette. When clean-up time comes, roll the paper up and that is it."

He realized early on that his customers rarely came with pictorial demands. "The more I showed them, the longer it took them to make up their minds, so I decided from now on in, no more than four [to select from] and if they are not satisfied, bring your own [picture] and I will be glad to do it."

His ideas come from a variety of printed sources.

I get so much mail around Christmas, Easter, and my birthday. And I never throw the cards away. They are all collected and taken out of the envelopes and put in cigar boxes. This is why when you go through the house you will see dozens and dozens of cigar boxes. Each box has its own category: Bungalows, white, blue roof. Mountains, trees, then come the animals. Quite a few people like animals. Mostly colored people like wild cats, tigers, lions, polar bears. And flowers…I wouldn't sit there and dream it up out of my head. Very few people do…Why should I make up a picture when it's already made? Greeting cards. I don't copy it exact. Change the house a little bit, move the chimney. But I don't paint people—little people walking around. Nope.

Johnny Eck was an avid letter writer, and relished receiving illustrated notes and cards of every description. His collection from friends nationwide not only built his catalog of potential sources for his artwork, but attested also to his "million-dollar" personality and a natural inclination to maintain friendships over years and miles. His lifelong fascination with epistolary forms may be attributable to a childhood game, "a little cardboard box that opened up and became a miniature post office complete with envelopes, stamps, paper." From their basement window's store/post office "we sold our cards, handmade, including an envelope for two cents apiece." Throughout his life, few missives left his hand that did not contain a caricature or full-color rendering with a personal reference. Along the perimeter of his living room studio he piled his cigar boxes brimming with greeting cards, seed catalogs, calendars, and magazine clippings. Stacks of *National Geographic* magazines lined the stairs of the slender rowhouse. A wooden artist's box disguised as his attaché case, overflowing with his favorite images, was always close by. Realism was his specialty. Action scenes were his calling card.

> Old mill with a boat, I make the wheel move. When the water is pouring out of the little buckets, it's splashing. The easiest picture to paint for me is an animal, like a tiger. Coming down a mountain getting ready to take a drink, or lazing up on an edge covered with snow and ice looking at you with his big green eyes and a paw ready to swat you…. This is a snow picture with big trees on each side of a frigid-looking creek running through the center and by looking at it, you can almost hear the water and ice crunching.

Among Eck's earliest screens was "a full red clipper ship bursting through the blue water and all the white sails puffed out. Big flying streamers on the top waving and a light blue sky. Clouds spilling across the air. It was beautiful." He remembers, "I've had requests to paint lighthouses … And it must have the light blinking. [He winks.] I've had buoys in the water with a yacht racing around it. With the buoys got to light up and sway." He had no need to invent scenes when they were readily available. If asked whether he drew his images from memory or copied them, he readily admitted to being "a cheater—like most people today." He used "a prompt sheet" to provide a rough outline. He longed to own a Project-A-Scope that cast images onto the surface of a painting from a transparency, another secret weapon he learned about by watching banner artists. He saw one in use in the able hands of the Oktavecs, father and sons.

Eck was proud that he never advertised, "Mouth to mouth advertising only." While his competition placed classifieds in the weekly *Guide,* he was content to let his work speak for itself. His home's oversized first-floor parlor window looked out on a busy street. Its location across from a post office and en route to the Monument Street shopping district made it the ultimate showcase for a screen painter. His business plan depended on quick turnaround, cash and carry only. He would no sooner place a newly completed screen in the window when someone would come and purchase it on the spot. He enjoyed the interaction and negotiation as much as the process of making art. "Truthfully I like to paint on screens because it's big. And the bigger the picture, the more detail you can put into it and it becomes third dimension. To me it's fun, it's easy and you get to know people. And everybody that gets a screen here, my customers, they always come back."

Eck was one of the few painters who put his "John Henry" on his screens, proudly signing his work. His customers came, not only from word of mouth, or having glimpsed his screens in nearby windows but from a stealth source as well. He had "a secret weapon" at the

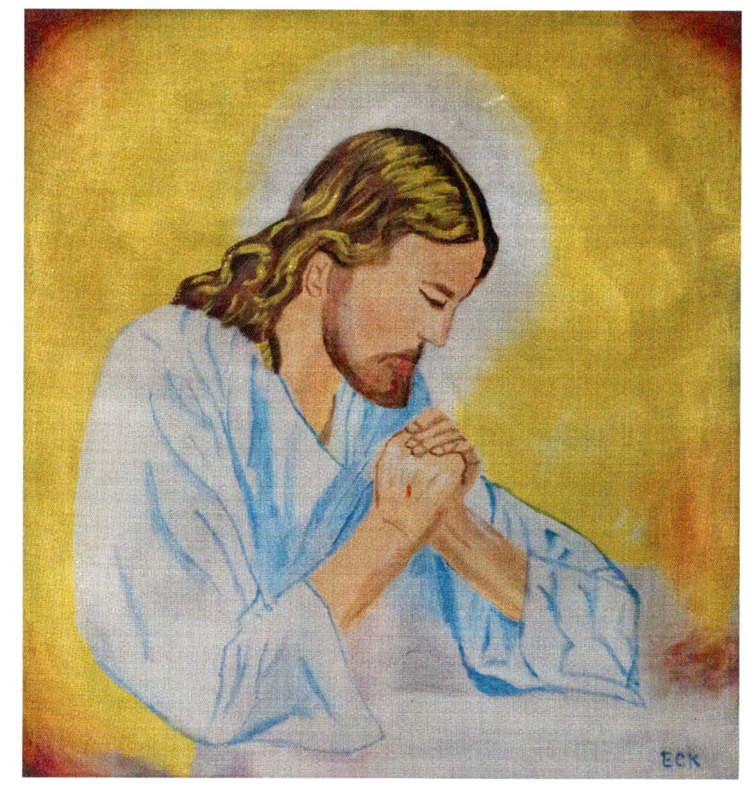

Jesus Christ was considered off-limits as a subject for screens by many of Johnny Eck's neighbors and other screen artists. He, however, considered Christ as a protector and an added crime deterrent in the increasingly unsavory environs of Milton Avenue. *Collection of the Painted Screen Society of Baltimore, Inc. Christine Fillat photograph.*

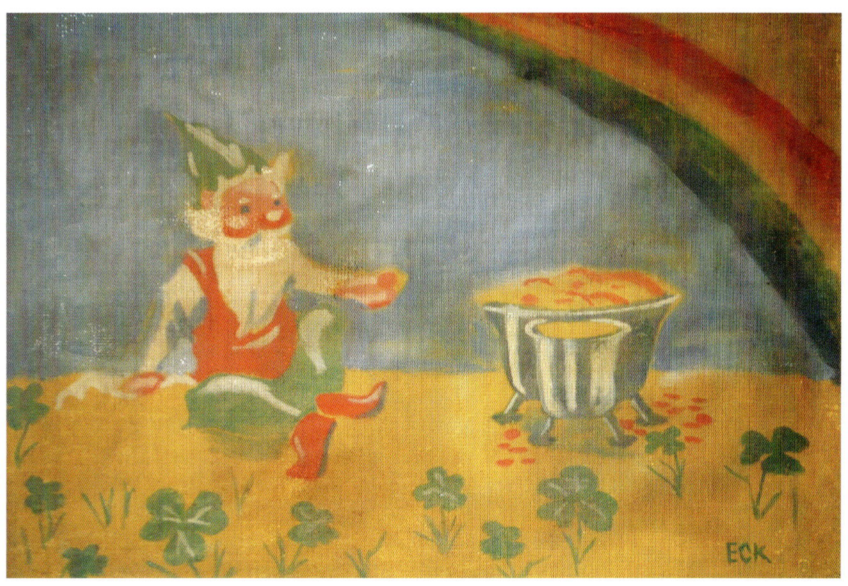

Johnny regularly displayed completed screens in his front window to attract buyers. His final screen portrayed omens for luck and wealth, both in short supply during his last years, 1989. *Courtesy of the Johnny Eck Museum.*

Art Shop. On numerous occasions, referrals came from brother Rob, who, while employed there, would either slip a hasty note with "622 North Milton" or discreetly whisper to "go around on Milton Avenue and there's a man who will paint it." Should a disappointed customer fail to find satisfaction at the hand of the Oktavecs, as on one occasion when excessive turpentine caused an artwork to fade in a matter of weeks, or if their desired subject matter was not in the Oktavec repertoire, Johnny was always eager to rise to the challenge.

Among his specifically requested pieces were snowscapes and religious scenes—which other artists avoided because winter scenes were tedious and religious topics invited criticism. Eck welcomed the neighborhood discussions that his depictions of Jesus Christ initiated. He painted numerous large door screens with imitations of Monet's water lilies for a San Francisco doctor and a Philadelphia lawyer. Few subjects were off-limits to him. However, he refused to paint nudes, considering them unacceptable for screens. Between fulfilling orders for upwards of forty screens a season and operating an active sign painting business out of the basement window, John patched together a livelihood in art that lasted a lifetime.

To enter the clutter of 622 North Milton Avenue and see the painter at floor level, brush in hand, using the stairway as his easel was to see a happy man. His living room studio served him well for decades. He welcomed visitors to watch him work, warning them "just don't kick the can of paint over." But he always imagined his ideal spot:

> Something that would be, oh, a little bigger than this. I would have a room, have my own studio where I could move around and have all my equipment on the side of the wall with, if I wanted, books or pictures or my paints. If you look around in here, you'll see paints spread all over the house, brushes here, brushes there. Course, I know where they are ... Course I would like to have a stream or pond or a little body of water.

In his later years, he limited the entertainment to the front stoop "stage" or outdoor salon, where he greeted youngsters and adult visitors from down the block and around the world with a musical "Hel-lo," a sky-high wave, and a smile that was unforgettable. Just over his right shoulder was the last screen he perched in his window, showing a leprechaun dancing alongside his pot of gold where a rainbow ended.

RUTH CHRYSAM
(NOVEMBER 5, 1913-FEBRUARY 5, 1998, BROOKLYN, NEW YORK)

Another of Oktavec's outstanding disciples was Ruth Chrysam, a neighborhood youngster of German descent who had great promise and even greater passion. She shared her story in a 1982 letter:

> I was born (in 1913) at 137 N. Montford Avenue in North East Baltimore. The youngest of nine children. Attended St. Michael's School at Lombard and Wolfe Streets. It was here the nuns discovered my aptitude for art and suggested to my mother further schooling at the Institute of Notre Dame. Here I majored in art under Sister M. Sabine. Upon graduation in 1930 the depression had set in. Employment opportunities were virtually non-existent, especially in the art field. I was fortunate in meeting Mr. Oktavec who operated an art store a few blocks from my home. I prevailed upon him to employ me as an apprentice to learn the fundamentals of Commercial Art. Some of the seasonal and year round art consisted of picture framing, religious statuary painting, gold leaf application, signs, air brushing, engrossing of diplomas, wood carving and window screen painting…. After working in Mr. Oktavec's shop for four years I opened my own business (Ruth's Art Shop) in the basement of my parents' home at 141 N. Montford Avenue. At least five months of the year were devoted entirely to screen painting. Forest scenes with lots of depth were my favorite subjects, although anything requested was painted. I took great pride in painting each screen for they had to be done to perfection before giving to the customer, plus typed instructions for preservation such as scrubbing with soap and water every two weeks during the summer. This is why my screens remained in good condition for years. Dirt eating into the paint makes it appear as if it's fading. Sunlight has nothing to do with fading as so many people think. There were often amateur painters who went from door to door painting screens. They offered low prices but very poor workmanship. I must add here each artist had their own particular style of painting…. Attended night school for four years at the Maryland Institute studying Costume Designing and graduated in 1939. Then in 1941 while visiting New York was offered a position of art director designing watercolors for Modern Art Picture Framing Co. This I accepted and remained doing until my marriage to William Fahey in 1946. Looking back I give thanks to Mr. Oktavec for making it possible to work at what I wanted to do—paint.[246]

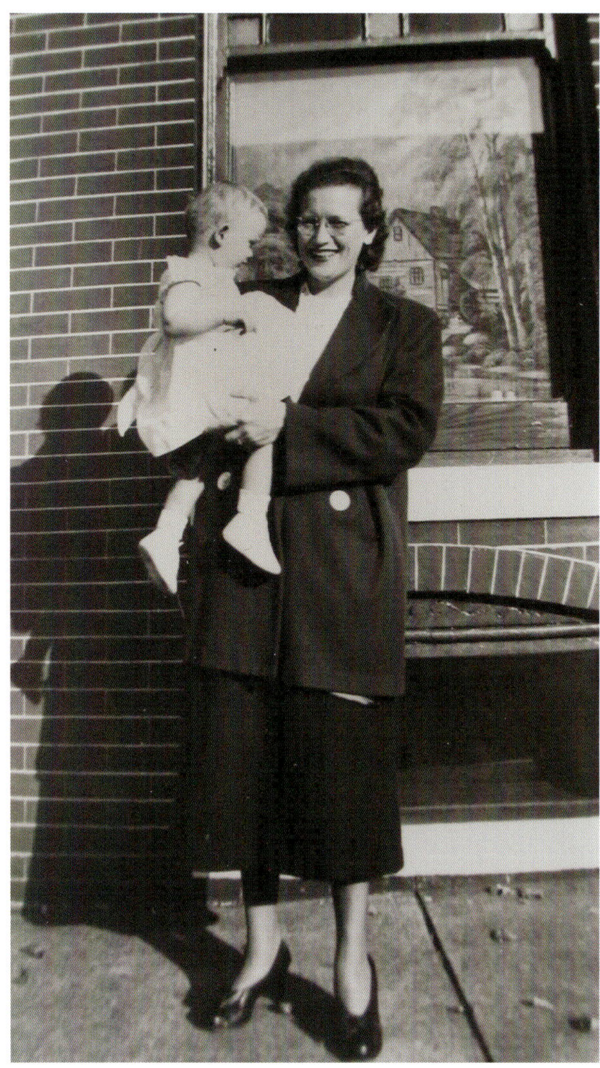

Ruth Chrysam Fahey, visiting from Brooklyn, New York, poses with her daughter Jane in front of the family home on North Montford Avenue, circa 1948. *Courtesy of Ruth Chrysam Fahey.*

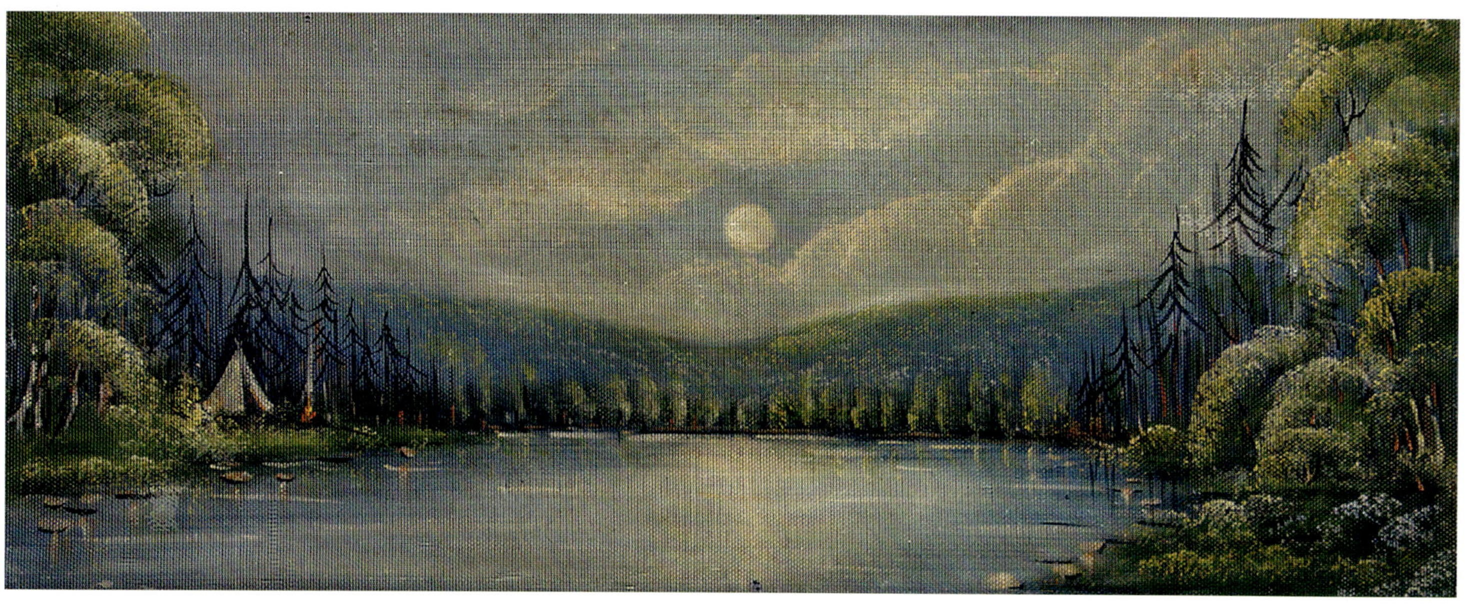

Moonlight on Lake by Ruth Chrysam. *Gift of Ruth Chrysam Fahey to the Painted Screen Society of Baltimore, Inc. Edwin Remsberg photograph.*

She remembers her neighborhood, filled with Eastern European and German families, for its parties held on the front pavement, an itinerant hurdy-gurdy player who made the rounds, and as a haven for roller skaters at a time when skates were used as much for transportation as for recreation. The block that she and many family members called home was for a time the most concentrated collection of her work.

Miss Ruth considered the itinerant artists who plied her neighborhood to be "a fixture during the Depression. They tried to finish a screen up immediately…which was impossible." Consequently she judged their output to have "no depth to it, like primitive faded looking paintings. They didn't charge hardly anything. I don't know how they paid for their paints."

She, in contrast, rendered exceptional work on screens. "I'm known as a perfectionist. I don't know if that's good or it's bad." Her unique style was both delicate and full of detail. The refinements in her handling of distance, especially sky and water, have never been equaled on woven wire. Her brushstrokes are worthy of the finest canvas. She was partial to moonlit scenes and reflections on water. Her admiration for the work of Renoir, who she says got his start painting on ceramic dishes, and her preference for pastels contribute to the lightness of her brushwork. According to her daughter, Jane, her subject matter was her own—land and waterscapes borrowed from copies of bits and pieces of fine German artworks she clipped from books and magazines and collected for inspiration. She took great pride in never having painted the red-roofed cottages, considering them to be "strictly Oktavec." She specifically chose not "to do his type of work." She considered her five-dollar charge "a pretty good price." In keeping with most of the artists of the time, she never signed her work.

Leroy Bennett, a screen painter and sign painter who specialized in painting signs on commercial vehicles and lived in the area, vividly recalled Chrysam's work decades later.

My favorites were that girl Ruth. She could paint an Indian girl leaning over in the water and the ripples would be just so. And the background would be the dark forest with a little bit of flowers and trees. She was the best screen artist I ever saw. You don't see her stuff around anymore. She worked for him. And she had to be good to work for Oktavec.

When Miss Ruth decamped for New York City in 1941, she suspended her screen-painting career except as special favors to family and close friends on her return visits to Baltimore. She always considered herself an artist above all, not compromising on a single stroke for her painted screens. "When I do it, I put my whole self in it. I really do. It's art."

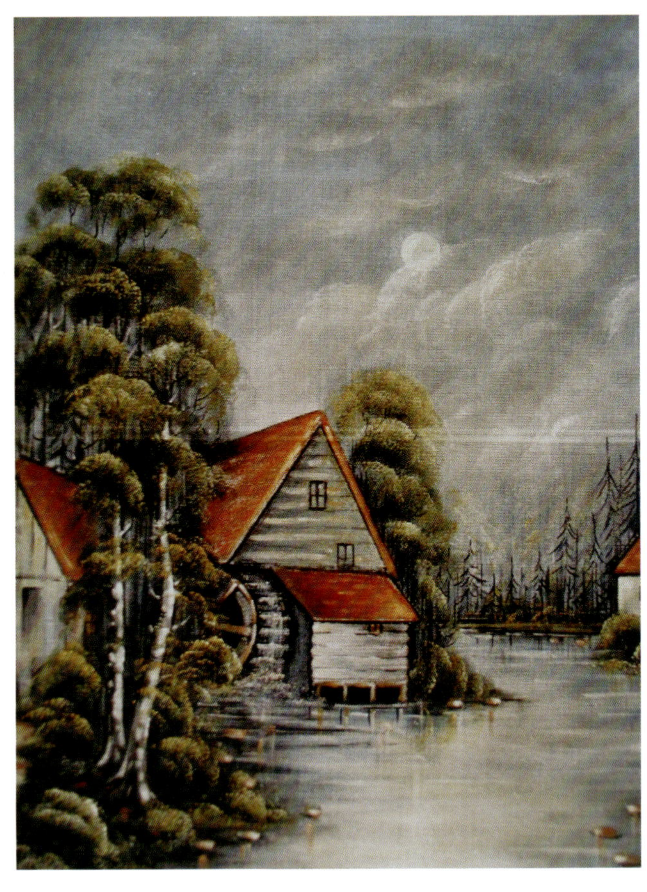

Red Mill by Ruth Chrysam. *Courtesy of the Chrysam family.*

HOW TO

MISS RUTH'S "MAIN FUNDAMENTALS OF SCREEN PAINTING"

"Get a quart of white enamel (oil base) undercoater (inside) paint. Use a good bristle brush about 2 ½" in diameter. Start painting on the wrong side of the screen in one corner. Cover about a six-inch area and work it in a circular motion until no holes are filled. Proceed across the screen. Then turn to the right side and do in the same manner working out any streaks that come through the back. This is worked very quickly. Then next day when dry repeat the process. Just remember the front of the screen is always done last. Now you have a good foundation to paint on, similar to a canvas. Take any kind of board and paint it black. Place this behind the screen when you're working...Must look up some paints to use, for now that the lead has been taken out of paint. I find the body is very poor for getting nice effects. Try to pick up any old bristle brushes that you can find (particularly if your neighbors are throwing some out). Clean them (soak with paint remover). Nylon brushes are no good. Sometimes you can pick these up in a Flea market."[247]

SIDEWALK ARTISTS

MAN ON THE STREET

ALONZO PARKS
(1898–1960)

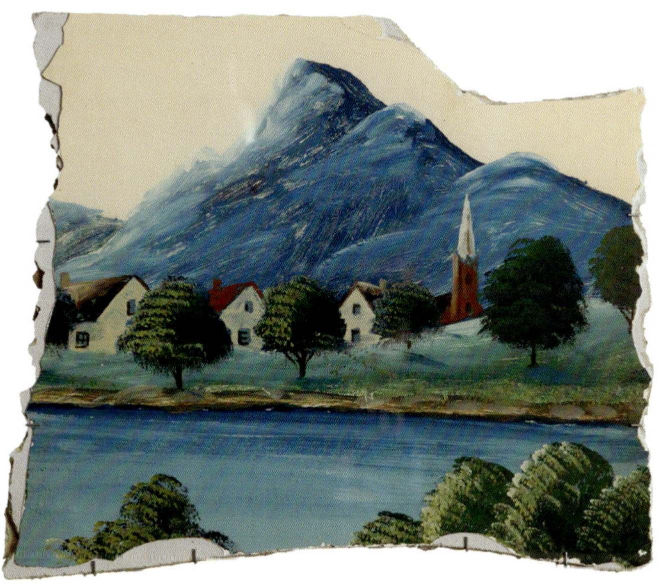

Alonzo Parks painted the interior of Beeche's Cafe Ladies' Dining Room. Only this fragment remained when paneling was removed in renovation. *Edwin Remsberg photograph.*

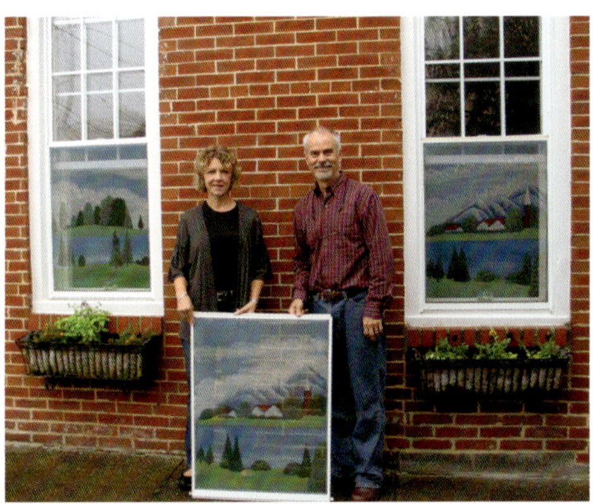

When Dave and Sue Wollner bought Beeche's Cafe, they attempted to save the painted walls. Unable to do so, they commissioned screen painter Dee Herget to replicate the few intact pieces they were able to document before they crumbled, an idea that would have pleased Alonzo Parks. *Edwin Remsberg photograph.*

"Free-lance artists" like Alonzo Aquilla Parks paid for paints out of pocket and usually took the daily profits directly to the nearest saloon. Everyone in southeast Baltimore seemed to know Parks—the artist, the virtuoso mouth organ player, the smokehound. He lived most of his life in the family rowhouse in the 900 block of South Linwood Avenue. He was described as a "short little fellow with a bit of hair on his head [who] shuffled his feet as he walked along."[248] "Guy had all the talent in the world. You'd look at him and think he could do nothin'."[249] He is listed in city directories as a sawyer, a box maker, and, in the 1920s, as a laborer. But most of his working life was spent spreading his art and music throughout southeast Baltimore until he came to a tragic end, suffering a fatal fall down a flight of stairs at home.[250]

There was a time when the name Alonzo Parks sparked memories among most neighborhood residents of a certain age. Stories abound of his impromptu performances at the outdoor Canton Market, playing as many as three harmonicas at a time, concealing miniature ones in his cheeks and playing "Yes, we have no bananas" while standing on his head.[251]

His skill as a painter of murals, ceilings, mirrors, vestibules, and screens was manifest throughout Canton, Fell's Point, and Highlandtown—neighborhoods that he could easily traverse on foot from home. Dozens of taverns and social halls benefited from wall paintings in the distinctive Parks style. Seascapes, landscapes, and alpine vistas graced taverns and eateries, including at least one "ladies dining room," later to be concealed under layers of remodelers' wallpaper and knotty pine paneling. His preferred form of payment was in drinks or bottles of whiskey. His reputation as a smokehound or "smokie" can be attributed to his habit, shared by many men of his era (particularly during Prohibition) of mixing low-grade or industrial standard alcohols with water to produce a hazy, intoxicating beverage. His mother, a widow whose home he shared, long and fruitlessly encouraged him to give up painting, mistakenly assuming that would keep him from frequenting bars.

Parks may have been the single most productive screen painter in the communities scattered with light industry and canneries along the city's bustling southeastern waterfront. He is responsible for hundreds, if not thousands of screens. His materials were of such high quality that many dating from the 1930s are still vibrant today. The presence of white lead, long a staple in artists' paint boxes, can be credited with the longevity of many early images on wire. Albert

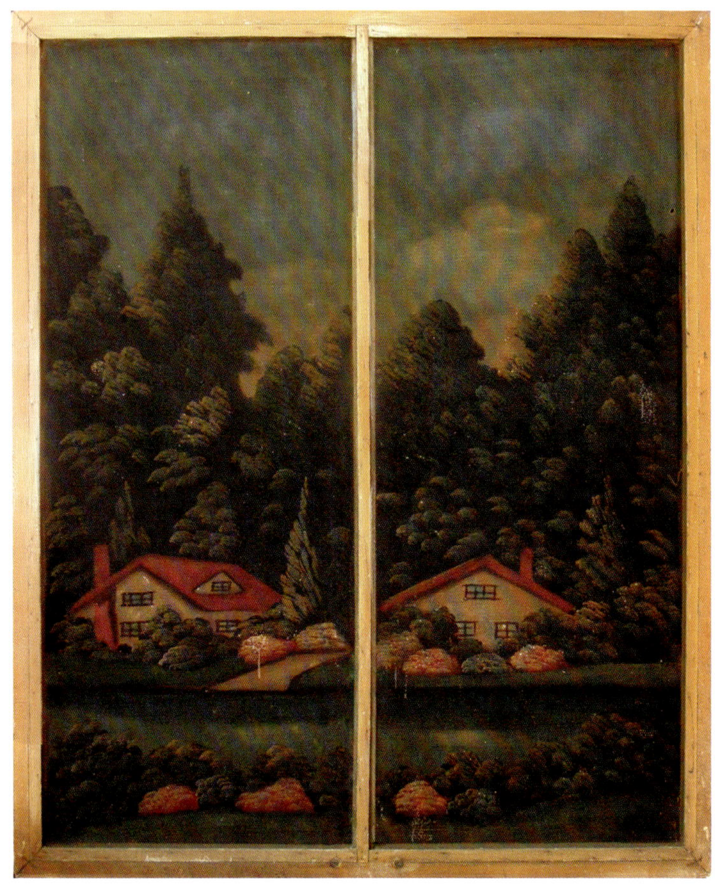

Oktavec claims to remember Parks's visits to the family Art Shop, spending hours watching Al's father, William Oktavec, paint screens. It is likely that Parks bought his painting supplies there and this was where he was inspired to apply his talent to screens.

His rather large body of work was unsigned, but his style was unmistakable. Parks's steeply roofed cottage was always beige (never white). The roof was a pinkish red or red orange. The building, window, and doors were always outlined in a confident black line. The chimney was especially elongated. His four-paned windows were painted a pale blue. Doors were often a missing detail. Towering fir trees were shaded in diagonal strokes, now white from the white lead residue in his palette that endured long after other colors had faded. The consistency of his style never seemed to waver, making one wonder whether his talent was enhanced or hampered by drink. Whatever his state, he was capable of producing his stock scene, bold and densely hued, with all manner of houses from Tudor to colonial to ranch. One pair of later screens found on a northeast Baltimore home even included contemporary styled homes with attached two-car garages, possibly a special order.

When duplicating a scene, he worked in an assembly-line fashion, according to his customers. He painted, not on an easel—he kept his traveling kit light—but directly on the screen in the window or propped up against the wall. He carried all of his supplies in a wooden box the size of a suitcase. His outdoor studio served as a classroom for a number of artists who followed him without ever learning his name.

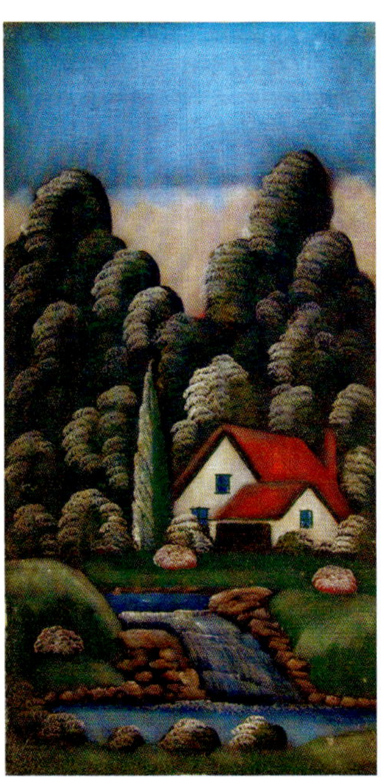

MOONLIGHTERS

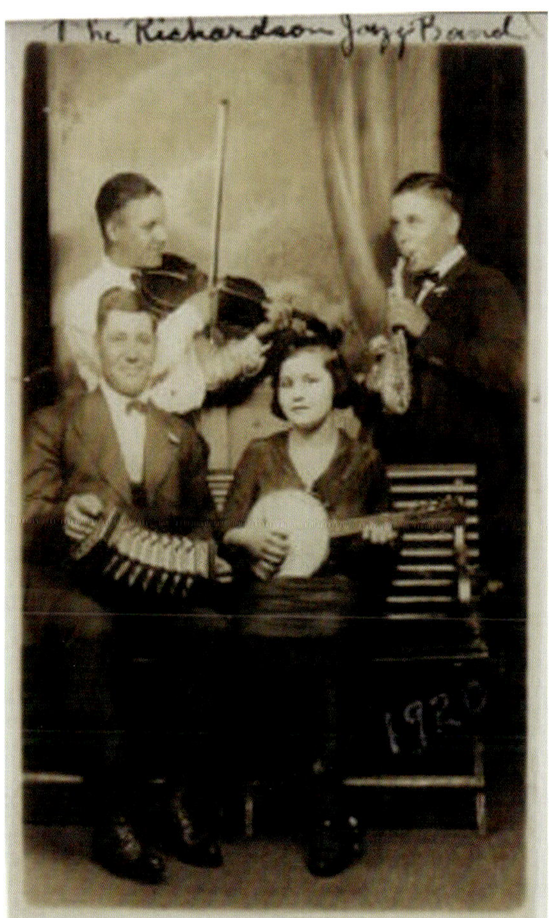

Ben and Ted Richardson playing together in a jazz band. The Richardson (family) Jazz Band featured children Ben on violin, Ted on saxophone, sister Myrtle on banjo, and father Arthur on concertina, 1920. Ben taught himself to fiddle after he severed his right hand in an industrial accident. Ted went on to play in orchestras and bands. *Richardson family photograph, Courtesy Edna Barney, "Richardsons of Hounslow Heath."*

BEN AND TED RICHARDSON

Although the earliest imitators lived relatively close to Oktavec's Little Bohemia, entrepreneurs like Ben and Ted Richardson traveled from across town to capture their part of the market. The Richardson brothers were born in England and raised among a family of self-taught artists and musicians. Their father, a brick mason, brought the family to North America to follow the building boom.

We first went to Toronto, Canada and stayed there until I was eleven [1915]. Then we went to Lake Worth, Florida, where my dad built a public school on Lake Avenue and then he built the courthouse in West Palm Beach while we lived there. We stayed in Florida for two and a half years and we left there when the boom stopped and we went to Macon, Georgia, where we got burned out [in a hotel fire.] We stayed here about three months and then went to Savannah. We only stayed there a short while and decided to come to Baltimore and we never got out. That was in 1917.[252]

A close-knit family, the Richardsons formed "a regular band," with Ted mastering banjo ukulele, clarinet, and saxophone while Ben, "a natural musician who couldn't read music but played it back if heard once," taught himself violin, mandolin, tenor banjo, and ukulele. Their sister played the tenor banjo and father played English concertina and sang, mostly old country hymns, while their mother joined in the vocals.

The boys credited their artistic talent to their "father [who] used to paint oil on canvas and would paint anything anybody would ask." A fierce rivalry from childhood pitted the boys against one another in everything they did. Whether it was vying for the affections of their parents, succeeding in careers as brick masons or musicians, painting the best version of an "English thatched cottage," they were always in competition. Ben claimed to be the first to paint screens and was instrumental in teaching his brother how to paint. Their styles, however, were easily differentiated:

EE: How can you tell the difference?

BR: By the way he clogged the holes up in the screens?

BEN RICHARDSON
(JANUARY 30, 1904, ESSEX, ENGLAND–FEBRUARY 22, 1991)

Ben started painting as a child, priding himself in doing his artwork in the dark under the dining room table. He bragged that he was able to enhance his eyesight in darkness by drinking large amounts of vinegar. He wanted to be "better than the rest" in whatever he tried. Although he claimed to have left school in the third grade, he studied mechanical drafting briefly at the Maryland Institute.

At age fifteen, while working with sheet metal at the Baltimore Gas Appliance Co., which later became Standard Gas Equipment Company (maker of Oriole stoves), he sheared four fingers from his right hand in an assembly-line accident. His intended career as a brick mason was dashed that day. Not to be deterred, he recalibrated his grip to play stringed instruments and taught himself to paint window screens. Rather than complain, he converted a series of jobs into showcases for his talents and a way to augment his salary.

For forty-two years, Ben was a "collector-salesman" for the Regal Shop, a men's haberdasher located on West Baltimore Street downtown. His job was to make regular rounds to the shop's customers to collect weekly installments on their bills. On any given day, his route brought him face to face with housewives in neighborhoods across Baltimore. He recited the list with pride: "Essex, Dundalk, Five Points, Colgate, Lorraine Park, Bengies, Turners Station, Harford Road, Old York Road, Belair Road, Pimlico, Pikesville, Reisterstown, down back, went towards the city. Annapolis, Eastport…Postal Zones, I knew every one of 'em. They didn't even have house numbers. Houseboats, got in a rowboat, rowed with one oar."

He was impressed by the tidiness of the East Baltimore neighborhoods, especially as he watched "the Polish women heading to the tomato packing plant at five o'clock in the morning in their aprons and little blue dresses and little white nurses' caps scrubbing down their steps before they left for work then again at twelve o'clock and then at five o'clock like they never tired and started scrubbing the steps again." Aware of his customers' reverence for cleanliness, he watched other collectors mount the marble steps in muddied shoes. "When I approach the peoples' houses to collect, I would stand on my tiptoes and touch [the doorbell] sometimes I used a stick to reach. I wouldn't even walk up those steps, because I didn't want to make them dirty. And I become the talk of the town in the churches and meetings over the area. 'How neat and clean Mr. Richardson was, the salesman that collected for the Regal Shop.' And it got to be a known thing that I was well liked over there."

While plying the Highlandtown and Canton neighborhoods near Patterson Park, Ben Richardson "saw different ones sitting on the pavement painting screens and that gave me the idea. If they can do it, so can I. I had just gotten married and I'm not making a whole lot of money here. I figured if I painted window screens I would be making something besides for when I wanted to pay my water bill or do some marketing, and that is how I got along. I never paid any interest to anybody in my lifetime. I always paid cash for everything I ever wanted. And I worked for a place that charged ten percent interest on thirty- and ninety-day accounts."

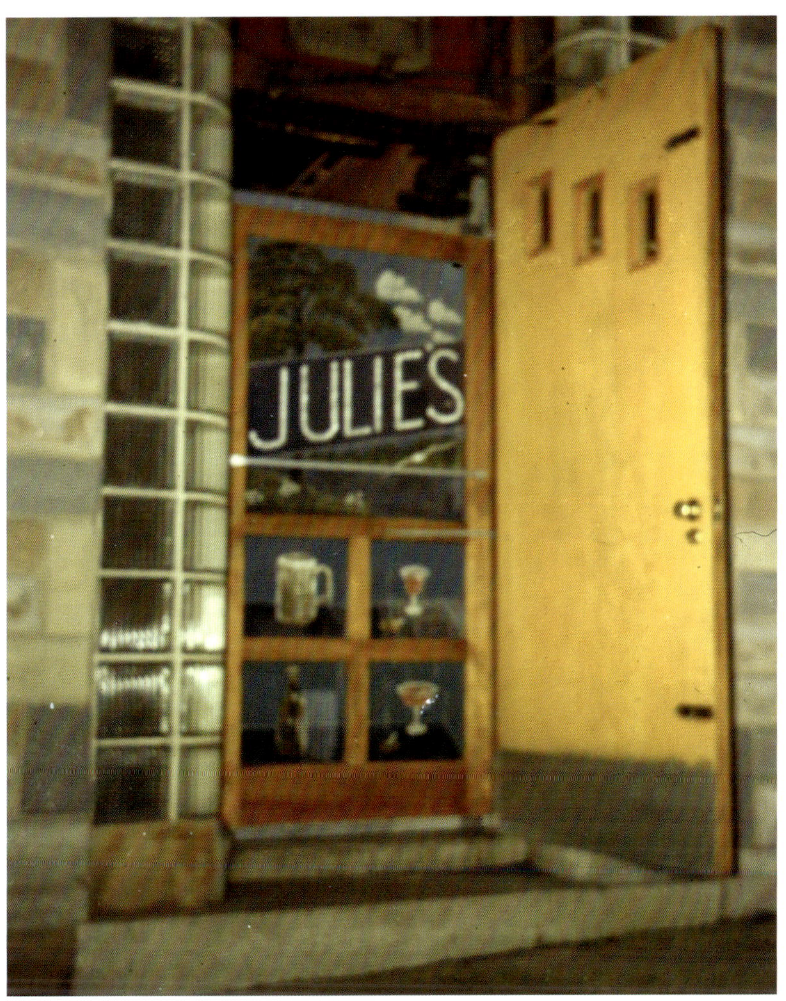

Tavern doors, like back bar mirrors and vestibules, were decorated by itinerant artists. This example painted by Ted Richardson was similar to the first screen painted by his brother Ben, which had taught him invaluable lessons about his craft.
Ted Richardson photograph.

I know I can draw and paint on canvas. You walk up any block and you see at least ten window screens in a row. I was living at 314 South Patterson Park Avenue. So I pulled my window screens out of the house and I set them up on the wall and painted them all and they turned out alright. I painted lighthouses, old Dutch windmills, moonlight scenes, sunset scenes, summer scenes, waterfalls, swans. Things I knew people liked around east Baltimore, I figured they could come around and they could look and see what I could do.

He found that his customers preferred scenes from their countries of origin. He claims to have introduced the snow scene in Highlandtown, "making the whole home look like it was cool or air conditioned." He noted, "I used to save all the calendars for years. Beautiful calendars. Typical marine scenes, I saved nudes. I got a bible, what I call my bible, where I got over 3,000 or 4,000 pictures in it."

When he decided to add screen painting to his eclectic repertoire of oil painting and fiddling, he jumped right in, learning by trial and error, with some unexpected consequences. He painted his first screen around 1934 for a Fell's Point tavern.

There was a fellow down on the corner had a saloon with two swinging doors. I took the screen doors off, took them up [to] the house, painted two Florida Everglades scenes on them. Looked real natural. I painted it and delivered it in one day. I was so proud of it that on my way home from work I wanted to look at them. I went by and you couldn't hardly see them. I said, "Holy Smoke, what happened to them?" I thought maybe he had something behind them that I can't see. Nope. Went over…and thought, "Well, that's funny." Went up to the owner, a real hot pot, and he says, "If that's the kind of work you do, get out." Well, it's the first time I ever painted a screen for somebody on the street. It really had me worried trying to figure out what caused it and I come to find out that I had been cleaning my brushes and was mixing in too much turpentine with the paint. And when the turpentine evaporated, the picture went with it. I went back with the intention of giving him his money back and giving him another set free. If I can't please anybody, I'd rather not do the work at all. But, he asked me to please leave. After that I never heard anybody ever say they was disappointed with any of my window screens in my whole life…. Experience is the best teacher after all, but it never stopped me. That's what made me start it. In fact, I asked people when I saw them, "How they do this and how they do that," but they wouldn't give me no information. I asked them what kind of paint they used and they wouldn't tell me. What kind of brushes they used and they wouldn't tell me. Anything I asked about their artwork they wouldn't tell me nothing.

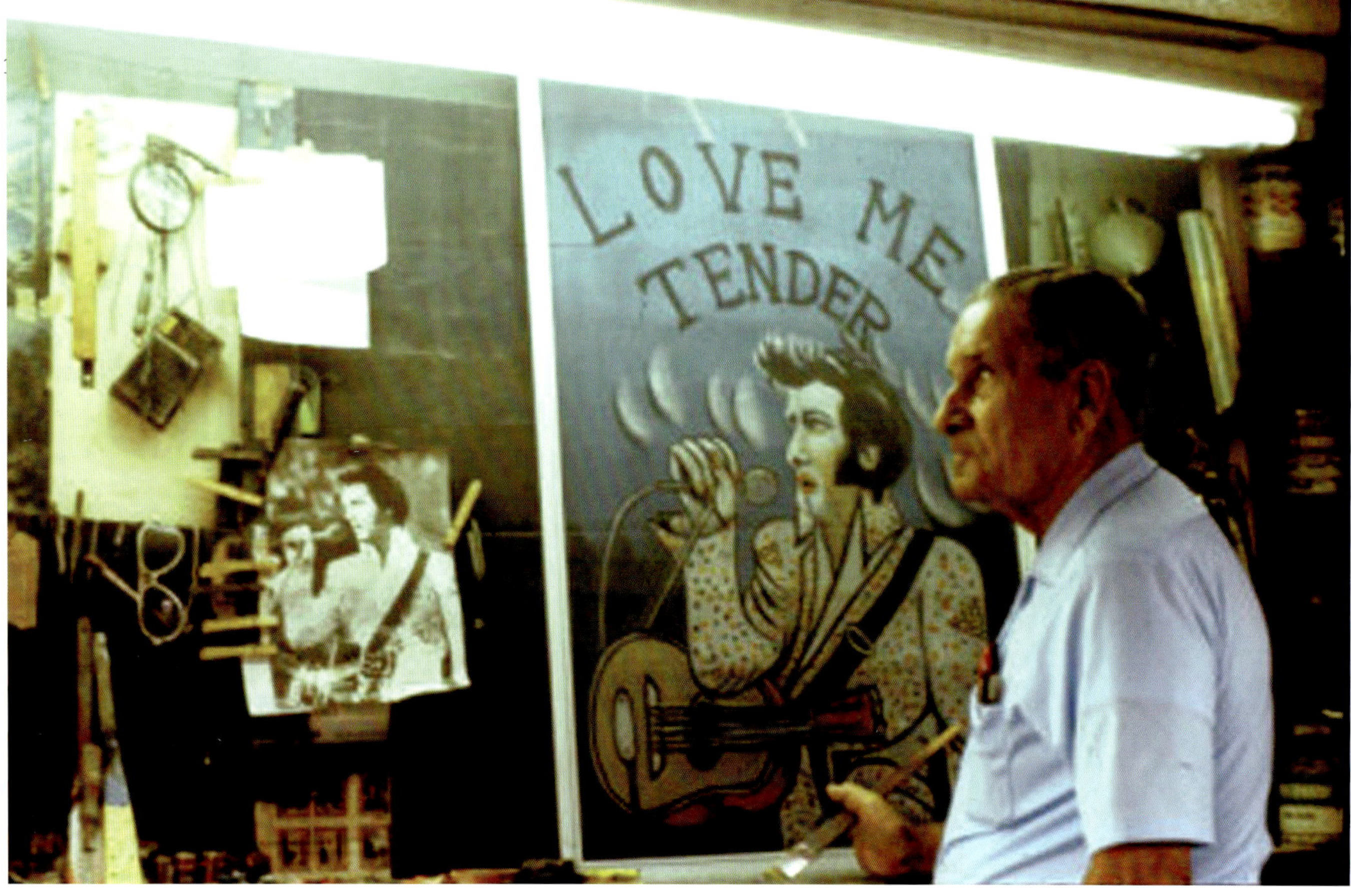

His visits to the Art Shop over many years were unrewarding. He never got to talk to William or Richard Oktavec. "So I decided I was going to learn anyway. I picked it up myself." Unable to avoid the "fad in East Baltimore," Ben asked his customers if they wanted theirs painted, no money down. "I take off the screen and mark the top inside with their name and address. The screen was the deposit." He provided a two-week turnaround, carefully removing and returning the screens as he made his rounds for the Regal Shop. He estimated he completed "ten screens a week for forty-two years, about six or seven months in a year."

In 1954, he bought a porch front rowhouse in West Baltimore's Morrell Park neighborhood. Within a few years he built a rectangular backyard workshop that he called a gazebo, because it was the one form that was not listed in the tax records. It stretched across the width of his wire-fenced yard where it meets the alley, built of "all marine plywood with four windows [running the length of the structure] that open up and fold into the ceiling, entirely screened to keep the dust out while painting screens. And it is nice and cool in there. Put an electric fan in and an electric heater and fluorescent light and a nice dark background and leaned my screens against it so I could see what I was doing much plainer than I could out there on the street. My gazebo has an all-brick floor, wall-to-wall carpet and a built-in amplifier where I played my music and tapes and I had crab parties and cookouts, a fiberglass roof that never needs any kind of repair, never leaked any water and the windows never blew off." When asked why he built it, he impishly replied, "Chicken feathers."

Ben Richardson puts the finishing touches on the Elvis screen that was displayed on his front porch as a sign for many years. *Author photograph, 1982.*

OPPOSITE, TOP

Ben Richardson was proud of the custom-built gazebo (the only structure type not listed in the Baltimore tax code) perched along the alley in the backyard of his Morrell Park home. It was outfitted for painting screens and used for eating crabs when the massive plywood side panels were lifted to reveal a screened-in room. *Author photograph, 1982.*

OPPOSITE, BOTTOM

A fearless pet painted by Ben Richardson for his front porch screen watches over the painted steps and walkway of the artist's tidy West Baltimore rowhome. *Author photograph, 1984.*

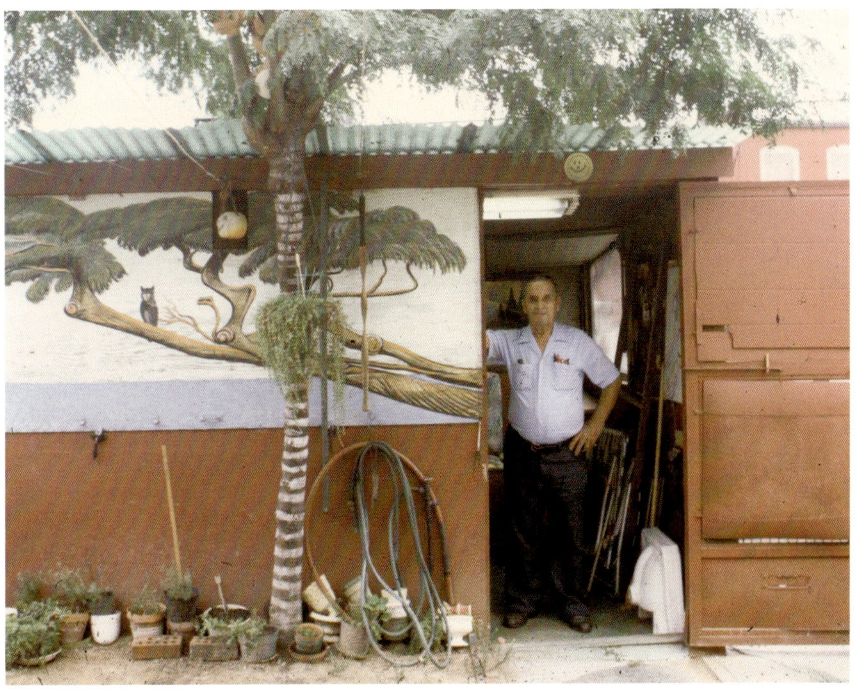

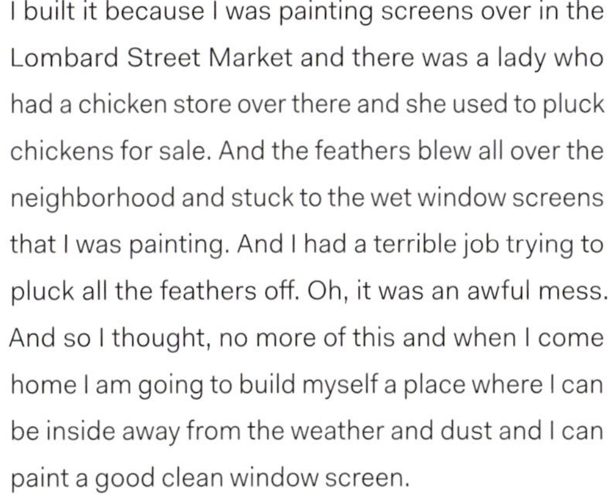

I built it because I was painting screens over in the Lombard Street Market and there was a lady who had a chicken store over there and she used to pluck chickens for sale. And the feathers blew all over the neighborhood and stuck to the wet window screens that I was painting. And I had a terrible job trying to pluck all the feathers off. Oh, it was an awful mess. And so I thought, no more of this and when I come home I am going to build myself a place where I can be inside away from the weather and dust and I can paint a good clean window screen.

Ben prided himself in providing scenes that went beyond the typical "house, tree, and lawn. Everywhere you went, house, tree, and lawn…. Somebody wanted a picture painted, they'll give me a picture I'll paint it. They tell me they used to live in Poland, I'll go home and look through my book and find different pictures of foreign countries and finally run into something that looks like Poland…or run to the library and see and go home and memory paint it on the window screen. I'll match up the same kind of trees they have in Poland, the same kind of building, not all the same."[253]

His hallmark was the white undercoat painted on both sides. "I put the picture on the paint instead of putting the paint on the wire." Taking it one step further, "I am the only one that ever painted a window screen on both sides. And I painted three of them."

Although he never signed a screen, he believed it was a good idea—an efficient form of advertising. He advertised briefly, but found it resulted in too much work.

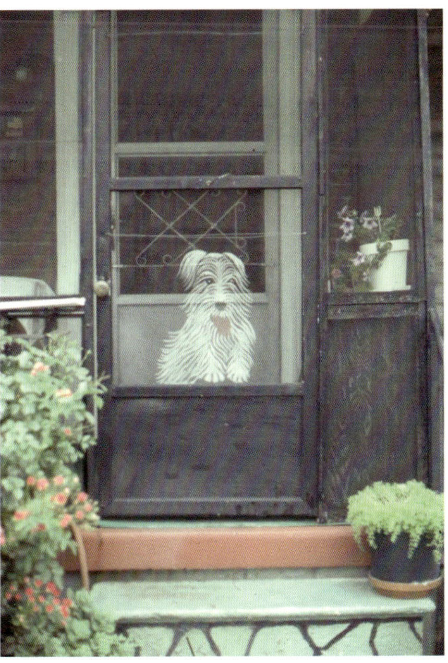

It was the worst thing I ever done in my life. I put the ad in the telephone book and the phone kept ringing every time I picked up the brush, so I quit advertising…. I used to go out and pick them up and deliver them. But I got away from that. I lost too much money traveling. Back and forth and you would lose too much time. So I told them that they had to bring their window screens to me. And the screen had to be wire not nylon. And you had to put a piece of tape marking the top outside of each screen…. My work came from the work I done. If I paint one window screen in the spring, that was a start for me for the rest of the season. As soon as you paint one that is when the season starts rolling. People would see it in somebody's house and they would all go over and ask who done it, what my name and phone number was.

Never wanting to be outdone, for a time Ben boasted of painting two window screens at once. "I would paint one with my right hand and set the other one beside it and paint it with my left hand. And then the pictures would be opposite—exactly the same picture."

Not all of his masterpieces were meant for public view.

I painted a picture of Lady Godiva when I was living at 314 South Patterson Park. And my daughter here she was going to the Salvation Army. They was trying to make her a missionary. And the preacher come down to see us and this Lady Godiva was on my back screen door and you couldn't get in the side door so they had to come to the back. So the preacher he comes around and my wife was in the house and he stood at the back door and when he went to rap on the door he looked up and there was Lady Godiva. With no clothes on. In all her glory. The horse was there too. And she had a real thin veil on. And the preacher, my wife was

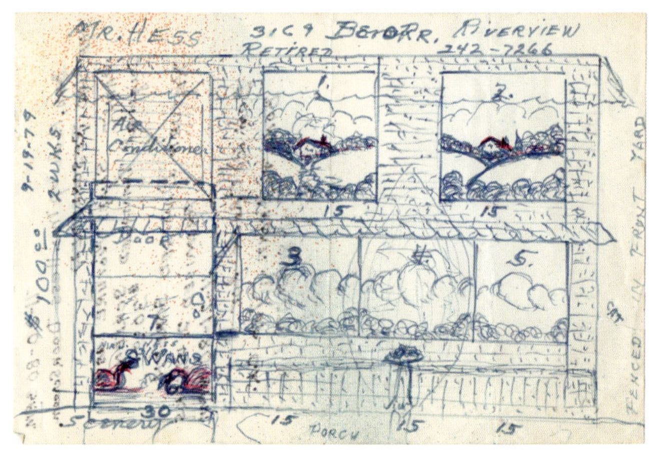

HOW TO

— ASSESORIES —
1— QUT. WHITE ENAMEL
1—   "   BLACK   "
1—   " DARK GREEN "
1—   " SKY BLUE   "
—1— GALLON VARNALINE
SET OF LARGE TUBE OIL COLORS
— — — — — — — — —
1— BEVELED CURTAIN PIN
TO UNCLOG HOLES 1 WEEK AFTER DRY
— — — — — — — — —
PAINT RAG — DARK CURTAIN
COLOR MIX LIDS — PAINT BOX — BOOK OF SUBJECTS
SCOTCH TAPE — TOP — FRONT
DON'T PAINT SCREEN UPSIDE DOWN OR BACKWARD
DON'T PAINT SCREENS while PLUCKING A CHICKEN ON A WINDY DAY.
DON'T KNOCK A HOLE IN COMPLETED SCREEN.
— HANDLE WITH CARE —

BRUSHES
ANGLE BRUSHES
BRISTEE
1/4" — 1/2" — 3/4" — 1"
3" FLAT BRISTLE

1/2 FULL VARNALINE
SCREENED BOTTOM
COFFEE CAN — 1 QT.

standing inside and he couldn't see her, but she could see him real plain. You could see out to him from the screen…So the preacher's mouth went open and he got scared and he left. —And I never became a missionary.[254]

Ben's repertoire may have been among the most varied. Few subjects were off-limits. His West Baltimore neighbors preferred images of dogs in their front door screens, suggesting to Ben that they loved their pets, but also that the screens served a secondary purpose as watchdogs. He was commissioned by a rabbi of a Park Heights Avenue Synagogue to paint a screen for the *mechitzah*, a traditional divider between men and women's seating areas. The subjects, "Mother Rachel's tomb, Bethlehem, Jerusalem, Wailing Wall" were taken from snapshots provided by the rabbi. "So women can see across but men cannot see in."

10/26/58
Mrs Ledderer
2nd Week in January
446 N Patterson
Likes Green
$23.00
(Take your time)
HEX SIGN
KEEPS JINX AWAY

#1.	#2.	#3.	#4.	#5.	#6.
WASH FRONT + BACK	"	"	"	"	"
STRAIGHTEN HOLES WITH BEVELED CURTAIN PIN	DARK CURTAIN BEHIND HELPS A LOT		BLACK UNDER SHADOWS	"	FILL IN COLORS
PAINT SKY BLUE	PAINT BOTH SIDES	WHITE CLOUDS-ETC.	GREEN LAWNS-ETC.	SHADING	OUT LINE IN BLACK
BEN PAINTS BOTH SIDES	BLACK " DESIGN	"	"	" YELLOW	" RE SHADE
BEN DON'T CLOG HOLES NEVER	"	BLACK UNDER SHADE	SHRUBS & TREE LEAVES	HIGH LIGHTS ON SUNNY SIDE	
CLEAN FRAMES	"				GO OVER INSPECT
DRY 2 DAYS	"				COMPLETED
DELIVER 2 WEEKS	"	— UNCLOG HOLES WHILE PAINTING —			"
SCOTCH TAPE TOP & FRONT	DON'T PAINT. OUT SIDE IN WIND BEN PAINTS IN SCREENED SHED	DARK CURTAIN SCREEN SUBJECT BENCH PAINT RAG	FOR BRUSHES SOAK IN TURPENTINE OR VARNALINE THINNER COFFEE CAN SCREEN	IT'S A NICE HOBBY — TRY IT -OVER-	COMPLIMENTS BY BENS ART SHOP 644-7755 SELF TAUGHT AGE-80 1-HAND

From Ben Richardson's "How to Paint Window Screens," a 1987 handwritten compendium of tips for the artist and the owner of painted screens. The information was "organized" when he retired from screen painting at the age of eighty-three. The manuscript's final words: "Don't tell my wife." *Collection of the Painted Screen Society of Baltimore, Inc.*

One of Ben's works was stolen soon after installation, as he recalled: "I painted one full-length life-size window screen of the Lord knocking on the door. And I painted it on this window screen in the 300 block of Madiera Street. They are a religious class of people over here, mostly Catholic. And I painted this window screen for this woman and I got it finished and then the next morning she came around to the house and she says to me, 'Mr. Richardson, what happened to my window screen?' She says, 'I paid you for it and it was in the window but it is not there now.' So I went around there and I saw that somebody had taken a razor blade and cut it out perfectly smooth all around and took the screen and who knows what they done with it. And then I looked down inside the storm door and there is a note down there that she didn't see. So I picked the note up and she asked me to read it because she [had] bad eyes and it said, 'The Lord is supposed to be displayed inside the house, not on the street.'"

Perhaps some of Ben's most iconic and Baltimore's most surprising and seemingly misplaced screens are located in the notorious downtown district known as The Block, famed for bars, strippers, and raucous male crowds. To mark America's Bicentennial, the owner of the Midway Bar, the rare watering hole without live entertainment, asked Ben to suggest scenes for the second- and third-floor windows. "I told him I think it would be a good idea to put historical scenes there. That was a second-floor apartment and he came up to my place. It was the owner of the bar and [he] gave me the job to paint it and Tattoo Charlie [whose emporium occupies the second floor] was with him to decide whether it was good work or not. The screens measure eight-foot tall and four-foot wide, with sturdy frames made of two by fours: Baltimore's George Washington Monument, Statue of Liberty, one boat of the constellation, one boat 'Full Speed Ahead,' one boat 'Before the Driving Wind,' and the Shot Tower. Painted the whole six window screens on my front patio. I would stand there and paint. That was the only way I could paint them."

The following year, Ben took on Dee Herget as his first student since teaching his brother. Although he never painted a screen in front of her, he considered her to be his best pupil. He told her what kind of brushes and paint he preferred while sharing a few tips as she took notes seated at his kitchen table.

She was a telephone operator and she says she has got to make a living somehow, so I felt sorry for her and she called me up and I says, "Yeah, come over any time." She come over here three times. But instead of her taking a paintbrush in her hand to paint, see, she used to paint on canvas and stuff like that at home. Or on old board or anything. She never painted no window screens here. But she wrote down everything that I told her on a pad and she went home and she bought all the materials that I had, the same kinds. And the same kind of paint and tried to follow my technique. Never come up to it. She would only paint one side and take an hour or two hours and charge four or five dollars. Well, I said, "You can charge thirty-five dollars for the same picture." But my pictures would take two weeks to paint. I can paint one picture in two weeks or I can paint ten pictures in two weeks. Because when I had ten screens, I was painting the same scene on every one of them, back and forth. I didn't have to keep opening up cans of paint and mixing different colors. I could do the whole ten at one [time]. That is where I made the money.

At some point Ben learned about Oktavec's prize student, Miss Ruth (Chrysam), who by that time was living in New York City. In 1980 he wrote her asking how she painted a screen, even though five decades had passed since she had last attempted one. Although Ben had already amassed quite a following for his work, he asked for her method, possibly in anticipation of expanding his career by teaching. Pained by his inability to get any information from the Oktavecs, he possibly and mistakenly thought he was circumventing them by going directly to one of their students. Her style and technique, however, was distinctly her own. She responded to him in a letter that shared the fundamentals she practiced in her brief and exacting career (see page 164) as a hands-on lesson. "Prepare an old screen so I can show you some tricks when in the future I get to Balto. Will try to give you a lesson next time I see you."[255] Although it was a little late for this seasoned painter to incorporate the secrets learned at the feet of the master into his own painting, Miss Ruth's generosity and the successful launch of his student Dee Herget encouraged Ben's willingness to teach friends, neighbors, and "total strangers." Ruth's unselfishness was likely responsible for Ben's late-life vision of a school for screen painters—and an inspiration for the documentary film *The Screen Painters*, which helped launch many would-be artists. His vivid comparison of clogged holes to "a buncha dead flies" continues to remind new generations that experience is the best teacher.

The Midway Bar on Baltimore's once notorious Block, dressed for the Bicentennial with screens of local and national symbols built and painted by Ben Richardson. The screens also brought privacy to the workplace of Tattoo Charlie on the second floor. *Edwin Remsberg photograph, 2011.*

TED RICHARDSON
(APRIL 1, 1901, ESSEX, ENGLAND–DECEMBER 29, 1986)

Ted Richardson liked to point out that he was born the year his namesake, King Edward VII, ascended to the throne of England. He might best be described as the P. T. Barnum of screen painting—an art he adopted at first sight and practiced for more than half a century. By the 1980s, driving around town in a blue sedan festooned with signs advertising his art, he was a bit of an anachronism.

A few decades earlier, he could be found drumming up business alongside an earlier-vintage station wagon, parked in a strategic East Baltimore location, possibly blaring music from a loudspeaker. During most of the 1960s, he was the only artist to operate a storefront dedicated exclusively to painted screens.

Not one to stick too closely to conventions, Ted strayed from the red-roofed bungalow whenever possible, lamenting, "Everybody wants a red roof." When given the license to improvise, he occasionally provided yellow or brown, but favored blue roofs, a feature that became a trademark. Ted was one of the few screen painters who consistently affixed his name to his work, using an inked stamp in his own script that read "By Ted Richardson" and later adding an adhesive label "Ted Richardson Screen Art" with his phone number.

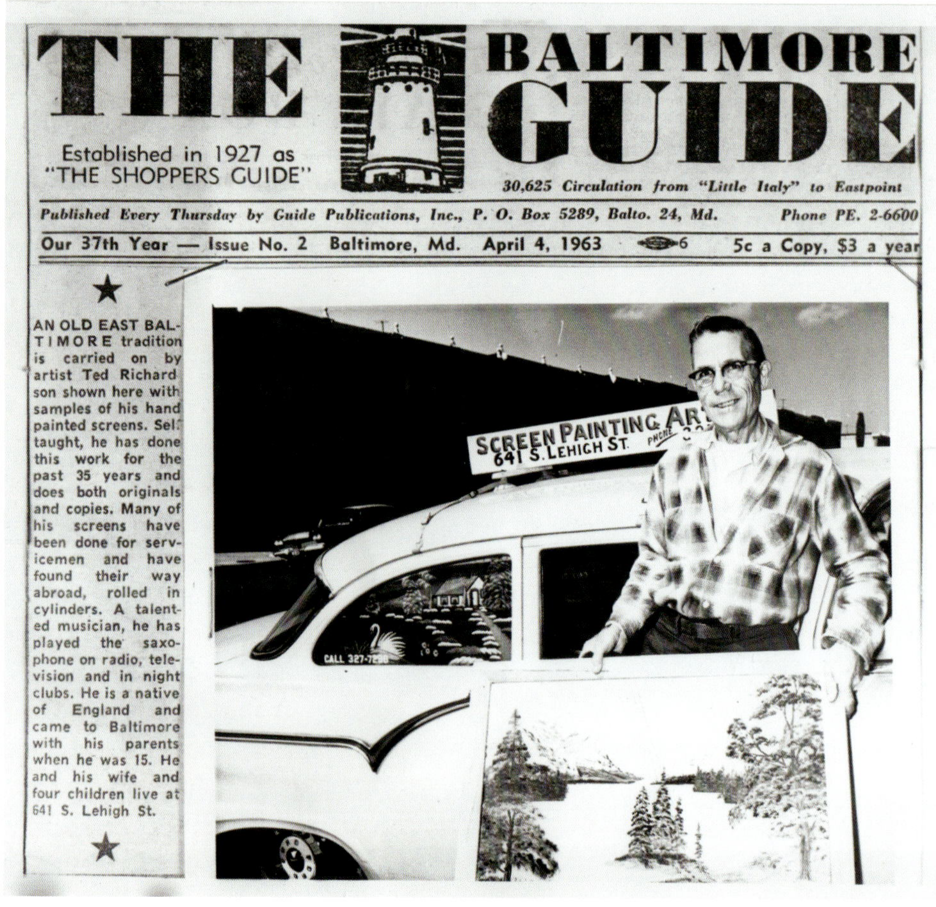

Although Ted's family lived primarily on the city's west side when he was a youngster, he tells one version of getting his start in screens by watching the smokehounds paint on the East Baltimore sidewalks as early as 1921. He recalled his Aha! moment:[256]

I was going through Canton one day and I happened to see a man coming down the street with a little box. He was staggering just a bit. I don't know whether he was drunk or not. And he knocked on this lady's door and asked her if he could paint a screen for her. So she told him he could paint the screen if he wanted to, she would like to have a picture. He says, "Well, I'll paint it for you if you will give me enough to buy a drink." So she gave him [money] and he went up to the saloon and bought a bottle and then came back and went to work. And he painted this screen for her on her window and I stood there and watched him do the whole thing. Then I started to think, "Why can't I do that?" And I got the idea that my dad used to be an artist. I used to watch him. He never let me use his oil paints, but I used to sketch a lot

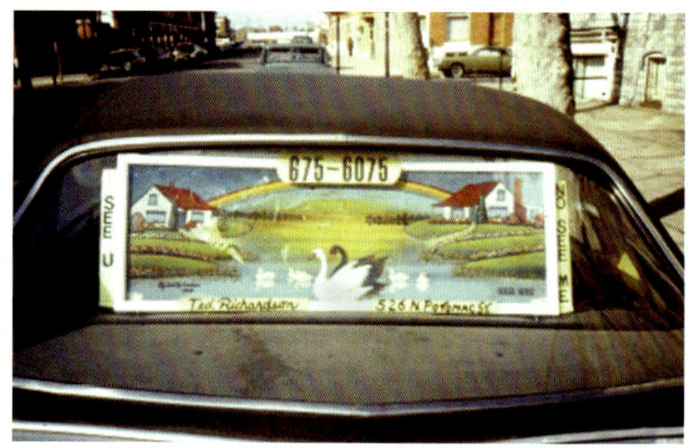

During the 1980s, Ted let the screen do the advertising as he moved the vehicle around East Baltimore. *Collection of the Painted Screen Society of Baltimore, Inc. Author photograph.*

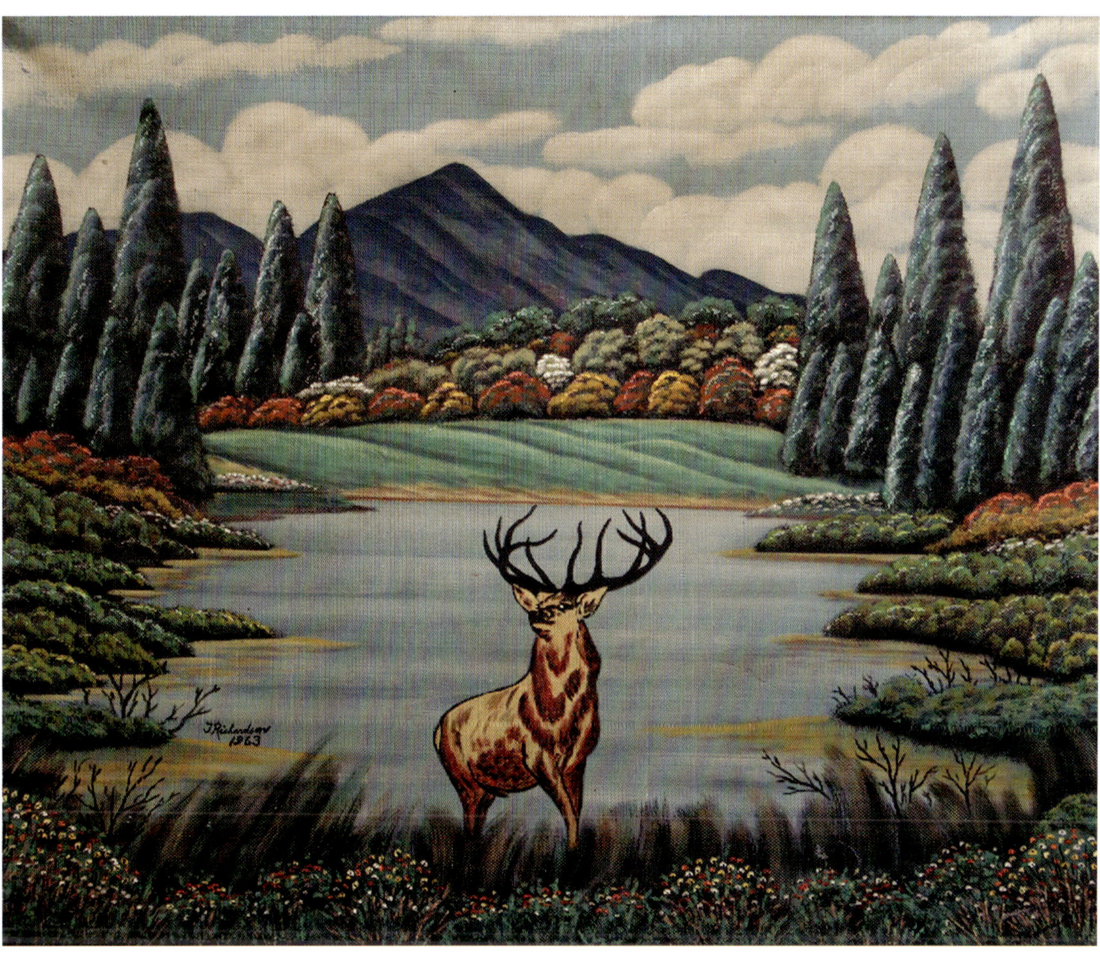

too. So I went home to my mother and said, "I saw a man painting pictures on screens today.
You've got screens in your window. Would you like me to try to paint on your screen? It keeps
people from looking in and you can still see outside." She said, "You go ahead and if you can,
do it." And it looked alright to me and everybody liked it. So I finally ended up practicing on
all the screens she had.[257]

Ted attempted a variety of occupations. Although he was preparing to follow in his father's
footsteps as a brick mason, completing his four-year apprenticeship in 1921, he was easily dis-
tracted. He strayed into work as a radio repairman, boatyard operator, country musician, dance
bandleader, graveyard manager, and screen painter. The common thread was the ability to be
his own boss. In the early years, his true passion was music. He preferred dates in clubs and
dance halls to any of his more reliable jobs. His "hillbilly band," Ranger Ted and His Blue Ridge

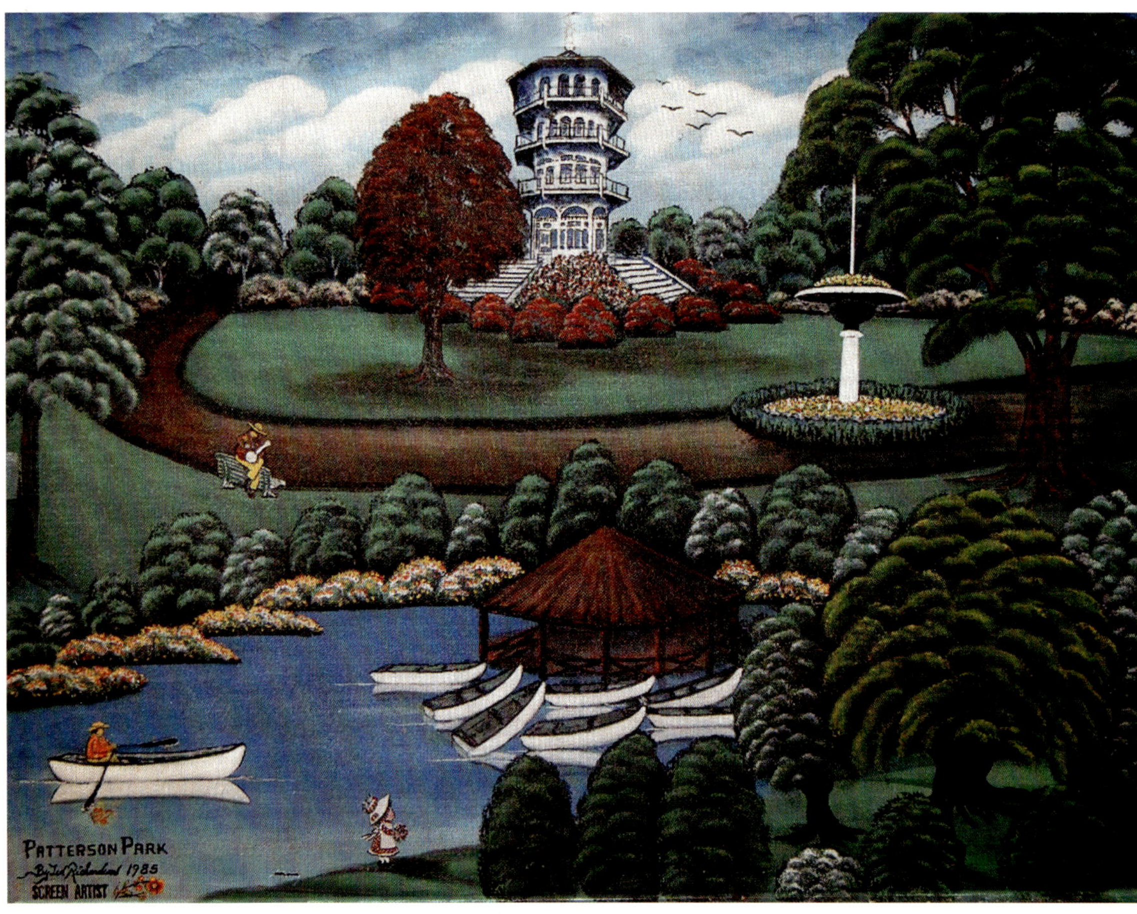

Rangers, which included brother Ben on fiddle, played regularly at Highlandtown's Slim Brow's tavern, where celebrities like Jimmy Dean sat in. For a short time, he had his own radio show on "Maryland's Capital Station, WANN Radio Annapolis." His playlist shows his versatility: "2 sax, 1 tenor banjo, Banjo and Baritone Uke, Washboard, Drums, 2 guitars, fiddle. All sound effects by Ranger Ted."[258] He also played with the Garden City Orchestra. But masonry supported him, off and on, into the late 1960s, always working under a dreaded boss. He turned to screen painting in fits and starts, until his death.

After a day of laying brick, he painted screens in the evenings "and then I would take them to work with me and stick them up on the job and let people see them as they walked by. That is how I picked up more work." While living on highly trafficked Hanover Street in South Baltimore, he "borrowed the fire department's nice brick wall and I would lay the screens right against it and you could see them real good while you were driving by." His days as an outdoor painter were numbered. "You could not stop flies from getting on the screens. And sometimes the kids would get around you and aggravate you while you were trying to paint. That's why I quit painting on the outside."

Ted Richardson's 1985 Patterson Park Pagoda screen was a showpiece created for Canton's Hatton Senior Center in the 700 block of South Linwood Avenue, where a gallery of screens grace the building's windows. He added self-portraits playing the banjo on a park bench and rowing a boat in the boat lake. The painting holds a special place inside the facility that Ted frequented. *Collection of the Charles F. Hatton Senior Center. Christine Fillat photograph.*

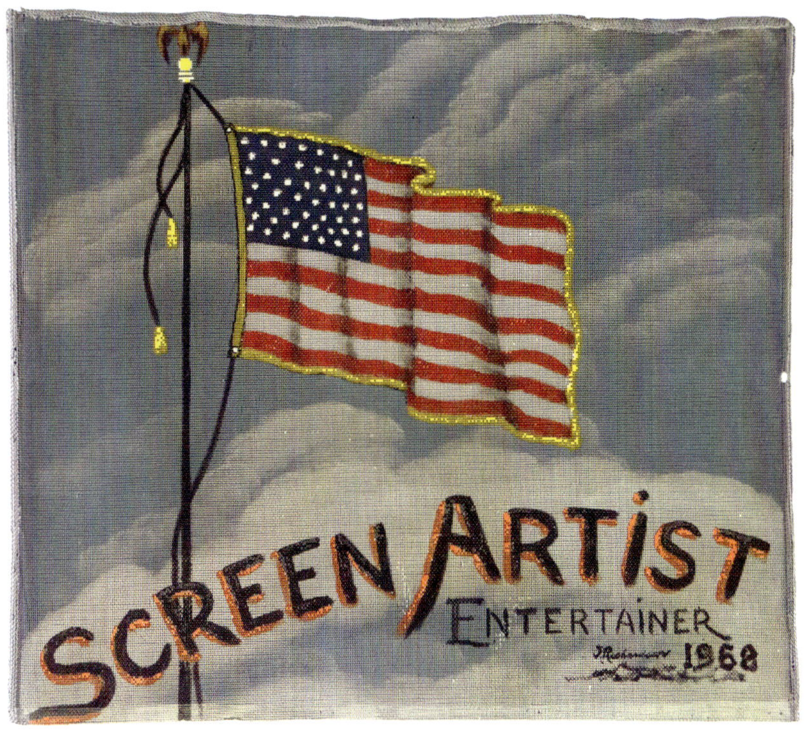

Ted Richardson's pride in place was apparent in much of his art, often serving multiple purposes. He dated and signed most of his screens, using a custom signature stamp. This 1968 screen was often displayed in his apartment window. *Gift of the artist. Collection of the Painted Screen Society of Baltimore, Inc. Christine Fillat photograph.*

Once he decided to work only indoors, he carved out workspaces in a succession of rented apartments. Although several of his surviving screens carry dates from the 1930s, another version of his story has his brother Ben schooling him in the finer points of screen painting in the 1960s in preparation for installing him in an Eastern Avenue storefront located two doors below Patterson Park. He closed the shop in 1969 after a successful, but brief, run on that busy commercial thoroughfare.

The number of different vocations Ted tackled rivaled his many addresses. Depending on the year, he is remembered as the painter from Hanover Street on the west side, or from Eastern Avenue, North Linwood, South Lehigh Street, or North Potomac Street in East Baltimore. His residences and on-again-off-again marriages were scattered among northern Anne Arundel County, West and South Baltimore, and Highlandtown. He may have lived longest, sixteen years, in the second floor of 526 North Potomac Street, with his companion of decades, Ginny Milstead. So he spent his last years solidly in painted-screen territory and directly across the street from the truck and sign painter turned screen artist, Leroy Bennett.

When he moved into the apartment, Ted padlocked his perfectly ordered paint supplies in an interior room, considering it "too much trouble to get it out and start all over again."

The reason I stopped painting in 1969 was that things started to get slack and I couldn't figure out the reason why. But when I did figure it out, I found it was nothing else but air conditioning. Because the people when they got an air conditioner would take the screen out of their window and put it in their cellars or attics. I would still be doing it today if it wasn't for air conditioning. A lot of the people don't think they need screens anymore. They keep their windows closed and the beautiful screens locked up.[259]

Following a hiatus of more than a decade, Ted Richardson realized that his avocation was once again finding an appreciative audience. As if unearthing a time capsule, he removed the lock, opened his paint cans, pulled out his chair, and sat once again at his easel, creating his signature screens for a grateful public.

CHARLES BOWMAN
(MARCH 19, 1896, LIMERICK, IRELAND–DECEMBER 29, 1987)

Timing and optimism were everything in Charles Bowman's long and colorful life. He left Ireland in 1913 with his father, a captain for the North German Lloyd Lines out of Bremen, Germany. He enrolled at Heidelberg University to study fine art and music shortly before the First World War exploded on the continent. Because he was an alien, he spent 1915–1918 in a German prisoner-of-war camp. Blessed with the gifts of charm and inquisitiveness, he turned that bleak situation into an opportunity to perfect his German and French language skills.

He returned to the university after the war, graduated, and headed to Paris to study commercial art. After only two months, he made contacts that brought him to New York City. He arrived in the United States in 1922 with little money. In his affable manner, he secured a job at a German-owned speakeasy, playing the piano for its wealthy, appreciative, and nostalgic clientele and making tips of up to "$100 a night from crazy drunks." After a year of sustaining himself with music, he determined that he would follow his other career path, art.

A patron urged him to complete a degree in commercial art at Cooper Union at his expense. Bowman accepted the largesse, celebrating "no more pictures and portraits." He immediately found work with the General Outdoor Advertising Company, rising to the position of assistant art director within a year.

At the time of the Stock Market Crash of 1929 he found himself in Philadelphia, where he had unwisely been influenced to transfer his savings. Once again, he found the bright side to his misfortune. While bemoaning the loss of his fortune in a local eatery, he met his future wife, Violet, an entertainer who was playing the East Coast circuit. When she played Baltimore in 1936, she and Bowman decided to marry, settle down, start a family, and make the city their home in the midst of the Depression.

He found his niche as a commercial artist during his long career in Baltimore, working for three companies, American Sign, Acme Stores, and Miller Brewing Company. He was proud to

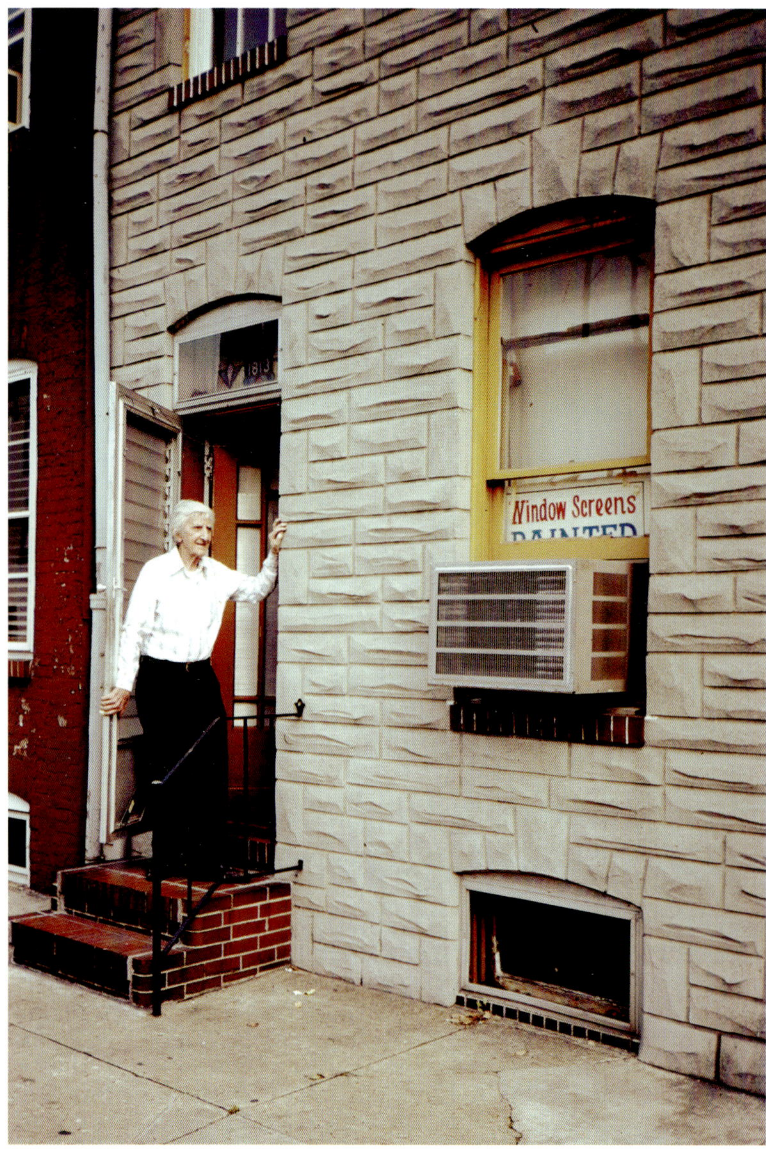

Charles Bowman, commercial artist, screen painter, musician, and violin repairman lived and worked in a pair of Fleet Street rowhouses, where he produced a single distinctive Red Bungalow image from the 1930s through the 1980s. *Author photograph, 1982.*

have designed slogans and logos for national brands including Camel cigarettes. While searching for a catchy phrase with his bosses, he related that during the war, "he'd walk a mile for a camel," won $800 and bragging rights for life.[260]

He and his wife bought a pair of rowhouses in the 1800 block of Fleet Street in Fell's Point, a rough-and-tumble community in East Baltimore where denizens of the waterfront encountered recent European émigrés like Bowman and their affiliated institutions. St Patrick's Irish Catholic Church and the German Methodist Church were a few blocks north on Broadway.

Charlie's first encounter with painted screens came shortly after his arrival in Baltimore. His wife wanted screens for her window and door to stop the rubberneckers from looking in her house, located on a busy sidewalk. He visited the library to see what he could learn, but found nothing. His best source was a "man in a blue apron," a street corner painter he met near Patterson Park. Bowman convinced him that as a fine artist he would be no competition. Based on his instructions, Bowman went back to his shop, added a black background to his sign table, and lettered a new sign for his window declaring "Window Screens Painted," seamlessly adding another competency to his already successful sign-painting business.

As a screen painter, Bowman quickly developed his own style, a simple and efficient design that could easily convert the requisite red-roofed bungalow into a church by elongating the roof or into a "Dutch" windmill by changing the roofline and adding the sails. This formula allowed him to paint eight to ten screens at once, adding one color at a time. Repetition "makes it cheaper and more effective." His secret was to "only paint the surface of the wire net with a soft touch" and to work from the dark color up to the highlights. Sky first, then dark, "You don't see a house on the outside with a heavy line on it."

Soon after arriving in Baltimore, Bowman became the much-sought-after Fell's Point screen painter, completing according to his accounting "about five hundred every summer. At the rate of five and ten dollars apiece they paid for my trip to Europe." In the mid-1970s he took on an apprentice, Darlene Grubb, an aspiring artist who lived with her family in an alley street nearby. She copied his style to the finest detail, using a deeper palette and thinner paint application.

Charlie was an accomplished fiddler and occupied himself with violin repair as well. Musicians regularly visited his studio where impromptu jam sessions were the norm. Before handing over his screen business to his protégé he remarked, "I'm not money hungry. I make a good living and I'm happy."[261]

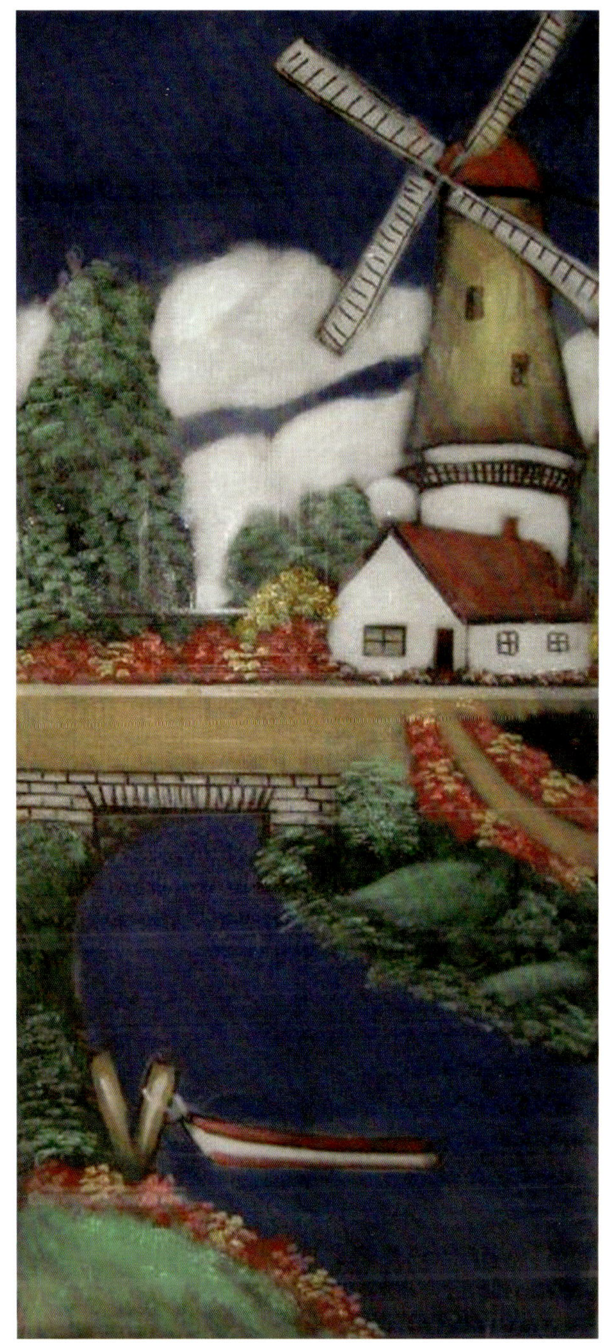

Bowman adapted his bungalow screen to a South Ann Street neighbor's request for a "spare" front door screen in the 1960s. This insert was never used. A mill was one of his favorite deviations from the simple cottage. *Photograph courtesy of Stan and Carla Thomaszewski.*

FRANK J. CIPOLLONI
(NOVEMBER 9, 1924–OCTOBER 22, 2002)

Baltimore's Little Italy claims Frank Cipolloni as its native son and "original and only" screen painter. He lived his entire life in the tiny three-and-a-half story, two-room-deep rowhouse on narrow Albemarle Street. This eleven-foot-wide, twenty-two-foot-deep house was where his mother raised him and his four siblings, surrounded by family members in adjoining and nearby homes. "Would you believe I was born up on the second floor and I still sleep in that same room?"[262] The house where sister Lena lived still shares the modest awning-covered porch atop half a dozen steep stone steps—the threshold having been refashioned in the Italian side-facing style by his next-door neighbor, Marsiglia the stone mason, to replace wooden steps that had sufficed since the mid-nineteenth century. His family's home, which included an uncommon raised basement, was originally red brick, then painted and striped on a regular basis, until it, along with the entire block, was covered with the synthetic Formstone.

Here Cipolloni and Mary, his wife of forty-nine years, raised a son and daughter in the heart of the local Italian cultural and religious scene. A stalwart of St. Leo's Roman Catholic Church a few blocks east, Frank was a regular at the bocce courts around the corner and proudly marched as grand marshal of the annual Saint Anthony's and Saint Gabriel's processions for fifty years. Charged with reminding Baltimoreans that the Great Fire of 1904 stopped at Little Italy's doorsteps in answer to their prayers, the saints' days are among the community's most-revered events.[263]

Art, in any form, was Frank's passion from an early age. He remembered visiting "a fellow three doors up who painted statues and I thought 'That would be nice to do when I grow up.'" But his neighbor counseled him "to do regular artwork that would help you out more." In grade school he applied Easter and Christmas art to the blackboards (analogous to the mirror art once popular in the city) and was always "encouraged by the nuns to do better." As a teenager, he painted numbers on houses, another Baltimore tradition essential for rowhouse wayfinding. One of his customers, not surprisingly, asked if he painted screens as well.

Like other aspiring screen painters, Cipolloni headed to the library and found very little information. As he traveled farther afield toward Fell's Point and Highlandtown, he studied the ever-present screens firsthand. He tried "to learn from the old-timers," who instead encouraged him "to find out the way I did." His growing familiarity with paint on any surface put him in a good position to do just that. Once he completed his first commission, his work was in demand, his title of "Little Italy's Screen Painter" was bestowed, and his quest for "date money" was fulfilled.

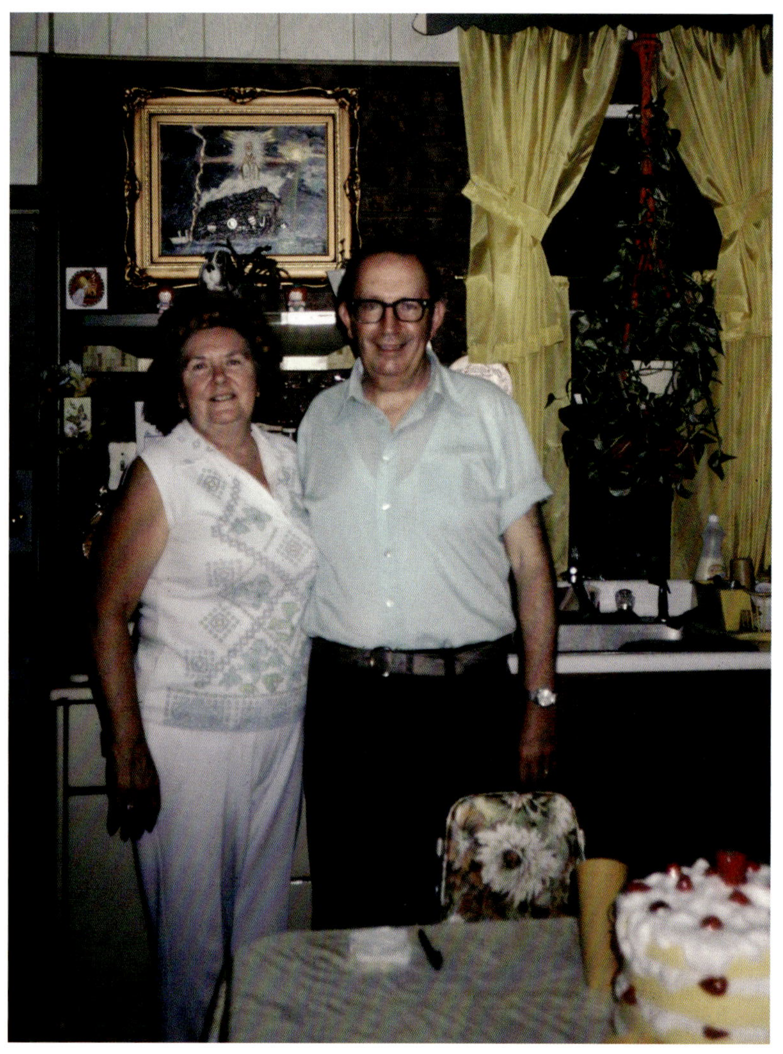

Mary and Frank Cipolloni in the kitchen of their Albemarle Street home, circa 1980. *Author photograph.*

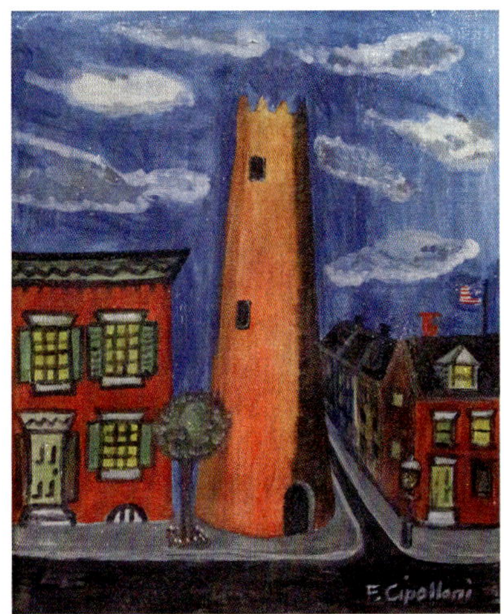

The Shot Tower, visible from Cipolloni's bedroom window, was a favorite landmark and motif. He finished the screen while demonstrating at a Patterson Park festival during the 1987 filming for *The Screen Painters. Gift of Frank and Mary Cipolloni. Collection of the Painted Screen Society of Baltimore, Inc. Christine Fillat photograph.*

But, operating in a vacuum, he was "free lancing" every aspect, including subject matter and pricing. "I didn't know what to charge. The first one gave me ten dollars and down in Highlandtown they were charging two dollars. But it didn't make no difference to me because I didn't know. I just figured if they like it that much, that's all right." Lacking space to work at home, he preferred to paint on site. Whenever possible he painted directly at the window. If there were no painted screens on the upper windows in Little Italy, it was because Cipolloni "never worked on second floors. I only worked on the first floors or where I could get a ladder."

His standard for a well-done screen required that it be "fast, colorful and no more than two of the same scene." Somehow he managed to steer his customers from the traditional red-roofed cottage, "just to be different." Since "all you ever see is a house, trees, and swans, I decided that I would like to try something else. So I did the Shot Tower," a landmark he could see from his house. Among his early offerings were "a chicken farm, a tulip garden, and a European-style bridge." "If you go down to Highlandtown you always see the same scene…But when you come by and see the American flag, planets, the Shot Tower, or even an Italian scene on the screens, you figure that's what catches the people's eye. They probably wondered, 'Why did he paint that?' Makes mine different from anyone else's." As a student, even as he copied the old masters, he questioned why he "had to do somebody else's. I want to do mine." He took immense pride that "every one you see is an original. No painting of mine is a copy."

FRANK CIPOLLONI'S "TECHNIQUES ON WINDOW AND DOOR SCREEN PAINTING" SECRETS REVEALED

"If you go to the library, here [Central Branch] you will find a brochure I did in 1960." Librarians were at a loss to direct the many requests they received for screen-painting instructions. They invited Frank, their own in-house artist, to write a concise, one-page sheet for distribution. It has been copied in many national publications. "It shows you all the tricks to paint a screen. This was a great secret. For some reason they just don't want to let it out, but I let it out." His simple, bare bones, seven-step approach "assures a satisfying and workmanlike job." The flyer enabled would-be painters "to sort of have your cake and eat it too…not only a joy to do, but also a beautiful expression of art."

· The screen must be cleaned from dirt and grease.
· Wash the screen with any type of <u>vinegar</u>.
· Give mesh a coat of <u>flat white paint</u>.
· Sketch scenery on white mesh with <u>charcoal</u>.
· VERY IMPORTANT—Use Fitch <u>brushes</u> (flats) or stiff brushes. Using a soft brush will cause clogging.
· USE <u>OIL PAINTS</u>—any outside colors. Do not use oils from tubes (Take too long to dry).
· When painting is dry give a good coat of <u>spar varnish</u>. In the winter wrap the [screens] in paper or cloth and they will last 2 or 3 years.[264]

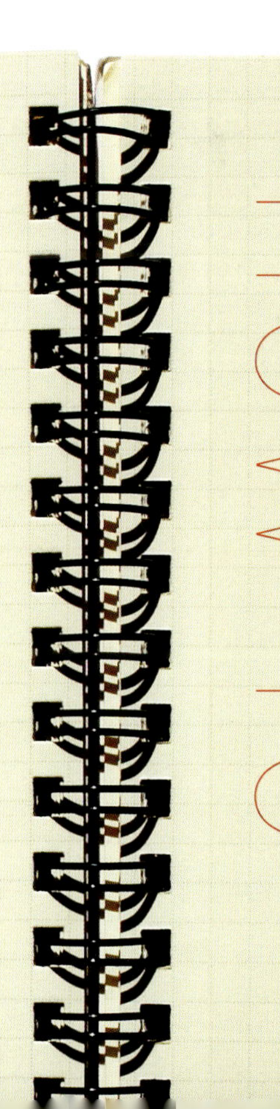

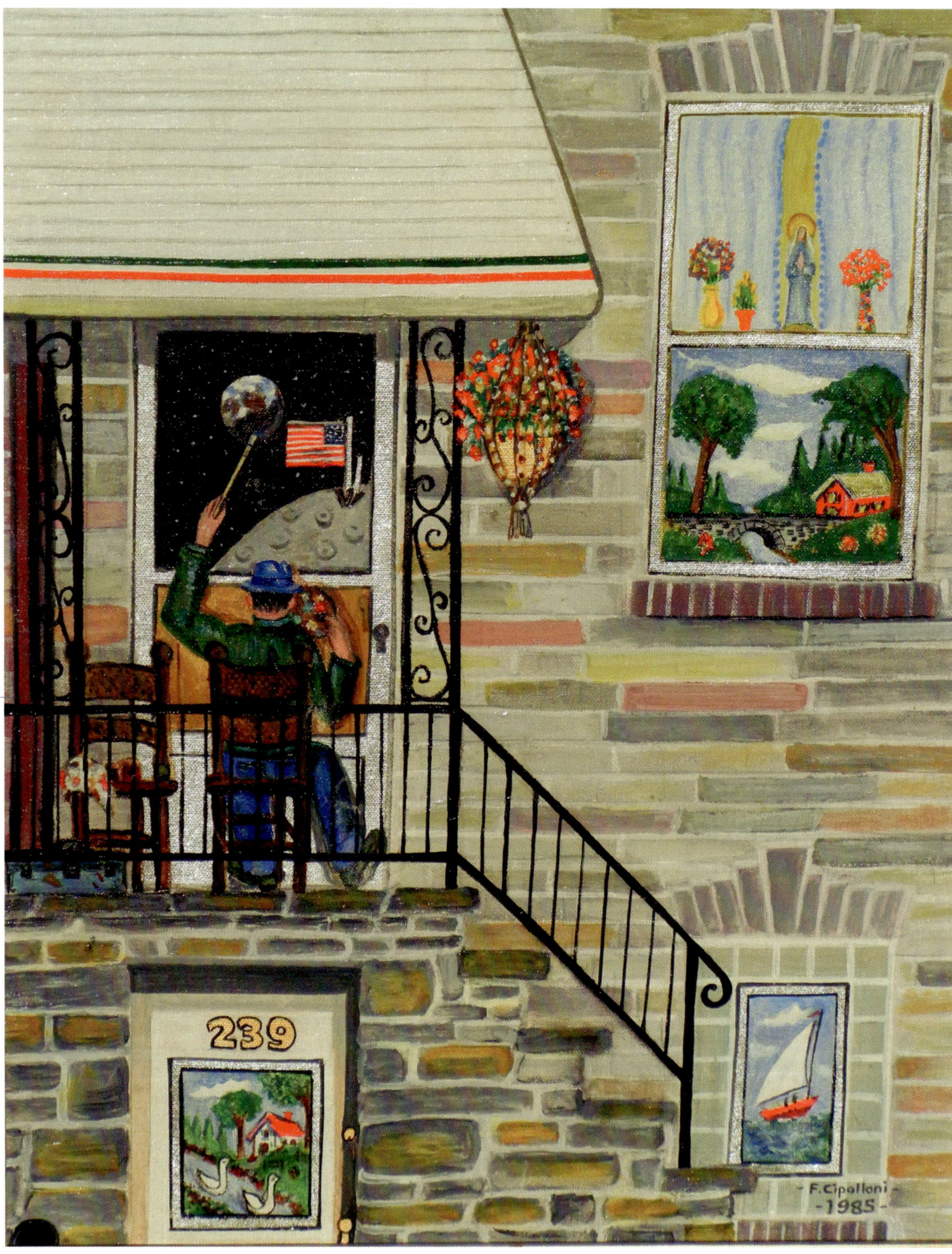

Frank Cipolloni painted himself painting the Planets screen on the front of his South Albemarle Street house in Little Italy. His canvas paintings found their way on to the family's annual Christmas cards. *Courtesy of the Cipolloni family.*

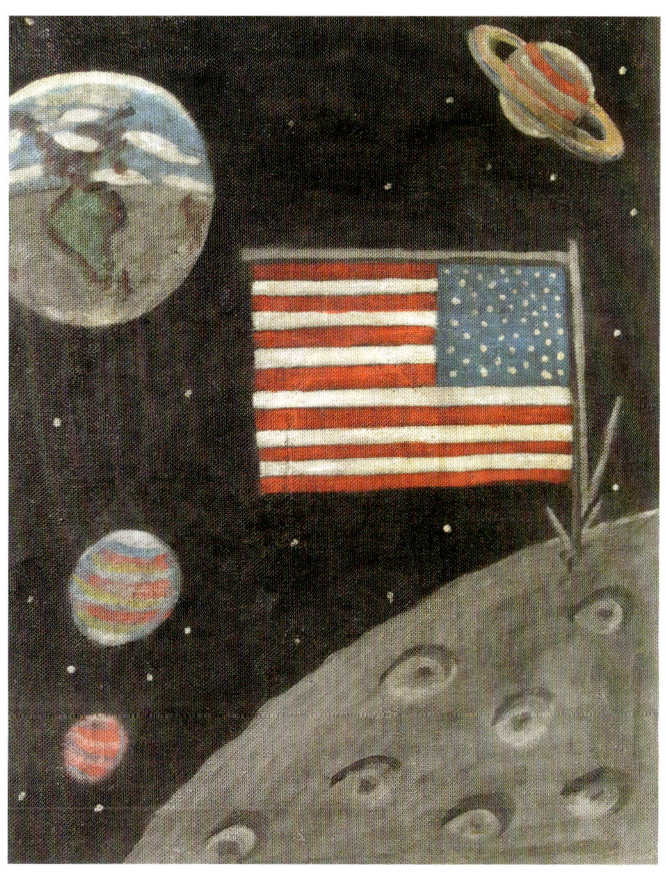

The Planets proved Frank Cipolloni's desire to break from the screen painter's mold and paint something other than the Red Bungalow. The reversed flag is how he remembers the U.S. moon landing in 1969. *Courtesy of the Cipolloni family.*

After serving in the armed forces, he took night courses, and eventually day classes, at the Maryland Institute. He and his older brother Charlie, always inseparable, found jobs together as illustrators in the Exhibit Department of the public relations office of the Central Branch of the Enoch Pratt Free Library. The commute was a short walk that he made daily for more than four decades. The library was nationally known for its prize-winning, oversized display windows facing Cathedral Street, which were significantly enhanced by Frank's inventive signs and lettering.

His home was similarly festooned with every manner of artistic endeavor. His annual holiday greeting card, lovingly created since 1968 with the original full-color version presented to Mary on an eight-and-a-half by eleven-inch show card, was copied in black ink on construction paper and reproduced to be mailed to family and friends. Some of his designs started as or became oil paintings, and all found space in the joyful but cramped basement quarters. His studio consisted of a four-foot by eight-foot sign table that could be shifted to accommodate any project. In addition to screens, he painted every kind of show card and sign, worked in oil on canvas and board, painted scenic murals in a number of Little Italy banks and restaurants, decorated scenic holiday mirrors, created logos and painted signs on trucks, signs for attorneys and doctors in reverse-painted black and gold, and banners of all sorts. He especially liked working with silver and gold leaf.

His personal repertoire had three themes: religious subjects, Baltimore scenes, and cosmological settings. His paintings chronicled immediately visible, remembered, and imagined worlds—and almost always included in the corner a line drawing of himself from the back, hat on head and brush and palette in hand.

When Frank was filmed for the 1988 documentary *The Screen Painters* he surprised everyone by painting over an aged bucolic scene on his Albemarle Street door screen with a scene of the planets, the American flag, and Halley's Comet as seen from the moon landing.

He told an inquisitive neighbor, "Don't copy. Do a new one. Be an artist." A few weeks earlier, he told a young disciple at a local arts festival, "The idea is the more you do it, the better you get at it. Practice makes perfect and perfect practice makes you an artist. And to be an artist, it has to be here in your heart, not just in your brains. You got to like it to do it."

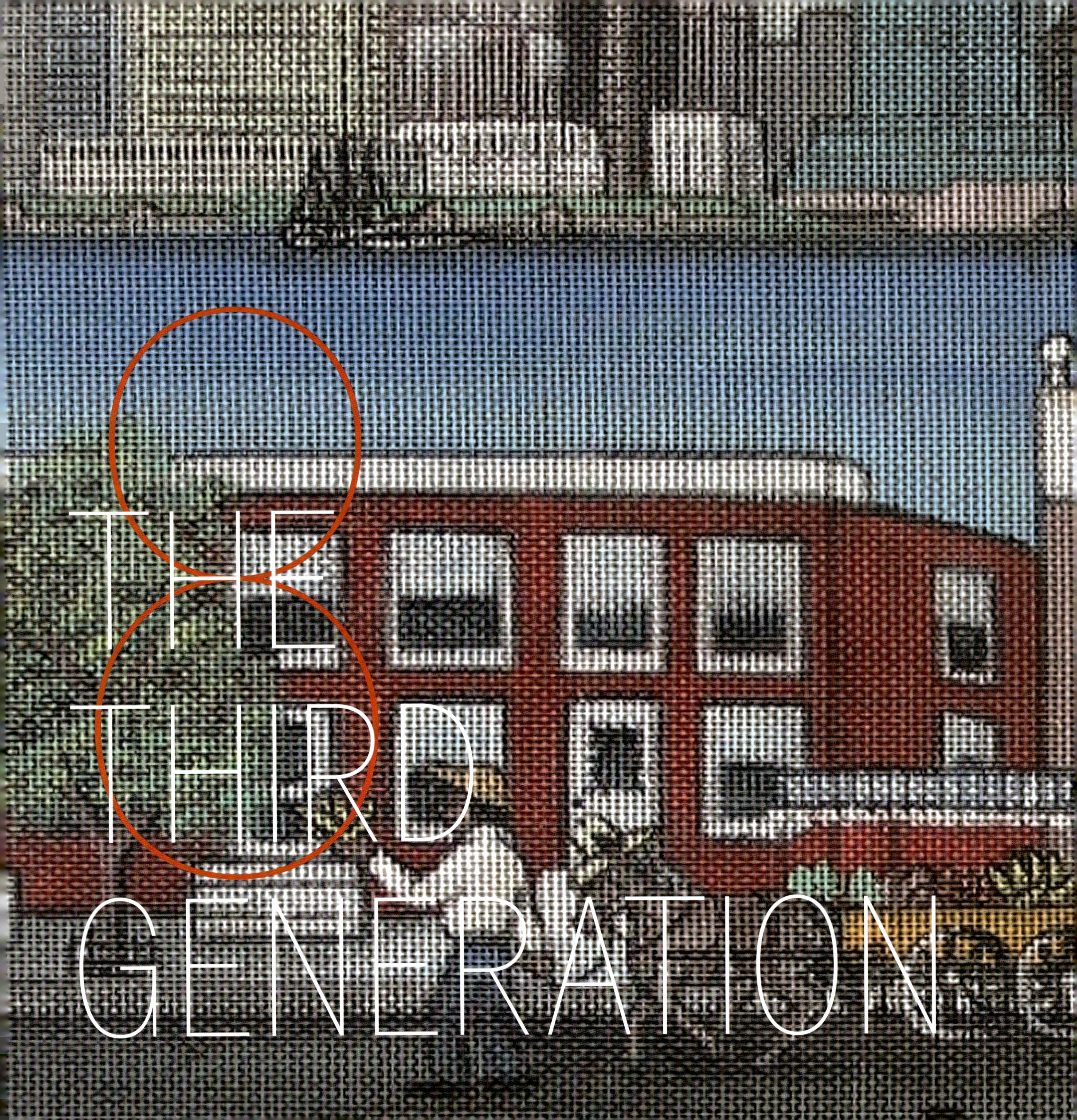
THE
THE THIRD
GENERATION

THE BASELINE FOR THIS STUDY (BOOK) AND THE YEAR MY RESEARCH BEGAN WAS 1974.
Screen painting was enjoying a stable existence at that time. An Oktavec (Richard) was resident screen painter at the Art Shop and new painters added their versions to the East Baltimore streetscapes with seasonal regularity. About a dozen active painters could consistently be found plying their trade. The lineage connecting the active screen painters to William Oktavec was now measured at one remove, reached through his sons or, in the case of "lifer" Tom Lipka, through an itinerant follower of William Oktavec. As this particular era of screen painting began, window air conditioners no longer seemed the threat that was going to make painted screens redundant, as they had begun to lose the battle to central air, and the windows were free to open once more.[265] The neighborhoods remained consistently white ethnic, just shy of 100 percent, with a majority of single or widowed women ruling the rowhouses. These same dwellings were where they had been raised in sizable families and, in many cases, where they had raised their own. Painted screens were only extraordinary to outsiders. The name Oktavec, however pronounced, was familiar to all. Screen painting was still an all-male club as the second generation was giving way to the next.

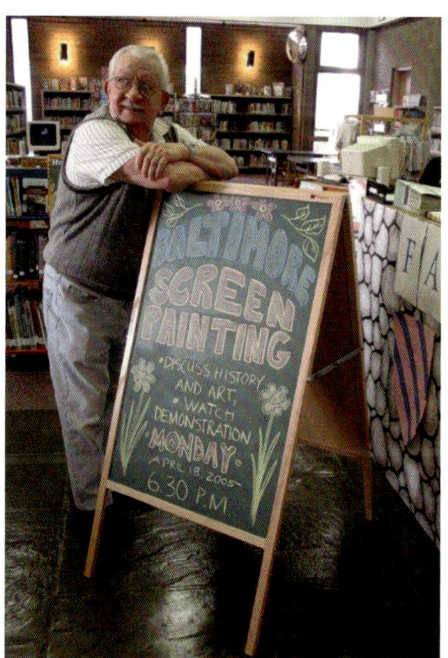

Tom Lipka prepares to share his art at the Light Street branch of The Enoch Pratt Free Library, 2005. *Author photograph.*

TOM LIPKA
(BORN SEPTEMBER 21, 1935)

"I was always in it," said Tom Lipka, who was born and raised in the same Canton neighborhood as Alonzo Parks. He vividly recalls "as a youngster in the 1940s, watching a real old man who could really paint. He just lined his work up right along the house or the alley. He could do a whole screen in a half hour. He could knock out ten in a couple of hours."[266] Tom claims to have actually seen the man, identified decades later as Parks, apply paint to wire only once, though Parks's screens would surely have been a part of the landscape young Tom navigated whenever he set out from home.

That inadvertent "lesson" took place on Lakewood Avenue, and "the owner of the home was a friend of my mother's, Mrs. Anuszewski. I asked her, 'How much are you paying him for this?' She said, 'He's painting the whole house for a pitcher of beer.'" When Tom begged his mother for a chance to try his hand, she gave him a few dollars "to go to Butts's hardware store to stock up on paint and brushes" and permission to experiment on her screens, and his career began. "Mom, being wise, realized of course that painting window screens could be a good venue to channel my untrained talents and excess energy, as well as keeping me busy, out of trouble and making the neighborhood a little safer from normally wild childhood escapades."[267]

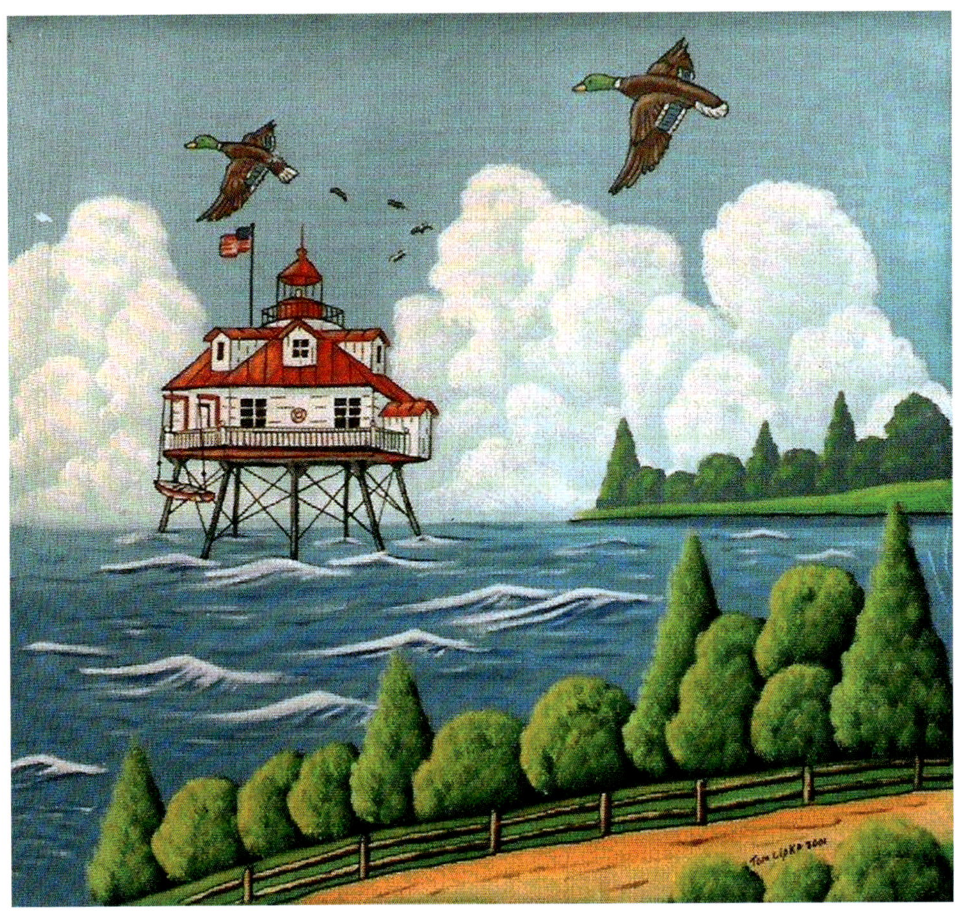

Despite its complexity, Thomas Point Light near Annapolis is one of Tom's favorite scenes. After the Red Bungalow, lighthouses are his most requested subject. *Courtesy of Tom Lipka. Christine Fillat photograph.*

With the technique and image firmly embedded in his mind, Tom recalls being further emboldened when he went with his sister Lil to Chicago at age eleven. There he executed an impressive rendering of an eagle in flight on screen, "which caused quite a stir." He returned home to paint for his family and neighbors in Canton, continuing a hobby and part-time or occasional job that lasted throughout his teenage years.

As the youngest of seven siblings, most of whom married and purchased houses nearby, he was never at a loss to find screens for practice. Two or three screens a day to start was a bonanza for him, allowing him to go bowling at Highland Lanes on Fleet Street, to Matthew's Pizza on Eastern Avenue, and to the local Linwood movie theater without asking his parents for cash. His career gained traction during his senior year, when he was featured in a *Baltimore Sun* article as one of a younger generation of screen painters alongside the master, William Oktavec.[268]

Although he recalls as a teenager painting a houseful of screens for neighbors depicting rocket ships and fantasy lunarscapes, when he resumed painting years later, he felt strongly about sticking with the traditional bungalow scene, specifically the one he saw being painted on the street. He did, however, help spark a late-twentieth-century boom in lighthouse scenes, catering to Chesapeake Bay-centric customers with images of most of the historic lighthouses of the region: Thomas Point Light, a multisided screwpile structure, was his favorite and the most difficult to execute.

Lipka's distinctive cottage style, borrowed directly from Parks, featured "a color called 'gold,' a cream color for the house and the road [while] others used white." He was especially gratified that his work added color to the relatively drab palette of his neighborhood. "Canton was kind of a sterile neighborhood in a way. The ladies scrubbing the steps. No trees. But they really loved those screens." Another image in Lipka's visual lexicon: colorful flowering bushes that some compared to gumdrops. He likened the vibrant bushes to Oktavec's red roof, which "made sense because it made the thing stand out...something to catch your eye because it was a bright color."

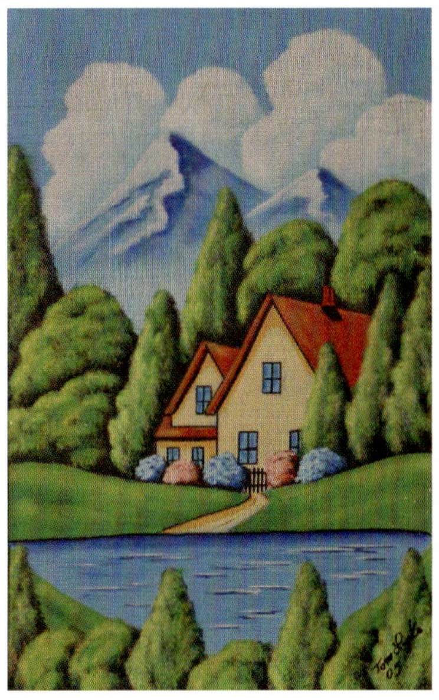

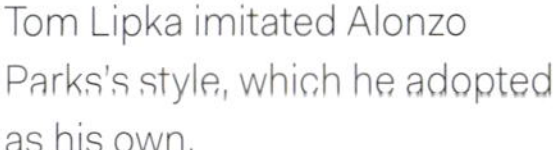

Tom Lipka imitated Alonzo Parks's style, which he adopted as his own.

LEFT

Tom Lipka screen, 2005. *Collection of the Painted Screen Society of Baltimore, Inc. Christine Fillat photograph.*

RIGHT

Alonzo Parks screen, circa 1960. *Collection of the Painted Screen Society of Baltimore, Inc. Christine Fillat photograph.*

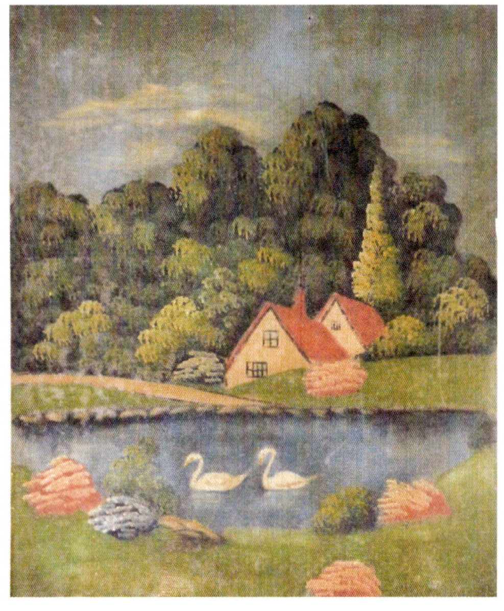

For Lipka, color was essential to a painted screen: "the paint in different colors on the screen acted like camouflage and it kind of distorted your vision. I didn't care why. As long as I made 25 or 50 cents a window I was happy."

What started as a way to earn date money eventually "spoiled my summers. I was too busy and my parents encouraged me to paint even more." After enlisting and serving in the U.S. Air Force in California, Labrador, and nearby Dover, Delaware, he married and moved with his wife, Ramona, in 1959 into the first of a series of rented rowhouses in Canton, all within a few blocks of his family's home.

From the backyard of the first of these homes, he could see Fort McHenry and watch the oil tankers load in the harbor. Within moments he could walk to the golden domes of St. Casimir's Catholic Church, the magnet for the second wave of Polish Americans, and shop at the outdoor Canton Market in the middle of O'Donnell Square. By this time, he began to notice that "the screens seemed to have disappeared, older people moving to the county, dying off. Houses being updated, windows modernized. Putting new storm doors and windows in, jalousies. It got very quiet [for screen painting]." This ebb and flow was a cycle that was to be repeated regularly in the one-hundred-year history of painted screens. Homeowners who didn't want to be branded as out-of-date embraced every remodeling trend, from the faux exterior stone to a single metal rail for the marble steps, to the newest replacement windows and storm doors. Tom's wife pressed him into service to paint screens for the few windows of their home. He was unable to resist requests for commissions from his neighbors, during another screen-painting phase that lasted only two years.

In 1962, he took a full-time job at the city's Department of Transit and Traffic, rising to the position of signal engineer. His responsibilities included timing lights, designing intersections, and managing the flow of traffic before and after sporting events. Meantime he continued his artwork. The city's cultural heritage museum, The Peale, had an annual art contest for city employees, and Tom's painted screen depicting a floral garden path, the only screen ever entered, won second place in 1964.

In 1966, his house, along with hundreds of others in southeast Baltimore, was slated for demolition to make way for "the expressway that was never built." This forced him to leave Canton.[269] He and his growing family relocated due north to the suburban Belair-Edison section of the city, a popular migration route for East Baltimoreans. The corner rowhouse built in the 1950s featured an oversized backyard with space for a large garden, outdoor play, and dining areas. His wife, a West Virginia native, insisted on painted screens for the dozen windows and doors of the end-of-row brick home. Tom complied, while helping to raise five children, working full time, bowling regularly, and coaching Little League. Otherwise, he gave up screen painting for close to two decades, but he stayed involved from the sidelines, driving around the city making a photographic record of screens he discovered and rescuing many victims of remodeling from local dumpsters.

His sister, Julia "Lil" Sims, maintained the Lipka family home on South Kenwood Avenue, dutifully keeping the windows and doors, front and back, fully decorated. Her commitment to the community art form was so strong that during the years that Tom was not active, she ordered her screens from Oktavec's Art Shop. Among the screens adorning her home was one bungalow scene painted by Johnny Eck when he was working under the Oktavec name. The Lipka family home continues to serve as a living museum of screen art, as it has for more than half a century. Lil dutifully cleaned her prized screens and stored them each winter. But more recently, she keeps them up year round as an act of pure pride, knowledgeably acting as docent for all who inquire about her brother's work and her growing and changing collection.[270] The late addition of cats to her household has wreaked more havoc on the fragile wire canvas than the passage of time or the elements. Tom's frequent visits to the house and to the nearby senior center where he conducts classes are encouragement not only to Lil but also to her neighbors. Across the street, at least one lifetime resident continued to regularly order a new set of screens featuring Tom's signature bungalows with each innovation in replacement window technology.

Tom's waning interest in painted screens was rekindled by a brief 1982 exhibition in Baltimore's City Hall Rotunda.[271] He was not invited to participate, but attended the show's opening and got the itch to paint again. Inspired by the excitement and the opportunity to meet other painters and members of the Oktavec family, he followed up with a visit to the Art Shop. He carried some of his own paintings to share with Al, who had only recently taken over the family franchise and showed Lipka a few of his recent screens.

When it was time to refresh his new screens at home, Tom unpacked the paints he had stored away for more than a dozen years. He used his remaining lead-based paints until the supply was exhausted. Realizing how much he enjoyed the diversion, he announced he was back in business. Word got out, and soon he had customers both in his new community and on his boyhood turf in Canton.

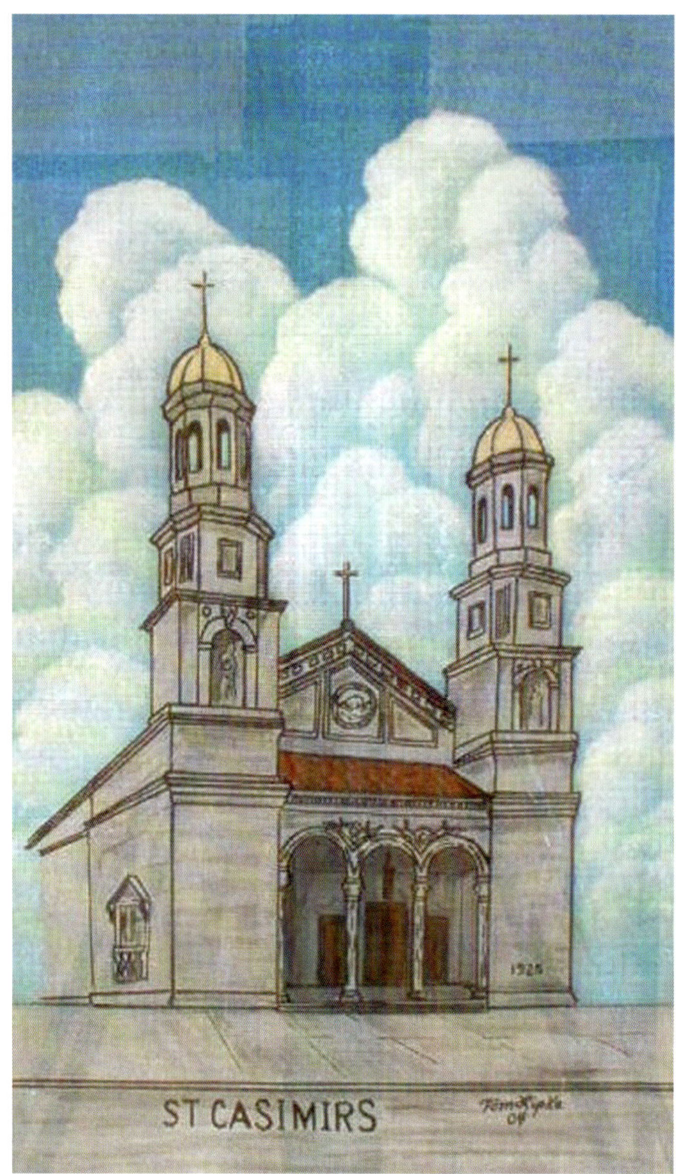

St. Casimir's Catholic Church is the centerpiece of the Polish community of Canton and Tom Lipka's family parish. Neighbors proudly display the local landmark on their screen doors. *Wayne Schaumburg photograph.*

An invitation to paint a landscape scene for the back door of the governor's mansion in 1991 marked both the highest and lowest point of Tom Lipka's painting career. William Donald Schaefer, Baltimore's longtime mayor and chief booster, newly elected as the state's chief executive, wanted to bring a bit of his hometown with him when he moved to Annapolis. A painted screen was his choice, honoring both his Baltimore constituency and his rowhouse roots. His lady friend, official hostess Hilda Mae Snoops, took the brunt of the conflict when decorators charged with the mansion's interior design took offense at the decidedly working-class artifact the governor had commissioned. An embattled ex-curator defended the house's historical integrity while starting a mild furor that pitted state preservationists against Baltimore's proud traditionalists:

> I'm a tremendous fan of the folk-genre of painted screens and they are a marvelous art form for Baltimore, but they couldn't be more incorrect for a Georgian revival mansion. If Hilda Mae wants to live in a row house on Eastern Avenue she should go back to Eastern Avenue and stop living in the governor's mansion.[272]

Despite the fact that the colorful scene was visible only within an enclosed rear basement courtyard, its presence in Annapolis was short lived. The tempest it stirred in the local media brought attention to the art form at a time when many of the oldest and most devoted screen owners were beginning to leave the old neighborhoods in a new wave of departures.

When the Lipkas themselves moved farther north along the Harford Road corridor in 1995 to a free-standing bungalow south of the county line, Tom's wife, Ramona, once again required that every screen be painted. This time Tom completed sixteen screens. While completing the job he was spotted by a local television station, which once again put him in the spotlight. "I was featured on a five-minute TV piece (Maryland by George). I'm still watching it and the damn phone started ringing off the hook. You want screens, bring 'em down. When I'm done with them, I'll call you. That's the way it worked. Get my crabbin' in, little league with the grandkids, go take 'em to the zoo. And it worked out."[273]

He never advertised but he did start a website when he retired. His classes and festival appearances probably provided his largest source of customers "If they want it, they call me. If I want to paint, I paint. If I don't want to paint, I don't paint."

When the Painted Screen Society was formed in 1985, Tom began teaching at multiple sites throughout the city. He regularly fills classes and is considered to be "screen-painter-in-residence" at Canton's Hatton Senior Center, a two-block walk from his birthplace. Five hundred students have passed through his classes in one-day workshops at senior centers and libraries and in weekly term-length classes at regional high schools organized through the Community College of Baltimore County. Required reading is his twenty-eight-page, densely descriptive and illustrated tome, *Tom Lipka's Screen Painting Instruction Manual*.[274] His students are required to copy his Alonzo Parks-inspired red-roofed cottage using acrylic paints. "Freelancing," or deviating from his model, is permitted but not encouraged. Though his students rarely sign their work, their lineage is never in doubt. Their finished screens pop up everywhere. At least one of his students was planning to teach screen painting in the Philippines. Regarding the scenes being painted today, he notes his students are doing "a lot of goofy things like underwater scenes, but I guess I'm from the old corps, I like the typical red-roofed bungalow 'cause that's the one that started it all."[275]

Further ensuring the survival of painted screens, in 2004 Lipka took on an apprentice through a state program to conserve traditional arts. Maryland Traditions, the folk arts program of the Maryland State Arts Council, enabled a year-long mentoring relationship between Lipka and his Caribbean born daughter-in-law Anna Ramos Lipka, the mother of young twins. Now living in the county, a good distance from her mentor, Anna also teaches, often substituting for her father-in-law. Tom considers teaching to be almost as important as selling screens: "I accomplished what I really wanted to do, keep screen painting alive."

Tom might be considered a reluctant screen painter, having entered and left the field four different times, but his tenure spans more than sixty years, a record that even William Oktavec did not approach. He has one foot in painted screens' past and a stake in their future, but observed, "What I'd really like to know, is what they're worth." For someone who started selling his work for a quarter, he will probably be pleased, whatever the figure.

Tom's mentorship of his daughter-in-law represented a shift in the art form from one that was male dominated to one that is today overwhelmingly practiced by women.

BOTTOM LEFT
Tom Lipka's Red Bungalow template made screen art an easy to follow paint-by-number exercise.

BOTTOM RIGHT
Cover of Tom Lipka's 2005 Screen Painting Instruction Manual.

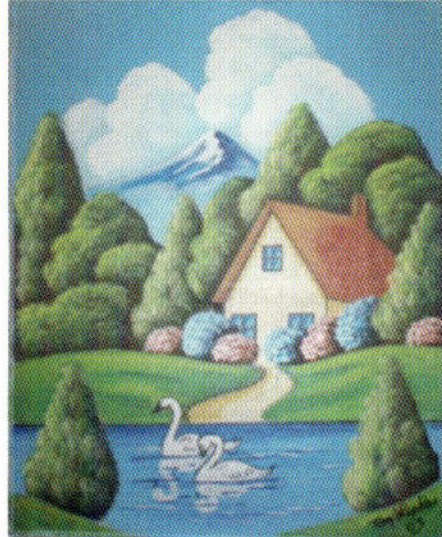

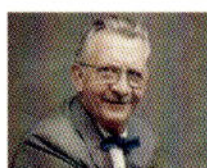

DEE HERGET
(BORN JANUARY 20, 1935)

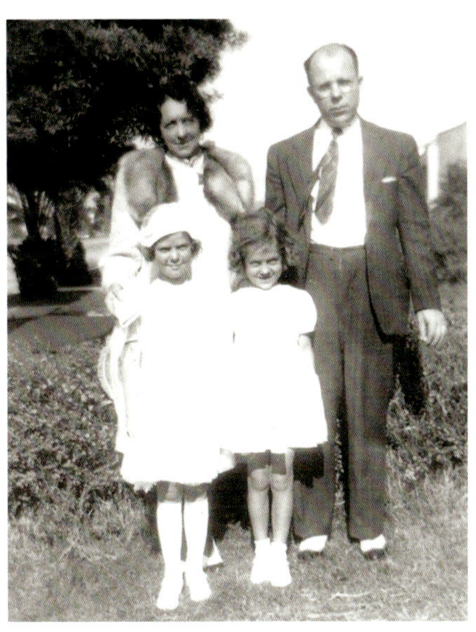

Dee Herget's family, the Amrheins, in Inglewood, California, their home until her mother's untimely death. When Dee was seven she moved to Baltimore to live among relatives. *Courtesy of Dee Herget.*

Another key member of the third generation, and a key force in promoting the art's revival, was a woman. For Dee Herget, "Art is the creation of someone's inspiration and people enjoy it. Whether it is singing, painting, a cake, anything. That is art. Thank God we have it." A native of northeast Baltimore City, Dee Amrhein moved to Inglewood, California, at age one and a half, with her parents and older sister. Her father, a metal worker, worked in the aircraft industry for a company that became North American Aviation. They returned to Baltimore, her parents' hometown, shortly before her mother's death at age forty in 1942. Her father was at first unable to keep the family together, so while he worked in the war effort for Glenn L. Martin, the aircraft manufacturer, the children lived first with a stern grandmother and several aunts and then in the Gardenville area (north of the city off Belair Road) with a wonderful and warm Aunt Dorothy.

It was during this period that Dee remembers her first sighting of painted screens and "the man with the collapsible stool and huge black board," hollering "Paint your screens" as he made his way down the block. As youngsters "all you could do in those stupid rowhouses was play on the sidewalk and marble steps. No toys." Her grandmother kept such a tight rein on her charges that they were forbidden from exploring their new neighborhood. So, of course, the girls were fascinated by the disheveled fellow as he took a chunk of their playground for his studio. "He barked, 'Don't crowd me, children.'" She did not recall him applying an undercoat to the screen placed on his handmade easel, "no background, just the necessary colors, a couple little clouds, a slash for a path." He was through in two minutes and went on to the next house. "Seventy-five cents." She "never saw him or thought about it again."[276]

Her father remarried at the urging of his sisters and gathered his daughters back under his roof. His new wife, a teacher, introduced Dee to classical music and art, but Dee ultimately chose to leave home before finishing high school, eloping at age sixteen and leaving Baltimore for her husband's U.S. Air Force postings in Texas, Florida, and Germany.[277] She returned to Baltimore ten years later with a failed marriage, two young children, and a taste for travel. She found a job she loved and excelled at, in "public relations" at City Hall, specifically as part of the Customer Service Division (read "complaint department"). During this period she married Carl Herget, a police officer she met when she summoned help for a minor fender bender. After thirteen years of being paid to listen to the woes of irate taxpayers, it is no surprise that she lost her hearing and left work on disability.

I came home and I did everything you say you are going to do when you don't have to work. All that sewing that piles up and all that dusting on the top bookshelves and all those things you are going to do, until I lived in a meticulously clean house. And I couldn't stand it. I was crawling the walls and I thought, "Well, I am going back to school."

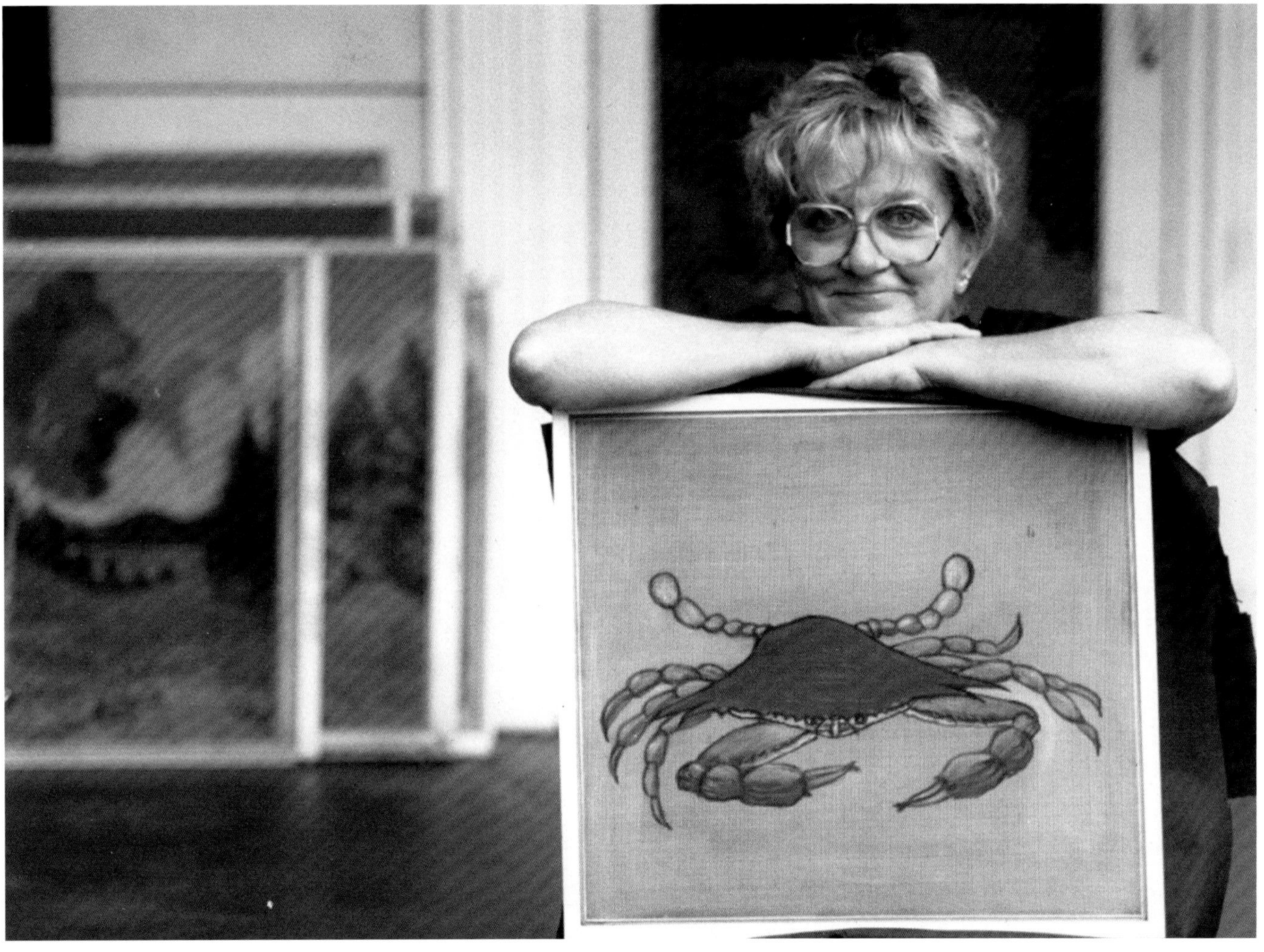

Dee Herget will paint almost anything on a screen, except abstracts, portraits, or automobiles. *Courtesy of Dee Herget. Jed Kirschbaum photograph.*

Having never attempted "any serious art," other than three years of summer classes at the Maryland Institute in her pre-teen years, she nonetheless considered herself artistic. "I use art in everything. In the colors you wear on your dress. Colors you make for your food for dinner. The sun going down and the colors in the sky can bring tears to your eyes. I would be sad if I couldn't see. It is bad enough not hearing, but I can live with that. But seeing, that is the ultimate of senses." She had kept her "art box" through all her travels, and now it came out of storage. She enrolled in Art 101 at the Baltimore City Community College: "So I went down, at that time I lived in Highlandtown and I was only a few miles from the Harbor Campus. And I used to come home every day and do homework and I would sit down at the dining room table and I thought, 'Gee, I can draw. I haven't lost anything.'"

She recalled the instant it occurred to her that the local art form in evidence all around her, screen painting, would be the perfect calling for an East Baltimore lady who loved art, home, and keeping busy.

I always tell people, at that moment I was sitting at the dining room table and lights should have flashed and bells should have rung. It was a magnificent idea. But I remember thinking, "artists are a dime a dozen and I should be able to have some kind of job where I could be able to make a little bit of money out of it." But I wanted to do something different. I didn't want to make handicrafts and I didn't want to do all the things that everybody does, because I am different. I knew I could draw. I do things quickly anyway. I talk quickly. I walk quickly. I cook quickly. Everything I do, I do quickly, so screen painting is nice because I can do that [quickly].

Little did she know that some of the home-based painters took days, often weeks, to complete a single screen.

So anyway, I got the idea. I walked up and down for half an hour thinking, "How do I find a screen painter?" I called the library and I called the Maryland Historic [sic] Society and I finally called our community newspaper and they gave me the name of [then retired seventy-six-year-old screen painter] Ben Richardson. He used to advertise years and years ago. That took me half an hour to get up the nerve to call him. And I called him and I said, "You don't know me but I would like to learn screen painting." "Well, come on over," he said, "come on over." And he gave me directions. Across town. It was like going to China. When I got there he sat me down at the dining room table and I wrote notes about what kind of paint and the brushes. I never did see the man paint until years later.

In the first of several meetings, Richardson talked her through the materials, technique, and studio set-up. Without ever lifting a brush, opening a can of paint, or inviting her into his gazebo work area, he advised her to go home and try her hand at it, then return. After one surprise visit to her house and critique by Ben, she was on her own.

And I went home and collected old beat-up screens and I went to the dump. I went to friends and neighbors and I got all these screens. That light up there, I bought that and a little bureau. I like my work high and I have to stand up doing it. And I started painting screens just like my job at City Hall, eight-thirty to four-thirty every day. Until about six weeks, my husband finally said to me… (I didn't say a word to him. He knew what I was doing but he didn't say anything). So he said to me one day, "When are you going to do something with this?" So I put an ad in *The Baltimore Sun,* "Screen Painting is not dead. It is alive and well and being painted in Baltimore," and waited for the phone to ring. And I write in my diary, "Grand Opening Dee's Art Shop. Not one call." And I think the next week, I got a call from a lady to retouch some. And then maybe the next week, another one to paint.

Dee Herget had high hopes for her screen-painting career when she opened for business. Work picked up after a brief mention of her by a local journalist, as the rare female screen artist. *Courtesy of Dee Herget.*

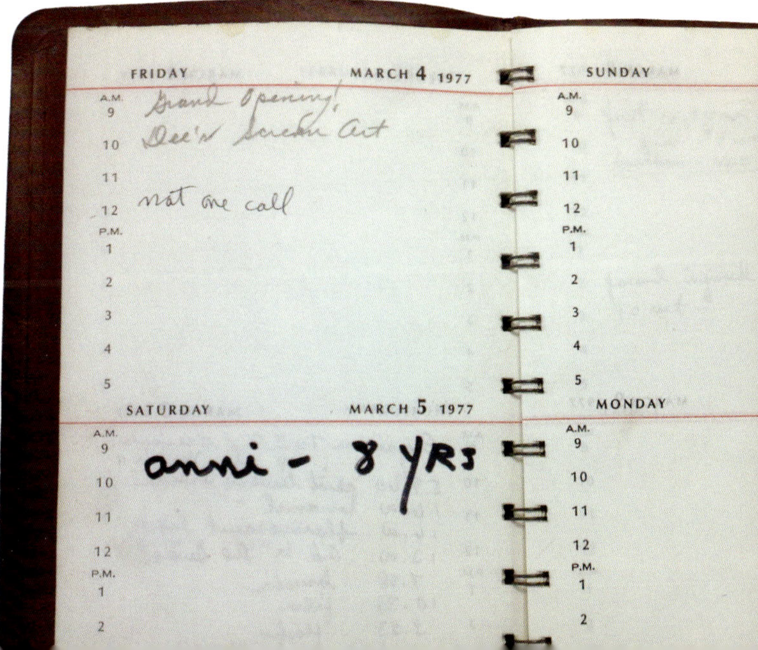

Her first customer brought an Oktavec screen to touch up. After several nerve-wracking weeks, the phone began to ring and she found that she had all the business she could handle. The listing also netted her a mention as an "effervescent redhead" in the *Sun Magazine* early in her career.[278] Callers were especially surprised to find a woman painting screens. She was among the first since Oktavec's apprentice Ruth Chrysam appeared on the scene in the 1920s. It had taken fifty years for females to re-enter the ranks of the exclusive male club.

Unfazed that she was breaking new ground, Dee's tireless interest in the art form included intense curiosity about her competition—past, present, and future; their materials, techniques, motivations, fees, and styles. She never questioned that screen painting was an all-male domain or the fact that she was opening doors for an avocation that would in short order come to be dominated by women.

She has continued to be in awe of the remarkable output of the Oktavec family, William, Richard, Albert, and John, and to consider them the epitome of screen art mastery. "Their trees— Oktavec was the best. No one could beat him." She has attempted to figure out some of his time- and paint-saving shortcuts, the cut of the brushes and application techniques, through close examination of individual screens. When a vintage Oktavec screen arrived at her studio for touch up, she used it as her personal tutorial, and most often sent it back after a cursory cleaning, advising the owners to leave it alone and treasure it. In her opinion, no other painters merited that level of respect, which for her bordered on reverence. On occasion she removed a faded Oktavec from its frame and replaced it with her own version, saving the original to add to her "study" collection, scattered in outbuildings and storage areas throughout her home and property. Collecting at yard sales and flea markets or through gifts from her customers, she has amassed a rag-tag museum-scavenger hunt that presents an impressive array of the work of the artists who paved the way for her esoteric avocation.

Her respect for screen painting's roots led her to my doorstep in 1978. She asked me to write a brief description of the history of screen painting for an outdoor festival where she was demonstrating and exhibiting screens to the public for the first time.[279] I agreed to write the requested piece, but wondered how someone barely two years in could call herself a traditional artist. Now she's well into her fourth decade as a screen painter.

It is no surprise that she became the most vocal advocate for honoring the *ur*-image of painted screens, Oktavec's red bungalow. According to Dee, "fancy work, like portraits or automobiles, doesn't belong on a screen. It would be like painting an abstract on a Polish Easter egg. It just is not done." She is a professed purist, a traditionalist who insists that only "the little cottage with lake and swans is real screen art." She is "a swan person. I have swans all over the house that I collect. [I have] swan pictures and put swans on my screens. You can't have a painted screen without a swan on it."[280] She nonetheless dutifully adds her own personal touch whenever possible—a tiny rabbit, squirrel, or deer, "something alive." She unapologetically adheres to a canon of proper subjects. Religious themes other than churches are strictly off-limits. When asked to paint the outlines and color code a screen with numbers, she was outraged. "Too much work, too much detail, too little money."

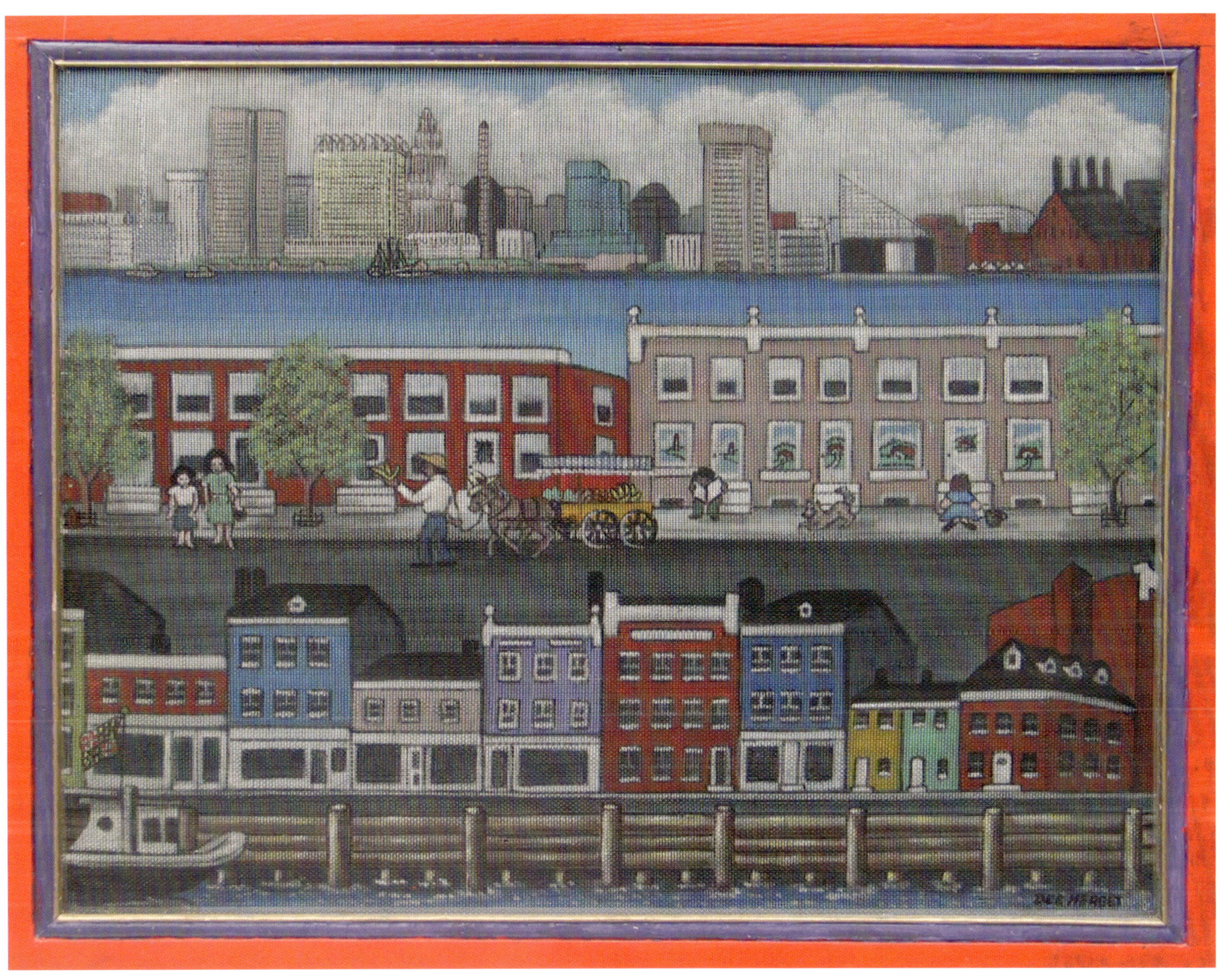

Herget painted her first "Cityscape" in 1994 as a commissioned gift from Baltimore to its Sister City, Odessa, Ukraine. The triptych shows (from top) the city's skyline, a typical rowhouse scene, and Fell's Point's Thames Street. *Courtesy of Dee Herget. Jed Kirschbaum photograph.*

Painting screens is a labor of love for Dee. In her heyday, she painted daily. When she and her husband moved from the city to the county in 1978, she despaired that she would lose her clientele that was "ninety-nine percent Highlandtown." Her continued advertisements in a number of local weeklies, the *East Baltimore Guide*, *Dundalk Eagle*, *The* (Essex) *Avenue*, and *Times*, word-of-mouth referrals, and the testament of highly visible screens installed throughout the city, have kept her busy as ever, with an expanded market northeast of the city, nationwide, and overseas. She regularly sends screens rolled in tubes with installation instructions for her mail-order clients. She has completed several wraparound porches that required scaffolding and days of outdoor work.

Perhaps the screen of which she is most proud is what she calls her "Cityscape." When invited to create an original and meaningful gift for Baltimore's Sister City, Odessa, Ukraine, she crafted and screened an oversized wooden frame with a vertically stacked colorful triptych of three streetscapes: Fell's Point from Thames Street, rowhouses with marble step scrubbers on the sidewalk and Arabbers and their horse cart passing along the street, topped by an Inner Harbor downtownscape.

Her home on a quarter-acre lot on Sue Creek in the eastern Baltimore County community of Essex is a cozy white bungalow with a green, she points out, "not red" roof. She shares it with her husband, Carl, and, depending on the day, as many as ten Yorkshire terriers, cats, egg-laying chickens, ducks, and a variety of tropical fish and songbirds.

My house is a painted screen. I decided that one day when I was coming down the street and it was sitting there and the light was shining on it just right. And I thought to myself, "What a cute cottage. All it needed was a thatched roof." So I decided I live in a red bungalow although the roof is not. As soon as I walked into that house, I knew. The walls said, "Man, you are home."

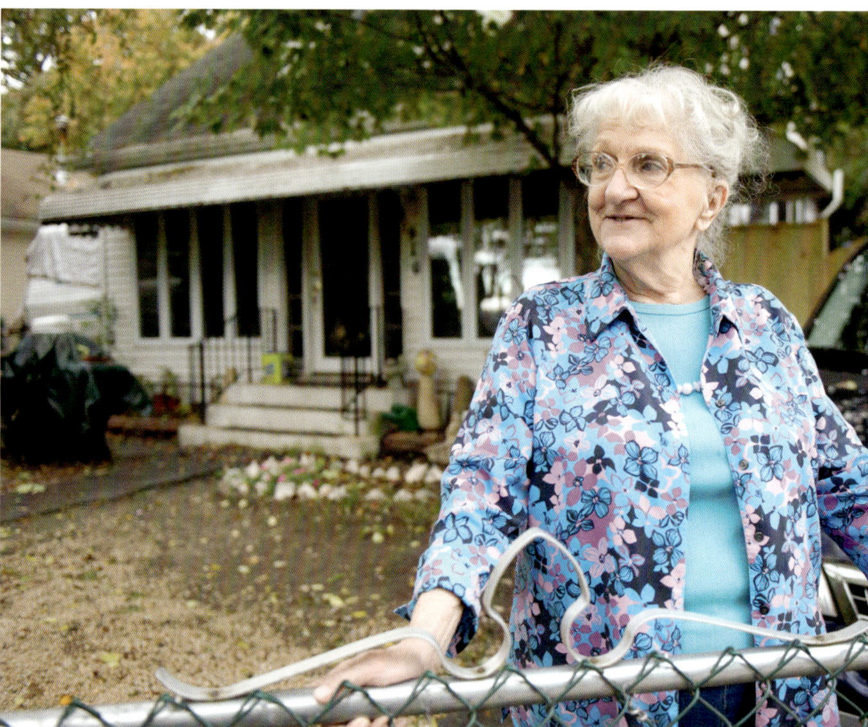

Dee Herget moved from a series of rowhomes to a cozy bungalow on Sue Creek in Essex, Maryland. She shares it with her husband, Carl, and a changing menagerie of small dogs, cats, birds, and an occasional duck, mostly rescued. No swans or red roofs may be found here. *Edwin Remsberg photograph, 2012.*

Eventually the front porch was enclosed to double as her display area. Customers once chose from among twenty screen samples arrayed there. She offered tidy little cottages, cabins of log or Tudor design—with thatch when appropriate, but red roofs dominated. Lighthouses, sailing ships, and wildlife were most always in stock. And "you always have to have a snow scene [even though] they are not that popular. But on a [hot] day like this, you look at it and you feel better." Once she tired of a particular style, having painted far too many or finding the execution too time consuming, she retired that image, temporarily or permanently. Now her porch houses plants in season and her latest flea market find, while her website, among the first screen-painting sites to go up more than a decade ago, serves as her virtual showroom.

When faced with multiple copies of a single scene, she sets up an assembly line. Her present record is twenty-two screens in a single day. "People just kept dropping them off and my studio was getting full. It comes in spurts like that. Nothing for two or three days and suddenly Saturday, Sunday, and Monday will come and you've got a house full. That's what's nice about it. You never know."

Her studio, aka pantry, is a former closet off the kitchen that doubles as the laundry. The room, barely ten feet square, is filled from floor to ceiling with the tools of the screen painter. Hanging fluorescent tubes provide illumination. A firm black vertical board forms the backdrop for a homemade table easel. Cans and bottles of paints, latex on one side, oil-based on the other, and well-worn brushes of every description in cans and bottles, borrow the horizontal surfaces. Shelves of books and clippings fill in the blanks for future images. File cabinets safeguard decades of memorabilia and free publicity from events, magazines, and newspapers. "It's crowded and I love it." Stacks of screens patiently await completion. "I used to finish them in a day. Now I ask them, 'What year?'" Notebooks and stacks of paper contain names of past and future customers with tidy piles of snapshots nearby. Everything is within arms' reach of the center of her paint-spattered universe.

She takes on students, researchers, curators, and reporters with a grumble and a wink. She has been invited to share her expertise at senior centers, elementary schools, and area colleges, at the State House and City Hall, formal galas and at least one gubernatorial inaugural ball. She has taken part in her fair share of museum exhibitions and scholarly meetings. She traveled to San Francisco as part of a museum opening that introduced screen painting to the west coast.[281] The audience for workshops and discussions was receptive, but the lack of screens on San Franciscans' windows was a sure sign that the Baltimore folk art would not find a welcoming home there.

At least one local tour guide regularly included a visit with Dee on her city bus tours, which featured lunch at one of the more venerable Baltimore institutions—Haussner's Restaurant in Highlandtown (living on now only in memory) or the Engineers' Club in Mount Vernon. The tour was always capped off with another local institution, Dee Herget, for a screen-painting demonstration.[282] Without interruptions, Dee could easily complete a prepared screen from start to finish in fifteen minutes.

Her first encounter teaching one-on-one was with Chrissy Lipka Maxwell (no relation to Tom Lipka), a young artist who was living and working in a newly converted Canton broom factory. Her grandmother had lived in the heart of screen-painting country above Fell's Point, and the persistent student in search of lessons "knocked on the door two or three times. She wouldn't go away. I brought her into the studio. Let her try a little."

When I met Dee, she was an eager newcomer to the art. She was honored in 2004 with a Maryland Traditions Master Apprenticeship Award from the State Arts Council. For almost a year, she mentored Jennifer Crouse, a widowed single mother more than thirty years her junior, whose story also included travels with a military spouse. Rather than follow Dee's lead down the path of traditional red bungalow imagery, Crouse adapted her screens to the medieval trappings of Renaissance fairs. Dee was not amused.

Dee can hardly remember when she was not a screen painter. Today her name is as widely known as the Oktavecs'. She still enjoys the shock of telling people what she does for a living. "I am a screen painter. And they will say, 'A what?' And they will put that in the same category as a cylinder engraver. And then they are excited to find out you paint pictures on window screens. And they say, 'Well, why not?'" Dee views every encounter as a teaching moment. Like Tom Lipka, she is determined to keep the tradition alive, "as long as there are rowhouses, screens, and a need for privacy, I think it will always be around."[283]

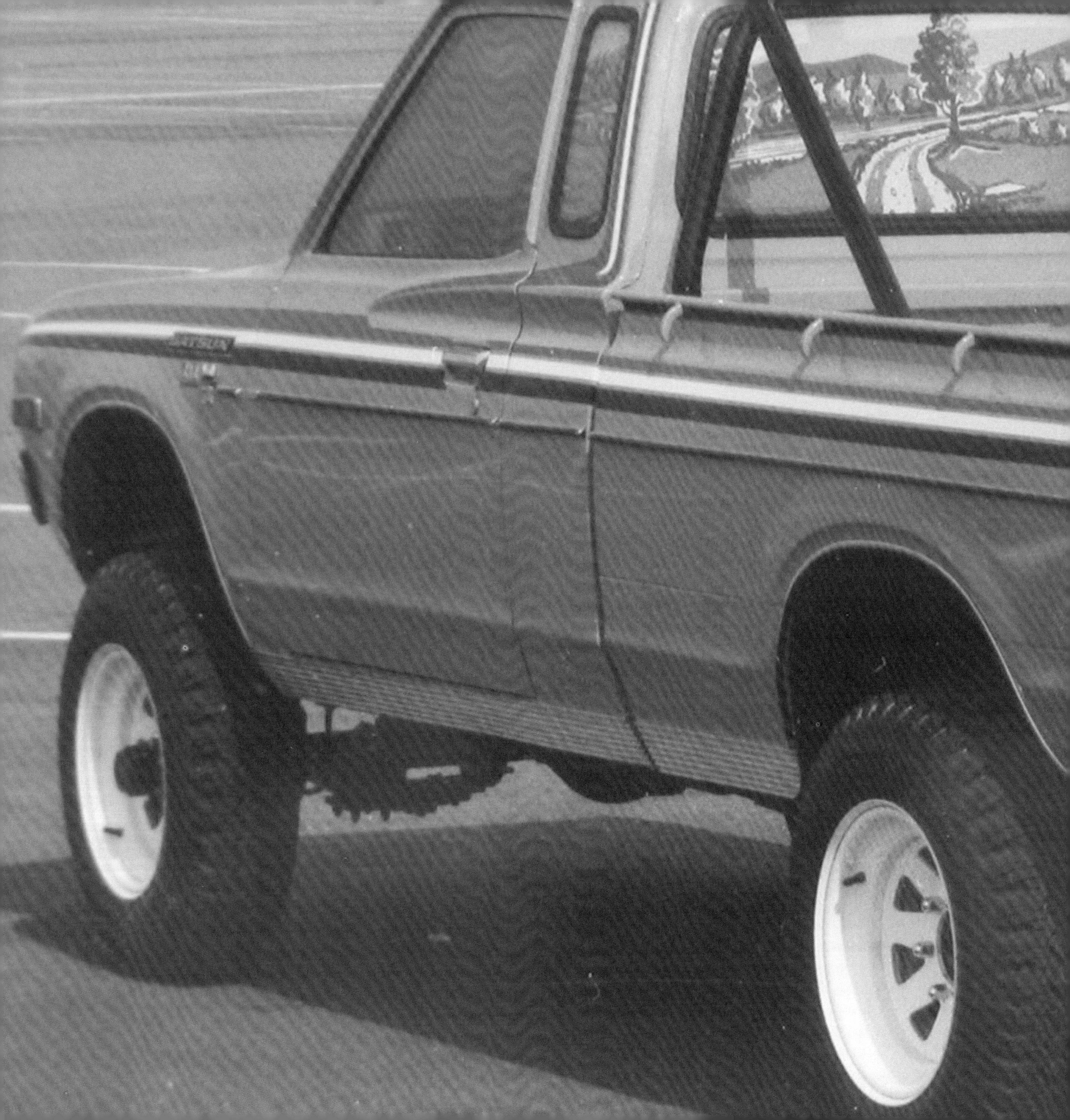

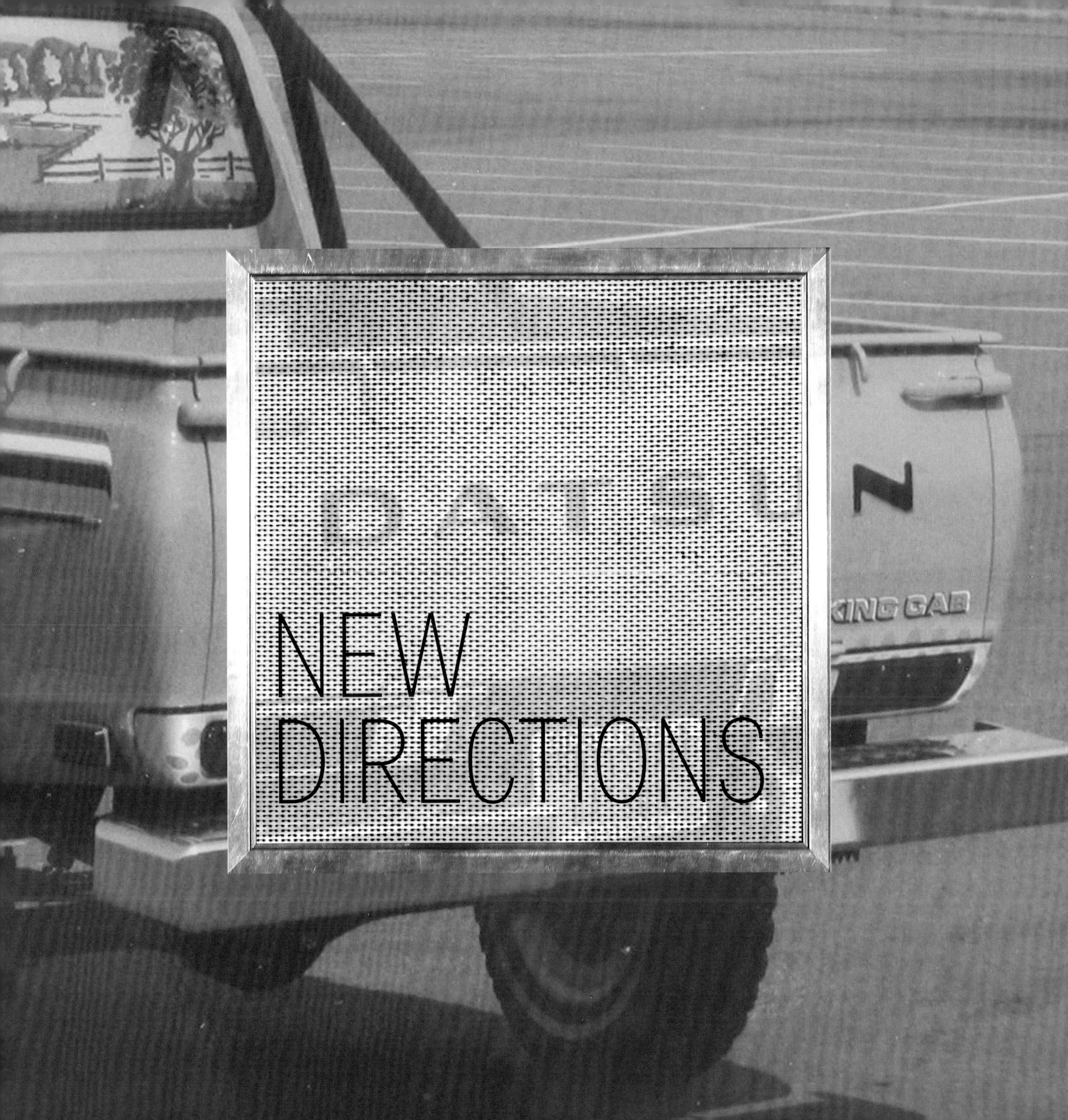

NEW
DIRECTIONS
KING CAB

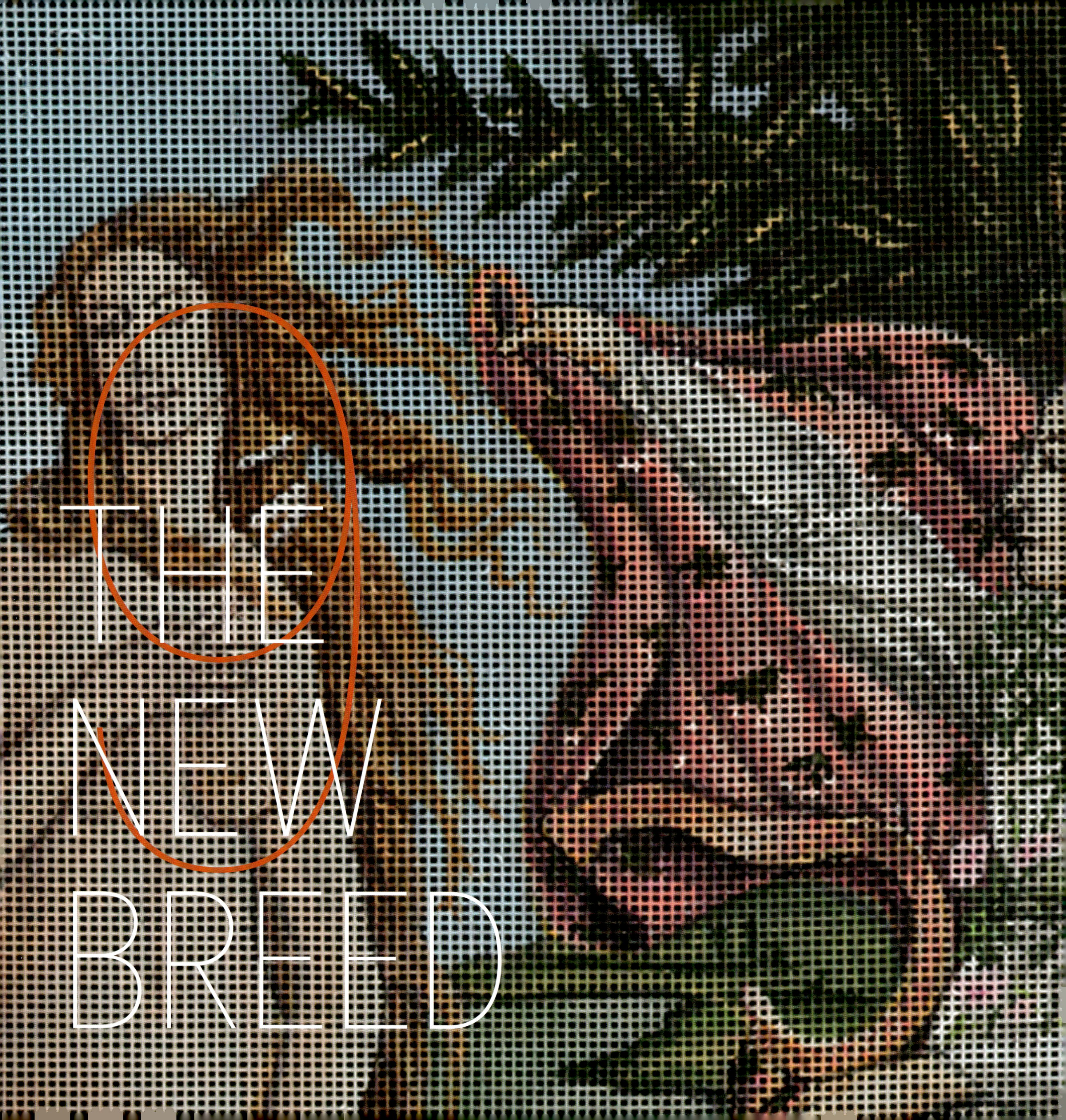

THE
NEW
BREED

IN THE NEW MILLENNIUM, BALTIMORE AND SCREEN PAINTING ARE BEING reinvented by creative individuals who are inspired by tradition but not constrained by it. While earlier generations picked up the aesthetic and technical foundation literally on the streets of Baltimore, the new generation of screen painters comes to it from many different directions. Some seek training from the masters. Others are self-taught independents. Many are introduced through grassroots workshops, films, and festivals. The new generation is the screen painting arm of the craft mob, young DIY artisans who have embraced and reimagined many folk art traditions. They set their own pace and styles, responding as much to a fading market and the void it created as to their own muses. One screen at a time, they build a new customer base, teach youngsters, elders, and peers, introduce new materials, offer new imagery, and bring the art form into the future.

After years of haunting the city's best-known female screen artist, Chrissy Maxwell showed up on Dee Herget's doorstep one day in 1995, and Dee finally agreed to take her on as a student. Chrissy's career as a screen painter was short lived, but her work can be found along Elliott Street in Canton. *Jed Kirschbaum photograph. Reprinted with permission of the Baltimore Sun Media Group. All rights reserved.*

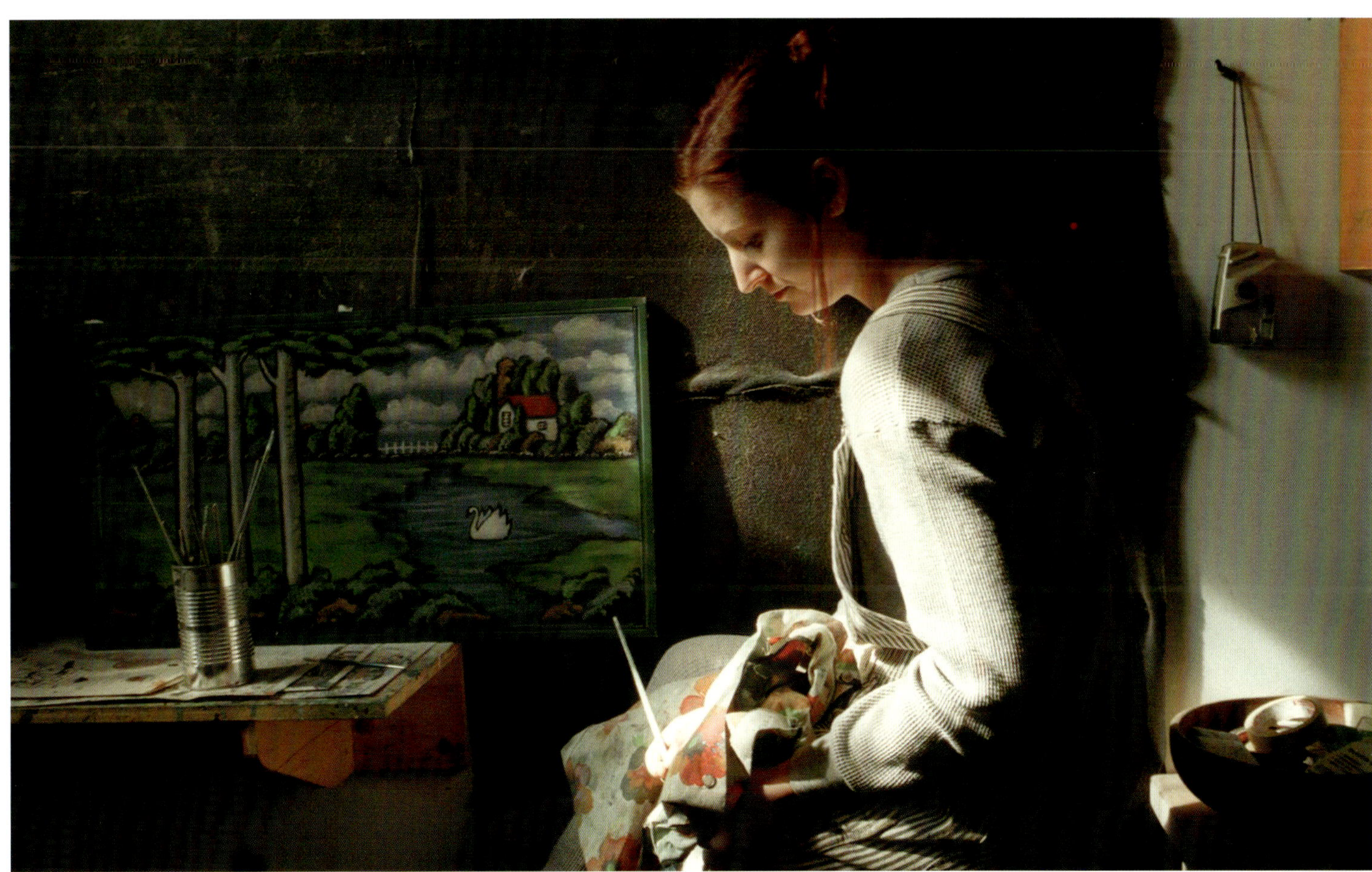

THE APPRENTICES

CHRISSY LIPKA MAXWELL (born 1968) had two grandmothers who lived over bars in painted-screen territory, one in Fell's Point and one in Highlandtown. (None were related to Tom Lipka's family.) Growing up in Highlandtown and Dundalk, Chrissy had always liked art in school. When she and her husband, a metal furniture designer, moved to the Southwestern Broom Company building in Canton, which had been converted to an arts incubator, she found creative work as a mannequin restorer for major department stores. In 1995 she joined a Painted Screen Society workshop taught by Dee Herget at the Canton Branch of the Enoch Pratt Free Library and thought, "I could do that." She was captivated "by the little old ladies there with their screens," who reminded her of her grandmothers. She attempted to coax Dee into taking her on as an apprentice. "Finally she let me come to her house and showed me how. We became friends."

Chrissy was among the first to deviate from the Red Bungalow scene and paint evocative scenes based on her patrons' stories and wishes. She started painting "the traditional pond and swan picture" but preferred special requests connected to clients' memories, like the man from California who requested two for his grandson: the rowhouse he grew up in and a dinosaur with a volcano. She likens screen painting to "doing a hairdo…. You come to me and tell me what you want. I am not an artist in the sense that I come up with ideas. It's about what THEY are after." She never advertised. She loved the way people tracked her down once they saw one of her signed screens in a neighbor's window: "They used the network from Mrs. Jones to Mrs. Smith to find me." She filled hundreds of commissions in her six years in Canton, including the oversized windows of the Canton library, which she decorated with scenes from favorite children's tales. Today many windows on nearby Elliott Street still sport her distinctive bold screens.

After leaving the neighborhood and starting her family, Chrissy realized that she favored the locals' stories more than the screens, and pursued a new vocation in occupational therapy. Her favorite clients continue to be the "ninety-plus"-year-olds. She recently moved from living "above the shop" to a house in the North Baltimore university neighborhood of Charles Village. For now, she has put her paints and brushes aside.

ANNA LIPKA (born 1959), a native of Trinidad, made Baltimore her home at age twenty-seven. She met her future husband, the son of screen painter Tom Lipka, in an art class in community college, where she was studying for a career in education. She worked as a travel agent and practiced art on the side. She became her father-in-law's apprentice only after her twins started school in 2004. That same year she moved from Parkville to Westminster in Maryland's Carroll County.

TOP

Anna Lipka's Red Bungalows both reflect memories of her native Trinidad and include the unmistakable trademark colors and geography of her mentor. *Courtesy of Anna Lipka.*

BOTTOM

Anna Lipka, daughter-in-law of Tom Lipka, took advantage of an opportunity to apprentice to the master artist through the Maryland State Arts Council. She lives in Carroll County, but continues teaching Tom's classes throughout the Baltimore area. *Author photograph, 2004.*

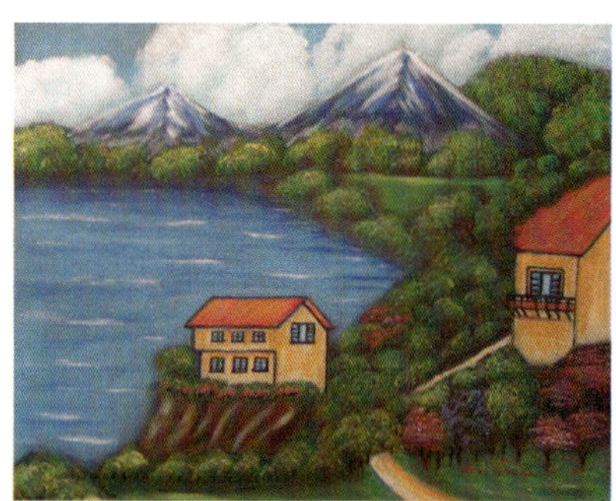

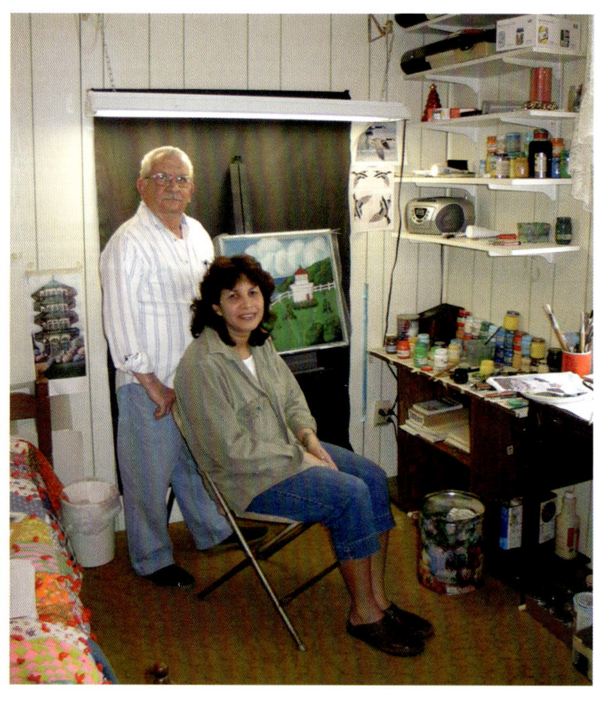

Originally a copyist, faithfully adopting Tom's style and palette, Anna ultimately developed her own style, which she calls "very country." Chickens and barns are often featured in her finished work. As her mentor paints less frequently, she has taken over his screen-painting classes in Baltimore County and the Hatton Center and has started offering her own at the Carroll County Farm Museum and senior centers nearer to her home. You can find her work at *www.annascreenart.com*.

MONICA BROERE (born 1954) "grew up on Long Island [New York], when it was still fairly rural. Then there was a housing explosion and people everywhere!" She came to Baltimore to attend the College of Notre Dame.[284] After one art course, she switched her major from English to art. She credits her drive toward self-sufficiency through making things with her hands to her independent and resourceful Depression-era parents. She discovered Fell's Point with "bars that exhibited people's paintings and drawings, and like any starving artist, I got a job as a bartender and moved to the area" where she was first exposed to painted screens.

Her first "real job" at age thirty was for a local advertising firm. She read all about painted screens, "how you could see out but not in," while doing paste-up for a client, the weekly *East Baltimore Guide*. She bought her first house in 1984, an alley house west of Patterson Park, "and was surrounded by painted screens in my new neighborhood.... I had put up a bird feeder in my backyard and wanted to watch the birds out the window [without the interference of a curtain]...so right out of the tube, I painted a wild colorful zebra stripey screen and loved it. Because I owned my own house, I started painting all the screens, but not following the traditional style. I was painting bold colors and shapes, still using my colors out of the tube. Being the renegade artist, I decided to intentionally clog the holes! And so I developed my 'wild style' painting animal spots and stripes, geometric shapes, splashes and spray-painted areas in bright and neon colors against black and white shapes, sliding screens with overlapping patterns." In her day job as an art teacher, she explored pottery, jewelry making, and printmaking. When she shared her screen-painting work in side-by-side rowhouse doors at a local festival, she began to attract retail clients, including one large commission for an unusual screen room inside a hip loft for the Hollywood film *Men Don't Leave*.

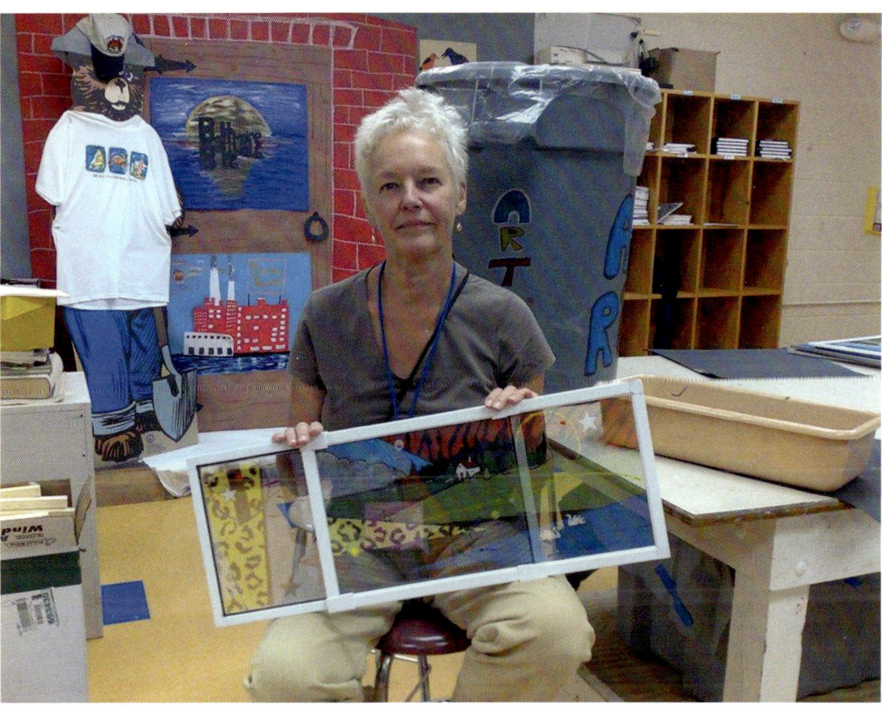

Monica Broere began painting "out there" screens for her kitchen window, beauty shops, and movie sets in the early 1980s in Fell's Point. She now creates her unique mash-up of abstract plus traditional art on items from flyswatters to wrist cuffs in her Highlandtown studio. Here she teaches a workshop to students at the Jemicy School. *Anna Pasqualucci photograph.*

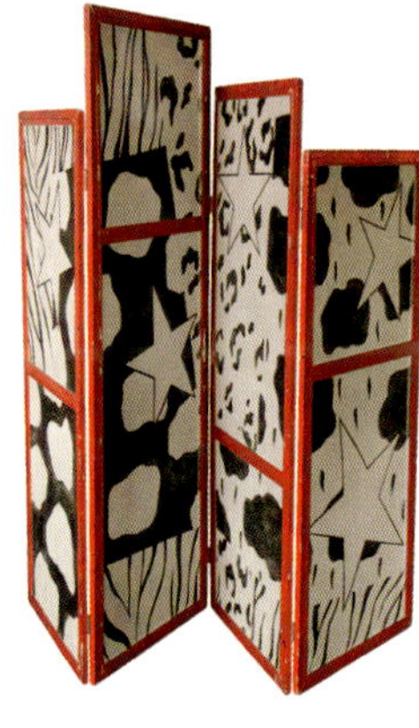

A free-standing screen by Monica Broere from the mid-1980s typifies her exuberant style. *Collection of Monica Broere.*

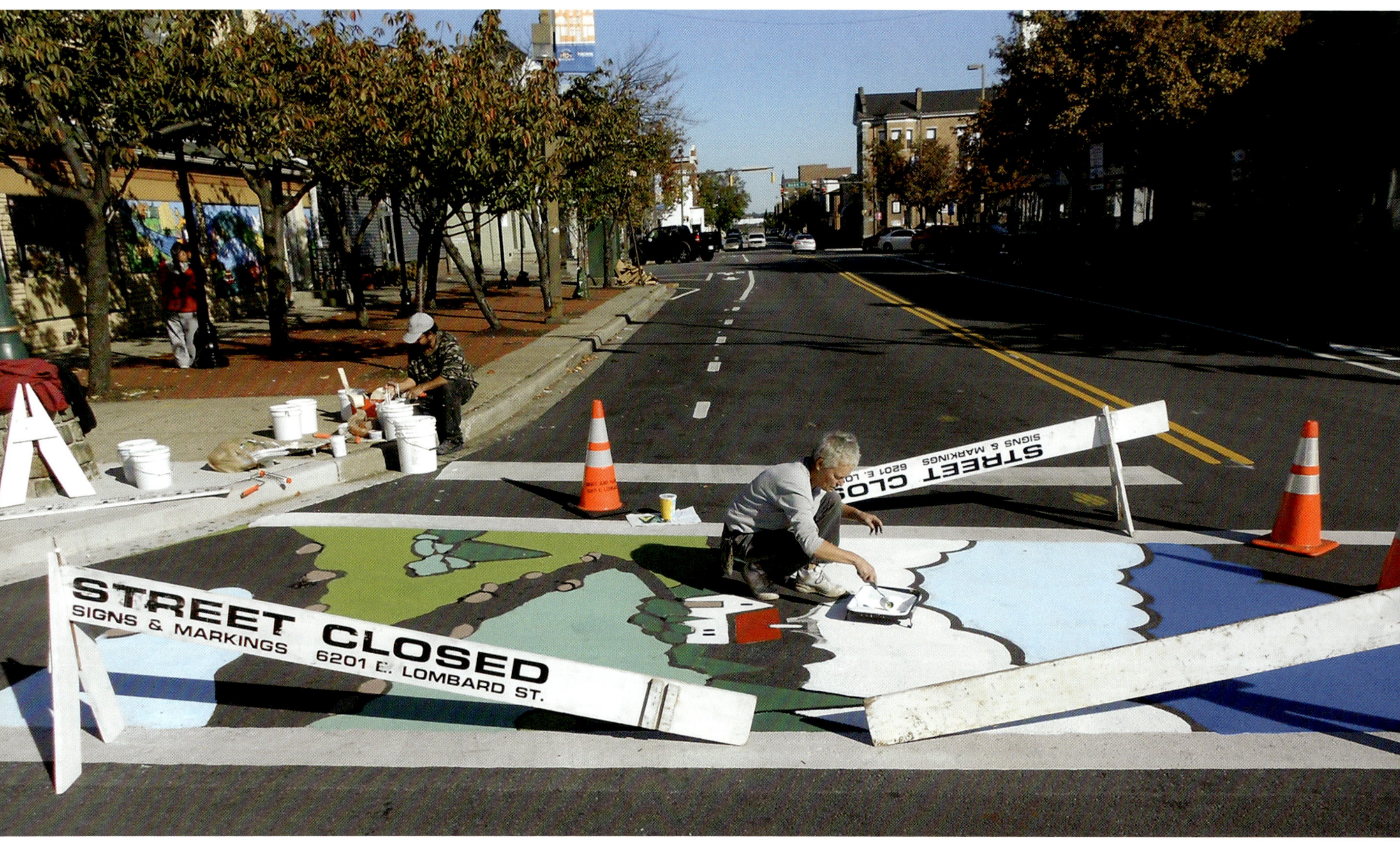

She has called several East Baltimore neighborhoods home, purchasing a Canton corner row-house with ironstone brick and second-floor bay window in 1989, and most recently a converted office supply store in Highlandtown. Her residence in the area for three decades, along with her position of more than twenty years as an art teacher at East Baltimore's Patterson High School, has engendered a commitment to her adopted communities and their endemic arts, particularly as she began to see how many screens had disappeared. Realizing a gap in her art education, she sampled a Painted Screen Society workshop with Dee Herget and volunteered at screen-painting events.

Broere determined to work backward to build the foundation of traditional screen-painting skills that she had bypassed earlier. In 2008, through Maryland Traditions, a program of the Maryland State Arts Council, she apprenticed to John Oktavec. With great pride, she has added to her skill set the ability to replicate Oktavec bungalows, trees, clouds, and swans.

Sprucing up Highlandtown's Arts and Entertainment District, Monica designed and completed a Painted Screen crosswalk as part of a design competition for the intersection of South Conkling Street and Eastern Avenue in 2011. *Courtesy of The Baltimore Guide.*

JENNIFER CROUSE (born 1961) was born in Havre de Grace, Maryland, and spent much of her life as a "military brat" and then as a military wife in Germany, Kansas, and Italy. Her Baltimore roots include living above a deli in Highlandtown and at her mother's home in Dundalk. Since grade school, art was her refuge. She started painting in oils, taking classes whenever she could. As her first marriage soured and, later, when she remarried and then became a young widow with two children, she periodically returned to Baltimore to be near family. During one home stay in 1987, she determined to buy painted screens as a gift to enliven the windows of her mother's rented house. Painted screens had always been a memorable constant in her life, providing a welcome backdrop to her love of art and need to nest. She located Dee Herget, paid a visit to her Essex cottage with screens in hand, and returned to complete the transaction.

When she came home for good to rebuild her life after her husband's death in 1999, she bought a small house on a cul de sac off Belair Road, in the Overlea section of Baltimore, and "let loose. I had put down the brushes to have babies," but that era was now over. She became "Queen of my own castle," painting whimsical scenes on the ceilings and walls—dragons, harbored sailing and fighting ships, Celtic borders. The cinderblock walls of the club basement became her faux stone "happy dungeon." A storage shed became her studio.

Jennifer wanted to paint her own screen door, but lacked the know-how. She found an old address book, resurrected Dee's phone number, and called, offering to pay for classes. Dee did her one better. After poring through Jennifer's portfolio, together they applied for the first Maryland Traditions Apprenticeship program and received a small grant that allowed them to meet once a week at Dee's tiny studio as master and apprentice. After trying her hand at "Dee's 'box of Crayola style' bungalow, which [she agreed] looks cheery on the house," her front door got the "Irish cottage with old English sheepdog and sheep" treatment. Her speed did not compare to that of Dee, who could execute a simple screen easily in under a half hour with water-based latex paints. Jennifer chose to work with slow-drying exterior oil-based enamels in a more classical style, using detail and blended colors, taking as long as two weeks to complete a screen.

As a regular at Renaissance fairs since 2000, she adapted appropriate subjects to woven wire. Expect to find angels and Madonnas among her repertoire. More of her screens are found indoors on walls than outdoors on windows, though she counts several porches among her finished works. She "would gladly go right to the door and paint [on site]" for anyone who wants one. She has recently moved to Baltimore County near Towson and will be looking for new markets for painted screens when she is not painting murals and other decorative touches in her own home.

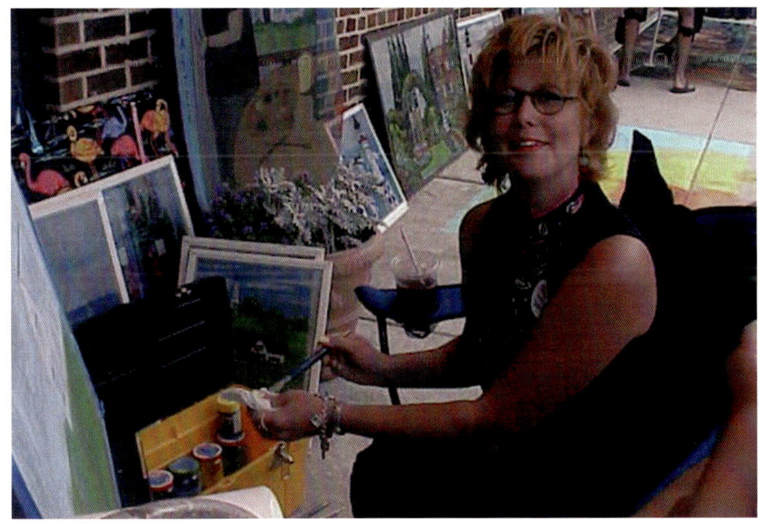

Jennifer Crouse apprenticed to Dee Herget through Maryland Traditions in 2004. She found a niche creating screens for the audiences at Virginia's Renaissance Faire. *Author photograph, 2011.*

SELF-TAUGHT

JENNY CAMPBELL (born 1965) believes screens are "one hundred percent my destiny." With family roots in Canton and Highlandtown, "I have always been aware of screens. I thought every neighborhood had them." Born and raised outside the city's eastern boundary, in Essex, she recalls regular sightings of painted screens savored from trips downtown via Eastern Avenue.

Art instruction began at home with the guidance of her artistic mother. She did not take formal art classes until her junior year of high school. She "stumbled upon" a career in photography thanks to a case of mistaken identity: the employer confused one of her early paintings for a photograph. As a newlywed she moved to "a house in Westminster with a white picket fence, my version of hell." To express her longing for Baltimore (despite her daily commute to the darkroom where she printed and archived images of works from the Walters Art Museum's collection for twenty years) and as a way of saying, "I'm not from here," she "tricked out" each window screen with a copy of a masterpiece. "I preferred the classics. I saw it as a great combination of my upbringing and my museum work. I tried the red-roofed cottage, but it was horrible." She started with the *Mona Lisa* in 1998. Her version of Grant Wood's *American Gothic* hung at her back door and confused people who thought someone was standing there. Botticelli's *Birth of Venus*, Hopper's *Nighthawks*, and *Whistler's Mother*—paintings "you are supposed to like"—completed her home away from home. She considers screens a friendly, neighborly art form. They "show identity in an approachable way." Around the same time she started painting screens, Jenny began making costumes—originally for her (now ex-) husband's band. She experimented with dresses and corsets of fiberglass screen and painted them to match her next whim. First she depicted pink flamingos (due to a windfall sale of discontinued hot-pink paint) on clothes and screens, and later Edie the Egg Lady (both in homage to hometown boy John Waters's film *Pink Flamingos*). For her first exhibition in 1999, held coincidentally on the same Canton streets (Potomac and O'Donnell) where her father's family had lived, she introduced framed postcard-sized "desktop" screens to the

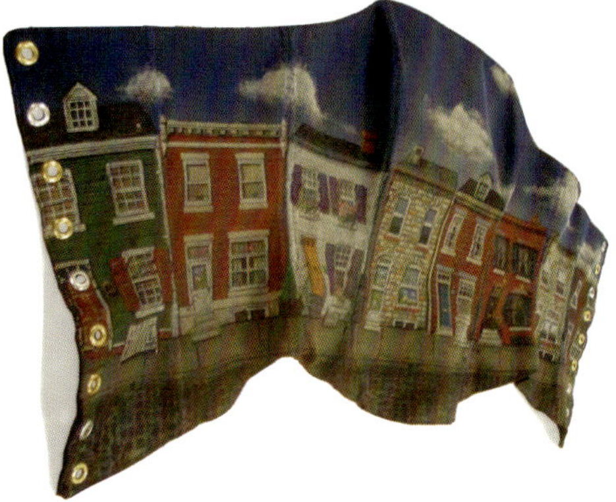

One of a series of screen corsets by Jenny Campbell show her love for Baltimore and interest in unusual forms. *Collection of the artist.*

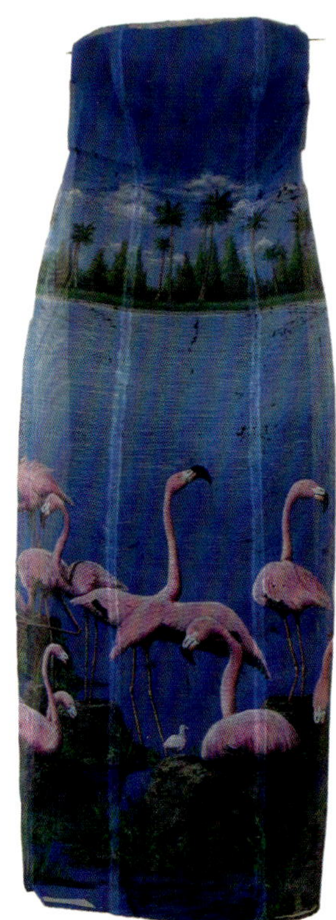

The pink flamingo screen dress was made by Campbell for the gala 1995 opening of the American Visionary Art Museum in Baltimore. Other dresses coinciding with AVAM occasions followed.

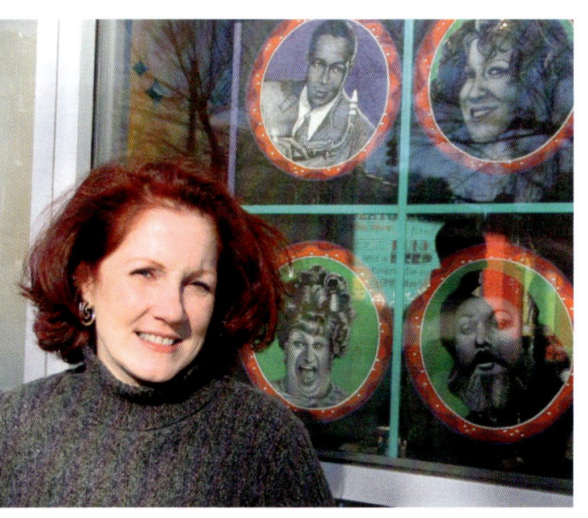

Jenny Campbell tried painting a Red Bungalow screen only once. She began with images from the great masters for her cottage in Westminster, Maryland, and graduated to iconic souvenirs and nontraditional forms. Her signage for Two Boots Pizza on Mount Royal Avenue merged her interest in portraits of famous Baltimoreans and the art of the unexpected, returning to the original function of screens for advertising. *Author photograph, 2011.*

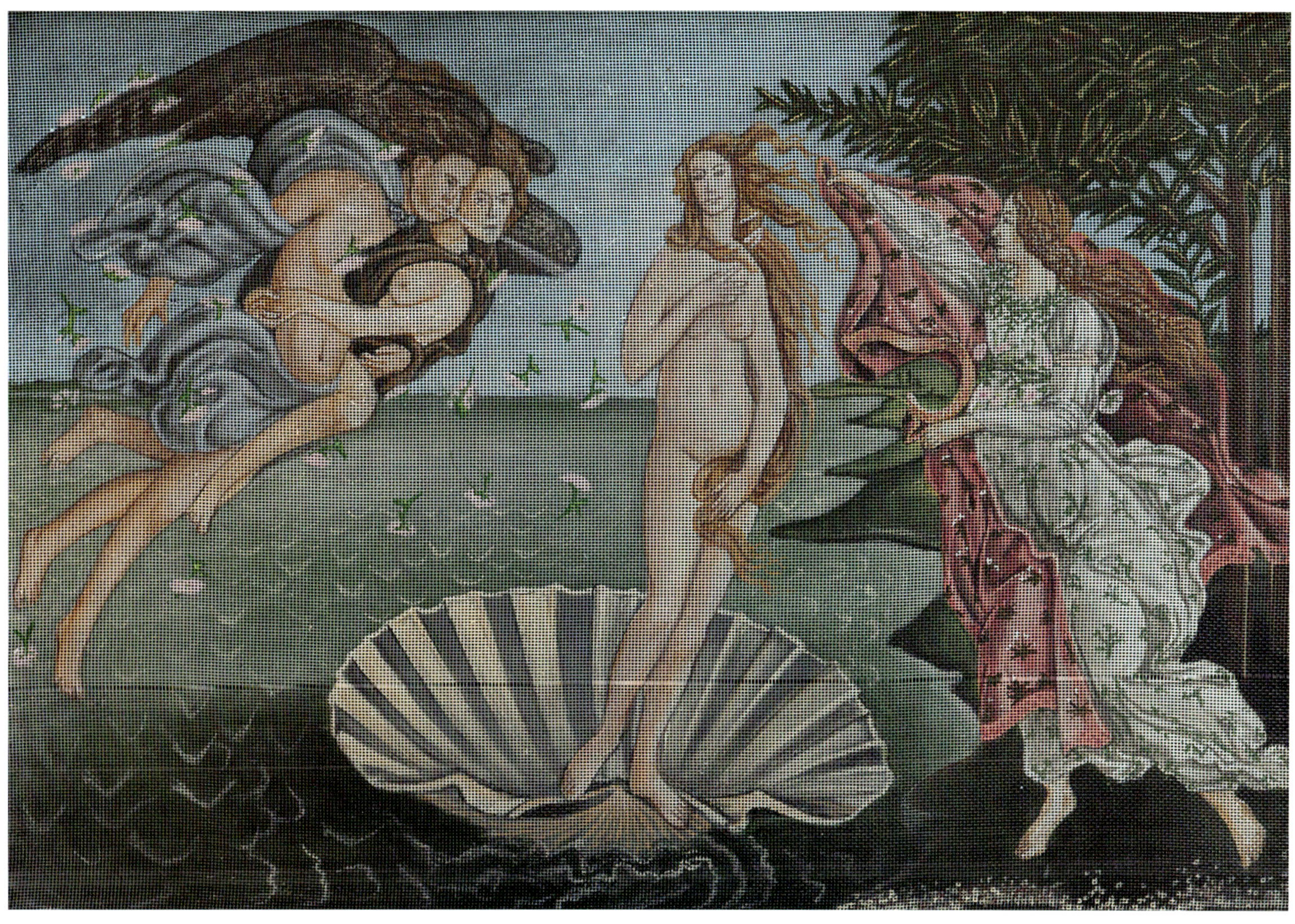

Botticelli's Venus by Jenny Campbell, circa 1998. *Author's collection. Edwin Remsberg photograph.*

Baltimore market. Her subject matter was "strictly Baltimore" landmarks and "personalities" like singer Billie Holliday, burlesque artist Blaze Starr, actor Divine, and jazz musicians Chick Webb and Eubie Blake.

Jenny is well known and loved in city art circles. She has contributed works on screen to numerous art and non-art venues including "Foodscape," an annual exhibition held at the Mt. Royal Tavern as an alternative to the annual arts festival Artscape. At the American Visionary Art Museum, she premiered her screen dresses and taught "anything goes" screen classes reminding her students that "there is no right way."

She admits to being "obsessed with glitter," one embellishment that finds its way onto her screens and clothes. Known as "the Bad Girl of Screen Painting"[285] she is moving toward what she calls "burlesque adult screens—a far way off from the red-roofed cottage." She recently completed interior art and signage for Two Boots, a New York–based pizzeria that opened an outlet in Baltimore. Known for their collection of works by outsider artists, the owners sought local artists working outside the mainstream for their new venture, and Jenny's postmodern spin on a traditional art fit the bill. Located between the campuses of Maryland Institute College of Art and the University of Baltimore and visible at all hours, this installation "is the only place I can come and visit my work," since she has sold or given away most of her screens. Her more conventional screens may not have been seen in windows since her early efforts, as her prices make people reconsider whether they should be placed outdoors.

Her innovative costume creations include award-winning entries in Coney Island's Mermaid Parade and the Mayor's Christmas Parade in Baltimore, costume-themed charity pub crawls, and, most recently, New Orleans's Mardi Gras, where she has been a reveler since 1997. She was taken by the fact that costuming there is a way of life. The place she calls a "sister city" to Baltimore instantly embraced her and her art. Long considering it a second home, she made the permanent move to New Orleans in 2012.

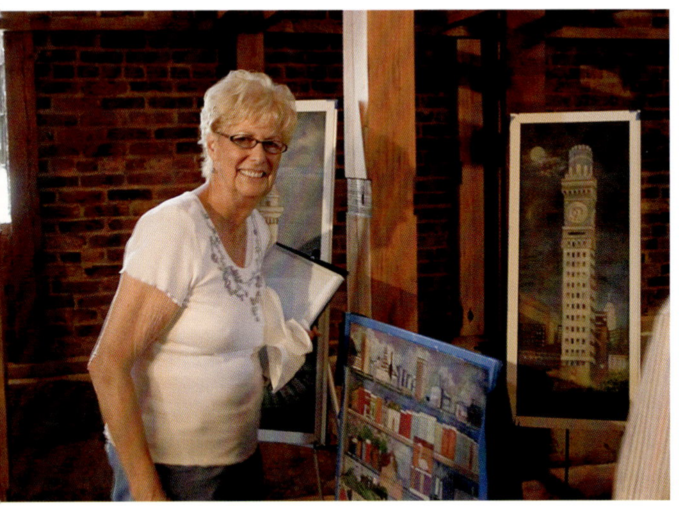

Catherine "Pat" Michalski teaches screen painting in craft shops and senior centers near her home in Anne Arundel County.

CATHERINE "PAT" MICHALSKI (born 1935) "always loved art, always painted, and always wanted to be an art teacher." After a career with the federal government and retiring as an instructor at the National Security Administration, she vowed to follow her dream. She took classes in a variety of media but was attracted to screens because they "are easier and quicker and dry faster than oils."

Pat was born and raised on Light Street in South Baltimore and though painted screens were not uncommon there, she first became aware of them when she saw them on "every house on the block" where Highlandtown's famed Haussner's Restaurant was located, when she celebrated a daughter's graduation there. Her immediate reaction was, "I want to do that." Curious, she began to seek out painters. To pick up pointers, Pat attended a workshop with Dee Herget at the American Visionary Art Museum. Soon after, she played a role in bringing John Oktavec from obscurity when she visited him in search of information that he willingly shared. Pat sold screens through Law Brothers, her neighborhood hardware store. But she finds teaching most rewarding: "[I'm] seventy-five percent teacher, twenty-five percent screen painter. I know I've taught over a thousand people [to paint]." Her classes are held at regional art and senior centers and craft shops in northern Anne Arundel County, near Glen Burnie where Pat currently lives.

You could say she has returned to her roots in more ways than one. Her daughter lives in a tiny alley street in the now-trendy Federal Hill, formerly South Baltimore. Pat's screens of Baltimore landmarks grace each of her windows.

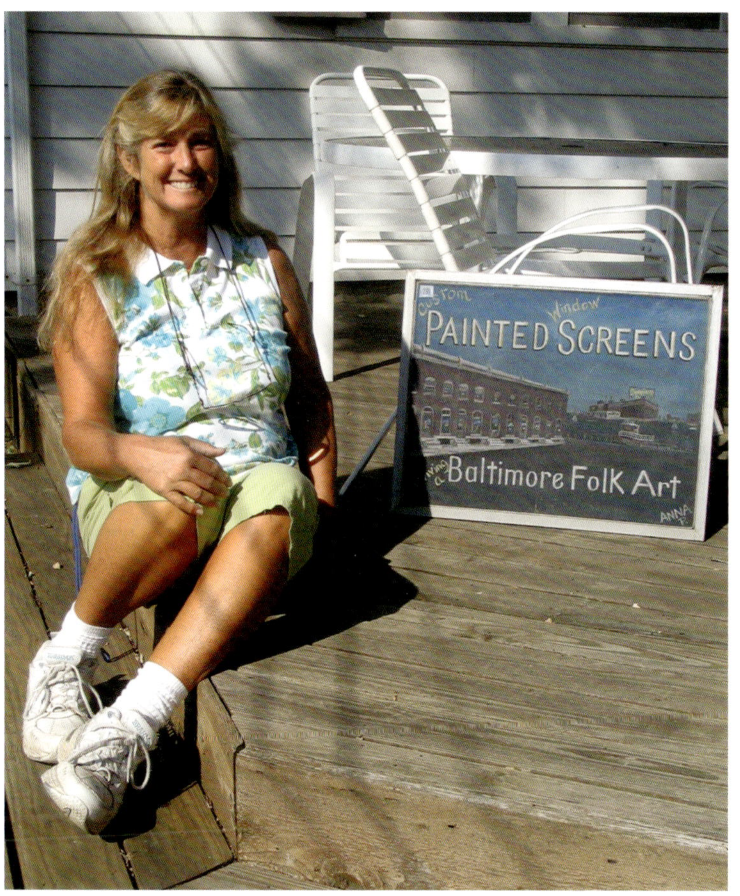

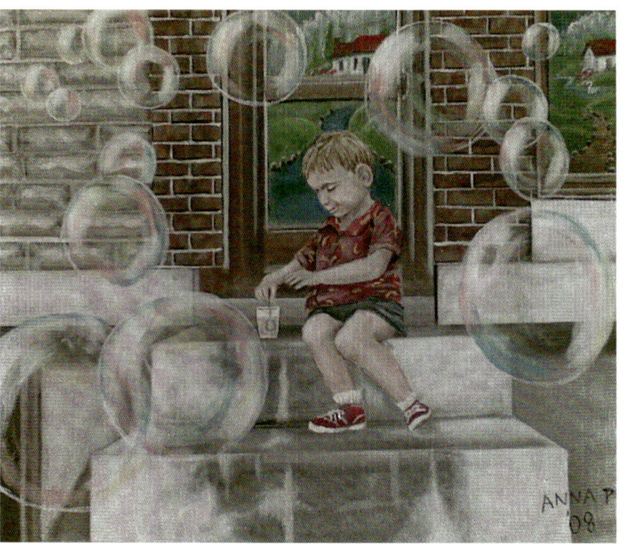

ANNA PASQUALUCCI'S (born 1954) great-grandfather Zuelke owned a corner bakery in Curtis Bay and great-grandfather Yurkewich owned a grocery store on South Hanover Street in South Baltimore. Yurkewich's son met his future wife, Anna's grandmother, while she was scrubbing her steps and immediately admired her as a hard worker. Anna's childhood memories of driving through the city in her dad's Dodge Phoenix included being mesmerized by the passing scene of colorful painted screens, one after another. She loved art from an early age and took every course she could in high school, but followed her graduation from Hood College in Frederick, Maryland, with a career in cell biology. Her laboratory work for several firms, including one prophetically called "NovaScreen," concentrated on scientific research, agricultural biotechnology, cancer, and pharmaceuticals. When in 2005 arthritis affected her hands and she could no longer perform certain fine-motor tasks, she sought an alternative career. She looked toward art, remembering that screens had "popped up through the years here and there."

She believes that "screen painting saved [her] life." Unable to hold a pencil but adept with a gentle brushstroke, she preferred the idea of screen painting to painting on canvas or murals. She quickly noticed that "people can relate better to being a screen painter than a cell biologist." She went out looking for screens in South Baltimore and returned "disheartened" by their absence. Part of the attraction for her was getting out beyond the four walls of a research facility and meeting new people. Her first painting was a sunset, although she admittedly "didn't know what I was doing."

Armed with information from the Painted Screen Society website, she methodically contacted or visited every practicing artist. "I cling to every word…when they offer tips and advice." She took classes at Canton's Hatton Senior Center with Tom and Anna Lipka after getting their advice by phone. She consulted Dee Herget, who advised her "not to work at your kitchen table and to use paints in cans rather than tubes." While vacationing in Ocean City, Anna paid a visit to John Iampieri, who shared ideas, and in 2009 she met John Oktavec as part of a Painted Screen Society presentation. She dedicated herself completely, showcasing her work at special events, exhibitions, and farmer's markets throughout Baltimore as well as on the Outer Banks of North Carolina and in West Ocean City, Maryland, where one house sports twenty-six of her screens. Her rise as a screen painter has been meteoric and her marketing skills are nothing short of phenomenal. Within five years she began teaching and helping to steward the future of the art form. Experimenting with imagery and forms, she has advanced the humble screen medium beyond windows to chairs, accessories, and "screen sculpting"—three-dimensional masks and landscapes. Her screens range from the traditional red bungalow scene to rowhouses and architectural landmarks topped by a winking "Natty Boh man," to trompe l'oeil to fantasy, to exquisite realism and detail. She is grateful that her "mistakes fall through the holes."

Adding to the "sense of purpose" that screens have provided her, she recently began teaching screen painting in schools and at public events. Anna lives in Linthicum, Maryland, where she was raised and where she raised her family.

JOHN IAMPIERI (born 1950) was a boy from suburban West Baltimore. He grew up just outside the city limits in Westowne, a modern postwar rowhouse community in Catonsville. His father ran a neighborhood women's and menswear store that became "the premier clothier of men's fine fashions in the 1950s and 1960s." On buying trips for the store and travels to visit the Iampieri's large extended family throughout Little Italy and Highlandtown, "it was not uncommon to get a glimpse of those special gems painted on doors and windows on the east side of town." Many years later, John's brother, who was considered the family artist, found a painted screen by Dee Herget at auction and added it to his Bolton Hill back door. John was so captivated and intrigued by that "magical" painted screen that he experimented and taught himself. He had found his passion.

At age twenty-five, Iampieri left Baltimore for Maryland's Eastern Shore, following a career in the food and beverage industry, and finally settled in Ocean City in 1987. While tending bar there, he had the urge to decorate interiors with paint—faux finishes and murals. When he suggested to his brother that he might like to go to art school, his brother only said, "Why?" Art had always come naturally to John. Once he determined to master a medium, he was "very tenacious." He started Bella Designs, where, his calling card announces, "art embraces your dreams." He added screens to his studio's offerings in 2003. His first screen featured a palm tree "like I was sitting on the beach with [it] shading me." He began with acrylics purchased at Walmart but quickly learned that "using cheap paints made for a bad mix if I was going to sell. So I started using only the best exterior latex paints available and figured I'd better seal them so they don't fade away." At some point, he bought a copy of the Painted Screen Society's *How to Paint a Baltimore Screen* video at a yard sale to add to his training. Though he has "never painted a traditional [red bungalow] scene," he still has "a certain reverence for them." His work is instead influenced by his life on the shore. His delicate palette features "combinations of tropical scenes, flowers, trees, natural Assateague settings, etc."

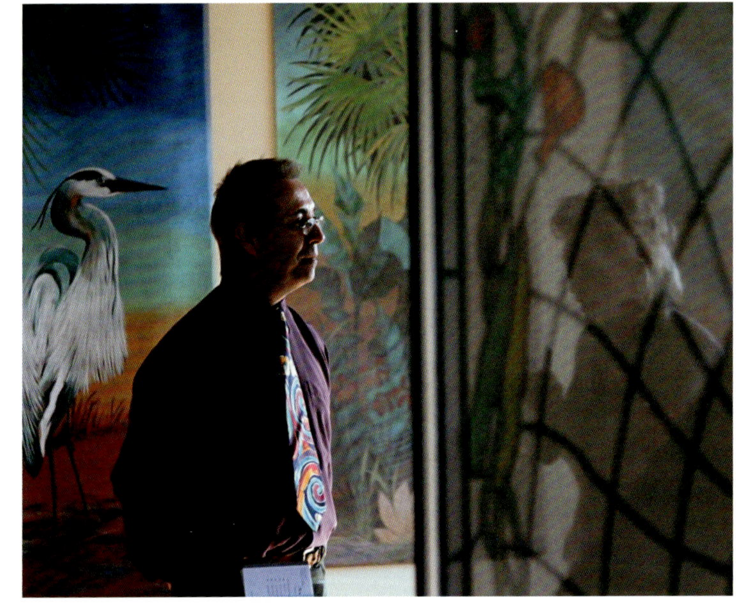

John Iampieri enjoys nothing more than sharing his love of decoration by teaching screen painting to young students as an artist in the schools. He participated in Baltimore's 2009 Artscape as a part of the Painted Screen Society's exposition at the Meyerhoff Symphony Hall but otherwise plies his trade from his home studio near Ocean City. *Photo courtesy of John Iampieri.*

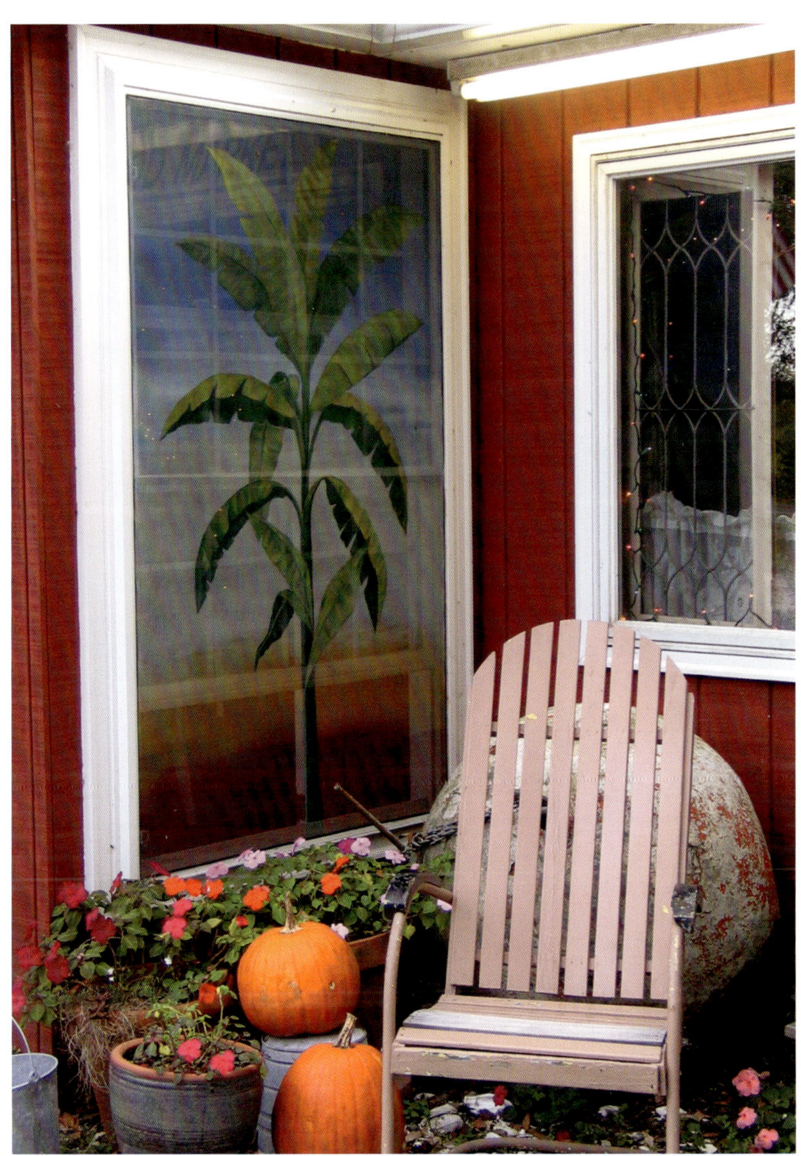

Iampieri's mural-like screens are installed at the Grove Market in Bishopville, Maryland, near his Eastern Shore home. *Author photograph.*

He balances his art business with teaching screen painting and other arts to youngsters and adults. He is certain to include the history of painted screens in the many classes he offers as part of the Maryland State Arts Council's Artist-in-Residence program. His love for painted screens is contagious. He engages students of all ages in schools on the Lower Shore and for Young Audiences throughout Maryland. He has "done everything from little tiny screens to a forty-five-foot-long mural on screen, and love[s] it all." He excels at large projects. His signed and dated screens can be found on porches, businesses, and restaurants throughout the Lower Eastern Shore and wherever his screen mobile (a vintage Volvo station wagon) can travel. John lives with his family in Bishopville, Maryland.

'THE MORE... THE BETTER'

Screen painters can now be found throughout the city of Baltimore and its surrounding region. From a storefront in Hampden in North Baltimore, beginning in 2003, a retired police officer, Tom "Razzo" Matarazzo, introduced screen painting to a constantly changing audience of locals and visitors who stroll The Avenue (Hampden's central artery and shopping district) in search of the real Baltimore. Bruce Barrett can be found at the North Point Flea Market selling his dog portraits on screen.

As in the early years, when itinerants were found on every street corner, painters eager to try their hand at a new medium can be found almost anywhere. But today they aren't guarding the art form's secrets. Instead, they're teaching others how to paint their own, offering classes in schools, community centers, and senior centers throughout the state. Over time, more names will join the ranks of the screen painters who have made their mark in Baltimore and beyond. And as Ben Richardson so aptly noted during the last big wave of screen painting, which he rode in the 1980s, "the more screens there are out there, the more people want them, and the more screen painters there are, the better it will be for everyone."[286]

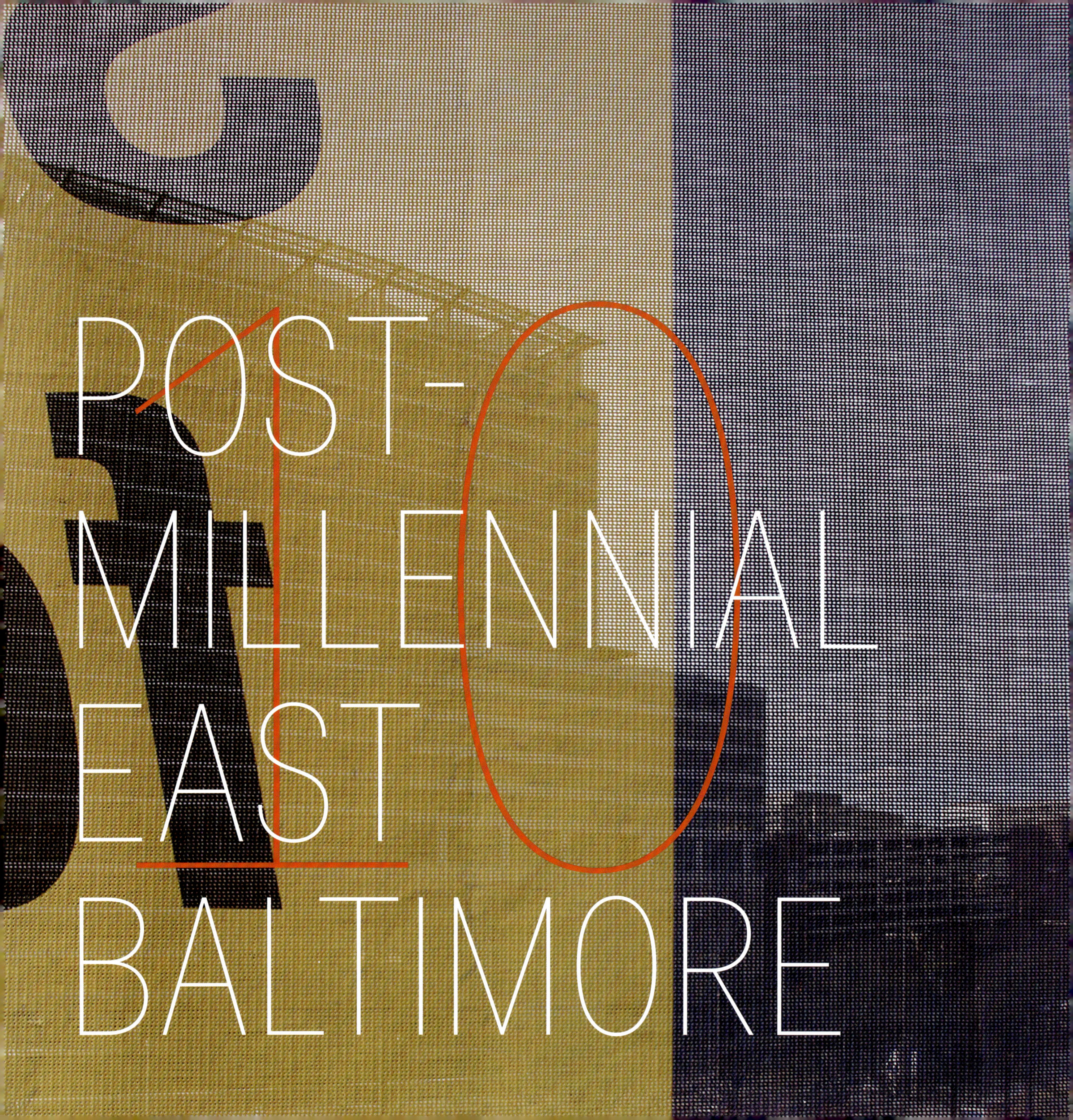
POST-
MILLENNIAL
EAST
BALTIMORE

THERE WAS A REASON THAT NO ONE LEFT EAST BALTIMORE UNTIL THE 1990S. GENERATIONS lived within shouting distance. Families stayed near the institutions that built and sustained their neighborhoods—church, school, library, bank, social club, newspaper, theater, barber, hairdresser, corner stores, and taverns. It was no coincidence that moving out most often meant heading north to the suburbs, following the city's main eastside avenues, Belair and Harford Roads—and making the journey north en masse. A national television show summed up eastside rowhouse life in a brief skit.

> Imagine a hair hopper (woman with high teased coif) sitting on her white marble steps, suitcase at her side in preparation for her move after a lifetime spent at the family home. Her incredulous father weeps over her imminent departure and loss as he peers from the partly open screen door. It is a sad day. He cannot bear the loss. She picks up her belongings and heads from the stoop, onto the sidewalk—to the house next door, up the marble steps. Opens the door…Her new home![287]

The dawning of the twenty-first century finds a very different and far less hospitable environment for painted screens and the screen painters. Although Baltimore's rowhouses remain intact, the last two decades have witnessed a major rearrangement of the residents who called these places home for generations and a shift in priorities for those who call these same rowhouses home today. A painted screen on every window is no longer a given. A screen that cost fifty cents to $5 through the 1940s, or $15 or $25 in the 1970s and 1980s, might now run $75 to $100, or more. Painted screens are now recognized as custom works of art, not attractive, but ultimately utilitarian, household amenities.

Of the few remaining master painters, the number who knew an Oktavec personally and visited the Art Shop is dwindling—only Oktavec's grandson John, approaching fifty years old, and Dee Herget and Tom Lipka, now in their seventies, remain. Dee paints fewer red bungalows and more custom screens with highly personalized subject matter, and she prefers scheduling demonstrations and classes that put her in the solitary spotlight. Her festival days are waning. Tom, a lifelong smoker despite his family's efforts to get him to stop, is on hiatus from painting and teaching while he recovers from the double whammy of a bout with throat cancer and losing his "sidekick Ramona," his wife of more than fifty years.

The neighborhoods, too, have done complete turnarounds—for better and worse. The changes range from subtle adjustments to major shifts that have rendered some areas unrecognizable. In the community once known as Little Bohemia, now Middle East, a vast open space sears the landscape where thousands of rowhouses once stood. Decades earlier, these rows were home to proud Germans and Bohemians. After the turbulent 1960s they were home to a wave of African American homeowners who built a vibrant and close-knit community of their own. In 2012, eighty-eight acres starting at the front door of St. Wenceslaus Church and the former Oktavec's Meats & Grocery were leveled as part of an ambitious and controversial partnership spearheaded by the Johns Hopkins Medical Institutions "to revitalize a once vibrant neighborhood that had become overwhelmed by poverty, abandoned housing, joblessness, crime and other social maladies." The houses were demolished to make way for mixed-use improvements in a new community centered on biotech innovation.[288] The first new school building constructed in the city in years is being built on seven acres directly across from St. Wenceslaus Church. Some neighbors, recalling how "it used to be rough, but now it's quiet," eagerly anticipate the change.[289]

A few miles south, a different kind of upheaval has transformed the waterfront communities of Canton and Fell's Point. Beginning in the 1980s, condominiums, luxury townhouses, marinas, restaurants, and offices began to replace the packinghouses, breweries, can companies, oil and copper works, and other industries that once provided employment to European émigrés who barely spoke English as a second language. The shells of buildings where canneries once disgorged tomatoes into the harbor now house high-tech incubators for digital enterprises and architectural and advertising firms. Two towering skyscrapers rise above a neighborhood previously distinguished by compact attached homes bursting at the seams with large families. These high-rises house empty nesters who have reversed the white flight trajectory, abandoning the suburbs for city life that offers the luxury of walking to shops and cafés.

During the real estate boom of the early 2000s, it was not unusual for original owners to leave the homes they had purchased for $1,500 when the price tags climbed above $250,000 in areas some realtors dubbed Baltimore's "Gold Coast." National chain stores tucked themselves into former factories. Strip malls created in the modern mold sprang up amid aging brick rows. The proximity of a quick meal or designer coffee was irresistible for a generation of young professionals that prefers gourmet-to-go to toiling over dinner from scratch in a basement kitchen. The area's parochial schools are seeing enrollment numbers grow, while some public schools are struggling to fill desks. Retired longtime residents have left, replaced by young families, and as the number of school-age children bounces back, the newest arrivals to this area are founding and supporting parent-involved charter schools, creating a new set of institutions to replace those that defined life in the neighborhoods for generations. Highlandtown's Patterson Theater has been successfully transformed into the Creative Alliance at the Patterson, a live-work arts venue, and the hub of a city Arts and Entertainment District. The libraries in Highlandtown and Canton promise to be among the most modern and up-to-date in the system while Fell's Point's library has been repurposed as a social service center for the neighborhood's growing Latino population.

In the 1960s the battle against "The Road" that threatened to bring an interstate across the harbor and through the hearts of Canton and Fell's Point displaced families like newlyweds Tom and Ramona Lipka. Theirs was one of 215 homes senselessly demolished. (The lots sat vacant for twenty years.) The grassroots opposition to that ill-fated public works project witnessed the rise of local activist Barbara Mikulski from hometown hero to the longest-serving woman in the United States Senate. It continues today in opposition to what may be an inevitable light rail line. The void that remained along Boston Street in Canton was developed to house retirees who have downsized, some to be near their boats docked along the waterfront, and young professionals who commute by kayak or water taxi to jobs across the harbor. That kind of daily maritime journey was once reserved for the local priest who served parishes in both Canton and Locust Point.

The two-story rowhouses of Canton, once considered the wrong side of town, precisely due to its proximity to the factories, could not be more right today. Inside the house, few separating walls remain on the first floor. At least one wall is exposed brick, undoing the sound baffle that extra layers of plaster originally provided. The Formstone façades have been removed, and the inferior, now pocked-and-pitted brick has been replaced or re-mortared, awaiting the next new life-extending technology. Conversely, a Formstone Preservation League has been established. Under the banner of "sustainability," windows and doors were replaced wholesale—by the thousands—as if a command required that all old windows of whatever vintage be unceremoniously tossed in back alley dumpsters and replaced by the latest white or brown man-made material. Alongside each front door, security lights announced a new era. Roofs are topped with decks that command water views and make backyard gathering spaces obsolete. Concrete and metal fences, raised-bed gardens, and anachronistic clotheslines have disappeared to make room for prized parking pads. The difficulty finding space for cars has become a chief complaint, as double-income families bring two and three automobiles apiece to crowded streets designed for a way of life dependent on bus and streetcar routes and a short daily walk to the neighborhood grocer. New parking patterns further erode the traditional patterns. The new residents do not relish walking many blocks at night. Stoop sitting as a means of socializing has been replaced by dog walking. The newest parks cater to canines rather than people.

This is not your grandmother's East Baltimore. Among the churches, Canton's St. Casimir's has seen a surge in membership. While many congregations closed or have been twinned with others, some share their space or have been replaced with new and growing Hispanic congregations. African and South Asian immigrants contribute to making East Baltimore the most diverse region of the city.[290] Book clubs and knitting groups replace bingos and polka bands. Front windows are increasingly covered with plantation shutters that provide only half the function of painted screens—keeping strangers from seeing in. Windows are otherwise bare. Infants of Prague and screen sightings are a cause for excitement. Entire blocks no longer seem to have been lifted from greeting cards and calendars.

NOT DEAD YET!

The story of screen painting's flowering and fall has been written dozens of times in Baltimore, throughout the United States, and abroad. Considering painted screens' roots in eighteenth-century London and the delicacy of the medium, the fact that screen painting as a decorative genre is practiced anywhere today would have to be deemed an amazing feat of survival. Despite continuing revivals and recurring reports of their demise, they hold on, but in diminished numbers.

At the end of the Victorian era in America, painted screens disappeared because they ceased to be produced. Wire companies had begun making them as a way to market their products, and they stopped making and marketing them when tastes changed, steering customers who continued to request them toward plainer, more fashionable substitutes. Individuals in random locations around the country, and especially New Englanders continued the tradition on a small scale, or started painting screens spontaneously for their own use and amusement, perhaps fueled by nostalgia for screens they had glimpsed at summer homes along the coast and among the commercial streets of their youth.

The most remarkable thread in the story of painted screens is that one man, William Oktavec, tried his hand at the art form in Bohemian Baltimore and started a fad that lingers even today, a fad that has become a cherished local folk art. That we know his name and the place and the time he introduced his innovation is even more fortuitous. Since that summer day in 1913 when Oktavec fulfilled his first commission, painted screens have been at various times omnipresent, beloved, endangered, vanished, revived, reviled, and reborn. The love-hate cycle has been repeated throughout their hundred-year run. "Painted screens" was a household phrase in East Baltimore in particular, and simply explained to the uninitiated with, "You see out. No one sees in."

The same mixed message that these artful dodgers communicated to the street, "Look at, but not in. See out, but remain unseen," has a parallel in their "here today, gone tomorrow, here today" existence. For as long as they have been a part of the city's streetscapes, their numbers have ranged from more than 100,000 to a pitiful low of under 1,000 spread over hundreds of blocks today. This census includes neglected, barely visible remnants left behind in forgotten windows, as well as fresh new takes on the historic form.

Nothing short of a miracle or a substantial outreach effort will restore screens in great numbers to the neighborhoods where screens and painters once thrived—but which are now devoid of both. A renaissance could be in the making now. One day painted screens might be commonplace again, but if not, we now know where and how to look for them, and who to thank for bringing a breath of fresh air, a blast of color, and a sense of privacy and well-being to the rowhouse neighborhoods of Baltimore past. Best of all, the secrets of screen painting are out and being brought forward by a new generation of artists who are making them their own.

TWENTY-FIRST-CENTURY STYLE: A PHOTO GALLERY

The best ideas are common property.
—Seneca

Painted screens' legacy continues today in new media, updated imagery, and timeless applications. The forms, like the painted screens themselves, at first seem to defy explanation, but upon careful examination make a world of sense. Likewise, many of these examples have increasingly become part of the everyday landscape, but in many cases are short lived, easily replaceable, and on the move.

This section provides a window into some of the most visible ways that enterprising creators are using new technologies and media to address the same challenge that led to the rise of painted screens again and again from the eighteenth century to the present. It offers a sampling of artifacts out there today and a glimpse into what the future may hold. Over time, the same idea meets changing needs or is reengineered thanks to new material and methods.

PRIVACY

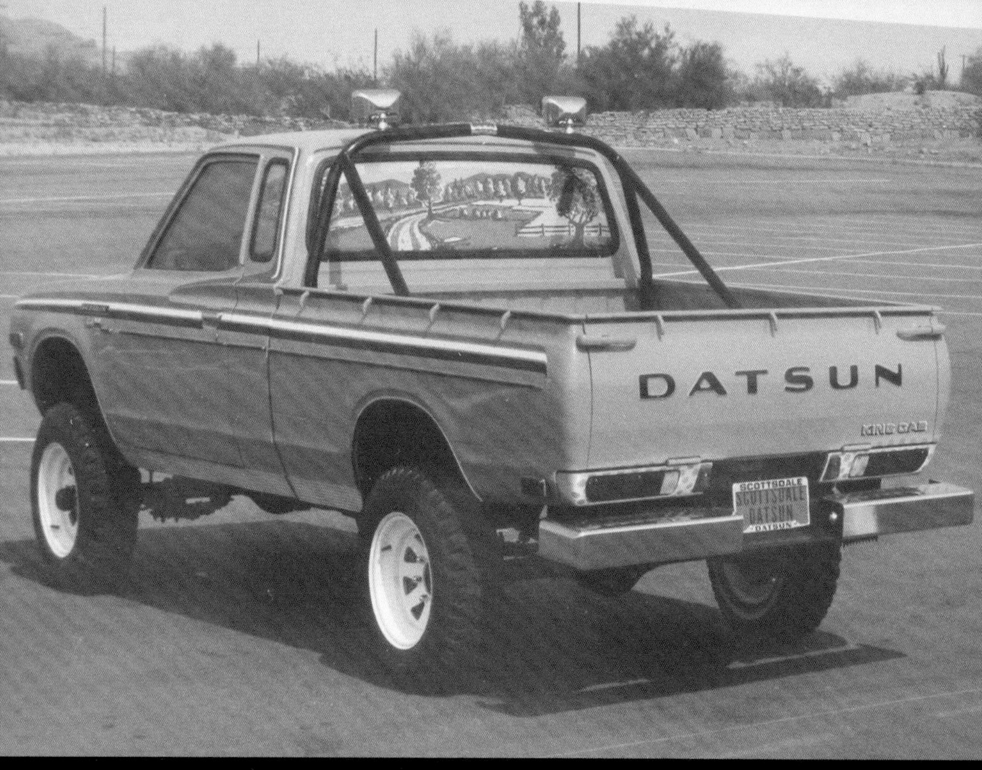

In 1973 George Berkner of Gila River Products introduced the original decorative sun screen, "with a brand-new design outlook for the vehicular market and later commercial and residential applications." The product, a perforated, metalized sun screen, reflects the heat out of a window and "provides privacy with excellent outward visibility." Originally intended for home use, "When first developed, the screen was undecorated. To make this product more aesthetically pleasing Mr. Berkner conceived the idea of [hand silk-screening] designs on these screens for use in the van market. It spread rapidly to the pick-up [truck] market." "The original designs were reminiscent of the early psychedelic type of art…and rapidly evolved into more generically acceptable scenic designs." The most popular designs? "Scenes with hills and trees."

Window film is still a popular inexpensive after-market accessory on pickup trucks. Colorful images of eagles, deer, landscapes, and American flags are still in demand. (Gila Window Film is now a product of Solutia Inc., a subsidiary of Eastman Chemical Company and specializes in DIY window tints.) *Courtesy of Gila Window Classics™, J. Calvin Hill, Gila River Products, Chandler, Arizona; correspondence with the author, December 22, 1982; and sales brochures, n.d.*

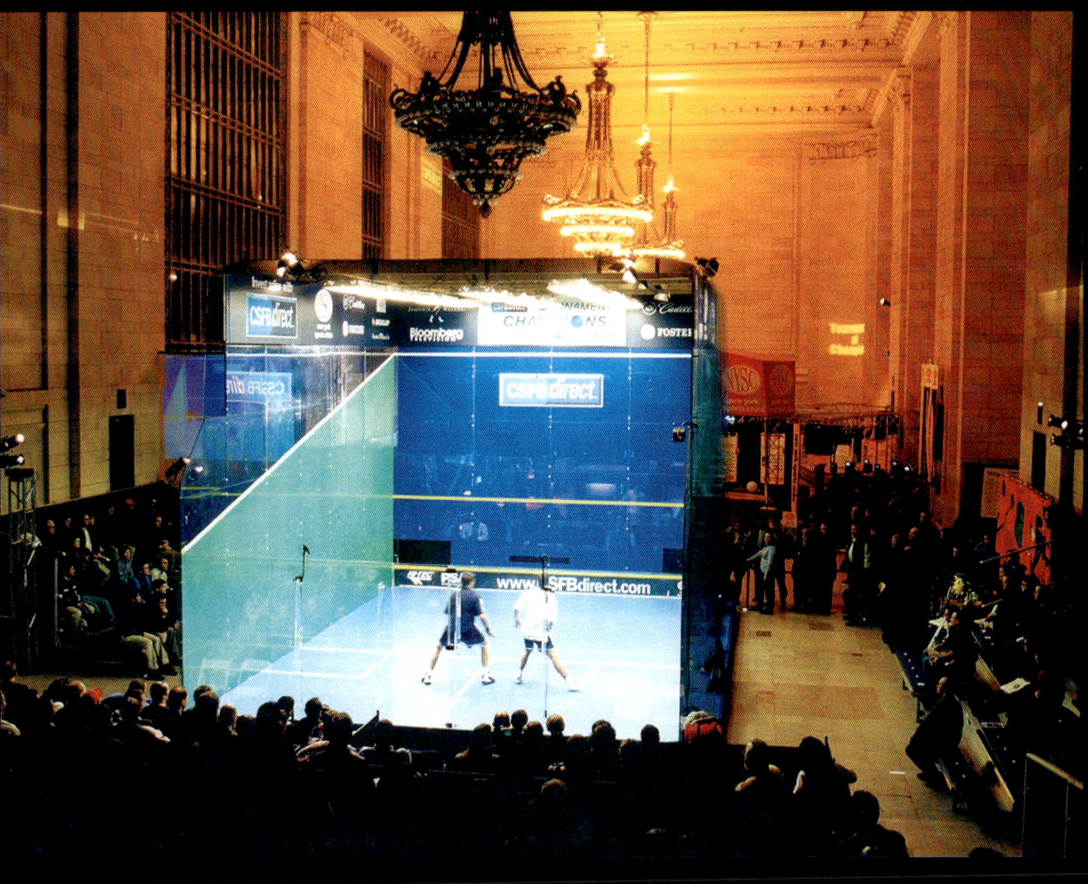

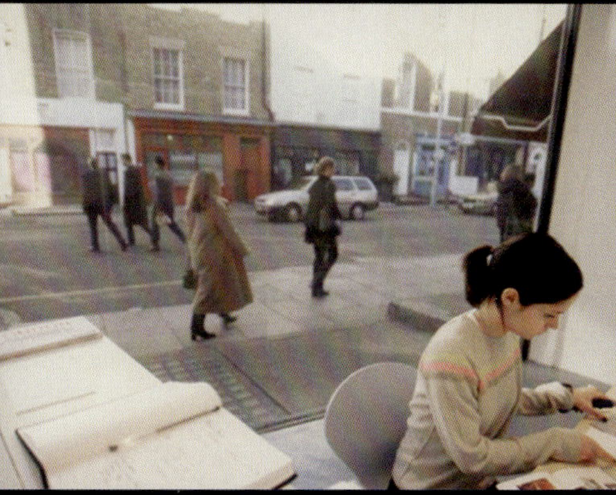

Interior View

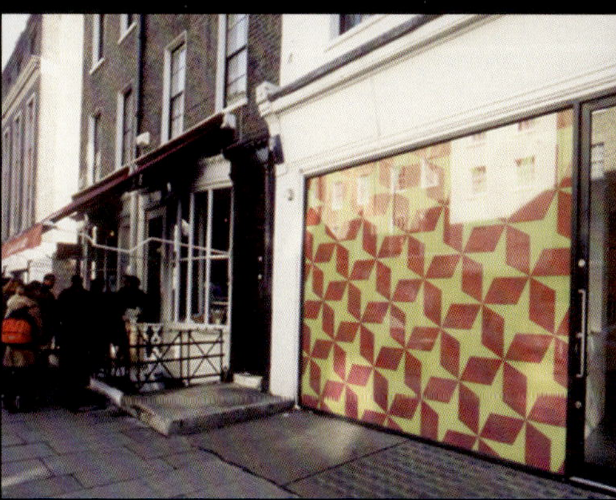

Exterior View

In the 1970s, engineer Roland Hill, "concerned only with one-way vision products," faced a challenge technically not unlike the one faced by the housewives of East Baltimore. Rather than search for a solution to domestic privacy, his charge was to create an all-glass squash court "first used for televised competition with 4 unobstructed, one-way vision walls" that would eliminate distractions to the players while allowing spectators to enjoy the action. His dilemma spurred the 1976 invention of custom-designed one-way graphic film that operated like the optics of a painted screen— only in the opposite direction. The public could see in, but the athletes were unable to see out. It eventually led to the first and dominant patent for see-through graphics in 1984 and the following year, the creation of Contra Vision®, an international corporation based in the United Kingdom. Perforated products were introduced in the mid-1990s.

According to one of the company's early lead North American partners, Donald "Duke" Zimmerman, formerly of Baltimore's Globe Screen Print, "a pure patent is not an improvement on any other, but a patent on something that does not appear in nature. There is nothing one way." Contra Vision's Type A products are composed of "print panels with an opaque silhouette pattern. The design is on one side and not visible from the other with illumination from the design side only." *Roland Hill Photograph, Contra Vision® XR™. Roland Hill, History of Contra Vision® and Contra Vision®, An Introduction, 2009. Roland Hill, conversation and correspondence with the author, 2012; Donald Zimmerman, conversation and correspondence with the author, 2012; Patrick Henrietta, conversation and correspondence with the author, 2013.*

One-way film, whether used inside offices or showrooms or on storefronts, is used to add impact to retail and office windows worldwide. Staff of the Robert Prime Gallery in London could work undisturbed by the passing scene outside. Of course, lighting within the building alters the effectiveness of the one-way vision. *Roland Hill photograph. Contra Vision® XR™.*

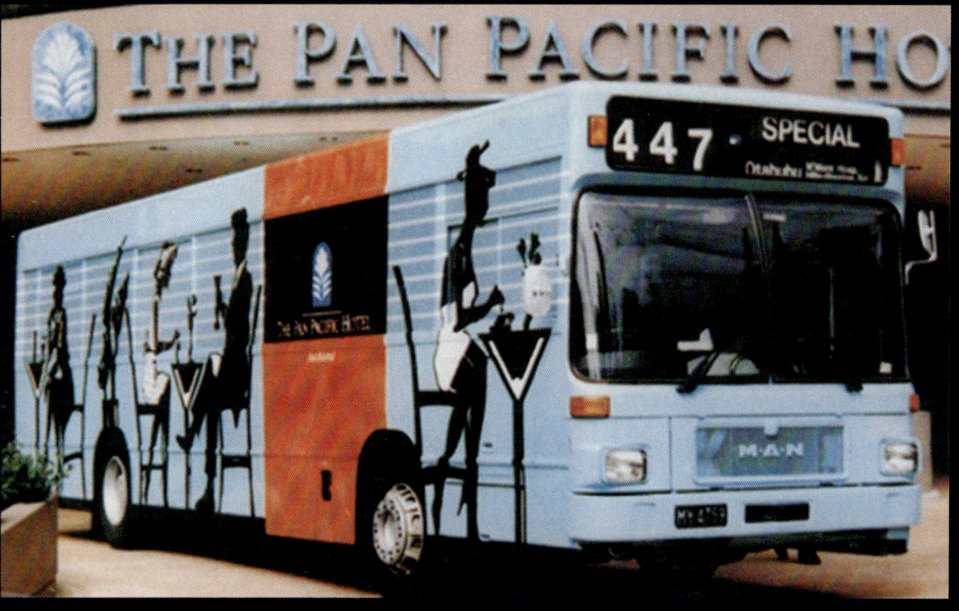

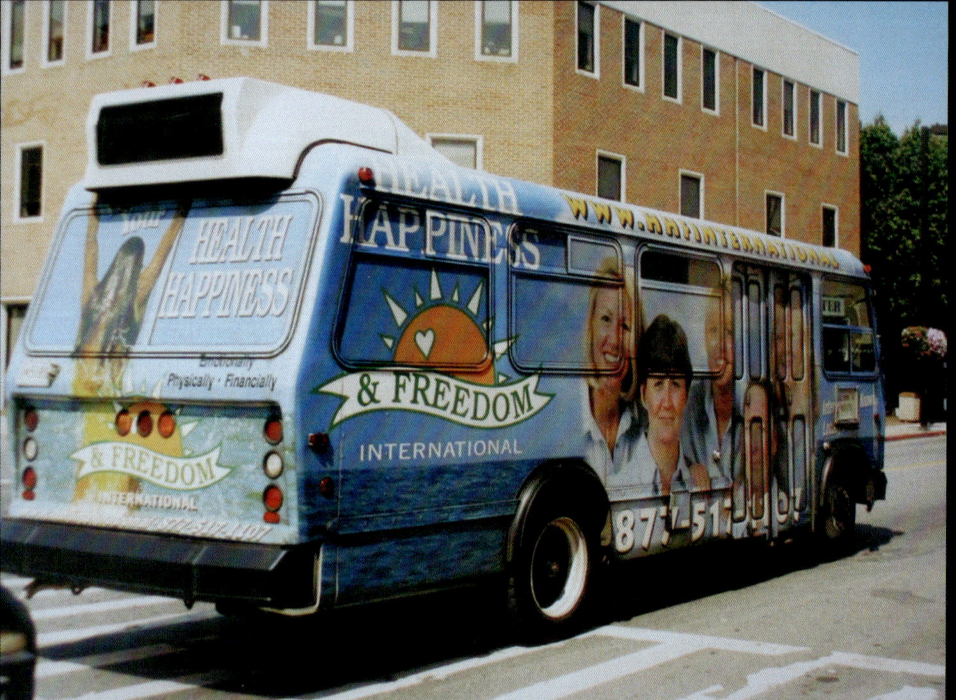

The world's first full bus wrap using exact registration one-way printed film was created and installed by Contra Vision® in 1991 on this bus for the Pan Pacific Hotel in New Zealand. This pilot effort led to the company's first $1 million order and a worldwide market for wrapped buses. *Courtesy of Contra Vision® XR™.*

Full or partial vinyl wraps for buses (and other large commercial vehicles) cover the bus body and the windows (without impeding the view) with computer-generated, full-color, perfectly registered designs known in the Baltimore region as "Jumbos" and "King Kongs." "This giant three-dimensional painted bulletin travels [city streets and highways].... Whether walking, jogging, riding your bike, or on your way to work, you cannot miss this eye-catching display." Passengers are still able to "view from the inside while maintaining a continuous design outside." *"Gateway/Mass Transit Administration, Baltimore, Maryland, Transit Advertising Information," 2003. Gateway Outdoor Advertising, Heard Communications, Inc., Lutherville, Maryland. Bottom photograph by author.*

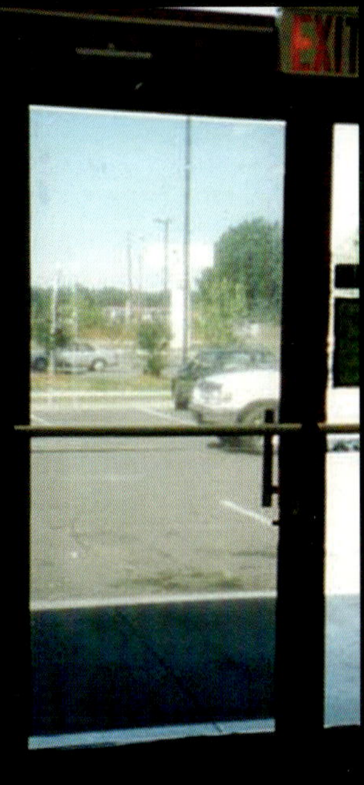

Interior View

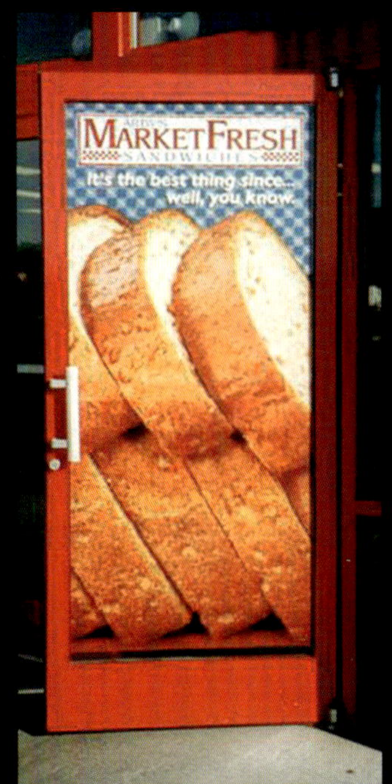

Exterior View

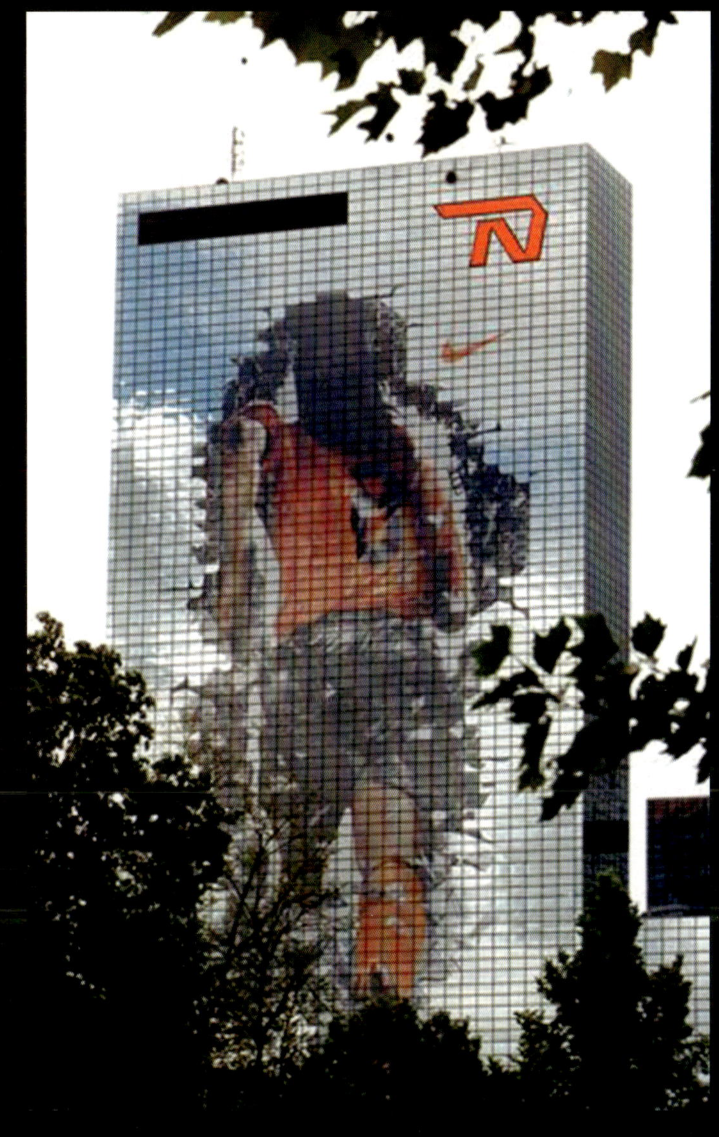

This modern take on the old commercial screen
door provides no airflow but does get the message
across while providing a view out from inside.
This updated version of the once-ubiquitous signs
on country and corner store doors promoting bread
(or soft drinks) could be found today at fast-food
purveyor Arby's throughout the United States.
This is one of millions of easy-on, easy-off graphics
that have become advertising staples worldwide.
*Linda Icard photograph. Courtesy of Donald
Zimmerman. Contra Vision® ORS™.*

RIGHT

Nike Building, London. This same technology
allows entire buildings to be covered with a
single graphic, which can be left in place for
years or for shorter durations. Often purely
decorative, the added feature of a sunscreen
may also be incorporated.

CAMOUFLAGE

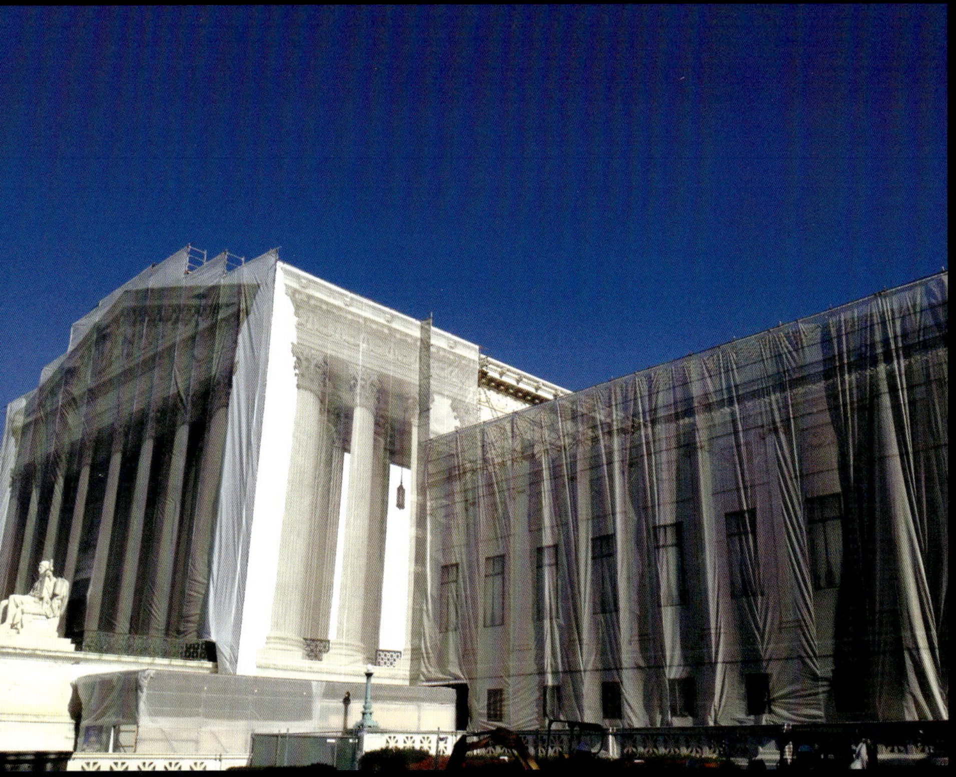

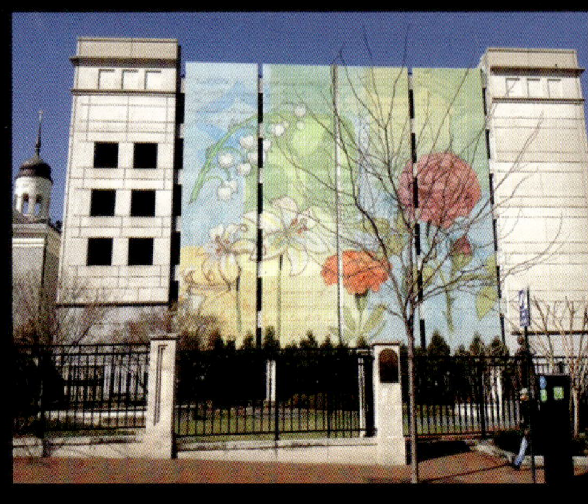

Exterior View

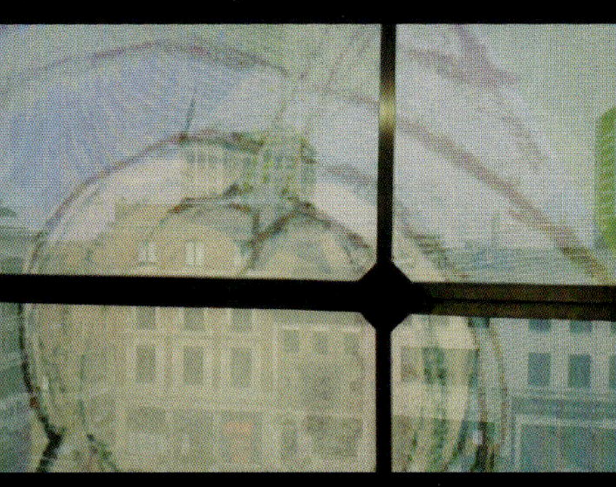

Interior View

The façade of the Supreme Court building in our nation's capital is covered with scaffolding, that in turn is covered with a transparent cloth replica of the project. Buildings under construction and renovation increasingly are required to apply temporary scaffolding to the entire structure, with a curtain of construction mesh to prevent debris from raining down on passersby. America was late in following Europe and Asia in using printed or painted fabrics in anticipation of the completed structure, for an art installation, or simply for commercial advertising. *Tim Kuczka photograph, 2012.*

In 2008, Baltimore's Basilica of the Assumption dedicated a contemplative refuge in the heart of the city for pedestrians to commemorate the Pope's 1995 visit. Located adjacent to America's first cathedral, a Catholic shrine and national landmark, Pope John Paul II Prayer Garden at Franklin and N. Charles Streets is at a major downtown intersection. To better frame the garden, an existing parking structure immediately behind it was tempered by adding digitally printed five-story fabric banners. Each panel bears modern interpretations of botanical drawings of flowers traditionally associated with Mary and excerpts of Pope John Paul II's writings on the environment. The illustration by Keith Kellner appears opaque in daylight, yet it is fully transparent from inside. He notes that "the mural not only conceals the garage but becomes an extension of the prayer garden, merging the façade with the ground plane." Phil Engelke, director of Environmental Graphics for RTKL Architects, oversaw the design installation, comparing its magical effect to a theater scrim and more recently to a painted screen. (Garden design by Scott Rykiel, Mahan Rykiel Associates.)

ARCHITECTURAL

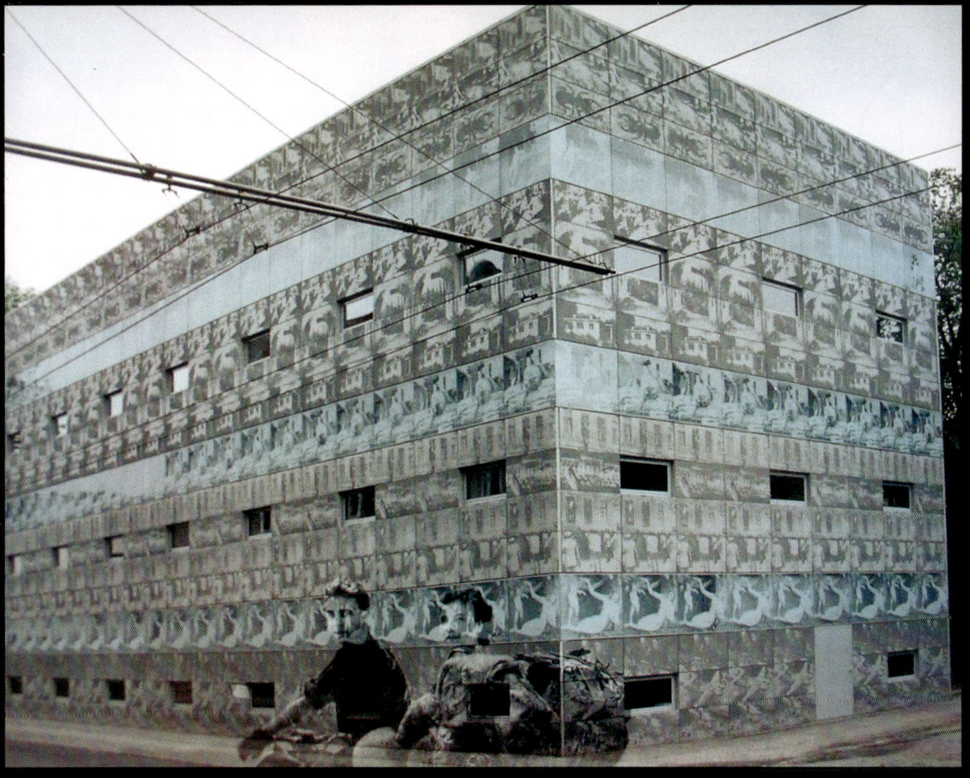

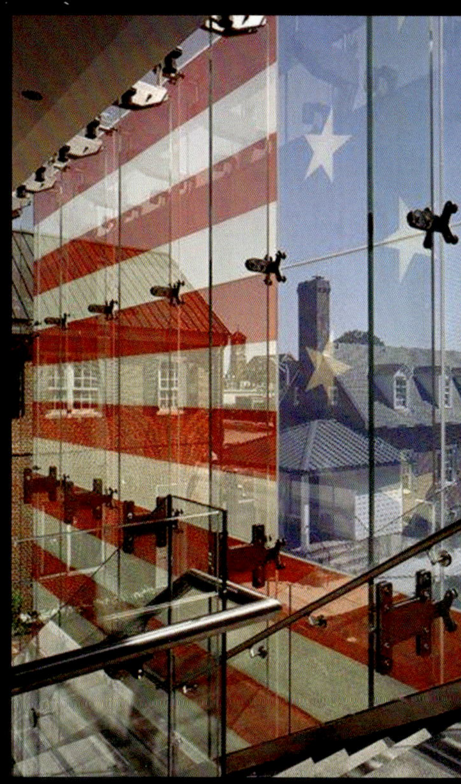

FRIT GLASS is increasingly found in architectural and interior applications. A patterned ceramic or enamel glaze is silkscreened on glass or related material to appear opaque from the outdoors and translucent from inside. It has been popular in the design of contemporary building exteriors since the 1980s. The original use of frit glass was in vehicle windshields to cut glare. A dotted band of this material may still be seen along the top edge of most cars' front windows.

The Bibliothek der Fachnochschule Eberswalde (Eberswalde Senior Technical School Library) in Brandenburg, Germany, was completed in 1999. Herzog & deMeuron Architects of Basel, Switzerland, designed the building with photographer Thomas Ruff, who designed the exterior motifs taken from his collection of evocative images. Herzog & deMeuron were pioneers in the use of printed pictorial curtain walls that become less visible as daylight diminishes. This treatment incorporating simple shapes or complex design is seen increasingly in buildings at every scale. *Thomas Ruff composite photograph © 2013 Artists Rights Society (ARS), New York/VG Bild Kunst, Conn.*

The 30x42-foot Star Spangled Banner, a local icon, was replicated at the Flag House Museum in Baltimore in 2003, using colored frit glass in a design for the building's exterior by architects Richter, Cornbrooks, Gribble. The image covers the addition to the 1793 home of Mary Pickersgill, the flag maker who made the banner that flew over Fort McHenry and inspired Francis Scott Key to write the poem that became our national anthem. *Alain Jaramillo photograph.*

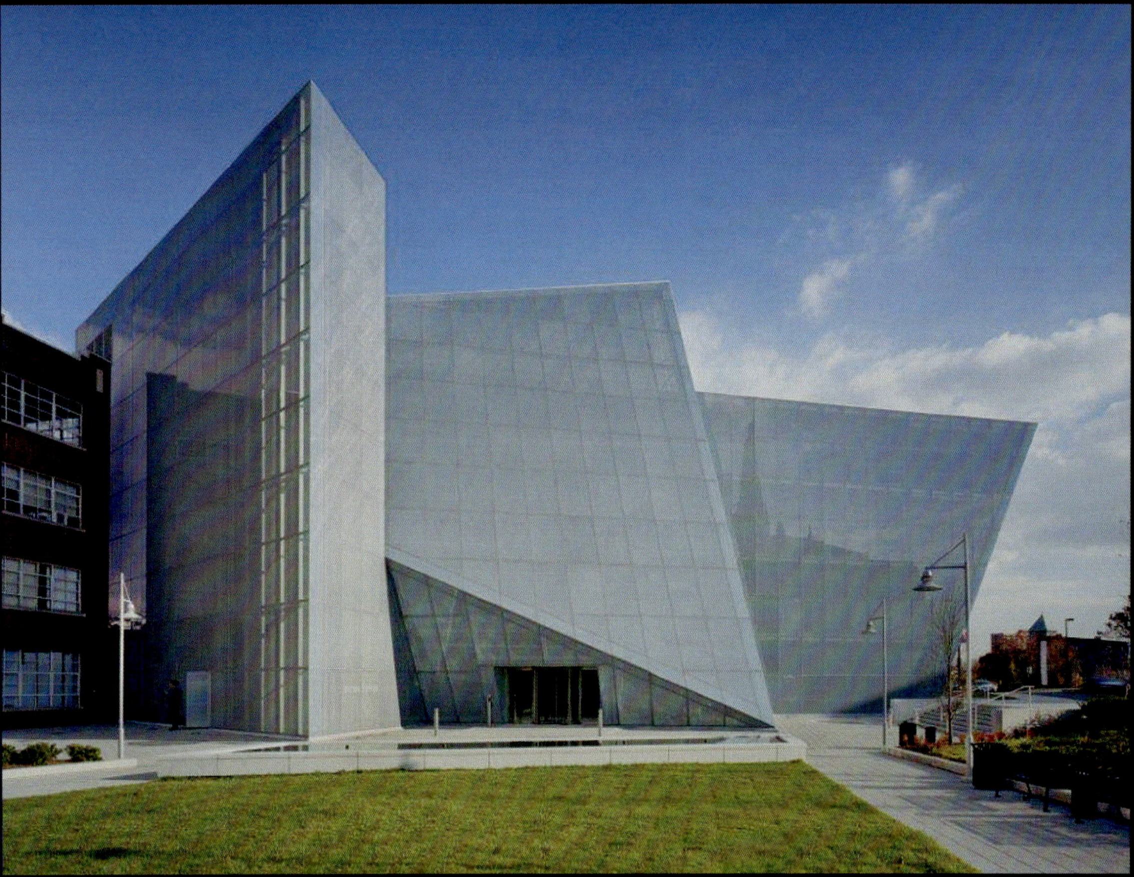

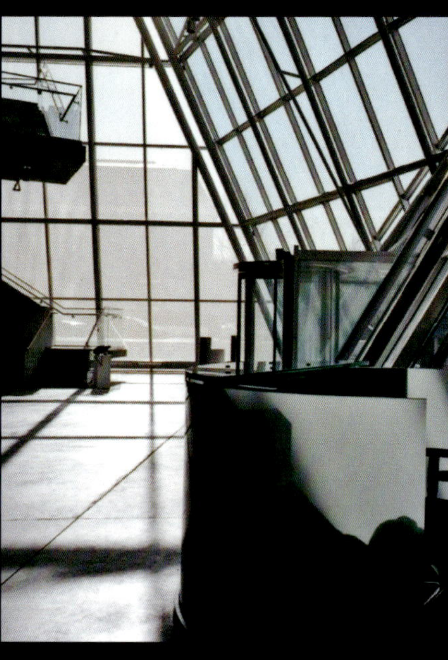

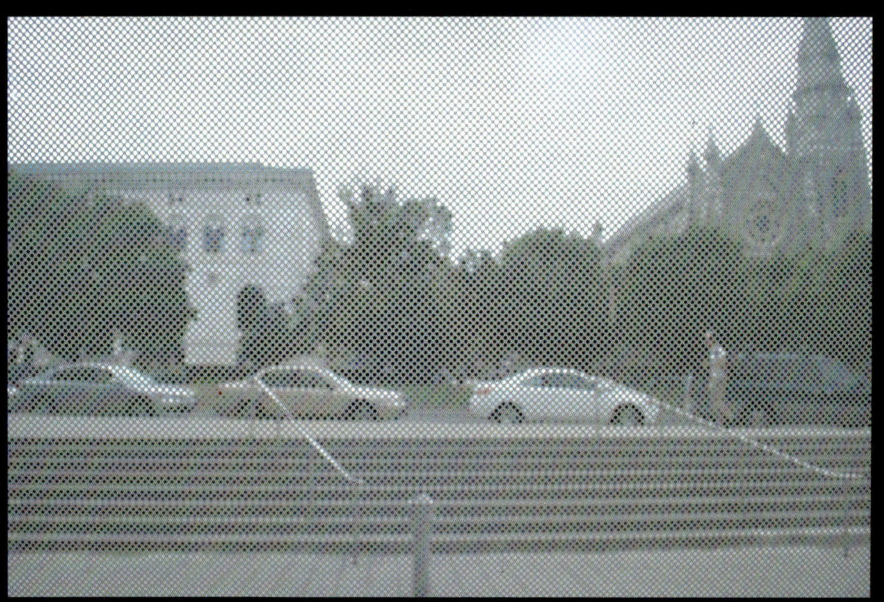

Brown Center, Maryland Institute College of Art (MICA), Baltimore (2004). The entire glass exterior of this signature building on MICA's urban campus, designed by Ziger/Snead and Charles Brickbauer, employs an overall enameled frit pattern, silk-screened and baked onto glass. It appears solid by day and translucent by night. It could be considered Baltimore's largest unpainted screen. *Eduard Heuber photograph, exterior. Ziger/Snead photograph, interior. Both courtesy of Maryland Institute College of Art.*

Interior View

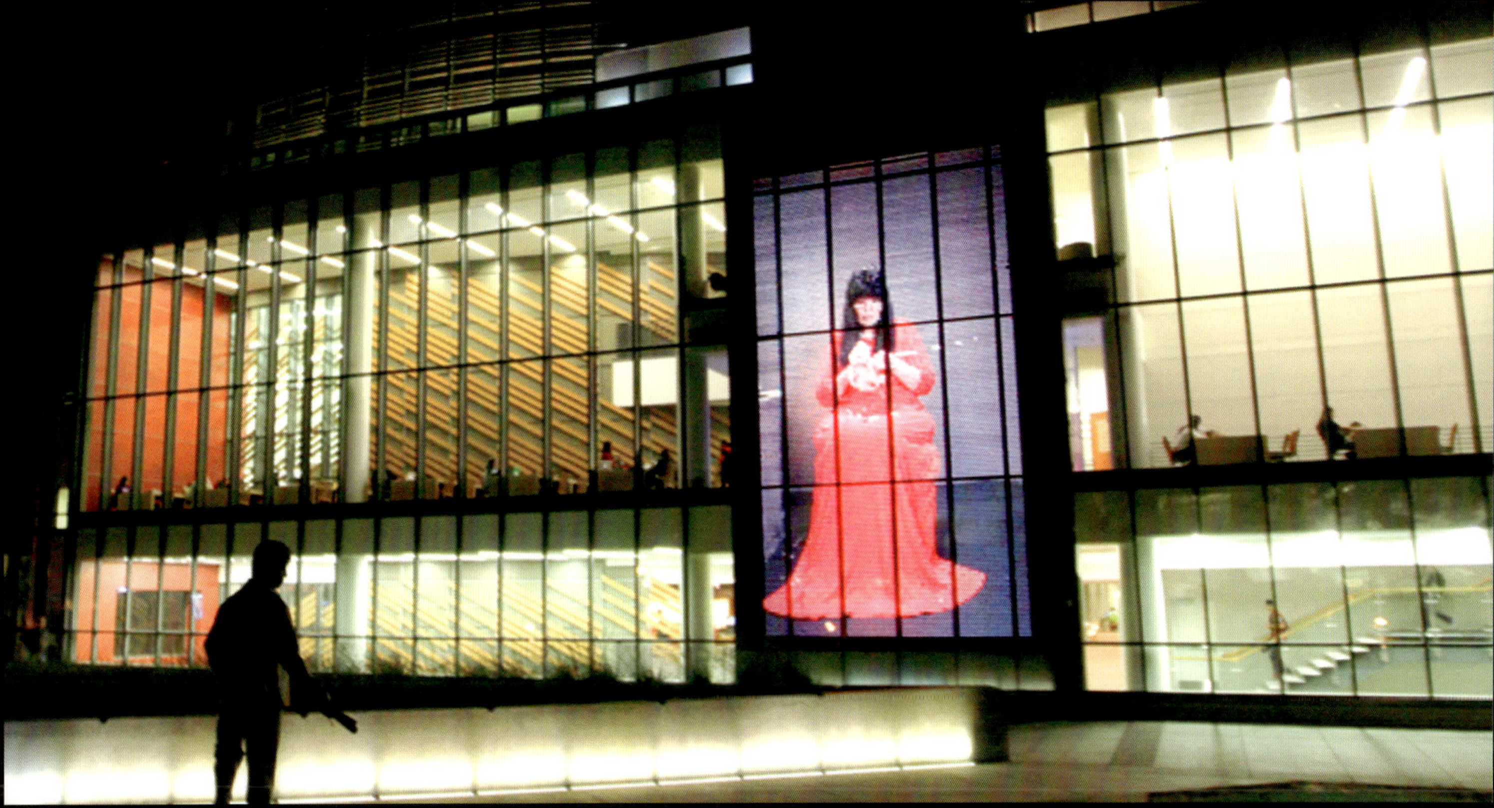

In a partnership between GKD Metal Fabrics of Germany and USA in Cambridge, Maryland, and ag4/mediatechture company of Cologne, Germany, a new class of flexible woven fabrics has been developed that integrate digital imagery with metal fabric in a truly twenty-first-century painted screen. Special LED strips are woven at regular intervals into GKD's stainless steel mesh. The LEDs display digital or static views, from logos to advertising and film clips, controlled remotely through a Web-based user interface. According to the company, GKD's flexible woven metal fabrics for building façades "create usable light, refreshing airflow, heat reduction and preserve outdoor views, all in a very sustainable fashion," as well as "ventilation and solar management for climate control and 'daylighting' applications for building comfort and operational costs." Their goal is to connect "the building's internal and external environments, achieve optimal functionality and stunning aesthetics." The digital version of a painted screen, Mediamesh®, is their most advanced product and today's state of the art in one-way applications, specifically viewing from inside to outside.

One of its most ambitious applications is at the Henry Madden Library at California State University, Fresno. Here the latest technology has been incorporated as the centerpiece of a new campus building. Mono-Chukchansi artisan Lois Connor was filmed in real time weaving a traditional basket from start to finish over the period of a year. The installation by artist and architect Susan Narduli used this footage to create a motion picture that shows the process from beginning to end. It can be viewed in its entirety over a two-week period, making this one of the longest art films made for a building. Unless they choose to linger, most viewers catch glimpses of the basket-in-process whenever they pass by. From the inside, library users are able to see outdoors. The building was a collaboration of AC Martin Partners/Narduli Studio, and the Table Mountain Racheria, a federally recognized American Indian tribe comprising members of the Mono-Chukchansi tribe. *Arthur Gray photograph. Courtesy of GKD-USA Inc. David Carduff, conversation with the author. See http://gkdmediamesh.com/category/type/educational/.*

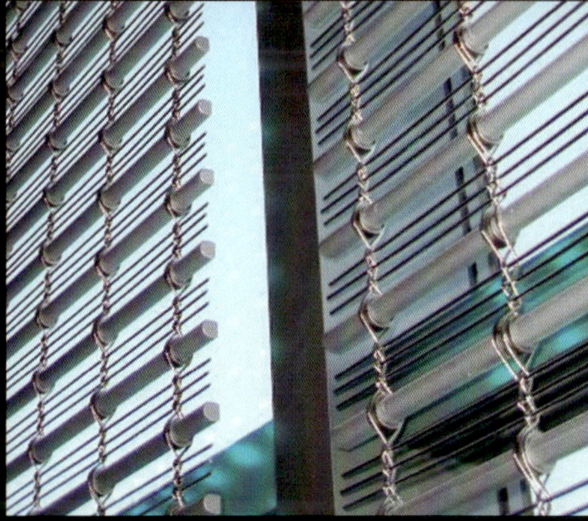

Mediamesh® detail

APPENDIX A:

BALTIMORE SCREEN PAINTERS: A CHRONOLOGY

1884   William Oktavec, born Vàclav (Wenceslaus) Anton Oktavec in Kasejovice, Bohemia, Austria (Czechoslovakia)

1901   Sails from Bremen, Germany, to NYC on *Kaiser Wilhelm der Grosse* (April 15–21)

Lives at 600 East 83rd Street, Manhattan (Yorkville)

Works as butcher for Zelenka Bros. (Brownsville)

Trains as draftsman in night school

Works for Eclipse Air Brush Company

Works for Western Electric Co. demonstrating airbrush, coating telephone wire

1909   Paints screen for harried secretary at Western Electric

1910   Screen wire for windows available to the mass market

1912   Weds Mary Theresa Soler in Valentine's Day double ceremony with brother Albert and wife's sister Agnes

First son William Jr. born

1913   Moves from New York to Little Bohemia, Northeast Baltimore

Opens grocery on North Collington and Ashland Avenues

Paints screen for shop door

Mrs. John (Emma) Schott commissions first screen for home (845 North Collington)

Petitions for naturalization on the Fourth of July

Enrolls in evening courses in mechanical drawing

1915   Sells grocery

Buys rowhouse at 906 North Luzerne Avenue

Works as draftsman and apprentice machinist for Slaysman Co. (manufacturer of dyes and tools for canning industry) Works at Naval Gun Factory in Washington during World War I

1916   Naturalized as U.S. citizen. Name changed to William Anton Oktavec

1922   Opens the Art Shop, lives in upstairs apartment

Alonzo Parks begins to paint in Canton

1930   Brothers Robert and Johnny Eckhardt (later Johnny Eck) begin to paint

1937   William Oktavec visits family in Kasejovice

Charles Bowman begins to paint in Fell's Point

1938   William Oktavec's father, John, dies in Kasejovice

1940   Ben and Ted Richardson begin to paint

1947   William Oktavec buys Boulevard Park (Pasadena) shore cottage, "Old Man's Nest," for $1,200 in back taxes

1950   Tom Lipka begins to paint

Formstone, synthetic stone façade, invades Baltimore

Aluminum replacement windows introduced

1954 *You Asked for It* TV show features William Oktavec

William Oktavec receives order for 800 screens for Germantown (Philadelphia) apartments; thousands for Atlantic City, Philadelphia, Miami hotel chains

Tom Lipka "retires"

1956 William Oktavec dies

Richard Oktavec assumes family screen-painting business

1959 Tom Lipka resumes painting

1961 Alonzo Parks dies

Johnny Eck returns to Baltimore for good and works with Oktavecs, paints screens

Film *Elysium* by Lincoln Johnson and Roland Reed features screen painting and Arabbers

Window air conditioners widely available

1965 Ted Richardson opens storefront art shop on Eastern Avenue

1969 Ted Richardson "retires," closes shop

1970 Frank Deoms paints screens on Ashland Avenue

Vinyl replacement windows and doors available

1974 Elaine Eff begins research on painted screens

1975 Darlene Grubb apprentices to Charles Bowman

1976 Ben Richardson paints bicentennial screens for Midway Bar on The Block

1977 Dee Herget begins screen painting after lessons from Ben Richardson

1979 Richard Oktavec dies

Albert Oktavec continues family screen-painting business

1982 Exhibition at Towson State University and Baltimore City Hall

Ted Richardson resumes painting

Baltimore Museum of Art engages painted screen research for exhibition

1982 *New York Times* article by Michael Wentzel

Screens experience upswing

Highlandtown Harvest Festival showcases screen painters

1984 *Windowscapes* exhibition at Artscape features painters, Lyric Theater lobby

Darlene Grubb publishes booklet, *How to Paint Window Screens*

Elaine Eff submits doctoral dissertation to University of Pennsylvania

1985 Painted Screen Society of Baltimore, Inc., founded

Hatton Center opens in Canton with screens by nine artists on exterior windows and one inside

Screen painters receive citations from Mayor William Donald Schaefer. Al Oktavec presents screen as gift

1986 Charles Bowman dies

Ted Richardson dies

1988 *The Screen Painters* documentary film premieres at Patterson Theater, Baltimore; AFI Washington; Maryland Public Television

The Art Shop closes

Johnny Eck retires

Screens surge

1989
Monica Broere paints screens for Hollywood film *Men Don't Leave*

Dee Herget paints screens for Hollywood film *Avalon*

Two Baltimore city schools offer screen painting

Ben Richardson retires, suffers stroke

Baltimore Visitors' Center commissions 100-square-foot screen

1990
Harborplace Tenth Anniversary features all-day screen-painting demonstrations and workshop

Smithsonian Associates feature film and tour of painted screens in Baltimore

1991
San Francisco Craft and Folk Art Museum exhibit "Sitting Pretty, Looking Fine" features screens and demonstrations by Dee Herget

Johnny Eck dies

1992
Al Oktavec dies

1996
Canton experiences demographic shift; ethnic community dispersing

New windows and doors installed, Formstone removed by new residents

How to Paint a Baltimore Screen Video/DVD is available

Tom Lipka offers screen painting in adult education courses through Baltimore County Community College

1999
John Oktavec begins screen painting

2004
American Visionary Art Museum (Baltimore) installation of painted screens opens in James Rouse Center for Visionary Art

Dee Herget and Jennifer Crouse win Maryland Traditions' Master and Apprenticeship

Tom Lipka and Anna Lipka win Maryland Traditions' Master and Apprenticeship

2008
Urbanite cover story by David Dudley on John Oktavec

John Oktavec featured in *Baltimore Magazine* story by Rafael Alvarez

Rowhouse Rembrandts at AVAM and Baltimore sites feature week of screen activities

Wire Guys displayed throughout city; auctioned for PSS benefit

Johnny Eck exhibition by Johnny Eck Museum (curated by Jeffrey Gordon) and *Freaks* featured at Creative Alliance

2009
John Oktavec and Monica Broere win Maryland Traditions' Master and Apprenticeship

2011
Anna Lipka organizes regular meetings of screen painters

2012
Dee Herget screen door exhibited in National Building Museum's (NBM) *House and Home*

Screen painters Anna Pasqualucci and Monica Broere participate in the Big Build

1,000 children make screen masks aided by NBM volunteers

Screen painters Catherine "Pat" Michalski, Anna Pasqualucci, and John Iampieri are selected to paint storefront screens for Harbor East's first Window Wonderland

2013
Painted screen exhibition at Maryland Institute College of Art Meyerhoff Gallery; with Johnny Eck Museum in Decker Gallery

The Painted Screens of Baltimore is published by University Press of Mississippi

Centennial of painted screens celebrated

RECOLLECTIONS OF SCREENS PAST

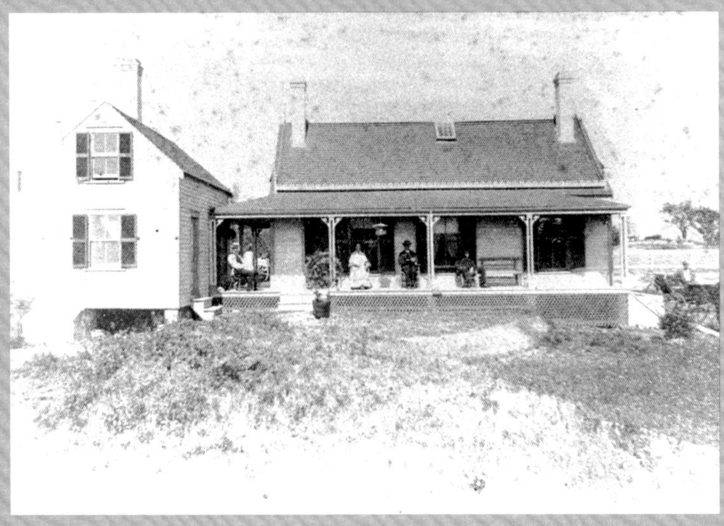 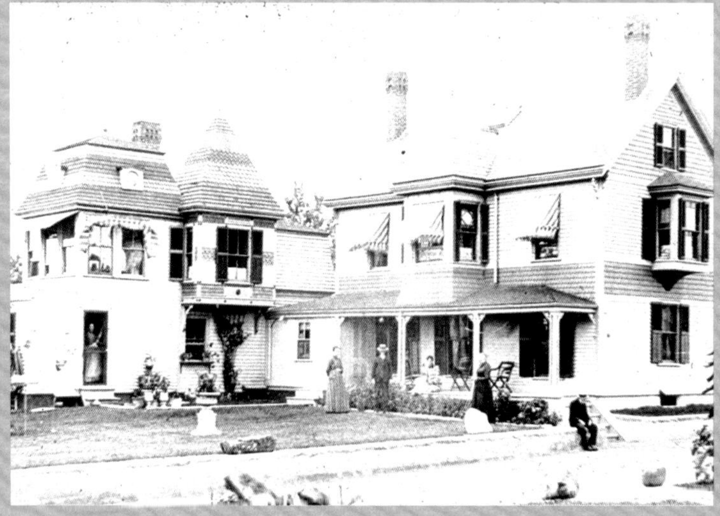

Haywood House, New Castle-by-the-Sea, New Hampshire, left: original residence, 1885; right: final expansion, circa 1900. *Courtesy of Douglas R. and Geraldine H. Woodward.*

RESEARCH INTO THE ROOTS OF PAINTED SCREENS UNCOVERED A number of homes in New England that have maintained their nineteenth-century screens in their original locations, and some that are gone, but have been well remembered or recorded.

The Haywood House, or Cerro Gordo as it was known in its heyday, was an oceanfront boardinghouse in Southern New Hampshire's Victorian playground New Castle-by-the-Sea. A series of photographs from the early 1800s to the present offers one of the best-preserved examples of a chronological (almost time-lapse) study of preferences in remodeling and adorning the exterior of a seaside retreat. These photographs show a simple vernacular one-story house evolving through a riot of additions, porches, and bays. The house eventually incorporated painted screens in every window, from the ground floor to the top, indicating their logical use to protect the guests from prying eyes while deterring flying insects. As the house became more of a showplace for period decorating styles, painted screens were simply another feature of its excessive outdoor enhancements. A family member shares her story:

I live in a house in New Castle, N.H., which was owned by my grandfather who lived in it from 1885–1900. He did extensive remodeling to the original house and made it Victorian. He had the painted screens on every window. They have walnut frames and we still have some of them, although not in use. They are very faded and the scenes which appear to be Italian landscapes are hardly discernible. My grandfather lived and worked for awhile in Boston. Most of the Victorian furniture came from Boston and the workmen who did the remodeling came from Boston. Perhaps that's where he got the screens. Also perhaps the screening was purchased and he had the screens made. The house is directly on the street and perhaps they were used for that reason.[291]

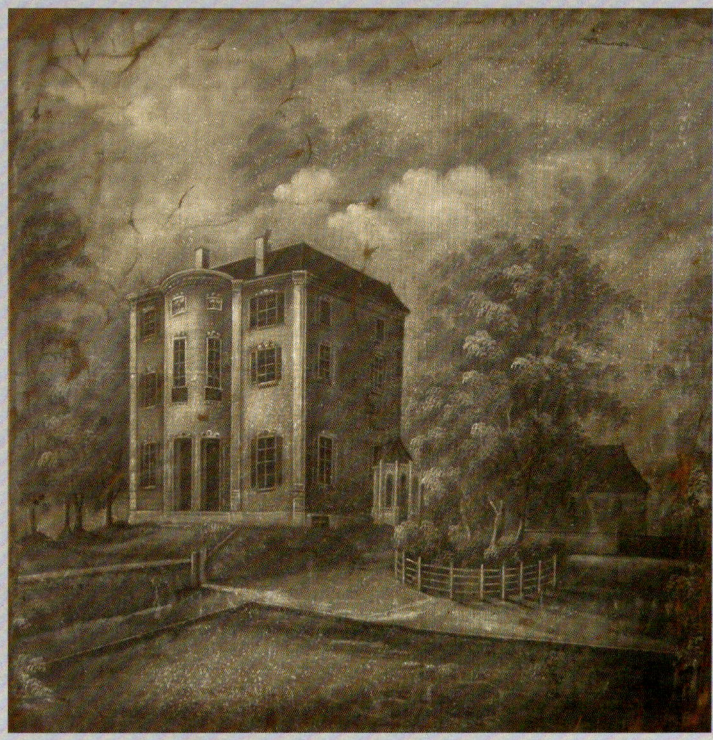

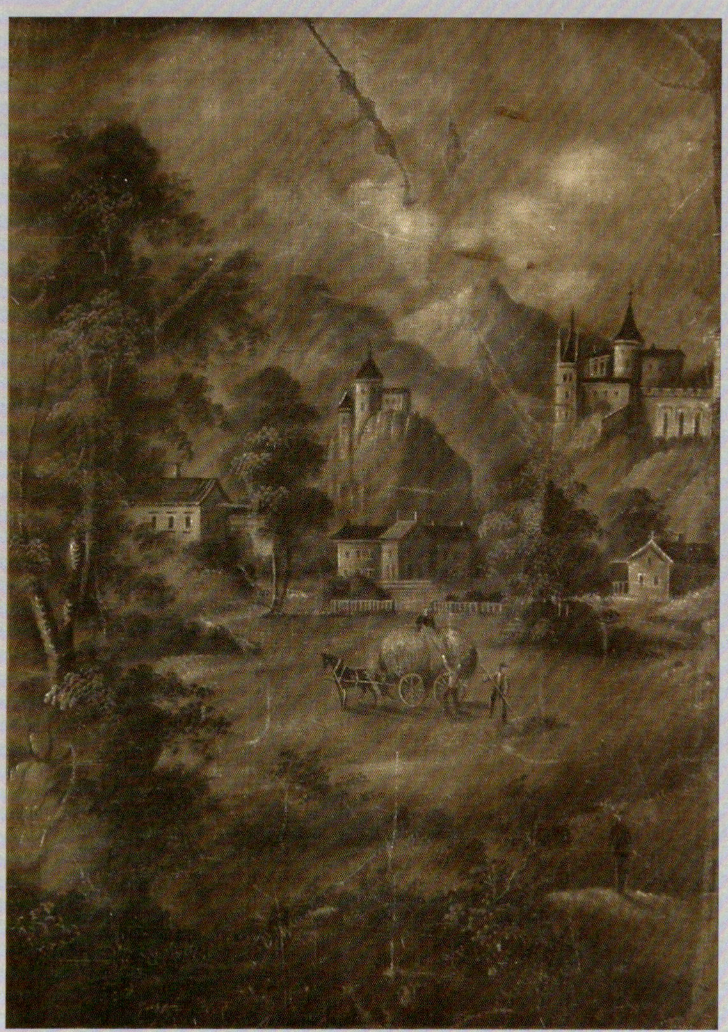

Likewise, a number of Massachusetts's oceanside communities reported painted screens that survived in place well into the twentieth century. The North Shore, in particular Manchester and Beverly, had abundant screens. On the island of Nantucket "possibly 1913 surely 1914 in the residential section of upper Main St. there was a house with the dining room and kitchen on the line with the brick side walk. Two large (3′ x 3′)...screens had oriental garden scenes on them. [They] were quite effective as deterrents to onlookers in bright light, or before dark. The owner of the house, Sidney Chase, married the daughter of Henry Rogers, a millionaire who was in with John D. Rockefeller. He lived in Fairhaven, Mass., and gave a church and library to the town Fairhaven."[292] Perhaps not coincidentally, landscape-painted screens were also placed on public buildings in Fairhaven.

LEFT
Charles Bulfinch's Jonathan Mason House appeared on a screen in a home in Nahant, Massachusetts, before 1900. *Collection of the Painted Screen Society of Baltimore, Inc. Christine Fillat photograph.*

RIGHT
Haying scene screen from Nahant, Massachusetts, before 1900. *Collection of The Painted Screen Society of Baltimore, Inc. Christine Fillat photograph.*

Closer to Boston, in the seaside town of Nahant, a group of three large, fine-meshed screens long separated from their frames and their house present a fascinating puzzle. Given the salty atmosphere of the oceanfront village, it is remarkable that the screens survive. One screen bears the scene of a distant castle. Another one shows similarly remote structures with an unusual foreground depicting haying activity with a horse-drawn wagon. The third and most unusual contains a reproduction of a pre-1836 lithograph of the Jonathan Mason House, since demolished, once located at the highest ridge on Mount Vernon Street in Boston's historic Beacon Hill neighborhood. The "elegant new…mansion house" was designed by Charles Bulfinch for Mason, a prominent lawyer, as early as 1799.[293] Two of Mason's five daughters had summer homes in Nahant. One, much altered, still stands and the other was recently taken down.[294]

Although most reported sightings of painted screens are on private residences, several were of screens in doctor's offices. A Glastonbury, Connecticut, homeowner described her house as "an old square Colonial built in 1735 and screens were found in the attic when we purchased the property…a former neighbor remembers seeing them in our kitchen windows." Louise Walker speculated that "as a doctor had lived here…possibly a patient had painted them in return for medical treatment." In fact the Walker screens, the scenic type found throughout the region executed by a trained painter, had been installed on the side of the house to shield the doctor's examination rooms, later a kitchen.[295]

Mary Gradolph's firsthand account confirms the use of the screens in home offices.

I lived in Norwich, Connecticut, from 1898 (at 3 years of age) until 1920, and during most of that time Dr. Patrick (J.?) Cassiday [*sic*], Sr. had an office (first floor) on Main Street, a door in the center, waiting room on the right, consultation room on the left. The front of the consultation room was just one large window which was covered with a wire screen depicting a scenic picture. I remember as a child that it fascinated me. Apparently there was no curtain behind it. I never did try to peek in, but I did wish I could go inside & see if I could see out. That day did come when I had measles or whooping cough or something & so was taken inside & found I *could* see through it.[296]

Screens have been reported in all parts of this country but in most cases little is known about the source of the screen or the artist. Advertisements in mail-order catalogs may have introduced the work of a Worcester or Cortland artist to Topeka, Kansas, or San Francisco. Also, images and samples might have encouraged local artists to try their hands and offer their efforts to hardware merchants or directly to homeowners. The recollections that resulted from inquiries in newspapers and magazines nationwide give insights to the kinds of people who took up a brush at the close of the nineteenth century and in the first decades of the twentieth century.

The following are a compendium of personal remembrances collected during research for this book.

Esther C. Goddard
WEBSTER, MASSACHUSETTS, DEC. 23, 1981

I am 88 years old but remember when about ten or twelve (ca. 1905) being taken to the farm home of a great uncle Andrew Walker who had a son who did sign painting and gold leafing. As I look back it seems to me "cousin John" had a talent that was wasted. I still have two scenes he painted. Also he did screen painting…The four windows in the front of the farmhouse had paintings of farm scenes. My grandfather's farm also had these works of art and I still wonder how it was done. The farm was in Dudley, Mass. and no longer exists.

Gloriana Gill Goodenough
POMFRET CENTER, CONNECTICUT, DEC. 24, 1981

My great uncle, Will Crowell, was an artist and master stenciller. His screen doors were painted by him, plus I was always fascinated by seeing the scene on the outside, but it disappeared when I went in to look at the other side. He used to paint these scenes with oil paint and worked directly on the screen itself, standing up to paint. I'm not sure if he did a preliminary sketch on the screen first.

Emily DeNyse Wright
LEXINGTON, MASSACHUSETTS, JAN. 16, 1981

One of my great-grandfathers and his brother were immigrants from Germany to Brooklyn, N.Y. …probably ca. 1854. According to my late father's recollection of family stories, the brother (last name Schenk, first name uncertain) had had some training in art, but finding that he could not support himself painting landscapes in oils, turned to the craft of screen painting. My father remembered seeing such screens in his childhood, for apparently they were much in demand over a period of time. I would suppose this was because many Brooklyn homes, like those in Baltimore, were row houses with windows close to the street. In 1955, when it became necessary for me to break up and empty the old family residence where 4 generations had lived, I found in the attic among many family treasures a couple of the screens with their colored landscape scenes well preserved—as if they had never been used. Having no place for them, and not knowing that anyone would be interested—I discarded them…In another storage area I came upon 2 other small oil landscapes—unframed and unsigned, but presumably his work…Perhaps they were models for scenes to be executed on the screens? The scenes are definitely European.

L. Robert Kling

CARVERSVILLE, PENNSYLVANIA

I have a painted window screen that was used in a house built in the 1870s here. The design is…a romantic landscape with a castle. Originally the colors were bright white, green and brown, and when new it must have presented quite a show to the street. The original owner of the house in which the screen was used was a tinsmith who may have had access to painted wire screening through his trade.

Mrs. Earl Whitcomb

WEST MEDFORD, MASSACHUSETTS, JAN. 18, 1982

…brought to mind the times I would go to the 17th of June parades in Charlestown, Massachusetts, on Bunker Hill St. As I walked along the sidewalk the houses flush with the street would have windows at eye level and I remember the screens with painted scenes on them. As this was some time ago—1914–16—I have no way of knowing what became of them.

Haven Andrews

KENNEBUNK, MAINE, DEC. 30, 1981

There are two such screens in this family, carefully cared for over the years. The screens were used by grand folks to provide privacy to the interior from one having entered the porch.

William K. Buxton

WILBRAHAM, MASSACHUSETTS, DEC. 26, 1981

I recall that about 1914 or 1915, when I was nine or ten years old, the family living across the street from us in Springfield, Massachusetts, had a painted dog on the front screen door of their home. As I remember, it appeared to be a short-haired dog much like a Boston Bull Terrier (or perhaps a little like the RCA Victor dog that is listening to the old-fashioned phonograph), in a seated position and looking out toward the street. It was in color, of course, and so life-like that from our front porch it really seemed to be the real thing. Not until approached closely did one realize it was only a painted scene. At the time I wondered who painted it and why but didn't know the family well enough to ask—or was too bashful. In all the years since I have never seen anything like it.

Clare Aylward

WABAN, MASSACHUSETTS, JAN. 4, 1982

As a child I lived in a very large house in Brookline, Massachusetts, where the big back porch was screened in three big sections of screening, on each section on which was painted in white a huge and graceful urn filled with flowers and leaves. In my naivete as a 9-year-old I thought someone had painted these just for the sake of painting and I did not understand the repetition of the subject and wished the three had been different, one from the other. Now I think I know what I was looking at. I am sure the screens have long since ceased to exist even though the house is still there. You've made me curious enough that the next time I am in that area I might just take a peek at the back of the house to check.

Whether these artists painted only for their own homes or shared their talents with wider audiences is lost to history. But more important is that the evidence confirms that screen painters, both amateurs and skilled, in city and county, contributed a beautiful distraction to the consuming public for almost two centuries.

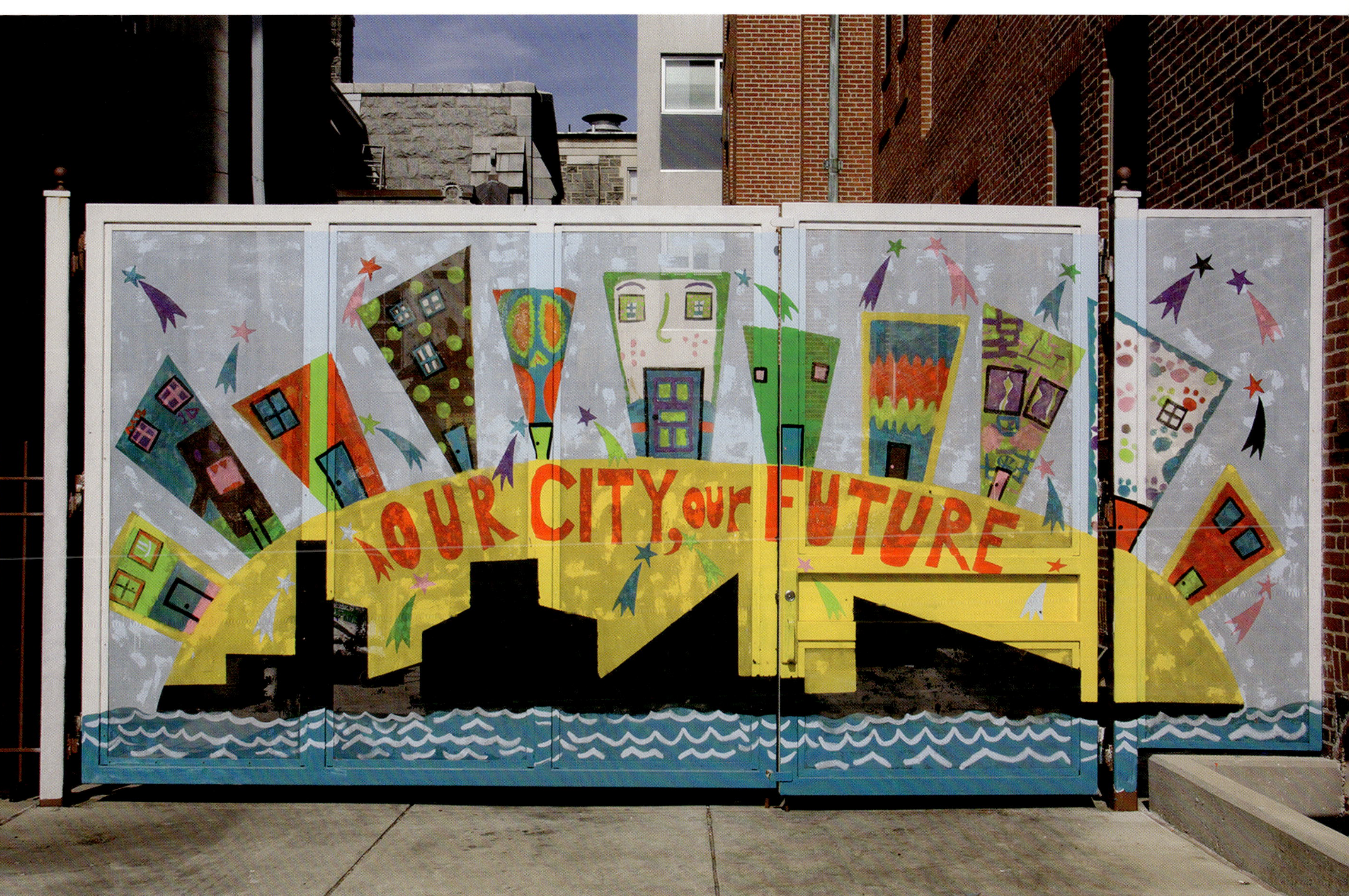

A new screen grows in Baltimore.

A protective perforated gate on the church/school property on Baltimore Street across from Patterson Park shields an entry and camouflages refuse bins. "Sixth through eighth graders from Patterson Park Public Charter School (formerly St. Elizabeth School) painted this screen during the 2011–2012 school year. As part of a Community Murals elective class, students brainstormed ideas, decided on a message, and designed the mural collaboratively. They included opinions from students throughout the school about what makes Baltimore so special. Each of the shooting stars is signed by one of the students who painted it." *Kristina Berdan, Dreamweavers project director, 2013.*

NOTES

1 *The Shopper's Guide* was established in 1927 in South Baltimore by Milton and Nelson Lasson. They moved the offices to the heart of Highlandtown where it became *The East Baltimore Guide* by 1935 and then *The Baltimore Guide* in 1998 but continues to be known locally as *The Guide*. The paper has been hand-delivered without charge to Southeast Baltimore doorsteps each Wednesday. In 2009 Ascend Communications, Inc., a Tennessee based family-owned media company, purchased the weekly.

2 Roland Hill, of British manufacturer Contra Vision, Ltd., and holder of a U.S. patent of a technology for one-way graphic film, suggested in a July 20, 2012, e-mail with the author that there is but "a sole inventor or group of co-inventors" of any product, and that "rediscovered or readapted" would be more apt terms for Mr. Oktavec's role in the history of painted screens "than re-inventor or inventor of a subsequent (or prior) iteration."

3 Building at 2 Dexter Row, Charlestown, Mass., the office of Mazow & Mazow, Attorneys.

4 Mrs. Earl Whitcomb, West Medford, Mass., letter to the author, December 30, 1981.

5 Geraldine Woodward, letter to the author, May 2, 1982.

6 William K. Buxton, Wilbraham, Mass., letter to the author, December 26, 1981.

7 Only one woman, Ruth Chrysam, was known to paint screens between 1913 and the mid-1970s, when Dee Herget and Darlene Grubb joined the ranks of screen painters. Today it is rare to find a male screen painter, as women dominate the field. See chapters 6 through 10.

8 Folklorist Henry Glassie's defining categories of creation, communication, and consumption, outlined in his 1999 book *Material Culture* (Bloomington: Indiana University Press), expand the notion of contexts and define the life history of the object.

9 Interview in *The Screen Painters*, Elaine Eff, director (Baltimore: Painted Screen Society, 1988).

10 Filmed interview with author, 1987, for *The Screen Painters*. Original 16mm film footage is archived at University of Baltimore's Langsdale Library.

11 Frank Bittner, e-mail to the author, July 29, 2012.

12 Kenneth B. Lewis, *Steel Wire in America* (Branford, Conn.: The Wire Association, 1952), 144.

13 Edwin T. Freedley, *Philadelphia and its Manufactures: A Hand-book Exhibiting the Development, Variety, and Statistics of the Manufacturing Industry of Philadelphia in 1857. Together with Sketches of Remarkable Manufactories; and a List of Articles Now Made in Philadelphia* (Philadelphia: King & Baird, 1858), 280.

14 John Leander Bishop, *A history of American manufactures from 1608 to 1860* (Philadelphia: Edward Young and Co., 1866), 205; Peter Igoe, *Three Score and Ten Years of Wire Making* (Newark, N.J.: Igoe Bros., 1952).

15 *Maryland Journal* 40, no. 87, vol. XL (No. 688) (November 2, 1784) p.4. In Louis C. Beers, "The Wire Fabric Industry in America," *A Collection of Papers Read Before the Bucks County Historical Society*. Volume V, 1926.

16 *The Gilbert & Bennett Manufacturing Company 1818–1968* (Georgetown, Conn.: The Gilbert & Bennett Manufacturing Company, 1968), 10.

17 Gilbert & Bennett Manufacturing Co. (Chicago, Ill.), Wire goods: Catalogue no. 115 (Chicago: The Company, 1890). The Winterthur Library: Printed Book and Periodical Collection, TS285 G46 TC.

18 Andrew Elmer Ford, *History of the Origin of the Town of Clinton, Massachusetts, 1653–1865* (Clinton, Mass.: Press of W. J. Coulter, 1896), 345. Erastus Bigelow named this town, located in the Blackstone Valley on the Nashua River, and the company for his favorite New York City hotel, the De Witt Clinton.

19 Ford, *History of the Origin of the Town of Clinton,* 345.

20 Charles C. Wickwire Sr., "History of Wickwire Brothers, Inc.," April 18, 1953. Unpublished MS. Collection of the Cortland County Historical Society, 3.

21 *The Standard and Journal* (Cortland, N.Y.), March 7, 1876.

22 Wickwire, "History of Wickwire Brothers, Inc.," 3.

23 Lalance and Grosjean, Importers of Hardware, advertising broadsheet, New York, n.d. The Winterthur Library: Joseph Downs Collection of Manuscripts and Printed Ephemera, Collection 214, misc. ads, accession number 74x253.

24 Continental Screen Goods Company, advertising broadside Detroit, Michigan, n.d. Hagley Museum and Library.

25 Howard & Morse, New York, Catalogue No. 16, [1880?] (New York: Henry W. Turner, Steam Mercantile Job Printer, [1880?]), 49. Collection of the Athenaeum of Philadelphia.

26 Boughton's advertisement, 1873. Warshaw Collection of Business Americana, Smithsonian Institution.

27 Laurence Farmer, "Moschetoes Were Uncommonly Numerous," *American Heritage* 7, no. 3 (April 1956): 54–57, 99.

28 Robert Cannon Bond, M.D., *American Journal of Science and the Arts* 18 (1830): 370–71.

29 Andrew Spielman and Michael D'Antoni, *Mosquito, A Natural History of Our Most Persistent and Deadly Foe* (New York: Hyperion, 2001), 62.

30 M. Foster Farley, "The Mighty Monarch of the South: Yellow Fever in Charleston and Savannah," *Georgia Review* 27, no. 1 (Spring 1973): 13.

31 "The History of Malaria, an Ancient Disease," Centers for Disease Control and Prevention. www.csc.gov/malaria/about/history/ross.html.

32 Burnette Vanstory, *Georgia's Land of the Golden Isle* (Athens: University of Georgia Press, 1956), 79.

33 Bern Dibner, *Luigi Galvani* (Norwalk, Conn.: Burndy Library, 1971.)

34 Wright Wire Company (Worcester, Mass.), Catalog (Worcester, Mass.: Wright Wire Co., 1912). Hagley Museum and Library.

35 Wright Wire Company (Worcester, Mass.), Catalog.

36 Harrison Rhodes, "Beyond the White Marble Steps," *Harper's*, February 1911.

37 Mrs. John W. Fraley, "I Remember … The Old Bohemian Community," *Sunday Sun Magazine*, November 1, 1953.

38 "Best Building/The 10-foot rowhouse," *Baltimore City Paper,* September 21, 2005.

39 Jacques Kelly, "Red Brick Rowhouses Are More Than Just Clay and Mortar," *News American*, September 16, 1974, p.1.

40 Wood-graining or grain-painting were the everyday equivalents of today's decorative faux painting, artistic techniques used to disguise common building materials as more valued exterior finishes. Do-it-yourselfers joined brick stripers, screen painters, and other handymen on the East Baltimore streets, going door-to-door to paint and re-paint wooden doors, window frames, and vestibules. The process required a base coat and a middle coat scratched through with combs or with other imprinting forms like corncobs or fingers. Preferred shades in East Baltimore were golden oak and "green wood." This decorative art form thrived up until the 1950s, when metal window frames requiring little upkeep replaced the original building material.

41 This East Baltimore church was named for Wenceslaus (ca. 903–935), Duke of Bohemia (and posthumously named king), who embraced Christianity and was murdered by his brother, named a martyr and sainted shortly after his death. Bohemia, Moravia, Slovakia, and Silesia incorporated into Czechoslovakia in 1918 gaining independence from the Austro-Hungarian Empire, and Bohemia became part of the Czech Republic in 1993. The names Czech and Bohemian have been used interchangeably, though nationalism among Bohemians has always been fierce, whether they were ruled by Poland, Germany, Austria-Hungary, or ancient duchies. Czechs began making Baltimore their home in large numbers in the area above Fell's Point beginning in the 1860s. Catholic Mass was first celebrated for them by priests of the Redemptorist order at a borrowed sanctuary (St. Michaels at Lombard and Wolfe Streets) in 1870. The first church building ministering to Czechs, Poles, and Lithuanians, located at East Baltimore and Central Avenues, was dedicated to St. Wenceslaus in 1872. A school there, under the auspices of the School Sisters of Notre Dame, was established seven years later. In 1882 a Czech-speaking priest took charge of the Bohemian congregation numbering 5,000. They purchased a building, rectory, and convent in this same area in 1886. As the community grew and moved further northeast, the church followed. A school and temporary church were built in 1903 on North Collington Avenue. The new and present church accommodating 700 worshipers (with a membership of 7,000) was dedicated January 24, 1915. The Lyceum, a social and recreation center, was added in 1925 around the corner on East Madison Street. Martin Oktavec (d. 1957), brother of screen painter William Oktavec, was the pastor from 1933 to 1939 and from 1950 to 1953. The school closed in 1986 and now houses MICA Place, community arts programs and residences for Maryland Institute College of Art. Sister Theresa's Missionaries of Charity now occupy the convent and minister to terminal AIDS patients. The Redemptorists, a dwindling order, were replaced by Franciscan Friars of the Third Order Regular. St. Wenceslaus's pastor shares duties with St. Ann's Church on Greenmount Avenue, two miles to the northwest.

42 Fraley, "I Remember…the Old Bohemian Community."

43 Mary Ellen Hayward, *Baltimore's Alley Houses: Homes for Working People since the 1780s* (Baltimore: Johns Hopkins University Press, 2008), 154–56, 162.

44 Board of Parks Commissioners, "Public Parks of Baltimore No. 2," December 10, 1927, 6.

45 Olmsted Brothers, *Report Upon the Development of Public Grounds for Greater Baltimore* (Baltimore: Lord Baltimore Press, 1904), 52–58.

46 William Patterson's heirs sold remaining parcels after 1890, increasing the park's acreage and the communities of Butchers Hill, Highlandtown, and Little Bohemia.

47 Olmsted Brothers.

48 By 1900, Baltimore had become the seventh-largest city in America, owing to the growing number of immigrants finding work in its industries. It rose to the sixth for much of the twentieth century until cities in the Sunbelt overtook it. Serious population declines after 1970 left the city with an abundance of vacant homes, specifically rowhouses. Between 1990 and 2010, the city fell from number 12 to number 21 in population rankings, reflecting its population of 620,961 in the most recent census.

49 The city has long been divided into four quadrants. Partisans hold on dearly to their origins in East, West, South, or North Baltimore and all intermediate compass points. Today, Charles Street is the city's east-west dividing line while Baltimore Street defines its north-south axis, as it has for centuries. Harris Creek, formerly Collett's Creek, at the foot of what is now South Lakewood Avenue in Canton, silted in by 1850 and within fifty years was submerged, "straightened out, covered over and made into a sewer." Board of Parks Commissioners, "Public Parks of Baltimore No. 2," December 10, 1927. The Jones Falls with its source north of the city in the Greenspring Valley became notorious for mosquito-infested swampland, unsanitary typhoid-bearing effluent and recurrent deadly floods. Though valued for powering grist and cotton mills upstream, which provided as many as 4,000 jobs by 1890, its unpredictable inundations took a toll on lives, animals, and real property. It continues in the twenty-first century to make brief unwelcome appearances when downpours cause it to emerge from the concrete tunnel and the Fallsway that replaced it.

50 West Baltimore similarly grew to house a surging immigrant population, primarily from Ireland. The Baltimore & Ohio Railroad was their primary employer. For a thorough discussion, see Hayward, *Alley Houses,* 63–109.

51 A few remaining frame homes from the late eighteenth century can be found in Fell's Point on Bethel, South Ann, and the 600 block of South Wolfe Street.

52 Ordinance No. 22 (approved June 11, 1799), *Ordinances of the Corporation of the City of Baltimore* (Baltimore: Thomas Dobbin, 1799); Ordinance No. 31 (approved February 9, 1826), *Ordinances of the Corporation of the City of Baltimore* (Baltimore: William Warner, 1826). The 1826 ordinance provided additional protection by requiring that masonry parapet walls extend above adjoining roofs and slope back toward the alley. The Great Baltimore Fire of 1904 stopped its destructive course at the Jones Falls due east of the city center. The residential communities of Little Italy, Fell's Point, and Canton hugged the shoreline above shipyards and industrial sites.

53 Sachse & Co., *Birdseye View of the City of Baltimore* (Baltimore: E. Sachse & Co., 1869; *George W. and Walter S. Bromley's "Atlas of the City of Baltimore Maryland from Actual Surveys and Official Plans, Part of Wards 6 & 7, 1906.*

54 Mary Ellen Hayward and Charles Belfoure, *The Baltimore Rowhouse* (New York: Princeton Architectural Press, 2001), 2–3.

55 Sally-ports or airy ways provided mid-block access to the rear in case of fire or other emergency.

56 The boundaries of Little Bohemia were Eager Street to the north, Orleans Street to the south, Chester Street to the west, and Edison Highway to the east. After the 1970s and the race riots of 1968, this community became known as Middle East. "Eager Park" is the most recent appellation. Today its majority population is African American, and it may be looking for a new name. Hundreds of rowhouses have been demolished in this area to make way for a new neighborhood under the auspices of East Baltimore Development, Inc., a Johns Hopkins Medical Institutions-related initiative originally intended to stem urban blight and bring biotech jobs to the region.

57   Hayward and Belfoure, *The Baltimore Rowhouse*, 73.

58   *Baltimore Sun*, November 19, 1844.

59   David Brown, "The longest city block: 54 row houses stretch into history," *The Sun*, March 27, 1983. Brown was speaking of West Baltimore's noted Wilkens Avenue row, with a record number of attached homes.

60   *Daily Record*, September 19, 1891.

61   The Baltimore Police Census of Buildings, reported in *Baltimore Sun*, January 1, 1908, and November 12, 1911. Hayward and Belfoure, *The Baltimore Rowhouse*, 139.

62   Sherry H. Olson, *Baltimore: The Building of an American City*, 214, 245ff.; Hayward, *Alley Houses*, 126ff.

63   *Baltimore Sun*, September 12, 1907, and June 20, 1908.

64   Rhodes, *White Marble Steps*.

65   John Wilber Jenkins, "The New City of Baltimore," *The World's Work. War Series*, ed. Arthur W. Page (Garden City, N.Y.: Doubleday Page & Co., 1914).

66   Hayward, *Alley Houses*, 144.

67   Sales Brochure, E. J. Gallagher Realty Company, Builders, n.d., Edward J. Gallagher Realty Company Collection, Langsdale Library, University of Baltimore (hereafter EJG).

68   The property anchoring the northeast corner of Ashland and North Collington Avenues became William Oktavec's home and grocery in 1913. Here he introduced painted screens to his shop's screen door, his neighborhood, and the city.

69   Hayward, *Alley Houses*.

70   Frank Novak was president and treasurer of Frank Novak Realty Company. He was a director of the Central Fire Insurance Company, the Maryland Title Guarantee Company, the Madison Square Building Bank, the National Central Bank, and the Metropolitan Savings Bank, and a member of the trust committee of the Maryland Trust Company. Edward J. Gallagher was president of St. James Savings and Loan Association. Highlandtown's M&T Bank, the present iteration of a national bank at the corner of Highland and Eastern Avenues, has long been known as the St. James Branch. For an in-depth study of the migration route of many East Baltimoreans north along Harford and Belair Roads to take up residence in porch-front homes and cottages built in large part by Novak's and Gallagher's companies, see Eric L. Holcomb, *City as Suburb: A History of Northeast Baltimore Since 1660* (Santa Fe, N.M., and Staunton, Va.: Center for American Places, 2008).

71   "Novak Buys Brick Co.," *The Sun*, November 27, 1919.

72   As the market for homes soared and residents aged and sold their homes, the community was resettled by a younger, hipper demographic in the mid-1990s. Gone was the protective community of neighbors who gathered on the steps or corners daily and treated one another like family, reporting any unusual activity within moments. Middle-class homeowners who gentrified neighborhoods were more interested in seeking grants for exterior lighting to improve neighborhood security than in preserving the culture of conformity represented by Formstone and painted screens.

73   Albert Knight and Lasting Products received Patent No. 2,095,644 in 1937 for a product known as FormStone. The patent expired in 1964, signaling the end of the industry.

74   Dean Krimmel, Baltimore historian formerly of the Baltimore City Life Museums and Peale Museum, interviewed in Lillian Bowers and Skizz Cyzyk, *Little Castles: A Formstone Phenomenon* (Baltimore: Formstone Productions, 1997).

75   Edward J. Gallagher, "Do You Want a Home?" n.d., builder brochure for 700 block of North Luzerne Street. EJG.

76   Hayward and Belfoure, *The Baltimore Rowhouse*, 101. Also E. J. Gallagher Realty Company, Builders, "McElderry Park Lifetime Homes," n.d., Sales brochure, EJG.

77   Henry "Sonny" Crowley, interview with author and Joseph "Turkey Joe" Trabert and Vince Cuffari, December 1, 1986.

78   In 1986, Baltimore boosters "Turkey Joe" and Sherry Trabert commissioned Crowley to stripe the front of their two-and-a-half-story Fell's Point 1840s rowhouse at 321 South Chester Street. They chose dark green paint with light yellow striping. For good measure they commissioned Ben Richardson to paint a scene of the tugboats at the nearby waterfront on their front window screen, a perfect complement to the colorful flourish of stained glass on the window's transom.

79   Barry Dressel, Peale Museum presentation, December 2, 1981.

80   Lee McCardell, "Those Rows of White Steps in City— They're a Mark of Respectability," *Baltimore Evening Sun*, June 5, 1940.

81   "Beaver Dam Quarry Historical for Edifices Built of its Stone," *Baltimore Sun*, April 28, 1942.

82   In addition to the hundreds of houses that he completed in East Baltimore, Miller was especially proud of having supplied and installed the marble for the 2600 block of Wilkens Avenue, Baltimore's longest block, with fifty-four attached homes. Frank W. Miller, "I Remember… How Many of Our White Steps Were Built," *The Sun*, July 17, 1955.

83   John O'Ren, "Down the Spillway," *The Sun*, April 29, 1942. O'Ren wrote, "Mrs. Frances Trollope, mother of Anthony Trollope, the English novelist, toured America [in 1827] with a notebook, recorded 'the abundance of white marble' with which the houses of Baltimore were then adorned." Also McCardell, "Those Rows."

84   O'Ren, "Down the Spillway," and McCardell, "Those Rows."

85   "Scrubbing Steps a Baltimore Joy," *The Sun*, April 13, 1913.

86   Eleanora Fagan (Billie Holliday) with William F. Dufty, *Lady Sings the Blues* (New York: Doubleday, 1956), 9. Thanks to John Szwed for sharing this information.

87   Ralph Reppert, "A Good Front in Baltimore," *The Sun*, November 14, 1948.

88   O'Ren, "Down the Spillway."

89   O'Ren, "Down the Spillway."

90   Ted Steinberg, *American Green: The Obsessive Quest for the Perfect Lawn* (New York: W. W. Norton & Co., 2006), 24. Also Rosalyn Baxandall and Elizabeth Ewen, *Picture Windows: How the Suburbs Happened* (New York: Basic Books, 2000).

91   Gail Cooper, *Air Conditioning America: Engineers and the Controlled Environment* (Baltimore: Johns Hopkins University Press, 1998). Also Marsha E. Ackerman, *Cool Comfort: America's Romance with Air Conditioning* (Washington, D.C.: Smithsonian Institution Press, 2002). Willis Carrier invented air conditioning for industrial use in 1902. The first (huge) home unit was installed in 1914 but was not perfected for window installations until the 1930s. Movie theaters were the earliest adopters. After World War II, air conditioners began to appear routinely in businesses and homes.

92 Stylish features borrowed from grand residences in down-town neighborhoods such as Mount Vernon and Bolton Hill, and in Butchers Hill just west of Patterson Park were incorporated in the modest rowhouses, but one by one these "touch[es] of class" fell victim to the need for more open spaces and a quest for light and air, ultimately leading to the "Daylight" houses introduced in 1915.

93 Gerald P. Gassinger, "I Remember…The Well-Top Icebox and the 'Weekend Rug,'" *Baltimore Sun*, June 10, 1973. Also Louise Taborsky, conversation with the author, March 1, 2010.

94 Betty Piskor, a crafter who specialized in *psanky*, the decoration of Easter eggs, and taught screen painting at a local senior center, was a pillar of the Polish community. She raised five children in a typical three-room-deep Gallagher home on Fait Avenue in Canton. Her windows were decorated seasonally. She kept a dedicated area of shelves and containers floor to ceiling in her basement, most recently plastic tubs, labeled for each display.

95 Jennifer M. Talken-Spaulding, "Authentic Baltimore: Defining the People and Places of an Urban Ethnoscape" (M.A. thesis, George Mason University, 2008).

96 The Baltimore Christmas Garden traces its roots to German families who carried the tradition of building villages and later train gardens under the family Christmas tree. What was for many years a household undertaking was later adopted by public institutions. Firehouses all over the city of Baltimore became showcases, and the layouts increased in size and complexity and began to reflect local landmarks and events. Firefighters and hobbyists created buildings, seasonal scenes, and animations in their spare time at the station. Visible from Thanksgiving through New Year's, the gardens attracted long lines to enjoy the spectacle. Engine 47 in the Mount Washington section of the city enjoys one of the longest running gardens.

97 "Most Attractive Painted Window Screen in East Baltimore Contest," *The Guide*, Baltimore: June 27, July 2, July 11, and July 18, 1940. Kalb's work can be found in the collection of Bill Steinmetz, a former neighbor who would go on to teach design at what is now Maryland Institute College of Art. Steinmetz, who with his wife, the jewelry designer Betty Cooke, is renowned for introducing Baltimore to goods by cutting-edge designers from around the world in their retail shop, The Store, Ltd. He was inspired by Kalb's work as a youngster and saved his family's screens for posterity.

98 William Sumner Appleton, "Editor's Attic: Victorian Window Embellishment," *The Magazine Antiques*, March 1940, 118–19.

99 Heal Collection, British Museum. See *The London Furniture Makers from the Restoration to the Victorian Era* (London: Batsford, 1953) and *London Tradesmen's Cards* (New York: Dover Publications, 1968).

100 Contemporaries of John Brown (active 1720s), whose trade cards can be found in the Heal Collection at the British Museum and other repositories, indicate similar offerings: "James Brown at the King's Arms, the South Side of St. Paul's Church Yard, London Makes & Sells…Blinds for Windows made & curiously painted on Canvas Silk & Wire" (Winterthur); "William Grinnell at the Looking Glass and South Side of St. Pauls"; "Charles Legg adjoining to Bishop's Gate London, Performs in the best manner… Coach, House & Sign Painting, Heraldry for Undertakers, Arms Painted on Vellum, Blinds for Windows"; Nathaniel Skinner featured "Painted-Window-Blinds At the Black Lyon and South Side of St Pauls"; Benjamin Rackstraw "makes and sells Window Blinds…after the newest fashion and at the most Reasonable Rates"; and "Richard Elliot at the Golden Head and Corner Queen Street Cheapside" added "Window Blinds done in the neatest manner" to his list of accomplishments.

101 T. J. S. Tidmarsh, letter to author, October 7, 1981.

102 Daniel Neal, *The History of New-England* (London, 1720).

103 Alfred Coxe Prime, ed., *The Arts and Crafts in Philadelphia, Maryland, and South Carolina 1721–1785, Gleanings from Newspapers* (New York: DaCapo, 1929), 13.

104 Correspondence and visits to southern historical societies, museums, archives, and collectors, as well as conversations with decorative arts historian Jesse Poesch, proved futile. Despite references to the contrary, no evidence of surviving painted screens in any of the urban centers or elsewhere in the region could be verified.

105 Hagen-Hohenlimburg was known as Limburg an der Lenne until 1903.

106 Wilhelm Bleicher and Peters Sohn, "Aus der Geschichte de Familie und der Firma Bernhard Boeckers" ["From the History of the Family and Company Bernhard Boeckers"], *Heimatblatter fur Hohenlimburg und Umgebung* 40 (Jg. 1979): 202. The Boecker firm became C. M. Pieper after 1831. Prior to fabricating wire cloth for

window screens, the company supplied finely woven wire mesh for miners' lamps and moulds for paper.

107 Bleicher and Sohn, translation unpaginated.

108 Wilhelm Bleicher, "Moskitofenster fur die Tropen: Uber die Technik der Drahtmalerei und Drahtweberei in Hohenlimburg" ["Mosquito Windows for the Tropics: About the Technique of Wire Painting and Wire Weaving in Hohenlimburg"], *Heimatbuch Hagen und Mark* 22 (Jg. 1981), translation unpaginated. The Schloss Hohenlimburg Museum and the Hemer Museum are the primary repositories for artifacts from Boecker's and Pieper's enterprises.

109 Bleicher, "Moskitofenster."

110 Bleicher, "Moskitofenster."

111 Paul Bornefeld, "Die Drahtweberei und Drahtmalerei in Hohenlimburg" ["Wire Weaving and Wire Painting in Hohenlimburg"], *Der Marker*, 4, 1960, 109.

112 Bornefeld, "Die Drahtweberei und Drahtmalerei in Hohenlimburg," 109. Many of Tilmann's paintings, drawings, watercolors, and postcard images are in the collections of the Schloss Museum of Hohenlimburg, along with a preserved portion of Tilmann's attic studio. The firm of Herman Boecker and Co. (est. ca. 1870) in Hemer, east of Iserlohn, employed the artist Raphael Clavel, who was known for his superior landscape paintings on wire. One roll is included in the collection of the museum in Hemer.

113 Wilhelm Bleicher, "Maler Tilmann," *Raum Iserlohn*, October 10, 1979.

114 Bleicher, "Moskitofenster," 277.

115 Bornefeld, "Die Drahtweberei und Drahtmalerei in Hohenlimburg," 108.

116 Ulrika Leander, conversation with author, August 9, 2010, Royal Oak, Md.

117 Karin Forsberg, "Gusums Bruks Historia 1653–1953," n.d. MS, 133. Gusums Bruk is best known today for brass candlesticks of a distinctly bulbous style, perhaps rooted in the city's origins as cannon makers.

118   Hazelius-Berg, *Der Gardiner* [*Curtains*], 85. Correspondence with curator Elisabet Hidemark, Nordisk Museet, January 20, 1981. Herman Hofberg, *Svensk Biografisk handlexicon efter tryckta kälor och medelst nya bidrag samlade ochutarbetrade* (Stockholm, 1876). Excerpted for Prins Eugens Waldemarsudde och Östergotlands Llinköpings Stads Museums (exhibitions), 1978. Although Hofberg dismisses Nils Andersson as a mere painter of screens who relied on stencils in addition to his freehand work, the full-time position at the wire mill allowed Andersson to pursue studies in literature and history, and he dreamed of being accepted by Stockholm's Art Academy. After five years at Gusums, Andersson sold all of his possessions and left for the capital city. There, he experienced years of deprivation, but continued to paint. With support from patrons, he traveled to Paris from 1854 to 1856. There he studied ancient and "new masterpieces" and was influenced by the work of French genre painter Thomas Couture. Though they were contemporaries and Couture was a well-known teacher, it is unclear if he personally taught Andersson. Upon returning to Stockholm in 1857 Andersson became a member of an independent art academy where he was asked to be the assistant and soon chief professor of drawing. He began his career as a history painter on wire cloth and moved into genre and landscapes on canvas for which he was noted. He died in 1865 at the age of forty-eight after "a very long and painful illness." His canvas paintings can be found in the collection of the National Museum in Stockholm. A copy of a 1773 engraving by the Polish Huguenot printmaker Daniel Chodowiecki, painted on a freestanding footed screen, attributed to Andersson, is in the Nordisk Museet, Sweden's folk art museum.

119   Appleton, "Victorian Window Embellishment," *Antiques*, March 1940.

120   "Maryland Journal," April 13, 1792, in Arthur Cox Prime, *Arts and Crafts of Philadelphia, Maryland And South Carolina 1786–1800*, ser. 2, 302.

121   Sumpter Priddy, *American Fancy: Exuberance in the Arts, 1790–1840* (Milwaukee: Chipstone Foundation, Milwaukee Art Museum, 2004), 128.

122   Frances Lichten, *Decorative Art of Victoria's Era* (New York: Scribner's, 1950), quoted in William J. Jedlick, *Landscape Window Shades of the 19th Century in New York State and New England* (M.A. thesis, State University of New York College at Oneonta, Cooperstown Graduate Programs, 1967), 74.

123   Jedlick, *Landscape Window Shades,* 78.

124   Priddy, *American Fancy*, 129.

125   Samuel F. Bartol, *Practical Hints on the Subject of Window Ornaments* (New York: C. Willets, Printer, 1849).

126   *The Rochester Republican*, May 28, 1839, quoted in Jedlick, *Landscape Window Shades*, 78.

127   Mary Clara Bowie, "Decorated Window Screens Regaining Vogue," *Baltimore Sun*, August 1, 1926. Part 2, Section 2, 13.

128   Murphy & Broom, Advertising broadsheet, Library Company of Philadelphia Centennial Scrapbook, Folio 2, 1876.

129   Mohler and Hurlbutt, Baltimore. Advertising broadsheet, 1893. The Winterthur Library: Joseph Downs Collection of Manuscripts and Printed Ephemera, 88x106.

130   William Henry Jackson, *Time Exposure: The Autobiography of William Henry Jackson* (New York: G. P. Putnam's Sons, 1940), 24.

131   E. T. Burrowes Co., *Wire Screen Catalogue* (Portland, Maine, 1878), 4. The Winterthur Library: Printed Book and Periodical Collection, TS285 G46 TC.

132   *Cortland Standard*, July 25, 1878, in Edith Steblecki, "Wickwire Brothers Inc., The Early Years," unpublished MS, Cortland County Historical Society, 1982.

133   *Ledger of Wickwire Brothers*, 1877, 592; March 1883, 26, 29, 32; May 1884, 59.

134   *Cortland City Directory*, 1879–81, 69; 1883, 97; 1887, 151; 1889, 125. Cortland County Historical Society.

135   Thelma Carpenter Congden, "Byron Ruel Carpenter Exhibit," n.d., Collection of Groton Historical Association, Groton, N.Y.

136   Edith Steblicki (compiler), "Wickwire Brothers, Inc. The Early Years," unpublished MS., Cortland, New York: 1890 House Museum, June 1982, p. 9; and ledgers of Wickwire Brothers Wire Company, January 1983, p. 19; February, 1883, p. 23; March, 1883, p. 26. Cortland County Historical Society.

137   *Cortland Standard*, 1886.

138   *Combination Atlas Map of Cortland County New York* (Philadelphia: Everts Ensign & Everts, 1876), 45. Carpenter's screens are now part of the collection of the Cortland County Historical Society, Cortland, N.Y.

139   Carolyn Ibbotson, Homer, N.Y., Cortland County Historical Society, conversation with the author, October 1, 1981. Also Thelma Carpenter Congden, "Byron Ruel Carpenter Exhibit," n.d., MS, Groton Historical Association, Groton, N.Y.

140   Morrill married Ruth Barrell Swann of Easton, Mass., Lawrence Wodehouse, "Senator Morrill's Gothic Cottage at Strafford, Vermont," *The Magazine Antiques*, August 1970, 239. The design source is truer to William Bailey Lang's Highland Cottage near Roxbury, Mass., featured as Bute Cottage (plate xxix) in Mrs. L. C. Tuthill's 1848 plans.

141   Wodehouse, "Senator Morrill's Gothic Cottage," 241. Also Andersen Thorpe, conversation with the author, August 11, 2010. The screens show a possible Japanesque influence, in favor at the time.

142   Letter from Ellen Harris Jennette to Ruth Morrill, May or June 1860, per Susan Cain and Gwenda Smith, researchers and historians at Justin Morrill Homestead for the Vermont Division for Historic Preservation, Montpelier, Vt.

143   Gwenda Smith pointed out the relationship between Ruth Morrill and the Johnsons of Enfield, N.H.

144   Nancy Diemond, Holicong, Pa., letter to the author, January 21, 1982.

145   State of Vermont, Agency of Development & Community Affairs, Vermont Division for Historic Preservation, Montpelier, Vt., 1982.

146   Andersen Thorp, researcher, artist, and former president of the Friends of the Morrill Homestead, is analyzing Morrill's screens for evidence of hand-painting style and technique, with special attention to the use of stencils.

147   E. T. Barnum, *Catalogue of Wire Goods* (Detroit, 1874), 8.

148   Elliot G. Storke, *History of Cayuga County, New York* (Syracuse, N.Y.: Mason & Co., 1879), 408–9.

149   E. T. Barnum, *Special catalogue of E. T. Barnum's wire goods, wire and iron work* (Detroit: The Company, 1881). The Winterthur Library: Printed Book and Periodical Collection. TS285 B26 TC, 8.

150 DeWitt Wire Cloth Co. had successive locations on John Street in New York. The firm was active well into the twentieth century.

151 Thanks to David Lintz, director of the Red Men Museum and Library in Waco, Texas, for insights shared in conversations and correspondence with author.

152 Judith Bettelheim, "Jonkonnu and other Christmas Masquerades," in *Caribbean Festival Arts*, ed. John W. Nunley and Judith Bettelheim (Seattle: University of Washington Press, 1988), 39–83.

153 Carl Lindahl and Carolyn Ware, *Cajun Mardi Gras Masks* (Jackson: University Press of Mississippi, 1997). Also Ronnie E. Roshto, "Georgie and Allen Manual and Cajun Wire Masks," *Louisiana Folklore Miscellany*, 1992.

154 Wickwire letters, transcribed by Anita N. Wright and Carolyn Ibbotson, Cortland County Historical Society, Cortland, N.Y.

155 *California Wire Works Catalogue* (San Francisco, 1892), 37.

156 Chicago Stamping Co., *Illustrated catalogue* (Chicago, 1874), Warshaw Collection of Business Americana, Smithsonian Institution.

157 Letter from Wickwire Brothers to Messer W. T. Buchanan & Son, Hillsdale, Michigan, March 27, 1889. In Wickwire file at Cortland County Historical Society.

158 San Francisco Wire Works.

159 Letter from Wickwire Brothers to Mrs. J. H. Crumb, DeRuyter, New York, June 21, 1889, in Wickwire file at Cortland County Historical Society.

160 Letter to Messr. Dorchester & Rose, Geneva, New York, June 21, 1889, in Wickwire file at Cortland County Historical Society.

161 Bowie, "Decorated Window Screens." This same theme was painted by Fell's Point painter Greg Reillo after 1975 and was displayed for decades in an Eastern Avenue window facing Patterson Park.

162 Margaret Millspaugh, "Ancient Lineage of Those Window Scenes," *Baltimore Sun*, September 7, 1947.

163 Richard Oktavec, interview with the author, November 7, 1974.

164 A star of the Norddeutscher (North German) Lloyd Line when launched four years earlier, the ship was, for a time, the largest and longest afloat and held numerous speed records.

165 William Oktavec Jr., interview with the author, April 11, 1976.

166 William Oktavec Jr., interview with the author, April 11, 1976.

167 Ralph Reppert, "Picture Windows that are Painted on," *Baltimore Sun*, August 9, 1953.

168 Stirling Graham, "Cleaning and Repairing Objets D'Art Provides a Livelihood for Czech Living Here," *Baltimore Sun*, December 4, 1938.

169 William Oktavec Jr., interview with the author, July 14, 1987.

170 William Anton Oktavec's naturalization as an American citizen and official name change from Vàclav Anton Oktavec were finalized on July 4, 1916.

171 Rhodes, "White Marble Steps."

172 Robert Irvin, ed., "The Bohemians of Baltimore," *Baltimore Municipal Journal*, 1929.

173 H.A.W., *Evening Sun*, July 10, 1944.

174 *Baltimore Sun*, March 18, 1938.

175 *Baltimore Sun*, March 18, 1938.

176 *Baltimore Sun*, March 18, 1938.

177 H.A.W. *Evening Sun*, July 10, 1944.

178 Margaret Millspaugh, "Ancient Lineage."

179 Albert Oktavec, interview with the author and Alix Litwack, July 17, 1987.

180 J.G., "Screen Painting Capital of The World," *Evening Sun*, July 22, 1960.

181 Albert Oktavec, interview with author, November 10, 1986. No evidence of silk-screened wire cloth remains. However, several examples of screens overlaid with lace and then rolled over with white paint were found in the Oktavec Boulevard Park studio.

182 Richard Oktavec, interview with the author, November 7, 1975.

183 David Hockney, *Secret Knowledge: Rediscovering the Lost Techniques of the Old Masters* (New York: Viking Studio, 2001). Fascinated by artists' aversion to sharing their methods, particularly concerning the use of optics (known earlier as "perspective") to translate reality onto their chosen medium, Hockney examined the work of empiricist Roger Bacon (1214–1294), who is credited by some with the invention of the telescope and microscope. Hockney looks at evidence of use of a camera obscura to replicate reality in the work and writings of Caravaggio, Leonardo, Durer, Bellini, Campin, VanEyck, and Van der Weyden. Oktavec was in good company.

184 Margaret Millspaugh, "Ancient Lineage."

185 "Baltimore's Picture Windows," *This Week*, January 24, 1954, 14.

186 *Baltimore Sun*, May 6, 1954.

187 "Baltimore's Picture Windows," *TV Guide*, May 7–13, 1954, A-16. Show No. 154, *You Asked for It* (Hollywood: Sandy Frank Productions, April 26, 1954).

188 Albert Oktavec, interview with the author and Alix Litwack for the documentary film *The Screen Painters*, November 10, 1986.

189 Every member of the Oktavec family and every article printed during his lifetime insisted that there was no connection between the red-roofed village of William Oktavec's childhood and the Red Bungalow scene that he applied to thousands of screens; nor was he familiar with any similar application of paint to wire as a child or a young man in Germany, New York, or elsewhere. His invention of the painted screen is wholly his own. On one occasion, sons Albert and Bernard were shown a ca. 1890 black-and-white, landscape-painted screen from New Hampshire. "That's Pop's work," Bernie confidently exclaimed.

190 "Rites Are Set for Oktavec," *Baltimore Sun*, June 5, 1956.

191 Richard Oktavec, interview with the author, November 7, 1974.

192 Richard Oktavec, "No. 2, Post War fighters," untitled bound notebook, 1944, Collection of John Oktavec.

193 Bernard Oktavec Jr., conversations with the author, December 2011 and January 2012. Nephew Bernard "Boh" Oktavec, who lived nearby as a youngster, shared Rich's love of motorcycles and recites every bike owned by Rich and his cohort. He distinguishes between motorcycles owned and those only test driven by Rich, which are shown in family photo collections. Photos are from the collection of John Oktavec.

194 Richard Oktavec, interview with the author, November 1974.

195 Albert Oktavec, interview with the author, 1986.

196 Richard Oktavec, interview with the author, 1974.

197 Richard Oktavec, interview with the author, 1974.

198 Doree Lovell, "Screen Star," *Baltimore Magazine*, September 1982, 129.

199 Al Oktavec, interview with the author, 1986.

200 Lovell, "Screen Star."

201 R. P. Harriss, "The Great Baltimore Cover-up," *The News American*, October 12, 1982.

202 Albert Oktavec, interview with the author, 1986.

203 Jessica I. Elfenbein, Thomas L. Hollowak, and Elizabeth M. Nix, eds., *Baltimore '68: Riots and Rebirth in an American City* (Philadelphia: Temple University Press, 2011). Although not directly dealt with in this volume, the tension experienced throughout the city of Baltimore was evident in the E. Monument Street business district. The book's accompanying tour does include this district, routing the curious to the 1700–2300 blocks of East Monument Street.

204 *The Catholic Review*, advertisement, February 22, 1989, B-5.

205 Jacques Kelly, "Images of Faith: Oktavec's plaster saints and virgins will soon go the way of all flesh," *Evening Sun*, August 20, 1987.

206 John Oktavec, interview with the author and Cliff Murphy, Pasadena, Md., April 6, 2009. Maryland Traditions Master Apprentice interviews are archived at Maryland State Arts Council, Baltimore.

207 Lovell, "Screen Star."

208 Obituary, *Baltimore Sun*, July 5, 1992.

209 Oktavec family screens of atypical subject matter were placed on windows throughout the family's detached home. There were enough excess finished screens around that Al's wife used them to fence the garden from the dog.

210 Christopher Oktavec had been in poor health for a number of years, suffering from a gradual loss of his eyesight from diabetes. Many times he expressed disappointment that his diminished vision prevented him from carrying on the family's signature art form. He died on December 30, 2011. The eulogy repeatedly used the refrain "his life was full of color."

211 Al and his wife, Therese, lost their oldest son, Anthony (1943–1972), before his thirtieth birthday.

212 All quotations in this section from John Oktavec, interview with the author, 2009.

213 Tom Lipka, "Tom Lipka's Screen Painting Instruction Manual," unpublished MS, Baltimore, 1985. Thomas S. Lipka, "Tom Lipka's Screen Painting Instruction Manual," unpublished manuscript, 2005.

214 Screens by William, Richard, Al, and John Oktavec have been on view in a special rowhouse installation in the James Rouse Center at the American Visionary Art Museum in Baltimore since 2004.

215 William Henry Jackson, *Time Exposure: The Autobiography of William Henry Jackson* (New York: G. P. Putnam's Sons, 1940), 24.

216 Arthur Danto, "Can it be the 'Most Wanted Painting' even if nobody wants it?" in JoAnn Wypijewski, *Painting by Numbers: Komar and Melamid's Scientific Guide to Art* (New York: Farrar Straus Giroux, 1997), 124–39.

217 "Painted Window Screens," *Evening Sun,* July 10, 1944.

218 Ruth Chrysam Fahey, interview with the author, July 15, 1987.

219 Richard Oktavec, taped interview with the author, November 1974.

220 Ben Richardson, taped interview with the author, August 13, 1982.

221 Ted Richardson, taped interview with the author, October 10, 1986.

222 Doree Lovell, "Screen Star," 129.

223 Dee Herget, taped interview with the author, August 3, 1987

224 Dee Herget, filmed interview with the author, July 30, 1987.

225 Frank Cipolloni, taped interview with the author, July 17, 1987.

226 Pure pigments mixed with linseed oil and driers by Ronan, "The House of Color Since 1889," have long been the first choice of sign painters, the Oktavec family, and Oktavec-trained artists. Johnny Eck swore by them his entire career.

227 *Evening Sun*, "Screen Painter Starts His Major Project," May 25, 1966, C19.

228 Frank Deoms, interview with the author, November 1974.

229 Ben Richardson, taped interview with the author, January 1982.

230 Ted Richardson, taped interview with the author, August 13, 1982.

231 Albert Baldwin, taped interview with the author, December 1982.

232 I spent many days visiting informally visiting with neighborhood elders in Baltimore senior centers where everyone had an Alonzo Parks story. Though they were eager to give up Parks's name, they often did not share their own.

233 Frank Deoms, interview with the author, 1974.

234 Greg Reillo, taped interview with the author, July 1982.

235 Johnny Eck, interview with the author, July 17, 1987.

236 Ben Richardson, "How to Paint Window Screens," February 13, 1987, unpublished MS. Collection of Painted Screen Society of Baltimore.

237 Ben Richardson, "How to Paint."

238 Ben Richardson, "How to Paint."

239 *How to Paint a Baltimore Screen* (Baltimore: Painted Screen Society of Baltimore, Inc., 1997).

240 Willam Oktavec Jr., in filmed interview for *The Screen Painters*, 1988.

241 Twenty hours of 16 mm footage is archived at the University of Baltimore Langsdale Library, Special Collections.

242 B. Drummond Ayres Jr., "Of White Marble Steps and Painted Screens," *New York Times*, June 7, 1988, A16; ProQuest Historical Newspapers; Jane A. Smith, "Screen paintings get film treatment: Documentary focus is E. Baltimore art," *The Sun,* July 20, 1987; ProQuest Historical Newspapers: pg. 1D.

243 All quotations from Frank Deoms in this section of the book are from an interview with the author, November 1974.

244 Frank Deoms unpublished MS. I first met Deoms after seeing his work on the street and knocking on his door to learn who the artist was. We talked at length. As we parted, he said, "I would like to write a good book." When I returned later that month with a tape recorder to record our conversation, he presented me with a 175-page handwritten manuscript telling his life story. See also, Elaine Eff, "'See Lizzie Stripped': A Bare Bones Approach to Oral and Written Narrative," paper presented at the American Folklore Society, Minneapolis, Minn., 1978.

245 All quotations in this section are from Johnny Eck, interviews with the author, December 28, 1981, January 7, 1982, August 12, 1982, July 17, 1987 (for *The Screen Painters*). Other sources include Fred and Mary Fried, *America's Forgotten Folk Arts* (New York: Pantheon Books, 1978). Johnny Eck, *Facts Concerning Johnny Eck, the Living Half Boy* (Baltimore: published by the author, ca. 1931) See also http://www.johnnyeckmuseum.com/photos/pitchBooks.html.

246 Ruth Chrysam Fahey, letter to the author, September 15, 1982. All quotations in this section from an interview with the author, September 29, 1982, as well as conversations with Jane Fahey Saunders, New Hope, Pa.; Farrell E. Fahey, Brooklyn, N.Y.; and Judy Chrysam, Baltimore.

247 Ruth Chrysam Fahey, letter to Ben Richardson, May 22, 1980.

248 Tiny Postherer, taped interview with the author, Abbott Senior Center, June 1982.

249 John Barnes, conversation with the author, Pasadena Senior Center, 1982.

250 Ethel Parks Seaton, sister of Alonzo Parks, conversation with the author, July 30, 1985.

251 Ethel Parks Seaton conversation, 1985.

252 Quotations in this section from Ben Richardson, taped interviews with the author, January 8, 1982; July 30, 1982; and July 15, 1987.

253 Painters consider the two sided screen to be the epitome of the art form. Whether the scenes be identical or two distinct scenes further defines their skill and competitiveness. The image on the inside screen provides an unexpected work of art after the sun sets.

254 Ben Richardson and Violet Felicio, his daughter, taped interview with the author, July 15, 1987.

255 Ruth Chrysam Fahey, letter to Ben Richardson, May 22, 1980.

256 Quotations in this section are from Ted Richardson, interviews with the author, November 10, 1986, and August 13, 1982.

257 This possibly apocryphal story may have its roots in get-togethers with groups of painters in public forums after 1983, where they shared stories about their roots in the art form. Tom Lipka and Dee Herget each related their first sightings of screens being painted by itinerants. Ted's version may have elements borrowed from their recollections.

258 Playlist typescript, Collection of the Painted Screen Society of Baltimore, Inc.

259 Ted Richardson, taped presentation to the Abbott Church Sunshine Club, April 24, 1984, and interview with the author, October 10, 1986.

260 Charles Bowman, interview with Nancy Andryszak, 1978.

261 Charles Bowman, interview with Nancy Andryszak, 1978.

262 Quotations in this section are from Frank Cipolloni Sr., interviews with the author, 1982 and July 17, 1987.

263 Cipolloni's son, Frank D., is still an active St. Leo's parishioner. He lives twenty-five miles from Little Italy, and "inherited" the tradition of leading both processions as grand marshal since his father's death. He and his wife, Paula, also continue to send his father's annual holiday cards in an updated and annotated digitized color version.

264 Frank Cipolloni, "Techniques on Window and Door Screen Painting," unpublished broadsheet for duplication, made for the Enoch Pratt Free Library Exhibit Department, August 3, 1960. Collection of the Painted Screen Society of Baltimore, Inc.

265 To learn about the technology and culture of air conditioning, the following volumes are well worth the read. See Gail Cooper, *Air-Conditioning in America. Engineers and the Controlled Environment, 1900–1960* (Baltimore: Johns Hopkins University Press, 1998), and Marsha E. Ackerman, *America's Romance with Air Conditioning* (Washington, D.C.: Smithsonian Institution Press, 2002).

266 Quotations in this section are from Tom Lipka, recorded interview with the author, September 20, 2011.

267 Thomas S. Lipka, "Tom Lipka's Screen Painting Instruction Manual," unpublished manuscript, 2005 edition, 1.

268 Ralph Reppert, "Picture Windows That Are Painted On," *Sunday Sun*, August 9, 1953.

269 A grassroots effort to save the ethnically rich rowhouse neighborhoods of Southeast Baltimore eventually stopped plans for a highway that would have destroyed their unique character, but not before 215 homes were demolished. As Lipka recalled in our 2011 interview: "Houses were in the way. They tore them all down and the road never came through. They gave me what I paid for it. And the bank charged me $100 for paying off early."

270 Andrea Siegel, "Screen Savers," Baltimore *Sun*, May 7, 2008.

271 "Baltimore's Painted Screens," exhibition and pamphlet with essay by Charles Camp. City Hall Rotunda, September 15–October 8, 1982, and University Union Gallery, Towson State University, October 15–November 5, 1982.

272 Stiles T. Colwill, a former curator with the Maryland Historical Society, reacting to Gov. William Donald Schaefer's friend Hilda Mae Snoops's desire to install painted screens at the governor's mansion. *Baltimore Sun*, March 1, 1991.

273 George Baumann, "Maryland by George," WJZ-TV, August, 1996.

274 Lipka, "Manual."

275 Maryland Traditions, a program of the Maryland State Arts Council was founded in 2001 by Rory Turner and Elaine Eff, at that time, state folklorists at the Arts Council and the Maryland Historical Trust respectively.

The Master Apprentice program was introduced in 2004 and has included three Baltimore screen painters among the exemplary artisans proficient in all aspects of traditional culture, and their apprentices from across the state who apply as a team and are selected annually by a professional panel.

276   Quotations in this section from Dee Herget, interviews with the author, July 30, 1987, and 2001.

277   Dee received a GED in 1960.

278   "Paintings for the People Passing By," *Sun Magazine,* January 22, 1978.

279   I remember being blindsided by her letter in mid-1978. Here was a newly minted screen painter who thought she was a folk artist. I, a newly minted folklorist, wondered where she got the audacity to think she had passed the test of time that warranted such a title. I was still in graduate school and had not yet mastered the notion of change over time, and that life, like tradition, is long.

280   *The Screen Painters* film. The Painted Screen Society of Baltimore, Inc. (1988).

281   *Catfish Dreamin',* exhibition organized by The Contemporary Museum, Baltimore, 1993; *Sitting Pretty, Looking Fine,* exhibition curated by John Turner, San Francisco Craft and Folk Art Museum, 1991.

282   Zippy Larson's Zippy Tours are another Baltimore institution.

283   Dee Herget, interview with the author, October 20, 2011.

284   Now Notre Dame of Maryland University.

285   See also Rachel Beckman, "It's Not Just a Screen, Hon; A Window on Baltimore Tradition," *Washington Post,* May 1, 2008, and Karol V. Menzie, "The art of screen painting: Artist Jenny Campbell, Baltimore," *Baltimore Sun,* May 16, 1999.

286   Ben Richardson, interview with the author, 1982.

287   "The Baltimore Stoops," *The Tracy Ullman Show,* Fox Network broadcast, November 19, 1989.

288   Joan Jacobson and Melody Simmons, "Daily Record Investigation: The muddled money trail of the EBDI project," *Daily Record,* January 31–February 4, 2011. And Tom Linthicum, Letter to the Editor, *Daily Record,* February 9, 2011, http://www.ebdi.org/ebdi_response_to_the_daily_record.

289   A North Collington Avenue resident interviewed by Maryland Institute College of Art student Edgar Reyes, October 2012.

290   The Refugee Resettlement Center is located in the heart of Highlandtown's commercial district.

291   Geraldine Woodward, New Castle, N.H., letter to the author, May 2, 1982.

292   Albert M. Lewis, Nantucket, Mass., letter to the author, December 31, 1981.

293   Harold Kirker, *The Architecture of Charles Bulfinch* (Cambridge, Mass.: Harvard University Press, 1969), 157.

294   Calantha D. Sears, curator, Nahant Historical Society, letter to the author, June 1, 2004.

295   Louise C. Walker, Glastonbury, Conn., letter to the author, December 27, 1981.

296   Mary (Maud May Ansell) Gradolph, Stow, Ohio, letter to the author, January 29, 1981.

SELECT BIBLIOGRAPHY

BALTIMORE

Almaguer, Tim, on behalf of the Friends of Patterson Park. *Images of America. Baltimore's Patterson Park*. Charleston, S.C.: Arcadia Publishing, 2006.

Arnold, Joseph. "Baltimore's Neighborhoods, 1800–1980." In Glenn Porter and William H. Mulligan, *Working Papers from the Regional Economic History Research Center*. 4:1, 2. Pp. 76–99. Greenville, Del.: Eleutherian Mills Hagley Foundation, 1981.

Canton Days. The First Hundred Years or so. Canton Company of Baltimore, 1928.

Deoms, Frank. Autobiography, unpublished ms., 1976.

Eck, Johnny. *Facts Concerning Johnny Eck, the Living Half Boy*: Baltimore: published by the author, circa 1931.

Fried, Fred and Mary. *America's Forgotten Folk Arts*. New York: Pantheon Books, 1978.

Gomez, Marisela B. *Race, Class, Power and Organizing in Middle East, Baltimore: Rebuilding Abandoned Communities in America*. Lanham, Md.: Lexington Books, 2013.

Hayward, Mary Ellen. *Baltimore's Alley Houses: Homes for Working People since the 1780s*. Baltimore: Johns Hopkins University Press, 2008.

Hayward, Mary Ellen, and Charles Belfoure. *The Baltimore Rowhouse*. New York: Princeton Architectural Press, 2001.

Helton, Gary. *Images of America: Highlandtown*. Charleston, S.C.: Arcadia Publishing, 2006.

Hisley, J. Edward. "A Brief History of St. Wenceslaus Church." Baltimore, n.d.

Olmsted Brothers. *Report Upon the Development of Public Grounds for Greater Baltimore*. Baltimore: Lord Baltimore Press, 1904.

Olson, Sherry H. *Baltimore: The Building of an American City*. Baltimore: Johns Hopkins University Press, 1980.

Rich, Linda G., Joan Clark Netherwood, and Elinor B. Cahn. *Neighborhood, a State of Mind*. Baltimore: Johns Hopkins University Press, 1981.

Rukert, Norman G. *Historic Canton*. Baltimore: Bodine & Assocates, Inc., 1978.

Sherwood, John, and Edwin Remsberg. *Maryland's Vanishing Lives*. Baltimore: Johns Hopkins University Press, 1994.

Talken-Spaulding, Jennifer M. "Authentic Baltimore: Defining the People and Places of an Urban Ethnoscape." M.A. thesis, George Mason University, 2008.

AESTHETICS

Becker, Howard S. *Art Worlds*. Berkeley and Los Angeles: University of California Press, 1982.

Danto, Arthur. "Can It Be the Most Wanted Painting, Even if Nobody Wants it?" In *Painting by Numbers: Komar and Melamid's Scientific Guide to Art*, ed. JoAnn Wypijewski. New York: Farrar, Straus and Giroux, 1997. 124–40.

DeWolfe, Elsie. *The House in Good Taste*. New York: Century Co., 1914.

Dutton, Denis. *The Art Instinct: Beauty, Pleasure and Human Evolution*. New York: Bloomsbury Press, 2009.

Earenfight, Phillip, and Nancy Siegel, eds. *Within the Landscape: Essays on Nineteenth-Century American Art and Culture*. Carlisle, Pa.: The Trout Gallery, Dickinson College, 2005.

Eastlake, Charles L. *Hints on Household Taste in Furniture, Upholstery and Other Details*. Boston: James R. Osgood and Co., 1876.

Hockney, David. *Secret Knowledge: Rediscovering the Lost Techniques of the Old Masters*. 2001; rpt., New York: Viking Studio, 2006.

Pilling, Ron. "Unmuddling…Removing Formstone and Other Indignities." *Old Home Journal* 10, no. 9 (September 1982): 179–82.

Steinberg, Ted. *American Green. The Obsessive Quest for the Perfect Lawn*. New York: W. W. Norton & Company, 2006.

CONVERSATIONS WITH THE AUTHOR, IN PERSON OR ON TELEPHONE

All conversations took place in Baltimore unless otherwise noted.

Barnes, John. Pasadena Senior Center, 2012.

Brill, Lewis. SBC Global, New York, July 17, 2012.

Campbell, Jenny. 2004, 2008, 2010. July 2012, New Orleans, LA.

Carduff, David J. GKD, Cambridge, MD. July 3, 2012.

Chrysam, Judy. September 15, 2011.

Deoms, Frank. December 1975.

Edmunds, Sheila. Aurora, NY. 1982. 2009.

Eshleman, Robin. June 1982.

Fahey, Farrell E., Brooklyn, NY. September 15, 2011.

Furness, Judy. Aurora, NY. 2009.

Herget, Dee. July 21, 1982, August 1982, March 12, 1984.

Hill, Roland. Contra Vision. 2012.

Ibex, Robert. June 2003, April 2004.

Ivers, Rob. July 12, 2012.

Kalb, Frances and Anna (children of Lawrence Kalb). September 1982.

Lewis, Ray. 2009.

Oktavec, Bernard, Jr. December 2011 and January 2012.

Pula, Jean (wife of Greg Reillo). 2011.

Saunders, Jane Fahey. New Hope, Pa. September 14, 2011.

Seaton, Ethel Parks (sister of Alonzo Parks). July 30, 1985.

Seaton, Jerry (great-nephew of Alonzo Parks). June 1985.

Singer, Annette. Lake Park, Florida, 2001.

Smith, Gwenda. Strafford, Vermont. 2011.

Steinmetz, William. 1985, 2001, 2012.

Taborsky, Louise. March 1, 2010.

Thorpe, Andersen. August 11, 2010.

Tomlinson, Liam. Van Wagner Communications, New York, July 16, 2012.

Wollen, Sue and Dave. 2010, 2011.

Zajdel, Jackie. 2008–2011.

Ziger, Steve. 2004, 2012.

Zimmerman, Donald "Duke." August 3, 2012.

CORRESPONDENCE

All correspondence was to author unless otherwise noted.

Broere, Monica. March 1989.

Carlsson, Hannes. Gusum Bruksmuseum. November 2010.

Carr, Marjorie. Enfield Historical Society. October 27, 2010. February 23, 2011.

Cipolloni, Frank and Mary. June 1982, December 1982.

Eck, Johnny. September 1981, August 21, 1981, February 2, 1983, July 29, 1983, March 30, 1984, August 5, 1984, November 4, 1984, February 26, 1985, March 30, 1985, August 21, 1985, September 3, 1985, October 19, 1986, January 7, 1987, May 23, 1987, November 14, 1987.

Fahey, Ruth Chrysam, to Ben Richardson. May 22, 1980.

Fahey, Ruth Chrysam. Summer 1982, September 15, 1982.

Gradolph, Mary (Maud May Ansell). Stow, Ohio. January 29, 1981.

Herget, Dee. October 23, 1979.

Hill, Calvin, Gila Products. December 22, 1982.

Hill, Roland. Contra Vision. London. 2012, 2013.

Iampieri, John. 2011.

Ibbotson, Carolyn. Cortland County Historical Society, October 1, 1981.

Idemark, Elisabeth. Nordisk Museet. January 20, 1981.

Lewis, Albert M., Nantucket, Mass. December 31, 1981.

Oktavec, Albert. November 1, 1982.

Oktavec, John. August 13, 1999.

Oktavec, Richard. December 1975, May 8, 1976.

Oktavec, William A., Jr. December 1982, July 14, 1985, December 23, 1987.

Richardson, Ted. November 1983. December 1986.

Sears, Calantha D. Nahant Historical Society, Mass. June 1, 2004.

Thorpe, Andersen. Strafford, Vt. 1982, 2011, 2012.

Walker, Louise C. Glastonbury, Conn. December 27, 1981.

Woodward, Geraldine. New Castle, N.H. May 2, 1982.

Wright, Anita. Cortland County Historical Society. 1983, 2009.

FILM AND OTHER MEDIA

Bowers, Lillian, and Skizz Cyzyk. *Little Castles: A Formstone Phenomenon.*" Baltimore: Formstone Foundation, 1999.

Eff, Elaine. *The Screen Painters*. Baltimore: The Painted Screen Society of Baltimore, Inc., 1988.

Eff, Elaine. *How to Paint a Baltimore Screen*. DVD. The Painted Screen Society of Baltimore, Inc., 1997.

Johnson, Lincoln, and Roland Reed. *Elysium*. Baltimore: Spectrum Films, 1961.

TRADITIONS

Eff, Elaine. "Behind Painted Screens." *Sunday Sun Magazine*, September 26, 1982.

Eff, Elaine. "Birth of a New Tradition." In *The Conservation of Culture*, ed. Burt Feintuch. Lexington: University Press of Kentucky, 1988.

Eff, Elaine. "Good Screens Make Good Neighbors: The Baltimore School of Landscape Artistry." In *Personal Spaces: Perspectives on Informal Art Environments*, ed. Dan Ward. Bowling Green, Ohio: The Popular Press, 1984.

Eff, Elaine. "Of Painted Screens and Butcher's Dreams." In *Catfish Crier*, for *Catfish Dreamin'*. Baltimore: The Contemporary, 1993.

Eff, Elaine. "The Painted Window Screens of Baltimore, Maryland." *The Clarion*, Spring 1976.

Eff, Elaine. "Rowhouse Rembrandts in Baltimore." In *Folk Arts Messenger*, Spring 2008.

Eff, Elaine. Producer, Director. *The Screen Painters*, film. Baltimore: Painted Screen Society of Baltimore, Inc., 1988.

Eff, Elaine. "The Secret Life of Screen Doors and Windows." *Old House Journal* (July/August 2001).

Eff, Elaine. *Sitting Pretty, Looking Fine*. Exhibition catalogue, San Francisco Craft and Folk Art Museum, 1993.

Eff, Elaine. "To Keep Tradition Going." In *Folklife Annual 1990*. Washington D.C.: American Folklife Center, Library of Congress, 1991.

Eff, Elaine. "Traditions for Sale: Marketing Mechanisms for Baltimore's Screen Art, 1913–1985." *New York Folklore* 12, no. 1–2 (Winter/Spring 1986).

Eff, Elaine, ed. *You Should Have Been Here Yesterday: A Guide to Cultural Documentation in Maryland*. Crownsville: Maryland Historical Trust Press, 1995.

HEALTH AND SANITATION

Ackerman, Marsha E. *Cool Comfort: America's Romance with Air Conditioning*. Washington, D.C.: Smithsonian Institution Press, 2002.

Humphreys, Margaret. *Yellow Fever and the South*. New Brunswick, N.J.: Rutgers University Press, 1992.

Spielman, Andrew, and Michael D'Antoni. *Mosquito, A Natural History of Our Most Persistent and Deadly Foe*. New York: Hyperion, 2001.

HISTORIC SCREENS, DECORATIVE ARTS

Appleton, William Sumner. "Editor's Attic: Victorian Window Embellishment." *The Magazine Antiques*, March 1940, 118–19.

Ayres, James. *Domestic Interiors: The British Tradition 1500–1850*. Yale University Press, 2003.

Bartol, Samuel F. *Practical Hints on the Subject of Window Ornaments*. New York: C. Willets, Printer, 1849.

Bleicher, Wilhelm. "Maler Tilman." *Raum Iser Iohn, Heft* 10 (October 1979): 181–93.

Bleicher, Wilhelm. "Moskitofenster fur die Tropen: Uber die Technik der Drahtmalerei und Drahtweberei in Hohenlimburg" ["Mosquito Windows for the Tropics: About the Technique of Wire Painting and Wire Weaving in Hohenlimburg"]. *Heimatbuch Hagen und Mark* 22 (Jg. 1981).

Bleicher, Wilhelm, and Peters Sohn. "Aus der Geschichte de Familie und der Firma Bernhard Boeckers" ["From the History of the Family and the Company of Bernhard Boeckers"]. *Heimatblatter fur Hohenlimburg und Umgebung* 40 (Jg. 1979).

Bornefeld, Paul. "Die Drahtweberei und Drahtmalerei in Hohenlimburg" ["The Wire Weaving and Wire Painting in Hohenlimburg"]. *Der Marker* 4 (1981).

Congden, Thelma Carpenter. "Byron Ruel Carpenter Exhibit." Groton, N.Y.: Groton Historical Association, n.d.

Cornforth, John. *English Interiors 1790–1848: The Quest for Comfort*. London: Barrie & Jenkins, 1978.

Cross, Coy F. *Justin Smith Morrill: Father of the Land Grant Colleges*. East Lansing: Michigan State University Press, 1999.

Downing, A. J. (Andrew Jackson). *The Architecture of Country Houses; including designs for cottages, farm-houses, and villas, with remarks on interiors, furniture, and the best modes of warming and ventilating. With three hundred and twenty illustrations.* New York: D. Appleton & Co., 1850.

Hazelius-Berg, Gunnel. *Gardiner Och Gardinuppsatiningar* [*Curtains and Satins*]. Stockholm: Nordisk Museet, 1962.

Heal, Ambrose. *London Tradesmen's Cards of the XVIII Century: An Account of Their Origin and Use*. London: B. T. Batsford, 1925; rpt., New York: Dover, 1968.

Hofberg, Herman. *Svensk Biografisk handlexicon efter tryckta kälor och medelst nya bidrag samlade ochutarbetrade* [*Swedish biographical lexicon printed after Kalor with new collected contributions*] (Stockholm, 1876). In Prins Eugens Waldemarsudde och Östergotlands Llinköpings Stads Museums, June–September 1978.

Hollcroft, Temple Rice. *A Brief History of Aurora, N.Y.* Ovid, N.Y.: W. E. Morrison & Co., 1976.

Jay, Robert. *The Trade Card in Nineteenth-Century America*. Columbia: University of Missouri Press, 1987.

Jedlick, William J. *Landscape Window Shades of the 19th Century in New York State and New England*. M.A. thesis,

State University of New York College at Oneonta, Cooperstown Graduate Programs, 1967.

Louw, Hentie. "The Development of the Window." In *Windows: History, Repair and Conservation,* ed. Michael Tutton and Elizabeth Hirst. Shaftsbury: Donhead, 2009.

Prime, Alfred Coxe, ed. *The Arts and Crafts in Philadelphia, Maryland, and South Carolina 1721–1785, Gleanings from Newspapers.* New York: DaCapo, 1929.

Priddy, Sumpter. *American Fancy: Exuberance in the Arts 1790–1840.* Milwaukee: Chipstone Foundation, 2004.

Romaine, Lawrence. *Guide to American Trade Catalogs, 1744–1900.* New York: Bowker, 1960.

Thornton, Peter. *Authentic Décor: The Domestic Interior 1620–1920.* New York: Viking Penguin, 1984.

Winkler, Gail Caskey, and Roger W. Moss. *Victorian Interior Decoration: American Interiors 1830–1900.* New York: Henry Holt and Company, 1992.

Wodehouse, Lawrence. "Senator Morrill's Gothic Cottage at Strafford, Vermont." *The Magazine Antiques,* August 1970.

INTERVIEWS

All interviews were conducted by the author in Baltimore, Maryland, unless otherwise noted.

Abremski, Frank. December 27, 1982.

Baldwin, Albert and Mollie. December 20, 1982.

Bennett, Leroy and Rita. June 15, 1982, July 20, 1987.

Bowman, Charles. Interviewed by Nancy Andryszak. December 1978.

Broere, Monica, with Cliff Murphy and Edwin Remsberg for Maryland Traditions. April 6, 2009.

Campbell, Jenny. December 28, 2011.

Cipolloni, Frank A., 1982, 1985, July 17, 1987.

Crowley, Henry "Sonny," with Joseph "Turkey Joe" Trabert and Vince Cuffari. December 1, 1986.

Deoms, Frank. November 8, 1974, December 1982.

Eck, Johnny. December 28, 1981, January 7, 1982, August 12, 1982, July 16, 1987; and July 18, 1987, with Alix Litwack.

Fahey, Ruth Chrysam. September 29, 1982, July 15, 1987.

Hemsley, Tilghman. June 12, 1984, July 28, 1987.

Herget, Dee. Essex, Md. December 1981, July 20, 1987, August 3, 1987; and October 20, 2011, with Clifford Murphy and Michelle Stefano.

Herget, Dee, and Ben Richardson. Essex, MD. July 30, 1982.

Lipka, Anna. 2011.

Lipka, Tom. July 14, 1987, September 20, 2011.

Michalski, Catherine "Pat." 2012.

Oktavec, Albert. November 10, 1986, July 17, 1987, and July 29, 1987, Interviewed with Alix Litwack.

Oktavec, Albert, and Bernard Oktavec. November 10, 1986.

Oktavec, Albert, and William Oktavec Jr. November 29, 1982.

Oktavec, John, with Cliff Murphy and Edwin Remsberg for Maryland Traditions. Pasadena, MD. April 6, 2009.

Oktavec, Richard. November 7, 1974, November 7, 1975.

Oktavec, Richard, by Barry Lanman for Maryland Historical Society #8031. 1972.

Oktavec, Richard, with William Oktavec Jr. June 1975, April 11, 1976.

Oktavec, William Jr. April 11, 1976, November 29, 1982, July 16, 1987.

Pasqualucci, Anna. 2012.

Philipoom, Jacobus and Mary. July 28, 1987.

Postherer, Tiny. Abbott Senior Center, 1982.

Reillo, Greg. July 17, 1982.

Richardson, Ben. January 8, 1982, June 30, 1982, July 1982, August 13, 1982, July 15, 1987, July 16, 1987.

Richardson, Ben, with Violet Felicio (daughter), July 15, 1987.

Richardson, Ted. August 13, 1982, April 24, 1984, October 10, 1986, November 10, 1986.

Scott, Joyce. July 28, 1987.

Sims, Julia "Lil," with Julia Walther. January 28. 1987.

Trocki, James. August 3, 1982.

800 block North Collington Avenue resident. Interviewed by Edgar Reyes, October 2012.

Waters, John. July 28, 1987.

NEWSPAPERS CITED

East Baltimore Guide

Baltimore Sun

Baltimore News American (1964–1986)

Baltimore News-Post (1936–1964)

Cortland (NY) *Standard*

PRESENTATIONS NOTED

Dressel, Barry. Peale Museum. December 2, 1981.

Herget, Dee. To Art Questers, Severna Park Library, March 10, 2009.

Richardson, Ted. To the Abbott Church Sunshine Club, April 24, 1984.

TRADITIONAL ARTS IN CONTEXT

Though not specifically cited in this book, numerous volumes on traditional arts and culture in a variety of settings, rural and urban, informed my own curiosity about handmade objects, the people who make them, and their communities. These studies may share similar documentary impulses and research methodologies. They are primarily the work of folklorists. They have been included to encourage further and deeper exploration of some of the most illuminating folk art and material culture research from an expanding corps of provocative and innovative thinkers.

Briggs, Charles L. *The Wood Carvers of Cordova, New Mexico: Social Dimensions of Artistic "Revival."* Knoxville: University of Tennessee Press, 1980.

Burrison, John A. *Shaping Traditions: Folk Arts in a Changing South.* Athens: University of Georgia Press, 2000.

Cashman, Ray, Tom Mould, and Pravina Shukla, eds. *The Individual and Tradition: Folkloristic Perspectives.* Bloomington: Indiana University Press, 2011.

Cerny, Charlene, and Suzanne Seriff, eds. *Recycled, Re-seen: Folk Art from the Global Scrap Heap.* New York: Museum of International Folk Art and Harry N. Abrams, 1996.

Dorst, John. *Looking West.* Philadelphia: University of Pennsylvania Press, 1999.

Feintuch, Burt, ed. *Eight Words for the Study of Expressive Culture.* Urbana: University of Illinois Press, 2003.

Ferris, William. *Local Color: A Sense of Place in Folk Art.* New York: McGraw-Hill, 1982.

Freeman, Roland L. *The Arabbers of Baltimore.* Centreville, Md.: Tidewater Publishers, 1989.

Freeman, Roland L. *A Communion of the Spirits: African American Quilters, Preservers and Their Stories.* Nashville, Tenn.: Rutledge Hill Press, 1996.

Glassie, Henry. *Pattern in the Material Folk Culture of the Eastern United States.* Philadelphia: University of Pennsylvania Press, 1968.

Glassie, Henry. *The Spirit of Folk Art.* New York: Abrams, 1995.

Glassie, Henry. *Material Culture.* Bloomington: Indiana University Press, 1999.

Glassie, Henry. *Prince Twins Seven Seven: His Art, His Life in*

Nigeria, His Exile in America. Bloomington: Indiana University Press, 2010.

Goldstone, Bud, and Arloa Paquin Goldstone. *The Watts Towers*. London: Thames and Hudson, 1997.

Green, Archie. *Tin Men*. Urbana: University of Illinois Press, 2002.

Hardin, James, ed. *Folklife Annual 90*. Washington, D.C.: American Folklife Center at the Library of Congress, 1991.

Holtzberg, Maggie. *Keepers of Tradition: Art and Folk Heritage in Massachusetts*. Amherst: University of Massachusetts Press, 2008.

Hunt, Marjorie. *The Stone Carvers: Master Craftsmen of Washington National Cathedral*. Washington, D.C.: Smithsonian Institution Press, 1999.

Jacob, Preminda. *Celluloid Deities: The Visual Culture of Cinema and Politics of South India*. Lanham, Md.: Lexington Books, 2009.

Jones, Michael Owen. *Craftsman of the Cumberlands: Tradition and Creativity*. Lexington: University Press of Kentucky, 1989.

Jones, Michael Owen. *Exploring Folk Art. Twenty Years of Thought on Craft, Work, and Aesthetics*. Logan: Utah State *University* Press, 1993.

Kirshenblatt, Mayer, and Barbara Kirshenblatt-Gimblett. *They Call Me Mayer July: Painted Memories of a Jewish Childhood in Poland Before the Holocaust*. Berkeley and Los Angeles: University of California Press, 2007.

Kitchener, Amy. *The Holiday Yards of Florencio Morales*. Jackson: University Press of Mississippi, 1994.

Pocius, Gerald. A *Place to Belong: Community Order and Everyday Space in Calvert, Newfoundland*. Athens: University of Georgia Press, 1991; Montreal: McGill-Queen's University Press, 2000.

Sciorra, Joseph, ed. *Italian Folk: Vernacular Culture in Italian-American Lives*. New York: Fordham University Press, 2011.

Sciorra, Joseph, and Martha Cooper. *R.I.P.: Memorial Wall Art*. New York: Henry Holt and Company, 1994; rpt., New York: Thames and Hudson, 2002.

Shukla, Pravina. The *Grace of Four Moons: Dress, Adornment, and the Art of the Body in Modern India*. Bloomington: Indiana University Press, 2008.

Siporin, Steve. *American Folk Masters: The National Heritage Fellows*. New York: Harry N. Abrams, 1992.

Vlach, John. *Charleston Blacksmith: The Work of Philip Simmons*. Athens: University of Georgia Press, 1981; rpt., Columbia: University of South Carolina Press, 1992.

Vlach, John and Simon Bronner. *Folk Art and Art Worlds*. Ann Arbor: UMI Research Press, 1986.

Ward, Daniel Franklin. *Personal Places: Perspectives on Informal Art Environments*. Bowling Green, Ohio: Bowling Green State University Popular Press, 1984.

WIRE

Beckmann, Johann. *A History of Inventions and Discoveries*. Vol. II. London: Longman, Hurst, Rees, Orme and Brown, 1817.

Bondeson, Gustaf. *Gusums Bruk. En kronika genomfyrasekler tgiven vid hundrarsminnett av brukets omvandling till aktiebolag* [*Gusum Factory: A chronicle of four centuries published on the 100th anniversary of the mill's conversion to limited liability companies*]. 1975.

Forsberg, Karin. *Gusums Bruks Historia* [*Gusum Factory History*] *1653–1953*. Stockholm, 1953.

Lewis, Kenneth B. *Steel Wire in America*. Branford, Conn.: The Wire Association, Inc., 1952.

Lindahl, Carl, and Carolyn Ware. *Cajun Mardi Gras Masks*. Jackson: University Press of Mississippi, 1997.

Miller, Raymond Curtis, and Phillip H. Knowles. *The Gilbert & Bennett Manufacturing Company 1818–1968*. Georgetown, Conn.: The Gilbert & Bennett Manufacturing Company, 1968.

Roshto, Ronnie E. "Georgie and Allen Manual and Cajun Wire Masks." *Louisiana Folklore Miscellany* (1992).

Steblecki, Edith. "Wickwire Brothers Inc., The Early Years." Unpublished MS, Cortland County Historical Society, 1982.

Welsh, Janie. "A History of Wickwire Brothers Inc., 1873–1972, Cortland, New York." Unpublished MS., September 7, 1976 (Hagley/University of Delaware), Collection of Cortland County Historical Society.

Wickwire, Charles C., Sr. "History of Wickwire Brothers, Inc. Talk Given before the Cortland County Historical Society." Unpublished MS. Collection of the Cortland County Historical Society, Cortland, N.Y., April 18, 1953.

INDEX

A

Abremski, Frank, 146, **148**

AC Martin Partners/Narduli Studio, 227

Acme Stores, 180

Adam, James, 43

Adam, Robert, 43

ag4/mediatechture company, 227

air conditioning, 179, 238n91

airy way, 143, 237n55

alley houses, **52**, 55, 65

American Express, 87

American Sign, 180

American Visionary Art Museum, 11, **208**, 209, 210

Andersson, Nils, **76**, 78, 126, 240n118

Andrews, Haven, 234

Annapolis, Maryland, 191

Appleton, William Sumner, 73

Arabbers, *33*, **124**

Art Shop, 18, **99**, 108–12, **105**, **108**, **109**, **110**, 114–16, **115**, **116**, 120, **120**, 122–24, 131, 136, 140, 141, 149, 152, 153, 154, 156, 157, 160–61, 162, 166, 170, 187, 190

Artscape, **148**, **212**

Aurora, New York, 87

Avenue, The, 213

Avenue, The (Essex), 197

awnings, 65

Aylward, Clare, 234

B

Baldwin, Albert, 142

Baldwin, Walter, 142

Ballard, Horatio, 83

Baltimore, modern history of, 216–17, 242n203

Baltimore Brick Company, 57

Baltimore City College, 115, 194

Baltimore Gas Appliance Co., 168

Baltimore Sun, 96, 146, 188, 195

Bank Street, **7**

Barrett, Bruce, 213

Bartol, Samuel F., 79

Basilica of the Assumption, **224**

Beaver Dam quarry, 63

Beeche's Café, **165**

Belair-Edison, 189

Bennett, Leroy, **139**, 146, 164, 179

Berkner, George, 220

Bethesda Fountain (New York Central Park), 106, **107**

Bigelow, Erastus, 38

Bittner, Frank, **57**

Bleicher, Wilhelm, 77

blinds (American). *See* window shades

Block, The, 174, **174**

Bodine, A. Aubrey, **118**

Boecker and Haver, 76

Bohemian Building Loan and Savings Association. *See* Slavie

Bohemians, 53

Bowie, Mary Clara, 96

Bowman, Charles, 136, **139**, 141, 144, 180–81, **180**, **181**

Bowman, Violet, 180

brick striping, 59, **59**, 238n76

Brickbauer, Charles, **226**

Britain, 35, 75

Broere, Monica, 205–6, **205**, **206**

Brown, John, **vi**, **73**, 74, 75

Bulfinch, Charles, 233

bus wrap, 222

business cards, 132

Butchers Hill, 237n46, 239n92

Buxton, William K., 234

C

C. M. Pieper, 76–77

Cajun Mardi Gras, 93

calendars, 126, 128, 136, 169

Campbell, Jenny, 208–10, **208**, **209**

Canoe, John, 93

Canton, 188, 189, 204, 217

Canton Company, 48

Canton Market, 165, 189

Carpenter, Byron Ruel, 83

carpet loom, 37, 38

Carroll County Farm Museum, 205

Cayuga Lake National Bank. *See* First National Bank of Aurora

Cerro Gordo. *See* Haywood House

Charleston, South Carolina, 75

Chase, Sidney, 232

Chicago Stamping Company, 94, **95**

Christmas garden, 69–70, **69**, 71, 239n96

Chrysam, Ruth (Ruth Chrysam Fahey), 135, 136, 141, 144, 162–64, **162**, **163**, **164**, 175, 196

Cipolloni, Charlie, 185

Cipolloni, Frank, 141, 146, 149, 182–85, **182**, **183**, **184**, **185**

Cipolloni, Mary, 182, **182**, 185

Civil War, 37

Clinton Wire Cloth mills, 38

Cole Brothers, 155, **155**

College of Notre Dame, 205

Community College of Baltimore County, 148, 191

Connor, Lois, 227

construction mesh, 224

Contra Vision, 221, 222, 236n2

Cooper, Peter, 48

Cooper Union, 180

Cortland, New York, 83

Cortland Wagon Company, 83

*Page numbers in **bold** indicate an illustration.*

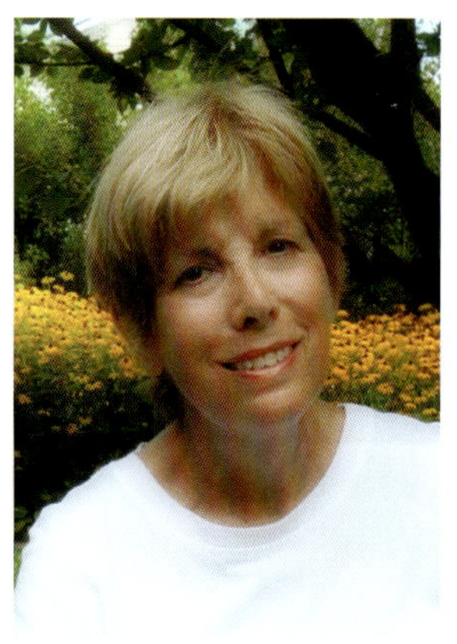

Photograph by Bill Thompson

ELAINE EFF, a Baltimore 'native' since age seven, first learned of painted screens upon heading north for graduate studies and again while working as a collections' assistant in a New York state museum. These coincidences culminated in this life's work, preceded by the documentary film *The Screen Painters*. Almost four decades of research were side-tracked by a career as a city and state folklorist, curator, oral historian, filmmaker, teacher, preservationist and arts administrator. She received degrees in International Affairs at George Washington University, in Folk Arts arts and Museum studies at Cooperstown Graduate Programs and a doctorate in Folklore and Folklife at The University of Pennsylvania. Her work has helped put other traditional artists and arts on the map including the state's heralded dessert, Smith Island cake. She has homes in Baltimore and Oxford, Maryland both featuring scenic painted screens on their front doors.